MW00598310

Netscape
Navigator Gold 3.0
WINDOWS EDITION
BOOK

OFFICIAL

Netscape
Navigator Gold 3.0
WINDOWS EDITION | BOOK

The official guide to the
premiere Web navigator
and HTML editor

Bestselling Author
ALAN SIMPSON

Official Netscape Navigator Gold 3.0 Book, Windows Edition
The official guide to the premiere Web navigator and HTML editor
Copyright ©1996 by Alan Simpson

Library of Congress Cataloging-in-Publication Data

Simpson, Alan.
 Official Netscape Navigator gold 3.0 book : the official guide to the premiere Web navigator & HTML editor / Alan Simpson. — Windows ed.
   p. cm.
  Includes index.
  ISBN 1-56604-420-0
  1. Netscape. 2. Internet (Computer network) 3. World Wide Web (Information retrieval system) I. Title.
  TK5105.882.T386 1996
  025.04—dc20   96-6204
                                                        CIP

First Edition 9 8 7 6 5 4 3 2 1
Printed in the United States of America

Published and distributed to the trade by Ventana Communications Group, Inc.
P.O. Box 13964, Research Triangle Park, NC 27709-3964
919/544-9404
FAX 919/544-9472
http://www.vmedia.com

Limits of Liability & Disclaimer of Warranty
The author and publisher of this book have used their best efforts in preparing the book and the programs contained in it. These efforts include the development, research, and testing of the theories and programs to determine their effectiveness. The author and publisher make no warranty of any kind, expressed or implied, with regard to these programs or the documentation contained in this book.

The author and publisher shall not be liable in the event of incidental or consequential damages in connection with, or arising out of, the furnishing, performance or use of the programs, associated instructions and/or claims of productivity gains.

Trademarks
Trademarked names appear throughout this book, and on the accompanying compact disk. Rather than list the names and entities that own the trademarks or insert a trademark symbol with each mention of the trademarked name, the publisher states that it is using the names only for editorial purposes and to the benefit of the trademark owner with no intention of infringing upon that trademark.

The Komputer Klinic "Kool Site" logo is used with permission from Kim Komando's Komputer Klinic ®: http://www.komando.com.

YAHOO! text and artwork copyright © 1996 by YAHOO!, Inc. All rights reserved. YAHOO! and the YAHOO! logo are trademarks of YAHOO!, Inc.

CHIEF EXECUTIVE OFFICER
Josef Woodman

VICE PRESIDENT OF CONTENT DEVELOPMENT
Karen A. Bluestein

MANAGING EDITOR
Lois J. Principe

PRODUCTION MANAGER
John Cotterman

TECHNOLOGY OPERATIONS MANAGER
Kerry L. B. Foster

PRODUCT MARKETING MANAGER
Jamie Jaeger

CREATIVE SERVICES MANAGER
Diane Lennox

ART DIRECTOR
Marcia Webb

ACQUISITIONS EDITOR
JJ Hohn

DEVELOPMENTAL EDITOR
Doug Lloyd

PROJECT EDITOR
Jessica A. Ryan

COPY EDITOR
Gail S. Burlakoff

ASSISTANT EDITOR
Patrick Bragg

TECHNICAL DIRECTOR
Dan Brown

TECHNICAL REVIEWER
Doug Lloyd

DESKTOP PUBLISHER
Scott Hosa

PROOFREADER
Ron Ferrell

INDEXER
Sharon Hilgenberg

COVER ILLUSTRATOR
Laura Stalzer

About the Author

Alan Simpson is the author of over 60 computer books covering Windows, word processing, databases, programming, the Internet, and publishing on the World Wide Web. His books are published throughout the world in over a dozen languages, and have sold millions of copies. Alan lives in San Diego, California, with his wife and their two young children.

Acknowledgments

Many thanks to Elizabeth Olson, my right-hand woman, for her many contributions to this book.

Many thanks to everyone at Netscape Press, including Karen Bluestein, JJ Hohn, Jessica Ryan, Doug Lloyd, Gail Burlakoff, and Scott Hosa.

Thanks to the gang at Waterside Productions, my literary agency.

And many thanks to Susan, Ashley, and Alec for their patience and support through yet another Daddy project.

DEDICATION

To my gang: Susan, Ashley, Alec, Tigger, Clifford, Tracker, and Lana.

Contents

PART II
CREATING CUSTOM WEB SITES

PART III
POWER PUBLISHING

PART IV
GETTING DOWN TO BUSINESS

Chapter 20 Doing Money on the Internet 479

Chapter 21 Creating Forms for Business 503

PART V
MORE GOLDEN INTERNET SERVICES

PART VI
THIS 'N' THAT, TECHNICAL STUFF

Introduction

When I first dipped into cyberspace a couple of years ago, everything was a hassle. Getting online was a hassle. After I was online I had to learn to use half a dozen different programs to access my e-mail, the World Wide Web, newsgroups, FTP, and all the rest. Getting a presence on the Web was even harder. It took forever to become fluent in HTML. And even when I gained a certain fluency, developing pages was a tedious, time-consuming process. Then *getting* those pages published on the Web—well, I don't even want to *think* about what a hassle that turned out to be.

Now, a mere two years later, that has all changed. A couple of mouse clicks and I'm online. Another couple of mouse clicks and I have instant access to my e-mail, the World Wide Web, newsgroups, FTP sites—the works. All from within one simple, intuitive Web browser.

Authoring and publishing on the World Wide Web is simple, too. Little or no HTML is required there anymore. I just design the page as I would a word processing document and let the computer worry about putting in all the appropriate tags. And publishing? Piece of cake. A couple of mouse clicks and those pages are available worldwide.

And the real miracle is that all of this capability is available from one simple-to-use program—Netscape Navigator Gold 3.0. Wow! And just for good measure, version 3.0 of Gold also gives me immediate access to multimedia Web sites, 3D Virtual Worlds, and a toll-free long-distance conference call system with voice, chat, and drawing board capability. It's all like some kind of dream come true.

What This Book Is About

As you probably know, this book is about Netscape Navigator Gold, version 3.0, the world's most popular Web browser. Well, actually, the term *Web browser* hardly seems appropriate anymore, because Navigator gives you access to virtually *all* the Internet services. I suppose we should call Navigator an Internet browser, now.

What's the "Gold" about? What makes Gold different from the non-Gold Navigator is this: Gold provides an intuitive WYSIWYG editor for creating Web pages without HTML. And a simple button for posting those complete pages to the World Wide Web without all the usual headaches.

Who Should Read This Book

Given the fact that you've chosen the Gold version of Navigator rather than the non-Gold version, I'm assuming that you're interested in publishing on the World Wide Web. Maybe you're just looking to put up a personal Web page. Maybe you want to promote a business. Perhaps you want to set up a virtual storefront and actually conduct a worldwide business on the Web. Regardless of what kind of presence you're looking to create, I'm sure you'll find this book helpful. I've dedicated at least two thirds of the book to business and to Web authoring and publishing.

What You Need to Know

Here's what you need to know before you can use this book effectively:

- You should already know Windows 95 basics, such as how to open and close programs, and what folders and files are all about.
- You should know that the Internet exists and basically what it's about.

WHAT YOU DON'T NEED TO KNOW

Things you *don't* need to know to use this book:

- You *don't* need to know anything about the Internet, other than the fact that it exists and you'd like to be a part of it.
- You *don't* need to know anything about Unix, HTML, programming, modems, or other "technical stuff."
- You *don't* even need to know how to get online. We know there are many newbies out there and we've got ya covered.

WHERE TO START

It's hard to write a single book that will cater to Internet "newbies" (people who have never been online), as well as to Internet gurus. But I've tried to organize the information such that you gurus (and aspiring gurus) could hop right in at Chapter 1. The newbies can do a quick catch-up to the gurus using some other, isolated chapters. Here's where I would recommend you start reading in this book based on your current Internet experience level:

- **If you have never been on the Internet** the first thing you want is access to the Net. After you skim the rest of this Introduction I suggest you go straight to Chapter 30, "Getting Online (for Newbies)." If necessary, use Chapter 31, "Windows 95 Tweaking & Troubleshooting" to work out any problems you have getting online. Then come back and start at Chapter 1.
- **If you are already comfortable cruising the Internet and World Wide Web** just finish the rest of this brief Introduction and start at Chapter 1.

HOW THIS BOOK IS ORGANIZED

This book is divided into several parts, with each part further divided into several chapters. There's no need to read the book cover-to-cover. You can pretty much hop in and out of parts and chapters to learn just what you want, or need, to learn at the moment. The parts are organized like this:

- **Part I:** *Being* **Online:** For those of you who are experienced with earlier versions of Netscape Navigator, this section provides a quick ramp-up to Gold 3.0's hottest new features, including multimedia and browsing 3D virtual worlds. Perhaps more important, this part of the book quickly takes you from being a Web "spectator" to being a Web author/publisher/businessperson.

- **Part II: Creating Custom Web Sites**: Right into the thick of it, this section teaches you just about everything you need to know to create cool Web pages in Netscape Navigator Gold. You can even add multimedia capabilities to your site. No prior experience required.

- **Part III: Power Publishing:** For the truly hard-core, this part of the book takes you beyond "basic" Web publishing and shows you how to jazz up your Web site with better graphics, clickable image maps, frames, and JavaScript.

- **Part IV: Getting Down to Business:** Here's where you can take your newfound Web publishing expertise from a hobby to a business. Learn about all the new ways in which the Internet supports secure financial transactions, create forms for interacting with customers and prospects, and promote your site to drum up business.

- **Part V: More Golden Internet Services:** As I said, Navigator is no longer just a Web browser—it's an Internet browser. And here's where you'll learn to use Navigator for toll-free long distance (CoolTalk), e-mail, newsgroups, FTP, Gopher, and Telnet. Advanced Web capabilities supported by Navigator—such as plug-ins, Java support, and LiveConnect—are covered here as well.

- **Part VI: This 'n' That, Technical Stuff**: Odds and ends are covered here, including getting online for you newbies, Windows 95 tweaking and troubleshooting, and personalizing Netscape Navigator.

- **Part VII: Appendices**: Take a look at the appendices for more useful information! Appendix A describes *Navigate!*, the official electronic publication of Netscape Press. Appendix B details the contents of the Companion CD-ROM. Appendix C gives important directions for installing Netscape Navigator Gold. Appendix D lists the special and foreign characters supported by Navigator. Appendix E identifies color names and triplets and Appendix F identifies all JavaScript's reserved words in a list for easy reference.

ABOUT THE CD-ROM

The CD-ROM that comes with this book offers many invaluable tools that will sharpen your Web authoring skills and help you make better, more compelling Web sites. See Appendix B for the whole enchilada, as well as installation instructions for the various programs.

LET ME KNOW...

I'm always open to suggestions and appreciate any feedback from readers that lets me know what I'm doing right and where I can make improvements. You can contact me at any of the following addresses and numbers:

Alan Simpson
P.O. Box 630
Rancho Santa Fe, CA 92067
Fax: (619)756-9320
E-mail: alan@coolnerds.com
Web: http://www.coolnerds.com

Thank you for buying this book. I hope it serves you well.

Alan Simpson

PART I:
Being Online

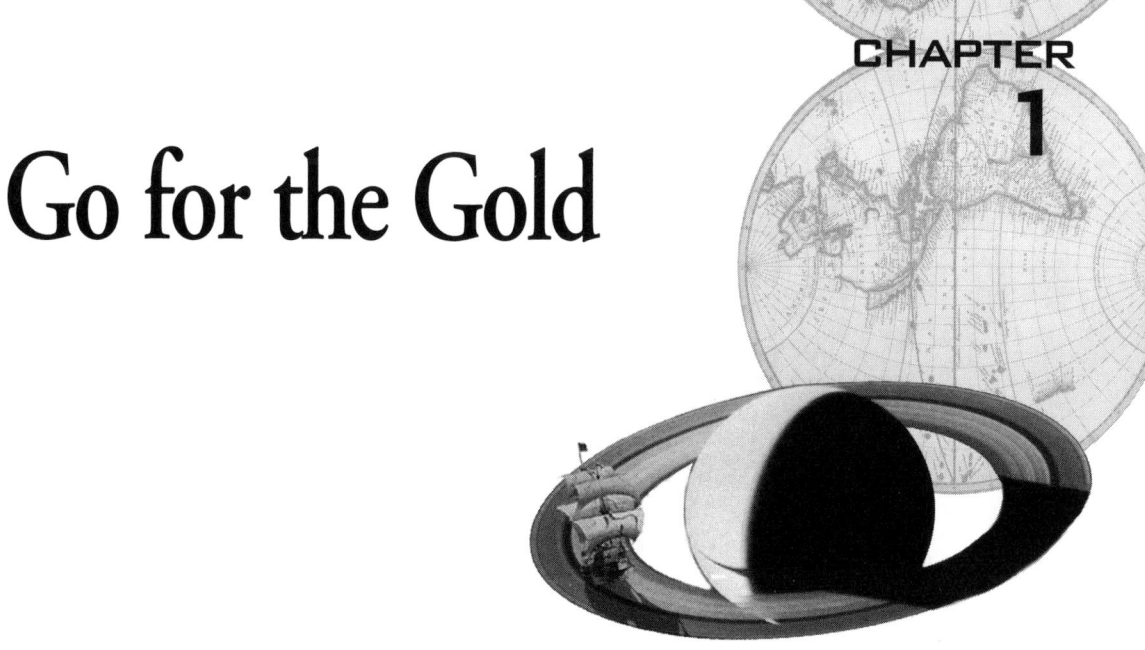

Go for the Gold

This chapter is for those of you who have already browsed the World Wide Web and other Internet services. Right now you're wondering just what is new in version 3.0, and what makes Gold different from Navigator. So here's what we're going to cover in this quick-and-easy warm-up chapter:

- The difference between Navigator and Navigator Gold
- Web page publishing without HTML
- One-button Web publishing
- New features in version 3.0

If you're new to the Internet, much of this chapter will be over your head. You'll need to back up a bit and read the section titled "Where to Start" in the Introduction.

WHAT'S DIFFERENT ABOUT GOLD?

The big difference between Netscape Navigator 3.0 and Netscape Navigator Gold 3.0 is this: Navigator, by itself, lets you experience the Internet as a "consumer" or "reader." Gold, on the other hand, lets you *participate* in the Internet as a publisher, information provider, business, virtual company—whatever. Perhaps an analogy to television would be a better way to describe the difference. Navigator lets you watch TV. Gold lets you *be on* TV.

WEB PUBLISHING WITH HTML

If you've been thinking about publishing on the World Wide Web, you probably know that Web pages are composed of text and HyperText Markup Language (HTML) tags. The tags tell the reader's Web browser how to format that text. For example, the line below contains two tags, <h1> and </h1>, and a short line of text:

```
<h1>Welcome to My Home Page</h1>
```

When a reader views the page that contains that line, his or her browser "knows" that <h1> means "start Heading 1 style" and </h1> means "end Heading 1 style." The browser doesn't display the tags, it just displays the text between the tags in large dark letters, as you can see near the top of the page in Figure 1-1.

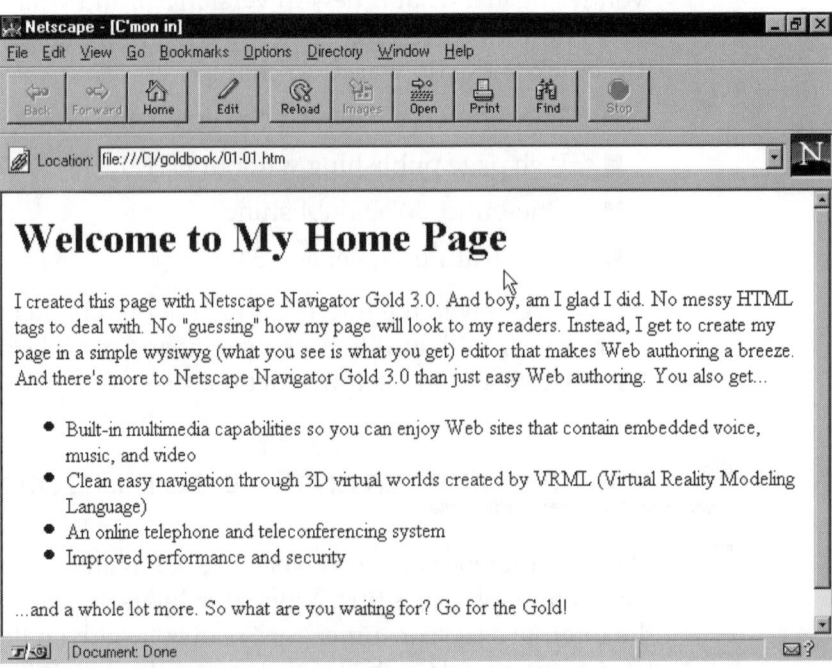

Figure 1-1: *A browser's interpretation of <h1>Welcome to My Home Page</h1>.*

In the olden days (which in Web time means "a few months ago"), authoring Web documents required that you actually type those tags in yourself. This created all kinds of headaches for Web authors. For starters, you had to learn the entire HyperText Markup Language first, so you'd know what tags are available. Then, you had to type in those tags manually as you're typing your text, which is a painstaking, slow, inefficient way to format text.

Furthermore, you really couldn't see how your page would look while you were editing it. That is, rather than seeing the page as your reader would see it, you would just see a bunch of tags and text, as in the example shown in Figure 1-2. So not only were you faced with the headache of manually typing in all those tags, it was nearly impossible to envision how your page was going to look to the reader as you were creating the page.

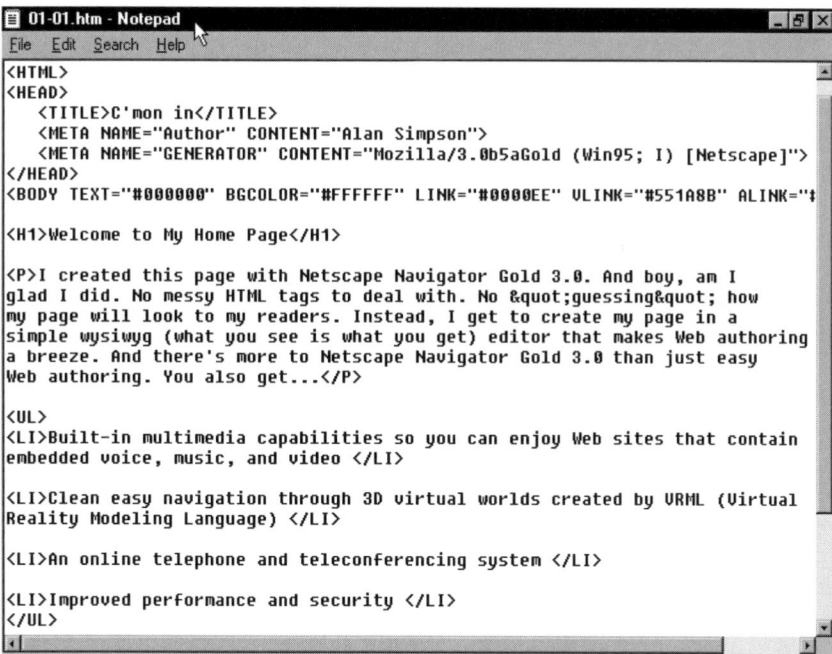

Figure 1-2: *The page back in Figure 1-1 in a simple text editor.*

Fortunately, the olden days are over and you don't have to mess with HTML tags. Navigator Gold provides a more natural, intuitive, WYSIWYG (What-You-See-Is-What-You-Get) editor that makes Web page formatting a cinch. For example, Figure 1-3 shows the page shown in Figure 1-2 as it appears in Gold's editor. As you can see, the page is virtually identical to the way the reader is going to see it in the browser. And the tags are hidden from you, so you can concentrate on the *content* of the page and not worry about the nitty-gritty details of every little HTML tag.

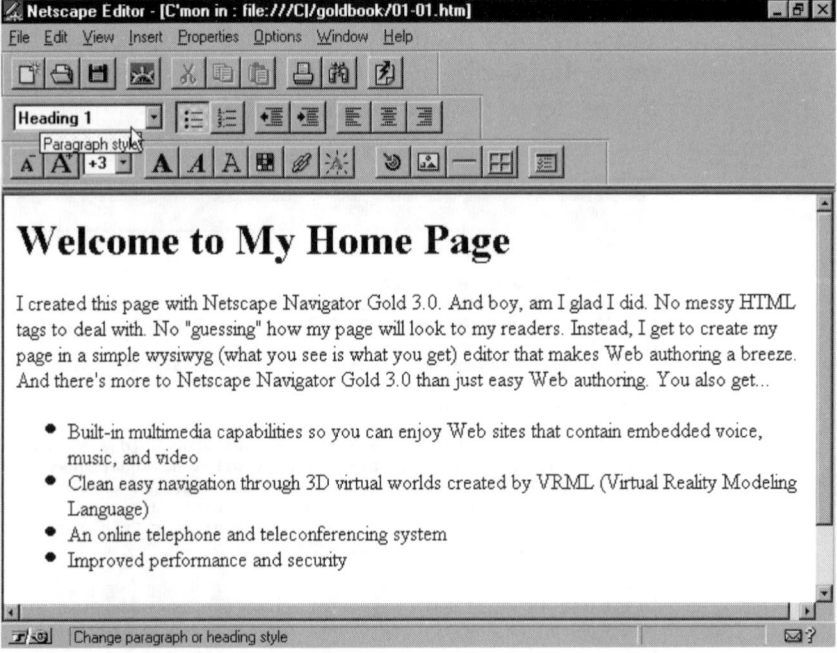

Figure 1-3: *The page back in Figure 1-2 being edited in Gold.*

The way in which you use the Gold editor is very much like the way you use any standard word processor. For instance, to format that top line in Figure 1-3 as a Heading 1, I didn't have to type any tags. Instead, I just clicked on that line of text, and then choose Heading 1 from the Paragraph style drop-down list in the toolbar, near the mouse pointer in Figure 1-3.

The whole business of creating tags takes place automatically, instantaneously, and quietly behind the scenes. You really don't have to think about tags at all. Just type what you want to say, and do a couple of mouse clicks to make the text look the way you want it to look. Take it from a professional author—this WYSIWYG approach is about a zillion times more efficient (not to mention easier) than wrestling with a bunch of little HTML tags.

ONE-BUTTON WEB PUBLISHING

A second major obstacle to publishing your own Web pages, in the olden days, was getting them from your own PC, where you created them, up to the Web server computer for all the world to see. The process often involved using tricky FTP (File Transfer Protocol) commands that most people found daunting (if not outright impossible!).

Gold's one-button publishing simplifies the process immensely. When you're ready to present your completed Web pages to the world, just click the Publish button in your toolbar (Figure 1-4), and Gold eases you through the process of getting all your materials onto the Web server in a jiffy.

Figure 1-4: *Just click a button to publish your Web pages.*

The one catch to one-button publishing is that you must find an Internet Service Provider that supports that Gold feature. But, there are plenty of them out there, and Chapter 5, "Finding a Home for Your Page," will lead you right to them.

WHAT'S NEW IN VERSION 3.0?

A great Web page creation and editing tool isn't the only thing that's new in version 3.0 of Netscape Navigator Gold. There are tons of new and improved features in the browsing side of things as well. Here's a quick summary of the hottest new features:

- LiveAudio: Hear music and voice directly from Web pages that contain embedded sound. Play external sounds with a simple intuituve audio control (see Figure 1-5).

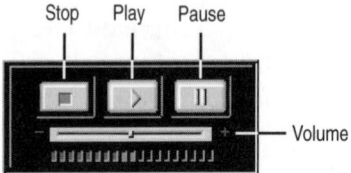

Figure 1-5: *Navigator's simple control for playing sounds.*

- LiveVideo: Watch embedded video and control video play-back (Figure 1-6) with a simple click of the mouse. Supports both the popular AVI and QuickTime formats.

Figure 1-6: *Right-clicking a video lets you pause, rewind, and so forth.*

■ Live 3D: Cruise through 3D virtual worlds (see Figure 1-7) without leaving the familiar Navigator browser.

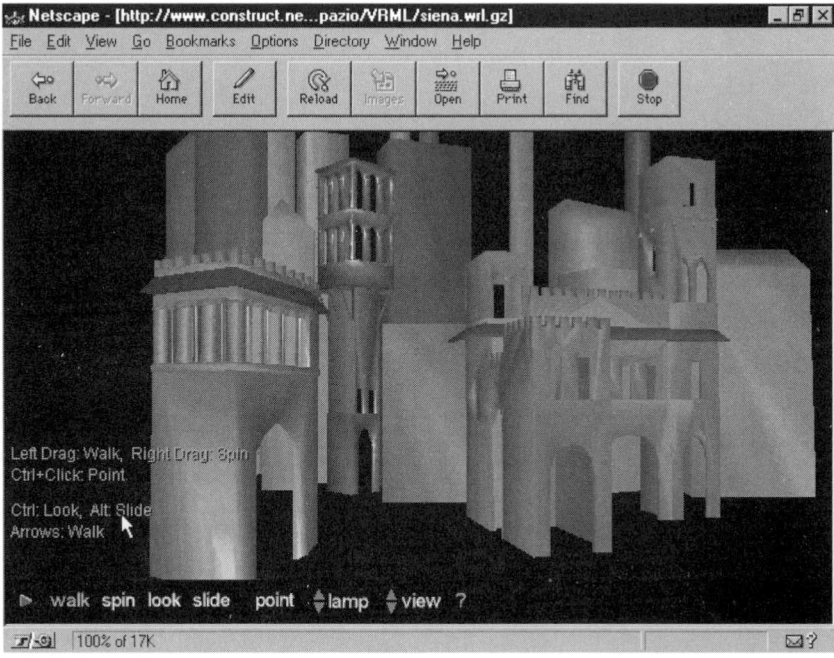

Figure 1-7: *A sample 3D virtual world.*

- LiveConnect: Enjoy a whole new level of interactivity that combines the capabilities of Navigator plug-ins, JavaScript, and Java.

- CoolTalk: Talk to anybody anywhere in the world without the long-distance charges from Ma Bell. Conduct conference calls with voice, chat (typing messages), and a white board for drawing (see Figure 1-8).

Figure 1-8: *Toll-free talk, chat, and white-boarding with CoolTalk.*

- High performance: Many performance improvements, including streaming audio and video, client-side image maps, intelligent LiveCaching, multiple simultaneous loading of pages, and native JPEG decompression reduce the time it takes to get information to your screen.

- Enhanced security: Set up a Personal Certificate to prove your online identity. Conduct business on the Internet with SSL 3.0 (*Secure Sockets Layer*) standards that guard against theft, vandalism, forgery, and invasion of privacy.

- Improved Internet-wide Browsing: Take advantage of virtually all the services the Internet offers—World Wide Web, e-mail, newsgroups, FTP, Gopher, and Telnet, without leaving the comfortable and familiar surroundings of Netscape Navigator.

- Netscape Administration Kit: Customize Navigator 3.0 by setting and locking-in personal preferences.

- Java and JavaScript enhancements: Run Java applets and JavaScript scripts automatically on Windows, Macintosh, AIX, and BSDI platforms.

In summary, Netscape Navigator is cooler than ever. If you're not exactly sure what some of those new and improved features are about, don't worry about it. Most of them are woven into the very fabric of Navigator, seamlessly. Which means that to enjoy these new features, you just have to start up Netscape Navigator Gold 3.0 and go about your normal routine on the Internet.

MOVING ON

Enough chit-chat *about* Netscape Navigator Gold 3.0. It's time to get online, get our hands dirty, and start putting this program through its paces. It's on to Chapter 2, "Browsing the Web, Gold Style."

Browsing the Web, Gold Style

You probably bought Netscape Navigator Gold because you want to create your own Internet presence on the World Wide Web. Smart move. But before you *present* on the Web, there's a very important step you need to take—you need to be really comfortable *using* the Web. In this chapter you'll learn about basic Web browsing and some new features in Navigator 3.0, including the following:

- Jacking into cyberspace
- Getting to a specific Web address (such as http:// www.wherever.com)
- Searching for specific information
- Browsing the new "framed" sites

I'm sure that many of you are already Web-browsing gurus to whom much of the information in this chapter will seem like old news. If you fall into that category, feel free to skim this chapter and then move on to Chapter 3.

Those of you who are new to the Web really need to spend some time learning how to browse the Web, for two reasons. First, you need to see other people's Web sites to get a feel for what Web pages are all about. Second, the Web itself is one of the best resources for the tools and information you need to create a successful Web presence. So, let's start at Step 1.

STEP 1: JACK INTO CYBERSPACE

Before you do anything else, you need to get online, using whatever method you set up (based on the information you gleaned from the "Where to Start " section in the Introduction to this book). I will be using a dial-up account and the Windows 95 Dial-Up Networking program, as many of you will. *Exactly* how you get online depends on what kind of Internet connection you have.

The typical way to connect through dial-up networking follows:

1. Double-click My Computer.

2. Double-click the Dial-Up Networking icon.

3. Double-click the icon for your Internet connection.

4. Click the Connect button.

The modem makes strange sounds, messages appear onscreen, and if all goes well, a little message similar to the one shown in Figure 2-1 lets you know you're connected to your Internet Service Provider (which means that you are on the Internet).

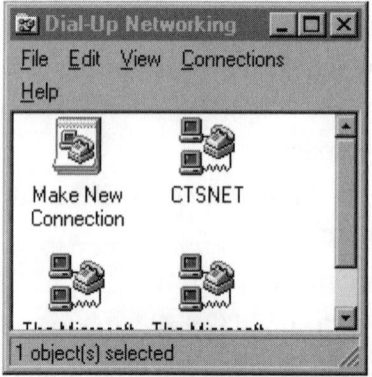

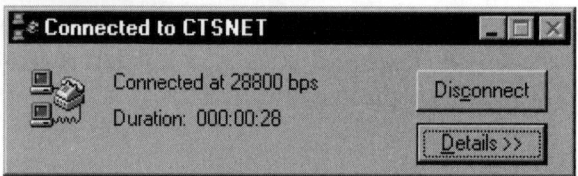

Figure 2-1: *Dial-Up Networking message indicates that I'm connected to my Internet Service Provider.*

TIP

If you don't know how to get your PC connected to the Internet, please refer to Chapters 30 and 31 for discussions of all the options available to you.

STEP 2: FIRE UP NETSCAPE NAVIGATOR

When you're online, you can start Netscape Navigator in either of two ways:

- If you have a shortcut to Navigator on your Windows 95 desktop, just double-click that icon.

- Or click the Windows 95 Start button and choose Programs | Netscape | Netscape Navigator Gold.

In a minute or so, Navigator displays the current contents of Netscape's own home page. Although the site changes daily, your screen will probably resemble Figure 2-2 after you've connected successfully.

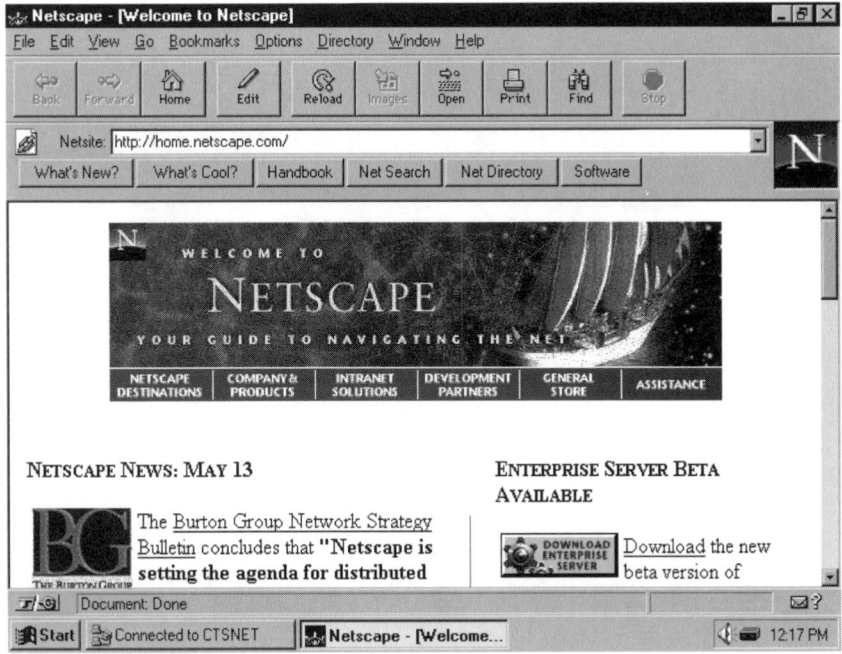

Figure 2-2: *Online, and viewing Netscape's Web site at http://home.netscape.com.*

WHAT'S ON THE SCREEN?

Before we start browsing the Web, let me point out the names of some of the features you see in Netscape Navigator's window, which I'll refer to as I talk about browsing the World Wide Web. Figure 2-3 shows Navigator with the Web page removed, so that you can see exactly which items are part of Netscape Navigator (and not part of the Web site you're viewing).

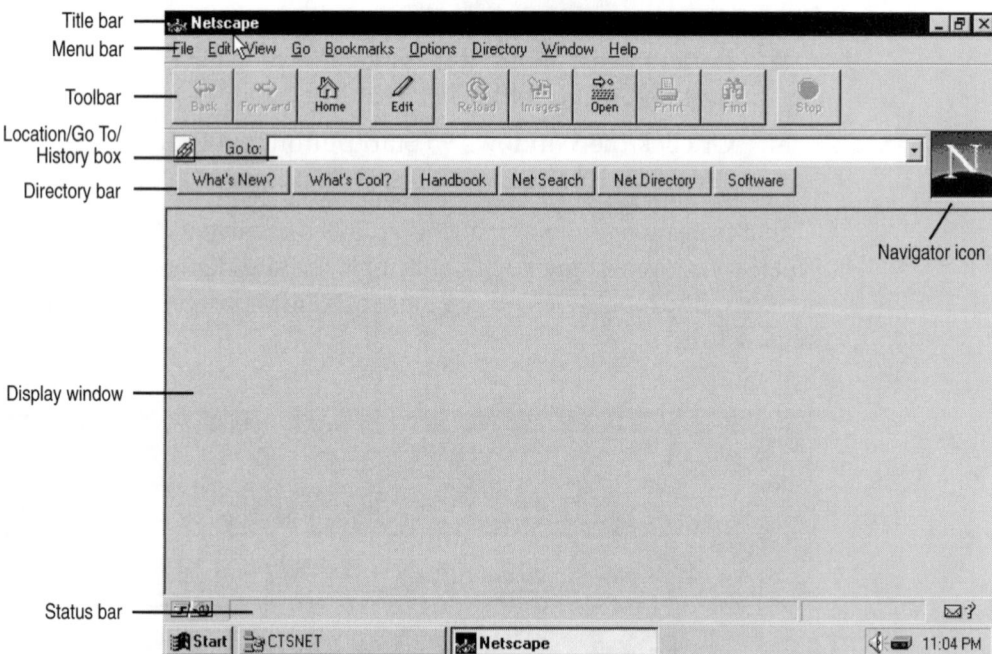

Figure 2-3: *The Netscape Navigator program, without a Web page showing.*

GETTING AROUND THE WORLD WIDE WEB

The World Wide Web is a collection of tens of thousands of Web sites on computers throughout the world. Each site has a unique address, or *Uniform Resource Locator* (URL). The URL of a Web site usually looks something like this: http://www.*somename*.com

Most Web sites consist of several *pages* of information, each of which resembles a short magazine article, or some other specific body of information. The first page you come to when you visit a Web site is that site's *home page*.

There are many ways to go from site to site, and from page to page within a site. All these ways are discussed in the sections that follow.

GOING TO A SPECIFIC SITE

If you know the address (URL) of the site you want to visit, you just need to type that URL in the Location box of Navigator and press Enter. Actually, you can take a couple of shortcuts so that you don't have to erase the URL currently in the Location box and then type the entire new URL.

TRAP

When you type a URL, be sure to use the same upper- and lowercase letters shown in this book. Do not insert any spaces. And be sure to use forward slashes (/), not backslashes (\).

- To erase the current URL and type a new one, first click on the current URL to select it (white text on a blue background). Then just start typing the new URL.
- If the URL you're typing starts with http://, you can omit the http://. For example, instead of typing **http://www.coolnerds.com**, you can just type **www.coolnerds.com**.

■ Optionally, if you want to keep some of the existing URL, just drag the mouse pointer through the part you want to change, and then type only the new part.

As an example of the last technique, let's suppose that you want to visit a site named http://www.weather.com. And let's say that the Location box currently shows http://www.coolnerds.com. Because both URLs have the same beginning and end, you can drag the mouse pointer through *coolnerds* to select that text, and then type **weather** to replace the selected text.

No matter which technique you use, you need to press Enter after you finish typing the URL. The site's home page might take a little while to appear onscreen. While the page is on its way to your computer, the Navigator icon displays a meteor shower, just to let you know it is working. The status bar, near the bottom of the screen, also keeps you posted on Navigator's progress.

TIP

If you omit the http://www *and* com *parts of the URL, you might still get a successful connection. You can get to Netscape's site, for example, by entering just* **netscape** *as a URL. To get to Microsoft's site, you can enter just* **microsoft** *as the URL. If you don't get the result you expected, you'll need to type in the complete URL.*

When you see Document: Done displayed in the status bar, you are "in" that site, and its entire home page is now in your computer and on your screen. Say, for example, that you enter **http://www.weather.com**, the URL for the Internet's Weather Channel, as the site you want to visit. When you press Enter the meteor shower rains down for a few seconds, the status bar flashes some messages, followed eventually by the Document: Done message, and the home page for the Weather Channel appears on your screen (see Figure 2-4).

Figure 2-4: *Entering **http://www.weather.com** in the Location box takes you to the Weather Channel's site.*

POINT MY WHAT WHERE?

You might often see or hear an instruction telling you to point your Web browser to http://www.*whatever*.com (*whatever* stands for an actual site address). What that means is to type the entire URL (http://www.*whatever*.com, in this example) in the Location box on your Web browser, and press Enter.

To return to the site you just came from, click the Back button in Navigator's toolbar.

USING HYPERLINKS

Most Web pages include *hyperlinks,* or little *hot spots,* of brightly colored, underlined text that, when clicked, take you to another page in the current Web site, or perhaps to an entirely different Web site. Netscape's home page, which is the first one you (probably) encountered when you started Navigator, contains many hyperlinks. For example, in Figure 2-5, the small "buttons" across the bottom of the headline (*Netscape Destinations, Company & Products,* and so forth), and the underlined text (*Burton Group...* and *Download*) are all clickable hot spots.

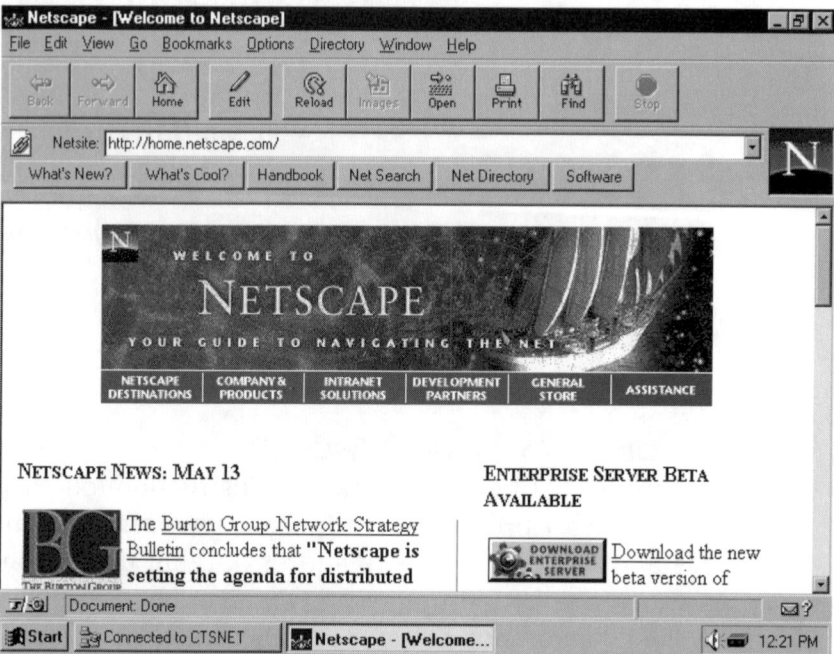

Figure 2-5: *You can see lots of hot spots on this page (http://home.netscape.com).*

It's not always easy to tell, at first glance, whether a chunk of text or a picture is a clickable hot spot. But there's a simple way to find out:

- When you move the mouse pointer to a hot spot, the mouse pointer turns into a pointing hand.

- The status bar displays the URL of the site you'll get to by clicking the hot spot.

When you click a hot spot, the meteor shower starts again and the status bar keeps you informed of Navigator's progress. But you don't have to take my word for it. If you're browsing the Web right now, go ahead and click any hot spot on your screen to see for yourself.

VISITED & UNVISITED LINKS

You might notice that some of the hyperlinks on a page are blue or have a blue border around them, and that others are red or have a red border. The difference between the two is as follows:

- A blue link indicates a site you've never visited.

- A red or magenta link indicates a site you have already visited.

It's possible that you'll see an entirely different color scheme, because the people who publish Web pages can color visited and unvisited links as they please. (And you can control the color scheme in your own copy of Netscape Navigator.) For more information, see Chapter 32.

TIP

When you're in a Web site that you think you'd like to visit again in the future, you can bookmark *that site. Just choose Bookmark | Add Bookmark from Navigator's menu bar. Then, to return to the site, choose Bookmark from Navigator's menu bar and click the name of the site you want to revisit. Chapter 24 will discuss techniques for managing a large collection of bookmarks.*

SEARCHING FOR SPECIFIC INFORMATION

It's fun to browse the Web, letting the hyperlinks take you where they may. Sometimes, however, you'll want to explore a particular topic or look for specific information. In that case, you can use a Web *search index* (also called a *search engine*) to look up sites in the same way you might look up pages in the index of a book.

Now for a quick crash course on using Yahoo, one of the more popular Web search indexes. Point Navigator to http://www.yahoo.com (just type **yahoo** in the Location box and press Enter). You'll come to Yahoo's home page, shown in Figure 2-6.

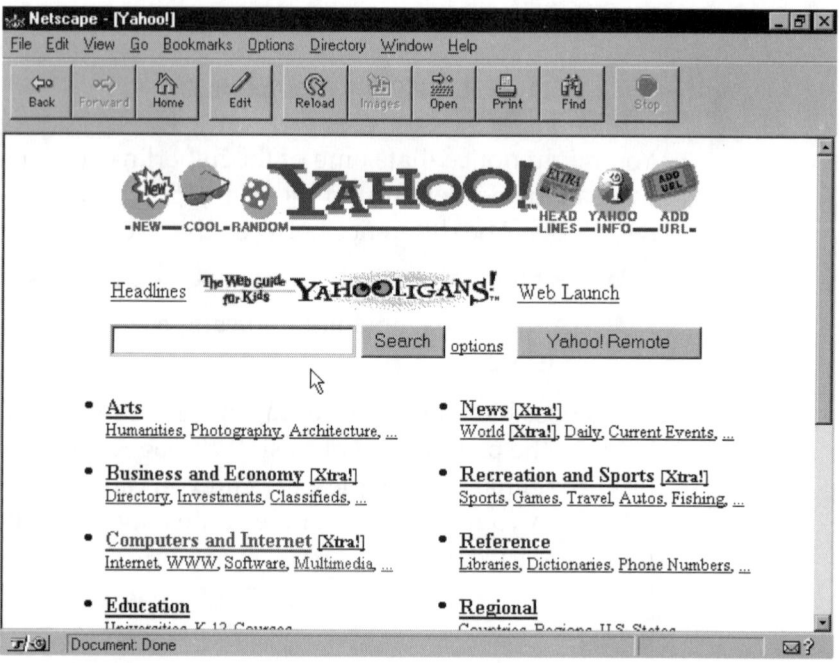

Figure 2-6: *Yahoo's home page.*

To use the index, type a word, or words, in the little text box, and then click the Search button. Say, for example, that you're thinking about getting a Great Dane (the canine variety) and want to see what information and resources you can find on the Web. Just type **great dane** and then click the Search button.

All the sites in the next page you see contain some information about Great Danes, as in the example shown in Figure 2-7. Because the list may include several pages of resources, be sure to browse down to the bottom of the page.

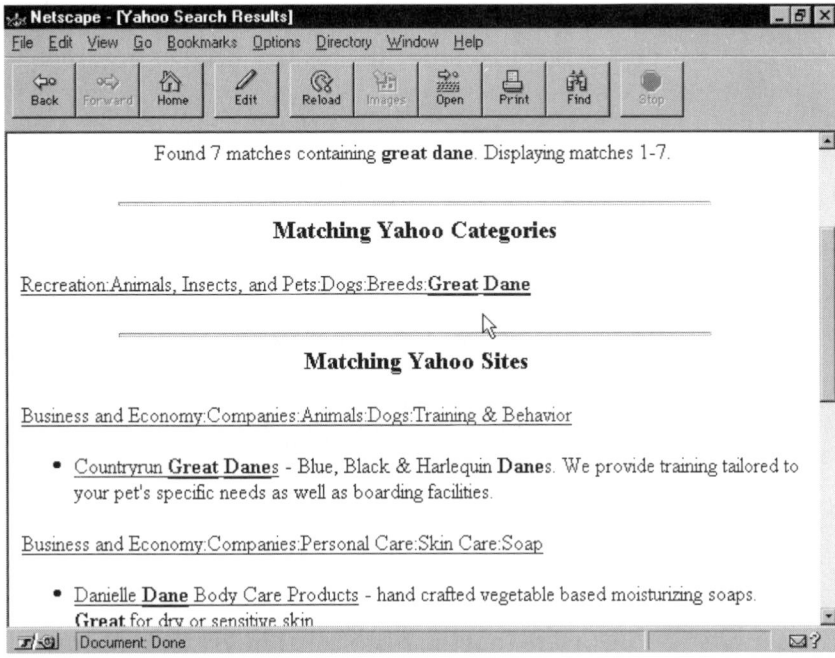

Figure 2-7: *Results of searching for great dane in Yahoo.*

If a site looks interesting, just click its hyperlink. You'll be taken right to the site. To get back to Yahoo, click the Back button in Navigator's toolbar until the Yahoo page is displayed. The process is quick, easy, and a terrific way to get a great deal of free information about *any* topic.

As mentioned earlier, Yahoo is just one of many search indices on the Web. For more information about searching the Web, see Chapter 24. Now, however, I want to tell you about some features (such as the Back button) on your Navigator screen.

POPPING BACK TO A RECENT PAGE

As you move from site to site and page to page, Navigator's *history list* keeps track of the places you've visited. The following steps show a simple way to return to a site that you've visited recently:

1. Click the drop-down list button to the right of the Location box to display the history list (see Figure 2-8).

2. Click the URL of the site you want to go to.

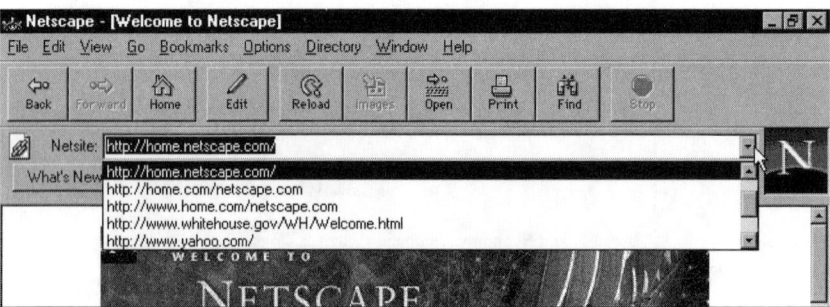

Figure 2-8: *You can revisit a recently visited site by choosing its name from the history list.*

Be aware that the history list might not show its entire content right away. If you see a scroll bar to the right of the list, you know that the list contains additional URLs. You can use the scroll bar to scroll up and down the list. When you see a URL that you want to revisit, just click on that URL.

TIP

The history list and its buttons refer to the current session only. Bookmarks, discussed in Chapter 24, let you keep track of favorite sites through multiple sessions.

The Back and Forward buttons in the toolbar provide a handy shortcut to cruising through the history list. To move back a page in the list, just click the Back button; to move forward again, click the Forward button.

In addition to using the drop-down list and buttons to move through recently visited sites, you can use the following techniques:

- Click Go in the menu bar, and choose a recently visited site from the bottom of the menu.

- Choose Window | History (or press Ctrl+H) to display the history list in a window. Then click on any site and click the Go To button. Click the Close button when you want to close the history window.

ALL THE WAY HOME

If you get lost and want to go all the way back to the very first page you saw at the start of the current session, click the Home button in the toolbar.

STOP! (THIS IS TAKING TOO LONG)

The millions of us who use telephone lines to connect to the Internet all share a common misery—getting to a Web site can be dreadfully slow. At peak hours, getting to a popular Web site can entail an unbearably long wait. If you reach a boiling point while trying to view a site and decide to give up and go somewhere else, all you have to do is click the Stop button in the toolbar. The meteor shower will stop, the hourglass (or other) indicator will disappear, and you'll be in control of your system again.

TIP

You can choose between slower browsing with *graphics, or faster browsing* without *graphics at any moment. Just choose Options | Auto Load Images to switch between the two modes. For more information, see "Speeding Up the Image Display " in Chapter 32.*

RELOAD THIS PAGE

You might notice that when you first go to a new Web site, the page can take a fairly long time to appear onscreen. When you revisit the page, using the Back button or history list, display of the page is much faster. The reason is described next.

When you visit a Web site for the first time, that site's home page is sent to your PC through the modem—a fairly slow process. As the page comes into your PC, Navigator automatically makes a copy of that page and stores it on your hard disk in a folder called the *cache* (pronounced *cash*).

When you revisit a recently visited page, Navigator doesn't bother to reload the entire page through the modem. Instead, it just reloads the page from the cache on your hard disk. This process helps speed things along as you're browsing the Web. The one slight disadvantage is that if the Web site has changed since your last visit, you won't see the latest changes.

You can easily overcome this problem by using the Reload button in Navigator's toolbar. When you click that button, you force Navigator to go to the original Web site and reload the entire current page. (If it can.)

"USING PREVIOUSLY CACHED COPY..."

When you fire up Netscape Navigator offline (i.e., without being connected to the Internet), Netscape displays a message that it is "Unable to locate the server...Using previously cached copy instead." What the message really means (usually) is, "You're not connected to the Internet right now, so I can't get that page for you. You do have a copy of that page from some previous session, however, so I'll display that copy."

The cache copy might not contain all the graphics of the original copy, because Navigator doesn't want to eat up too much disk space storing old pages, and large graphics, sound, and other multimedia files take up huge amounts of disk space.

A couple of scenarios will prevent the Reload button from doing its job. The first (and perhaps most obvious) is when you're working offline (when you're using Navigator without being connected to the Internet via your modem).

A second possible scenario is that the *server*—the computer that contains the page you want to view—is down (not working). In either case, clicking the Reload button simply reloads the cached copy from the hard disk.

NAVIGATING FRAMED SITES

Some Web sites offer *frames*, wherein your browser screen is divided into two or more windows or frames, each of which can display independently its own Web site, page, or section of a page. To see an example of a framed site, follow these steps:

1. Point your Web browser to http://home.netscape.com.

2. Scroll down to the bottom of the page.

3. Click the Show Frames button at the far right of the on-screen toolbar.

Your browser window will be divided into five frames, as in Figure 2-9.

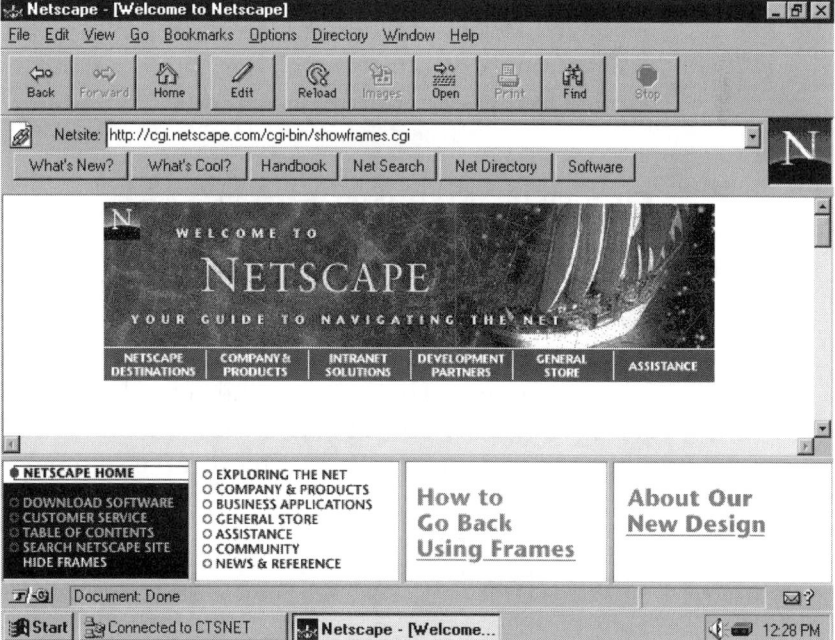

Figure 2-9: *Netscape's home page, with frames turned on.*

The topmost, largest frame is the "normal" display window for the Netscape site. It has its own scroll bar, off to the right. The bottom frames offer a table of contents and a couple of tutorials (*How to Go Back Using Frames* and *About Our New Design*). You can jump to any topic in the table of contents by clicking that topic. Click either of the tutorial links for information on those topics.

Navigating in a framed site is pretty much the same as navigating in any other site. The Back and Forward buttons take you back and forward in the current frame. You can also move through frames independently by right-clicking in the frame and choosing an option from the pop-up menu that appears.

TIP

Many framed sites offer the option to turn off the frames. In Netscape's site, the Hide Frames button is in the frame nearest the lower left corner of the screen.

If you don't find the command you're looking for in the pop-up menu, then just click (with the left mouse button) the frame you want to work with. That frame becomes the active one (indicated by a thin black border around the frame). When you choose commands from Navigator's menu bar, the commands you choose are applied to that currently active frame.

GETTING ONLINE HELP

As a Windows user, you're probably familiar with online help—that you press the F1 key to get help right on your screen. Online help in Netscape Navigator is a little different, in the sense that it is literally online. That is to say, the help files for Netscape Navigator are actually on Netscape's Web site, and are available only when you're connected to the Internet (i.e., online).

Navigator's help is also unique in that it's set up more like a
Web site, with hyperlinks, than a typical Windows help file. To get
online help in Navigator, follow these steps:

1. Make sure you're online (connected to the Internet).

2. Click Help in Navigator's menu bar (see Figure 2-10).

3. Choose whatever topic in the menu seems appropriate. If
    you're just looking for general help, click on Handbook.

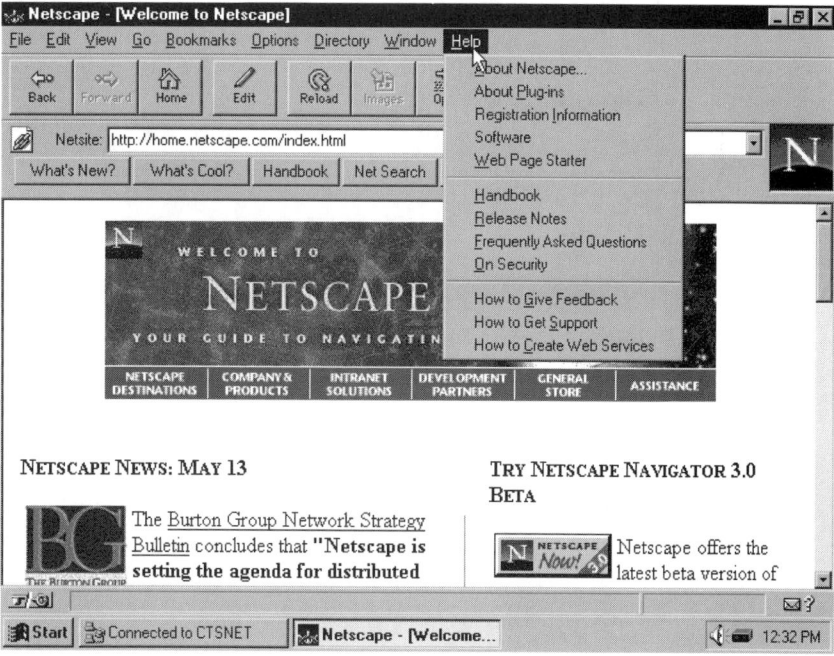

Figure 2-10: *Navigator's Help menu.*

In the online Handbook you can scroll down to the Tutorial and
Reference sections (see Figure 2-11). The Tutorial options present
information in lesson format. In the Reference section you can
look up information by topic.

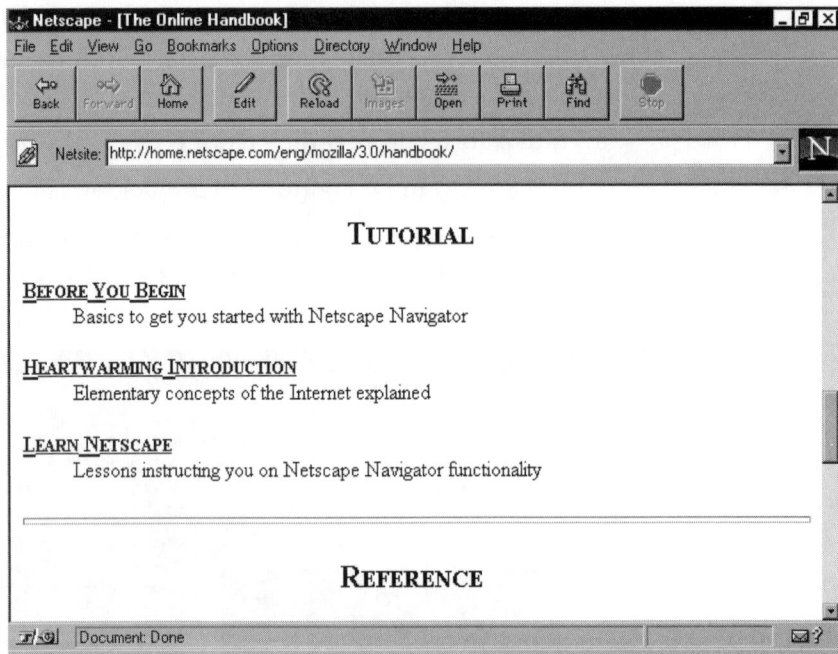

Figure 2-11: *The Tutorial and Reference sections of the online Handbook.*

An index (see Figure 2-12) follows the handbook section. Feel free to use the online Handbook to supplement what you learn here, and to get some hands-on experience while you're learning.

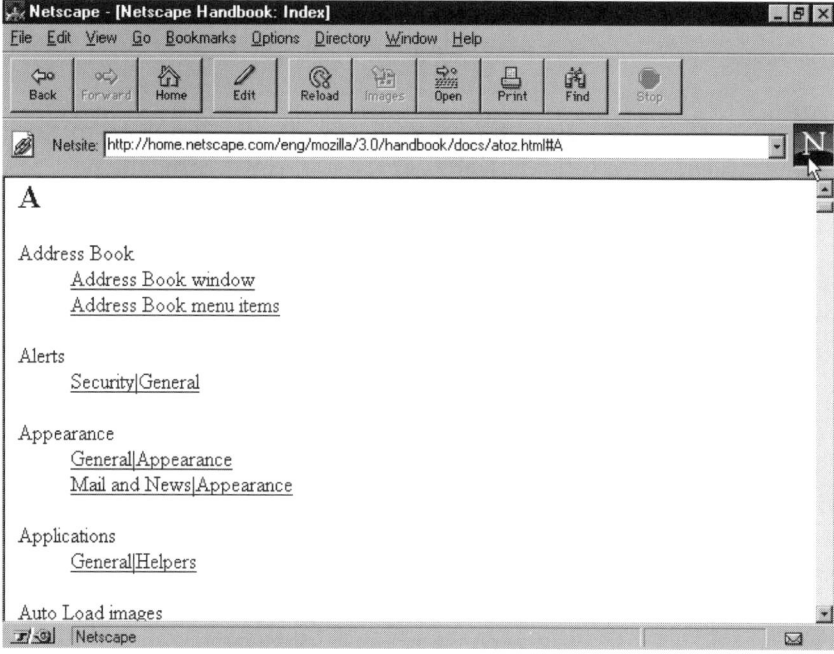

Figure 2-12: *The online Handbook has its own index.*

SITE SEEING

Not everything on the Internet is *about* the Internet. There are Web sites covering every topic imaginable. When you want to take a break from all the technical stuff on the Internet, and get good practice, try pointing your Web browser to any of the following sites that interest you:

- Art: Why not start with a tour of the WebMuseum at http://sunsite.unc.edu/louvre? Or visit the Andy Warhol Museum at http://www.warhol.org/warhol/warhol/html. Or search Yahoo for *art*.

- Business: Grab the latest business info from Reuters at http://www.bizinfo.reuters.com/index.html. Or check out Business Opportunities Online at http://www.trinidad.net/cartis.

- Education: Try CyberKids at http://www.cyberkids.com. Or maybe cruise by Apple Computer's Virtual Campus at http://hed.info.apple.com/home.html.

- Entertainment: How about a laugh from Rodney Danger-field at http://www.rodney.com/rodney/joke.of.the.day/joke.html? Or swing by http://www.movielink.com.

- Government: Bill and Hillary currently host http://www.whitehouse.gov. Or check out the Fed Center at http://199.171.16.49.home.html.

- Health: For traditional medicine, check out Physicians Online at http://www.po.com. If you're into alternative medicines and herbs, take a gander at http://www.herbweb.com.

- News: CNN Interactive is always at your beck and call at http://www.cnn.com. Or how about WorldNews Online at http://worldnews.net?

- Recreation: If you're into thrill rides, zoom to http://www.coasters.net/Coasters. If gardening is more your speed, take a peek at the American Horticultural Society's site at http://eMall.com/ahs/ahs.html.

- Sports: It's hard to beat http://espnet.sportszone.com for sports coverage. But there are some other great resources out there. Take a swing at http://www.sportsline.com, for starters.

MOVING ON

I hope you'll take a few minutes to click around and browse the Web, just to see some sites. And maybe take a crack at searching Yahoo (www.yahoo.com) for topics that interest you. The practice is good, and will help you feel comfortable with the World Wide Web. In the next chapter, I talk a little more about Web browsing and focus on new capabilities in Version 3.0 of Netscape Navigator Gold 3.0.

Multimedia & 3D Virtual Worlds

Multimedia *Web sites* are those that contain sound and/or video in addition to the standard text and pictures. *Virtual worlds* are Web sites that offer 3D space in which you can move around freely. Instead of being limited to scrolling up and down, you can also "scroll" closer in, farther out, and all around.

Historically, to enjoy multimedia and 3D you had to download and install special software, perhaps do some tweaking, and go through other inconveniences. But now it's all sort of a no-brainer, because Netscape Navigator has all the tools you need built right in. In this chapter you'll learn to use the tools. Specifically, you'll learn about the following:

- Enjoying sound with LiveAudio
- Viewing video with LiveVideo
- Exploring 3D virtual worlds with Live3D

 ## ENJOYING SOUND WITH LIVEAUDIO

Navigator 3.0 comes with LiveAudio, a built-in tool that can play inline audio and external sound files without special helper apps. To take advantage of LiveAudio you need the following:

- A multimedia PC, or PC with an MPC-2-capable sound card (i.e., one that can play 16-bit sounds and general MIDI)
- At least a 486 processor, running at 50mHz
- Windows 95
- At least 8MB RAM (16MB recommended)

BEFORE YOU BEGIN

If you haven't used your sound card recently, you should check to make sure that it's working. Here's a little checklist to go through:

- Are the speakers turned on, and the volume turned up?
- Is the volume in Windows 95 turned up? Click the little speaker icon in the taskbar, or choose Start | Programs | Accessories | Multimedia | Volume Control, and make sure that the sound is not muted or turned down too low to hear.
- Is any program other than Navigator using the sound card at the moment? If so, close that program.

If the answer to all of these questions is Yes, and you're sure that the sound card is installed correctly and the speakers are connected correctly, you should be able to play a sound right from the Windows 95 desktop. If you want to conduct a test, follow these steps:

1. Click the Start button and choose Settings | Control Panel.
2. Double-click the Sounds icon.
3. In the Sound section of the dialog box that appears, use the Name or Browse button to locate any sound file.
4. When the Preview box shows a sound file's icon, click the Play button (a right-pointing triangle just to the right of the Preview icon).

You should hear the selected sound. If you don't, go through the preceding checklist again. You might also want to see if you're having a hardware conflict, because sound cards are known to conflict occasionally with other devices. To check for and resolve hardware conflicts, click the Windows 95 Start button. Then choose Help | Contents | Troubleshooting | If you have a hardware conflict.

USING LIVEAUDIO

You don't have to do anything special to use LiveAudio, because it's already integrated into Netscape Navigator 3.0. When you come across a Web site that contains background music (or voice), LiveAudio just kicks in automatically and plays the sound.

You might also encounter "external" sounds—sounds that don't play automatically. In these cases, however, you'll see a link or icon that you can click to start the sound and bring up the LiveAudio controls (see Figure 3-1). In some cases, you might even see the LiveAudio controls right on the page, ready to go.

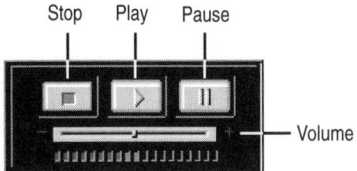

Figure 3-1: *LiveAudio controls.*

To use the LiveAudio controls:

1. Click the Play button to start playing.
2. Click the Stop button to stop playing and rewind to the beginning.
3. Click the Pause button to pause play (and to resume paused play).
4. Use the Volume slider to adjust the volume.

Navigator 3.0 has made audio webbing that simple. But be aware that downloading a sound file can take time. If you don't hear sound when you expect to, take a look at Navigator's status bar. The problem might simply be that you haven't fully downloaded the sound file yet.

Multimedia is so popular that, in your day-to-day Web browsing, you'll probably stumble across plenty of Web sites that include sound. Just in case you don't, the "Site Seeing" section near the end of this chapter points out some good audio sites.

USING LIVEVIDEO

LiveVideo plays video AVI files (movies) in Web sites. To use LiveVideo, you need a multimedia PC. LiveVideo is built right into Netscape Navigator 3.0, and thus doesn't require any special setup or installation.

TIP

If you want to play MPEG and other video formats, see Chapter 25, "Plug-Ins, Java & LiveConnect," for information about plug-ins.

When you're browsing the Web, you may come across sites that offer *inline video*—the movie starts playing as soon as you open the Web page. You might also come across external video images that you start by clicking a link or icon. Keep in mind that because video files can be *huge*, downloading them to your PC can take several minutes.

After you get a video playing, or see a video frame on your screen, you can use these simple techniques to control the play:

- Click the video to start playing it.
- If the video is already playing, you can click it to stop.
- To rewind, fast forward, or move through the video one frame at a time, right-click the video and choose an option from the pop-up menu that appears (see Figure 3-2).

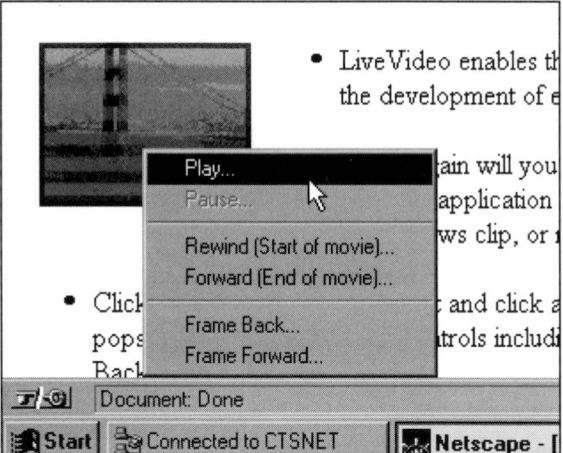

Figure 3-2: *Right-click a video to view LiveVideo's pop-up menu.*

Because video, like sound, is becoming very popular on the Web, chances are you'll come across some video sites in your day-to-day browsing. To check out some video right now, point your browser to some of the sites listed in the "Site Seeing" section of this chapter.

USING LIVE3D FOR VIRTUAL WORLDS

Netscape Navigator 3.0 also comes with Live3D built in. This new feature lets you experience 3D virtual worlds, and also lets you interact with text, images, animation, sound, music, and video—all on a single Web page. Here are some specific features of Live3D:

- 3D navigation: Walk and fly through virtual worlds. Point to destinations. Select camera viewpoints, collision detection, and gravity to add realism to your navigation.

- 3D applications: Play tomorrow's 3D games, participate in chat environments, geographical information systems, interactive systems, authoring environments, online presentations, and database visualizations.

- Animation: Experience the rich lifelike behaviors offered by objects in many 3D worlds.

- Multimedia: Full integration with LiveMedia supports audio and video in 3D worlds.

- High-performance VRML viewing: *Virtual Reality Modeling Language* (VRML) allows Web publishers to create 3D virtual worlds that readers can explore. Live3D allows you, the reader, to explore those worlds at maximum speed through adaptive rendering, background processing, GZIP data compression, and hardware acceleration.

CRUISING VIRTUAL WORLDS

When you point Navigator to a site that offers virtual 3D space, Live3D kicks in automatically and presents a navigation bar along the bottom of the space, as in the example shown in Figure 3-3.

Figure 3-3: *The jeep drives around this 3D space.*

There are several ways to navigate within a 3D space. For example, you can click on an option in the navigation bar, then drag the mouse (with the left mouse pointer held down) in the direction you want to go. Or you can hold down various keys while using the mouse to move. Here's a summary of the various ways to get around the 3D space:

TIP

To hide/display the navigation bar, right-click the 3D space and choose Options | Navigation Bar. To hide/display onscreen navigation help, click the question mark in the navigation bar, or right-click the 3D space and choose Heads up Display | Navigation Help.

- Walk: To "walk" toward an object, choose Walk from the Navigation bar or pop-up menu, then drag the mouse pointer in the direction you want to walk. Or press an arrow key to indicate which direction you want to walk.

TIP

You can get a bird's eye view of most spaces by walking backward. Hold down the Down arrow key for a few seconds to see what I mean.

- Spin: Hold down the right mouse button and drag in the direction you want to go. Or choose Spin from the Navigation bar or pop-up menu, and use the left mouse button to spin.
- Point (zoom in): Hold down the Ctrl key and click where you want to go. Or choose Point from the Navigation bar or pop-up menu, and click where you want to zoom to.
- Look (turn your head to change your viewing angle): Hold down the Ctrl key and drag in the direction you want to look. Or choose Look from the Navigation bar or pop-up menu, and use the left mouse button to "turn your head."

- Slide: Hold down the Alt key and drag in the direction you want to slide. Or choose Slide from the Navigation bar or pop-up menu, and use the left mouse button to slide.

VIRTUAL WORLD OPTIONS

You can also right-click within a virtual 3D space to see a pop-up menu of options (see Figure 3-4) that give you even more control over your view and navigation. Options in this menu are summarized below:

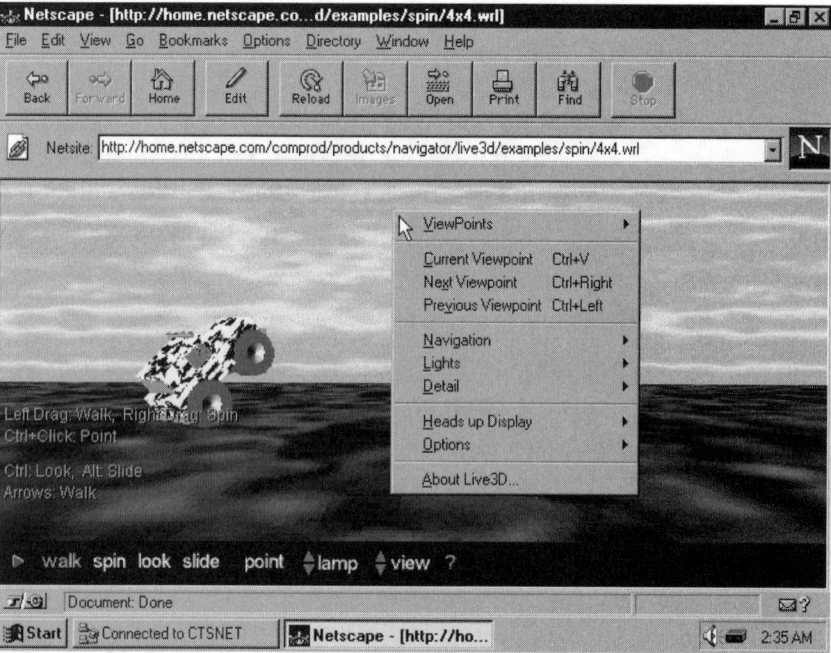

Figure 3-4: *Virtual 3D space pop-up (right-click) menu.*

- ViewPoints: If the space offers multiple viewpoints, the ViewPoints, Current Viewpoint, Next Viewpoint, and Previous Viewpoint options let you change your viewpoint.

■ Navigation: Lets you choose a navigation style for the left mouse button. Also offers Straighten (to get "unlost" if you lose track of where you are), Stay on Ground... (a.k.a. gravity), Bank while Flying, and Collision Detection (which prevents you from walking through walls and other objects).

■ Lights: Presents options for controlling the lighting within the space.

■ Detail: Lets you choose between full-render, wireframe, and point cloud views of the space.

■ Heads up Display: Hide or display pointer cross hairs, onscreen Navigation help, and download status.

■ Options: Choose a rendering style, hide or display the Navigation bar along the bottom of the window, Optimize window size, or choose to make your current settings the default settings for Live3D.

■ About Live3D: Copyright and version information for Live3D.

Simply reading about 3D navigation won't get you very far. The only way to really learn 3D navigation is to go into a 3D space and try everything. You'll probably feel pretty klutzy at first—few of us are accustomed to navigating in 3D space on a 2D computer monitor. But trust me—if you experiment and practice, you'll get the hang of it. Try out some of the virtual worlds listed in the following section.

SITE SEEING

Here are some cool multimedia and 3D sites you can visit, to play with multimedia and get some hands-on experience exploring 3D virtual worlds.

AUDIO SITES

You'll find all kinds of sounds to play with in these sites:

- Headspace Offworld: Inline audio, "Myst"-style navigation. Also offers Shockwave demos (Chapter 25). If you want to maximize your cache settings as recommended in this site, see "Keeping Your Cache on Hand" in Chapter 32. http://www.headspace.com/offworld

- Jerky Boys: Wacky voice clips from the Jerky Boys albums. http://web.mit.edu/tweather/www/wackyass.html

- Music Previews: Preview music from hundreds of labels and artists. http://www.mpmusic.com

- The MIDI Farm: Cool samples and lots of links. http://www.midifarm.com

- Movie Sounds: Sound clips from your favorite movies. http://www.moviesounds.com

- The Verve Pipe: Lyrics, photos, tour info and, of course, sound samples. http://www.thevervepipe.com/music.html

- The Zone: MIDI files of different music genres. http://www.concentric.net/~venom666

AVI VIDEO

Explore these sites to check out some AVI videos:

- Jesse's Movies: All kinds of clips in formats. You can view the AVIs right now. You may need to add some plug-ins (Chapter 25) to view the other formats. http://www.uslink.net/~edgerton/index.html

- Jesse's Sports Movies: Great moments in sports. http://www.uslink.net/~edgerton/sport.html

- Multimedia Movies Archive: More movies. http://tausq.resnet.cornell.edu/mmedia.htm

- Multimedia Page: Videos in .avi format, plus some cool sound files in .wav and .au formats. http://www.wintermute.net

- Netscape's Media Showcase: A little of this, a little of that, all in one place. http://home.netscape.com/comprod/products/navigator/version_3.0/showcase/index.html

VIRTUAL WORLDS

To try out Live3D, just point Navigator to some of these awesome sites:

- Cool Worlds: A great place to learn and practice 3D navigation. http://home.netscape.com/comprod/products/navigator/live3d/cool_worlds.html

- VRML Legit List: Over 50 sites, offering VRML virtual objects and worlds. http://www.geom.umn.edu/~daeron/bin/legitlist.cgi

- Ziff-Davis Terminal Reality: Takes a long time to download, but quite the site for 3D navigation. http://www.zdnet.com/zdi/vrml/content/vrmlsite/outside.wrl

MOVING ON

In this chapter you've learned about multimedia webbing (sound and video), and 3D virtual worlds. As you've seen, Netscape Navigator comes with LiveAudio, LiveVideo, and Live3D already built right in and ready to go, which makes it very easy to enjoy sites that offer multimedia and 3D space.

I know that most of you bought Netscape Navigator Gold for a reason, other than its cool multimedia and 3D capabilities. You bought Gold because it lets you *create* your own Web site—not just enjoy other peoples' sites. So let's get right to the heart of the matter and take a look at what Web *publishing* is all about.

Golden Opportunities (or, Why Create a Web Site?)

No doubt you've heard—from all the people who have done it already, and all the companies trying to sell you products to make it easier still—that creating a Web site is *easy*. But just how easy is it? Well, it's not as easy as, say, falling off a log. You do have to put some time and effort into the process, and you need a *reason* to put in that time and effort.

In this chapter, I want to give you some reasons to contemplate so that, hopefully, you'll start thinking about how you can benefit from the Internet and World Wide Web. Right off the bat I can think of three main reasons to create a Web site:

- Web publishing for fun
- Web publishing for profit
- Great things happen when preparation meets opportunity

WEB PUBLISHING FOR THE FUN OF IT

Most Web sites are created and maintained by individuals, just for the fun of it. Some of these people want to share a hobby, craft, or collection. Some want to socialize—meet people. Many want to publish their own creative works. And some are looking to drum up a little freelance business.

SHARING HOBBIES, COLLECTIONS & INTERESTS

Many people publish information about their favorite hobby, a collection they maintain, or a passion for art. In that way, they meet (online) other people who share the same interest. They can exchange ideas, get good tips from one another, generate a support network, find good products, memorabilia, collectibles, or whatever. In short, they can converse with people, worldwide, who share the same passions. And that's just plain fun. Figure 4-1 shows someone sharing a Teddy Bear collection on the Web.

Figure 4-1: *Sharing a collection or hobby is a good way to meet people with similar interests.*

MEETING PEOPLE

Meeting people, in and of itself, is a perfectly good reason to publish a Web site. Many people post Web sites just to tell who they are and what they're interested in. Interested parties can send e-mail, strike up an electronic conversation, and before you know it, new friendships and relationships are born.

Is it safe to meet people this way? Well, I suppose it's exactly as safe to meet people via the Internet as through any other means. The fact that the Internet is a new technology doesn't mean that it has *more* than its share of deadbeats, morons, and wackos. But because it is open to the public (and is not an exclusive club) the Internet—like any other place where people gather—has its fair share of winners, losers, and regular folk.

If you're interested, you can participate in a wealth of dating services, matchmaking services, and the like. The Get Met home page, shown in Figure 4-2, is an example of one of these services.

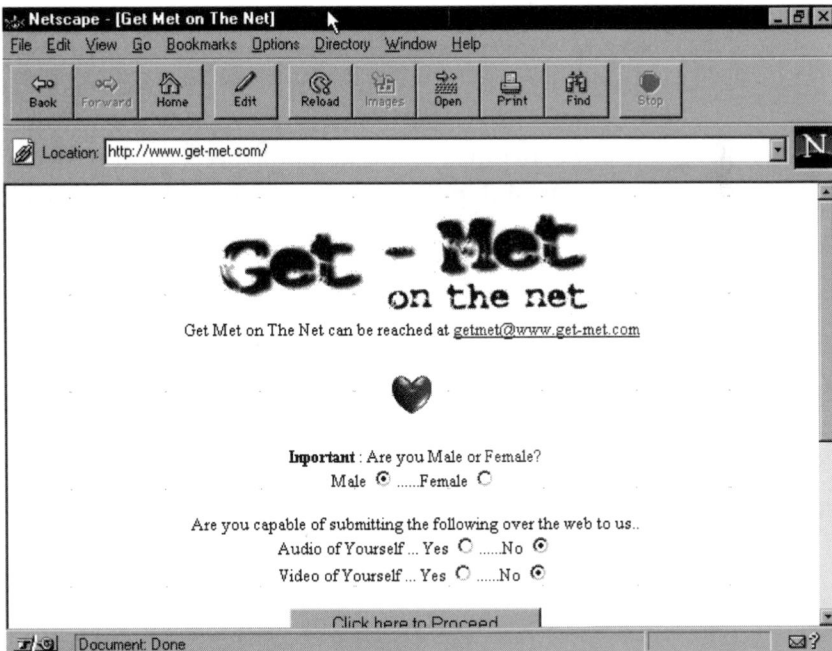

Figure 4-2: *Home page for Get Met on the Net.*

> ### TIP
>
> *Much of the bad press about the Internet centers around adult-oriented newsgroups and chats. These are entirely separate from the Word Wide Web. However, there are also some Web sites that present material that's not appropriate for children, and material that most adults will find distasteful. But, we live in a "freedom of speech" society, so that kind of material will be published.*

BEING PUBLISHED

If you have creative aspirations—perhaps you're an author, poet, artist, photographer, or musician—you probably know how difficult it is to be published through traditional channels. But there are *no* barriers to publishing your works on the World Wide Web. Sure, you may have to shell out a little money to get your Web site started and invest some time in learning how to publish on the Web. But the investment is a good one, because you get instant worldwide exposure. (And it will probably be a heck of a lot cheaper than hiring a public relations firm or talent agency.)

In fact, you could publish your own work and that of others. Be the publish*er* instead of the publish*ee*. Gandolf's Poetry Exchange (see Figure 4-3) publishes works by freelance poets, for example.

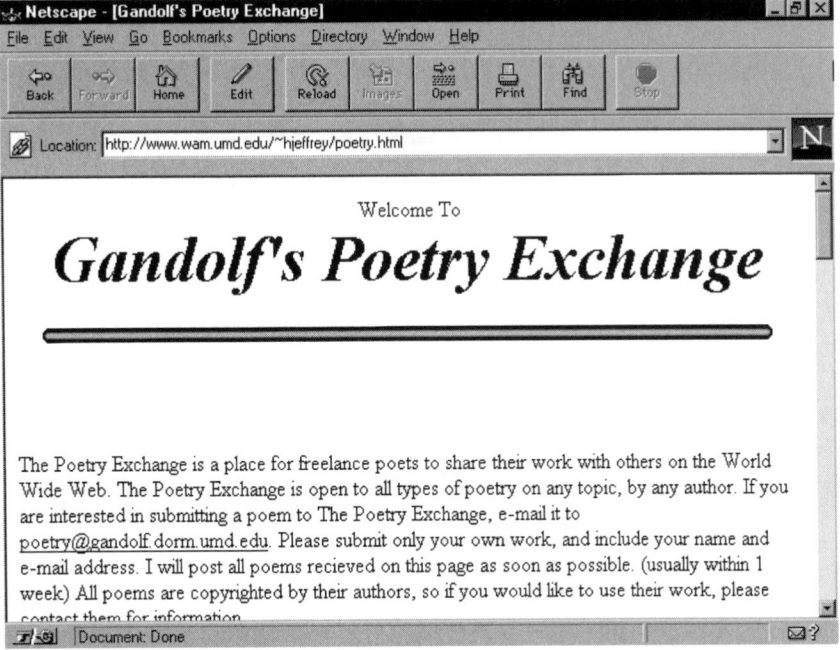

Figure 4-3: *Gandolf's Poetry Exchange publishes the work of freelance poets.*

PROMOTING A SKILL OR SERVICE

If you're looking for a job, or just some freelance work, the World Wide Web is a great place to post your resumé or portfolio. The instant worldwide exposure that the Web provides makes it an ideal place to hang your shingle. Figure 4-4 shows a sample Web site whose author is promoting a freelance graphic design service.

Figure 4-4: *A freelance graphic artist displays his talent.*

Not all sites are as fancy as Josh's. As you browse the Web, you may come across sites that are little more than a business card. But sometimes a business card is all it takes to generate some new business.

WEB PUBLISHING FOR PROFIT

A big question on everyone's mind these days is, "Can I make money doing business on the Net?" The answer is, "Maybe." Although I know of *tons* of people and large companies who are *spending* lots of money doing business on the Net, I don't know of anyone who's actually *making* any serious money. At least, not yet.

A major reason for modest sales via the Web may well be that the Internet is such a new technology. Although people are comfortable exploring the Net and having fun with the technology, they clam up when asked to part with money for goods or services. Some

Internauts are afraid of fraud. Others are (rightfully) leery of sending credit card account numbers and other financial information over the all-too-public Internet. And let's face it—we all feel most comfortable with transactions in which the goods and the money are exchanged, on the spot, with our own hands.

TIP

Chapter 20, "Doing Money on the Internet," explores issues surrounding, and alternatives to, using credit cards for financial transactions on the Internet.

But don't be discouraged. I'm not trying to dissuade you from taking a shot at making your fortune on the Internet. To the contrary, I think the Internet is ripe with opportunity, and that many fortunes will be made. I'm only telling you the downside first, because so many people believe that the minute they post their Web site, the money is going to start rolling in. Sorry, but it just doesn't work that way. I don't know of any easy money and, like everyone else, I'm still *earning* mine. The three ways you might be able to earn some money from a Web site are by selling advertising space, by selling products, or by creating a subscription service.

SELLING ADVERTISING SPACE

If you've spent much time on the Web, you've no doubt seen the little advertising banners that some companies are putting up. What these companies are doing, essentially, is renting space for their banners from the owner of the Web site. Thus, if you have a Web site, you might be able to generate some income by renting out a little advertising space. Sportsline, for example, rents a little "click-me" space in Yahoo's Sports section (see Figure 4-5).

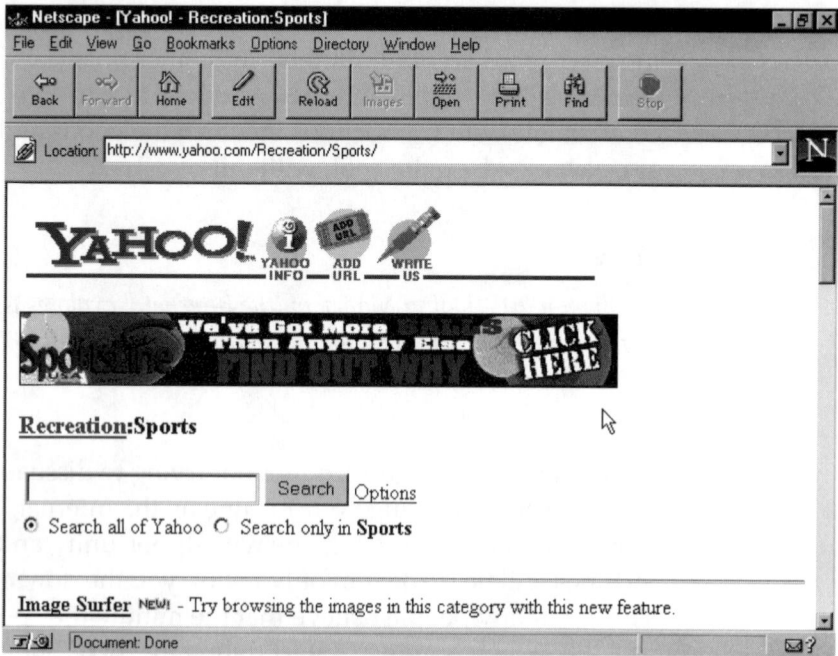

Figure 4-5: *Sportsline rents this ad space from Yahoo.*

Sponsorship is another possibility. If you don't like the idea of plastering your site with ads, some companies may be willing to sponsor you. You just have to give them some subtle sponsorship credit somewhere in your site, with a hyperlink that takes the reader to their sites.

SELLING PRODUCTS ONLINE

If you have a product to sell, you may be able to sell it online. You're not limited to selling software, not by a long shot. For example, GeekGeer (see Figure 4-6) sells T-shirts, hats, pocket protectors, mouse pads, mugs, glasses, pens, and other items for accomplished and aspiring geeks.

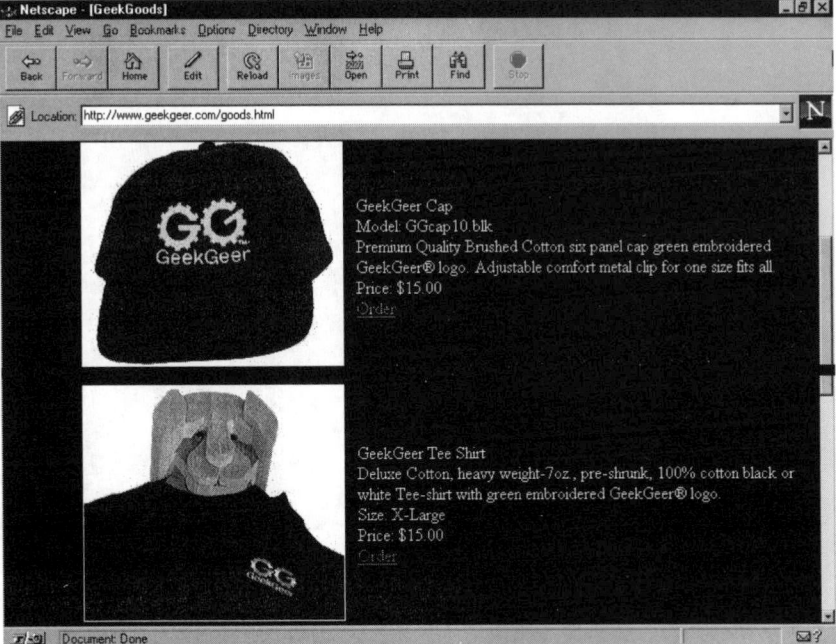

Figure 4-6: *GeekGeer sells hats, T-shirts, and other products from their Web site.*

MARKETING, PROMOTION & INDIRECT SALES

It's not necessary to exchange money over the Internet to make money from the Internet. If you offer a service, post a Web site describing that service. Make it easy for people to find you and contact you. For example, Webs Are Us designs, develops, and hosts Web sites. Figure 4-7 shows their nice Web site.

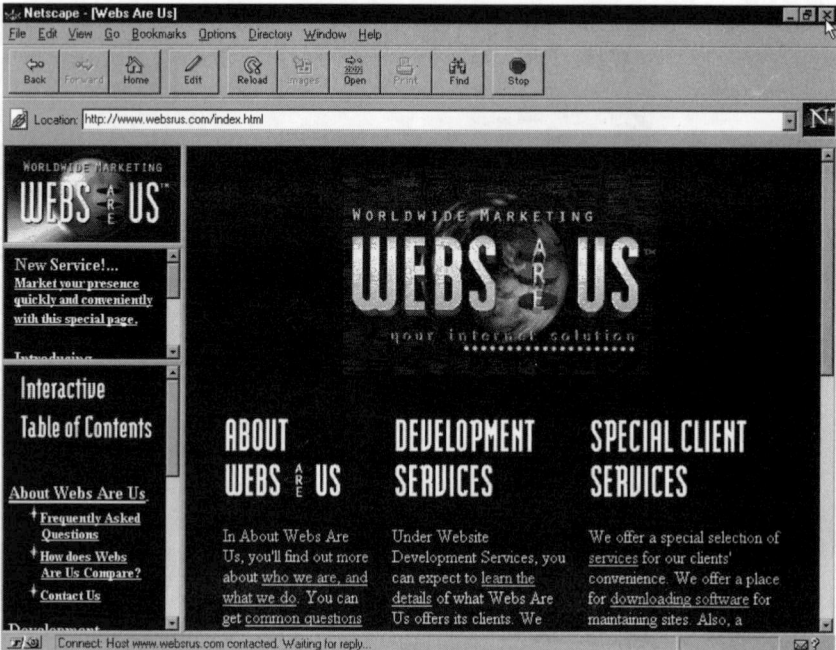

Figure 4-7: *Use the Web to promote your company's goods and services.*

CREATING A SUBSCRIPTION NEWSLETTER

There is no law that says you must give away your information (free) on the World Wide Web. If you have information of value to readers, consider setting up a subscription service and marketing the product on the Web. The Cabot Market Letter (see Figure 4-8) is a subscription newsletter that's sent via e-mail.

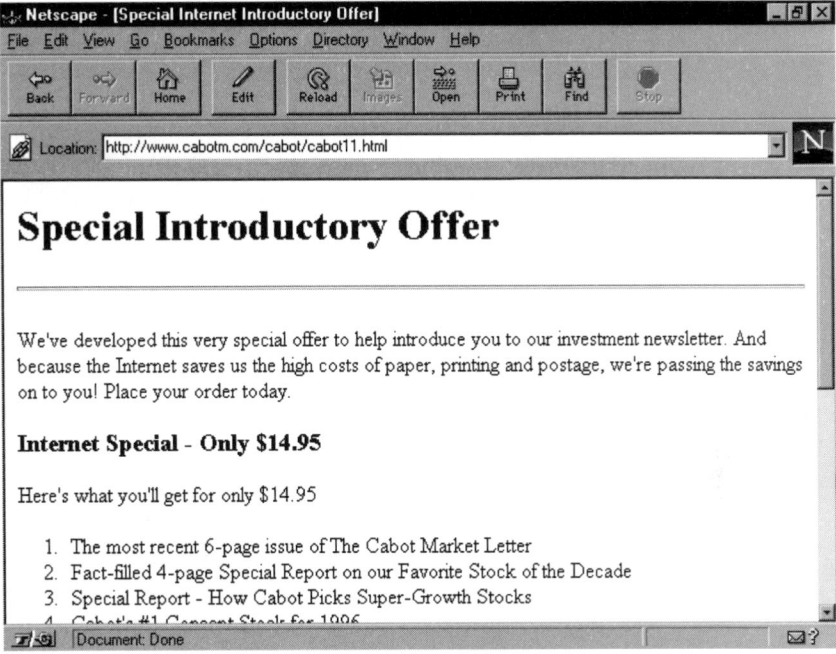

Figure 4-8: *The Cabot Market Letter is an e-mailed subscription newsletter.*

There are many reasons to get involved with the Internet today and ways to earn some money from it. And although nobody can predict the future, the general feeling is that it's all going to get even bigger, better, and more profitable very soon.

PREPARE FOR THE BEST

Although this may sound a little strange, another good reason to get your Web site out there is that you really don't know *what's* going to happen with the Internet. I do know, however, that this whole Internet phenomenon is a tiny sprout emerging from a seed of opportunity. Nobody can predict how big it's going to get, how many fortunes will be made and lost, or even whether it will last. But one juicy scenario, if it plays out, is going to make a good many fortunes.

The process, called *microcharging,* will (theoretically) work something like this: Each person who visits your Web site is automatically charged a dime, a nickel, a penny, or whatever, and that money goes to you, the owner of the Web site.

Now before you say, "Big deal, a penny," do the math. Tens of millions of people are online right now, with 15,000 newbies joining up every day. Plenty of Web sites are already getting 100 to 1,000 hits a day. Some sites are getting 10,000 to 100,000 hits a day. And some of the really big boys get a million hits a day. That's a lotta pennies.

And remember, microcharging is just one scenario. Others might not have been thought of just yet. And, my friend, this big unknown is a really good reason for establishing a presence on the Internet now. To create a Web site, all you need is the know-how, some spare time, and a little cash.

By getting started now on a Web site, you have time to learn what you're doing and to get a feel for what will make your site popular enough for people to drop you a dime, nickel, or penny each time they visit. Then, should the opportunity to start charging a penny arrive, you will be fully prepared to take advantage of the opportunity. And remember—great things can happen when preparation meets opportunity.

SITE SEEING

To look at some of the sample sites shown in this chapter, and explore similar sites, point Navigator to these URLs:

- Bearly a Page Teddy Bears: http://www.aa.net/~urizen/bears.html. For other collections, search Yahoo for the type of collection you're interested in, or for the word *collecting*.

- Get Met on the Net can be found at http://www.getmet.com. Or search Yahoo for *personals* or *dating*.

- Gandolf's Poetry Exchange is at http://www.wam.umd.edu/~hjeffrey/poetry.html. Or search Yahoo for the type of publishing you're interested in, such as *fiction, sci-fi,* or *photography.*

- Josh Designs is at http://village.ios.com/~josh4. To see what other freelancers are up to, search Yahoo for *freelance*.

- Yahoo is at http://www.yahoo.com. To explore current trends and opinions on Web advertising, search Yahoo for *advertising on Web*.

- GeekGeer conducts business at http://www.geekgeer.com. If you're looking for a particular product, search Yahoo for the product name (*tshirt*, for example).

- Webs Are Us appears at http://www.websrus.com. To check out similar services, search Yahoo for *internet presence providers*.

- The Cabot Market Letter is offered at http://www.cabotm.com/cabot.html. Search Yahoo for *newsletter* or *subscription* to check out other subscription services.

MOVING ON

So—what do you think? Interested? Ready to find your place on the Web? I hope so, because Chapter 5, "Finding a Home for Your Page," is going to show you how.

Finding a Home for Your Page

After you've given some thought to what kind of material you'd like to publish on the Web, the next step is to find someone to *host* your Web site. Which is to say, you need to find some space on a *Web server*—a computer that's connected to the Internet 24 hours a day, seven days a week.

If the company you work for has its own Web server, then you probably can put your pages right on that computer. Just ask the company's network administrator how to do so. Those of us with dial-up connections to the Internet will need to "rent" some space on a Web server. This chapter focuses on how to get that Web server space. It explores the following topics:

- Choosing between a personal and commercial site
- Considering optional "extras"
- Shopping around for Web server space

DEFINING YOUR NEEDS

When you're looking for Web space, you'll need to decide whether you want to create a *personal* Web site or a *commercial* Web site. The differences between them involve what the site is likely to cost you, as well as the kind of "extras" you can get with your site. Let's look first at the personal site.

PERSONAL WEB SITE

From the Internet Service Providers' viewpoint, a personal Web site generally is one that doesn't eat up a lot of network resources. For example, a site that uses only a megabyte or so of disk space, doesn't get thousands of hits per day, and doesn't sell products over the Net would probably be considered a personal Web site by most ISPs. The sample site shown in Figure 5-1 certainly qualifies as a personal site.

Figure 5-1: *A sample personal Web site.*

Many Internet Service Providers offer a megabyte of "free" personal Web publishing space as part of the basic package. America Online, CompuServe, and some of the other large commercial online services also offer free personal Web publishing space. If you already have access to the Internet, you might also already have space for publishing your Web pages. To find out, just check with your Internet Service Provider.

Even if your Internet Service Provider doesn't offer Web publishing, you might be able to publish (free) on someone else's Web space. To find someone to give you that free space, you might have to do some digging around: just point your Web browser to http://www/yahoo.com, and search for *Free Web Pages*.

If you can't find some free space just waiting to be filled, you'll need to shop around for an ISP that can give you Web space. You might want to explore services that support Netscape Navigator Gold's one-button publishing, just to make things simpler for yourself. I discuss those services in the "One-Button Publishers" section, a little later in this chapter.

COMMERCIAL WEB SITE

A commercial (or business) Web site is generally one that conducts business on the Internet. This type of service is likely to cost you some money. Depending on your Service Provider, you may also have several options to choose from, including the following:

- Virtual hosting: Lets you give your site a clean, simple URL in the format http://www.*yournamehere*.com. This service can cost from $10 to $100 per month.

- Statistics reporting: Daily reports of the number of visitors you've had.

- Electronic forms: Fill-in-the-blank forms that your readers can use to request information or to place orders.

- One-button publishing: Lets you update your site with a simple click of a button in Netscape Navigator Gold.

- FTP site: A place to store large files that readers can download to their PCs. If you add an FTP drop box, readers will be able to *upload* (send) files to you, as well.

- Toll-free access: The telephone company is involved *only* in the connection between your PC and your ISP. After that, the Internet takes over. If you can find an ISP that can give you toll-free access from your PC, you won't even have to pay for the local call to your ISP.

> **TIP**
>
> *You can start your Web publishing endeavors with free or inexpensive personal Web space. If and when your site outgrows what the ISP considers "personal," you can easily upgrade to a commercial account.*

Any of the sample sites described in "Web Publishing for Profit," in Chapter 4, "Golden Opportunities (or, Why Create a Web Site?)," would qualify as a commercial Web site. The WinZip site shown in Figure 5-2 is another example of a commercial site. Note the custom domain name, http://www.winzip.com, which is the same as the product name. And there's no mistaking that you can do business (place an order) from this home page.

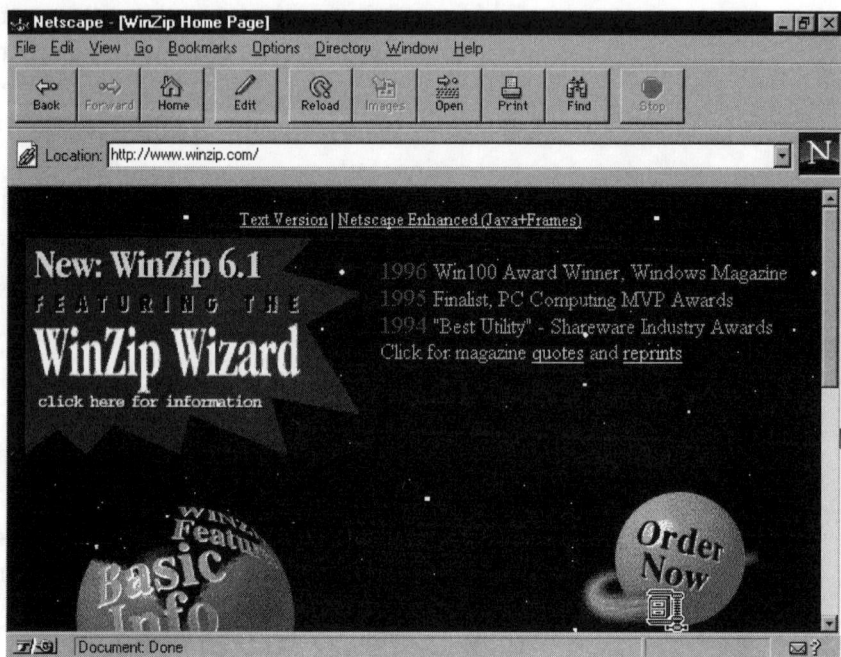

Figure 5-2: *A sample commercial Web site.*

As I said earlier, a commercial Web site isn't likely to come free. If you don't already have some means of publishing a commercial site, you might want to start shopping around. You can start by looking into the services discussed in the next section, "One-Button Publishers."

BUILDING YOUR OWN SERVER

Yet another alternative to publishing on the World Wide Web is to build your own Web server. Although that option is beyond the scope of this book, suffice it to say that you're probably looking at an initial investment of $10,000 or more for hardware and software. Add to that several hundred (or several thousand) dollars a month for a dedicated full-time connection to the Internet. Also, be prepared to invest some serious time and/or hire a full-time person or staff to help out.

I strongly suggest that before you even consider building your own Web server, you create your pages and get them posted on the Web, using an Internet Service Provider. Chances are that the ISP will provide everything you need at a tiny fraction of the cost (and headache) of building your own Web server.

ONE-BUTTON PUBLISHERS

If you have *any* Internet access at all, a good place to look for potential Web server space would be Netscape's list of ISPs that support Netscape Navigator Gold. Here's how to get to that list:

1. Connect to the Internet and start up Netscape Navigator in the usual manner.

2. Go to Netscape's home page at http://home.netscape.com.

3. Scroll down to the Welcome to Netscape! area (see Figure 5-3) and click Creating Net Sites (under the "Assistance" heading).

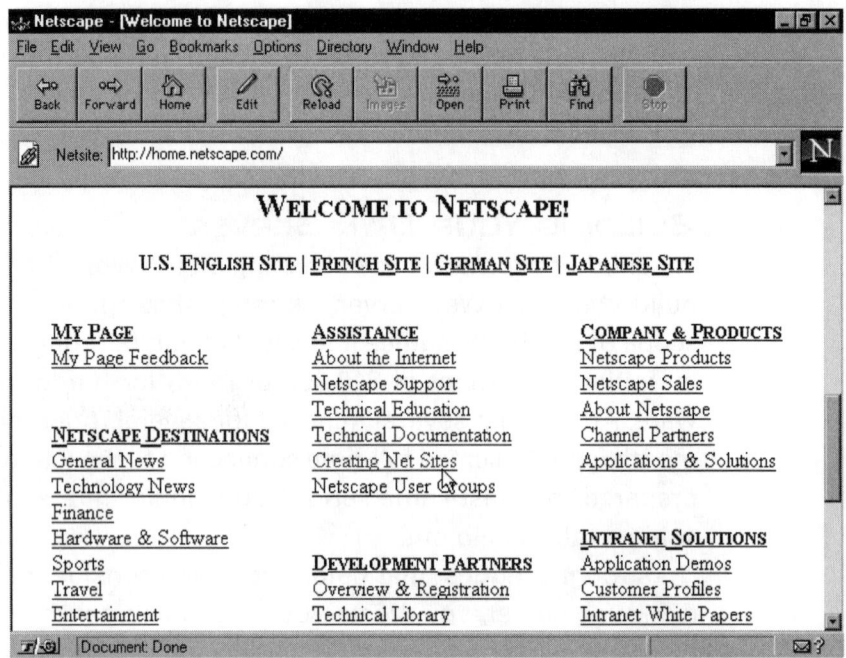

Figure 5-3: *The Welcome to Netscape! page.*

4. Scroll down to the *Netscape Page Starter Site* link, and click it.

5. Scroll down to, and click, *Get Your Page On the Web.*

6. Scroll down the list of ISPs that currently support Netscape Navigator Gold (see Figure 5-4).

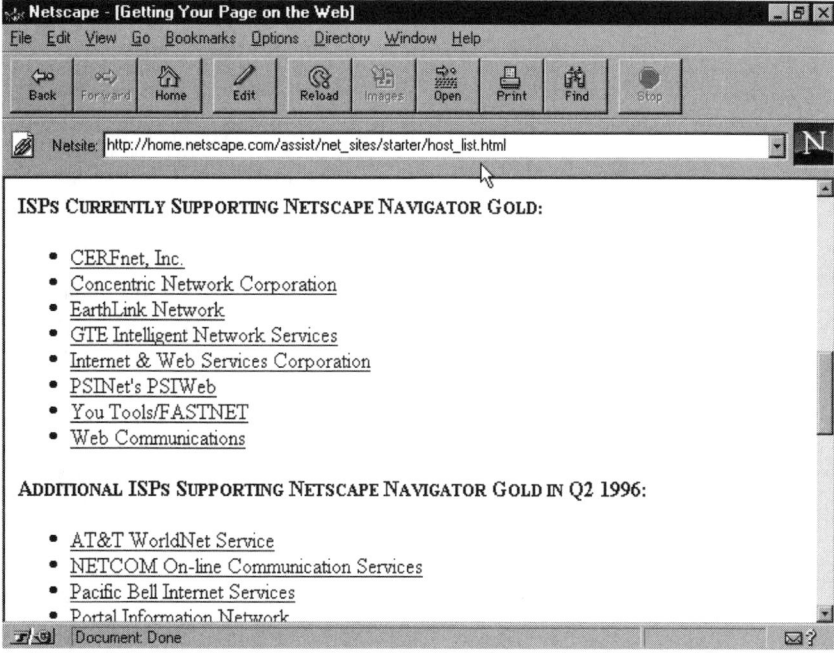

Figure 5-4: *Internet Service Providers that support Navigator Gold.*

NETWORK TRAFFIC CHARGES

Some ISPs charge for *network traffic*, the amount of activity your Web site creates. Traffic is defined in *megabytes*, with one megabyte equal to a million bytes.

To understand how network traffic is calculated, suppose that your Web site contains a couple pages of text and a few graphic images, and occupies 10K (10,000 bytes) of disk space. After 1,000 people have viewed that 10K page, you have generated 1,000×10,000 bytes of traffic. When you do the math, the result is 10,000,000 bytes, which is 10MB of traffic. (To convert to MB, just knock the *,000,000* off the larger number.)

If possible, try to find an ISP that doesn't charge for network traffic, or one that allows for a substantial amount of free network traffic per month.

By the time you read this chapter, the list shown in Figure 5-4 will probably be much longer. So you'll have many vendors to choose from. If you don't have an Internet connection, and can't view that list of ISPs, here are some other resources you can try:

- Check your local newspaper, computer circulars, computer stores, and Yellow Pages for Internet Service Providers in your area.

- Call the one-button publishers listed under "Connecting Through a National or Local ISP" in Chapter 30 to see what kinds of services you can get.

SETTING UP YOUR ACCOUNT

After you've shopped around and decided on an ISP to host your Web site, you'll need to set up an account. The ISP will then set up Web server space for your pages, and provide you with specific instructions on *posting* your pages (copying the pages you create on your PC to the Web server space, for all the world to see).

Unfortunately, I can't offer much help here. How you go about setting up an account with an ISP is entirely up to the ISP. I'm sure, however, that they'll be more than willing to make the process as easy and painless for you as possible. After all, these ISPs are competing heavily for the chance to host *your* Web pages. They would be foolish to do anything that might cause them to lose you as a customer.

MOVING ON

After you have decided on an ISP to host your Web site, you can begin creating your Web pages. Don't worry if your ISP needs a few days to set up your account. The whole process of *authoring* (i.e., creating) your Web pages can take place offline. You don't need the Web server space until *after* you've created, tested, and refined those pages on your own PC.

Creating Your First Home Page

When you have (or will soon have) a place to publish your pages, the next step is to create the pages. You'll probably want to start with a *home page*—the first page visitors see when they point their browsers to your Web site. This chapter shows you how to create your first Web page the easy way—using Netscape's Page Wizard. I'll also overview a couple of other methods. Here's what we'll cover:

- Creating your first home page using Netscape's Page Wizard

- Overview of using Netscape's templates to create a home page

- Overview of creating a home page from scratch

The process of creating even a simple plain-vanilla page will probably take anywhere from 30 to 60 minutes. Ideally, you should try to set aside that much time so that you can concentrate without distractions. If you have only a couple minutes to spare right now, perhaps you should come back to this chapter when you have more time available.

CREATE A FOLDER FOR YOUR SITE

You'll create and work with all your Web pages on your own PC before you send them to the Web server for publication. To keep life simple, you should create on your hard disk a single folder in which to store all the files you'll upload to your Web server. That way, when it comes time to publish, you'll just need to copy the files in that folder to a directory on the Web server computer. Use the standard Windows techniques to create the folder, as follows:

1. Close all windows, and get to the Windows 95 desktop (if you aren't already there).

2. Double-click the My Computer icon.

3. Double-click the icon for your local hard disk (C:), or any other local drive of your choosing.

4. In the folder window that appears, choose File | New | Folder from the menu bar.

5. Type **My Web Site** as the name of this new folder.

6. Click anywhere just outside the new icon to save that new name.

7. To organize your folders, choose View | Arrange Icons | by Name.

That should do it. You should see your folder in with the other top-level folders on your hard drive. In Figure 6-1 you can see mine near the mouse pointer.

Figure 6-1: *Your My Web Site folder will hold the files that you want to publish on the Web.*

WHAT TO NAME YOUR HOME PAGE

Your ISP may require that you give your home page a specific filename. For example, many ISPs require that you name your home page index.html or index.htm. Check with your ISP to find out exactly what filename to give your home page—and jot it down! Keep in mind that, on many servers, filenames are case-sensitive. Be sure to use the correct upper- and lowercase letters when you jot down that home page name.

THREE WAYS TO CREATE YOUR FIRST PAGE

Now you're ready to create your first Web page. You can use any one of the following techniques—based on your current skill level—to create that page:

- Use the Netscape Page Wizard: This is by far the easiest approach, especially for a beginner, but to use it you must connect to Netscape's Web site.

- Use a Netscape template: Slightly easier than starting from scratch, this method creates a preformatted "dummy" page that you can modify by using Gold's editor. You need to connect to Netscape's Web site if you want to use this method. Also, prior experience with any Windows word processing program will be required.

TIP

In this chapter I'll overview techniques for creating Web pages from scratch, and editing the pre-defined templates. Those of you with some Windows word processing experience under your belt will probably find this overview a sufficient head-start. Keep in mind, however, that the real discussion of creating/editing Web pages spans Parts II, III, and to some extent, Part IV in this book!

- Create the page from scratch: This technique is virtually identical to that used for creating a word processing document from scratch. You don't need to be online to take this approach. But once again, prior experience with a Windows word processing program is required.

I'll let you decide for yourself which approach to take to create your own Web page. If you're a beginner, I recommend the Page Wizard. If you're comfortable with basic Windows editing (word processing) techniques, you might try the template instead. If you already have experience creating Web pages, or you can't get connected to Netscape's Web site, you can create your first page from scratch.

USING THE NETSCAPE PAGE WIZARD

Netscape's Page Wizard is the easiest way to create your first home page. To use it you will just get online and fill in a few blanks on the screen. The time you spend online, however, will be more productive if you plan ahead a little.

PLANNING FOR THE WIZARD

Netscape's Page Wizard gives you the opportunity to include some information about yourself, your site, and your favorite Web sites. Think about what you might want to say, and write down your thoughts on a piece of paper, using the guidelines in the sections that follow.

WEB PAGE TITLE & INTRODUCTORY TEXT

Jot down a title for your Web page, as well as some introductory text. The title can be *Your Name's* Home Page, or *Your Name's* Personal Web Page, or anything else you want it to be. You're the one creating this page, and you can come up with any title you like. Just be sure to make it short (a few words).

Next, to introduce readers to your site, include some information. Tell readers a little about yourself, your interests, why you have a Web page, what your page offers. And because you can give visitors links to your favorite Web sites, you might want to mention something about the sites to which you'll be linking them.

FAVORITE WEB SITES

The Page Wizard lets you put up to four links to other pages in your page. While you jot down your notes, be sure to write down the names and URLs of those four favorite sites. If you don't remember the URLs for those sites, but have bookmarked them, you can get online and visit the site from your bookmarks. After you're in a site, its URL will appear in the Location box in Navigator. Just jot down the name and URL of up to four of your favorite sites, as in the example below:

Coolnerds   http://www.coolnerds.com

Netscape   http://home.netscape.com

Ski America   http://www.skiamerica.com

Web Comics   http://www.webcomics.com

CLOSING TEXT & E-MAIL ADDRESS

The Wizard also gives you the opportunity to type a closing paragraph for your page and a hot link to your e-mail address. Write down anything that comes to mind for a closing sentence or two. And include your e-mail address.

VISIT THE WIZARD

Having planned what information you want to put on your page, you're ready to go online and fire up the Wizard. Here's how:

1. Connect to the Internet, and start up Netscape Navigator as you usually do.

2. From Navigator's menu bar choose File | New Document | From Wizard. Your screen will look something like Figure 6-2.

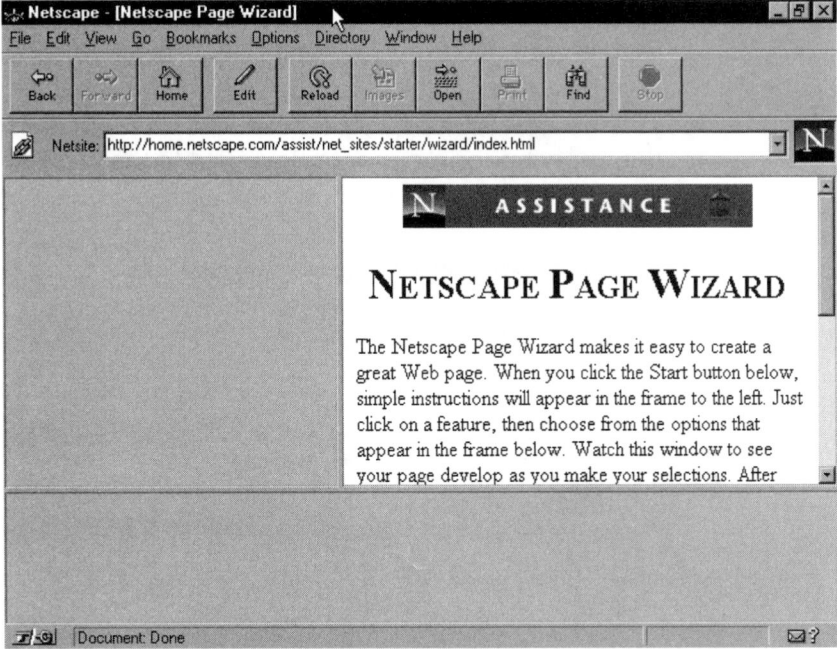

Figure 6-2: *First peek at the Netscape Page Wizard.*

TIP

The reason I say "...will look something like..." is that the Netscape Page Wizard is on Netscape's Web site, which could change its appearance at any time. Should that happen, just be sure to follow the instructions that the Wizard displays.

Notice that the frame on the right has its own scroll bar. You should scroll through and read the instructions in that frame. When you get to the bottom, click the Start button to start building your page.

The rest is pretty easy. The left frame provides instructions, as well as links to options. For example, when you click the link to give your page a title, the lower frame displays a text box in which you can type your page title. Go ahead and type the title, then click the Apply button. Your entry is copied to the preview frame (upper right), as in the example shown in Figure 6-3.

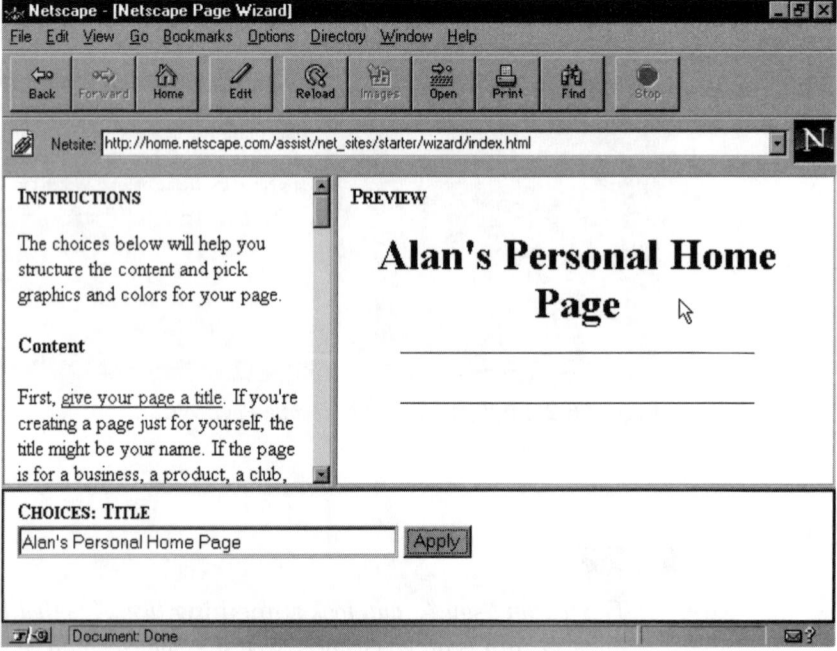

Figure 6-3: *I've typed my title into My Web Site.*

To replace text that's already in the text box, drag the mouse pointer through that text to select it. Then type your own title. Use the Back-space and Delete (Del) keys to make corrections as you type.

After you finish typing the title, you can scroll down through the Instructions frame (upper left) until you get to the next link, *type an introduction.* Click on that link, then fill in the text box displayed in the lower frame. Click the Apply button.

Just keep repeating those basic steps—scrolling to and clicking the next link in the instructions. Fill in the blanks that appear in the bottom frame, then click the Apply button. If you don't see your new entry in the Preview (upper right) frame right away, just scroll down in that frame.

In the section in which you can type hot links, type a site name and a URL, following the instructions near the bottom of the screen (see Figure 6-4). Each time you click the Apply button, your previous entry is cleared from the text box, and you can type another site name and URL. After you've typed as many as four such links, go back to the Instructions frame and scroll down to the next link.

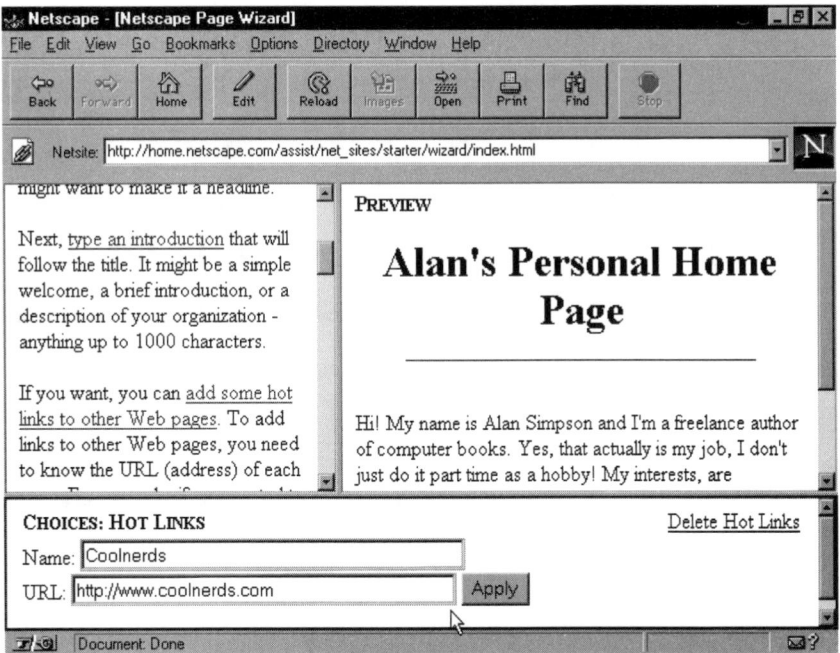

Figure 6-4: *Sample site name and URL typed into the Wizard.*

Finally, type your closing sentence(s) and your e-mail address.

When all the text and links are done, you can start working on the look and feel of your page. You can choose a color scheme, a background pattern, bullet style, and horizontal rule style. Play around, try out some things. Have some fun. Remember, you can scroll up and down through the Preview (upper right) frame to get an idea of the way your page is shaping up.

SAVE YOUR PAGE LOCALLY

When you've finished with the Wizard, you need to save the newly created page to your hard disk. Scroll down to the bottom of the Instructions frame, click on the Build button, and wait a few minutes while the Wizard builds your page. When the Wizard is done, you'll see the full-screen version of your creation, as in the example shown in Figure 6-5. You can scroll through the entire page, using the scroll bar at the right side of the Navigator window.

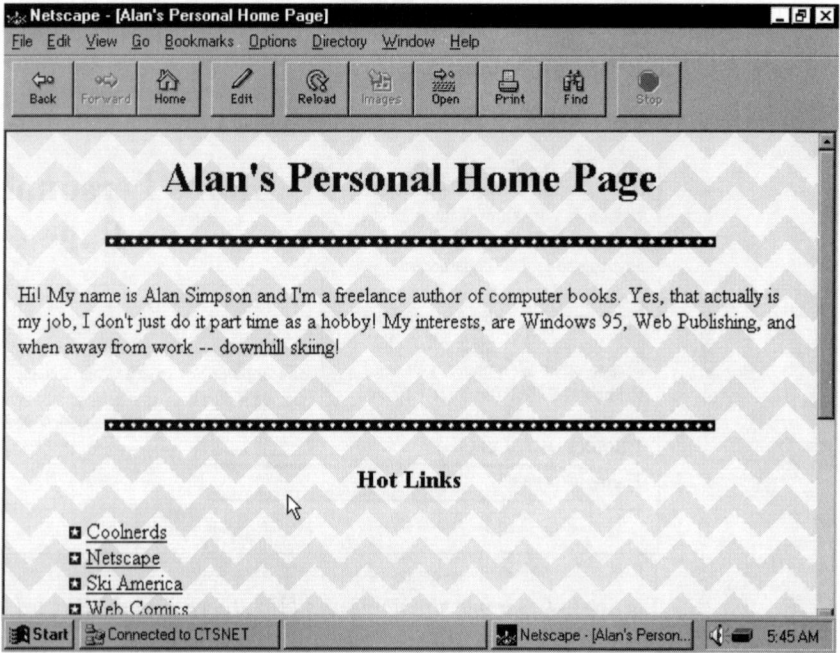

Figure 6-5: *A first home page, ready for saving.*

It's very important to save this page locally, on your own hard disk, so that later you can send it to your Web server for publication. Follow these steps:

1. In Navigator's menu bar choose File | Edit Document. You'll see the dialog box shown in Figure 6-6.

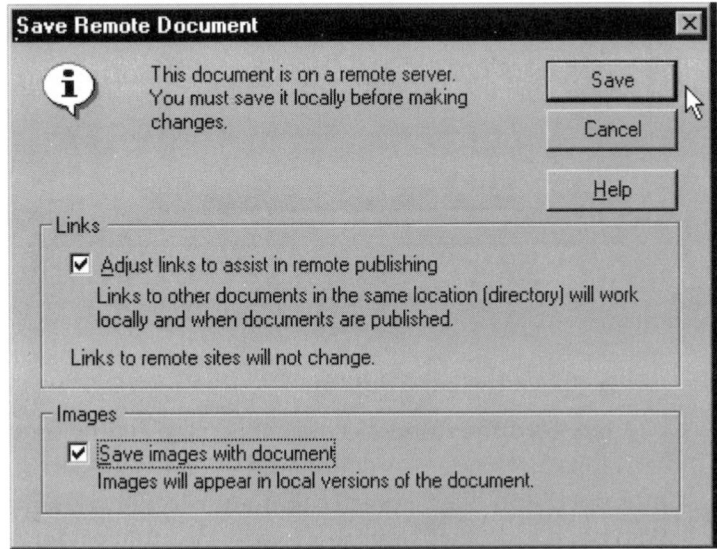

Figure 6-6: *The first dialog box you see when saving your first home page.*

2. You can't edit this page right now because it's on Netscape's Web server, not on your PC. Make sure that both check boxes are checked, then click the Save button.

3. You may see another message, telling you that you're about to download a remote document. (We know that, and it's OK.) If you see such a message, click the OK button.

4. In the Save As dialog box that appears, browse to the folder in which you want to store your page, then type whatever filename your ISP recommends that you assign to your home page. In Figure 6-7, for example, I've chosen My Web Site as the folder, and have named the page index.html.

Figure 6-7: *Saving my first home page as index.html in my My Web Site folder.*

    5. Click the Save button.

There—you're done. Because this page is now on your PC, you can close Netscape Navigator, and even disconnect from the Internet if you like. To verify that your folder contains your new Web page, use My Computer to open up that folder. You should see at least one file for the page you created. If you opted to use custom bullets, lines, or a background pattern, you'll see additional files that represent those objects.

WHY SO MANY FILES?

When you open the My Web Site folder on your PC, you might be surprised to see that it contains several files—not just a single file for your Web page. The reason is that any pictures, bullets, or lines you chose for the page are graphic images, and in Web publishing the graphics are always stored in their own separate files, outside the page. Tags in the Web page tell the browser which pictures to display where on the reader's screen.

When it comes time to upload your pages to your Web server, it's important to copy all the files, including the graphics, to the server. This is why we recommend that you keep your pages and graphics all together in a single folder.

REVIEWING YOUR WIZARD-GENERATED PAGE

Now that the page is on your own PC, you can browse it at any time—even when you're not connected to the Internet. To browse the page, just double-click its icon (index.html, in my example). The page will open right up in your Web browser, as in Figure 6-8. (Note that in that figure, I've changed my screen resolution to give you a better view of the overall page.)

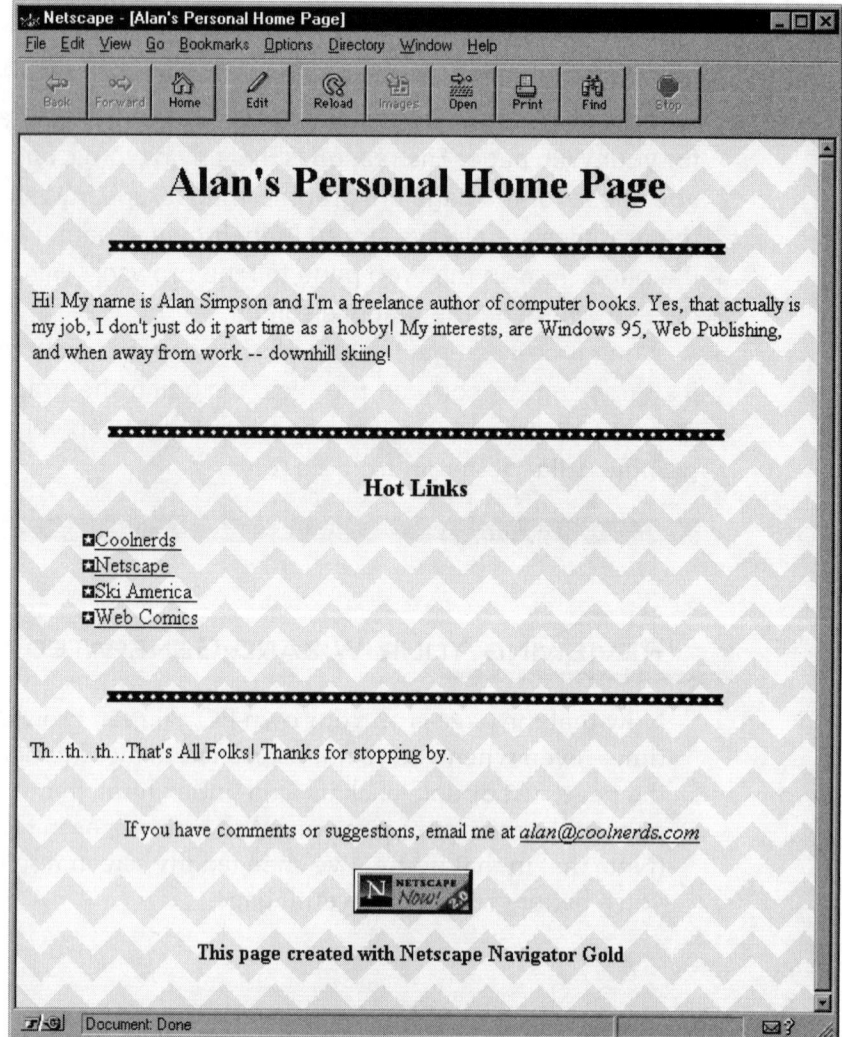

Figure 6-8: *Browsing my home page on my own PC.*

Be aware that if you click one of the hot links in your Web page while you're offline, you'll see a little dialog box like the one shown in Figure 6-9. Don't worry. After you get this page posted on the World Wide Web, those links should work just fine. When you've finished viewing your page, just close the Navigator window again.

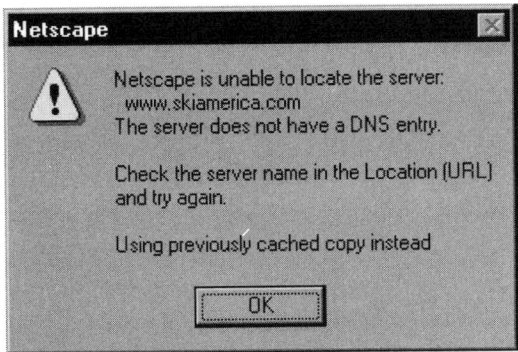

Figure 6-9: *Hyperlinks display this message if you try to browse offline.*

To publish this page for all the world to see, go straight to Chapter 7, "Presenting Your Page to the World," now. If you're not in a hurry, stick around (in this chapter) and explore other alternatives for creating Web pages.

USING A TEMPLATE TO CREATE YOUR FIRST PAGE

As an alternative to using the Page Wizard to create your first Web page, you might consider using one of Netscape's templates. The templates, which don't use a fill-in-the-blanks approach, are a bit more challenging than the Wizard but give you several designs to choose from. After you choose a design, the template gives you a complete, formatted Web page with "dummy" content. Which is to say, the page contains generic text (that has nothing to do with what *you* want to write), pictures of total strangers, and links that go absolutely nowhere.

After you download a template, it's up to you to change the dummy text, pictures, and links to real content. Use Gold's editor to do that. I can't teach you everything about Gold right here and now—Chapters 8 and beyond do that—but I can give you a crash course in editing a page prepared for you by a template. And if you have any experience with Windows word processing programs, many of the techniques covered will be very familiar to you already.

CHOOSING A TEMPLATE

To create a home page from one of Netscape's templates, follow these steps:

1. Connect to the Internet in the usual way, and start Netscape Navigator.

2. From Navigator's menu bar, choose File | New Document | From Template.

3. Scroll down to the list of templates (see Figure 6-10) and look at all your options.

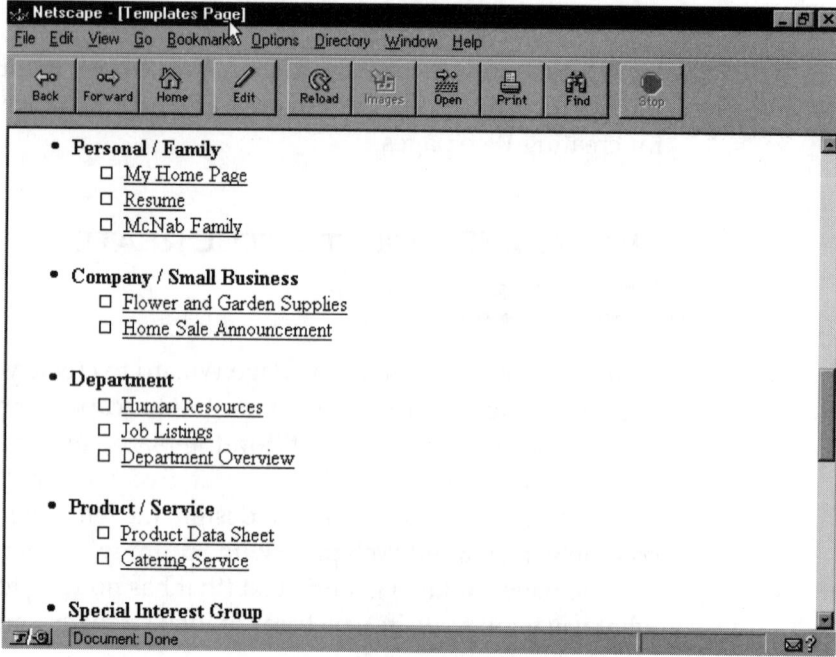

Figure 6-10: *Some of the preformatted templates at Netscape's site.*

4. After reviewing the list of templates, click on the one you think best exemplifies the type of page you're trying to create.

5. Now save a copy of the template to your hard disk. First,
   choose File | Edit document from Navigator's menu bar.
   You'll see the dialog box shown in Figure 6-11.

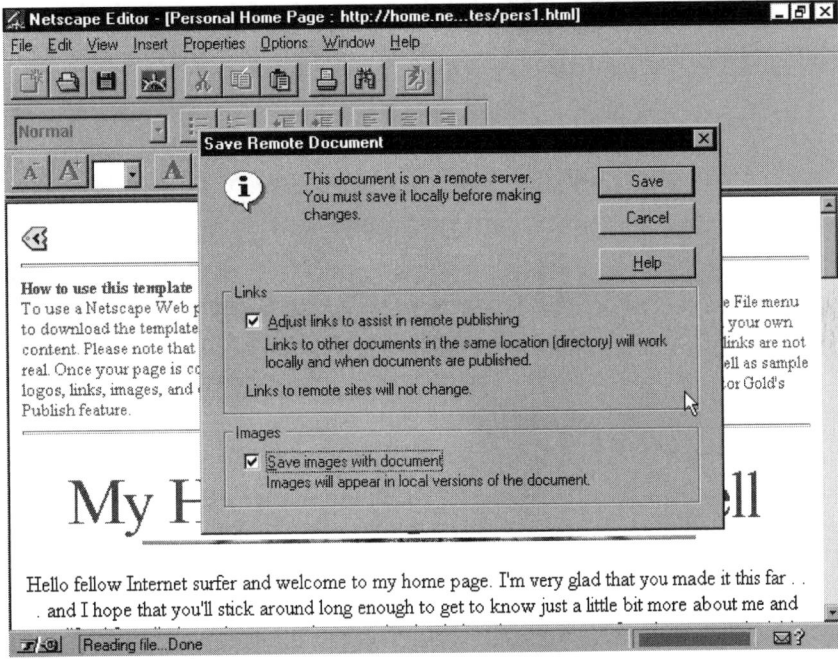

Figure 6-11: *Ready to save a copy of a template to your own hard disk.*

6. Make sure that both check boxes in the Save Remote Document dialog box are checked, then click the Save button. In
   the Hint box that appears next, just click the OK button.

7. In the Save As dialog box, choose a folder (e.g., My Web
   Site) and an appropriate filename for the page, then click
   the Save button.

TIP

*If you've already created a page named index.html and don't want to
lose it now, be sure to give this new page a different filename.*

Now that you have finished copying the template, you can modify it to your heart's content with some basic word processing skills in Gold's editor.

TEMPLATE EDITING CRASH COURSE

You must be working in Gold's editor (Navigator's title bar shows Netscape Editor) to edit the page that the template created for you. If you're working in the browser, just click the large Edit button in the toolbar to switch to the editor. Now, here's a crash course for changing the dummy content in the page that the template handed you:

- To change text, select (drag the mouse pointer through) the text you want to change, and type your new text. (See Chapter 8, "Basic Skills for Gold Authors," for details.)

- To delete the light blue and light green instructions that appear in the page, select whatever you want to delete and then press the Delete (Del) key, or choose Edit | Delete from the menu bar.

- To change a picture, double-click the picture and browse to, and open, the .GIF or .JPEG file that contains the picture you want to display. Then choose OK. (See Chapter 10, "Spice It Up With Lines & Pictures," for details.)

- To change a link, first delete the existing link by dragging the mouse pointer through it and then pressing Delete (Del). Then click the Make Link button in the toolbar, or choose Insert | Link from the menu bar, and fill in the dialog box that appears. Then choose OK. (See Chapter 11, "Adding Hyperlinks," for details.)

When you've finished, choose File | Save from the Editor's menu bar to save your changes. If you want to browse the page, to see it as your readers will, click the View in Browser button in the toolbar.

If you'd like to publish the page now, go straight to Chapter 7, "Presenting Your Page to the World." To try your hand at creating a home page from scratch, continue reading this chapter.

CREATING A PAGE FROM SCRATCH

The skills required to create a Web page from scratch are identical to those required to create a document with a word processing program. If you have word processing experience, creating a new Web page in Gold will be fairly easy. Just follow these steps to get started:

1. If you're online and being charged for it, feel free to disconnect. You don't need to be online to create a page from scratch.

2. Start Netscape Navigator in the usual way.

3. When Navigator complains about not being able to locate the server, just click the OK button. (We don't need the server right now.)

4. From Navigator's menu bar, choose File | New Document | Blank. Gold's editor is displayed, with a blank page to start on (see Figure 6-12).

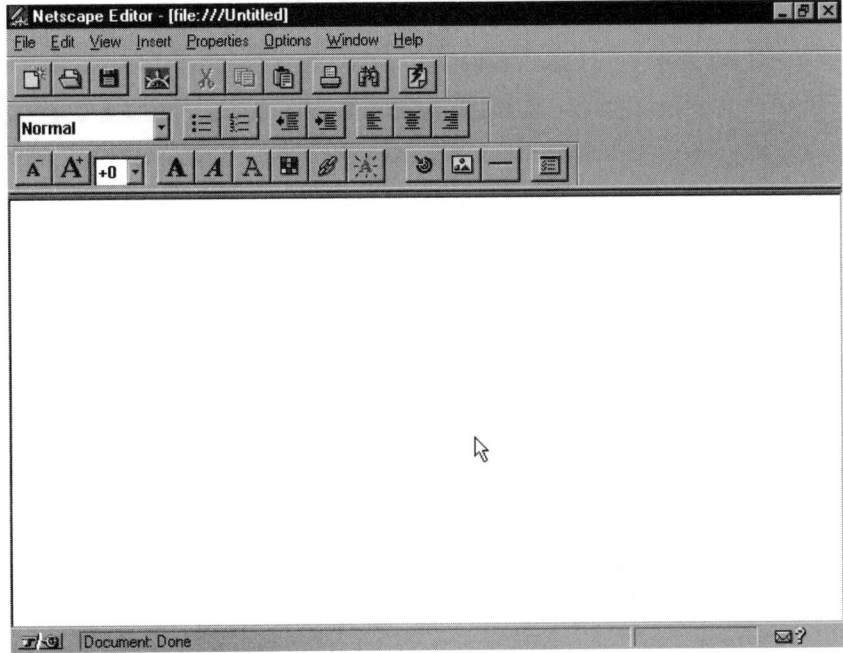

Figure 6-12: *Gold's editor, with a blank page displayed.*

5. Now type as you would in any word processor. For example, press Enter only to end short lines, entire paragraphs, or to insert blank lines. Use the Backspace and Delete keys to make corrections.

TRAP

If you have experience with earlier Web page editors, you might be inclined to start typing HTML tags. You'll have to break that habit right away. Gold's editor doesn't "understand" manually typed HTML tags!

Figure 6-13 shows the start of a simple document typed in from scratch. There I typed the short title, pressed Enter, then typed a paragraph. Same as I would have typed them in Microsoft Word, WordPerfect, or just about any other Windows word processing program.

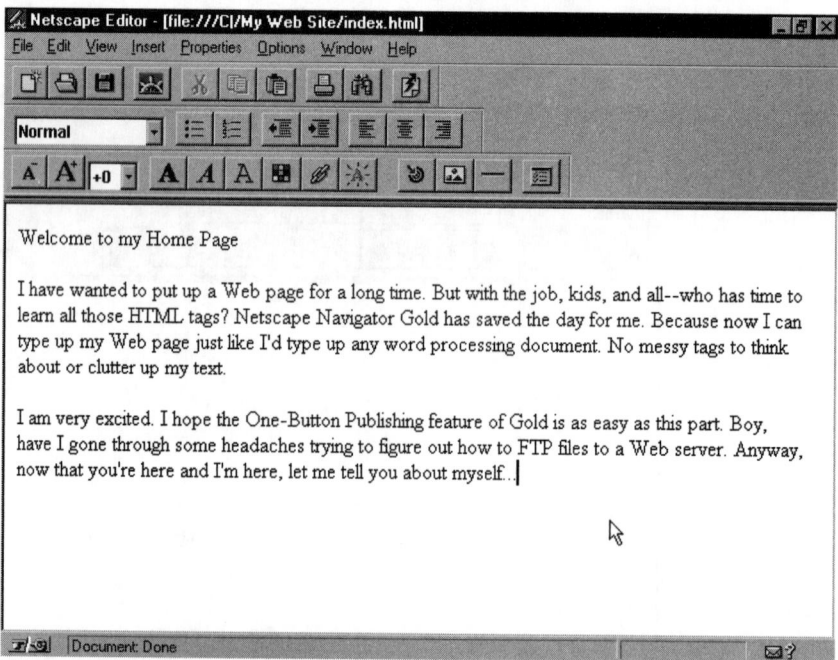

Figure 6-13: *A little text typed in a Web page.*

FORMATTING YOUR WEB PAGE

Formatting text in a Web page is easy in Gold. In most cases you just click on the text you want to format, then click on a toolbar button, or choose a style from the Paragraph style drop-down list in the toolbar. For example, to enlarge and center the top line in Figure 6-14 I clicked that line, then chose Heading 1 from the Paragraph style list (near the mouse pointer in the figure). Then I clicked the Center button in the toolbar.

Figure 6-14: *First line is centered and displayed in Heading 1 style.*

Other toolbar buttons make it easy to insert lines, pictures, and links. Just click where you want to insert some object to get the mouse pointer to that location, then use these toolbar buttons to insert objects:

- Insert Horiz. Line: Inserts a horizontal rule.
- Insert Image: Inserts a .GIF or .JPEG file.
- Make Link: Lets you define a hyperlink

> **TIP**
>
> *To see the name of a toolbar button, just rest the mouse pointer on the button for a couple of seconds.*

As I said earlier, we get into the real nitty-gritty of editing Web pages in Chapters 8 and beyond. Here, I just wanted to give you a feel for how Web page editing works in Gold.

SAVING YOUR MASTERPIECE

Save your Web page (locally) at any time, just as you'd save any other document. Choose File | Save from Navigator's menu bar, choose a folder (e.g., My Web Site), and enter a filename with a .html or .htm extension. After you save the page, you can upload it to your Web server, for all the world to see, as you'll learn in the next chapter.

MOVING ON

Let's take a moment to review where we've been recently. In Chapter 5, "Finding a Home for Your Page," you learned how to go about getting a place on the Internet to publish your pages. In this chapter you've learned three different ways to create Web pages. After you've created one or more Web pages, and are happy with their content and appearance, you can send them on up to the Web server. You'll learn how to do that in the next chapter.

Presenting Your Page to the World

If you've been following along since Chapter 5, "Finding a Home for Your Page," you now have a place to publish your Web page and a Web page to publish. Now the question is, "How do you get that page from your PC onto the Web server, for all the world to see?" The answer to this question is a resounding—and typical— "It depends." Mainly, it depends on whether your ISP supports Gold's one-button publishing. If so, great. If not, you have to use FTP (File Transfer Protocol). This chapter covers the following topics:

- Setting up Navigator for one-button publishing
- Posting your pages with one click
- How to post your pages, using FTP
- Viewing your own site "live"
- How to change pages after you've posted them

Let's start with the easiest scenario.

ONE-BUTTON PUBLISHING

If you signed up with an ISP that offers one-button publishing, posting your pages to the Web is easy. First, you need to get the following information (provided after you sign up for an account) from your ISP:

Publish To (FTP or HTTP):_____

Browse To (HTTP): _____

User name: _____

Password: _____

Jot down the information right here in the book—and perhaps make a copy to store in your files.

SETTING UP YOUR PUBLISHING PREFERENCES

When you have the information you need from your ISP, follow these steps to bring your completed Web page into Navigator, and set up your one-button publishing preferences:

1. Using My Computer, Find, or Windows Explorer, open the folder that contains your Web page (My First Page, in the example), then double-click the name of the home page (index.html, in the example). The page will open in Netscape Navigator.

TIP

In this chapter I'll post the sample page I created using the Page Wizard, back in Chapter 6, "Creating Your First Home Page." You, of course, can post whatever pages you please.

2. Switch to the Editor (click the Edit button in the toolbar or choose File | Edit Document).

3. From the menu bar choose Options | Editor Options, and click the Publish tab. You'll see the dialog box shown in Figure 7-1.

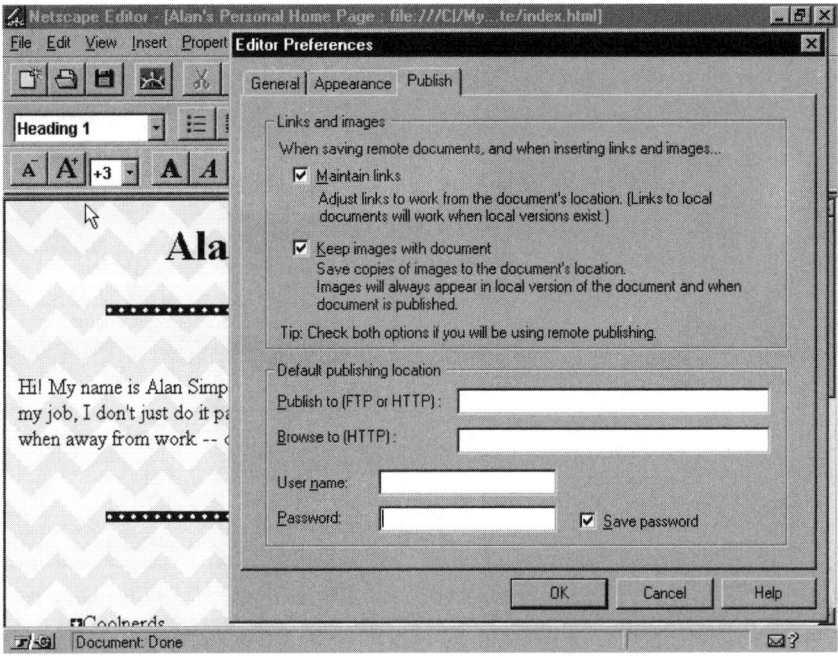

Figure 7-1: *The Editor Preferences dialog box.*

4. Fill in the blanks, using information provided by your ISP. Figure 7-2 shows an example (your entries will be different).

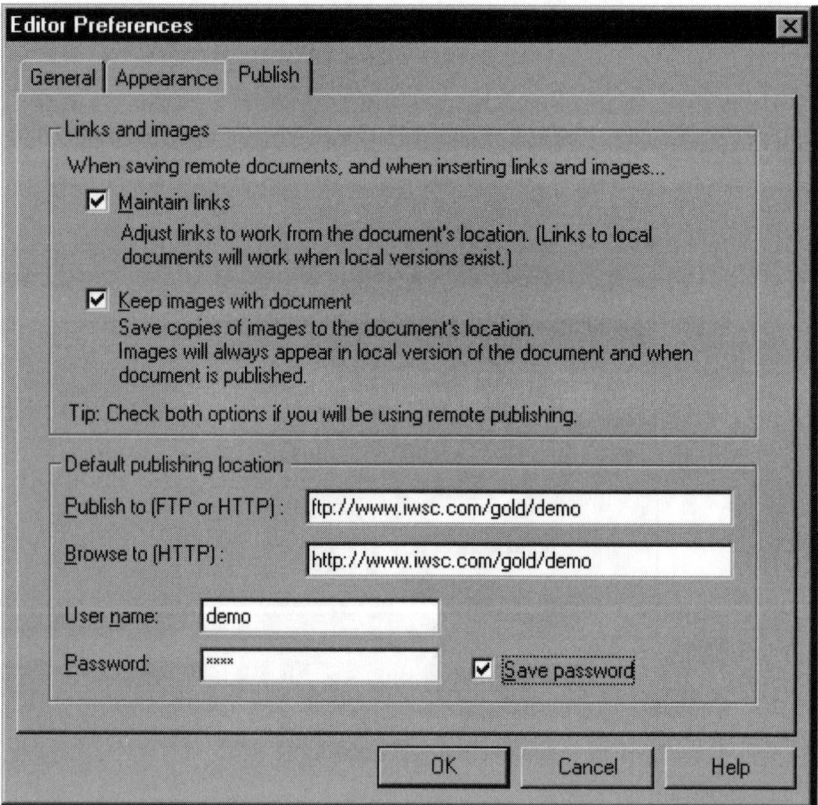

Figure 7-2: *Sample entries in the Editor Preferences dialog box.*

TIP

If you don't share your PC with other people, you can select the Save Password check box to have your password entered automatically when you want to post Web pages. If you do share your PC, and you want to prevent others who use it from posting files, clear the Save Password check box.

5. Choose OK to save your entries and close the dialog box. You'll be returned to your Web page.

ONE-BUTTON PUBLISH YOUR PAGES

When you're ready to show your pages to the world, follow these simple steps:

1. If you're not already online, get online as you usually do.

2. Choose File | Publish from the Navigator Editor's menu bar. You'll see the Publish Files dialog box shown in Figure 7-3.

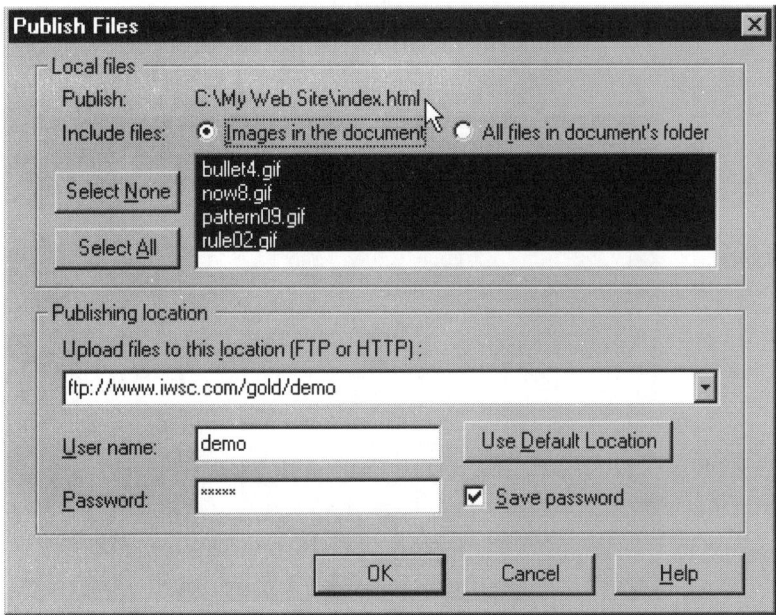

Figure 7-3: *The Publish Files dialog box.*

3. By default, the page you're currently viewing in the Editor is listed as the home page to publish (*c:\My Web Site\ index.html*, in this example). Any graphic images in that page are listed and already selected under *Include Files*.

4. If you have more than one page (i.e., more than one .html or .htm file) in your site, choose All files in document's folder to display all the files in the folder. To publish all those files, click the Select All button.

TIP

If your folder contains some files that you were just experimenting with and don't care to upload, you can just click on the files you don't want to upload to de-select them. (Or, click on Select None then click on the files you do want to upload.)

5. Click the OK button.

6. You may see a brief security reminder, as in Figure 7-4. Just click the Continue button to proceed.

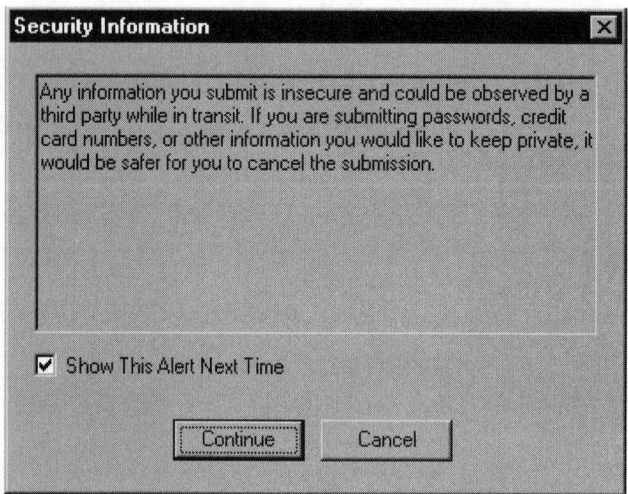

Figure 7-4: *You can choose Continue to get past this message.*

7. You'll see some progress indicators as your pages are up-
    loaded to the Web server directory. When the job is done
    you'll see a message like the one shown in Figure 7-5.

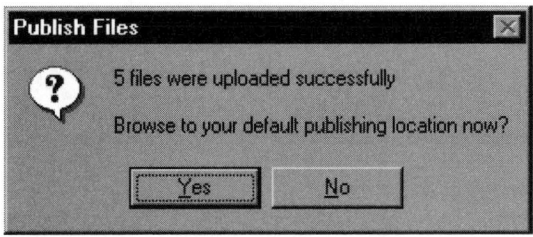

Figure 7-5: *Files successfully posted to the Web server.*

8. Choose Yes if you'd like to see what your page looks like on
    the World Wide Web.

At this point, you're done. If you chose Yes in Step 8, you're now
viewing your Web page, live, on the World Wide Web. The Location box shows the URL of your Web page, as in Figure 7-6.

TIP

*If you haven't already done so, be sure to write down the URL of your
Web page!*

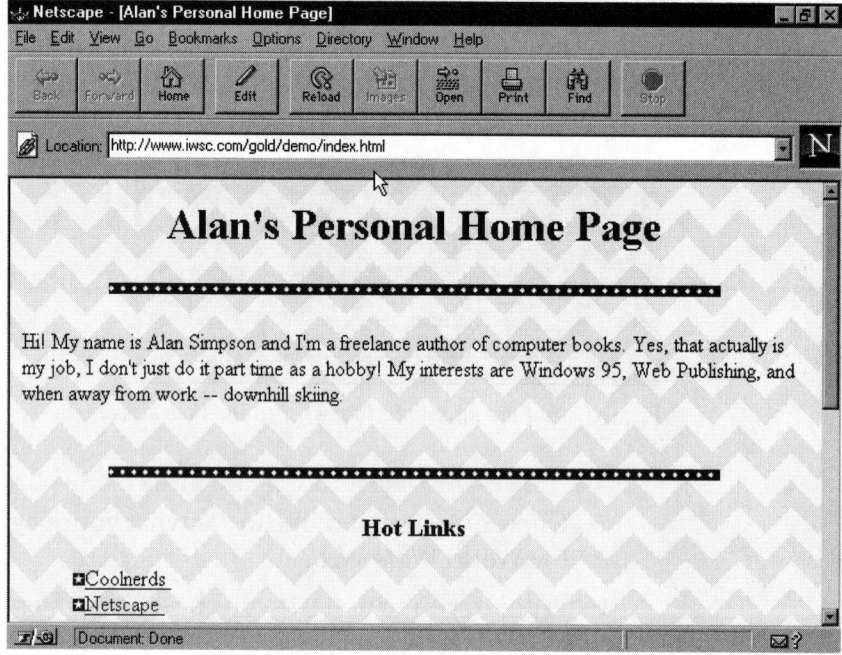

Figure 7-6: *My first Web page, live on the Web.*

Any hot links you put in your page now work, because you're viewing your page on the Web. To get back to your page after you view another site, click the Back button.

TIP

You can change Gold's preferences to make your own home page your default startup page. See "Changing Netscape's General Appearance" in Chapter 32, "Personalizing Netscape Navigator." You can exit Navigator and disconnect at any time. You, or anyone else on the Internet, can now view your Web page by connecting to the Internet, starting up a Web browser, and entering your URL in the Location box.

Congratulations. You're done! You are an officially published Web author, a Web publisher, and a Webmaster all rolled into one. You can skip down to "Changing Your Posted Page(s)" now, if you like. The FTP stuff that follows isn't relevant to you.

POSTING YOUR PAGES WITH FTP

If your ISP doesn't support Gold's one-button publishing, they probably will provide you with exact step-by-step instructions for posting your pages. But just in case they don't, I'd like to take you through a sample scenario for uploading pages the "old-fashioned" way—by using the Internet's FTP service.

DON'T ASSUME TOO MUCH!

Don't assume that your ISP *doesn't* support one-button publishing. Ask them directly whether they support Netscape's one-button publishing. If they do, they can send you the information you need to fill in the Publish tab of the Editor Preferences dialog box. Then you can post your pages to their server by using File|Publish, as discussed earlier in this chapter, rather than all this FTP stuff.

You will need some information from your ISP. Ideally, if they give you the exact URL to connect to, and a password to use, you can just use that information in the FTP program. On the other hand, if your ISP assumes that all their Web publishers are Internet gurus, they might divide the necessary information into four components: host name, path, username, and password, as in the following example:

Host name: crash.cts.com
Path to use: public_html
Username: alan
Password: yeahright

TIP

The preceding example is a real one, but needless to say, the password isn't really yeahright. *Don't bother trying to upload your pages there!*

Let's suppose that you have the preceding information for *your* account and Web server directory, and now you want to post your pages to that directory. The next session takes you through a scenario that should get the job done.

PUBLISHING VIA AMERICA ONLINE & COMPUSERVE

If you plan to publish your Web pages via the free space provided by America Online, CompuServe, or some other commercial online service, you'll need to follow that service's instructions to upload your pages. At CompuServe, visit GO OURWORLD for information. In America Online, look up the keyword *home page*.

GETTING TO YOUR WEB SERVER DIRECTORY

You can use Netscape Navigator to connect to your Web server folder and upload your pages. Typically, you need to supply a *nonanonymous* FTP address, in the form:

`ftp://username@ftp.host`

In this form, *username* is the name assigned to you by your ISP, and *host* is their host name. Referring to my earlier example, I would use the address:

`ftp://alan@crash.cts.com`

You can include the password in the URL if you like. To do so, use the following format:

`ftp://username:password@ftp.host`

For instance, I could use the URL:

`ftp://alan:yeahright@crash.cts.com`

If you omit the password, no big deal—the program prompts you for it at the appropriate time.

Here's how to get to the address, using Netscape Navigator:

1. Get online and start Netscape Navigator Gold in the usual way.

2. In the Go to: box, enter the nonanonymous FTP address you need to get to your Web server directory. (For example, I would enter **ftp://alan@crash.cts.com**.)

3. Press Enter. If you didn't include a password in the URL, you'll be prompted for that password now, as in the example shown in Figure 7-7. Type your password and click the OK button.

Figure 7-7: *You need to enter your password when you want to upload pages.*

4. You should see a list of files and folders that resembles the one shown in Figure 7-8.

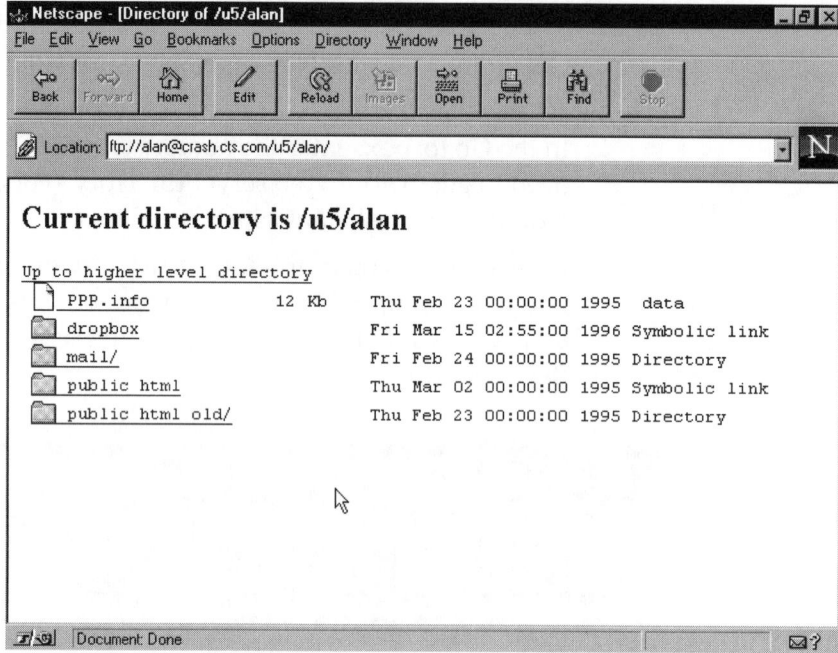

Figure 7-8: *Connected to my general FTP site.*

5. If your ISP specified a directory (or folder, or path) to post your pages to, you should select the directory now. (In my situation, for instance, I would select the public_html directory.)

6. When you get to the appropriate directory, shrink the Navigator window a little so that you can get to the Windows 95 desktop. Then use My Computer, Explorer, or Find to open the folder that contains the pages you want to post (My Web Site, in this example).

7. Select all the files you want to post. For example, in Figure 7-9 I've selected all the files that the Netscape Page Wizard sent when I created my first home page (in Chapter 6).

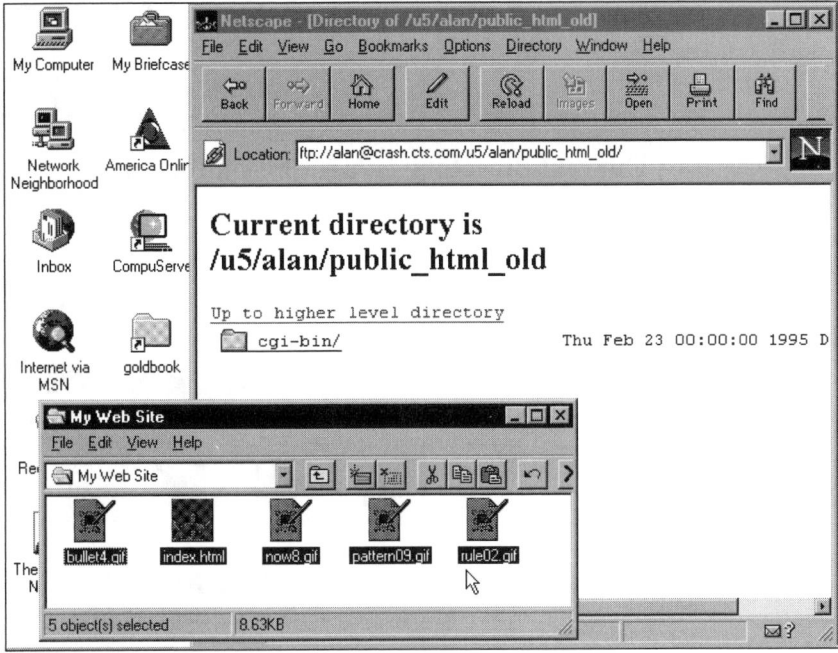

Figure 7-9: *Files to upload are selected.*

8. Drag and drop the selected files into the Navigator window. When you see the "Do you want to upload the dragged files to the FTP Server?" message, click the OK button.

9. You may see a security reminder. Click on Continue to proceed. You'll see a progress meter, and a message that tells you when the upload is finished.

When you've finished, all the files you dragged into the Navigator window should now appear in your FTP list, as in the example shown in Figure 7-10.

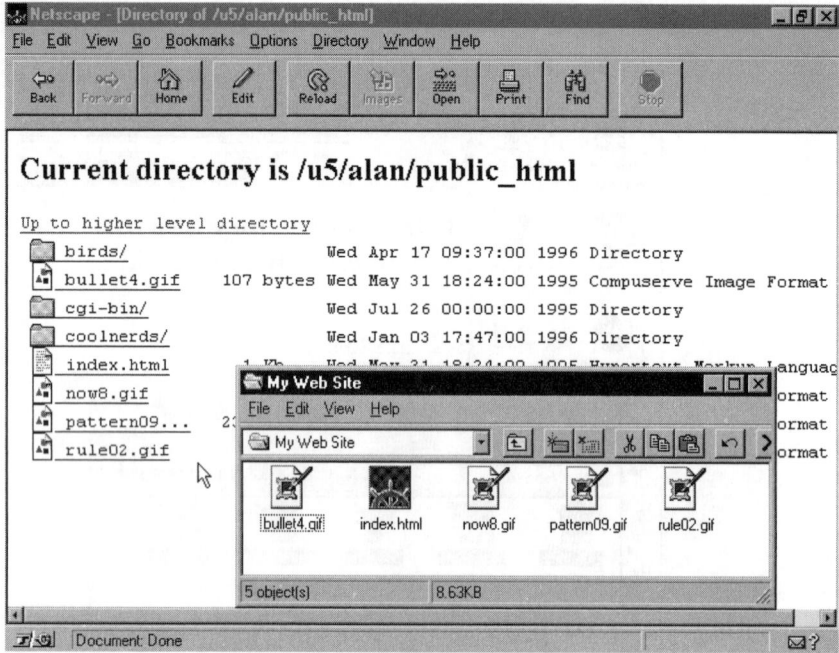

Figure 7-10: *Web pages, successfully posted to FTP address.*

TIP

Navigator's FTP capabilities are modest compared to some dedicated FTP programs. For example, Gold won't let you rename or delete files on the remote computer. For more information on Navigator's FTP capabilities, and alternative FTP programs, see Chapter 29, "FTP, Gopher & Telnet."

VIEWING YOUR SITE

Unless your ISP tells you otherwise, your uploaded page(s) should be available immediately for viewing. (Just type the appropriate URL in Navigator's Location box and press Enter.) For instance, when I enter the URL for my Web site—http://www.coolnerds.com—I see my Web page as everyone else on the Web will see it, as shown in Figure 7-11.

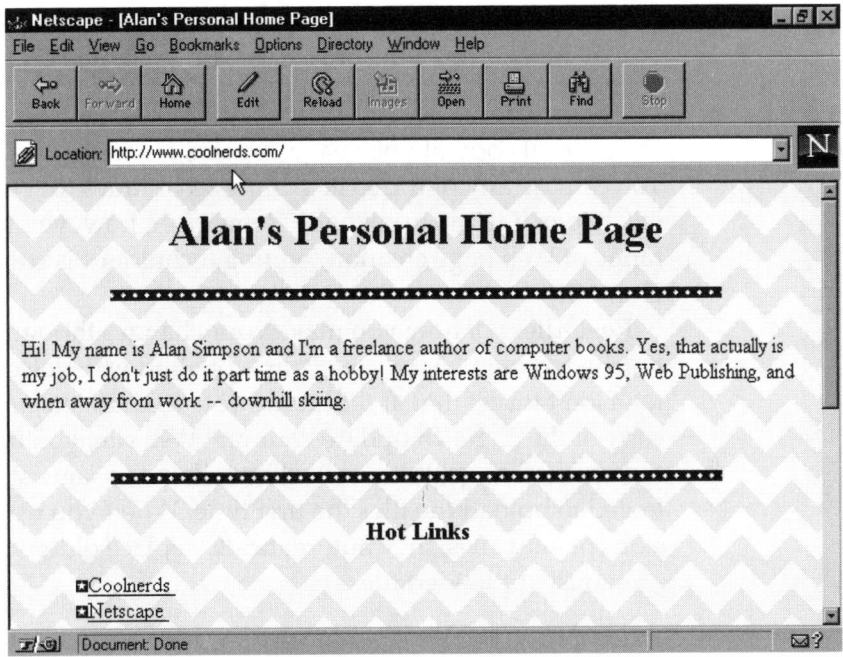

Figure 7-11: *Browsing my posted Web page.*

Because this page is "live," the hot links, Back, and Forward buttons work normally.

Changing Your Posted Page(s)

Do keep in mind that there are now two complete, and separate, copies of your Web site: one on the World Wide Web, and one on your own PC. If you want to make any changes to your pages, you need to make those changes on your own PC. First, you'll need to open the page for editing. This is pretty easy. Just follow these steps:

1. Using My Computer, Explorer, or Find, open the (local) folder that contains your Web material (My Web Site, in the current example).

2. Double-click the page you want to edit (in this example, index.html—the only page we've created).

3. Click the Edit button in Navigator's toolbar.

The local copy of your page appears onscreen, ready for editing. You can use any of the basic editing techniques that we overviewed in Chapter 7 to make changes. Remember, however, that the full range of Web page creation/editing techniques is covered in Parts II and III.

Regardless of how you make your changes though, when you've finished, remember to save your work and exit Netscape Navigator. Don't forget that at this point, you've changed *only* the local copy of the page. To update your real Web site, you need to upload the updated file(s) to that site. Just follow the same steps you followed to upload the files the first time. When you upload new versions of your files, they automatically replace older versions of any previously uploaded files.

MOVING ON

Congratulations. You have created and published your first Web page. Where you go from here depends on what you want to do:

■ If you want to change your Web page, or start building bigger and better sites, proceed to the next chapter.

■ If you're happy with the page you've created, and want to start publicizing it, see Chapter 23, "Promoting Your New Web Site."

PART II:
Creating Custom
Web Sites

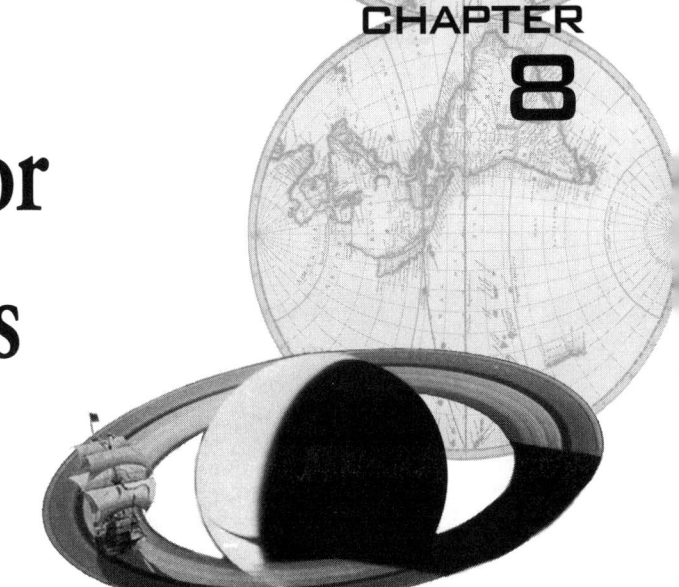

Basic Skills for Gold Authors

By now you've probably created and posted your first Web page, using the Netscape Page Wizard to make things easy. Many of you are probably wondering how to create something more dazzling than a single-page site with four hyperlinks. Well, in this chapter, you're going to start learning to do just that. We begin with an in-depth discussion of a great Web authoring tool—Netscape Navigator Gold's editor—and the skills you need to use it creatively. In summary, you'll learn:

- How to get around in Gold's editor
- How to type a Web page
- How to make changes and corrections
- Different ways to view your page

WHAT'S SO SPECIAL ABOUT THE EDITOR?

Those of you who have used PCs for a while probably know that an *editor* is a program that lets you create and change text. Netscape Navigator's editor is just such a program. But it's different from most other editors in that it is designed specifically to help you create and edit Web pages for publication on the World Wide Web.

Here's another way to look at it. You probably already know Navigator as a Web browser that lets you view other people's Web sites. The editor has the same basic look and feel as the browser, but unlike the browser, which just lets you look at stuff, the editor lets you create and change (edit) stuff.

Much of the work you do with the editor can be done offline, on your own PC. If you're paying for connect time, you'll be glad to know that authoring your pages involves very little connect time.

OPENING THE EDITOR

To get to the editor—as though you were going to create a new Web page from scratch—just follow these steps:

1. If you haven't already done so, start Netscape Navigator Gold.

2. From Navigator's menu bar, choose File | New Document | Blank.

That's all there is to it. The bright red line across the top of the large editing area is your visual cue that you are in the editor—but many other things in this editor window also are different from things in the browser.

WHAT'S ON THE SCREEN

Let's take a moment to identify the various parts of the editor screen so that you'll know what I'm talking about when I refer to these items later in the chapter. Figure 8-1 shows the main parts of the editing screen.

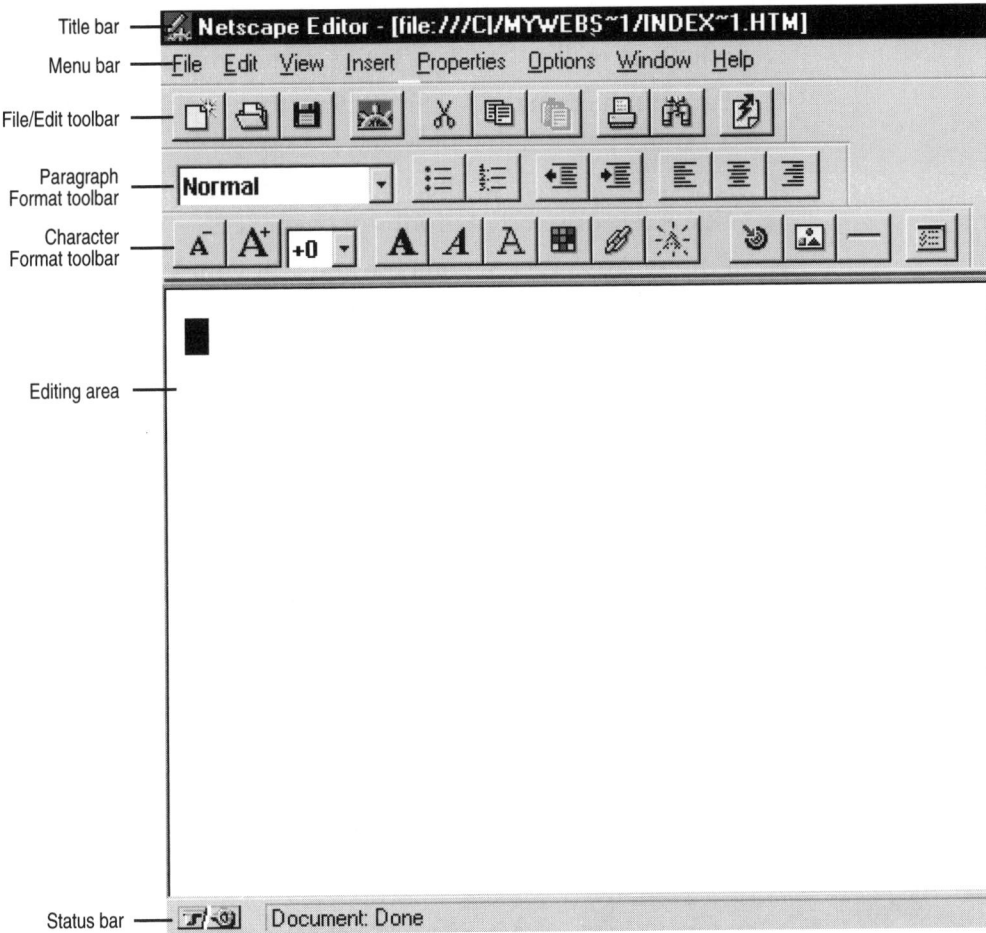

Figure 8-1: *Main parts of the editor's screen.*

More detailed descriptions follow:

■ Title Bar: Standard Windows title bar, shows the name of the document currently being edited and standard Windows buttons.

■ Menu Bar: Standard Windows menu bar with commands that operate on the page currently being edited.

- File/Edit Toolbar: Buttons for working on the document as a whole, as well as Cut, Copy, and Paste buttons.

- Paragraph Format Toolbar: Buttons that apply formatting to an entire paragraph or selected paragraphs.

- Character Format Toolbar: Buttons for formatting individual characters or selected groups of characters.

- Editing Area: Where you type and edit your Web page. Right-click in this area for context-relevant pop-up menus.

- Status Bar: Standard Netscape Navigator status bar.

Here are a few little tricks you can do with the toolbars:

- To see the name of a button, rest the mouse pointer on the button for a second.

- To join two toolbars horizontally, drag one so that it overlaps another.

- You can hide or display the toolbars by choosing Options | Show *whichever* Toolbar.

- To *float* a toolbar, point to a space between buttons and drag the toolbar toward the center of the screen. To reanchor the toolbar, drag it up above the red line.

BASIC WEB-AUTHORING SKILLS

If you know how to use Microsoft Word, WordPerfect, or some other Windows word processing program, you know about all the basic skills you need to type and edit a Web page in Navigator's editor. For those of you who are not familiar with word processing, the sections that follow present the basic skills you need for typing and editing.

No HTML Allowed!

Those of you who are accustomed to creating Web pages with earlier editors might feel compelled to type HTML tags right into your page. Sorry—it doesn't work that way in Netscape's editor! All the necessary tags are created automatically and put in place behind the scenes, as you type. Any tags you type in Navigator's editor are treated as regular text rather than as HTML tags.

If you want to go in and work directly with tags, you'll need to use a separate text editor. We'll get to that in Chapter 15, "Tuning HTML Tags." Chances are, you won't have to bother with HTML before then.

Basic Typing Skills

Typing a Web page is similar to typing a page with a typewriter or word processing program. The basic rules are as follows:

- When typing a paragraph, don't press Enter until you get to the end of the paragraph.

- To end a short line, and put a blank line below it, press Enter.

- To end a short line without putting a blank line below it, press Shift+Enter, or choose Insert | New Line Break from the menus.

- To rejoin two lines that you broke accidentally, move the cursor to the end of the top line and press the Delete (Del) key.

Figure 8-2 shows an example in which the typed text explains how I did the typing. Notice that the lines in the "poem" are broken, but that there is no blank line between them.

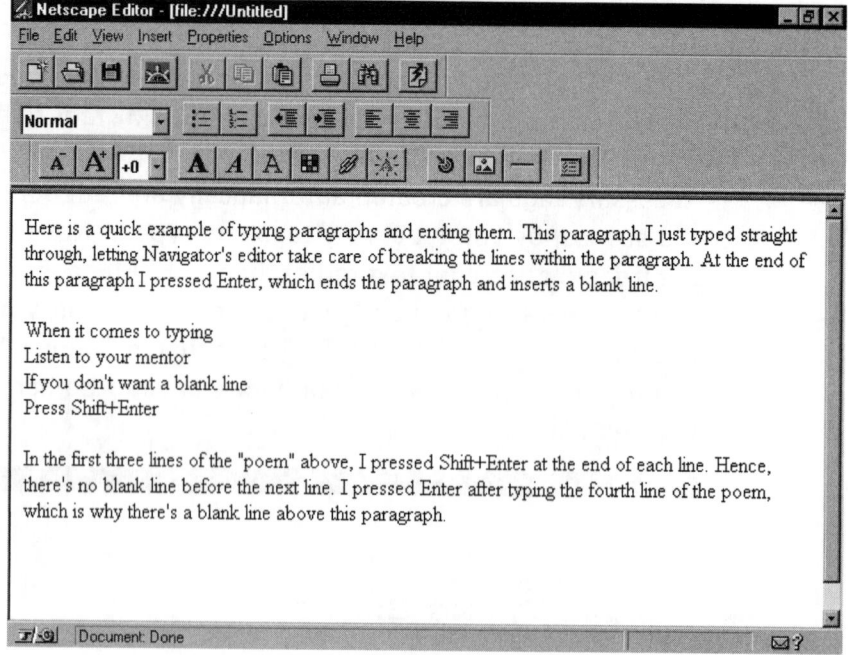

Figure 8-2: *A simple document, typed in the editor.*

TIP

You can use the Windows Character Map to insert foreign language characters and special characters like ©. See Appendix D for information.

BASIC NAVIGATION SKILLS

Whenever you type something, the text you type appears at the blinking cursor. To make changes and corrections, you first need to move the cursor to the point at which you want to make the change or corrections. You can do so by using either the mouse or the keyboard.

To position the cursor using the mouse, move the mouse pointer to the place you want the cursor to land, then click on that spot. Table 8.1 lists the keys you can use to position the cursor using the keyboard.

TRAP

Using the mouse and keyboard to position the cursor works only in text that's already onscreen. To get below the last line of text, you must move the cursor to the bottom of the page (Press Ctrl+End) and then press Enter or Shift+Enter to insert blank lines.

To move the cursor	Press
Left one character	Left arrow
Right one character	Right arrow
Down one line	Down arrow
Up one line	Up arrow
Right one word	Ctrl+Right arrow
Left one word	Ctrl+Left arrow
Start of line	Home
End of line	End
Top of document	Ctrl+Home
Bottom of document	Ctrl+End

Table 8-1: *Navigation keys.*

SELECTING TEXT

For many operations, you must *select, then do*. To delete a chunk of text, for example, you select the text you want to delete, then press the Delete (Del) key (or choose Edit | Delete). You can select text by using either the mouse or the keyboard.

SELECTING TEXT WITH THE MOUSE

To select text with the mouse, point to the place you want to begin the selection. Then hold down the mouse button and drag the mouse pointer to the place you want to end the selection. Selected text is always displayed as white letters against a dark background, as in the example shown in Figure 8-3.

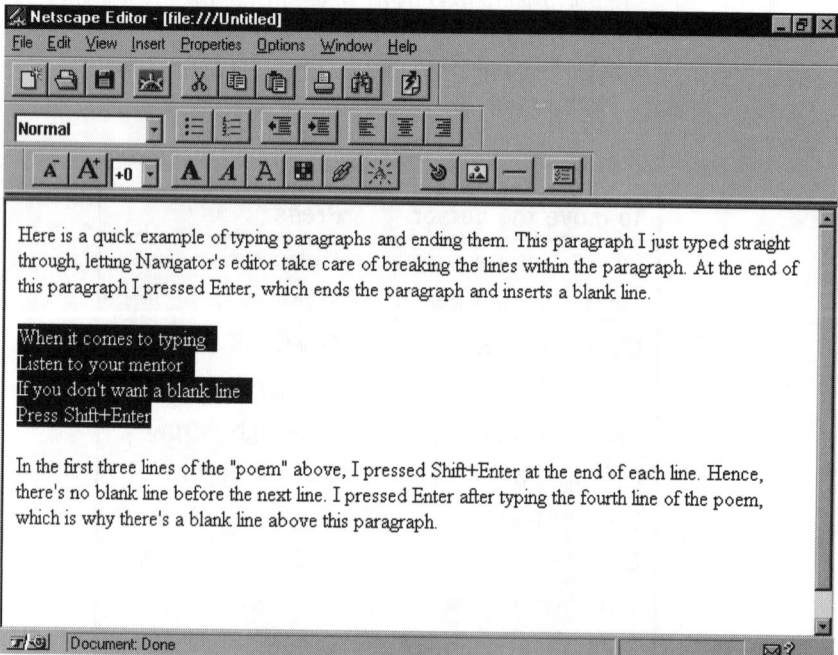

Figure 8-3: *Selected text appears as white letters against a dark background.*

Here are some handy shortcuts for selecting text, using the mouse:

- To select a word, double-click the word.
- To select a line, click in the left margin next to the line.
- To select a paragraph, double-click in the left margin next to the paragraph.

Here's yet another way to select text using the mouse. Click where you want to start the selection, point to the place where you want to end the selection, and then hold down the Shift key as you click the ending location.

You can use any of the Shift+*key* techniques described in the next section to expand or shrink the selection area.

SELECTING TEXT WITH THE KEYBOARD

To select text by using the keyboard rather than the mouse, hold down the Shift key as you press an arrow key (or any other key listed in Table 8-1). For example, to select all the text from the current position of the cursor to the end of the document, press Shift+Ctrl+End.

To select the entire document, press Ctrl+A, or choose Edit | Select All from the menu bar.

TRAP

If you select text, then start typing, the new text will replace the selected text! *If you do this by accident, you can reclaim the replaced text by choosing Edit | Undo.*

UNSELECTING TEXT

If you select some text, then decide to start over, just press Escape (Esc) to clear the current selection without changing any of that text.

DELETING TEXT

You can delete text in any of three ways:

- To delete characters to the left of the cursor, press Backspace.
- To delete characters to the right of the cursor, press the Delete (Del) key.

■ Or select the text you want to delete, then press Delete (Del) or choose Edit | Delete.

You can also delete text and replace it with new text in one fell swoop. Just select the text you want to get rid of, then start typing the new text. The selected text is instantly replaced by the new text you type. (If you do this by accident, just undo the action, as discussed next.)

UNDO & REDO

If you delete or change text, and then change your mind, choose Edit | Undo (or press Ctrl+Z) to undo the change. (Undo works only on your most recent action.) If you change your mind again, choose Edit | Redo (or press Ctrl+Shift+Z).

MOVING & COPYING TEXT

You can easily move and copy text in your page, as follows:

1. Select the text you want to move or copy.

   ■ If you want to *copy* the selected text, click the Copy button in the File/Edit toolbar, or press Ctrl+C, or click the right mouse button and choose Copy, or choose Edit | Copy from the menu bar. A copy of the selected text will be placed in the Windows clipboard.

   ■ If you want to *move* the selected text, click the Cut button in the File/Edit toolbar, or press Ctrl+X, or click the right mouse button and choose Cut, or choose Edit | Cut from the menu bar. The selected text will be moved to the Windows clipboard.

2. Click wherever you want to place the moved or copied text.

3. Click the Paste button in the File/Edit toolbar, or press Ctrl+V, or click the right mouse button and choose Paste, or choose Edit | Paste from the menu bar.

You can use the same technique to move or copy text between Navigator Gold's editor and any Windows text editor or word processor. For example, you could copy all the text from a Web page into Microsoft Word to do a spelling check or whatever. Then you could copy the text from Word back to Navigator's editor.

You should do this only during the earliest stages of development—after typing text but before applying any formatting to the text—because the text will transfer back and forth, but very little (if any) of the formatting will. In fact, you might even lose line breaks—those places where you pressed Shift+Enter to end a line without adding a new blank line beneath it.

> **TIP**
>
> *I often type the first draft of a Web page in Microsoft Word 7.0, because Word automatically corrects certain typos, underlines misspellings, and has a built-in thesaurus. When I'm happy with the text, I cut and paste it from Word into Navigator's editor. Then I use Navigator's editor to do all the formatting.*

FORMATTING TEXT

The chapters that follow explain the many different ways you can format the text in your Web page, and when each type of format is appropriate. Now, however, I just want to show you the basic skills necessary for applying a format to text:

To apply a paragraph format to a single paragraph, click anywhere in the paragraph and choose an option from the Paragraph Format toolbar. The format is applied automatically to the entire paragraph.

> **TIP**
>
> *In word processing jargon, a* paragraph *is any text that ends with a hard return—added by pressing Enter. For example, even a short line like a title is considered a paragraph.*

To apply a paragraph format to several paragraphs, select all the paragraphs you want to format (before you choose an option from the Paragraph Format toolbar).

A character format is one that's generally applied to a chunk of text that's smaller than a paragraph. For example, you might apply the boldface or italics character format to a single word or phrase within a paragraph. To apply a character format, you must first select the text you want to format. Then choose a format from the Character Format toolbar.

To undo a format, choose Edit | Undo. Or, if it's too late for that, click the paragraph or select the text that you want to unformat. Then choose Normal from the Paragraph Style drop-down list in the Paragraph Format toolbar. (If I'm going a little too fast for you, don't worry. As I said, the chapters that follow discuss formatting in greater detail and present many examples.)

SAVING YOUR WORK

As with all programs, nothing you do in Netscape's editor is permanent until you save your work. For this reason, you should *save your work often*. How often is up to you, but a good rule of thumb is that any time you make a change to your page, and want to *keep* that change, save the entire document. It takes only a second, and you can do so using any one of these techniques:

1. Choose File | Save.

2. Press Ctrl+S.

3. Click the Save button in the File/Edit Toolbar.

If you've never saved this document before, you'll be prompted to choose a folder and enter a filename. Try to get in the habit of saving all your Web pages to a single folder so that finding all of them will be easier when it's time to post them to your Web server.

Also, be aware that many Web servers can handle only eight-character filenames, with a .htm or .html extension tacked on. And remember that, on may servers, *filenames are case sensitive*. This last caveat is a real bane to Windows users. Try to get in the habit of using either all lowercase letters or all uppercase letters whenever you save a Web page. Then you won't have to remember which letters in the filename are upper- and which are lowercase.

UMPTEEN WAYS TO VIEW YOUR DOCUMENT

Most of the time, what you see in the editor is pretty close to what your document will look like to your readers. For a truly accurate view, however, you should browse your own document. And, as the sections that follow explain, there are other ways to view your document.

BROWSE YOUR LOCAL DOCUMENT

To see your document exactly as readers on the World Wide Web will see it, just switch to the browse view. To do so:

- Click the View in Browser button in the toolbar.
- Or choose File | Browse Document from the menus.

Because Navigator's editor is WYSIWYG (what you see is what you get), the browser view is similar to the editor's view. (Until you start adding pictures. But we'll get to that later.) Because the browser view *is* your Navigator browser, you can't edit anything in your page from this view. When you want to make a change, you need to switch back to the editor. To do so, just click the Edit button in the toolbar, or choose File | Edit Document.

By the way, I should mention that if you haven't saved your work, you'll be prompted to do so before Navigator switches to the browser view. You should choose Yes to save your current changes. Then, when the browser reads a copy of the page from your hard disk, you'll be sure to get the most recent version of that page.

SHOW/HIDE PARAGRAPH MARKS

When you start creating more complex pages, being able to see the paragraph and line-break marks in your document can be useful. As you may recall, a paragraph mark shows where you pressed Enter to end a line. A line-break mark shows where you pressed Shift+Enter to end a line.

To view the marks, choose View | Display Paragraph Marks (in the editor, of course). Tall dark rectangles indicate paragraph marks; smaller dark squares indicate line breaks (see Figure 8-4).

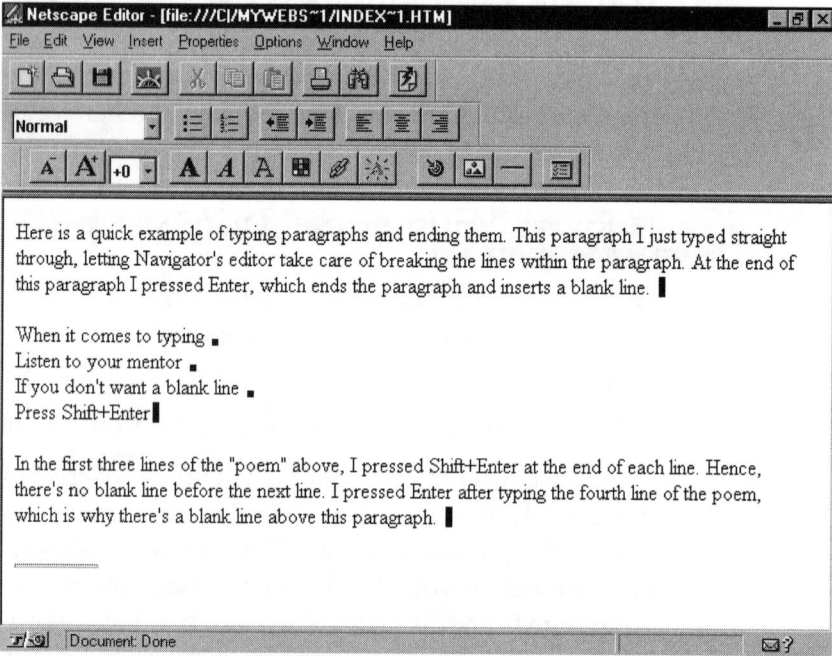

Figure 8-4: *My sample document, with paragraph marks and line breaks visible.*

You can edit normally in this view. For example, to delete a paragraph mark place the blinking cursor just to the left of the mark you want to delete, and press the Delete (Del) key. To insert a paragraph mark press Enter. To insert a line break, press Shift+Enter.

To hide the paragraph marks, choose View | Display Paragraph Marks again.

VIEW THE DOCUMENT SOURCE

When you create a Web page using Navigator Gold, you are creating an HTML document for the World Wide Web. An *HTML document* is one that contains *tags* that tell the browser how to format the document. Normally, neither you nor your readers will see those tags, which are just there for the browser. If you want to look at the tags, just choose View | View Document Source from the menu. Figure 8.5 shows my small sample page in this view.

```
Netscape - [View Document Source]                            _ 🗗 ✕
<html>
<head>
   <title></title>
   <meta name="Author" content="Alan Simpson">
   <meta name="GENERATOR" content="Mozilla/3.0b3Gold (Win32)">
</head>
<body text="#000000" bgcolor="#FFFFFF" link="#0000EE" vlink="#551A8B" alink="#
Here is a quick example of typing paragraphs and ending them. This paragraph
I just typed straight through, letting Navigator's editor take care of
breaking the lines within the paragraph. At the end of this paragraph I
pressed Enter, which ends the paragraph and inserts a blank line.
<p>When it comes to typing
<br>Listen to your mentor
<br>If you don't want a blank line
<br>Press Shift+Enter</p>

<p>In the first three lines of the &quot;poem&quot; above, I pressed Shift+Ent
at the end of each line. Hence, there's no blank line before the next line.
I pressed Enter after typing the fourth line of the poem, which is why
there's a blank line above this paragraph. </p>

</body>
</html>
```

Figure 8-5: *My little sample page in Document Source view.*

If you're not familiar with HTML, much of what you see in that view will appear to be gibberish. Don't worry about it. You don't really need to know anything about HTML at this stage. But in case you're really curious, I'll tell you what some of those tags mean:

- **<p>** marks the beginning of a new paragraph.
- **
** marks a line break (where you pressed Shift+Enter).

- </p> marks the end of a paragraph (where you pressed Enter).

- &quot; indicates quotation marks (") like the ones surrounding the word *poem* in my sample document.

You can't edit the document while you view the HTML source. When you want to resume normal editing, just close the View Document Source window. (Click the X in the upper right corner of the window, or press Alt+F4.)

GETTING HELP

The online help available for Netscape Navigator's editor is truly "online" in the sense that much if it is stored in Netscape's Web site. To access it, you must first be connected to the Internet. Then, in Netscape Navigator, follow these steps:

1. Choose Help | Handbook from Navigator's menu bar.

2. For help creating Web pages, look for the Authoring Guide link.

3. When you click on the Authoring Guide link, you should see a screen that looks something like Figure 8-6.

TIP

The reason I always say "...that looks something like..." when referring to online documents is that those documents can change at any time. And I have no control over if and when their authors will change them.

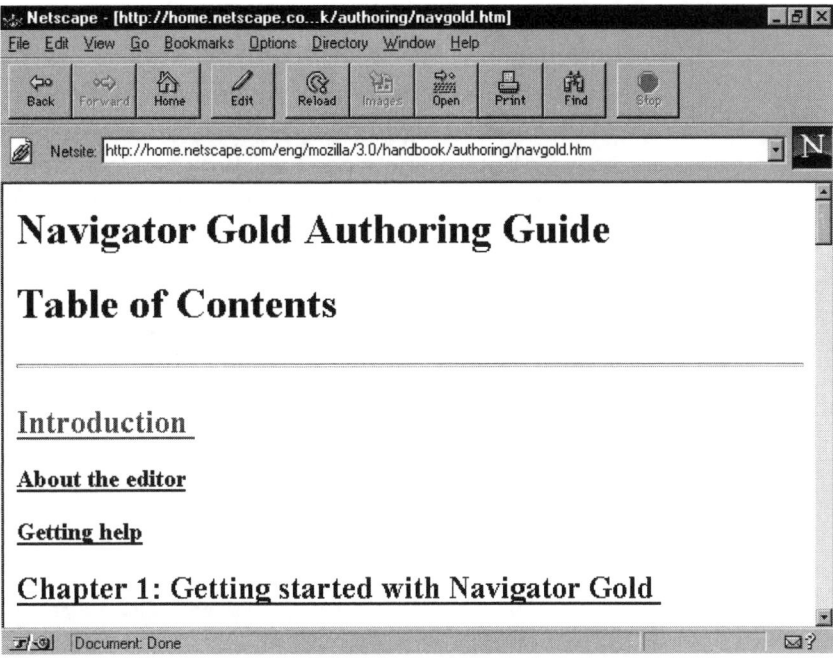

Figure 8-6: *Netscape's online Authoring Guide.*

You can browse through the online documentation as a supplement to this book. Or you can look up a specific topic by scrolling down to the index at the bottom of the Authoring Guide.

When you finish viewing the online help, click the Back button in the toolbar until you get back to your document. You'll probably be in browser view, but you can resume editing by clicking the Edit button or by choosing File | Edit Document.

TIP

From any a dialog box that has a Help button, you can get help (even when you're not connected to the Internet) by clicking that button.

If you're charged for connect time and want to disconnect from the Internet, you can do so. You'll still have access to the cached copy of the handbook that Navigator downloaded to your PC. To get to that cached copy, switch back to browser view (click the View in Browser button or choose File | Browse Document). Then, to access cached information, use the Back and Forward buttons and links in the handbook.

ABOUT REMOTE DOCUMENTS

If you try to switch to the editor while viewing a document on the Web—as opposed to a document you've created and saved on your own hard disk—you'll see the Save Remote Document dialog box shown in Figure 8-7.

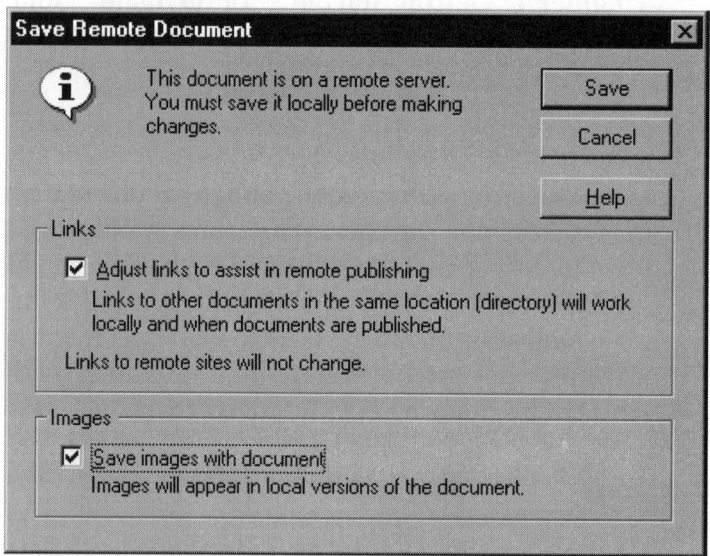

Figure 8-7: *The Save Remote Document dialog box.*

It's important to keep in mind that when you switch to the editor you're telling Navigator that you want to edit (change) the page that's visible on your screen right now. If someone else's page (not one you created) happens to be on your screen at the moment, the Save Remote Document dialog box appears to warn you that you really can't edit this page. And for good reason.

Just imagine that you publish your own Web site. What would happen if anyone who visits that Web site—including all the hackers, cybervandals, knuckleheads, and so forth—were free to make changes to your Web pages? You would have virtually no control over the contents of your own Web site. Fortunately, it's impossible for other people on the Web to mess with your pages. If they try to change your Web page, all they get is that Save Remote Document dialog box.

When the Save Remote Dialog box shows up on your screen, it's telling you that you can't mess with other people's pages either. You can copy someone else's page to your own hard disk, and edit that copy, if you want. But there's no way to get your edited copy uploaded to the owner's Web server.

I suspect that, often, you'll get to this dialog box by accident. For example, you might intend to edit your own page, but accidentally try to switch to the editor while someone else's page is visible on your screen. Should that occur, you can click the Cancel button in the dialog box, then use the Back key in the toolbar to get back to your own Web page—the one you want to edit. *Then* you can click the Edit button or choose File | Edit document to switch to the editor, without getting that Save Remote Document dialog box.

SAVE, EXIT, THEN EDIT AGAIN LATER

When you've finished with a document for the time being, you can save it and exit Navigator. First, choose File | Exit from Navigator's menu bar. When you see a message asking whether you want to close all windows and exit Netscape, choose Yes. If you've changed the document since you last saved it, you'll see a message asking whether you want to save those recent changes. Choose Yes (unless you made a mess of the document and don't want to save the changes). If you've never given the current document a filename, you'll be prompted to choose a folder and enter one. When Navigator finally closes, you'll be returned to the Windows 95 desktop.

To open the page again in Navigator, just do any of the following:

- Click the Windows 95 Start button, point to Documents, and if you see the name of the Web page, click on it.

- Or, open the folder that contains the document, then double-click the name of the page you want to view.

- Or, start Navigator in the usual manner (there's no need to go online, however). In the editor, choose File I Open File, choose the appropriate folder and filename from the Open dialog box, then click the Open button.

- Or, if you remember the name of a page you saved, but not its location, you can click the Start button and choose Find I Files or Folders. Type the name of the file you're look-ing for, and click the Find Now button. When you see the name of the file you want to open, double-click it.

Depending on how you open the file, it may open in Navigator's browser rather than in the editor. Remember, you can't make any changes to the document in the browser. You can easily switch to the editor, using either of these techniques:

- Click the Edit button in the toolbar.

- Or choose File I Edit document.

MOVING ON

And that, my friend, pretty much covers the basic skills needed to create and edit your own custom Web pages, using Netscape Navigator Gold (without using the Page Wizard). I realize that if you're new to text editing, this may seem like a lot to remember, but you can always flip back to this chapter whenever you need a reminder. Now it's time to really get your hands dirty, and create that first Web page.

Headings, Lists, Fonts & Indents

In this chapter we're going to look at the most commonly used formats in Navigator Gold's editor. These formats (also called *styles*, and *design elements*) are so common that you can probably find hundreds of examples of their use just by browsing around the World Wide Web. In fact, you can find countless examples just by flipping through the pages of this book—or any other book or magazine, for that matter. The design elements discussed in this chapter include:

- Titles and headings
- Left, center, and right alignment
- Boldface, italic, and other common text styles
- Numbered, bulleted, and other lists
- Indented text
- Sized and colored text

Don't forget that you must apply these formats from Gold's editor. You can't change or format text in Navigator's browser.

TITLING YOUR PAGE

As a Windows user, you're probably familiar with the title bar that appears across the top of every Windows application. It contains the application name and the Minimize, Restore, and Close buttons. (See Figure 8-1 back in Chapter 8 if you need a reminder.) You can also add to your page a title that will appear only in this title bar—not within the body of the page. To add such a title:

1. Choose Properties | Document from Navigator's menu bar.

2. In the dialog box that appears, type the title, exactly as you want it to appear in the title bar, in the Title text box.

3. If you like, fill in other options (discussed next).

4. Choose OK to exit the dialog box.

Let's take a moment to review the first three options presented in the Document Properties dialog box:

■ Title: The title as it will appear in the Web browser's title bar.

■ Author: Your name. Appears only in the document source (not in the browser).

■ Description: A brief description of the page (copyright information, last date edited, and so forth). Visible only in the document source (not in the browser).

The two options under *Other Attributes* are used by search engines, such as Yahoo, to help readers find your pages. You can leave these blank until you're ready to start promoting your site, as discussed in Chapter 23, "Promoting Your New Web Site."

In the example shown in Figure 9-1, I've filled in the title, author name, and description of my Web page.

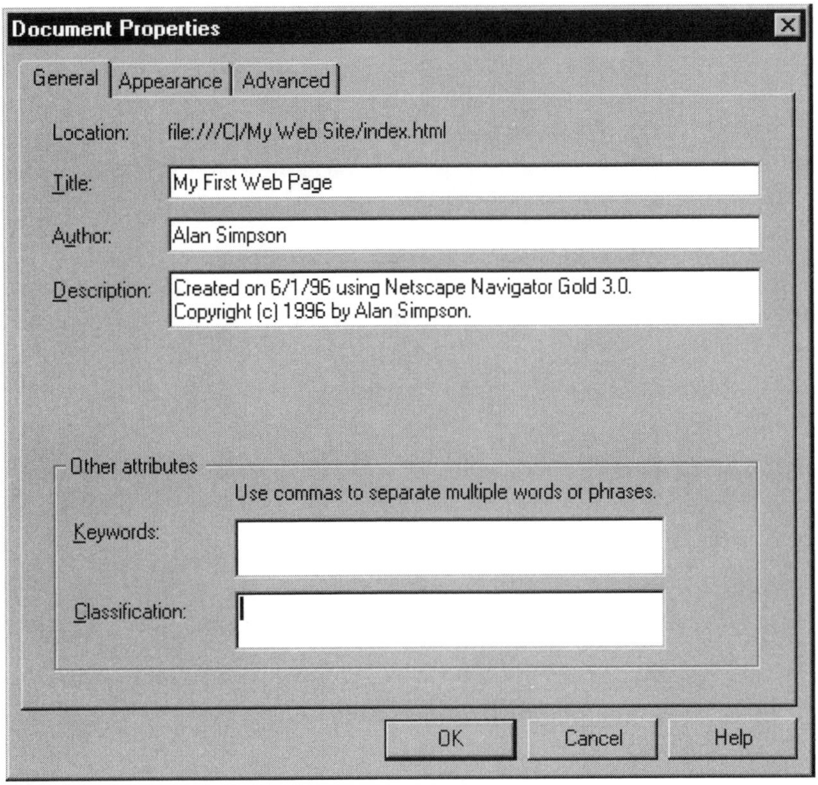

Figure 9-1: *The Document Properties dialog box with some sample entries.*

After you close the Document Properties dialog box you won't notice any big difference in your document. If you browse the document, however, you'll see the title you entered displayed in the title bar of the Navigator window. If you view the document source, you'll see the information between the <head> and </head> tags in the document (see Figure 9-2). Those HTML tags mark the informational part of the document that the average reader never sees. We'll talk more about HTML tags as we move along through these chapters. Don't worry about them now.

```
Netscape - [Source of: file:///C|/My Web Site/index.html]                    _ 🗗 ✕

<html>
<head>
   <title>My First Web Page</title>
   <meta name="Author" content="Alan Simpson">
   <meta name="GENERATOR" content="Mozilla/3.0b3Gold (Win32)">
   <meta name="Description" content="Created on 6/1/96 using Netscape Navigato

Copyright (c) 1996 by Alan Simpson.">
</head>
<body text="#000000" bgcolor="#FFFFFF" link="#0000EE" vlink="#551A8B" alink="#

</body>
</html>
```

Figure 9-2: *The document source for my page after I filled in some blanks in the Document Properties dialog box.*

If you're following along here on your own PC, don't forget that when you want to continue editing your document, you'll need to close the Document Source view window.

CREATING HEADINGS

Headings identify major sections, subsections within a major section, sub-subsections, and so forth within a larger body of text. This book, as you've probably noticed, is also loaded with headings that help you find specific information. For example, the heading for this section is "Creating Headings." You can use headings in your Web pages as well, to help readers find specific information.

Navigator offers six levels of headings named Heading 1, Heading 2, and so forth. The first-level heading is the largest text. Heading 2 is the next largest, and so forth, down to Heading 6, which is the smallest (see Figure 9-3).

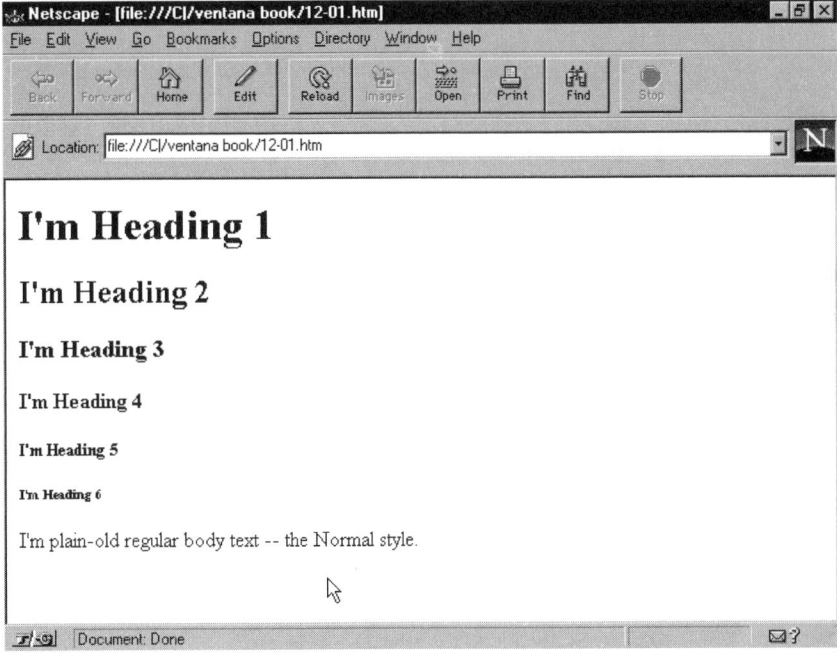

Figure 9-3: *Relative sizes of Heading 1 through Heading 6.*

There's no rule that says you *have to* use headings in any particular way. But when you design your own page you might want to use Heading 1 for the first line on the page—the page "headline." Then use Heading 2 to identify major sections in the page. Use Heading 3 to identify subsections within each section, and so forth, as in the example shown in Figure 9-4.

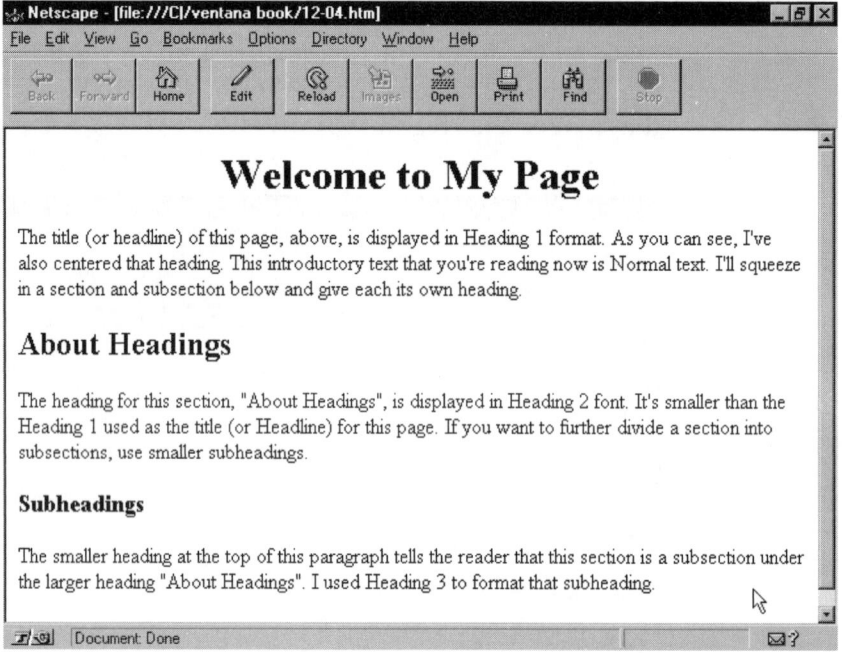

Figure 9-4: *Examples of ways to use a few headings.*

ALIGNING TEXT

You can easily align text on your Web page. Your choices are illustrated in Figure 9-5 and summarized here:

- Left-aligned: Text aligns with the left margin.
- Centered: Text is centered between the margins.
- Right-aligned: Text is flush right.

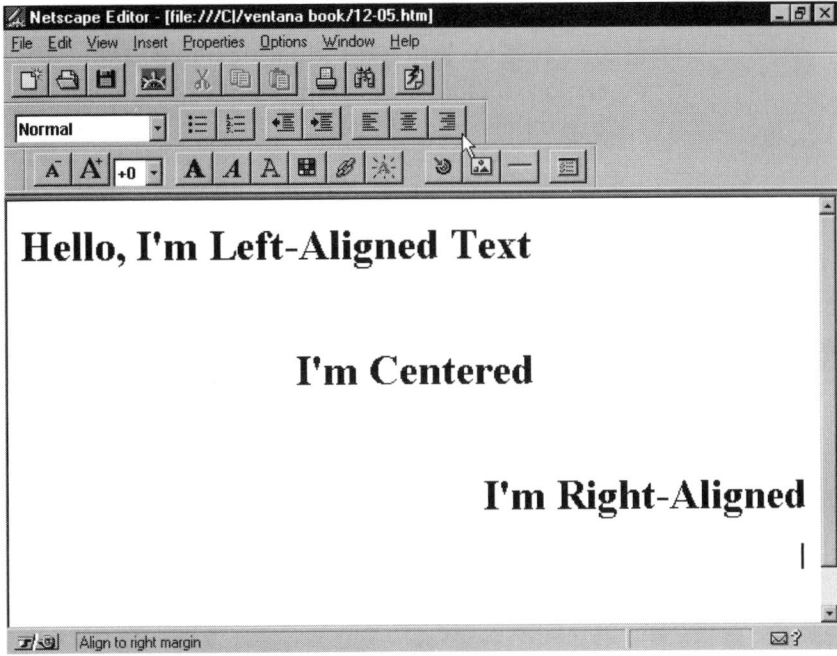

Figure 9-5: *Examples of left-aligned, centered, and right-aligned text.*

The basic procedure for aligning text is simple. Just follow these steps:

1. Click on the line (or paragraph) you want to align, or select multiple lines.

2. Click the Align Left, Center, or Align Right button in the Paragraph Format toolbar. Or choose Properties | Text | Paragraph, then choose Left, Center, or Right from the Align options, and then choose OK to close the dialog box.

If you change your mind, choose Edit | Undo, or repeat Step 1 and choose left alignment in Step 2.

Note that the alignment you choose affects the entire line or paragraph. You can't individually align certain parts of a line, but you can use a table (see Chapter 12, "Get It Straight With Tables") to achieve that kind of effect.

BOLDFACE, ITALIC & SUCH

You can apply boldface, italic, and other common *weights* and styles to text in your Web page. Figure 9-6 shows examples of these design elements. Applying these elements is pretty easy:

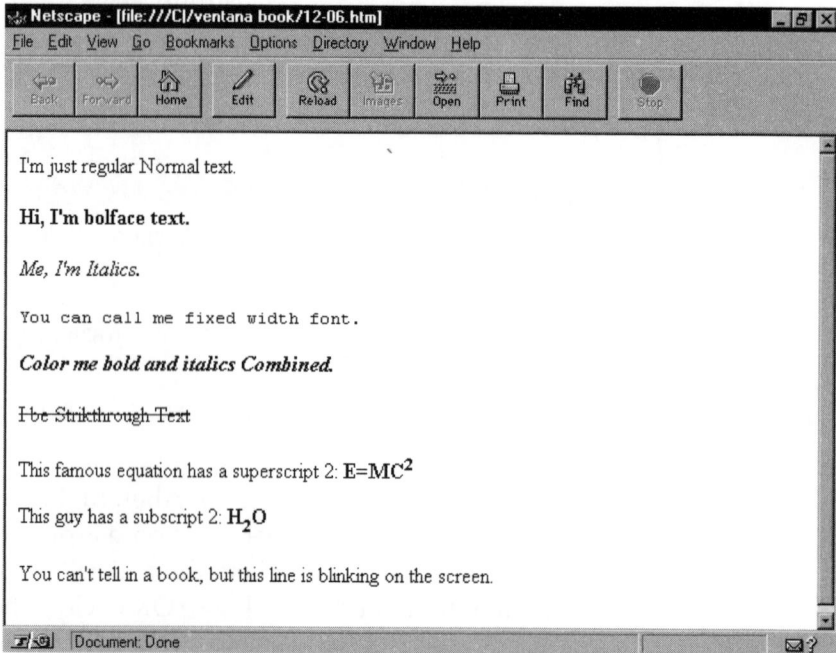

Figure 9-6: *A sample page with boldface, italic, and such.*

Select the text to which you want to apply the format. If you want to apply the format to a single word, you can just double-click that word to select it. Then do one of the following:

■ If you want to apply boldface, italic, or fixed width to
   the text, just click the appropriate button in the Character Formatting toolbar.

TIP

*Keyboard Shortcuts: You can press Ctrl+I to italicize selected text.
Press Ctrl+B to boldface text.*

■ To apply other formats, choose Properties | Text, click
   the Character tab, and then choose any combination of
   options from the Style group (see Figure 9-7).

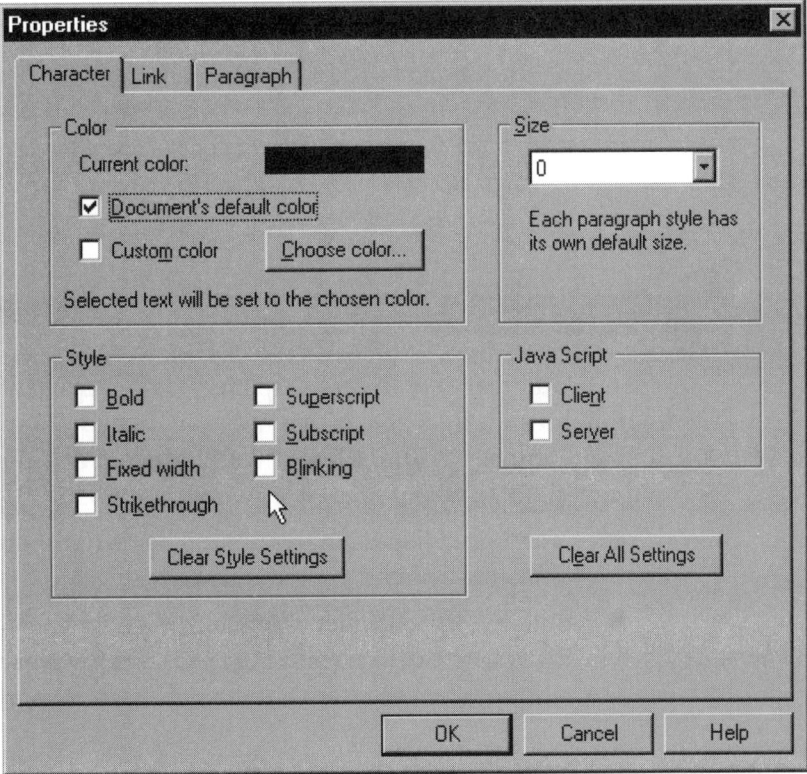

Figure 9-7: *The Character tab in Properties offers several text styles.*

If you change your mind after applying one of these styles, you can clear the selection by using any of these methods:

■ If you haven't done anything else since applying the style, just choose Edit | Undo.

■ Or, reselect the text you want to "unstyle," and click the Clear All Styles button in the toolbar.

■ Or, reselect the text you want to "unstyle," choose Properties | Text, click the Character tab, and then click the Clear Style Settings button.

TRAP

You might wonder why there's no underline option. Well, because hyperlinks in Web pages are underlined, using underlines for regular text is discouraged. You can underline regular text, but to do so you'll have to insert a couple of HTML tags manually (see Chapter 15, "Tuning HTML Tags"). Insert a <u> tag in front of the text you want to underline, then insert a </u> tag where you want the underlining to stop.

CREATING LISTS

Lists are a great way to break up large paragraphs into less intimidating little chunks of text that are easy to read. If you thumb through the pages of this book, you'll see that I'm a big fan of lists. You might also notice that I use two types of lists:

■ Numbered list: Each item in the list is numbered. Good for presenting step-by-step instructions.

■ Bulleted list: A bullet character precedes each item (as in the list you're reading right now). Useful for presenting information when the items in the list are in no particular order.

TIP

For future reference, a numbered list is also called an ordered list, *and the HTML tag for such a list is <ol>. A bulleted list is called an* unordered list *and its HTML tag is <ul>.*

CREATING A NUMBERED LIST

Typing a numbered list is as easy as pie:

1. Type each item in the list *without the number*. Press Enter after you type each item.

2. Select all the items that make up the list, as I've done in the example shown in Figure 9-8.

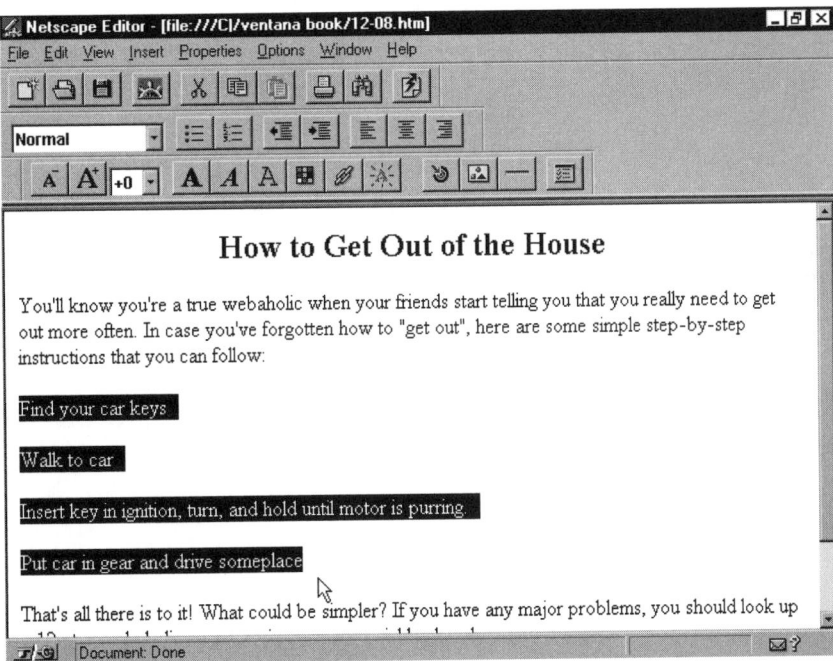

Figure 9-8: *Items to be numbered are selected.*

3. Click the Numbered List button in the Paragraph Format toolbar.

Your list will change instantly. The blank lines between items will disappear, the list will be indented a little, and ## symbols will appear to indicate that numbers will be visible in the browser. To verify the numbers, just view your page in the browser (click the View in Browser button or choose File | Browse Document). Your list will look more like the one in Figure 9-9.

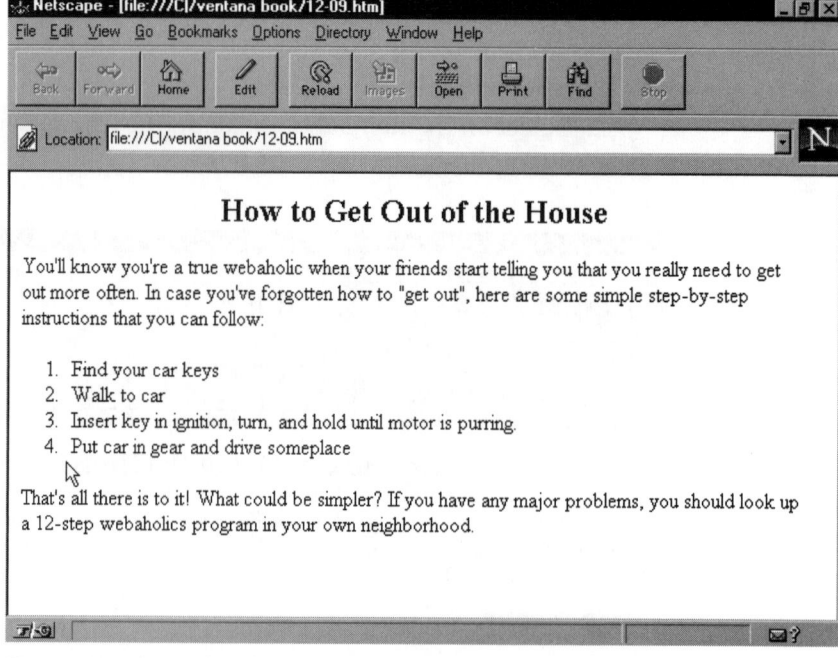

Figure 9-9: *A numbered list as it appears in a browser.*

HEY, STOP LISTING. WOULD YA?

When you get a list going, stopping it may seem difficult. Say, for example, that the cursor is at the end of the last item on the list, and you press Enter with the intention of typing "normal" text. But the darn ### or bullet or whatever appears anyway. What are ya gonna do?

Easy—just leave the cursor right next to the ### or bullet character, and then choose Normal from the Paragraph Style drop-down list in the Paragraph Format toolbar. Or right-click the ### or bullet, choose Paragraph/List properties, choose Normal under Paragraph style, and click OK.

CREATING A BULLETED LIST

As I mentioned earlier, a bulleted list is one that uses a bullet character, rather than a number, to identify each item. Use a bulleted list when the items in a list are separate from one another and need not be read in any particular order.

To create a bulleted list, start with the same basic procedure you used for a numbered list. That is:

1. Type each item in the list, pressing Enter after you type each item.

2. Select all the items in the list, as in my example in Figure 9-10.

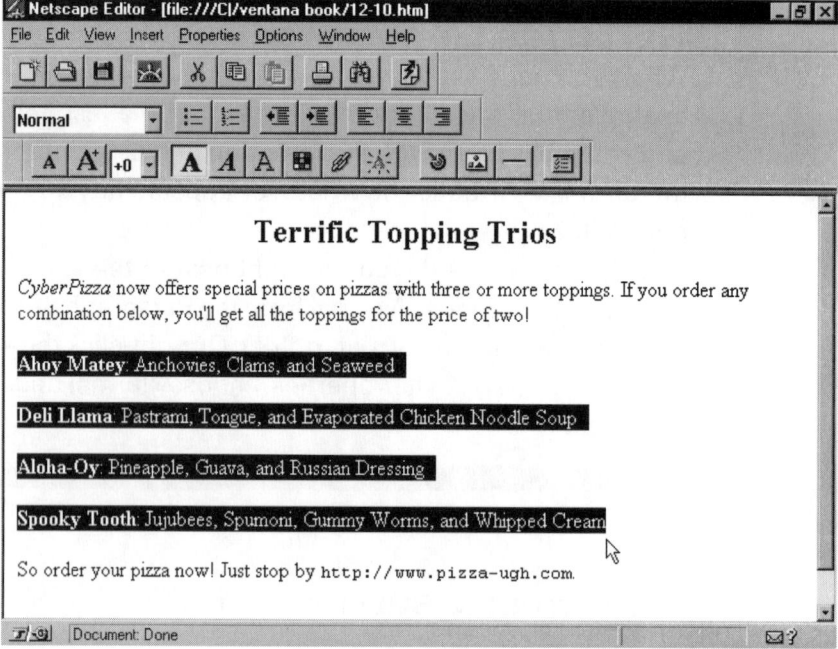

Figure 9-10: *Items for a bulleted list are selected.*

3. Click the Bullet List button in the Paragraph Format toolbar.

Instantly, the list is converted to single-space (no blank line between the items), indented, and each item is marked with a round bullet character, as in Figure 9-11.

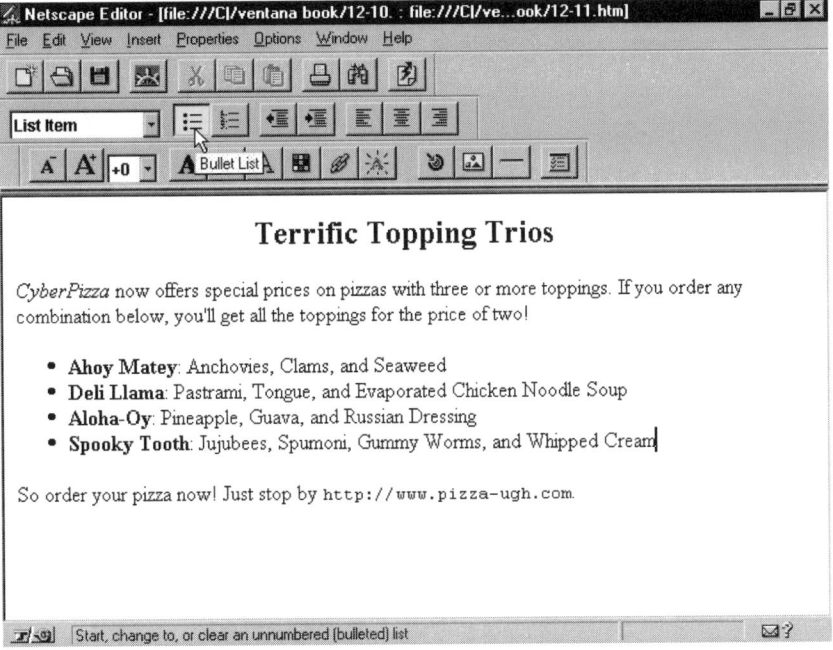

Figure 9-11: *An example of a bulleted list.*

TIP

For added pizzazz, you can use a small graphic image instead of a bullet character to mark each item in a bulleted list. I'll show you how in the next chapter.

MORE ON LISTS

The basic numbered and bulleted list formats just described can be used for almost any list. But you can get much fancier, if you wish, as you'll see in the sections that follow.

CUSTOMIZING NUMBERS & BULLETS

You don't have to stick with the 1, 2, 3, 4 . . . numbering, nor with standard round bullets. You can customize either by following these steps:

1. After making sure that you are working in the editor (not the browser), right-click the first item in the list.

2. Choose Paragraph/List properties from the pop-up menu that appears.

3. In the Properties dialog box, choose an option from the Bullet Style or Number Style drop-down list.

4. If you're customizing a numbered list, you can also change the starting number for the list.

5. Choose OK to close the dialog box and save your changes.

For an accurate view of a numbered list, be sure to switch to the browser view.

TIP

If you're using A, B, C or a, b, c to mark items in the list, the starting number must still be expressed as a number. For example, if you want the list to start with the letter m, the starting number would be 13 (because m is the 13th letter of the alphabet).

INDENTING WITHIN LISTS

As a general rule, indenting anything in a Web page is tricky business. Most of the time, you can't really do it. You can, however, easily indent (and unindent) lists. Here's how:

1. Select the entire list.

2. To indent the list, click the Increase Indent button in the Paragraph Format toolbar, or press Tab.

3. If you go too far and want to "outdent," click the Decrease Indent button in the toolbar, or press Shift+Tab.

Those steps let you control the level of indentation for the entire list. You can also indent selected items within a list. Essentially, when you indent within a list, you create a new, separate list within the outer list. This new list can have its own numbering scheme, bullet style, or whatever. Let me show you a couple of examples.

COMBINED NUMBERS & BULLETS

Figure 9-12 shows a simple numbered list (in browser view) that I created, using the basic technique described in this chapter's "Creating a Numbered List" section.

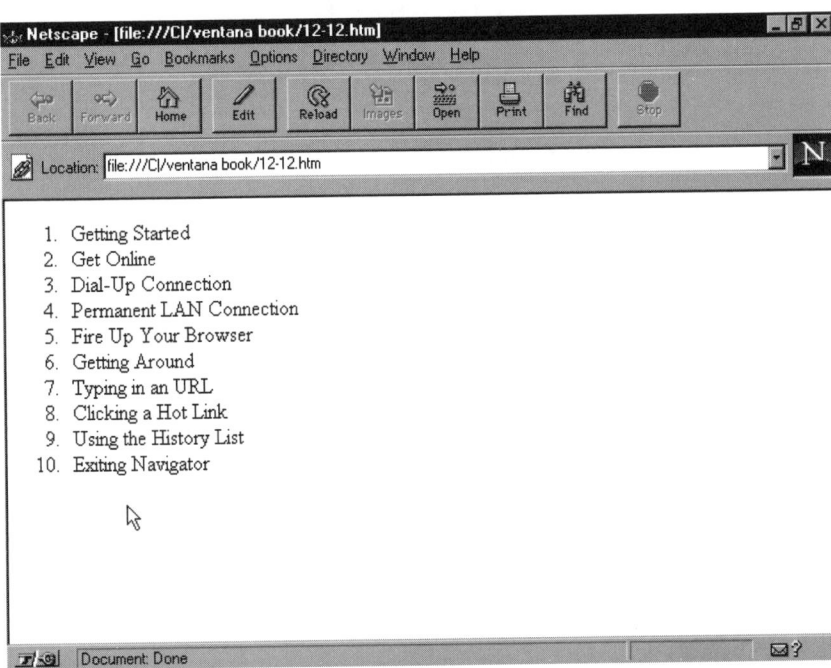

Figure 9-12: *A simple numbered list, in browser view.*

Now observe what happens when I indent portions of the list, and convert them to bulleted lists. First, I switch to the editor. Then I select two items that I want to indent, and I indent those items. While they are still selected, I click the Bulleted List button in the toolbar. The selected items are now indented and marked by bullets rather than numbers (which appear as ## in the editor), as shown in Figure 9-13.

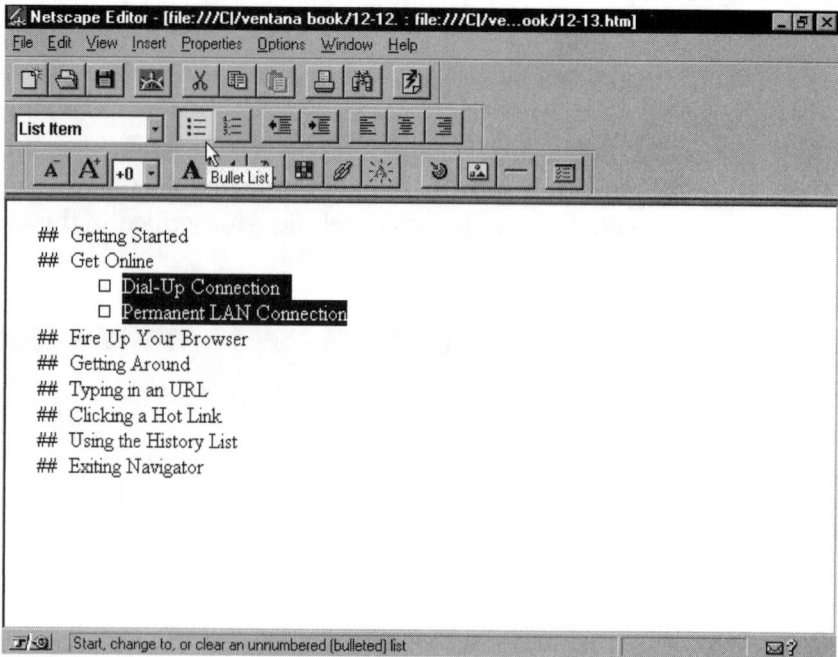

Figure 9-13: *Two lines in the larger list, indented and converted to a bulleted list.*

As another example, let's say that I do the same thing for the three items under "Getting Around," and then switch to browser view for an accurate picture of the modified list (see Figure 9-14).

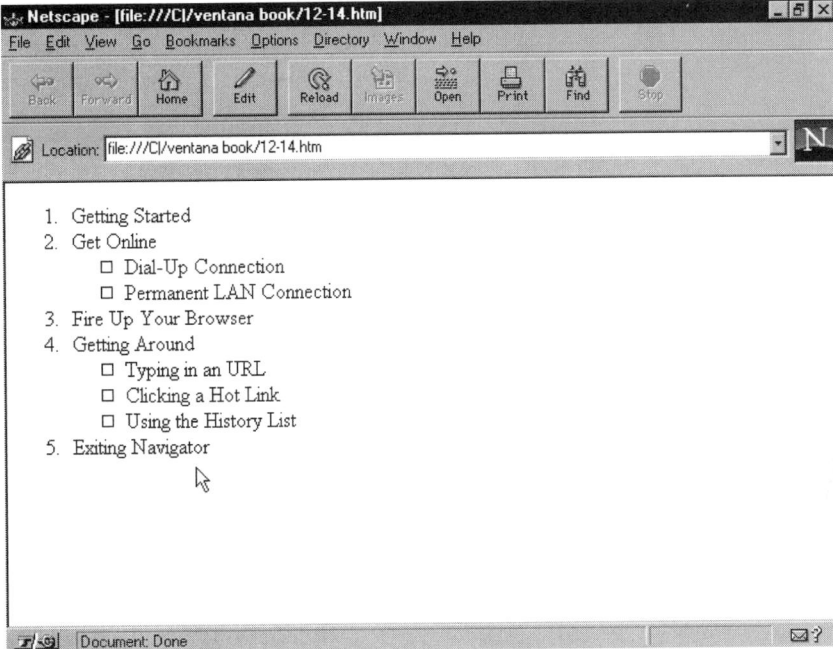

Figure 9-14: *A numbered list with bulleted subitems.*

As you can see in Figure 9-14, Navigator handled the job quite nicely. The numbered items are in proper order, from 1 to 5. The indented bulleted items do not affect the numbers.

AN OUTLINE-STYLE LIST

Now let's look at another example. This time we'll indent some list items, but instead of making them bulleted items, we'll keep them as numbered items. We're going to give each level of indentation its own numbering style, however, to give the list the appearance of a standard outline.

Figure 9-15 shows a sample numbered list. I created this list using the same technique as in earlier numbered lists. After I created the list, however, I changed the number style to I, II, III style. As you can see in browser view, the entire list is numbered with these Roman numerals.

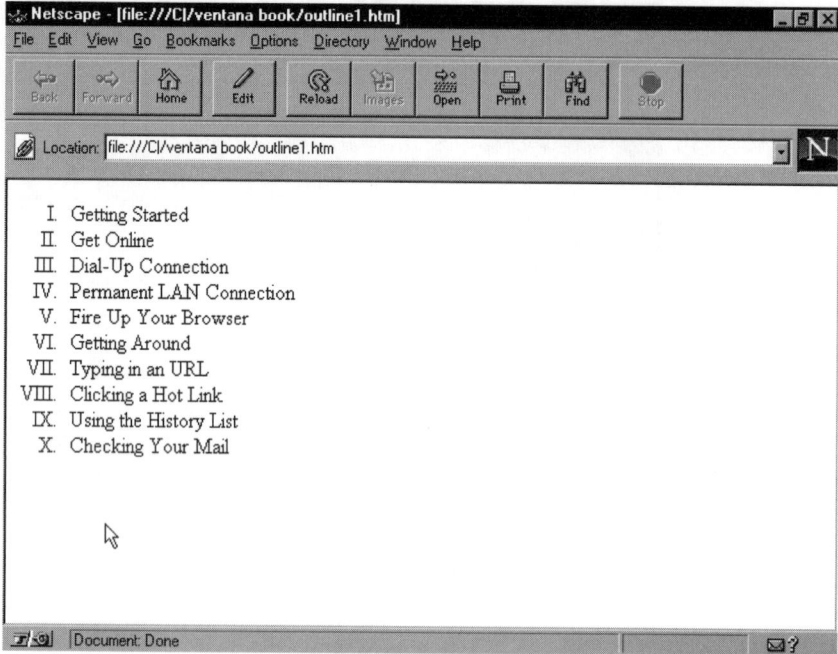

Figure 9-15: *A numbered list, using a Roman-numeral number style.*

Now let's say that I switch to the editor, select three items under "Getting Started," and indent them. Then I select four items under "Fire Up Your Browser," and indent them. Next, I change the Number Style for each of those indented lists to the 1, 2, 3 style. In the editor, my list now looks like the one in Figure 9-16. Notice that Roman numerals are represented by *XX*, and numbers are represented by ##.

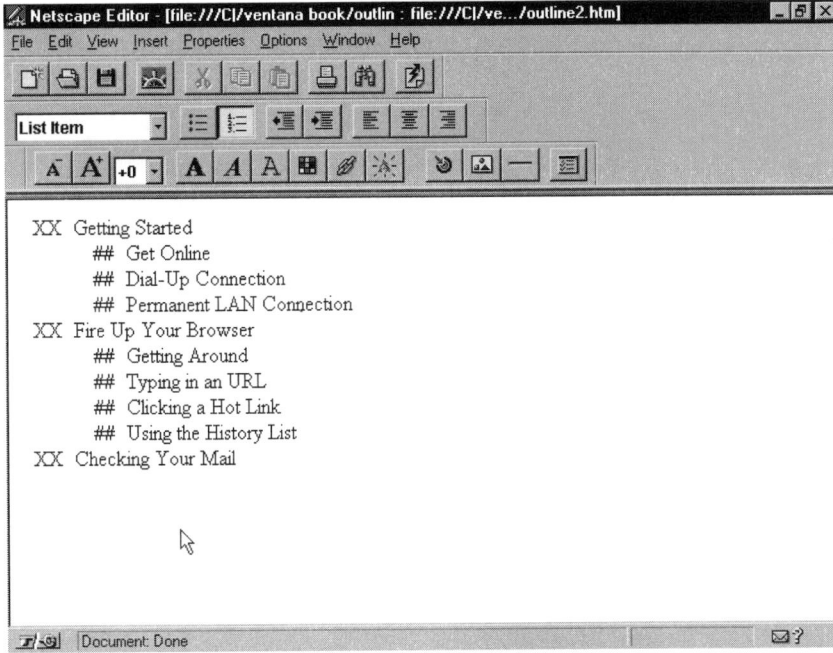

Figure 9-16: *Some items are indented and changed to 1, 2, 3 number style.*

Now, taking it one step further, I indent the two items under "Getting Online," and change their number scheme to a, b, c. Then I do the same for the three items under "Getting Around." You can see the result in Figure 9-17, where the innermost indented items are marked by the letter *A*.

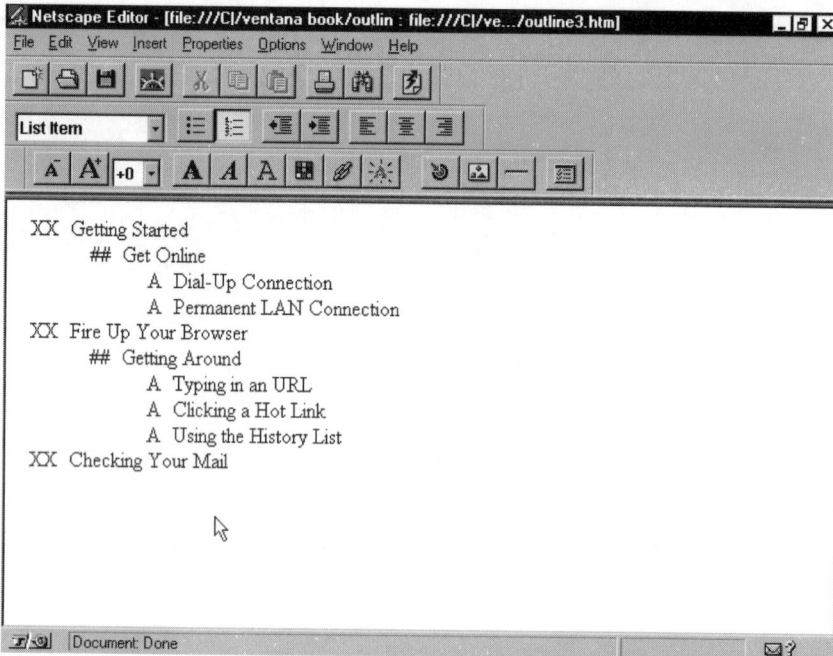

Figure 9-17: *Items indented to a third level, with the numbering style set to a, b, c.*

How will all this look in the Web browser? Well, fortunately, it will look exactly the way you (probably) want it to. The outermost items are numbered sequentially I, II, III. Subitems in each level are numbered correctly, as Figure 9-18 shows.

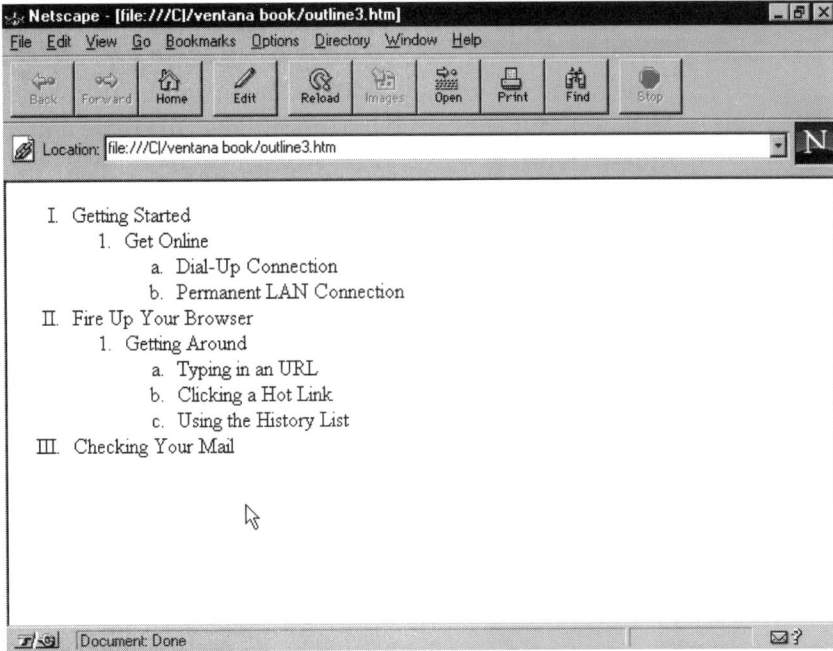

Figure 9-18: *The list from Figure 9-17, in Web browser view.*

The moral of the story is that although indentations seem very difficult to create in Navigator's editor, they're not so bad provided that you make the items to be indented list items.

Which perhaps brings us to the question, "Yeah, but what if I don't want to mark these items with numbers *or* bullets?" Well, you can create another kind of list, called the *menu list*. Its items are not marked by either bullets or numbers.

TRAP

Not all browsers support menu lists. Even the beta (prerelease) version of Netscape Navigator Gold didn't properly support these lists. I'm hoping it will by the time you read this!

CREATING A MENU LIST

The menu list gives you all the benefits of a numbered or bulleted list, without the numbers and bullets. To create a menu list, follow these steps:

1. Type each item in the list, pressing Enter after you type each item.
2. Select all the items in the list.
3. Choose Properties | Text, and click the Paragraph tab.
4. Under Paragraph Style, choose List Item.
5. In the section titled List, choose Menu List from the Style drop-down list.
6. Choose OK.

You can indent items within the list, as in the examples presented earlier.

TRAP

Browsers that don't support the menu list display them as regular bulleted lists.

CREATING A DIRECTORY LIST

The directory list succinctly presents short list items in three columns across the page. Each item in the list should be a short word or phrase (up to 20 characters). To create a directory list, follow the same basic steps you'd follow to create a menu list:

TRAP

Like menu lists, directory lists aren't widely supported and appear as bulleted lists in many Web browsers.

1. Type each item in the list (up to 20 characters), pressing Enter after each item.

2. Select all the items in the list.

3. Choose Properties | Text, and click the Paragraph tab.

4. Under Paragraph Style, choose List Item.

5. In the section titled List, choose Directory List from the Style drop-down list.

6. Choose OK.

CREATING A DESCRIPTION LIST

The description list—also called a *definition list* or *glossary list*—is generally used to list brief words or phrases and their definitions or descriptions. The idea is to present information like that presented in the Glossary of this book.

Creating a description list is not at all like creating the other lists described in this chapter. You can't select an entire list and apply a list style to it. Instead, you define a definition term (a word or short phrase) and then press Enter. Then type the lengthier definition or description, and press Enter. To format that text as an item in a definition list, follow these steps:

1. Click on the definition term (the short text).

3. Choose Description Title from the Paragraph Style drop-down list in the toolbar.

2. Click in the lengthier definition (the longer chunk of text).

4. Choose Description Text from the Paragraph Style drop-down list in the toolbar.

5. Repeat Steps 1 through 4 for every item in the list.

Figure 9-19 shows an example of a description list, used to format a glossary. In this example, I've also boldfaced the Description Titles (short text) by selecting that short text and clicking the Bold button in the toolbar.

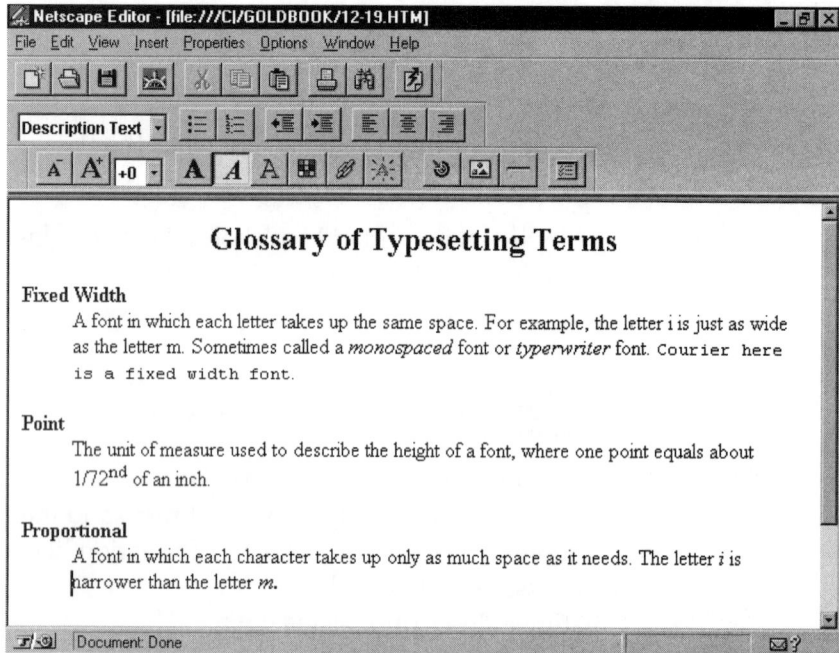

Figure 9-19: *A sample description list in Web browser view.*

USING FONTS IN YOUR PAGE

For those of you who are new to publishing, let me first describe
what a font *is*. In the real world, a *font* is a combination of a typeface, weight, and size. The *typeface* has a name, such as Times Roman or Courier. The *weights* are things like **boldface** and *italic*. And
the size is measured in *points*, with one point equal to 1/72 inch.
Thus, in a font shown at 72 points, the largest letters are about an
inch tall. Figure 9-20 shows some examples of fonts.

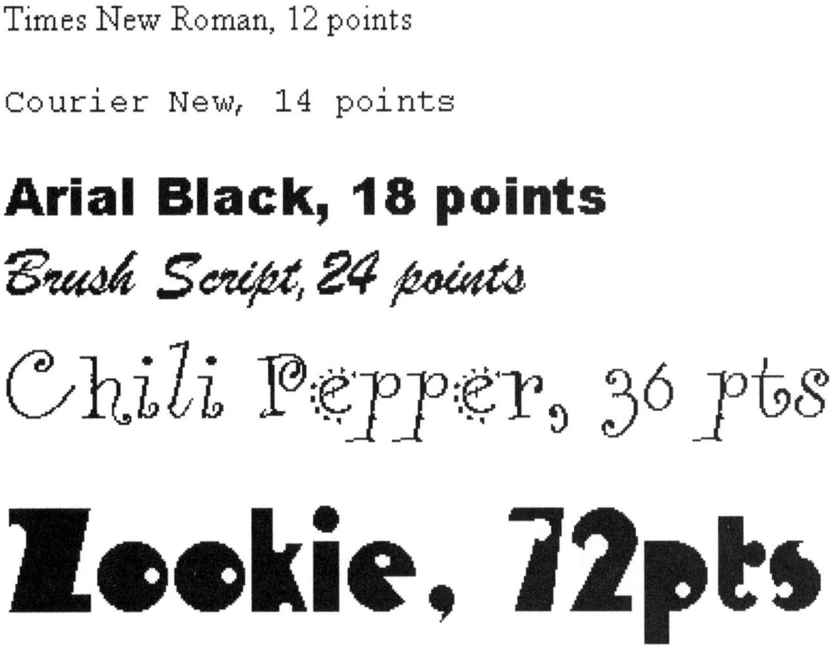

Times New Roman, 12 points

Courier New, 14 points

Arial Black, 18 points

Brush Script, 24 points

Chili Pepper, 36 pts

Zookie, 72pts

Figure 9-20: *Some examples of fonts.*

I used the phrase "in the real world" because you can't always choose a specific typeface or point size when you author Web pages. There are a couple of reasons for these limitations. First, fonts exist on the *reader's* PC. Your Web page can show only the fonts on the reader's PC. Second, the reader has more control over fonts than you do. While the reader is browsing your page with Netscape Navigator, he or she can choose Options | General Preferences and click the Fonts tab to choose a proportional font and fixed-width font for viewing *your* page.

In short, it wouldn't make sense for Navigator to give you *too* much control over fonts, because you can't predict which fonts a particular reader can see. Navigator does, however, let you control the *relative size* of fonts, their colors, and their weight. (Changing the weight of a font is discussed in "Boldface, Italic & Such," earlier in this chapter.)

TWO WAYS TO CONTROL TYPEFACE

Actually, there are a couple of ways that you can control which font appears on a reader's screen. For absolute control, you can use a graphic image to display text in some fancy font. See Chapter 14, "Power Image Publishing," for more information.

A second alternative would be to use the new FACE= attribute of the <font> tag. While this doesn't give you *exact* control these days, the situation is improving. See "Cutting-Edge Design Tools" later in this chapter for more information.

CHANGING THE RELATIVE FONT SIZE

You can change the relative size of a font to any value in the range of –2 to +4 (–2 is very fine print, 0 is the same as the normal text on the page, and +4 is very large). To see for yourself, follow these steps:

1. Select the text that you want to resize.

2. In the Character formatting toolbar, use any of the following tools to change the font size:

   ■ Click the Decrease font size button to shrink the text.

   ■ Click the Increase font size button to enlarge the text.

   ■ Or, choose a value (–2 to +4) from the Font Size drop-down list.

   ■ Or, choose Properties | Font Size and whatever size you want.

Figure 9-21 shows you the relative sizes, –2 to +4, in a Web browser screen.

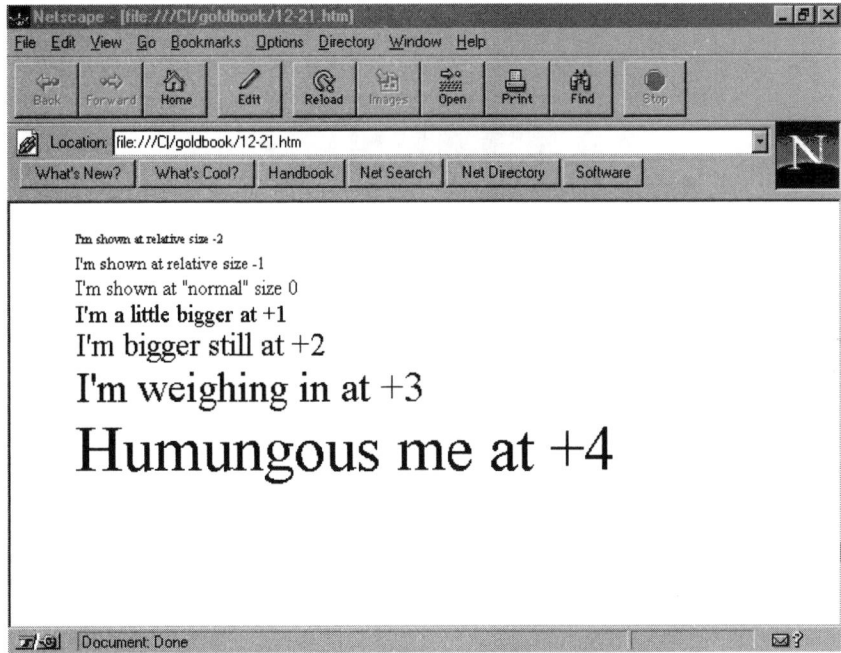

Figure 9-21: *Examples of relative font sizes.*

CHANGING THE FONT COLOR

You can choose a color for any chunk of text, as follows:

1. Select the text you want to color. Then...

   ■ Click the Font Color button in the Character Format toolbar.

   ■ Or right-click on the selection and choose Character Properties | Custom Color | Choose Color.

2. In the Color dialog box shown in Figure 9-22, choose a color.

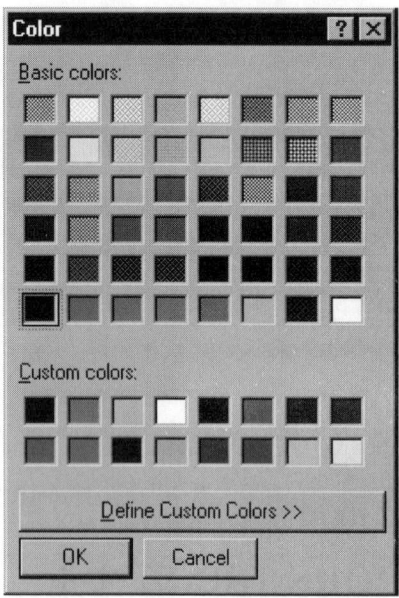

Figure 9-22: *The Color dialog box lets you choose a color for text.*

3. Click OK to work your way to back to the document.

At first, the colored text will look strange because it's still selected. If you just click anywhere on or near the selected text, you'll
see the text in its correct new color.

DEFINING A CUSTOM COLOR

You may have noticed that there's a Define Custom Colors button
in the Color dialog box. As the name implies, clicking this button
lets you define your own custom color. When you click the button
you see an expanded Color dialog box that looks like Figure 9-23.

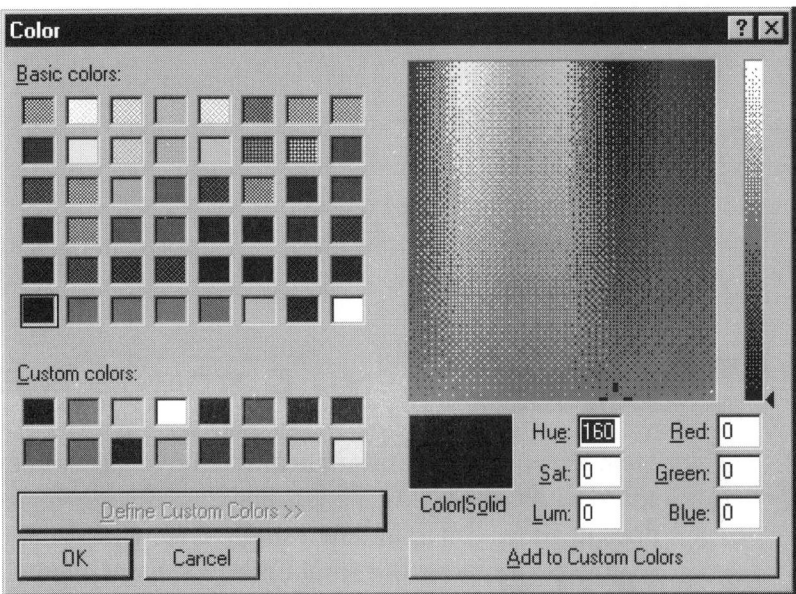

Figure 9-23: *Color dialog box expanded to allow custom colors.*

To add a new custom color, first click on an empty (white) color box. (To replace an existing custom color, click on the color you want to replace.) Then create your color, using the palette and slider bar (over to the right). Click anywhere in the large color matrix to get in the ballpark. Then, to add black or white, drag the slider to the right of the color matrix up or down. Watch the Color | Solid indicator for an accurate view of the color you're creating.

When you've created a color you like, you'll need to choose between the actual color or the nearest solid, which has no black-and-white in it. If you want to use the solid, double-click the Solid side of the Color | Solid options.

Even though there's no Help button in the Color dialog box, you can right-click any option and choose What's This? for more information.

When you're happy with your color, click the Add to Custom Colors button. Your new color will appear in the selected box under Custom Colors.

MORE ON INDENT, OUTDENTS & SPACES

Most Web browsers automatically remove tabs and extra white space when displaying a page. For this reason, Navigator's editor doesn't allow you to indent a single line by pressing the Tab key or typing extra spaces. But sometimes you want a few lines to be indented or spaced a certain way. If you can't accomplish what you want by using a list and the Increase Indent button, try using Formatted style, or a fixed-width font. Let me give you an example.

Suppose that I'm writing a Web page for techno-nerds, one that discusses the JavaScript programming language in relation to the BASIC programming language. I want to show a couple of little snippets of code from each language, as in Figure 9-24.

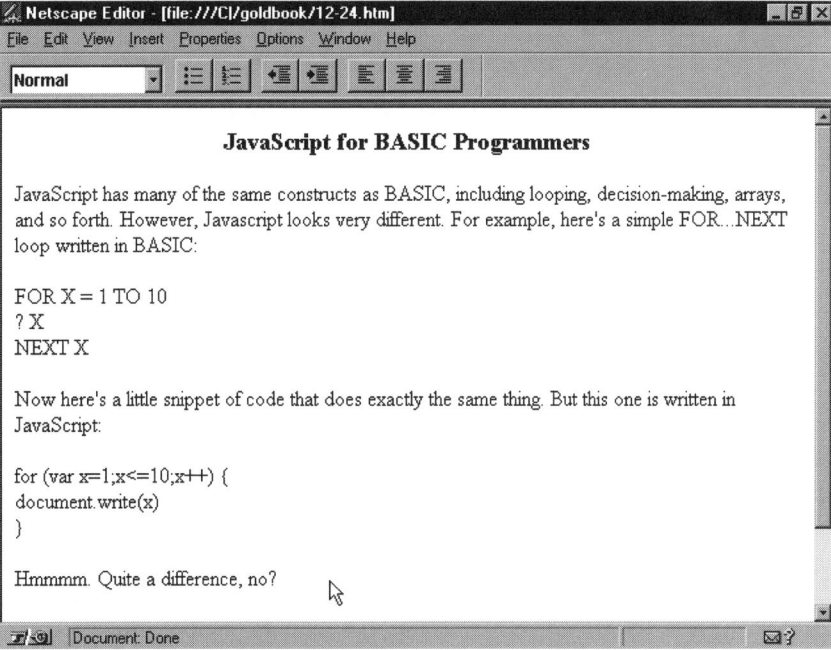

Figure 9-24: *First draft of a Web page that will need a couple of single-line indents.*

I was able to single-space the code examples by pressing Shift+Enter, rather than Enter, to end each line. But to really do the job right, I need to indent some lines within the code snippets. Trying to do so by using the Tab key or Increase Indent button indents the entire snippet—not just the current line. If I try to indent a line by inserting blank spaces at the beginning of the line, the editor just ignores those spaces. What's a body to do?

Well, the Formatted design element (also called the *preformatted* element) can help here because it *does* allow you to type in extra white spaces (and also ensures that the reader's Web browser doesn't remove them). To apply the Formatted format, select the text that you want to format. Then choose Formatted from the Paragraph Style drop-down list.

> **TIP**
>
> *If you're trying to organize text into rows and columns, I recommend that you use Tables (discussed in Chapter 12, "Get It Straight With Tables") rather than the Formatted paragraph format.*

In my example, I would select the BASIC sample code and apply the Formatted style to it. Then I'd do the same to the JavaScript sample code. Having applied the formatted style, I could indent individual lines by moving the cursor to the beginning of a line and pressing the spacebar to my heart's content. In Figure 9-25, I've actually indented both examples in their entirety, and further indented the middle line in each code snippet. To help the code stand out a little more I slightly increased the font size of each snippet and applied boldface.

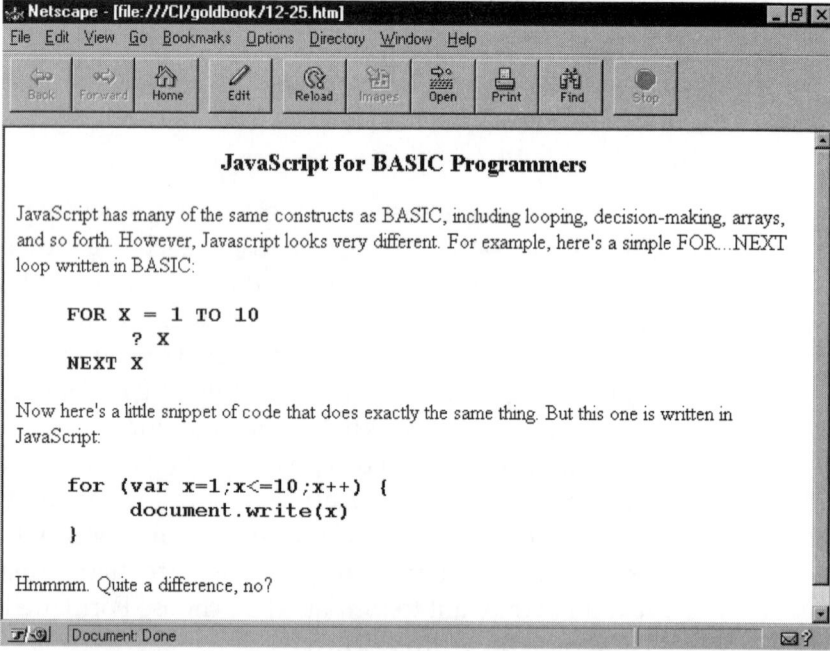

Figure 9-25: *The Formatted paragraph format lets me use the spacebar to indent individual lines.*

BLOCK QUOTATION

Yet another way to indent text is with the Block Quotation format. This format is typically used to identify lengthy quotes. Use the standard techniques to apply the Block Quotation format to text, as follows:

1. Right-click the paragraph that you want to format, and choose Paragraph/List properties.
2. Choose Normal from the Paragraph Style drop-down list.
3. Choose Block Quote from the Additional Style drop-down list.
4. Click the OK button.

The paragraph is indented equally from both the left and right margins. You can click the Increase Indent and Decrease Indent buttons in the Paragraph Format toolbar to increase and decrease the level of indentation. In the example shown in Figure 9-26, I've indented the block quotation a few extra spaces.

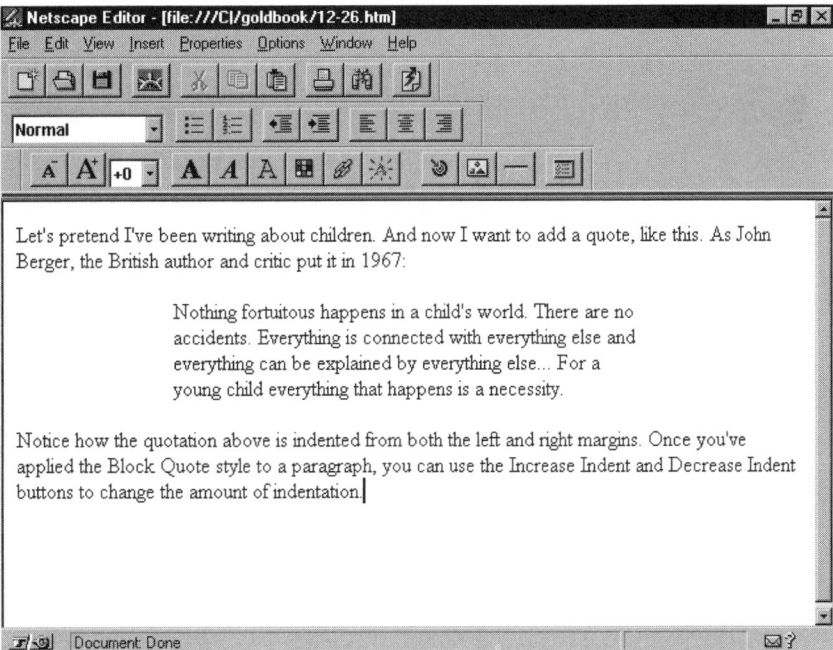

Figure 9-26: *The indented paragraph is formatted as a block quote.*

NONBREAKING SPACES

All Web browsers *wrap* text in paragraphs. In other words, when a line in a paragraph reaches the right margin, the browser breaks the line at a space between words, rather than smack in the middle of a word.

You may come across a situation in which you want to add a blank space but *not* let the browser break apart text at the space. For example, if you type a telephone number in the format *(619) 555-1434*, you might want to make sure that the number doesn't get broken between the area code and the telephone number.

In such a situation, just replace the regular blank space with a nonbreaking space. To do so, delete the space. Then press Shift+Spacebar. Optionally, you can choose Insert | Nonbreaking Space from the menus.

SIGNING OFF

It's customary to end each Web page with a *signature* that describes who wrote the page, and who to contact for more information. You can also include copyright information, a hot link to your own e-mail address (see Chapter 11, "Adding Hyperlinks"), and other useful information.

The signature line is so common that there's even a built-in style for it. This style, called the Address style, typically displays text in italics. To add a signature line to the bottom of your Web page, follow these steps:

1. Move the cursor to the bottom of the page (press Ctrl+End).

2. If you want to insert a blank line or two, press Enter.

3. If you want to insert a horizontal line, click the Insert Horiz Line button in the Character Format toolbar. (You'll learn more about lines in the next chapter.)

4. Type your author name, e-mail address, and any other information you feel is pertinent.

5. Select all the text you just typed, then select Address from the Paragraph style drop-down list.

In the example shown in Figure 9-27, I've put a signature at the end of one of my own pages, and applied the Address style.

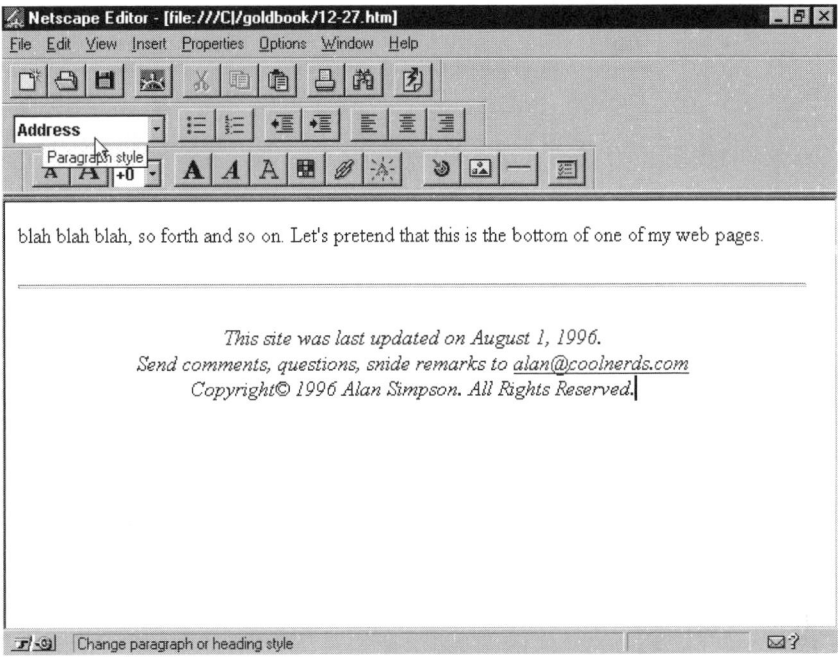

Figure 9-27: *Last line on a page, formatted with the Address style.*

HTML TAGS YOU HAVE MET

As I've mentioned, the Web browsers use HTML tags to determine how to format text in pages. Fortunately, you don't have to think about HTML because Navigator's editor automatically puts in all the right tags, behind the scenes. The only time you even see the tags is when you view the document source behind a page (by choosing View | View Document Source).

Just in case you do go peeking behind the scenes, Table 9-1 summarizes some of the tags you might encounter. These tags are just the ones that are relevant to styles you've learned about in this chapter and the previous one. There are other tags, as you'll learn in later chapters.

Tag	Formats text as
	Nonbreaking space
<address>...</address>	Address style (italics)
...	Boldface
<blink>...</blink>	Blinking
<blockquote>...</blockquote>	Block quotation
 	Line break (Shift+Enter)
<center>...</center>	Centered
<dd>...<dd>	Description list description
<dir>...</dir>	Directory list
<div align=right>...</div>	Right-aligned
<dl>...</dl>	Description list
<dt>...</dt>	Description title (short text)
<font>...</font>	Relative size and/or color
<h1>...</h1> through <h6>...</h6>	Headings
<i>...</i>	Italics
<li>...</li>	List item (a single item in a list)
<menu>...</menu>	Menu list
<ol>...</ol>	Ordered (numbered) list
<p>...</p>	Paragraph
<pre>...</pre>	Formatted (preformatted)
<strike>...</strike>	Strikethrough
_{...}	Subscript
^{...}	Superscript
<title>...</title>	Title as it appears in title bar
<tt>...</tt>	Fixed-width (typewriter) font
<ul>...</ul>	Unordered (bulleted) list

Table 9-1: *Some HTML tags that the editor types for you.*

CUTTING-EDGE DESIGN TOOLS

The Internet is constantly evolving, bringing new and better ways to format your Web pages. Netscape Navigator Gold 3.0 offers many of these cutting-edge design tools, including font face, multi-column layouts, and spacers. As I write this chapter, Gold's editor, unfortunately, doesn't offer any WYSIWYG tools for adding these features to your Web page. But you can go "behind the scenes" and add the required HTML tags manually, if you want to try out some.

One thing to keep in mind before you start using these new features is that not all browsers will be able to support them. Most browsers just ignore tags that they don't support. Still, you'll want to see how your page looks to browsers that do, and do not, support these features. So after you add any of the features I'm about to discuss in these next sections, I recommend you try to view the page using as many different browsers as you have available.

BEFORE YOU TRY THESE

Before you try any of these new formatting techniques, make sure you have some means of editing the HTML source of your pages. To do so, start in Gold's editor and follow these steps:

1. Choose Options | Editor Preferences.
2. Click the General tab.
3. Next to HTML source type **c:\windows\notepad.exe** or browse to the Windows directory and choose notepad.exe.
4. Choose OK.

That should do the trick. You'll be able to edit your HTML source code in a moment. If you have any problems, or want to learn more about editing HTML tags directly, see Chapter 15, "Tuning HTML Tags."

CHOOSING A TYPEFACE

A new attribute, FACE=, has been added to the <FONT> tag to specify a typeface for a font. Currently, the only two browsers that support this tag are the latest versions of Netscape Navigator and Microsoft Internet Explorer. However, other browsers will probably follow suit soon.

There is a catch to using the FACE= attribute. The attribute works only if the requested font is available on the reader's PC. If the requested font isn't available on that PC, then the FACE= attribute has no effect.

You can even specify a series of font faces, separated by commas, in the attribute. For example <FONT FACE="Arial,Helvetica"> tells the Web browser to use the Arial typeface if it's available. If Arial isn't available, use the Helvetica typeface. If that's not available either, then just ignore this request and use the font you've been using up to now. Whichever font is selected stays in effect up to the closing </FONT> tag.

To add a FACE= attribute to a <FONT> tag, you need to first edit the document source. Let's look at an example. Suppose that, in Gold's editor, I type a title like *Hi, I am A Title* near the top of Figure 9-28. Let's say I've also selected that text and increased its font size to +3 using the Font Size drop-down list. Now I want to change the typeface of that font to Arial.

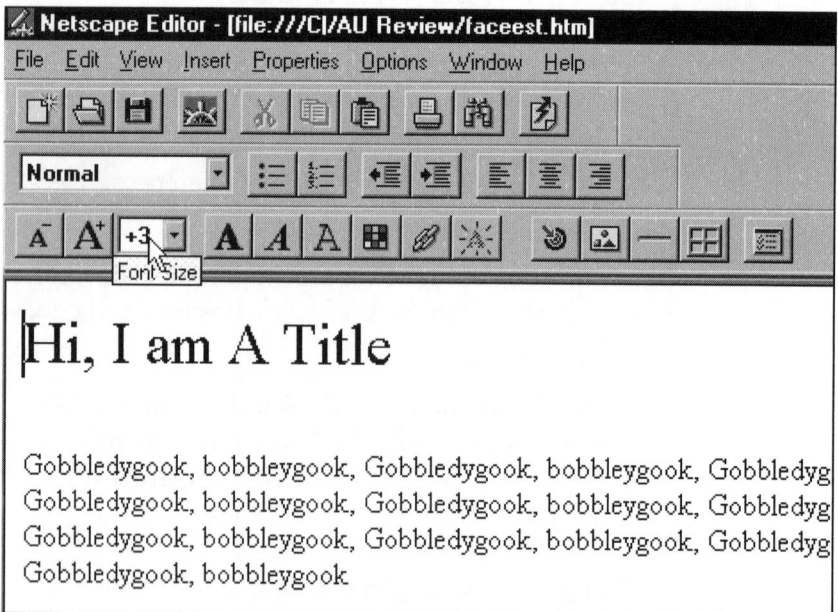

Figure 9-28: *Sample text with title in "regular" (Times) font, at +3 size.*

To add the FACE= attribute I need to get to the document source. To do that I choose View | Edit Document Source. You may be prompted to save the document. If so, choose Save and name the file, if necessary.

The HTML source code will appear in a Notepad editing window. You'll need to look around for the <FONT> tag to which you want to add the FACE= attribute. Once found, type in **FACE="Arial"** to the right of **<FONT** but still within the brackets, as below and in Figure 9-29.

```
<FONT FACE="Arial" SIZE=+3>
```

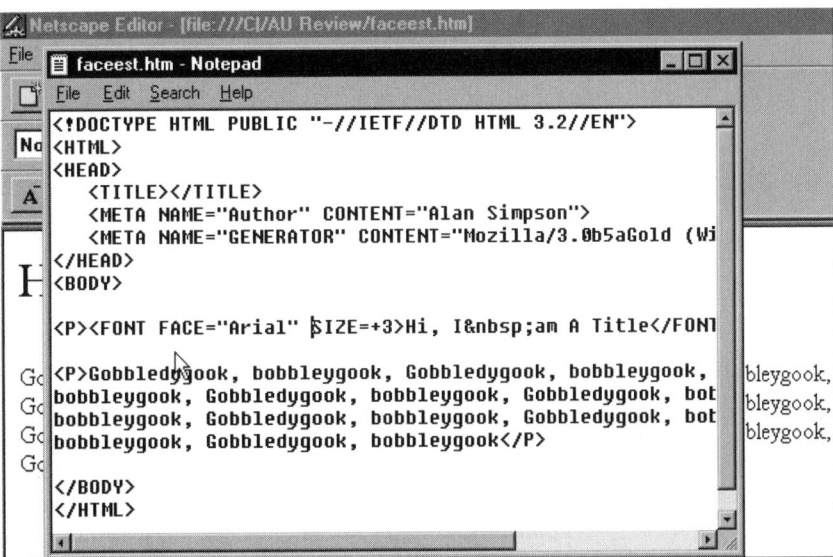

Figure 9-29: *The FACE="Arial" attribute added to a <FONT> tag.*

Then you can close the Notepad window by choosing File | Exit from its menu bar, or by clicking its Close (X) button. Prompts will appear asking if you want to save the change and reload the document. Choose Yes as your response to each prompt. Figure 9-30 shows the result. The large title text is no displayed in the Arial font. Of course, it works here because it just so happens that my system has the Arial font on it, as do most other Windows systems.

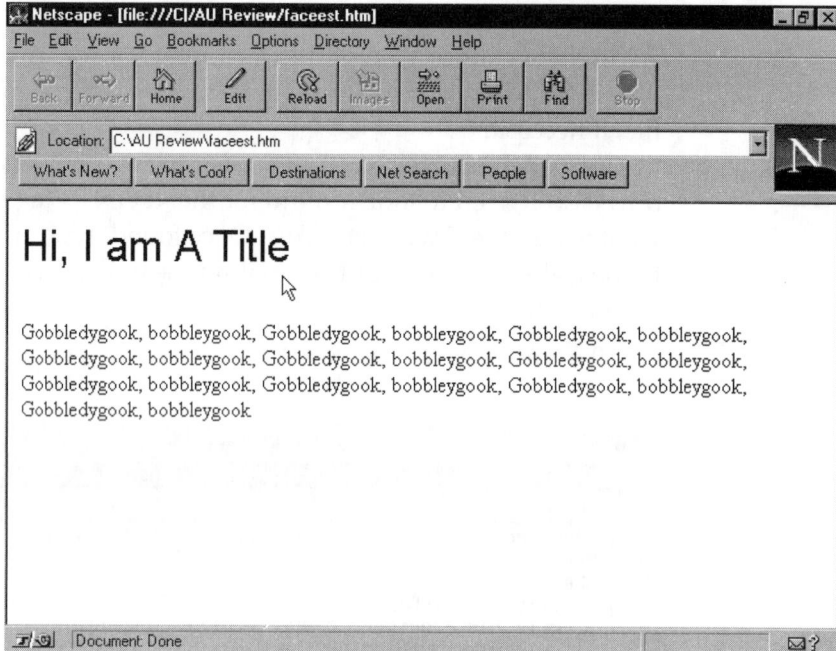

Figure 9-30: *Large heading now displayed in Arial typeface.*

TIP

To review all the fonts available on your own PC, click the Windows 95 Start button and choose Settings | Control Panel. Then double-click the Fonts folder icon.

As I mentioned, one of the weaknesses to specifying a typeface is that it assumes that the requested typeface is installed on the reader's PC. But that situation will improve in the near future because some vendors (Microsoft and Netscape, I think, but don't quote me on it) are planning to put universal font sets out on the Web. If a reader's PC doesn't have the font you want to show your text in, the browser will know to grab the font from that universal font set out on the Web. So you won't have to worry anymore about which fonts your readers do or don't have on their PC.

USING THE NEW <SPACER> TAG

The new <SPACER> tag lets you add blank space to (or around) body text. As far as I know, only Netscape Navigator 3.0 supports this tag right now. And, there appears to be no direct support in Gold's editor; you have to manually insert the tag as I'll explain in a minute.

TIP

If all this business of "tags" and "attributes" has your head spinning, consider reading Chapter 15, "Tuning HTML Tags." There you'll get a quick overview of what HTML tags are all about.

The <SPACER...> tag offers the following attributes:

- TYPE = HORIZONTAL/VERTICAL/BLOCK
- SIZE= *number of pixels*
- WIDTH=, HEIGHT= *number of pixels*
- ALIGN = LEFT/RIGHT

Figure 9-31 shows an example of using a couple of simple <SPACER> tags to indent a lower paragraph. Though you can't see the tags in the browser, you can see that the first line of the third paragraph is indented. Furthermore, there is extra space above that paragraph.

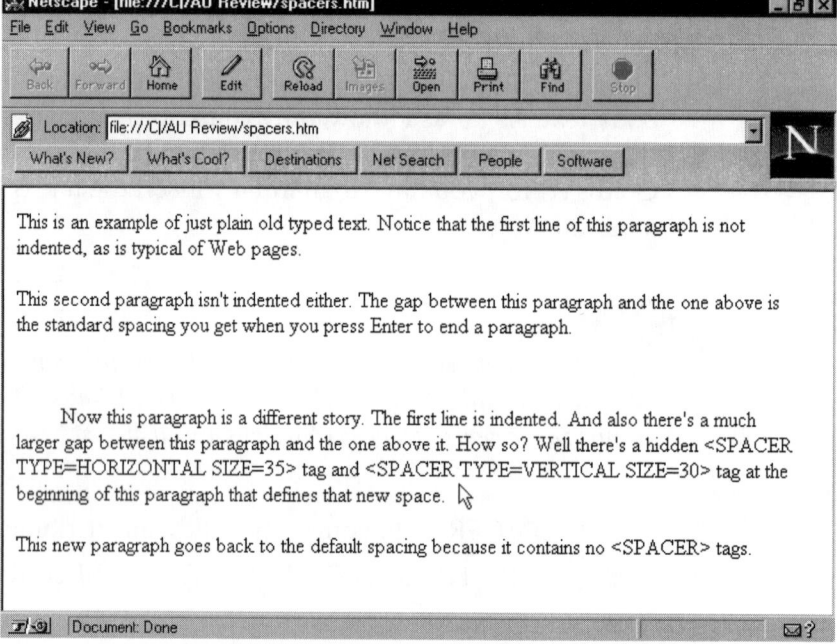

Figure 9-31: *Third paragraph indented and lowered using hidden <SPACER> tags.*

Now if I were to show you the document source "behind the scenes" in Figure 9-31 you'd be able to see the <SPACER...> tags, as in Figure 9-32. Notice that the first one creates a horizontal space that's 35 pixels wide (the indentation) using the syntax:

```
<SPACER TYPE=HORIZONTAL SIZE=35>
```

Right after that tag comes the next spacer tag that creates a vertical space of 30 pixels, above the current paragraph:

```
<SPACER TYPE=VERTICAL SIZE=30>
```

```
Netscape - [Source of: file:///C|/AU Review/spacers.htm]

<!DOCTYPE HTML PUBLIC "-//IETF//DTD HTML 3.2//EN">
<HTML>
<HEAD>
    <TITLE></TITLE>
    <META NAME="Author" CONTENT="Alan Simpson">
    <META NAME="GENERATOR" CONTENT="Mozilla/3.0b5aGold (Win95; I) [Netscape]">
</HEAD>
<BODY>

<P>This is an example of just plain old typed text. Notice that the first
line of this paragraph is not indented, as is typical of Web pages. </P>

<P>This second paragraph isn't indented either. The gap between this paragraph
and the one above is the standard spacing you get when you press Enter
to end a paragraph.</P>

<P><SPACER TYPE=HORIZONTAL SIZE=35><SPACER TYPE=VERTICAL SIZE=30>Now this
paragraph is a different story. The first line is indented. And also there's
a much larger gap between this paragraph and the one above it. How so?
Well there's a hidden &lt;SPACER TYPE=HORIZONTAL SIZE=35&gt; tag and &lt;SPAC
TYPE=VERTICAL SIZE=30&gt; tag at the beginning of this paragraph that defines
that new space.</P>

<P>This new paragraph goes back to the default spacing because it contains
no &lt;SPACER&gt; tags.</P>

</BODY>
```

Figure 9-32: *Document source view of the page shown in Figure 9-31.*

So now you may be wondering how one goes about inserting a spacer into a page. Simple! First, open your Web page in Gold's editor. Then:

1. Click where you want the space to appear.

2. Choose Insert | HTML Tag from Gold's menu bar.

3. Type in one (and only one) complete tag. For example in Figure 9-32 I've typed in the tag for making the vertical space.

4. Choose OK.

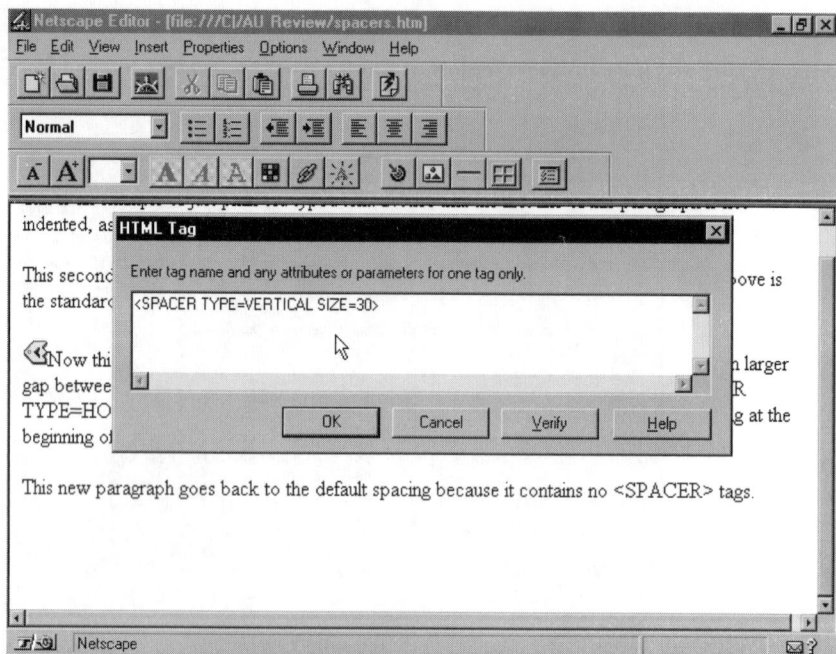

Figure 9-33: *Typing a single HTML tag via Gold's editor.*

Initially, all you'll see is a tag icon where you placed the new HTML tag. To see the effect of the tag, you'll need to switch to the browser view.

Figure 9-34 shows an example of using spacers to indent one or more paragraphs in a "block quotation" format, i.e., from both the left and right margins. I used spacers to define the empty blocks of white space that act as the margins, which allows me to define the level of indentation right down to the pixel.

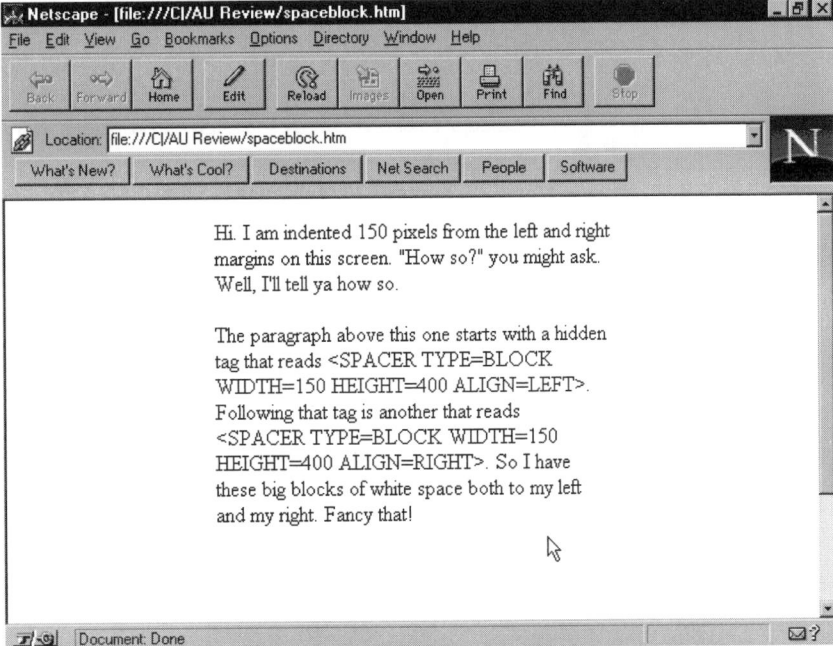

Figure 9-34: *Sample page with paragraphs indented using spacers.*

Figure 9-35 shows the document source for the page in Figure 9-34. You can see the two <SPACER...> tags just under the <P> tag that starts the first paragraph. I inserted both of those tags using the Insert | HTML Tag commands from Gold's menu bar, exactly as I inserted the <SPACER> tags in the example that preceded this one.

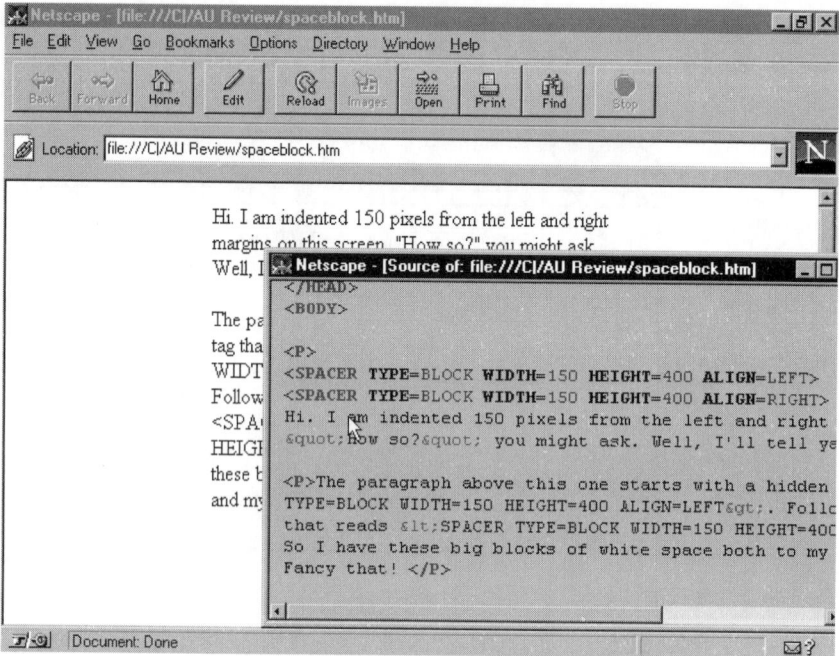

Figure 9-35: *Some of the document source for the page shown in Figure 9-34.*

REAL NEWSPAPER COLUMNS

Hot on the presses for future Web pages are real newspaper columns (also called *snaking columns*). You're no doubt familiar with this style of column from newspapers and magazines where you read down one column and, when you get to the end of the column, you resume reading at the top of the next column. As I write this chapter, only Netscape Navigator 3.0 supports newspaper columns. And as with other cutting-edge features, there are no simple WYSIWYG approach to creating newspaper columns in Gold's editor. So to use newspaper columns you'll need to insert some HTML tags manually.

The tags you'll use are as follows:

- <MULTICOL>...</MULTICOL>: These tags surround the text that is to be displayed in multiple columns.

- COLS=: Used within the <MULTICOL> tag to define how many columns the text will be split into.
- GUTTER=: Defines the gap between columns, in pixels. If omitted, defaults to 10 pixels.
- WIDTH=: Defines the width of an individual column, in pixels. If omitted, each column is the same width.

Figure 9-36 shows an example of a Web page before applying the <MULTICOL> tags to it.

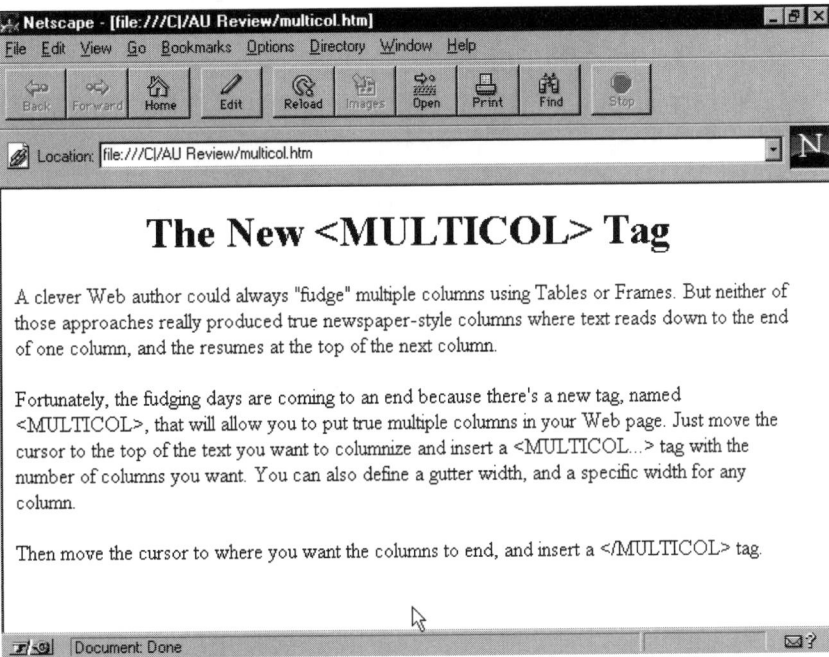

Figure 9-36: *A standard Web page before applying multiple columns.*

Now let me show you how to columnize this page. First, I would go to Gold's editor. Then I would click where I want the columns to begin—just to the left of the letter *A* that starts the sentence *A clever....* Then I would choose Insert | HTML Tag from the menu bar and type in the tag <MULTICOL COLS=2> as in Figure 9-37.

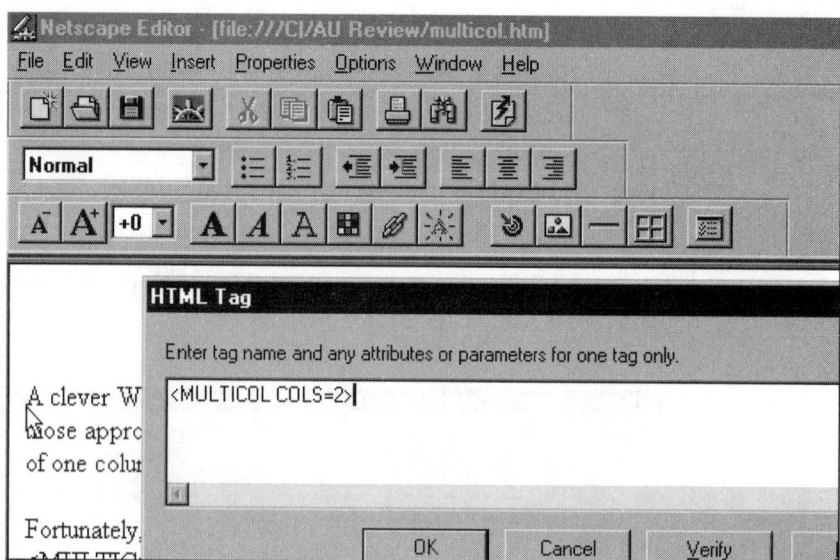

Figure 9-37: *Adding a <MULTICOL> tag to the top of some body text.*

Next, I would move the cursor to the end of the text to be columnized. There I would use Insert | HTML Tag to insert a </MULTICOL> tag. Initially, nothing would look any different in Gold's editor, other than the fact that little tag icons would appear where I inserted the custom tags. However, switching over to the browser view would show that the main body of text in my page is indeed in two columns, as in Figure 9-38.

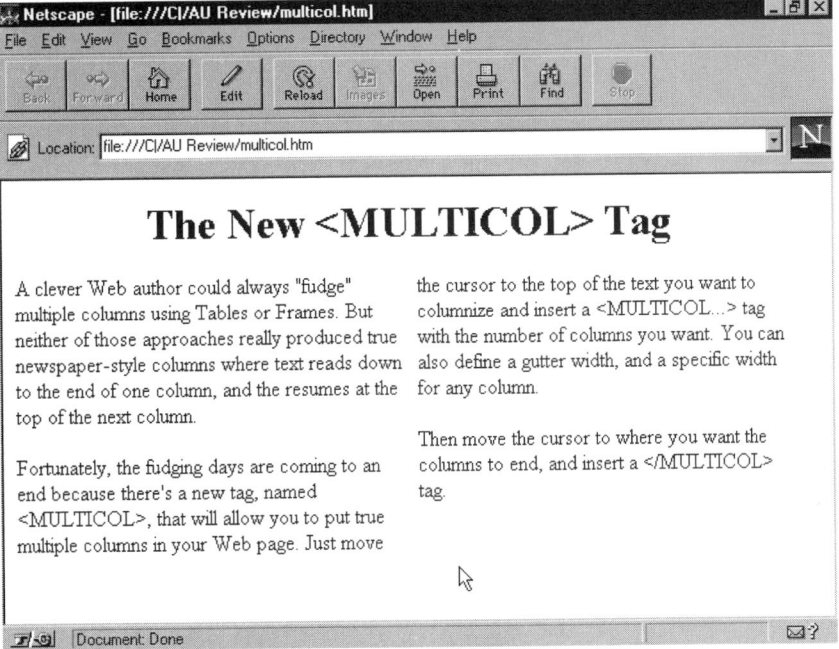

Figure 9-38: *Text is now displayed in two columns.*

I could fancy this page up a bit in Gold's editor. For example, I might start by inserting a horizontal line under the main title (using the Insert Horiz. Line button or Insert I Horizontal Line in Gold's editor). Then I could double-click the icon that represents the <MULTICOL> tag, and add a GUTTER=40 attribute, as in Figure 9-39.

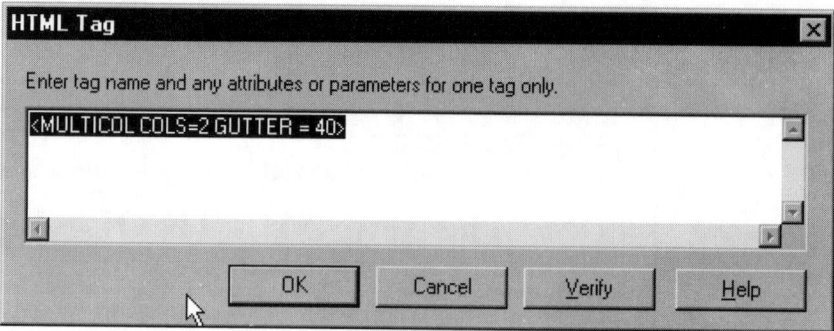

Figure 9-39: *Expanding the gutter space to 40 pixels.*

Switching to the browser view now shows my page with the horizontal underline under the title and the wider gap between the columns (Figure 9-40).

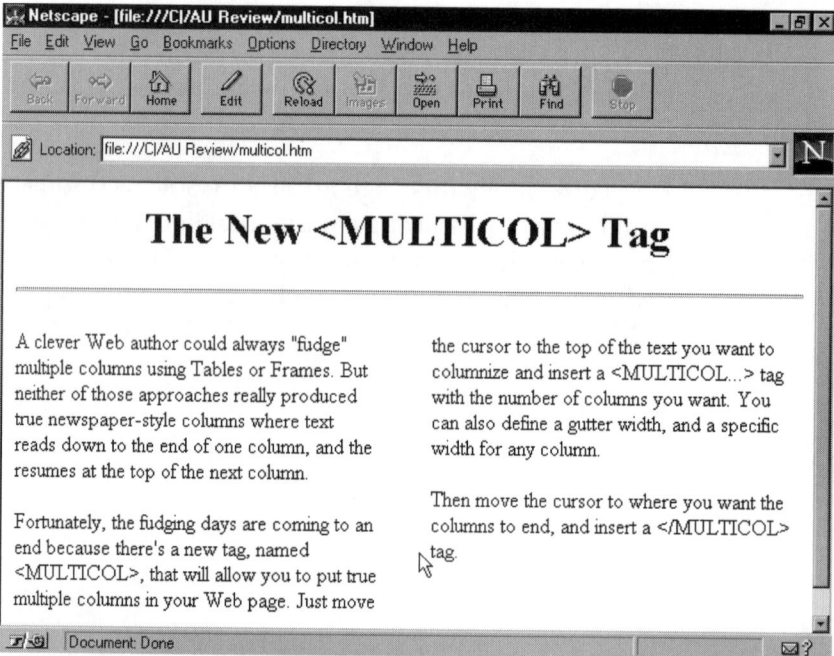

Figure 9-40: *Multicolumn page with horizontal line and wider gutter.*

Hmmm, I wonder what the page would look like if I changed the <MULTICOL> tag to this?:

```
<MULTICOL COLS=40 GUTTER=20>
```

Figure 9-41 shows the result.

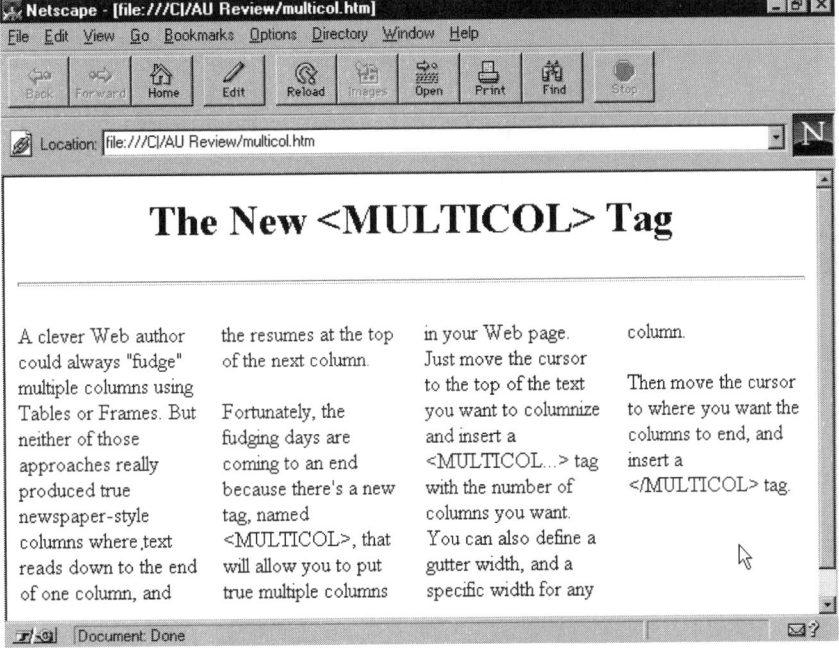

Figure 9-41: *Four columns with a gutter space of 20 pixels between each column.*

Once you get the hang of it, it's easy to try out different column styles. Just get to Gold's editor, double-click the tag icon that represents the <MULTICOL> tag, make your changes, choose OK, and switch back to the browser view.

There are a couple of other ways to do columns, though neither of them really gives you the smooth simple snaking columns that the <MULTICOL> tag offers. To see other "columnized" text see Chapter 12, "Get It Straight With Tables," and Chapter 17, "Get Framed."

CASCADING STYLE SHEETS

A new method of creating Web pages, called Cascading Style Sheets (or CSS for short) is currently being proposed. CSS will make it possible to format all the pages in a Web site with a single design spec. And, CSS promises to bring us even more control over fonts, line spacing, indentations, and multicolumn layouts.

To keep abreast of this developing technology just swing by the Web Publishing section of my Web site at http://www.coolnerds.com.

MOVING ON

Nicely formatted text makes for a good Web page. In this chapter you've learned to use all the major design elements that make up a Web page—or any printed page, for that matter. Now to really add some pizzazz to your Web pages, you'll need to add some pictures, and maybe some lines. Chapter 10 shows you how to do that.

Spice It Up With Lines & Pictures

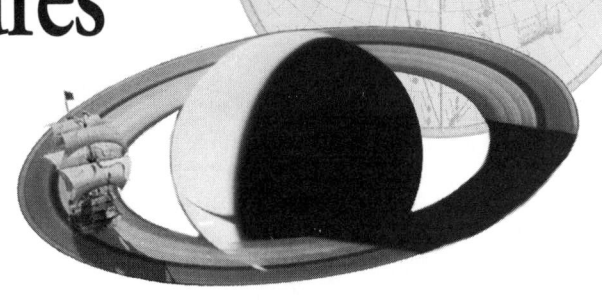

Organizing and formatting the text in your Web page is certainly important, but the real fun and dazzle comes when you start adding lines and pictures to your page. In this chapter you'll learn, among other things, how to do the following:

- Put lines and pictures in your Web page
- Position and size your pictures
- Align pictures with nearby text
- Add a background picture, texture, or color to your page
- Use pictures as bullets and horizontal lines

INSERTING LINES

To insert a horizontal line, you don't type a series of hyphens or underlines. Rather, the process is similar to that used to insert a picture:

1. Click at about the place you want the horizontal line.
2. Click the Insert Horiz. Line button in the Character Format toolbar, or choose Insert | Horizontal Line from the menus.

That's all there is to it. The line will extend across the full width of the page, as in the example shown just below the headline of the Web page in Figure 10-1.

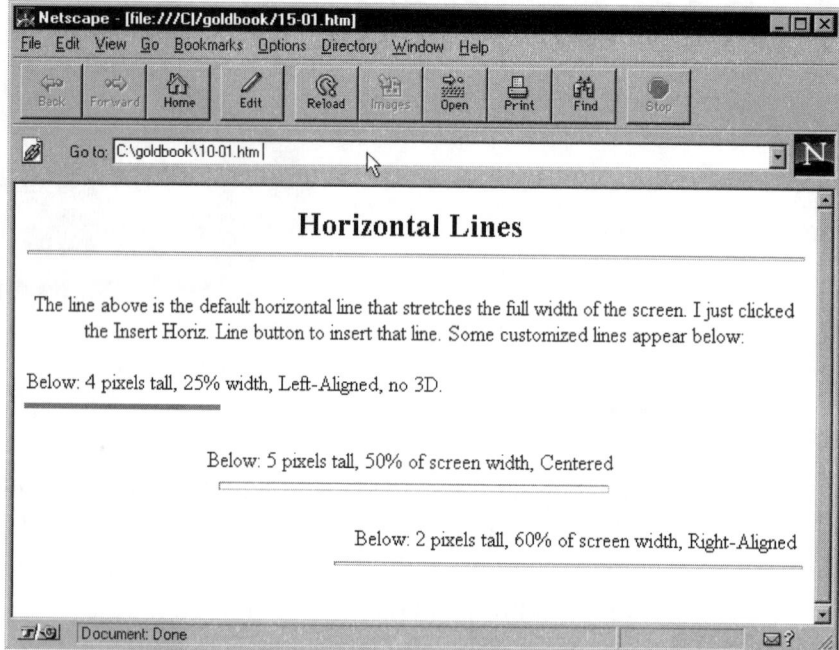

Figure 10-1: *A "default" horizontal line under the headline and some custom lines.*

CUSTOMIZING A LINE

You can alter the length, height, alignment, and appearance of a horizontal line by following these simple steps:

1. Right-click the line you want to change and choose Horizontal Line properties from the pop-up menu. You'll see the dialog box shown in Figure 10-2.

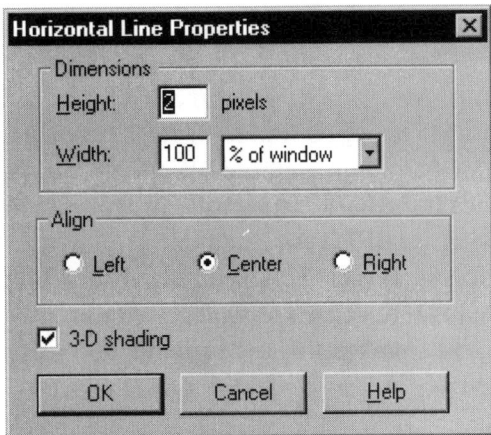

Figure 10-2: *The Horizontal Line Properties dialog box.*

2. Make whatever selections you wish and then click the OK button.

The customized horizontal lines in Figure 10-1 should give you an idea of what the various options offer. Easy enough, don't you think?

ABOUT PICTURES

The old saying that "A picture is worth a thousand words" holds true (doubly) for Web pages. Yes, one picture can convey as much information as a thousand words. But one picture can also take as long to download as 1,000 words—or even longer. Therefore, as a Web publisher, you need to use pictures sparingly and effectively. In Chapter 14, "Power Image Publishing," I point out some ways to fine-tune your pictures for maximum download speed. Before getting into that level of detail, however, you need to know what kinds of pictures you can put in your Web site, where you can find pictures, and how to get those pictures into your pages.

ACCEPTABLE PICTURE FORMATS

Pictures on computers come in hundreds of formats, including these: bitmap (.BMP), tagged image file (.TIF), computer graphics metafile (.CGM), Windows metafile (.WMF), WordPerfect graphics (.WPG), graphics information format (.GIF), and joint photographic experts group format (JPEG)—just to name a few.

Of all these formats, you can use only GIF and JPEG in your Web site, mainly because those two formats compress the pictures into a very small file size to minimize the time needed to send the picture across the Internet.

TIP

Actually, you can use any picture format you like. But only readers with appropriate plug-ins will be able to view the non-GIF and non-JPEG images. Plug-ins are covered in Chapter 25, "Plug-ins, Java & LiveConnect."

GIF files, which are good for general-purpose artwork, can contain up to 256 colors, and can have transparent backgrounds. JPEGs, which can contain millions of colors, are preferred for photographs and other very-high resolution color images.

TIP

If a picture that you want to use in your Web site is not in GIF or JPEG format, you can probably convert it to GIF or JPEG by using Paint Shop Pro. See Chapter 14, "Power Image Publishing," for more information.

INLINE IMAGES VERSUS EXTERNAL IMAGES

You can present an image in your Web site in two ways:

- Inline image: Displayed automatically when the reader opens your page. Most images you see are inline.

- External graphic: Only a hyperlink appears in your page. The reader must click the link to view the image. Preferred for large pictures that are not critical to your general presentation, and which might take a long time to download.

The sample page shown in Figure 10-3 includes both inline images and links to external images. This chapter focuses on inline images. External images are treated the same as multimedia files, which are discussed in Chapter 13, "Multimedia Madness."

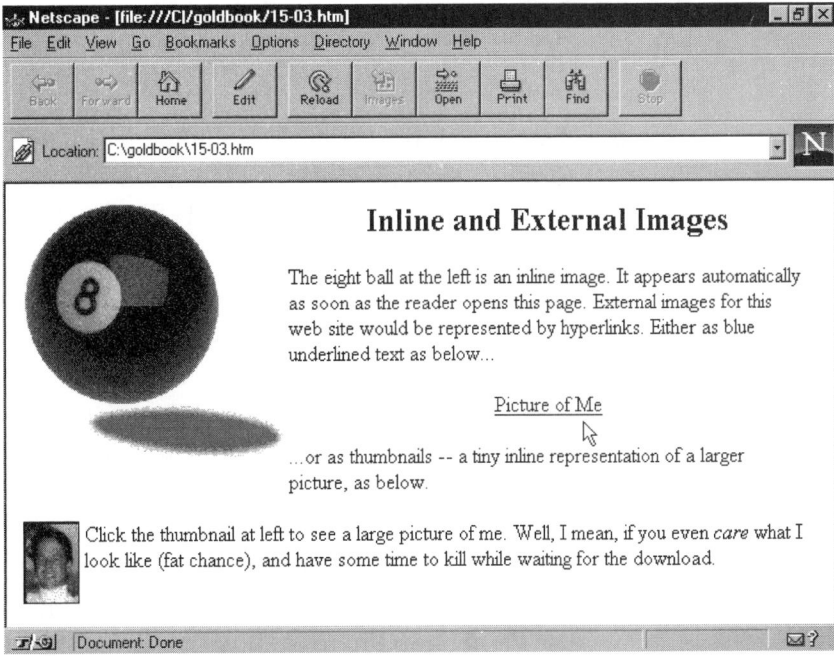

Figure 10-3: *A sample Web page with an inline image and links to external images.*

■ SOURCES OF IMAGES

The many sources of pictures for your Web site include the following:

- Royalty-free clip-art packages: You can buy huge clip-art collections at computer stores and through mail-order ads in computer magazines.

- Image archives: Some sites on the Web offer free clip art that you can download and use. (See the "Site Seeing" section near the end of this chapter.)

TRAP

Don't assume that all images on the Internet are free for one-and-all to use. Many graphic images are copyrighted. You can't use them unless you have permission from the holder of the copyright.

- Animated GIFs: You've probably seen small animated pictures (called *animated GIFs*) in some Web sites. To learn where to find some, see the "Site Seeing" section near the end of this chapter.

- Custom artwork: You can use a drawing program to draw your own pictures, or hire graphic artists to create custom artwork for you.

- Word art, equations, business charts: If you have Microsoft Office—or one of the programs that's included in the Microsoft Office suite—you can create a variety of picture "objects," and then use Paint Shop Pro to convert them to GIF and JPEG files (see Chapter 14, "Power Image Publishing").

- Screen shots: You can capture any image on your screen and use Paint Shop Pro (or another program) to crop and save it as a GIF or JPEG file (see Chapter 14).

- Scanned images: Any printed image can be *scanned* (digitized) and saved to a computer file for inclusion in your page.

SCANNING TIPS

You can scan virtually anything that's printed—logos, printed documents, photos, your signature, whatever—and put that scanned image in your Web page. If you don't own a scanner, you can probably find someone locally to scan a picture for you. Check your local print shops, copy centers, and desktop publishing bureaus.

When you scan pictures for your Web site, you can do a couple of things to ensure high-quality results. First, while scanning, try to size the picture to the exact dimensions you want to use in your page, so that you don't have to resize it after you've copied it to your hard disk. Second, if possible, save the picture in JPEG (for a photograph) or GIF format so that you don't have to convert it later.

ORGANIZING YOUR PICTURES

It's important to understand that even though pictures appear to be "in your Web page," they're not. Your Web pages contains only text and HTML tags. When you put a picture in a Web page, you're really just inserting an HTML tag that tells the browser to display a particular picture. The tag "expects" to find the picture on the Web server hard disk. If the tag doesn't find the picture, the Web browser screen shows only the "missing image" icon (see Figure 10-4).

Figure 10-4: *Icon for a missing image.*

As a Web publisher, you are responsible for making sure that pictures are where the Web pages expect to find them. You need to remember to upload all the appropriate GIF and JPEG image files when you upload your Web pages to your Web server. It's easy to forget to do this! To avoid mistakes, your best bet is to always put copies of pictures that will be used in your site in the same folder as your Web pages.

DOWNLOADING PICTURES FROM THE WEB

If, in some Web site, you find a picture that you want to use in your own Web pages, and you're sure you can do so without stepping on any toes (i.e., without infringing on anyone's copyright), you can follow these steps to download the picture:

TIP

Remember, this chapter's "Site Seeing" section points out some places to pick up free clip art.

1. Right-click the picture you want to download to your own PC, then choose Save Image As from the pop-up menu (see Figure 10-5).

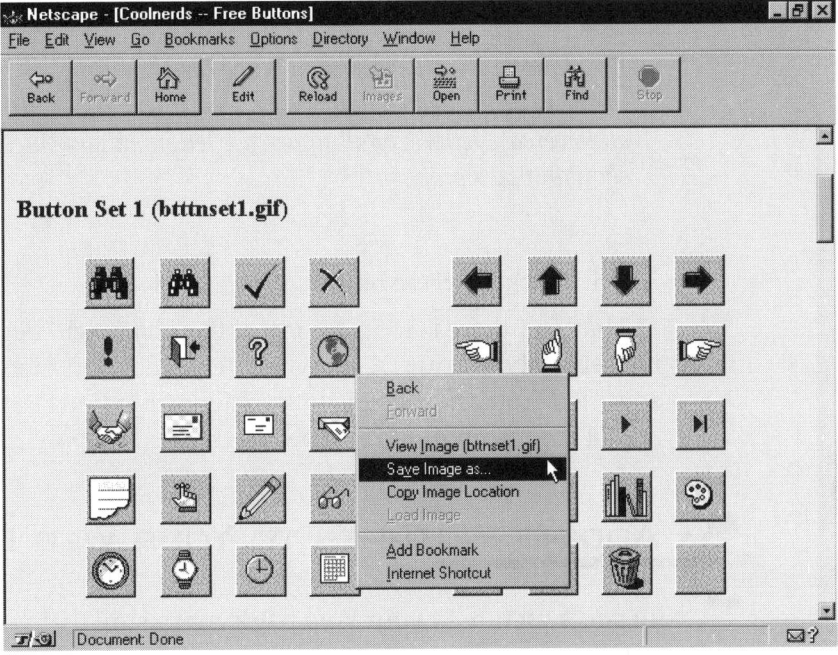

Figure 10-5: *To download a picture from the Web, first right-click on the picture.*

2. In the Save Image as dialog box, choose a folder in which to store the image (preferably the same folder that your pages are stored in).

3. Optionally, enter a new filename in the File name text box. Be sure to use the same extension used in the original filename.

TRAP

Don't forget that filenames might be case-sensitive on your Web server and may be limited to eight characters. If you stick with short names of all lowercase letters, or all uppercase letters in your filenames, this shouldn't be a problem.

4. Click the Save button.

That's all there is to it. A copy of the image will be downloaded immediately to your PC, to whatever folder and filename you specified. You can then insert the image into your Web page, using any of the techniques described in the next section.

ADDING PICTURES TO YOUR WEB PAGE

To add a picture to your Web page, make sure that your page is in Gold's editor. Then follow these steps:

1. Click the Insert Image button in the Character Format toolbar, or choose Insert | Image from the menus.

2. If you've never saved this document before, you'll be prompted to do so now. Choose Save, and save the document to whatever folder you want to store your pages in.

3. In the dialog box shown in Figure 10-6, click the top Browse button.

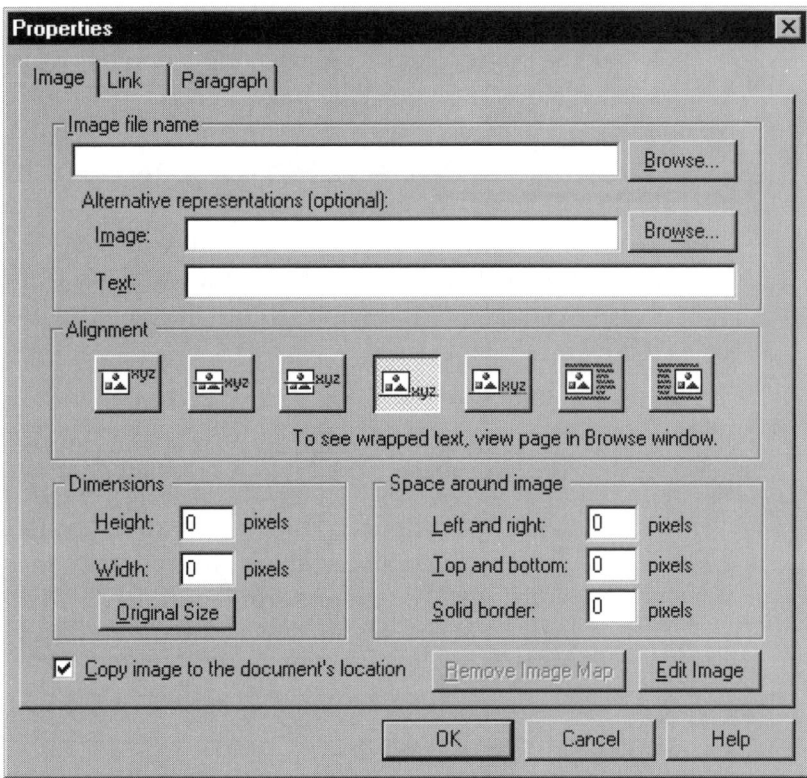

Figure 10-6: *The Image Properties dialog box.*

4. In the Select Image File dialog box, browse to the image you want to insert. That is, choose its folder from the Look in drop-down list, then click the name of the specific image you want. Click the Open button.

5. If the image you selected is *not* in the same folder as the Web page you're editing, make sure that the *Copy image to the document's location* check box is selected (checked).

6. You can now choose additional options in the dialog box, as described under "Formatting Your Pictures," later in this chapter. Or you can leave all those options as-is and change them later if you like.

7. Choose OK.

The picture appears in your Web page. Before we look at ways to tweak the picture, let's look at a couple of other ways you can insert a picture into your Web page.

DRAG AND DROP A PICTURE INTO YOUR PAGE

Yet another way to insert a picture into your page is to simply drag the picture's filename from the Windows 95 My Computer, Windows Explorer, or Find window into the page. To use this method, follow these steps:

1. Make sure that your Web page is open in Gold's editor.

2. Size Navigator's window so that you can see some of the Windows 95 desktop.

3. Use My Computer, Find, or Windows Explorer to open the folder that contains the picture you want to insert in your Web page. For example, in Figure 10-7 I've opened a folder named My Web Site, which already contains some GIF and JPEG images.

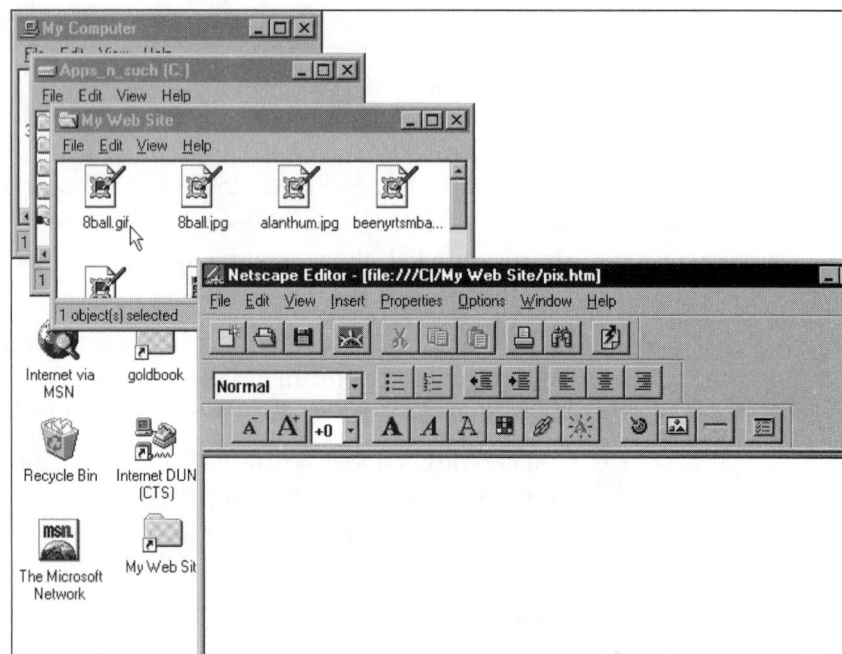

Figure 10-7: *Gold's Editor and Windows's My Computer are both open.*

4. Drag the icon or filename of the image you want to put in your page to wherever you want to place the picture in your Web page.

5. If you haven't saved the current Web page yet, do so, as prompted.

When you release the mouse button, the picture will appear in your page. If you need to change the picture's properties, you can double-click the picture and make your selections (see "Formatting Your Pictures," later in this chapter).

You can also drag and drop a picture from the Navigator Web browser into your own page in Gold's editor. This is a handy way to copy a picture from someone else's Web site right into your own page (assuming that you have permission to do so). The scenario for this kind of drag and drop follows:

1. Connect to the Internet in the usual manner.

2. Open Netscape Navigator.

3. Open a Web page you've already created (choose File | Open File in Editor) or, if you prefer, create a new document (choose File | New Document | Blank).

4. Size and arrange the windows so that you can see not only the Web site you're visiting, but also your own page, as in Figure 10-8. For starters, try right-clicking the taskbar and choosing Tile Vertically.

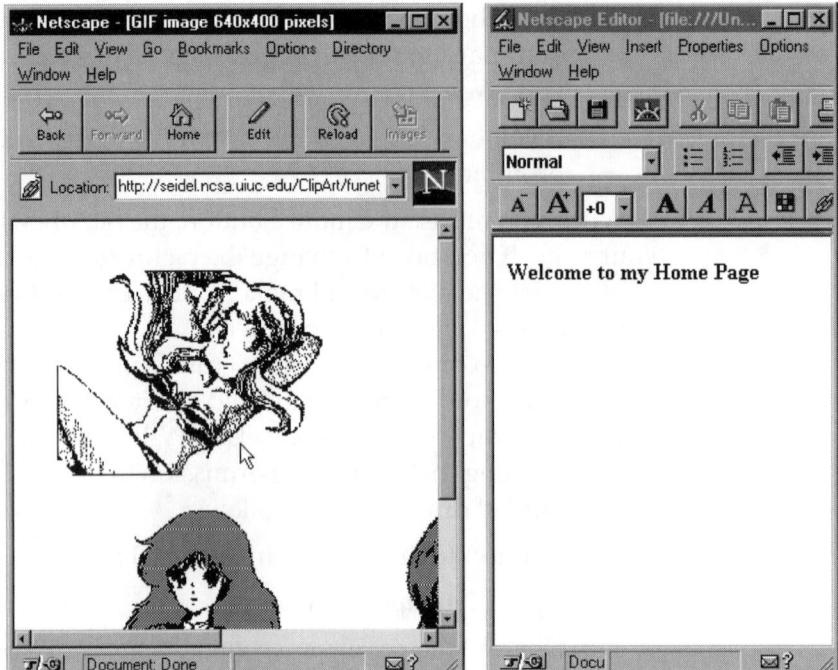

Figure 10-8: *Navigator as Web browser, and as Editor, on the screen in two separate windows.*

5. Drag the image you want to use from the Navigator browser window into your own document.

TIP

Sometimes when you download images from the Internet, you actually get a little collection of images in a single file. You can use Paint Shop Pro (see Chapter 14, "Power Image Publishing") to crop out the individual picture you want.

6. If you've never saved your page before, do so (as prompted).

The image will appear in your page. To make sure that a copy is placed on your own PC, double-click the picture and look at the Copy image to document's location option. If that option is *not* selected, select (check) it now. Then choose OK.

POSITIONING A PICTURE

When the picture is on your page, you can easily align it with either the left or right margin, or center it. Just click the picture (once) to select it. Then position the picture on the page by clicking the Align Left, Center, or Align Right button in the Paragraph Format toolbar.

If you need to move the picture to some other area on the page, click the picture once, then click the Cut button in the toolbar, or choose Edit I Cut (or press Ctrl+X). The picture will disappear, but a copy will remain in the Windows clipboard. Next, click at about the place you want to put the picture, then click the Paste button, or choose Edit I Paste (or press Ctrl+V).

Don't worry if text near the picture doesn't align or wrap exactly as you'd like it to. You can refine that alignment in the Image Properties dialog box, discussed next.

FORMATTING YOUR PICTURES

With your picture on your page, in roughly the right place, you can use the techniques described in this section to fine-tune the picture to perfection. First, you need to get to the Image Properties dialog box (refer to Figure 10-6). To do so, just double-click the picture.

ALTERNATIVE REPRESENTATIONS

The Alternative representations area in the Image Properties dialog box lets you specify an alternative image and alternative text. Many commercial clip-art packages provide both low- and high-resolution versions of their images. Typically, the alternative image is a low-resolution version of the larger image. This low-resolution image is smaller, and therefore faster to download. If you specify the low-resolution image as the alternative image, your readers will see that picture fairly quickly. The larger resolution image will follow.

From the reader's perspective, the picture displayed improves with time—but readers don't have to wait around for the high-resolution image, if they don't want to.

You should also type a brief description of the picture in the Alternative Text box, so that readers who are browsing with nongraphical browsers, or who have graphics turned off, will at least see a description of what's in the picture. Also, many browsers display the alternative text as the picture is downloading, so that readers have an idea of what's coming, and can move to another page if they don't want to wait for the picture.

ALIGNMENT

The Alignment options in the Image Properties dialog box let you decide how neighboring text in the document aligns with the picture. If you plan to have one line of text next to the picture, you should choose one of the first five buttons to specify how you want that one line to align with the picture.

If you plan to have a larger body of text (one or more paragraphs) next to the picture, you should pick one of the last two options to wrap text around the left or right side of the picture.

WHAT YOU SEE ISN'T WHAT YOU GET

Be aware that Gold's editor may not give you an accurate representation of what the page will *really* look like to your readers. Specifically, the editor never shows text wrapping around a picture. (Bummer, I know.)

To see the picture and text as your readers will see them, choose OK from the Image Properties dialog box. Then switch to browse view (click the View In Browser button), the view readers will see. For example, Figure 10-9 shows what a picture (a beanie, in this example) looks like in the Editor and in the browser after you choose a wrapped text alignment option. The browser window, in which the text really does wrap around the beanie, is the view the reader sees.

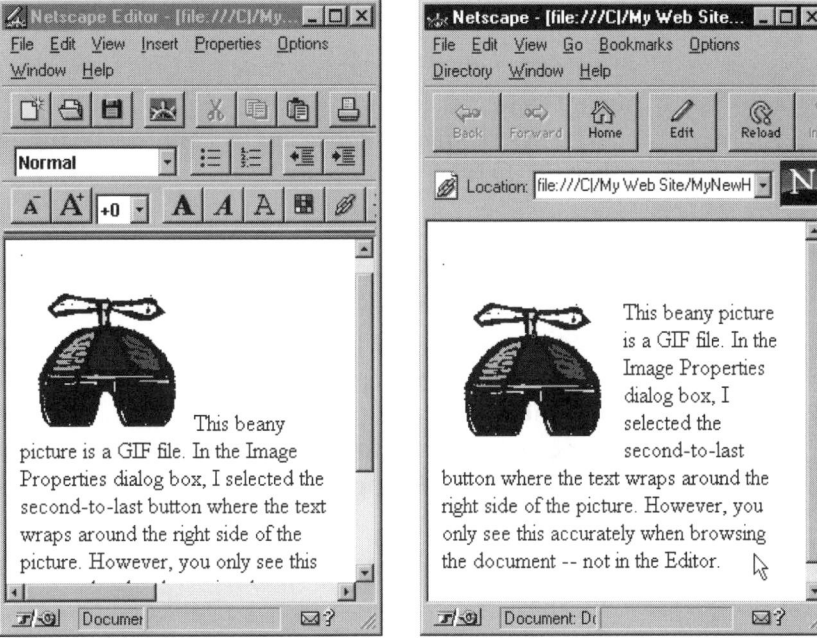

Figure 10-9: *The Wrap alignment options look right only when you browse the page.*

To return to picture editing, click the Edit button in the browser's toolbar. Or choose File | Edit Document. Then, to get back to the Image Properties dialog box, double-click on the picture once again.

SIZING A PICTURE: DIMENSIONS

The Dimensions option is an important one because it determines the size of the picture, in pixels. When you place a picture in your Web page, the dimensions of that picture are filled in automatically. You should leave those settings as-is, unless you *must* show a larger or smaller version of the picture.

> **TIP**
>
> *As an alternative to sizing an image in Gold's editor, try using the Image | Resize or Image | Resample option in Paint Shop Pro (see Chapter 14, "Power Image Publishing"). For instructions, search Paint Shop's Help function for resize.*

Be aware that if you do use the Dimensions options in the Image Properties dialog box to change the size of a picture, you risk distorting the picture. You can avoid the distortion, however, by maintaining the same *aspect ratio* when defining the new size. By "aspect ratio," I mean the ratio of the length as compared to the width.

Suppose, for example, that I want to put the photo shown in Figure 10-10 in my Web page. Currently, I'm viewing that photo in Paint Shop Pro. If you look at the status bar in that figure, you can see that the photo measures 100 pixels (wide) by 150 pixels (tall).

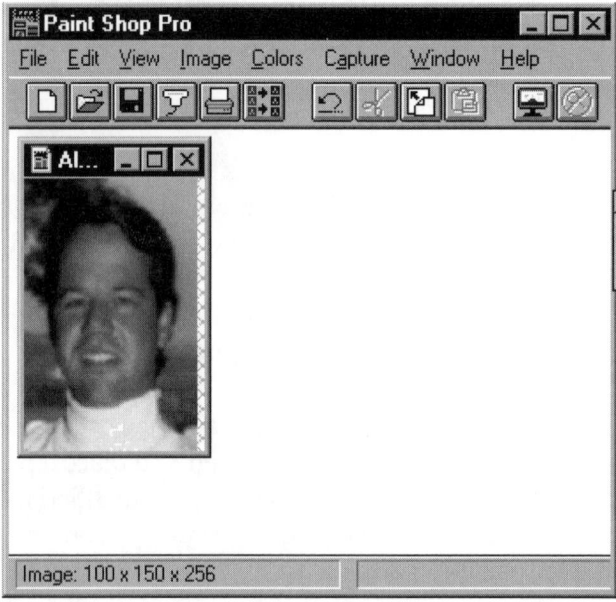

Figure 10-10: *A photo in Paint Shop Pro.*

In my Web page, I want this picture to be a little larger—say, 200 pixels wide. Well, if I arbitrarily set both the height and the width of the picture to 200 pixels each, the picture has to stretch to fit those dimensions. As a result, the picture becomes distorted, as in the upper portion of Figure 10-11. (When my daughter saw that picture onscreen, she exclaimed, "It's Mr. Fat Head!")

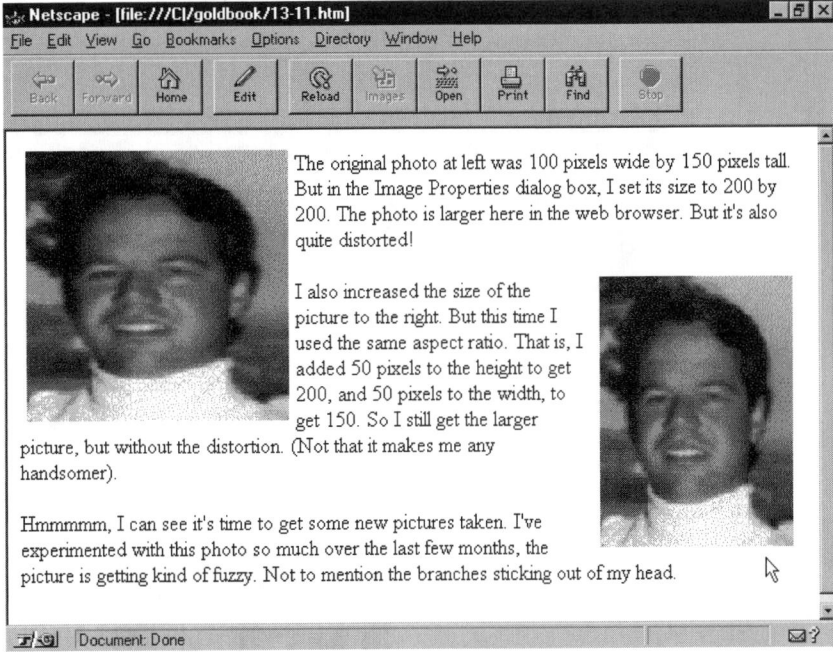

Figure 10-11: *The photo enlarged without, and with, using the same aspect ratio.*

If, on the other hand, I maintain the same aspect ratio, by adding 50 to the current height (changing it from 150 to 200), and 50 to the current width (changing it from 100 to 150), the enlarged picture is not distorted (as in the lower part of Figure 10-11).

SPACE AROUND IMAGE

The Space Around Image option lets you determine how much blank space to put between a picture and its neighboring text. If you leave all the settings at zero, the text comes in very close to the picture, as in the upper-left picture in Figure 10-12. By increasing the space you put a wider gap between the picture and text. You can also place a solid black border around the picture, as in the bottom picture in Figure 10-12.

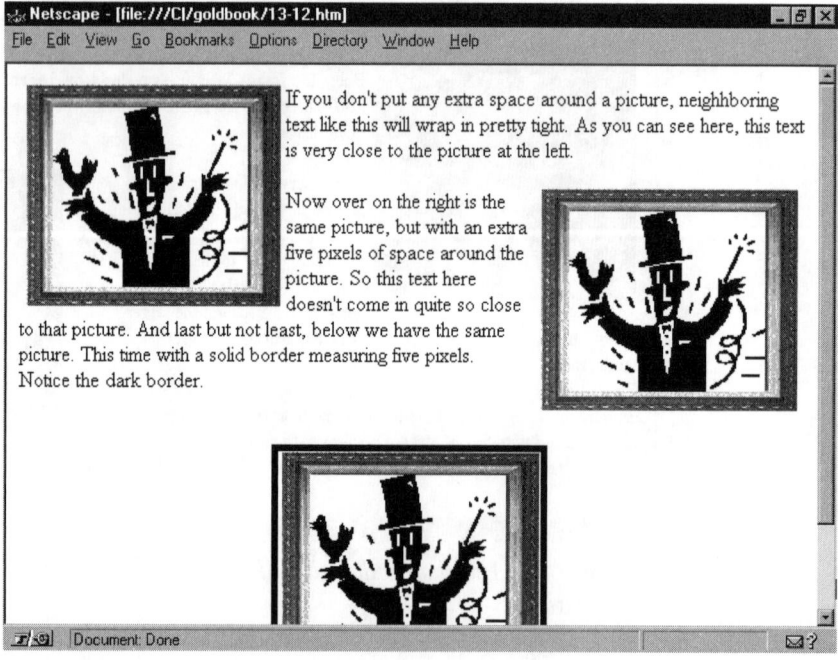

Figure 10-12: *You can add empty space or a solid border around a picture.*

Copy Image to Document's Location

The Copy Image to Document's Location option ensures that any pictures you put in your Web page are copied to the same folder that holds the page itself. As mentioned earlier, you probably will want to put all your pages and pictures in a single folder to ensure that you don't forget anything when you upload your files to the Web server. By leaving the Copy Image to Document's Location check box checked, you ensure that if you forget to copy a picture to that folder, Navigator will copy it for you.

Edit Image

The Edit Image button opens the current image in whatever program you've chosen as your image editor. Chapter 14, "Power Image Publishing," shows you how to designate Paint Shop Pro as that graphics editor. You can use Paint Shop Pro not only to do all kinds of graphics editing, but also to create transparent-background GIFs and interlaced fade-in GIFs.

Unwrapping Text From an Image

Suppose that you have some text wrapping around an image, but you want to start a new paragraph beneath that image, as in the second paragraph shown in Figure 10-13. What to do? Simple. Move the cursor to the start of the text you *don't* want to wrap. Then choose Insert | Break Below Image(s) from Navigator's menu bar.

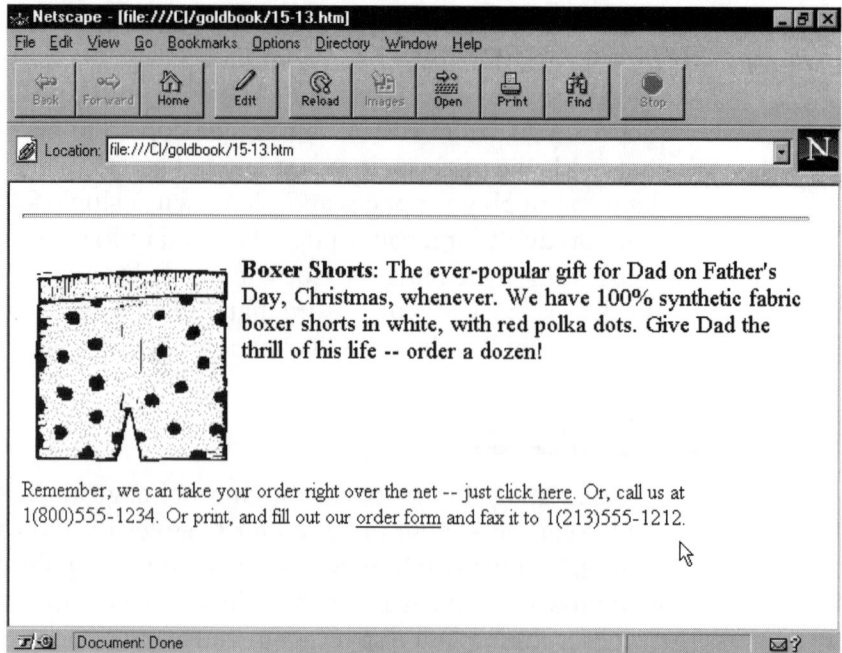

Figure 10-13: *The first paragraph wraps around the image, but the second paragraph doesn't.*

You can use the same technique to ensure that text starts below an image that you're using as a headline, and to prevent two images from lining up side-by-side.

BACKGROUND TEXTURES, IMAGES, & COLORS

You're not limited to plain white or dreary gray backgrounds in your Web pages. You can color the background, or even add a picture or texture. As an example, The Ultimate Collection of Windows Software (TUCOWS) sports its logo as a sort of background image (see Figure 10-14). (Do you suppose that TUCOWS is pronounced *two cows*?)

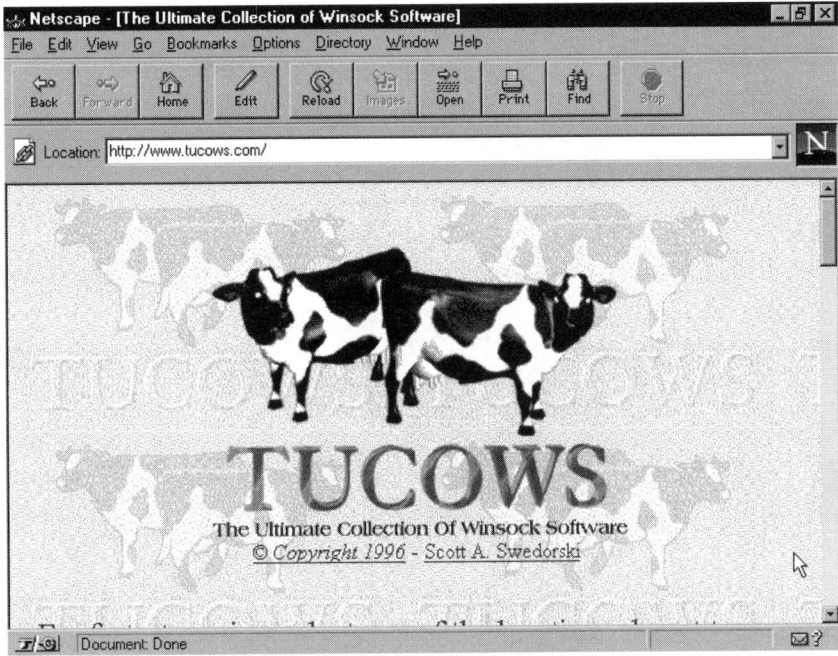

Figure 10-14: *This site uses its own logo as a background.*

Background images and textures are just regular GIF and JPEG files. Usually they're pretty small—no more than 100-by-100 pixels. When you define such an image as a background, Navigator "knows" to tile the image so that it fills the entire screen.

To add a background texture or picture to your Web site, you must first create, or find, the GIF or JPEG image you want to use. (See the "Site Seeing" section later in this chapter for some resources.) Put the GIF or JPEG image in the same folder as the page that will display the image. Then follow these steps:

1. Open your Web page in Gold's editor.

2. Choose Properties I Document, and click the Appearance tab to get to the dialog box shown in Figure 10-15.

3. Click the Use Custom Colors option button, then . . .

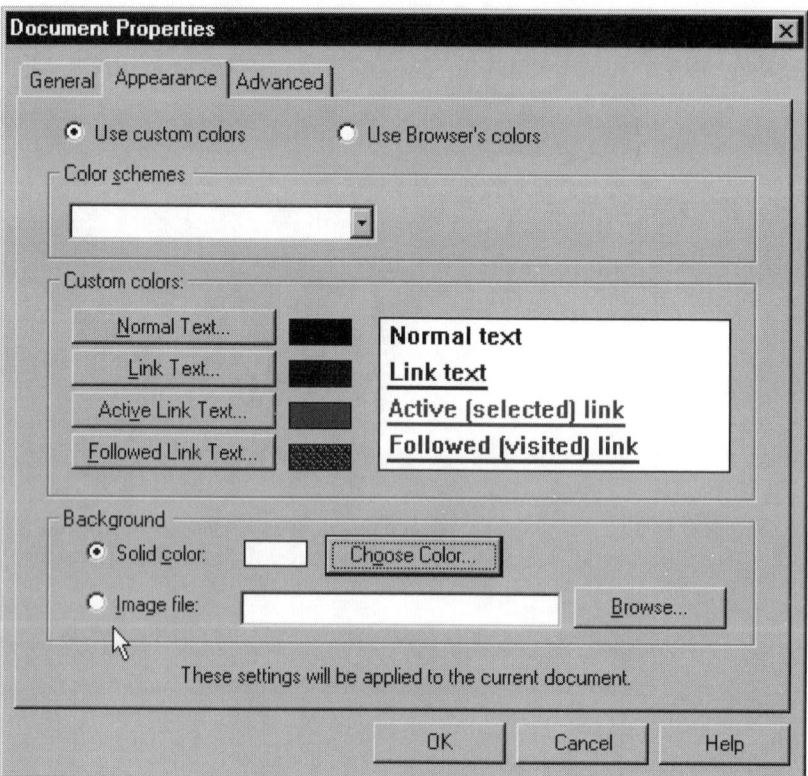

Figure 10-15: *The Background area lets you choose a background color or image.*

- To give the page a solid background, click the Solid color option button, then click the Choose Color button and select a color from the palette that appears.

- If you prefer to use an image file, click the Image file option and use the Browse button to open your image file.

4. Choose OK to close the Document Properties dialog box.

Your new background color or image will be displayed immediately, both in the Editor and when you browse the page.

FADING YOUR LOGO TO USE AS A BACKGROUND

If you have a logo or photo that you'd like to use as a background image, keep in mind that you'll need to fade the image. Otherwise, readers will have difficulty seeing the text on the page. You can use Paint Shop Pro (Chapter 14) to create a faded version of your picture.

Open the Picture in Paint Shop Pro, and use File|Save As to save this copy with a new name. Then choose Colors|Adjust|Brightness/Contrast. Crank up the brightness and reduce the contrast to suit your taste. Then choose OK, and save the image.

SWIPING BACKGROUND IMAGES

When you shop around for background images, you'll find that most are presented on your screen as regular graphics images. To download an image as a normal graphic, you right-click the image, then choose Save Image As, as in Figure 10-16, where I'm about to copy a background pattern from Netscape's Gold Rush Toolkit. Copy the file to the folder in which you're storing all your other Web site files. After you've copied the file to your PC, you can use the preceding steps to put it in your page as a background.

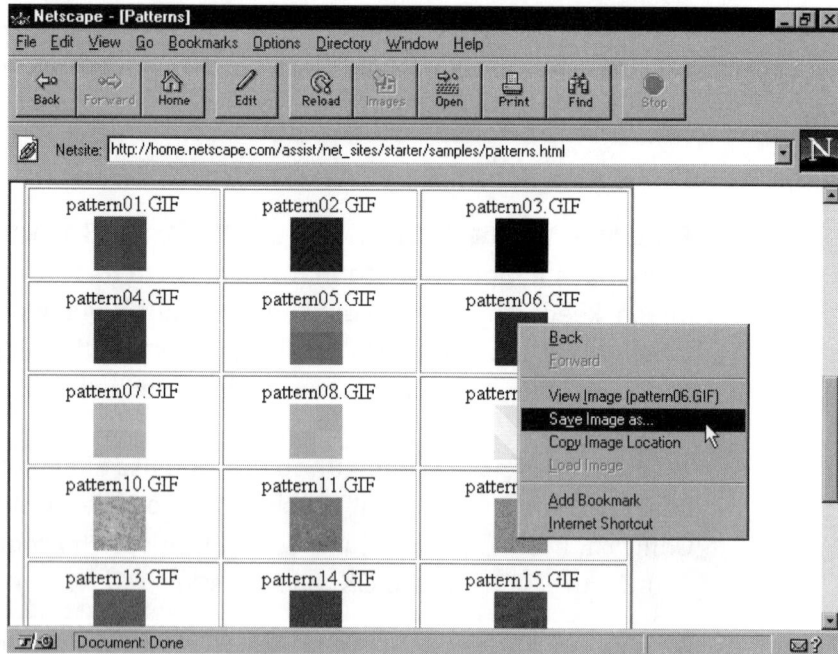

Figure 10-16: *Free background patterns are available from Netscape.*

Now let's suppose that you come across a page with a back-ground image you want to swipe. You can't copy the background by right-clicking on a background image. Hmmm, what are you going to do?

Well, first you're going to check with the owner of that Web site to see whether it's OK to swipe the background image. Right? Then grab a copy of that background image by following these steps:

1. In your browser, click View | View Document Source.

2. Look for the <body text...> HTML tag, just under the <HEAD>...</HEAD> section. It will look something like this:

```
<body bgcolor=...background="pinktile.gif">
```

3. Select (drag the mouse pointer through) the filename defined within the quotation marks to the right of the background = part. For instance, in this case you'd want to select *pinktile.gif.*

4. Press Ctrl+C to copy the selected filename.

5. Close the View Document Source window by clicking its Close (X) button.

6. Now, in the Location box, select the filename at the end of the current URL. For example, if the URL in the Location box is http:\\www.howdy.com\index.html, you should select index.html.

7. Press Ctrl+V to replace that filename with the one you just copied. (In our example, the URL in the Location box would now be http:\\www.howdy.com\pinktile.gif.)

8. Press Enter.

The graphic image being used for the background will appear, all alone, in your Web browser screen. *Now* you can right-click that image, choose Save Image As, and save a copy to your local hard disk, along with all your other Web files. Click the Back button to return to the previous page.

It's kind of a neat trick. But please don't abuse it. If you get busted swiping someone else's background graphic, and they get miffed, don't be telling them, "But Alan Simpson said it's OK." I'll deny it, and show them this paragraph. Hah!

USING PICTURES AS BULLETS

If you want to jazz up your Web page a little, consider using little GIF images as bullets in your bulleted lists. You can also put a little *burst*—a message like *new!* or *cool!*—in line with the text, as in the example shown in Figure 10-17.

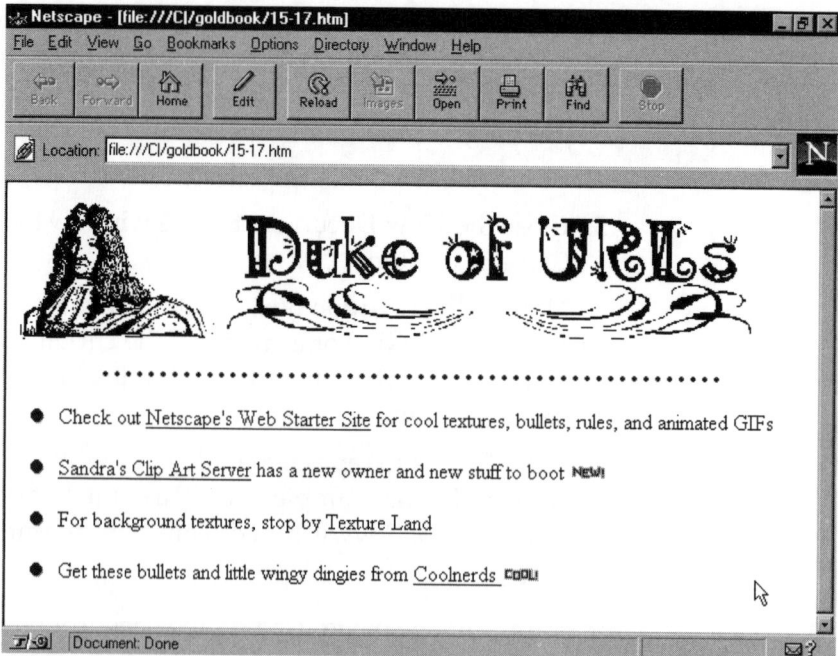

Figure 10-17: *This page uses tiny graphics as bullets and banners.*

You can find little bullets and bursts on many sites on the World Wide Web. I point out some good resources in the "Site Seeing" section near the end of this chapter. After you've copied one of these small graphics to your local Web folder, you can insert it as you would any other picture:

TIP

If you've already typed your list and defined it as a bulleted list, you should get rid of the current bullets before you substitute graphics. To do that, select the list, then choose Normal from the Paragraph style drop-down list.

1. In Gold's editor, click about where you want to place the little graphic.
2. Click the Insert Image button or choose Insert | Image.

3. Use the Browse button to open the file that contains the small image.

4. Select other options as appropriate. In particular, you'll probably want to use one of the first five alignment options, as in the example shown in Figure 10-18.

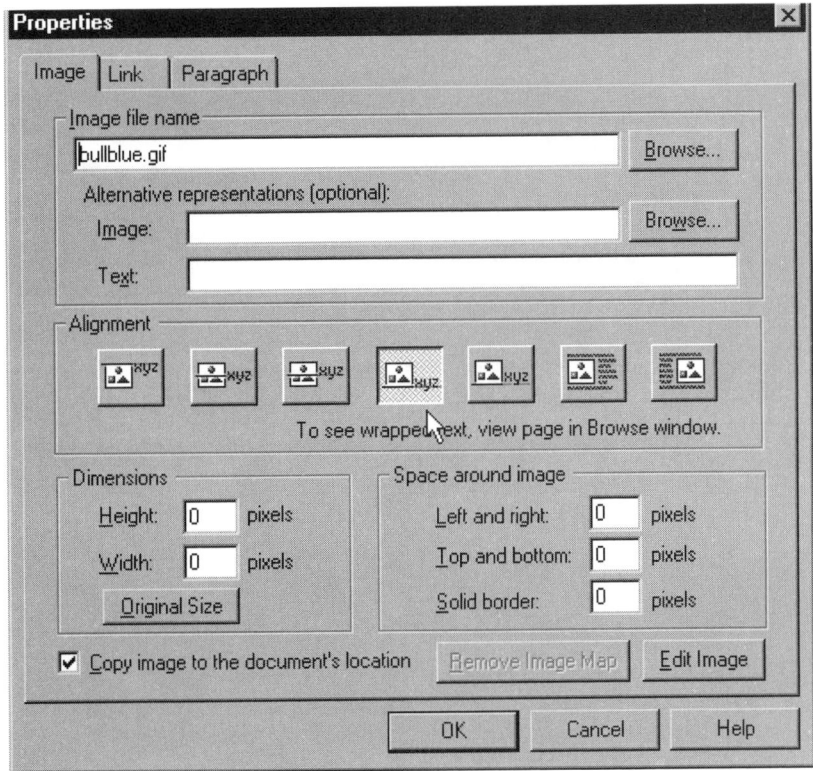

Figure 10-18: *Image properties with alignment set for small inline graphic image.*

5. Choose OK.

You can type text near the graphic image. If you have any trouble with text alignment, just double-click the graphic image to get back to the Properties dialog box. Then try a different alignment option and choose OK.

USING PICTURES AS LINES

You can also use graphic images in place of the built-in horizontal rule that Navigator offers. The Web offers many nice lines you can choose from. Those shown in Figure 10-19 are available from Netscape's site. (See the "Site Seeing" section for several other resources.)

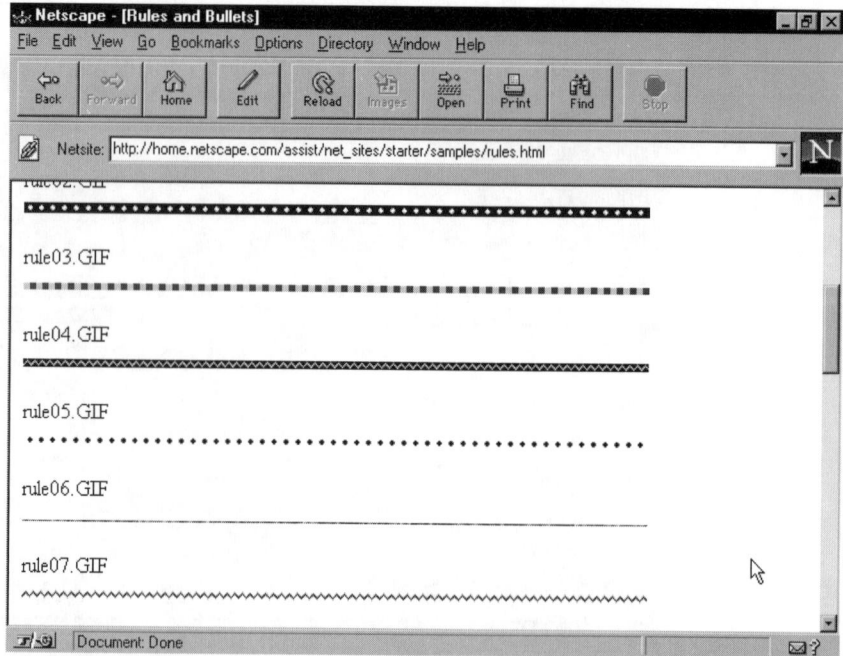

Figure 10-19: *Cool rules at Netscape's site.*

Graphic images used as horizontal rules are just like any other graphic image. To copy a line from the Web, right-click the line and use the Save Image As option to save a copy to your local hard disk. In Gold's editor, click about where you want the line to appear. Click the Insert Image button, and open the file that contains the line. If you want to center the rule on the page, click it and then click the Center button in the Paragraph Format toolbar.

NEW HTML TAGS YOU'LL MEET

As you know, while you're creating your page in Golds's editor, the editor is quietly converting your formatting decisions to HTML tags for the World Wide Web. As I've said before, you really needn't concern yourself with HTML tags right now. We'll look at tags in more detail in Chapter 15, "Tuning HTML Tags."

Just in case you decide to peek at the document source, and wonder what some of the tags are, Table 10-1 provides a quick summary.

Tag	Purpose
<hr>	Horizontal rule.
<br clear = both>	Ends a line and gets past all images before typing the next line of text (Break below Image(s)).
<body... bgcolor= "#XXXXXX">	Specifies background color of page as an RGB triplet (see Appendix E).
<body...background= "filename.ext">	Specifies a background image where filename.ext is the file name of the image.
<img src ="filename.ext".>	Displays a graphic image where filename.ext is the name of the file in which the image is stored.

Table 10-1: *HTML tags for lines, pictures, and background color.*

SITE SEEING FOR IMAGES

The sites mentioned in this section offer different kinds of graphics images that you can use in your Web site. Many (but certainly not all) offer free images that you can download on the spot. For easy one-click access to these sites, and others, check out the Web Publishing section of my Web site at http://www.ccolnerds.com.

ANIMATED GIFS

Animated GIFs are animated graphics images. As you author your pages, you insert an animated GIF as you would a nonanimated GIF—by using drag and drop or the Insert Image button. To see some cool animated GIFs, check out these sites:

- GIF Animation on the WWW: http://members.aol.com/royalef/gifanim.htm
- Netscape Animated GIFs: http://home.netscape.com/assist/net_sites/starter/samples/animate.html

CLIP ART

Clip art is predrawn generic art that's widely used in all types of publishing. Because people don't give away clip art as freely as they do small bullets, lines, and backgrounds, be careful about copying images, and always check to see whether the publisher is *selling* the art, or giving it away. Some of these sites offer free clip art, some have clip art for sale:

- Clip Art: http://www.n-vision.com/panda/c
- Image Club: http://www.imageclub.com
- Mozilla Illustrations: http://home.netscape.com/assist/net_sites/starter/samples/mozilla.html
- Publisher's Depot: http://www.publishersdepot.com

LINES, BULLETS & SUCH

You can find many small graphic images, both regular and animated, in several Web sites. Take a gander at these sites:

- Coolnerds Images: http://www.coolnerds.com
- Netscape Rules and Bullets: http://home.netscape.com/assist/net_sites/starter/samples/rules.html

BACKGROUND TEXTURES

These sites offer some neat background images and textures:

- Netscape Patterns: http://home.netscape.com/assist/ net_sites/starter/samples/patterns.html

- RadioActive Textures: http://www.radzone.org/textures

- Texture Land: http://www.meat.com/textures

MOVING ON

Now that you know how to format the text of your Web page, and embellish it with lines and pictures, you can do anything an author of a book or magazine can do. What really differentiates the Web from standard print media, though, are hyperlinks—which give you the ability to go from one place to any other place (on the planet) with just the click of a mouse. In the next chapter, you'll learn how to add hyperlinks to your own Web pages.

Adding Hyperlinks

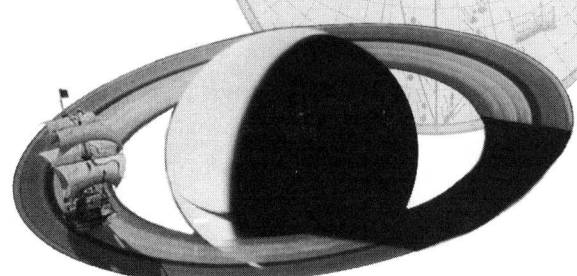

The title of Chapter 3 of Netscape's online Authoring Guide is "The Hyperlink's the Thing." What a great title! Wish I'd thought of it first. It's a great title because, ultimately, *hypertext* is what Web publishing is all about. And the *hyperlink* is what makes hypertext "hyper." This chapter covers everything you need to know about hyperlinks to make your page work, including the following topics:

- What is a hyperlink?
- How to create *targets* (named anchors) in your pages
- How to link to targets in your pages
- How to link to other pages in your site
- How to link to other sites on the World Wide Web
- How to link to e-mail

WHAT IS A HYPERLINK?

A *hyperlink* is a "hot spot" in a Web page. When you click on a hyperlink, your browser takes you to some other page on the World Wide Web. You've no doubt come across dozens of hyperlinks in your own Web browsing. Some hyperlinks are colored, underlined text. Some pictures act as hyperlinks. And you've probably come across situations in which a single picture contains multiple hot spots, each of which takes you to some other page.

> **TIP**
>
> *A single picture that offers multiple hot spots is called a* clickable image map. *You'll learn how to create those in Chapter 16, "Creating Clickable Image Maps."*

As a Web author and publisher, you can create hyperlinks for others to follow. The process is *really* easy. But because you do need to understand a little about what you can link *to,* I need to give you some background information before I show you how to plop hyperlinks into your pages.

A "REAL" WEB SITE

The "Your Very First Home Page" that you created back in Part I of this book was just that—a single Web page. In real life, most Web sites consist of several pages: a home page (the first page the reader sees when entering a site) and some additional pages.

Dividing a site into several small pages makes the site easier to manage. Also, the larger a single page is, the longer it takes to download to the reader's computer. Because you want your home page to get to the reader as quickly as possible, it's to your advantage to keep that home page small.

The home page should display hyperlinks to other pages in the site. For example, the page in Figure 11-1 has hyperlinks to several areas in that site (including Current Issue, Back Issues, and Late-Breaking News). Clicking on one of those hyperlinks takes the reader to a particular page in the site.

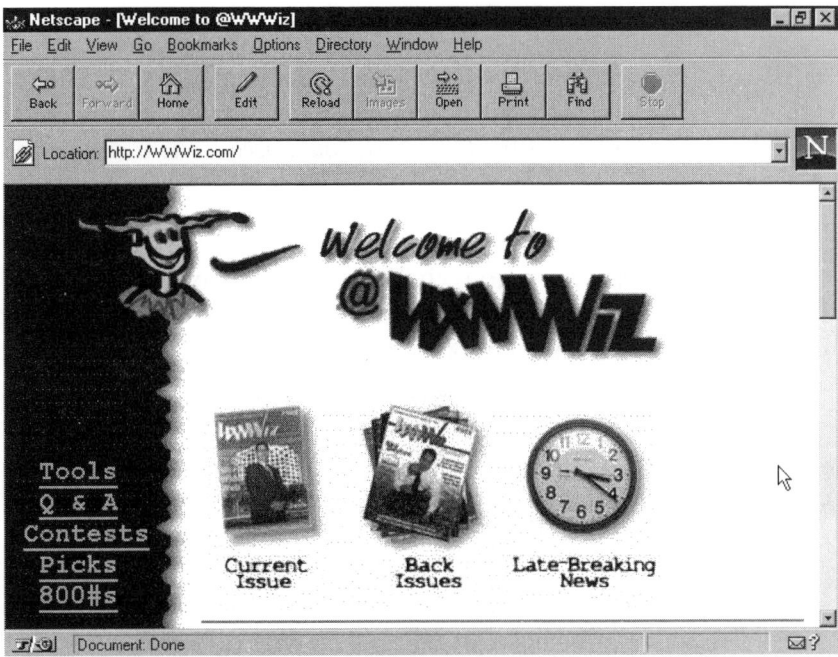

Figure 11-1: *A sample home page, with hyperlinks to other pages in the site.*

If you were to go behind the scenes and see how this site is structured, you'd probably find that each hot spot takes the reader to a separate page. Figure 11-2 shows the relationship between the home page and the site's other pages.

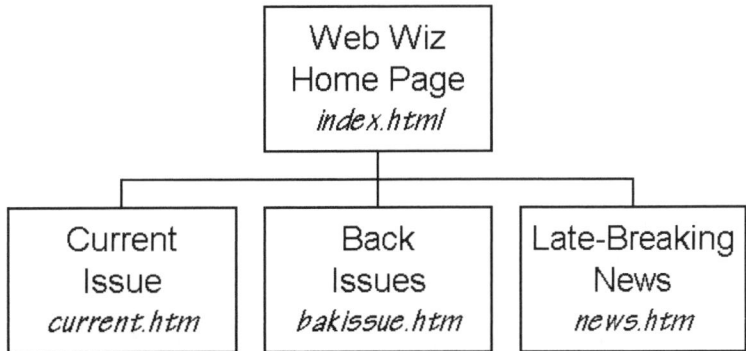

Figure 11-2: *A sample Web site, with a home page and three subordinate pages.*

> **TIP**
>
> *Actually, the Tools, Q & A, Contests, Picks, and 800#s links on the sample page probably have subordinate pages also. But if I put all that into my little Org chart, you'd need a microscope to read the print!*

The beauty of splitting the site into several smaller pages is this: When the reader clicks a link to get some specific information, *only* that information is sent. The reader doesn't need to wait while irrelevant information is downloaded.

ABOUT URLS

As you know, every site on the World Wide Web has its own unique address, or URL. In the example shown in Figure 11-1, the URL is http://WWWiz.com. Netscape Press, the publishers of this book, have their site at http://www.netscapepress.com. My personal Web site is at http://www.coolnerds.com. Netscape's URL is http://home.netscape.com.

Each *page* on the Web also has its own URL. The specific page is identified by the URL, followed by a slash and the name of the page. For example:

http://www.coolnerds.com/index.html

is the URL for the page named *index.html* in the Coolnerds site.

A large site, such as Netscape's, might be divided into several subdirectories—just as your PC is probably divided into folders and subfolders. If a particular page in a site isn't in the root directory of that site, then the URL for that page will include the directory path to the page. For example, the following URL:

http://home.netscape.com/comprod/index.html

points to the index.html page in the comprod directory at Netscape's Web site.

Some sites have complicated directory structures, which is why you sometimes come across really long URLs like this one:

http://home.netscape.com/assist/net_sites/starter/samples/index.html

As you'll learn in this chapter, a Web page can contain *targets* (also called *named anchors),* which are "target points" the reader can jump to within the page. A link can take a reader directly to a specific place (target) in a page. In the URL for such a link, the name of the target follows a # symbol at the end of the URL. For example, the following URL points to a target named *Funstuff* in a page named urls.htm in the root directory of the site at http://www.coolnerds.com:

http://www.coolnerds.com/urls.htm#Funstuff

What this all boils down to for you, as Web publisher, is that you can create a hyperlink that takes any reader to any place in the World Wide Web—even to a particular place in a particular page on the Web. That's pretty potent stuff!

LOCAL VERSUS REMOTE LINKS

When you create a hyperlink, you can have the link point to a page in your own Web site. That kind of link is called a *local link.* Or, you can have the hyperlink point to someone else's Web site. And that kind of link is called a *remote link.*

TIP

Some people use the term relative link *to refer to a link to a local document, and* absolute link *to refer to a link to a document outside the current Web site.*

The URL to which a link points doesn't need to have all the parts that typically make up a URL. For example, just *news.htm* alone is a valid URL in a hyperlink. So is *#Funstuff.* The reason these mini-URLs are valid in hyperlinks has to do with assumptions that Navigator makes about the different parts of the URL. Following are the "official" names of the different parts of a URL, and the assumptions Navigator makes when told to go to a URL:

- Protocol: The first part of the name is the *protocol,* which defines how information in the URL is to be accessed. Web documents are accessed through the *hypertext transfer protocol* (http://). Files can be accessed through the *file transfer protocol* (ftp://). When the protocol is omitted, the same protocol as the current page is assumed.

- Host Name: The second part of the URL is the *host name,* the name of the computer as the Internet sees it. For example, *home.netscape.com* is the host name for Netscape's Web site. When the host name is omitted, the current host name is assumed.

- Directory: If the URL refers to a particular directory on the host computer, the directory path follows the host name. When the directory path is omitted in a local link, the current directory is assumed; in a remote link, the default (root) directory of that computer is assumed.

- Filename: The filename portion, if any, of the URL refers to a specific file. When the filename is omitted in a local link, the current document is assumed; in a remote link, the default page for that server (usually a file named *index.html*) is assumed.

- Target: If the URL points to a specific target in a page, that target name appears at the end of the URL, preceded by a pound (#) symbol. When no target is specified, the top of the page is assumed.

Fortunately, you don't have to remember all of this information. You just need to keep in mind that the place a hyperlink jumps to doesn't necessarily have to be a complete URL in the *http:// www.whatever.com/yippe/yiyo.html* format. Short names also work, as long as they point to something that Navigator can find.

ABOUT TARGETS (NAMED ANCHORS)

One last thing I need to explain before I show you how to create hyperlinks is what a *target* (or *named anchor*) is. Targets are entirely optional—there's no rule that says your Web page must contain targets. If you're presenting a lengthy page to a reader, however, you might want to include targets so that the reader can access things near the bottom of the page with a single mouse click, rather than by scrolling.

For example, Figure 11-3 shows the top of a page that offers the reader links to other sites on the Web. Rather than just present a long list of links, the top of the page lets the reader pick a category by clicking on a hyperlink.

Figure 11-3: *The top of a page that offers links to other sites.*

When the reader clicks on one of those category links, he or she is taken immediately to that part of the list. For example, clicking Background Art takes the reader directly to the Background Art section of the page shown in Figure 11-4. Other categories also appear on the page, simply because each of the categories in this example is rather small.

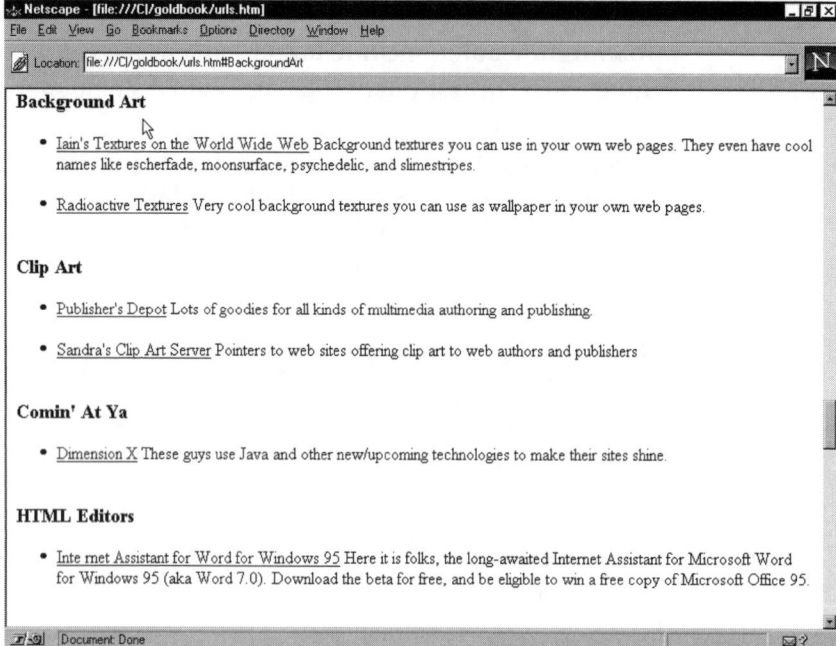

Figure 11-4: *By clicking a category link, I jumped right to the Background Art section (at the top of the page).*

In short, a target allows the reader to jump from point A to point B in a page, without scrolling. Most readers would rather jump than scroll, because jumping is faster and easier.

 ## ADDING TARGETS TO YOUR PAGES

Adding a target to a Web page is easy. Just follow these steps:

1. Open, in Gold's editor, the page in which you want to place the named target.

2. Move the cursor to the location at which you want to place the target.

3. Optionally, select a small chunk of text (up to 30 characters) that will act as the target name.

4. Click the Insert Target (Named Anchor) button in the Character Format toolbar. Or choose Insert | Target (Named Anchor). You'll see the simple dialog box shown in Figure 11-5.

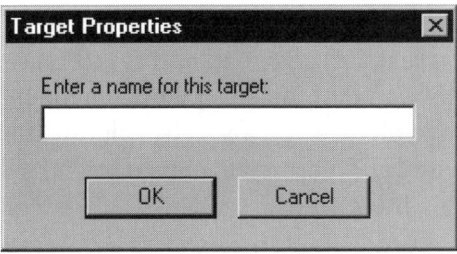

Figure 11-5: *The Target Properties dialog box.*

5. If you selected text in Step 3, that text appears in the dialog box. You can use that text as the anchor name or, if you want to use a different name, just type that name (up to 30 characters).

6. Choose OK.

A small target icon appears at the cursor position. When you point to that icon, the name of the target is displayed in the status bar, as in the example shown in Figure 11-6.

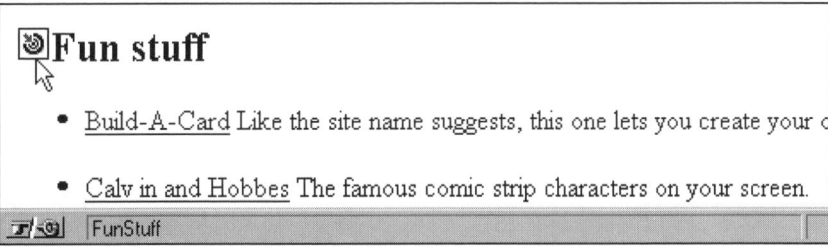

Figure 11-6: *A sample target in the editor.*

In the browser, although the targets are invisible (no icon representing the target appears on the reader's screen), a hyperlink will still take the reader to a target.

ADDING HYPERLINKS

Now comes the fun part—adding the hyperlink. First, make sure that the page in which you want to place the link is open in Gold's editor. If you want to use a little chunk of text as the hyperlink, but haven't typed that text yet, go ahead and type that text right into your Web page. If you want to use a picture as the hyperlink, but haven't inserted the picture yet, insert the picture, using any of the techniques discussed in Chapter 10, "Spice It Up With Lines & Pictures." Then follow these steps:

1. Select the text or picture that will act as the hot spot. (To select a picture, just click it once.)

2. Click the Make Link button in the Character Format toolbar, or choose Insert | Link. (Or just press Ctrl+L.) The dialog box shown in Figure 11-7 appears.

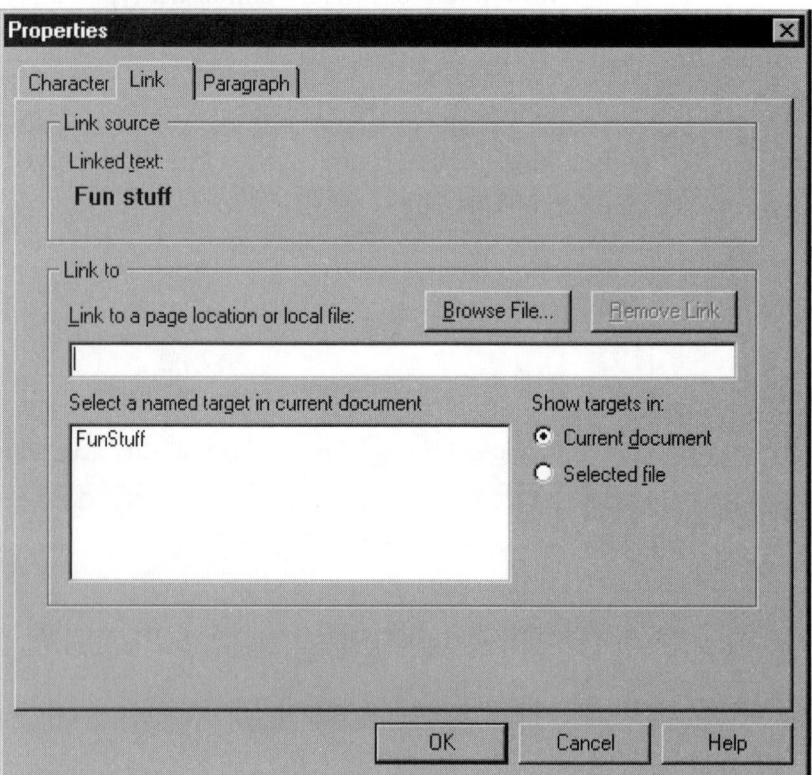

Figure 11-7: *The Properties dialog box, for creating a hyperlink.*

3. Next, specify where you want this link to take the reader, as follows:

   ■ If you're linking the reader to a different Web site, type the complete URL of that site (e.g., **http:// www.coolnerds.com**) under *Link to a page location or local file.*

   ■ If you're linking the reader to another page in this site, click the Browse File button and then, in the Link to File dialog box that appears, select (open) the file you want to link to.

   ■ If you're linking to a target in the current page, leave the *Link to a page location or local file* option blank, and just select (click) the named target that you want this link to point to.

4. Choose OK.

The selected text turns blue and is underlined. (If you selected a picture as the hot spot, the picture is now enclosed in a blue frame.) Note that nothing happens when you click the hot spot in the editor. To test the hyperlink, you need to switch to the browser. (Click the View in Browser button, and select Yes when asked whether you want to save your changes.)

LINKING TO A TARGET IN A DIFFERENT PAGE

To link to a specific target in some page other than the one you're editing at the moment, you must include both the filename and the target name in your selection. Suppose, for example, that I'm currently editing a page named index.htm, and that I want to add links to another page, which I've named travel.htm. Let's say I've also put two targets in travel.htm; one named *Domestic* and the other named *Foreign.*

In index.htm, I need to type the link text and select one of the links. Then I click the Make Link button to get to the Link Properties dialog box. There, I use Browse File to open the document I want the link to open—travel.htm, in this example. Now all I have to do is find the target I want in the list of targets in that document (see Figure 11-8), click on that target, then click on OK.

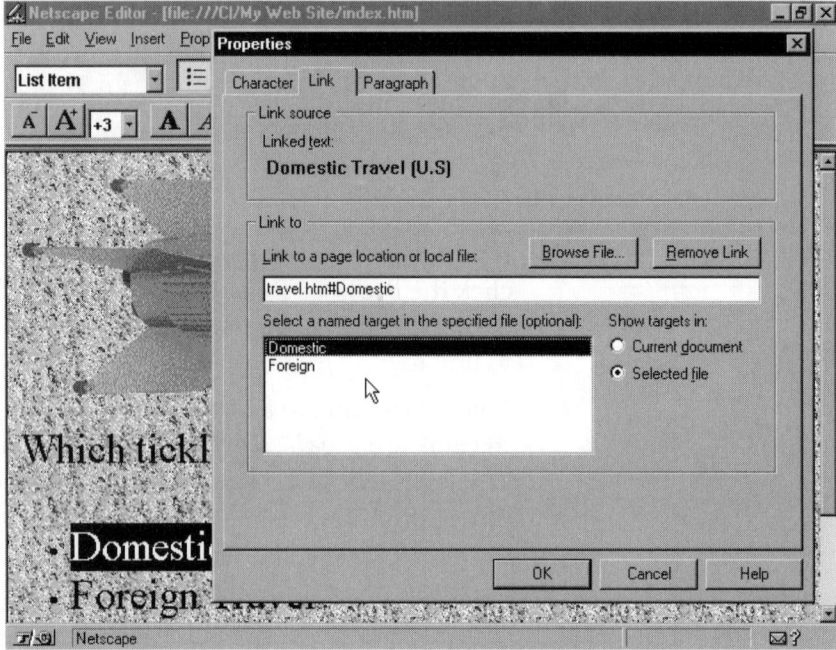

Figure 11-8: *When you link to another document, any targets in that document are displayed in the lower window.*

DRAG-AND-DROP HYPERLINKS

You can use some great drag-and-drop shortcuts to create links in your own pages. For example, let's say that you're editing a page you've created (named myurls.htm), and you want to browse around the Web and point your readers to some other sites.

First, open another Navigator window (File | New Web Browser). Get online (if you aren't already), and use one of the windows to browse the Web. Leave the document you're editing in the other window. You may want to size the windows so that you can see both of them.

When you come to a site to which you'd like to create a hyperlink, point to the little link icon next to the Location box in the browsing window. Then drag that little icon into the Web page you're editing. Instantly, the title of the site appears in your page, already underlined and "hot," as in the example shown on Figure 11-9.

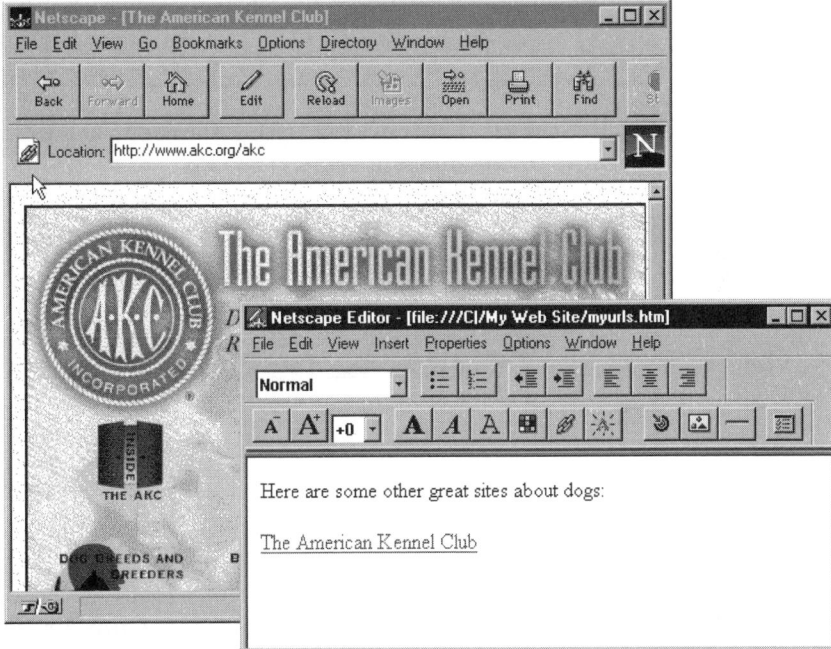

Figure 11-9: *By dragging the link icon to the editor's lower window, you create an instant hyperlink.*

You can also drag a link from a bookmark window, newsgroup, or mail window to create a link to that URL. For example, to make a hyperlink to any one of the underlined newsgroups in Figure 11-10, you could just drag the link from the news window right into your editor window.

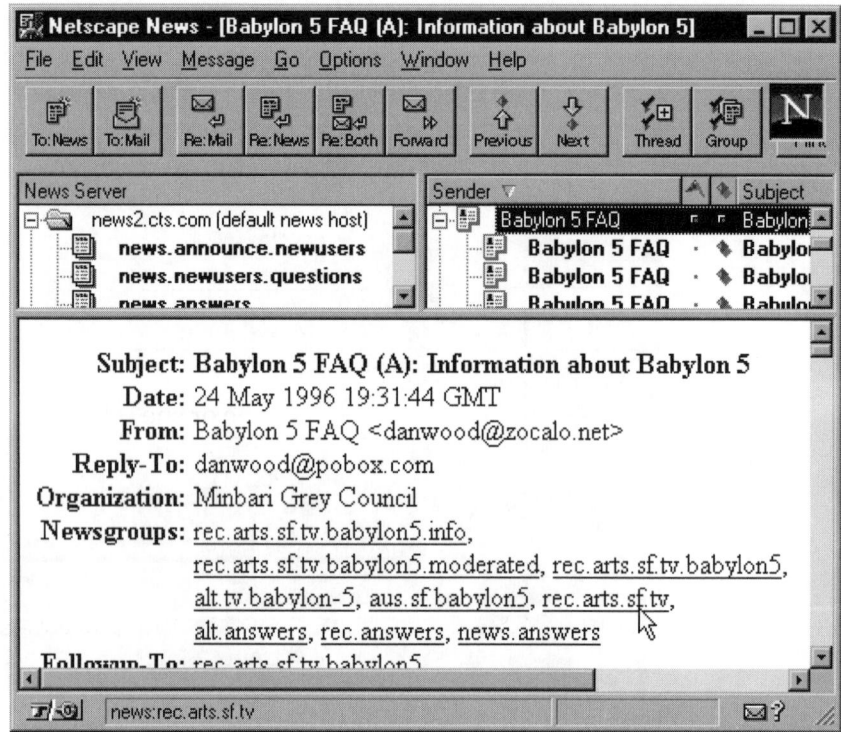

Figure 11-10: *Drag and drop a newsgroup link to create an instant hyperlink.*

Similarly, you can drag the name of any .htm or .html file from the Windows 95 My Computer, Find, or Explorer window to make an instant hyperlink to that file. Be sure, however, to create links only to files that you plan to upload to the Web server.

CHANGING OR DELETING A HYPERLINK

Should you need to change or delete a hyperlink, just right-click that link (in the editor) and choose Link Properties. Make your changes in the Link Properties dialog box (or select Remove Link to remove the link), then click on OK.

ADDING A "HOT" RETURN ADDRESS

To put a "hot" return address at the bottom of a Web page, select the text that will act as the link, then click the Make Link button. In the *Link to a page location or local file* box, type **mailto:** followed by your e-mail address, or whatever e-mail address you want the reader's message sent to. In Figure 11-11, for example, you can see that I've selected some text and set the link to my own e-mail address like this:

```
mailto:alan@coolnerds.com
```

When a reader clicks that link, he or she is taken to an e-mail form. My mail address is already typed in the Mail To portion of the form.

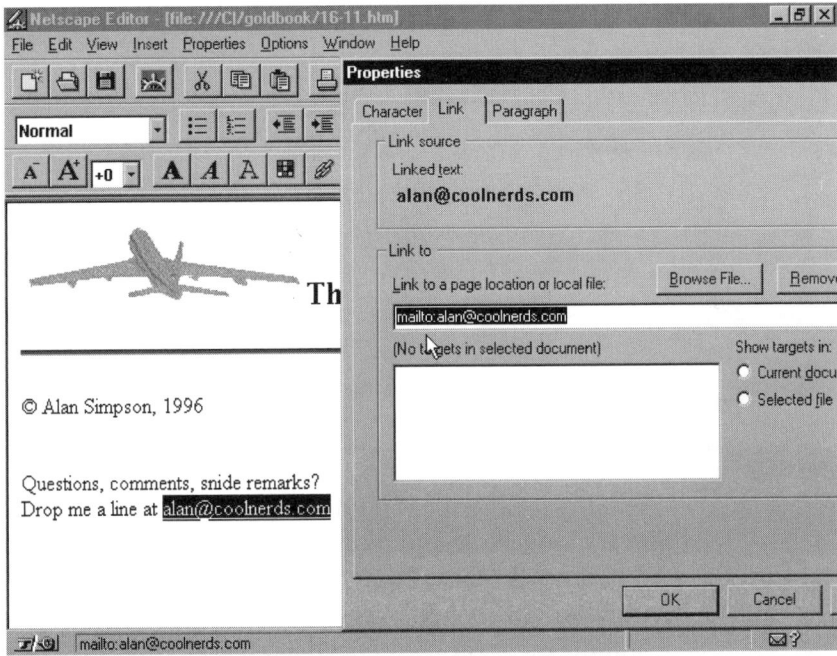

Figure 11-11: *Linking a chunk of text to my e-mail address.*

NEW HTML TAGS

Should you ever be tempted to peek behind the scenes at the document source, to see what these hyperlinks look like in HTML, you'll find that both targets and links are defined by the <A>...</A> tags summarized in Table 11-1. The *A* stands for *anchor*, the generic term in HTML for a place to or from which the reader can jump.

HTML Tag	Purpose
<A NAME="name">...</A>	Defines a target with the name specified in *name*.
<A HREF="URL">...</A>	Specifies a hyperlink in which *URL* is the destination (target) of the link.

Table 11-1: *HTML tags that define targets and links.*

TIP

In local (relative) links, the URL might start with two periods and a slash (../). That symbol stands for the parent directory (the directory above the current directory).

MOVING ON

Well, my friend, that about wraps it up for hyperlinks. You now have all the skills and tools necessary to create some darn good Web pages. In fact, if you browse around the World Wide Web on your own for a while, you'll see that almost every page you visit contains the three elements described in the last three chapters: text, graphics, and hyperlinks.

You may also come across some fancy pages in which tables are used to organize text and pictures into neat little columns and rows. In fact, in the next chapter, you'll learn how to create tables.

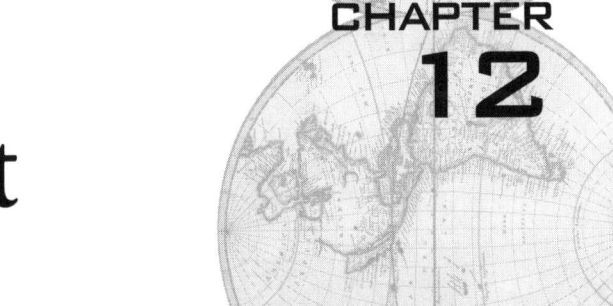

Get It Straight With Tables

Tables let you organize text and pictures into nice neat rows and columns. With a little fudging, you can use tables to give your Web pages a multicolumn format. In this chapter you'll learn everything you need to know about creating tables with Gold's editor, including:

- What is a table?
- How to create a table
- How to fill a table
- How to format a table

WHAT IS A TABLE?

In its simplest form, a table in a Web page is just like a table in a book or any other printed document—it is used to align text into rows and columns. For example, if I were to publish this chapter on the World Wide Web, I might present the table shown near the end of this chapter as in Figure 12-1.

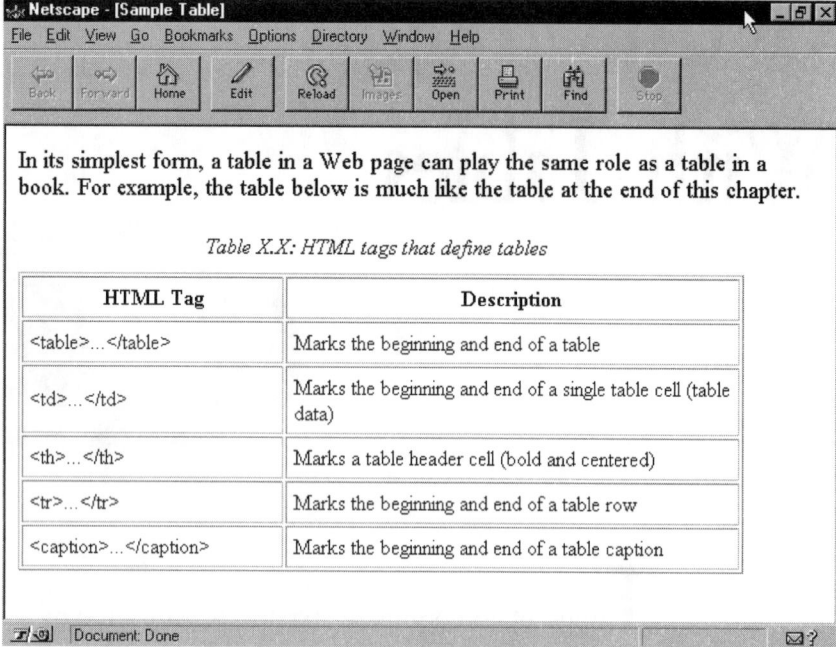

Figure 12-1: *A simple table.*

You're not limited to putting text in a table. You can put pictures in as well—even pictures that act as hyperlinks. Figure 12-2 shows some pictures organized into a table.

Figure 12-2: *A table that contains pictures.*

The borders within the table are optional. You can turn them off to give the presentation a different look and feel. In Figure 12-3, for example, you can see the previous table (the one shown in Figure 12-2) with the borders turned off. In this rendition, the table looks more like a clickable image map, with several little individual hot spots.

Figure 12-3: *Table from Figure 12-2, without the borders.*

Now take a look at Figure 12-4, from Netscape's site. How do you think they got that multicolumn look, with all those pictures and text blurbs lined up so nicely and so evenly spaced?

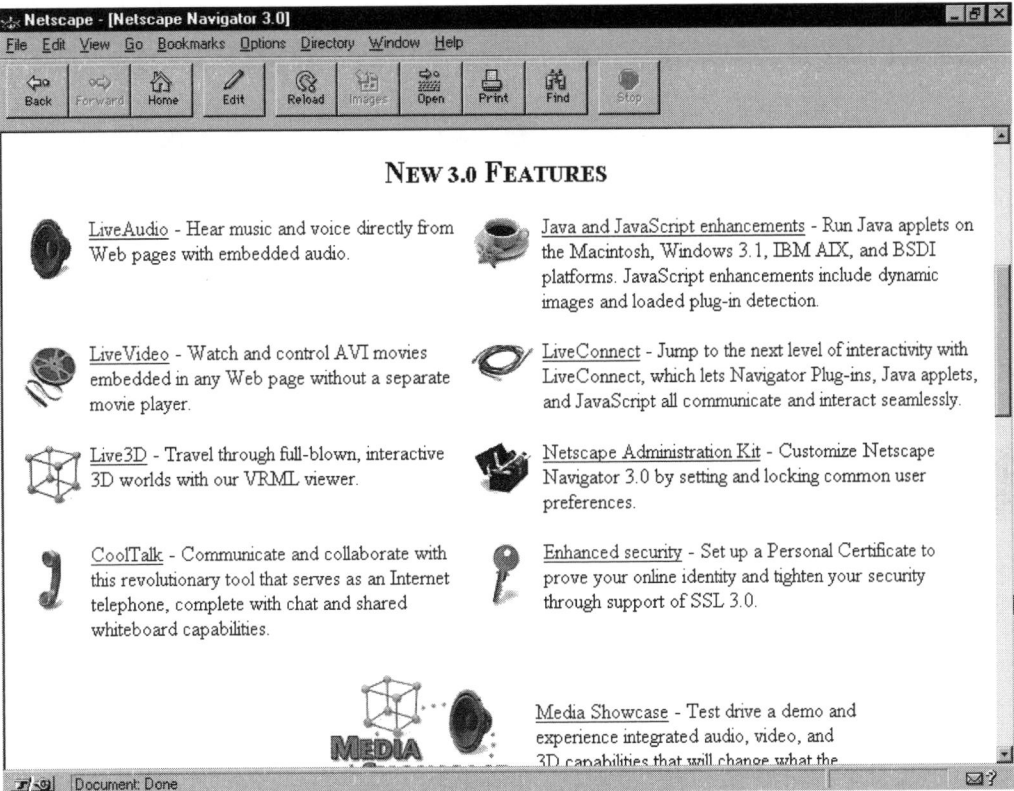

Figure 12-4: *A sample multicolumn page from Netscape's site.*

I know exactly how they did it. But I'm not telling. (Just kidding!) They did it with a table, of course. To prove it, I can download a copy of that entire page and all its graphics to my PC (by using File | Edit Document). Then I can switch to the editor, click in the general vicinity of the table, then turn on the table borders. And sure enough, those clever guys and gals at Netscape used a table to present that page so nicely. Figure 12-5 gives you the inside look.

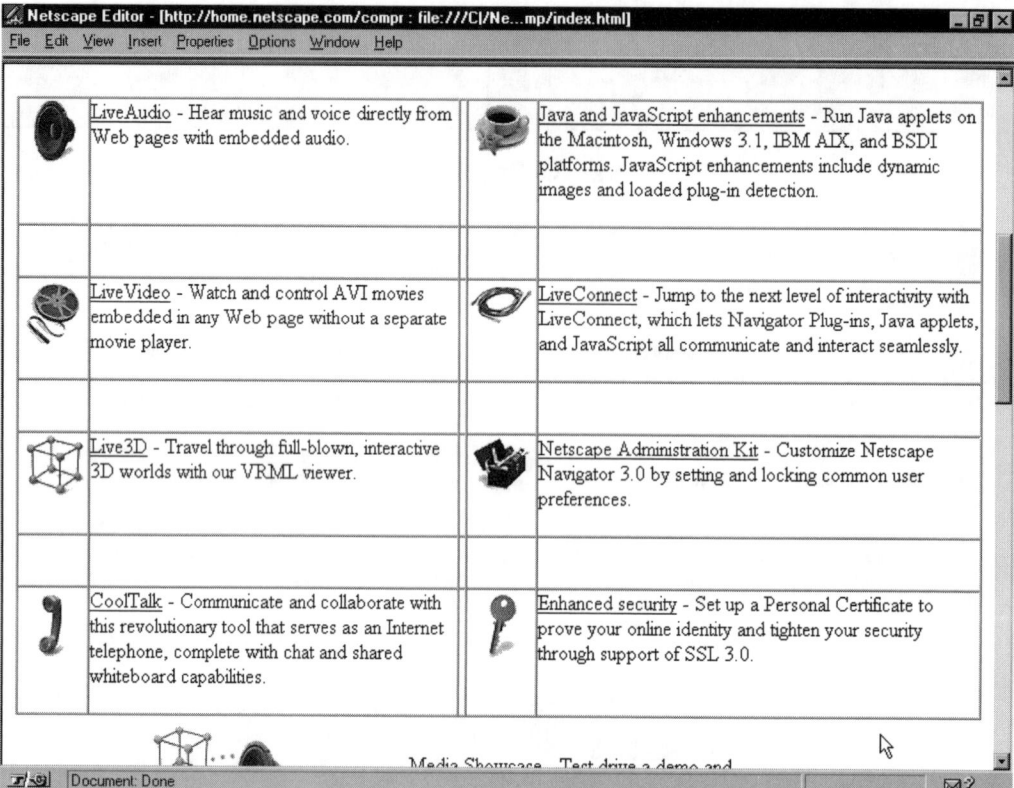

Figure 12-5: *The page shown in Figure 12-4, but with table borders turned on (in Gold's editor).*

TABLE JARGON

A little jargon goes along with tables. *Rows* go across the table, *columns* go up and down. The place at which a row and column meet is called a *cell*. The lines that separate the cells are called *borders*. A table's *caption* is a line of descriptive text above or below the table. Tables can also have *header cells*, which are the same as any other cells except that text within the header cells is automatically centered and boldfaced. Figure 12-6 illustrates the basic anatomy of a table.

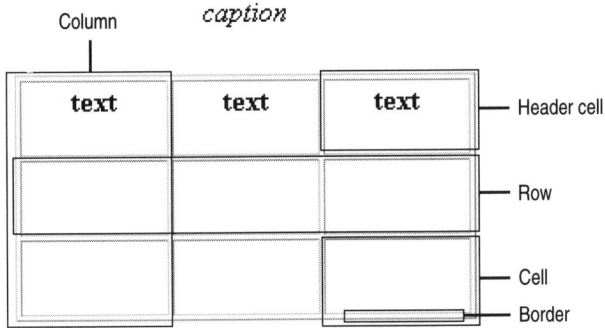

Figure 12-6: *Table jargon illustrated.*

HOW TO CREATE A TABLE

To create a table open your Web page in Gold's editor. Click approximately where you want the table to appear. If you need some extra space above the table, you can add some blank lines by pressing Enter as many times as necessary. Then follow these steps:

1. Choose Insert | Table from the menus. The Create Table dialog box shown in Figure 12-7 appears.

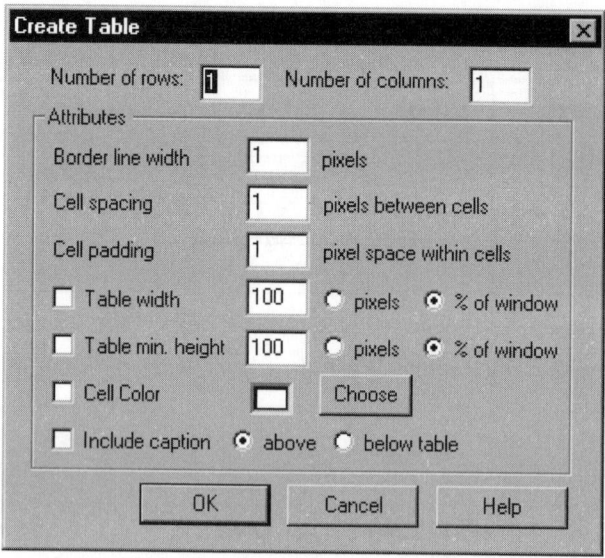

Figure 12-7: *The Create Table dialog box.*

2. Specify the number of rows and columns you want the table to contain.

3. You can choose other options if you wish, as described in this chapter's "Formatting a Table" section. Personally, however, I think you'll find it easier to start with just the default settings.

4. Click the OK button.

An empty (and kind of strange-looking) table appears. For example, Figure 12-8 shows a newly created table that has four rows and two columns.

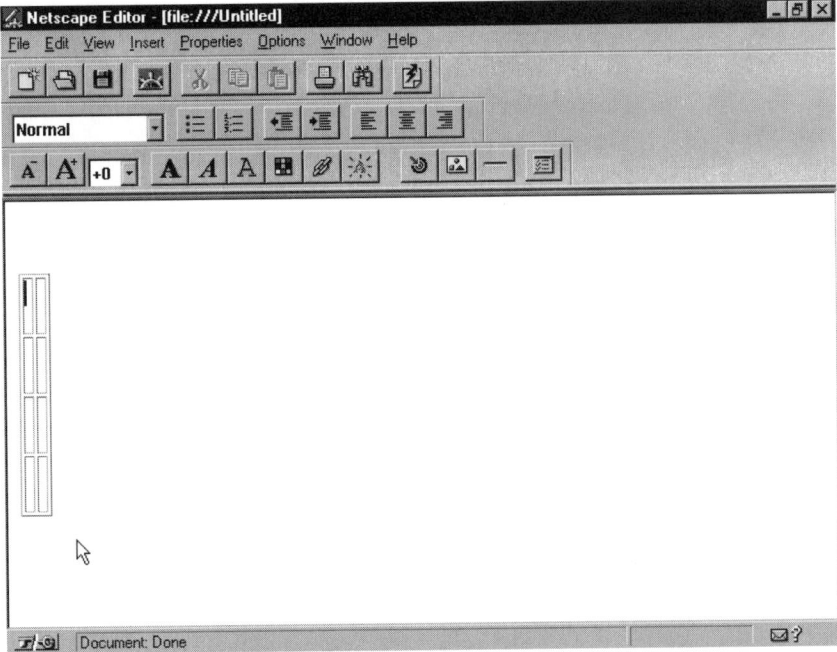

Figure 12-8: *A new, empty table with four rows and two columns.*

FILLING A TABLE

After you've created a table, you can easily start filling it. Just click the cell where you want to type something, and start typing. Or, if you want to insert a picture, click the cell and then click the Insert Image button. The height and width of the row and column grow, as necessary, to accommodate what you put into the cell. As you fill other cells, some columns may shrink to balance out the column widths.

TRAP

Make sure that you get the blinking cursor in the correct cell before you start typing. It can be a little tricky when you first start filling those tiny cells in an empty table.

Let's take a look at a quick example. In Figure 12-9 I clicked in the first cell and used the Insert Image button to insert a small graphic image. Then, in the cell to the right, I typed a paragraph of text. The column containing the picture widened automatically to accommodate the picture. The column with the text widened until it reached the width of the page, and then word-wrapped the text within the cell.

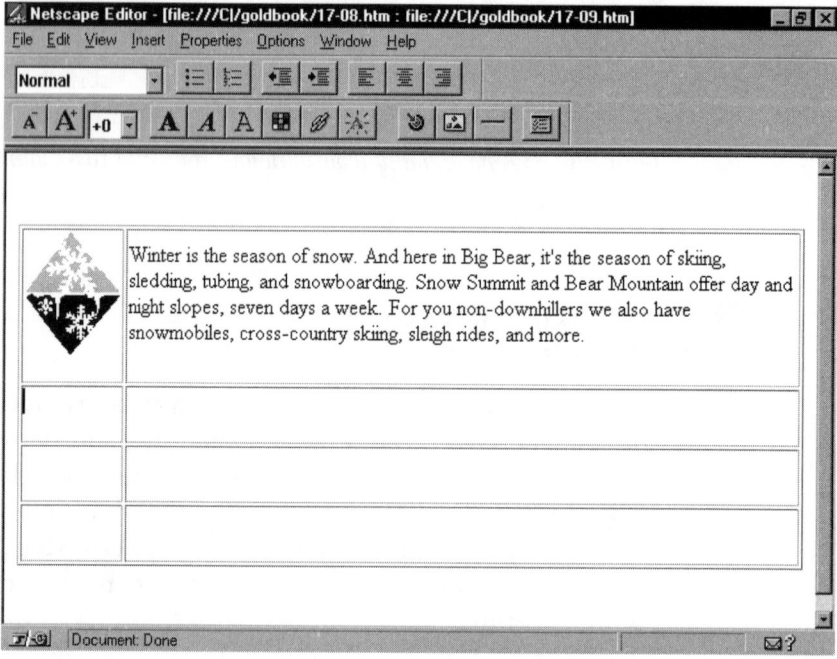

Figure 12-9: *A picture and some text in the first sample table.*

SELECTING & EDITING WITHIN A TABLE

Typing, navigating, selecting, and editing within a table is pretty straightforward. The simplest way to get the cursor into a specific cell is to just click in that cell. You can also use the arrow keys to move from cell to cell.

TIP

To force a line break within a cell without adding a blank line, press Shift+Enter at the end of each line, just as you would outside a table.

You select text and graphics in a table in much the same way as you do outside a table. To select a graphic image, click it once. A dark border appears around the image. To select text, just drag the mouse pointer through the text you want to select.

After you have selected a picture or text, you can perform most of the normal formatting and editing operations on it. For example, when text is selected in a table cell, the Align Left, Center, Align Right, Font, Font Color, Bold, Italic, Fixed Width, Cut, Copy, and Make Link toolbar buttons all work normally on that selected text. You can also right-click a picture, text, or selected text to get to the appropriate Properties box to make changes or to cut or copy to the Windows clipboard.

In addition to being able to do all the normal editing and formatting in a table, you also have many options for formatting the table itself, individual rows, or even individual cells.

FORMATTING A TABLE

To format the table as a whole, click anywhere in the table and choose Properties | Table from the menus. You'll come to the Table dialog box shown in Figure 12-10.

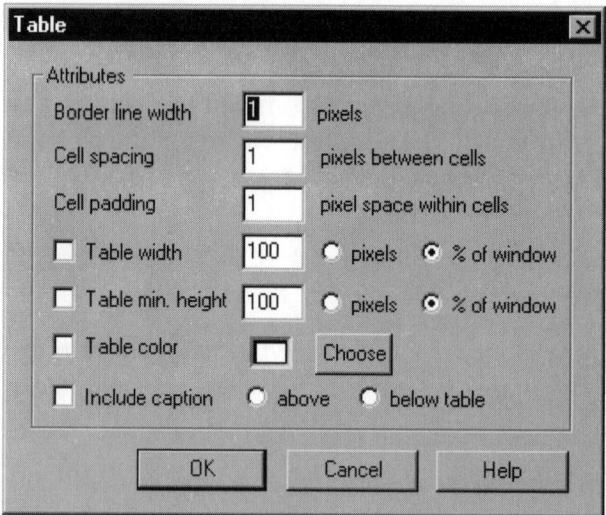

Figure 12-10: *Table dialog box.*

Brief descriptions of the options in this dialog box follow:

- Border line width: Defines the width of the border around the table, in pixels. Setting this value to zero hides the borders.

- Cell spacing: Provides extra spacing, measured in pixels, between the cells.

- Cell padding: Defines a margin, measured in pixels, within the cells.

- Table width: Defines the width of the table. When this option is not checked, the table automatically widens to accommodate its contents (up to a maximum of the total screen width). Optionally, you can assign a fixed width in pixels or as a percentage of the Navigator window's width.

- Table min. height: Defines the minimum height of the table. If this option is not checked, the table height is determined automatically, based on its contents. Optionally, you can assign a minimum height in pixels or as a percentage of the Navigator window height.

- Table color: If this option is not checked, the table is transparent. If checked, you can click the Choose button to define a color for the table.

- Include caption: If this option is checked, an extra row is added to the table to accommodate a caption. You can choose to place this row above or below the table.

To give you examples of some of these settings, I filled in the sample table shown in Figure 12-9, and then applied some table formatting to it. Specifically, I did the following:

- Set the border line width to 5 pixels.

- Set the cell padding to 5 pixels, putting some margin space in each cell.

- Set the table color to gray.

Figure 12-11 shows the results of applying these formatting options.

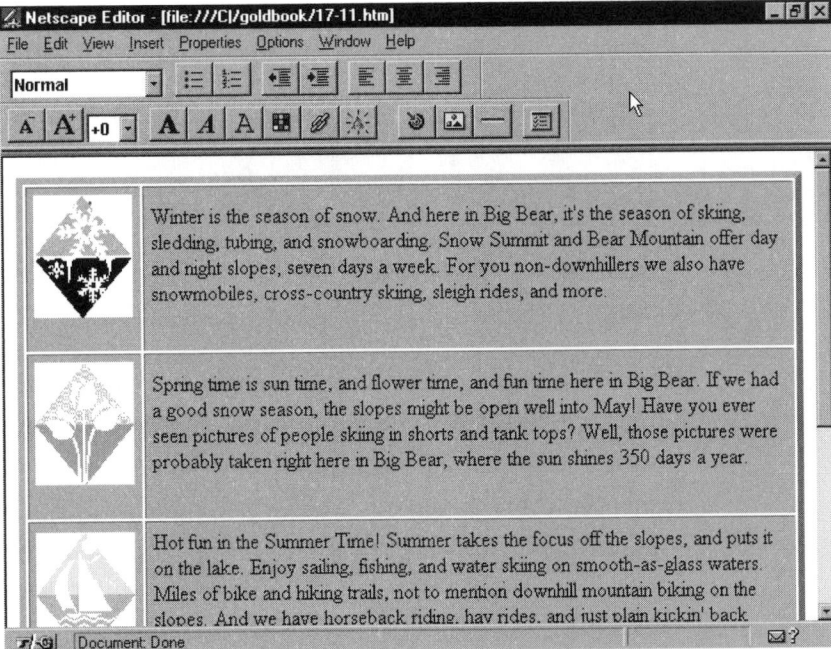

Figure 12-11: *Sample table with some table formatting options applied.*

FORMATTING ROWS

The row-formatting options let you align text within cells and choose colors for individual rows. To format one or more rows, follow these steps:

1. Click anywhere in the row you want to format, or select multiple rows to format.

2. Choose Properties | Row from the menu bar to get to the Row dialog box shown in Figure 12-12.

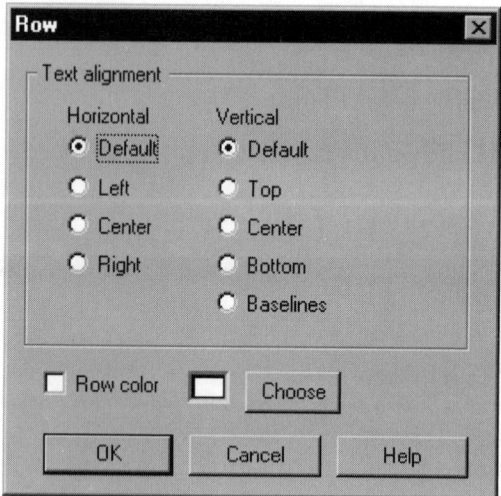

Figure 12-12: *The Row dialog box.*

3. Choose options for Horizontal and Vertical text alignment, and (optionally) a color for the selected row(s).

4. Click on the OK button.

Figure 12-13 shows an example of the various text-alignment features in action. Note that the default format aligns text to the left of the cell and centers it vertically. I've also alternated the colors of the rows.

Horizontal Alignment	Vertical Alignment	Sample Lengthy Text
Default	Default	Howdy Howdy Howdy. I'm a long chunk of text that needs to wrap inside it cell. The first and second columns are each 100 pixels wide.
Left	Top	Howdy Howdy Howdy. I'm a long chunk of text that needs to wrap inside it cell. The first and second columns are each 100 pixels wide.
Center	Center	Howdy Howdy Howdy. I'm a long chunk of text that needs to wrap inside it cell. The first and second columns are each 100 pixels wide.
Right	Bottom	Howdy Howdy Howdy. I'm a long chunk of text that needs to wrap inside it cell. The first and second columns are each 100 pixels wide.
Right	Baselines	Howdy Howdy Howdy. I'm a long chunk of text that needs to wrap inside it cell. The first and second columns are each 100 pixels wide. My column is 300 pixels wide.

Figure 12-13: *Examples of text alignment and individual row coloring.*

I also fixed the width of the first two columns to 100 pixels each. To set column widths, you just need to set the width of one cell in the column, as described in the next section.

FORMATTING CELLS

You can format individual cells or groups of cells. Click the cell you want to format, or select the cells you want to format. Then choose Properties | Cell from the menu bar to get to the Cell dialog box shown in Figure 12-14. Summaries of the options in that dialog box follow:

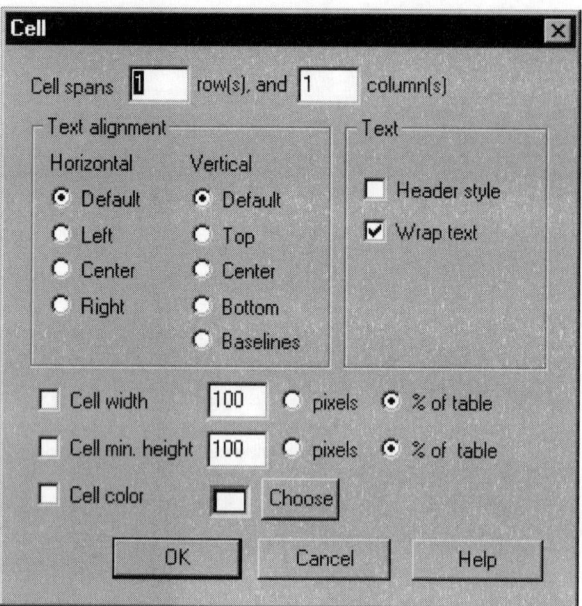

Figure 12-14: *The Cell dialog box.*

- Cell spans: Makes a cell span two or more rows, or two or more columns. See "Spanning Rows & Columns," later in this chapter, for an example.

- Text alignment: Overrides the table and row formatting, if any, for the currently selected cell(s) only.

- Text: Header style automatically centers and boldfaces text in the cell. Wrap text, when disabled, prevents text from word-wrapping within the cell.

- Cell width, min. height, color: Same as equivalent options in the Table dialog box, but applied only to the currently selected cell(s). Changing the width of a cell sets the width of the entire column.

Figure 12-15 shows a small sample table that illustrates some cell formatting. Each cell is set to 50 pixels wide and a minimum of 50 pixels tall, so that each cell is identical in size. Alternating cells have a gray color assigned to them.

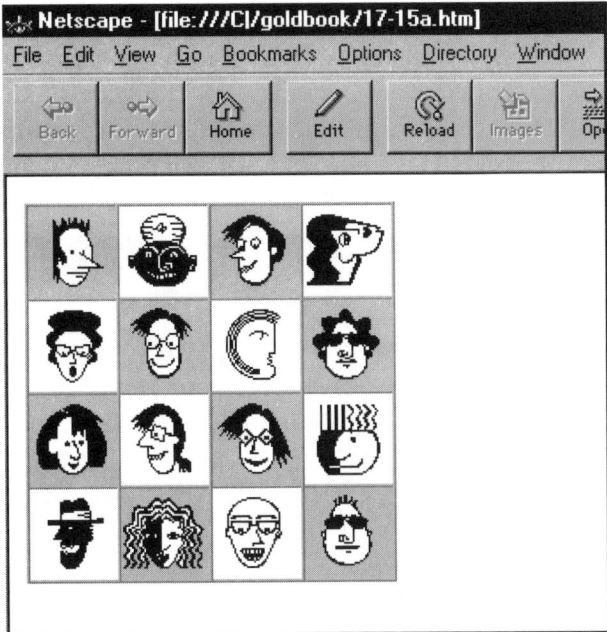

Figure 12-15: *Individual cells formatted in this table.*

INSERTING & DELETING ROWS & COLUMNS

You can easily insert and delete entire rows and columns in a table. First, click anywhere in the row or column you want to delete, or where you want to insert a row or column. Then:

- To insert a row or column, select Insert from the menu bar and choose either Row or Column.

- To delete the row or column, click on Properties in the menu bar, then choose Delete Row or Delete Column.

If you change your mind after the fact, you can choose Edit | Undo to undo the most recent change.

A newly inserted row is always placed *below* the current row, and a newly inserted column is always placed *to the right of* the current column. If you're trying to add a new row at the top of the table, or a new column to the left of the table, and you've already filled the table, you'll probably need to cut and paste after you insert the new row or column. For example, in Figure 12-16 I put the cursor in the first column and then inserted a new column. Thus, the new empty column is to the right of that column.

Figure 12-16: *The second column is the newly inserted column.*

Now let's suppose that I really had intended to make this new column the first column in the table. A simple solution here would be to right-click the Art & Artists picture and choose Cut from the pop-up menu. Then right-click the next cell over to the right, and choose Paste. Repeat that procedure to move the Uncle Sam picture over a cell. Now the new column contains the two pictures, and the first column in the table is empty (see Figure 12-17).

Figure 12-17: *The table from Figure 12-16, after two pictures have been moved to the right.*

Incidentally, to delete an entire table, just click anywhere inside the table and choose Properties | Delete table from the menus.

SPANNING ROWS & COLUMNS

A single cell can span two or more rows, or two or more columns—which allows you to do some neat formatting tricks. To make a cell span more (or fewer) rows and columns:

1. Click anywhere in the cell that you want to expand or shrink.

2. Choose Properties | Cell to get to the Cell dialog box shown in Figure 12-18.

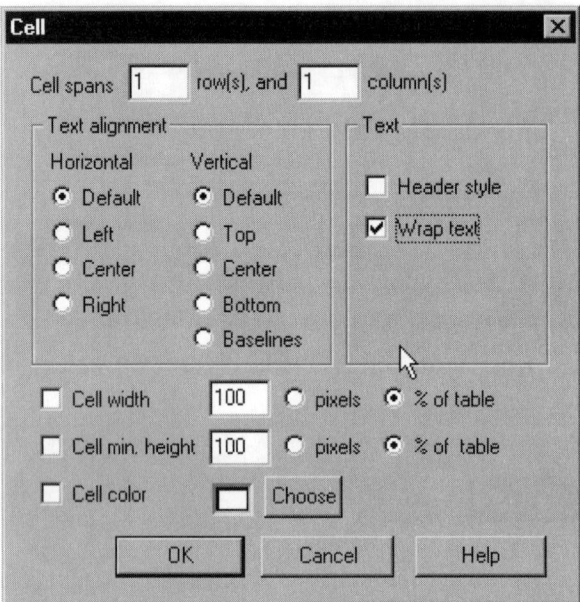

Figure 12-18: *The first option lets you determine how many rows or columns a single cell spans.*

3. In the *Cell spans* options, specify the number of row(s) and the number of column(s) that you want the cell to span.

4. Choose OK.

Because the results can be a little confusing at first, let me take you through an example. Look back at Figure 12-17, and notice that the first column is split into two rows, just like the columns to the right of it.

Now let's suppose that I put the cursor in the top left cell, choose Properties | Cell, and change that cell so that it spans two rows. Initially, the result looks like Figure 12-19. The leftmost (skinny) cell does indeed span two columns. But what's with that new empty cell under Arts & Artists?

Figure 12-19: *Initial result of making first cell span two rows.*

Well, actually, it kind of makes sense that the extra cell ended up where it did, because the top left cell grew downward. So it had to push the cell that was already there over to the right. In this particular scenario, however, we don't really want that extra cell. I click inside that new, empty cell under Art & Artists, then choose Properties | Delete Cell from the menu bars, and without any major headaches—thank goodness—things look much better (see Figure 12-20).

Figure 12-20: *The extra blank cell under Art & Artists has been deleted.*

Now what can I do with the tall cell in the first column? Well, I can put a tall skinny picture in it, as in Figure 12-21. Because the cell is already tall enough to accommodate the picture, none of the other cells needs to be resized.

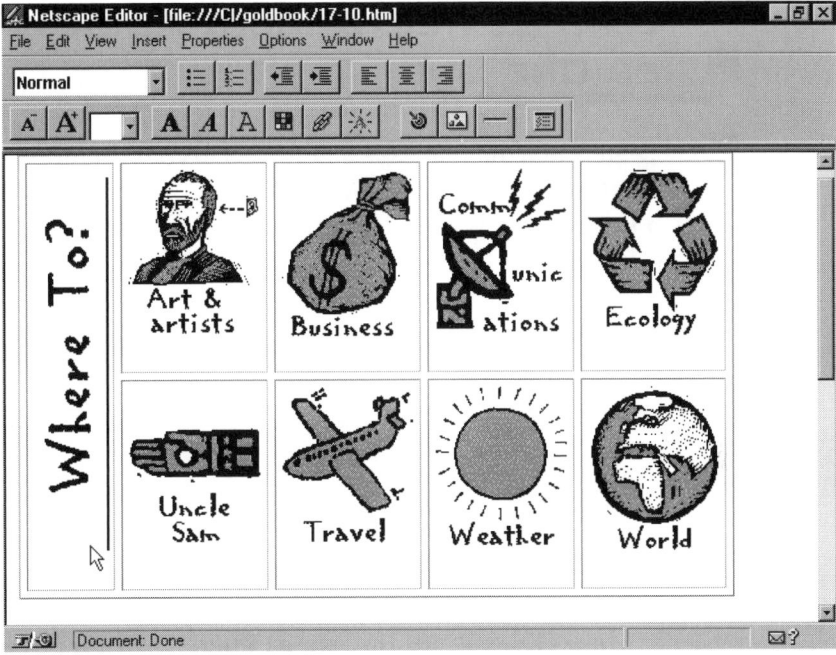

Figure 12-21: *Tall skinny picture in first column.*

In case you're curious, I created the pictures shown in Figures 12-16 through 12-21 in Paint Shop Pro, which is discussed in Chapter 14, "Power Image Publishing." The clip art and "Regular Joe" font are from the Art Parts collection, which I purchased from Image Club at http://www.imageclub.com or (800)387-9193.

LEFT, CENTER, & RIGHT ALIGN ON ONE LINE

There's no rule that says a table has to contain more than a single column or a single row. You can use a single-row table with hidden borders to show left-aligned, centered, and right-aligned text on a single line, as in the example just under the headline in Figure 12-22.

Figure 12-22: *Text under the headline appears to use left, center, and right alignment in a single line.*

When I switch to Edit mode and turn on the borders, you can see that the line is really a table. Text in the first cell is left-aligned, text in the center cell is centered, and text in the third cell is right-aligned. Each cell is set to 33 percent of the screen width.

Figure 12-23: *Text from Figure 12-22, behind the scenes.*

As you can see in Figures 12-22 and 12-23, the stories on the page appear to be in columns. Actually, however, they're in a separate table that has three columns and one row. To ensure that each story starts at the top of its column, the vertical text alignment for the row is set to Top.

Figure 12-23 uses a table to display three stories in three separate columns. As an alternative, try the <multicol> tag discussed under "Cutting-Edge Design Tools" in Chapter 9. Or take a look at the Webhead Examiner example (see Figure 17-4).

OTHER COOL TABLE TOOLS

I guess that Netscape and Microsoft are pretty heavy-duty competitors these days. Those of you who have chosen sides in the battle might think it somehow blasphemous for me to mention this. But I'll mention it anyway. Microsoft's Internet Assistants for Word and Excel offer some great tools for creating and managing tables in Web pages.

If you have Microsoft Word or Excel, and want more information and free software, point your Web browser to http://www.microsoft.com/internet, and check out the Authoring Tools (see Figure 12-24).

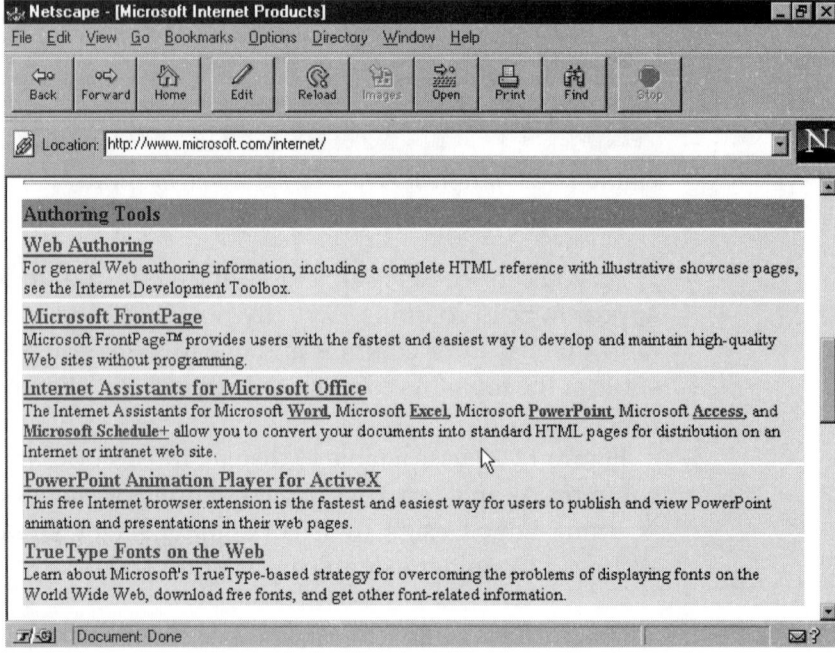

Figure 12-24: *Supplement your Gold editor with authoring tools from Microsoft.*

HTML Tags for Tables

If you take a look behind the scenes at any Web page that contains a table, you'll see a mind-boggling array of HTML tags that start with the letter *t*. Just be thankful that you don't have to create tables by typing in those tags *manually*! Ugh. Table 12-1 summarizes the HTML table-formatting tags.

HTML Tag	Description
<table>...</table>	Marks the beginning and end of a table.
<td>...</td>	Marks the beginning and end of a single table cell (table data).
<th>...</th>	Marks a table header cell (bold and centered).
<tr>...</tr>	Marks the beginning and end of a table row.
<caption>...</caption>	Marks the beginning and end of a table caption.

Table 12-1: *HTML table-formatting tags.*

Moving On

You are definitely getting into some pretty fancy Web page formatting skills now. How about we spice things up a little more with some multimedia? On to Chapter 13, "Multimedia Madness"!

Multimedia Madness

Nothing jazzes up a Web site like *multimedia*—some sound and video. You've probably already seen examples of sound and video in other people's Web sites. In this chapter you learn how to incorporate multimedia into your own site. Here's what we'll cover:

- Two ways to present sound and video
- Finding and creating sound and video clips
- Adding external sound and video to your site
- Adding inline multimedia to a page

Make sure that your sound equipment is working properly before you try anything in this chapter. You wouldn't want to spend an hour trying to get a sound file to work, only to discover that your speakers are turned down low or turned off!

TWO WAYS TO PRESENT SOUND

Sound can add a whole new dimension to your site. You can present sound in either of the following ways:

- External sound: When the reader clicks a hyperlink that your page presents to the reader, the sound or video is played.

■ Inline sound: A sound clip plays automatically when the reader opens your page.

Whether external or inline, the sound clip itself can be music, voice, or both.

Small music clips are often used as inline sounds to present background music for a page when the page is opened. External sound clips are often used to let readers sample bits of music. For example, many record companies offer sound clips that let you experience some part of a song, so that you can get a feel for the artist's style.

Windham Hill's site (see Figure 13-1) provides such external clips. When the reader clicks the link marked with the musical note, the sound file is downloaded and played. Note that the publishers of this site inform the reader of the clip's duration (28 sec) and size (311,446 bytes), so that readers know what to expect and can gauge, roughly, how long the download will take.

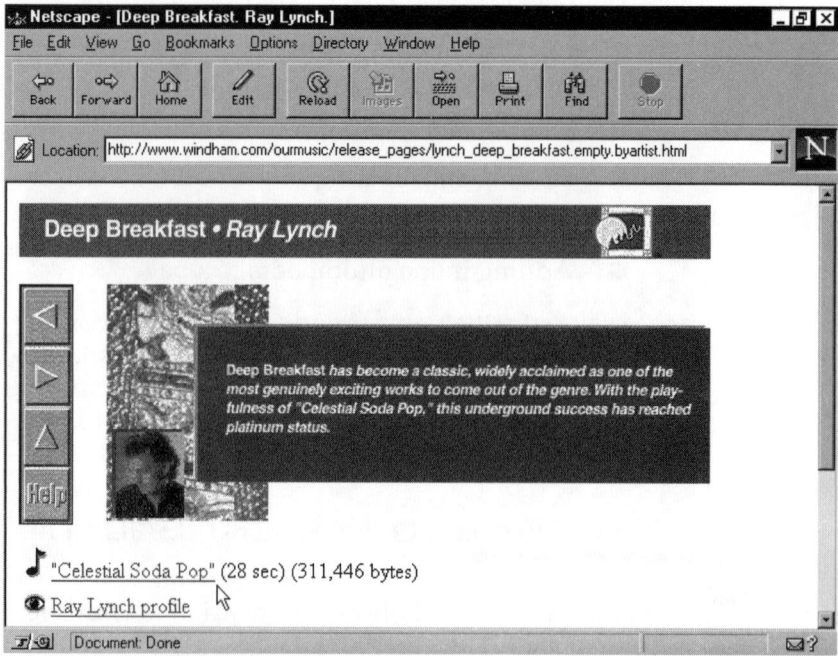

Figure 13-1: *Windham Hill's site (http://www.windham.com) lets browsers experience samples of their artists' work.*

Voice can be used to present spoken instructions on the screen, or for celebrity voices. For example, Rock the Web (http://www.rockweb.com) offers taped interviews. The interviewer's question is displayed as a hyperlink (see Figure 13-2). By clicking on a question you download the interviewee's response, in his or her own voice, to your PC (so that you can hear it).

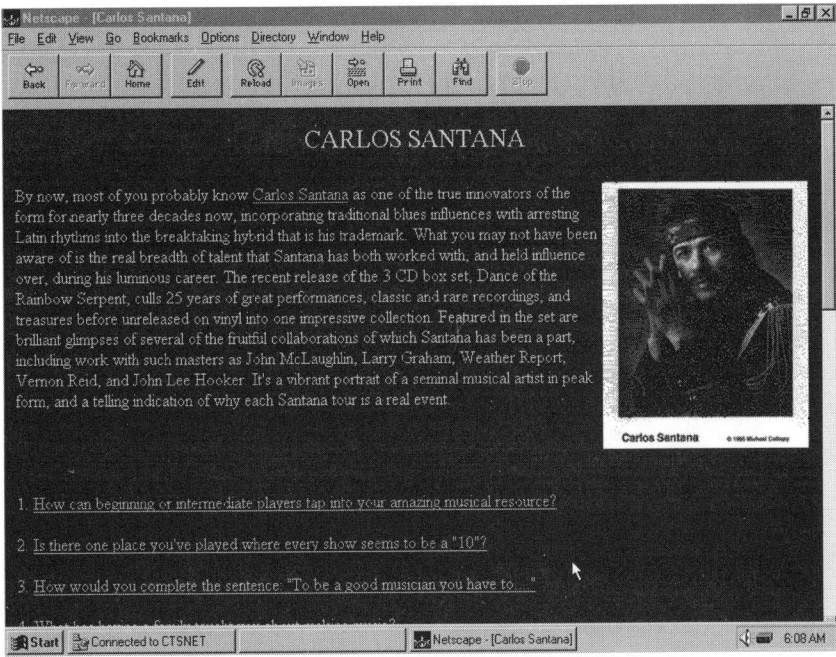

Figure 13-2: *Rock the Web (http://www.rockweb.com) offers taped interviews.*

TIP

Carlos Santana's voice is stored in RealAudio format, which Navigator doesn't support on its own. But you can easily install a plug-in (see Chapter 25, "Plug-Ins, Java & LiveConnect") to play RealAudio files.

GIVE READERS AN ESTIMATE

While we're looking at examples of ways to use sound on the Web, you should be aware of this important point: When you offer multimedia files for your readers to download, you should tell them the size of the files so that they can estimate how long the download will take. You can easily discover the size of each sound file by opening, in My Computer, the folder that contains the sound files.

There, switch to Detail view (View I Details), then click the Type column heading to group all the sound files together in the list of filenames. The size of each file is displayed in the Size column. In Figure 13-3, for example, you can see that BECK.WAV is 232K, DIMEOLA.WAV is 170K, and so forth. Jot down those sizes for future reference.

TIP

Inline sounds are sent to your reader automatically, which means they don't really have a choice in the matter. Therefore, you should keep inline sound files as small as possible.

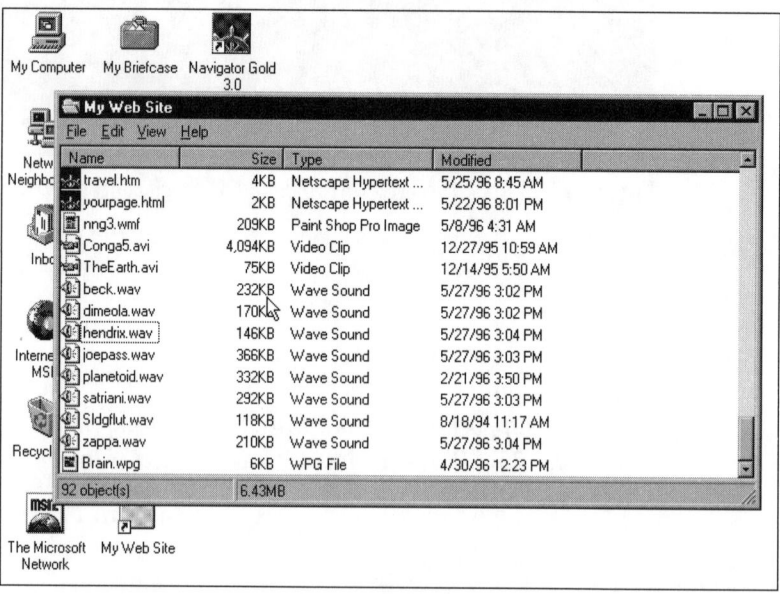

Figure 13-3: *Use My Computer's detail view to determine the size of each multimedia file.*

WHERE TO GET SOUND FILES

Several sound archives on the Web contain sound effects and small sound clips from famous movies and characters. For example, Joe's Original Wave Files at http://www.sky.net/~jdeshon/joewav.html (see Figure 13-4) offers a variety of original sound effects in .WAV format for your listening pleasure.

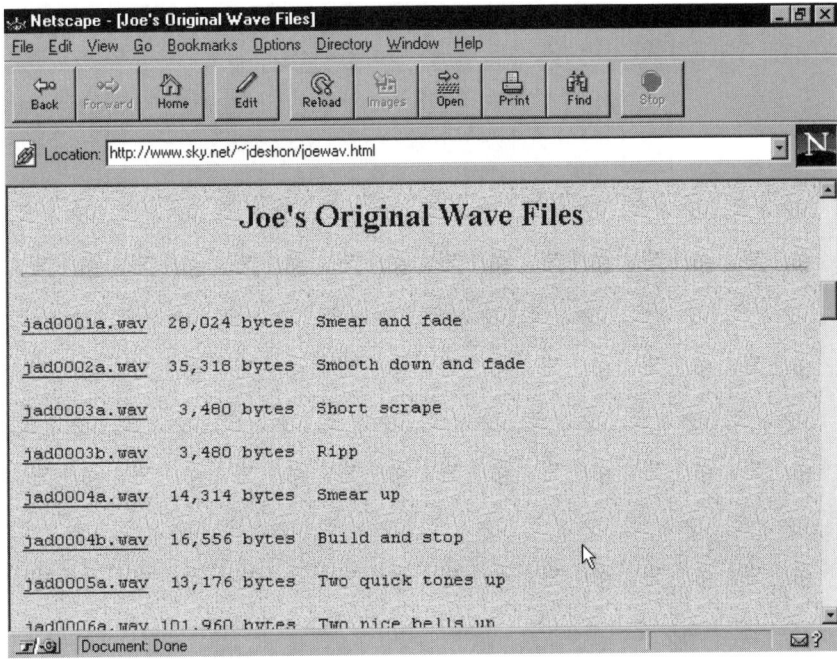

Figure 13-4: *Joe's Original Wave Files offers some fun sound effects.*

In the "Site Seeing" section near the end of this chapter, I point out some other sites that contain sound clips. As with pictures, however, don't assume that all sound clips are up for grabs and royalty free. Unless you're sure that it's OK to use a particular sound clip in your Web site, you should get permission from the holder of the copyright before you use a sound clip in your site.

DOWNLOADING A SOUND FILE FROM THE WEB

When you find a sound file that you want to copy (and are *allowed* to copy), follow these steps to copy the sound file to your PC:

1. Click on the link that plays the sound. If it's a WAV, AU, or AIFF sound, you are taken to Navigator's LiveAudio player, which looks like Figure 13-5.

Figure 13-5: *Navigator's LiveAudio player.*

2. To hear the sound, click the Play (middle) button in the player.

3. If you want to save this sound, choose File | Save As from Navigator's menu bar, choose a folder and filename, then click the Save button. The file will be saved to your hard disk.

4. To return to the previous page, click the Back button.

Sound files that you play with plug-ins other than LiveAudio can usually be saved in a similar manner (usually just by choosing File | Save from the player's menu bar). I'll talk in a moment about using a downloaded sound clip in your Web page. But first, I'd like to discuss an alternative to downloading prerecorded sound clips—creating your own clips.

RECORDING YOUR OWN SOUND

Most multimedia PCs and sound cards have the capability to record from a microphone, from an external source (such as a stereo), and from the PC's built-in CD-ROM player. I can give you some general pointers for recording your own sounds, using the built-in audio capabilities of Windows 95. But dozens of makes and models of sound cards and programs are out there on the market. I can't guarantee that these instructions will work on *all* PCs. If the procedures outlined here won't work, you'll need to refer to the documentation that came with your sound card or PC. (Bummer, I know.)

Be forewarned—sound files can become very large, very fast. If you're planning to use a recorded sound in your Web site, you'll want to limit the length of the recording to just a few seconds. Otherwise, the file will be so large that nobody will want to download it!

To record sounds, you don't need to be connected to the Internet or even have Navigator running. Your starting point is the Windows 95 desktop. The first thing you want to do is get to your Volume (playback) and recording controls, which you can do on most Windows 95 systems by using either of these approaches:

- Double-click the little speaker icon in the Windows 95 taskbar.

- Or, click the Start button and choose Programs | Accessories | Multimedia | Volume Control.

The Volume Control dialog box that pops up will resemble Figure 13-6. I need to warn you that this dialog box is critical to successful recording and playback, and is also a little tricky to use. Don't skim too lightly here, or you may pull your hair out trying to record and play back sounds later!

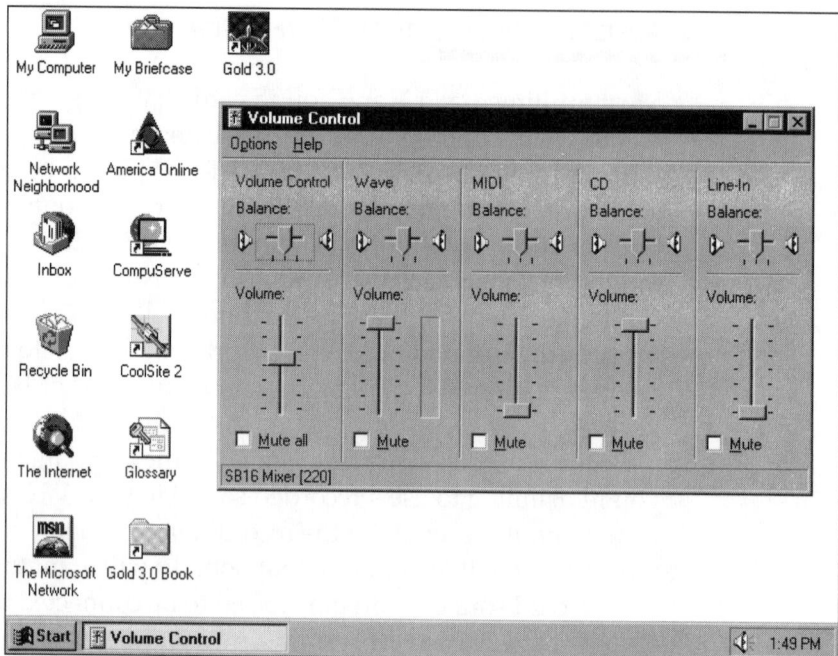

Figure 13-6: *Volume Control dialog box for playback.*

Notice that the title bar shows Volume Control. These controls apply *only* to playback. They have nothing to do with recording. The leftmost slider controls the general playback volume. The other sliders control the volume of different types of sounds, as follows:

- Wave: Controls the volume of .WAV (and other general) sound coming from files on your PC or from the Internet.

- MIDI: Controls the volume of MIDI output coming from MIDI files or a MIDI device.

- CD: Controls the volume of sound coming from your built-in CD-ROM drive.

- Line-In: Controls the volume of sound coming from an external device, such as a stereo, that's connected to your computer via the Line-In jack on your PC.

As a general rule, you can set all these sliders to about the middle, as shown in Figure 13-6. The only reason to do otherwise would be to make one device play louder than another while playing multiple devices simultaneously.

TRAP

If the Mute check box on any of the playback devices is checked, you won't hear any sound coming from that device.

To repeat—the Volume Control sliders have nothing to do with recording. To control recording, you must switch to the Recording Controls. Choose Options | Properties | Recording | OK from the menu bar. The Recording Control dialog box (see Figure 13-7) resembles the Volume Control dialog box. But when you look closely, you can see that the title bar now shows Recording Control, and you might see a slider for the Microphone input.

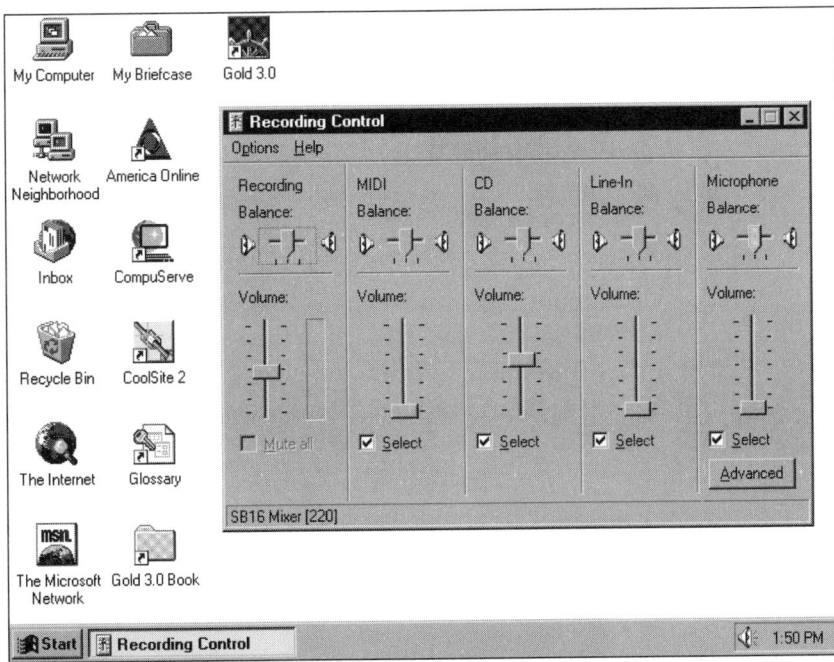

Figure 13-7: *Recording Control dialog box.*

For the cleanest possible recording, your best bet is to select *only* the device you'll be recording from. Clear the Select check box on any devices that you're not recording from at the moment.

You'd do well to leave this Recording Control dialog box open and onscreen whenever you record something (so that you can always see exactly where your sound card thinks it's recording *from*).

Spend a little time practicing with the sliders in Volume Control and Recording Control while you record and play sounds. Seeing them in action makes it easier to remember what each one does.

Next, we'll look at some specific pointers for recording from your microphone, built-in CD-ROM drive, and an external source such as a stereo.

RECORDING FROM A MICROPHONE

To record from your microphone, make sure that the microphone is plugged into the Mic jack of your sound card. Make sure also that the microphone is close to the source of the sound. If you're recording your own voice, for example, the microphone must be near your mouth.

Next, if the Recording Control dialog box isn't open on your screen, open it. Then fire up the Windows 95 Sound Recorder by clicking the Start button, and choosing Programs | Accessories | Multimedia | Sound Recorder. Size and position the windows so that you can see both the Recording Controls and Sound Recorder. Make sure that the Select check box for the Microphone is checked, then clear all the others (see Figure 13-8).

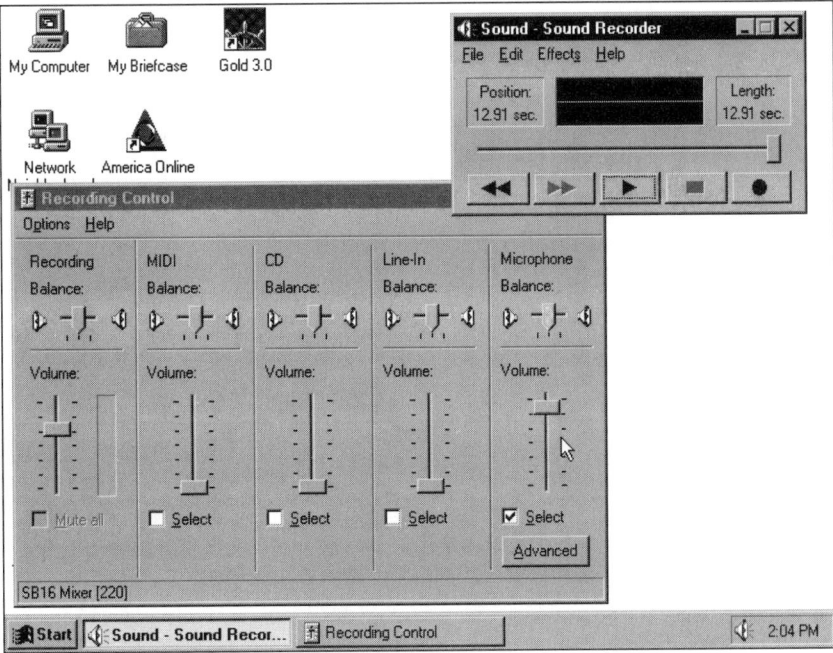

Figure 13-8: *Ready to record from a microphone.*

To record a sound, follow these steps:

1. Choose File | New from Sound Recorder's menu bar.

2. When you're ready to record, click the record button (the one with the Red dot).

3. Speak clearly into the microphone.

4. To stop recording, click the Stop button in Sound Recorder.

To hear the sound you recorded, click Sound Recorder's Seek to Start (rewind) button, then click the Play button. If you don't hear anything, see "Troubleshooting Recording & Playback," later in this section.

After you've made a successful recording, choose File | Save from Sound Recorder's menu bar, and save the file. If you plan to use the sound in a Web page, you might want to save the file to the folder that contains your other Web materials.

RECORDING FROM YOUR CD-ROM DRIVE

You can also record from regular audio CDs (the kind you buy in music stores) using your PCs internal CD-ROM drive. To record from your built-in CD-ROM drive, open Volume Control. Make sure that the CD device isn't muted, and that its volume isn't turned down too low. Then switch to the recording controls (Options | Properties | Recording | OK). Make sure that the general recording slider and CD sliders are turned up, and that the Select box for the CD player is checked. Finally, clear all the other Select check boxes (see Figure 13-9). To start recording, follow these steps:

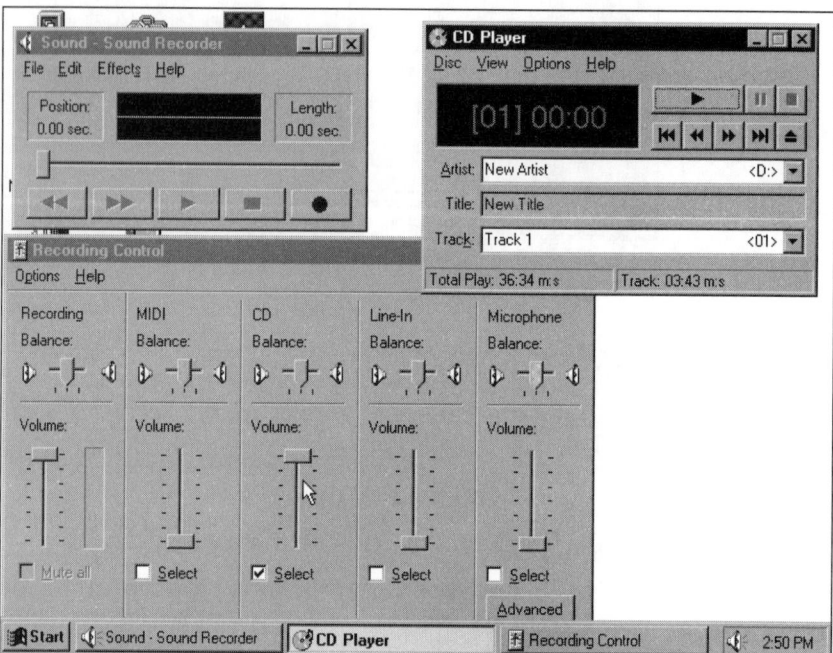

Figure 13-9: *Ready to record from an audio CD in the PC's CD-ROM drive.*

1. Open Sound Recorder by clicking the Start button and choosing Programs | Accessories | Multimedia | Sound Recorder.

2. Pop the audio CD into your CD-ROM drive. Most likely, it will start to play on its own, and you'll see the CD Player on screen. If you don't see the CD Player, click the Start button and choose Programs I Accessories I Multimedia I CD Player. Position the windows so that you can see all three, as in Figure 13-9.

3. Use the Play and Stop buttons in CD Player to start and stop playing. You can use the Previous Track, Skip Backwards, Skip Forwards, and Next Track buttons to get in the vicinity of the music you want to record.

4. As the sound you want to record approaches, click the Record (red dot) button in Sound Recorder. To stop recording, click Sound Recorder's Stop button.

To check your recording, stop the CD by clicking the Stop button in CD-player. Then click the Seek to Start and Play buttons in Sound Recorder. If you don't hear the recorded music, see "Troubleshooting Recording & Playback" later in this chapter.

TIP

When you play back a recorded sound, you're playing a Wave file—not the CD. So adjust your Playback volume accordingly.

To save the recorded sound byte, choose File I Save from the Sound Recorder menu bar, and choose a folder and filename for the recorded sound.

RECORDING FROM YOUR STEREO

To record sounds from an external source, such as your stereo, you must first connect the stereo's Line-Out jack(s) to your sound card's Line-In jack. If your stereo has two RCA-style Line-Out plugs, as most do, you'll need to purchase a special cable. This cable—sometimes called a *Y adapter*, or just a sound-card-to-stereo cable—is available at most computer stores.

After you hook up the cables correctly, open the Volume Control dialog box. Make sure that the Line In slider is turned up and not muted. (Even if you're recording from a CD in your stereo, the CD slider doesn't apply here because the sound source is coming into your Line In plug, *not* your internal CD-ROM drive!)

Switch to the Recording Controls dialog box (Options | Properties | Recording | OK). Make sure that the Line-In device is selected and that its slider is turned up. You can clear all the other Select check boxes. (Even the CD Select box, because your sound source is the Line-In jack on your sound card, *not* your internal CD-ROM drive.) Next, start Sound Recorder (Start | Programs | Accessories | Multimedia | Sound Recorder). Your screen should look something like Figure 13-10. Note that Line In is the selected recording device in Recording Control.

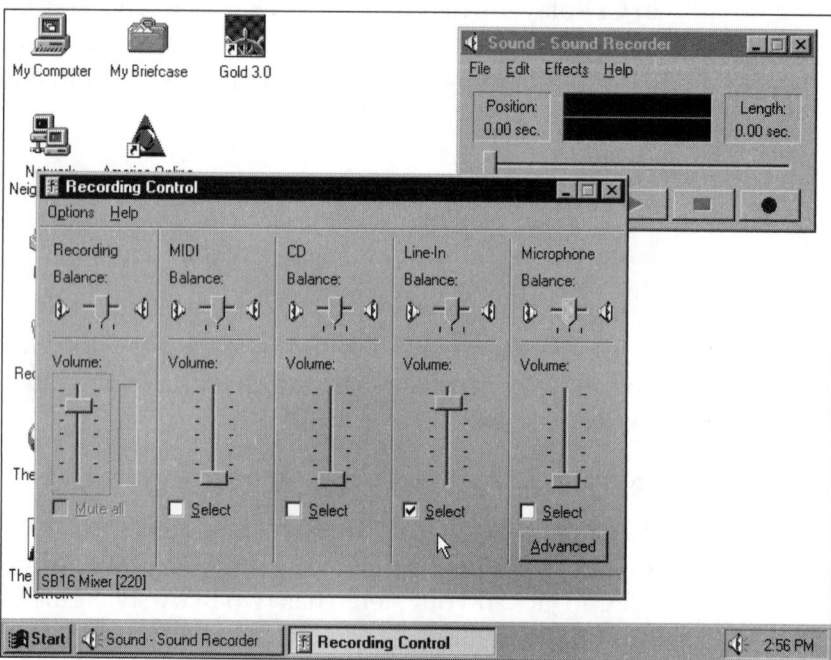

Figure 13-10: *Ready to record from an external sound source.*

To record from your stereo, follow these steps:

1. Start playing music from your stereo, near where you want to record.

2. Click the Record button in Sound Recorder when you're ready to start recording. Then click the Stop button in Sound Recorder when you finish recording.

To test the recorded sound, turn off the stereo, click the Seek to Start button in Sound Recorder, then click the Play button. If you have any problems, see "Troubleshooting Recording & Playback."

To save the recording, choose File | Save from Sound Recorder's menu bar, then choose a folder and filename for the sound file.

TROUBLESHOOTING RECORDING & PLAYBACK

Because there are so many different sound cards and programs on the market, and many different ways to control sounds, sound on a PC can be confusing. If you have any problems recording or playing back, check first to see whether you can get *any* sound from your PC, as discussed in the "Before You Begin" section of Chapter 3, "Multimedia & 3D Virtual Worlds."

Then, during recording and playback, be sure to set the appropriate sliders in Volume Control and Recording Control. The first slider in Volume Control and Recording Control is the primary control, which must be turned up no matter what device you use to record and play sounds.

Other sliders in Volume Control and Recording Control control the relative volume of individual devices. Table 13-1 summarizes which slider (in addition to the main slider) is important during each play, record, and recorded playback activity.

	Volume Control Original Play	Recording Control Recording	Volume Control Recorded Playback
Microphone	n/a	Microphone	Wave
Internal CD ROM	CD	CD	Wave
External stereo	Line In	Line In	Wave

Table 13-1: *Volume Control and Recording Control during various stages of playing and recording.*

EDITING RECORDED SOUNDS

Any sound file—whether it's one you've downloaded or one you've created yourself—can be edited. You can clip off any extraneous sounds from the beginning or end of the clip. You can combine two or more sound files. You can add special effects, such as echo. Here are a couple of tools you can use to edit sound files:

- Sound Recorder: The Windows 95 Sound Recorder program discussed in preceding sections has an Edit menu and Effects menu that let you refine your recorded sound.

- Cool Edit: The CD-ROM that comes with this book includes a shareware version of Cool Edit, which provides much more editing capability than the Windows 95 Sound Recorder. See Appendix B.

Unfortunately, space prevents me from discussing these programs in any depth here. Both programs are easy, fun, and pretty intuitive to use. You can probably get all the information you need just by choosing Help from each program's menu bar. You can also get more information about Cool Edit, and the latest shareware version of that program, from http://www.syntrillium.com.

ADDING EXTERNAL SOUND TO YOUR WEB PAGE

When you have one or more sound files to put into your Web site, making them accessible to your readers is as easy as creating a link to the sound file, like this:

1. If you haven't already done so, move or copy (to the folder that contains your Web pages and images) all the sound files that you want to offer your reader.

2. In Gold's editor, create or open the Web page that will offer the reader links to play these sound files.

3. Select the text or graphic that will act as the hot spot for launching the sound file.

4. Click the Make Link button in the toolbar, then click the Browse File button.

5. Set the Look in option to the folder that contains your sound files. And set the Files of type option to WAV (*.WAV) or whatever format you've recorded, as in Figure 13-11.

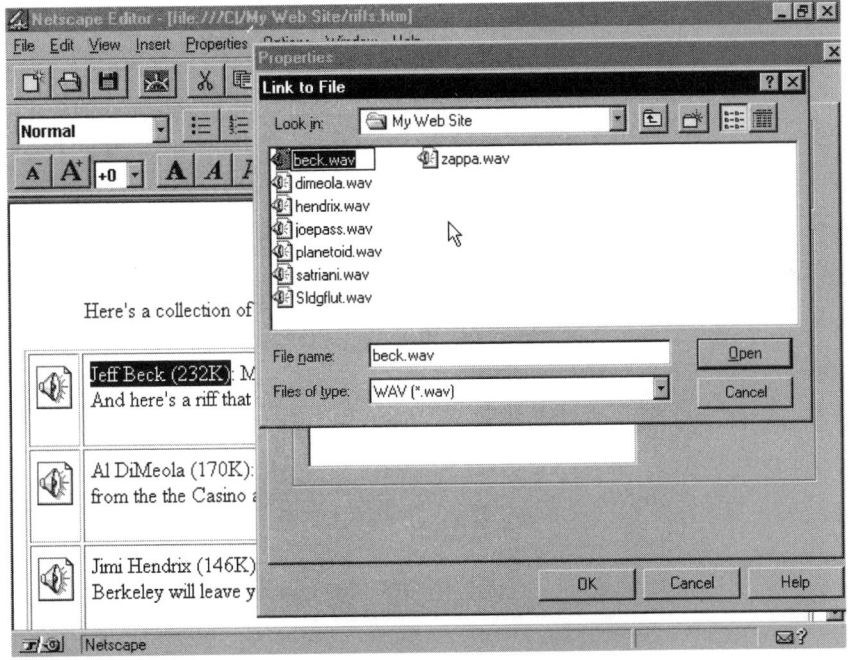

Figure 13-11: *Just about to make a link to the file named beck.wav.*

6. Click on the name of the sound file you want to associate with the current link. Then click the Open and OK buttons.

To test the link, just switch to browser view by clicking the View in Browser button, or by choosing File I Browse document. Save the edited file, then click on the link you want to test. When the LiveAudio control appears, click its Play button to play its sound. To return to your page after you complete the test, click the Back button.

When the time comes to upload the page to your Web server, don't forget to include all the sound files with your page!

Adding External Video to Your Presentation

Video can be another exciting way to communicate on the Web. The downside, however, is that video files tend to be *huge*, and take a long time to download. You're not going to win any popularity contests if you make a reader wait half an hour to see a few minutes of Fifi playing fetch (no matter how much you love the dog). If you're going to offer video, make it short and sweet.

Personally, I'd be leery of offering any kind of home video on the Web, unless it's to share with other relatives across the country. On the other hand, if you have some interesting stuff on video—such as lighting a barbecue with three gallons of liquid oxygen (http://ghg.ecn.purdue.edu), or the infamous exploding whale at http://www.xmission.com/~grue/whale (see Figure 13-12)—some people might consider it worth the wait. (By the way, don't worry about the whale. It was dead long before they blew it up.)

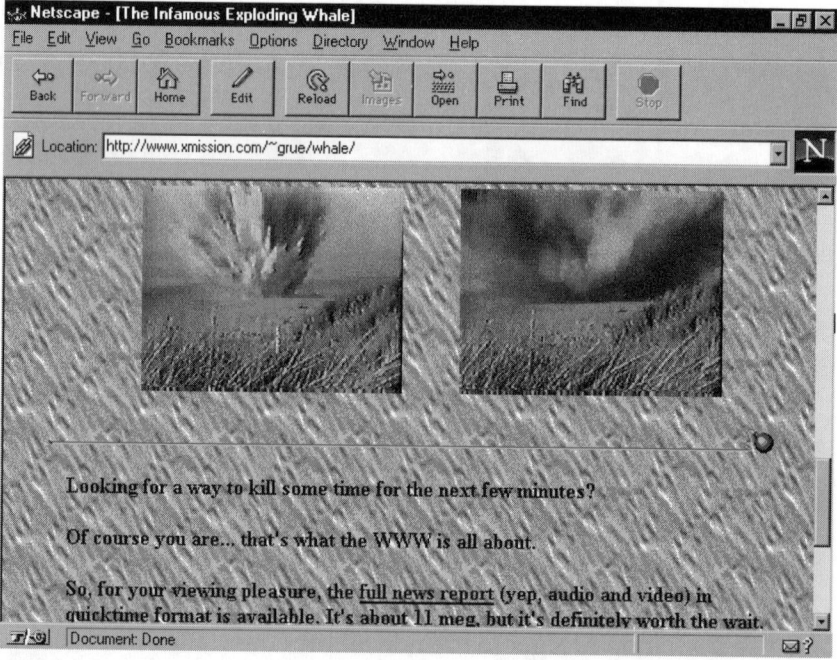

Figure 13-12: *A piece from the Infamous Exploding Whale site.*

TIP

If you just want to put a little animation in your Web site, your best bet is probably an animated GIF (see Chapter 10, "Spice It Up With Lines & Pictures"). The animation plays automatically when the page opens, and (compared to video) the download time is trivial.

Creating your own digital video is no trivial task. You need considerable expertise, special hardware, and some software. The good video editing programs generally cost between $500 and $1,000. Two of the more popular programs used by digital video aficionados are Adobe Premiere (http://www.adobe.com) and Macromedia Director (http://www.macromedia.com).

As an alternative to creating digital video from video tape, several programs are available that let you create digital animations right on your PC. One of my personal favorites is CrystalGraphics' Flying Fonts Pro. It's fun and easy, even if you don't know anything about digital video. For more information, take a peek at http://www.interdine.com/ff.

VIDEO FORMATS

If you have some resources for video that you want to present in your Web site, remember that Navigator can play Video for Windows (.AVI) and QuickTime (.MOV) files all on its own. If you're offering up any other video format, you should refer your Navigator readers to some sites where they can download an appropriate plug-in. (See Chapter 25, "Plug-Ins, Java & LiveConnect," for more information on plug-ins.)

PUTTING EXTERNAL VIDEO IN YOUR PAGE

You add video to your site in the same way that you add sound: by creating a link from a regular Web page to the video file. You can use text or an image as the link. One good trick is to make a screen shot of a frame from the video, and use that as the hot spot for launching the video.

TIP

You'll learn how to create and edit screen shots in Chapter 14, "Power Image Publishing."

No matter how you present the link in your page, the steps for adding the video to your page are as follows:

1. Move or copy the video file to the same folder that holds your other Web materials.

2. In Gold's editor, create or open the page that contains the link to the video.

3. Select the text or picture that will act as the hot spot, then click the Make Link button, or choose Insert | Link.

4. Click the Browse File button.

5. Set the Look in option to the folder that contains your sound files, and set the Files of type option to All Files (*.*) or to the format of your video, as in Figure 13-13.

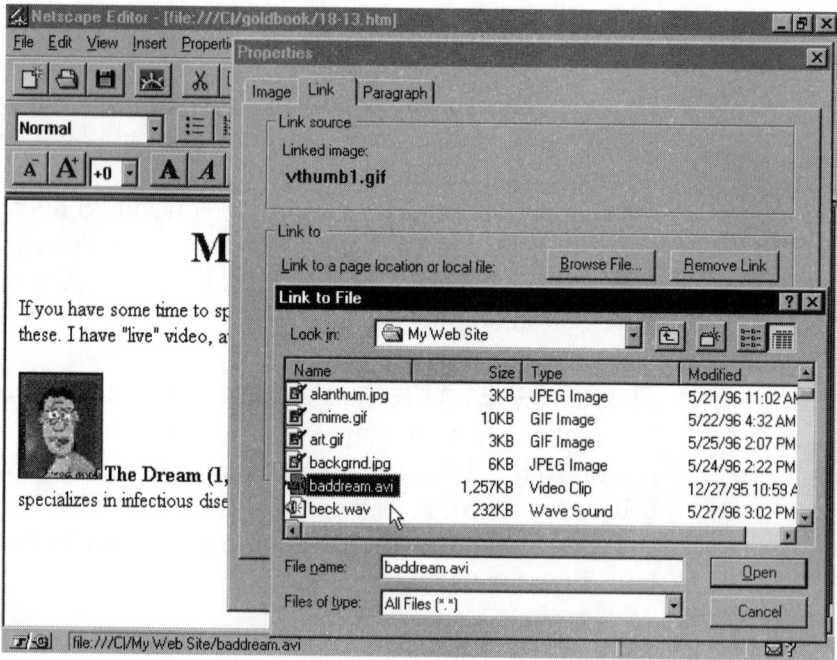

Figure 13-13: *Just about to make a link to a video clip stored as baddream.avi.*

6. Click on the name of the video file that you want to show your reader. Then click the Open and OK buttons.

To test the link, just switch to browser view by clicking the View in Browser button, or by choosing File | Browse document. Save the edited file, then click on the video link you want to test. Initially, you'll see the first frame in a new Navigator window. Click that frame to watch the video. You can right-click the video to pause, rewind, fast-forward, and so on. After the video plays, click the Back button to return to your page.

ABOUT EXTERNAL IMAGES

Before I show you how to add inline sound and inline video to your Web page, I'd like to address the issue of adding external pictures to your page. As discussed in Chapter 10, "Spice It Up With Lines & Pictures," any large photos or other pictures that you want to present should be presented as links so that the reader can decide whether to download the entire large picture file.

Let's suppose that you're an artist or photographer, and that you want to exhibit some of your works on the Web. To really show off these works, you want to present them full-screen, and in high resolution. Instead of forcing readers to wait while the better pictures download, you can give them a sampling and let them choose which pictures to look at. Show them the size of each picture, so they will know what they're going to get and can gauge how long the download will take.

You'll probably want to store the image in a JPEG file, as this format supports the high-quality 24-bit color you're probably looking for. Furthermore, your readers will be able to view the JPEG file without having to add any plug-ins. Let's look at an example.

LINKING TO AN EXTERNAL PHOTO

Suppose that you want to display in your Web site the photo shown in Figure 13-14, and several others like it. First, save them all as JPEG files in the same folder as the rest of your Web materials. You might name them myphoto1.jpg, myphoto2.jpg, myphoto3.jpg, and so forth.

Figure 13-14: *A sample large, high-resolution photo.*

Then you use Paint Shop Pro (see Chapter 14, "Power Image Publishing") to create some miniature *thumbnail* versions of these photos (naming them thumb1.gif, thumb2.gif, thumb3.gif, and so forth). You store these small thumbnail photos in the folder with the rest of your Web materials.

Finally, you're ready to create your gallery page. After you create a new page, using Gold's editor, you use the Insert Image button to insert a copy of the first small picture (thumb1.gif) into this page. Next to that small picture you type a description of the picture, noting its size, as in the example shown in Figure 13-15.

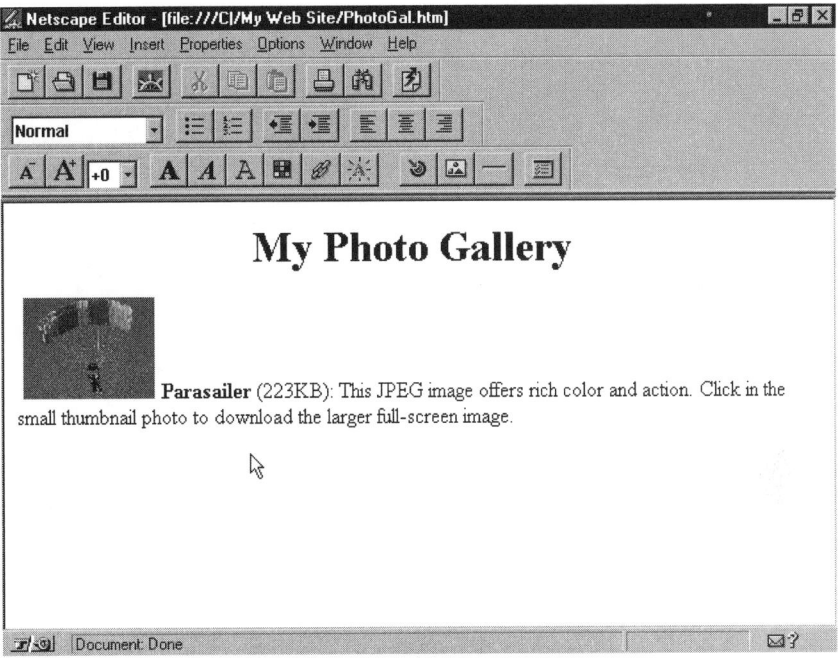

Figure 13-15: *Thumbnail photo and text in a Web page.*

To make a thumbnail picture the link to a larger picture, follow these steps:

1. Making sure that you're working in Gold's editor, click the thumbnail picture once. A frame around the picture indicates that it's now selected.

2. Click the Make Link button in the toolbar, or choose Insert | Link from the menus.

3. Next to Look in, choose the folder that contains the larger photo.

4. Under Files of type, choose All Files (*.*) or whatever file type matches the file type of your large photo.

5. Click the name of the larger photo, then click the Open button.

6. Choose OK to return to your document.

To test the link, first switch to browser mode (click the View in Browser button in the toolbar). Choose Yes when asked about saving. When you see your page in the browser, click the thumbnail. The larger photo will fill Navigator's display window (see Figure 13-16). To return to the previous page, click the Back button in the toolbar.

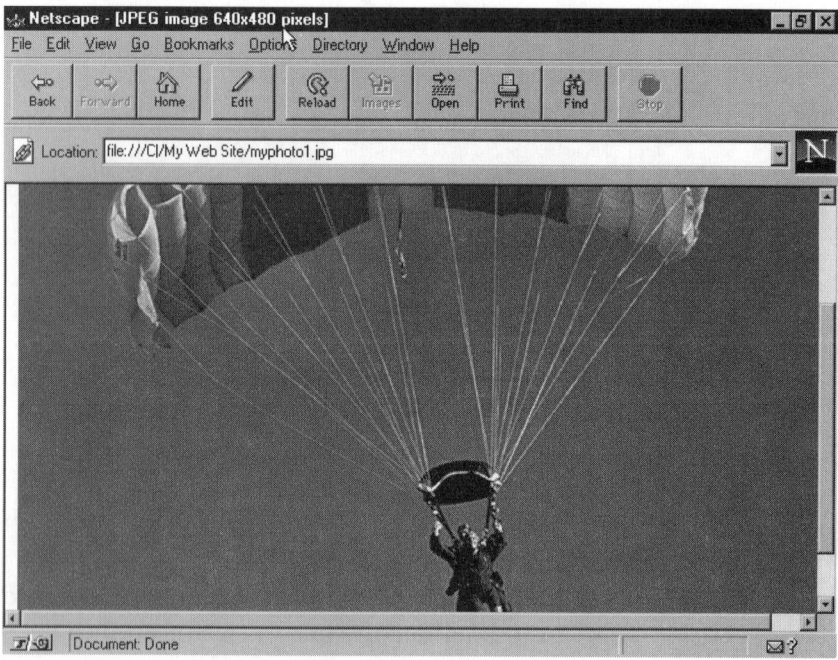

Figure 13-16: *The full-screen version of the thumbnail picture.*

INLINE MULTIMEDIA

Inline sound and video, as you may recall, are sound and video clips that play automatically as soon as the reader opens the Web page. Both are unique, in that there are no toolbar buttons or menu commands to insert these files into your page. Instead, you have to work directly with HTML tags—specifically, the <embed> tag.

You've seen many examples of HTML tags in previous chapters. Though in those examples Gold's editor automatically created the HTML tags for you. There is no menu command or dialog box for placing the <embed> tag in your page. So you'll have to type in the tag manually. I'll show you exactly how to do that here. Then we'll get deeper into tags in Chapter 15, "Tuning HTML Tags."

ADDING BACKGROUND SOUND

To add a background sound to your Web page, first copy the .WAV, .AU, or .AIFF file that contains the sound to the folder that contains your Web pages, graphic files, and other files (My Web Site, in this example). Then follow these steps to insert the embedded sound:

1. If you haven't already done so, create or open, in Gold's editor, the page that will play the background sound.

TIP

You can embed sound in formats other than .wav, .au, and .aiff. However, these are the only three formats that Navigator can read on its own. If you use other sound file formats, only readers with appropriate plug-ins will be able to hear those embedded sounds.

2. Click anywhere near the top of the page as though you were going to insert some text or a picture. (Don't *select* a picture or any text.)
3. Choose Insert I HTML Tag from the menus. You'll see the dialog box shown in Figure 13-17.

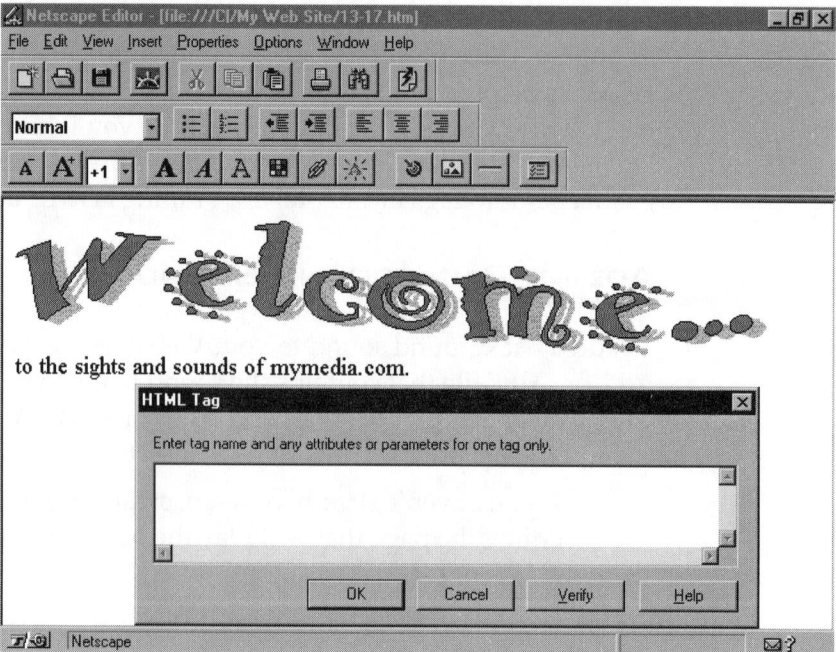

Figure 13-17: *The dialog box for inserting raw HTML into a Web page.*

4. Type the following tag *exactly* as shown, replacing *bkgdsnd.wav* with the name of your sound file:

```
<embed src="bkgdsnd.wav" hidden=true autostart=true>
```

Figure 13-18 shows the tag in the dialog box. Be sure to type the angle brackets (<>), quotation marks, and use spaces exactly as shown when you type your own tag.

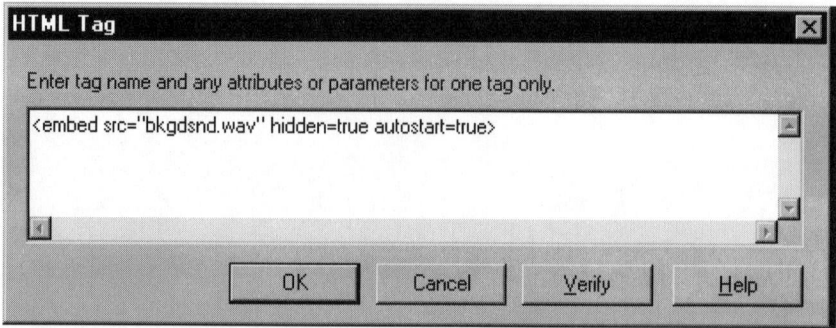

Figure 13-18: *An <embed> tag for playing a background sound.*

5. Click the OK button.

A small tag icon is displayed where you inserted the tag. To test the tag, just view it in the browser, as follows:

1. Click the View in Browser button.

2. Choose Yes when asked about saving the changes to the page.

Although nothing on the page looks different, the background sound will play automatically. If you don't hear any sound, either you need to increase the volume on your sound system or you typed something incorrectly in the tag. If you need to modify the <embed> tag, return to the Gold editor and double-click the tag icon.

SHOWING CONTROLS FOR AN INLINE SOUND

You can have the LiveAudio sound control appear automatically when the background sound is played. You might want to do this to give the reader a chance to replay the sound and to adjust the volume.

You'll need to think about where on the page you want the control displayed. As an example, suppose that I delete the tag I put into my sample page in the previous section. (To do that, I click the tag icon and press Delete.) Then I move the cursor to the bottom of that sample page, and I click the Center button in the toolbar. The blinking cursor appears, centered on its own new line in the page.

Once again, I choose Insert | HTML tag, but this time I enter the tag shown below and in Figure 13-19:

```
<embed src="bkgdsnd.wav" width=145 height=65 autostart=true>
```

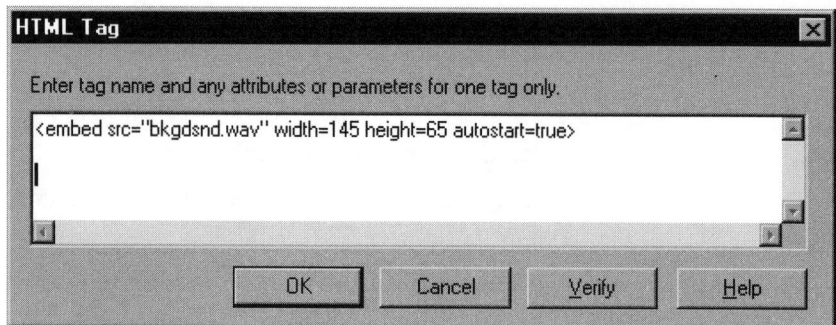

Figure.13-19: *Autoplay a background sound, don't hide the LiveAudio controls.*

Again, the tag icon appears in the page. This time, when I view the page in the browser, I not only hear the background sound, but also get a LiveAudio player that lets me replay the sound as many times as I wish (see Figure 13-20).

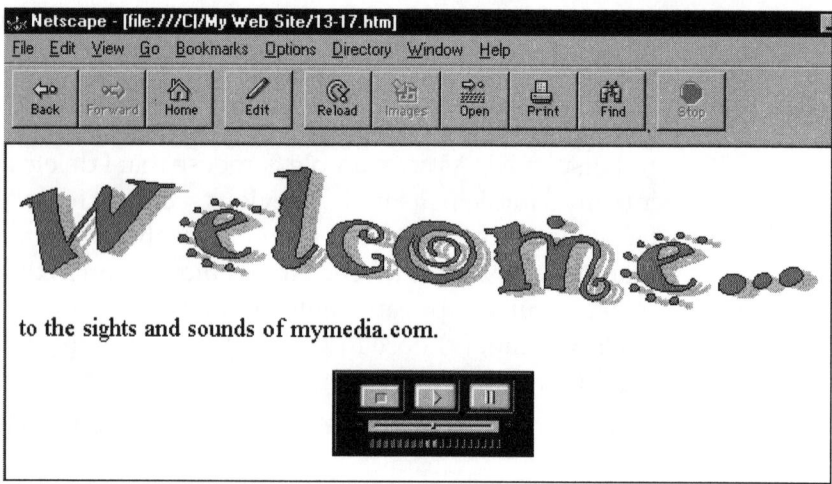

Figure 13-20: *The LiveAudio control lets the reader replay the sound and adjust the volume.*

ADDING INLINE VIDEO

Inline video is a video clip that is *downloaded* automatically as soon as the reader opens the page. Notice that I didn't say it's *played* as soon as the reader opens the page—the reason being that video files tend to be large, and the reader may need to wait a few minutes before any video action takes place onscreen.

> **TIP**
>
> *Most of the small animated pictures you see in Web sites are animated GIFs, not video clips. When you create a Web page, you treat an animated GIF as you would any other inline graphic image. In other words, you use the Insert Image button in the editor's toolbar to insert the animation.*

If you're not concerned about the wait (perhaps because the video clip is in a very small file), you can follow these steps to insert a .AVI file into your page as an inline video:

1. If you haven't already done so, create or open, in Gold's editor, the page that will play the background sound.

2. Click wherever you want the video to appear in your page. If you want to center the video, click the Center button in the toolbar.

3. Choose Insert | HTML Tag from the menus.

4. Type the following tag *exactly* as shown (here and in Figure 13-21), but replace *betty.avi* with the name of your sound file. Also substitute the height and width of your video frame, if known, for the measurements (162 and 120) shown:

```
<embed src="betty.avi " width=162 height=120
autostart=true>
```

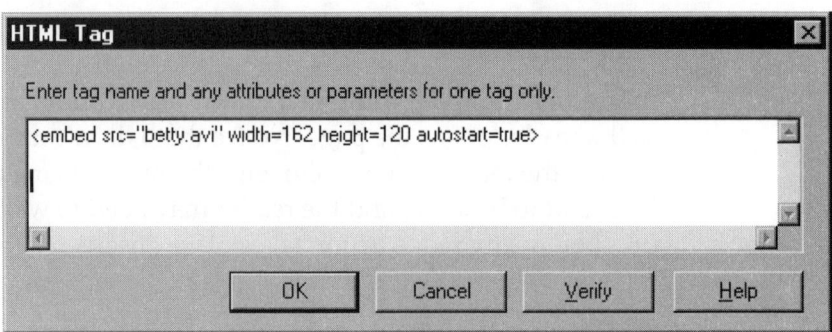

Figure 13-21: *An <embed> tag for playing an inline video.*

5. Click the OK button.

TIP

You can use Paint Shop Pro to determine the size of your video frame. Capture your screen while the video is playing, and then paste it into Paint Shop Pro. Crop the video frame to a new window. The status bar displays the width x length *measurement of the frame. See Chapter 14, "Power Image Publishing," for more information.*

The HTML tag icon appears where you inserted the tag. To view the video, open the page in the browser. In Figure 13-22, I put a video clip from an old Betty Boop movie near the center of the page (after first deleting the tags presented in the two previous examples). The reader can right-click the video to pause, rewind, play, and so forth.

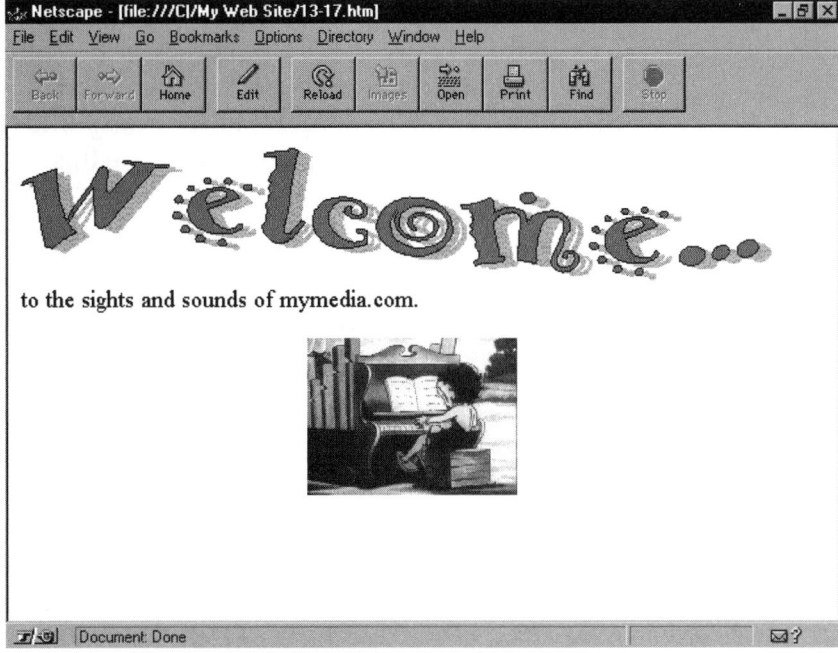

Figure 13-22: *Video clip near the center of the page plays automatically.*

SUPPORTING MICROSOFT INTERNET EXPLORER

Microsoft Internet Explorer (Version 2.0) supports inline sound and video, but doesn't use the <embed> tags that Navigator uses. Instead, Explorer supports a <bgsound> tag for background sound, and an <img dynsrc=...> tag for displaying inline video. If you want people who are browsing with Internet Explorer to experience your inline sound and video, you'll need to add these tags to your page, along with the <embed> tags you inserted for Navigator browsers.

Use the same technique you used for inserting the <embed> tags. Open the page in Gold's editor, click near where you inserted an <embed> tag, then insert the equivalent Internet Explorer tag for the sound or video. For example, the <bgsound> tag for playing the sample bkgdsnd.wav file would look like this:

```
<bgsound src="bkgdsnd.wav">
```

The tag for playing the inline betty.avi video would look like this:

```
<img dynsrc="betty.avi" start="fileopen">
```

After you insert these tags and save the page, you can open the page with Microsoft Internet Explorer. Explorer will ignore all <embed> tags, but will execute any <bgsound> and <img dynsrc...> tags that it finds in the page.

When you open the same page in Netscape Navigator, Navigator will ignore the <bgsound> tag, but execute any <embed> tags it finds. Unfortunately, Navigator won't completely ignore the <img dynsrc...> tags. Instead, it will display a small picture icon, as in Figure 13-23.

Figure 13-23: *The picture icon is Explorer's <img dynsrc...> tag.*

There is a forthcoming solution to this problem. As I write this chapter, Internet Explorer version 3.0, due for release soon and will support JavaScript. So you'll be able to write a little script that determines which browser your reader is using, and then plays the video accordingly. The section titled "JavaScript Decision Making" in Chapter 18, "An Introduction to JavaScript," shows the script you'd need.

SITE SEEING

When you're ready to see how some authors are using sound and video, or you want to search for clips or want more information about <embed>, <bgsound>, and <img dynsrc...> tags, check out some of these sites:

- <embed> Tag Syntax: A page from Netscape's *Creating Net Sites* page discussing the HTML <embed> tag: http://home.netscape.com/assist/net_sites/embed_tag.html. See also *Plug-Ins and HTML* at http://home.netscape.com/eng/mozilla/3.0/handbook/plugins/index.html.

- Ashley's Sound Files: Lots of .WAV files at http://netspace.net.au/~pirovich/sounds.html.

- Caddyshack Sound Archive: Clips from the movie: http://www.ee.duke.edu/~ceh/caddy/caddy.html.

- IWIN Weather Videos: You'll find tornadoes, hurricanes, and floods cut from NOAA Weather video tapes at http://iwin/nws/noaa.gov/iwin/videos/videos.html.

- Jesse's Movies: Lots of video clips from sports, movies, and TV, plus links to other sites offering video: http://www.uslink.net/~edgerton/index.html.

- MADwork's Web Site: Lots of multimedia to explore here at http://www.madworks.com.

- Microsoft Multimedia: Explanations of Internet Explorer <bgsound> and <img dynsrc> tags appear at http://198.105.232.5:80/ie.

- MultiMedia Music: Archives of sound effects and music loops for multimedia projects: http://www.wavenet.com/~axgrindr/quimby.html.

- Netscape Media Showcase: Check out the possibilities at http://home.netscape.com/comprod/products/navigator/version_3.0/showcase/index.html.

- The WAV Place: Sound files galore at http://lincoln.midcoast.com/~harr/kim2.htm.

- WAV Files: Sound clips from popular movies and TV shows: http://www.softfarm.com/personal/chrisbland/wavs.htm.

MOVING ON

Multimedia has brought us to some new concepts and techniques that creep beyond what you do with simple "point-and-click" in Gold. For example, creating a custom sound file required using external programs such as Volume Control and Sound Recorder. Inline multimedia required manually inserting HTML <embed> tags. Part III, which begins in the next Chapter, will take you more fully into the realm beyond Gold's editor. Starting with a discussion of using Paint Shop Pro as an external graphics editor.

PART III

Power Publishing

Power Image Publishing

In this chapter I want to extend your Web authoring capabilities beyond Gold and into Paint Shop Pro. As you'll learn in this chapter, you can use Paint Shop Pro to create and edit GIF and JPEG images for your Web site. Here you'll learn how to:

- Set up Paint Shop Pro as your default image editor
- Convert just about any image to GIF or JPEG format
- Crop pictures
- Add equations, word art, and various business charts to your Web pages
- Control the size and color depth of pictures to minimize download time
- Create fade-in and transparent-background GIFs

INSTALLING & STARTING PAINT SHOP PRO

There are two ways to install the evaluation version of Paint Shop Pro. If you *don't* have a CD-ROM drive, or don't have the CD that came with this book, you can download and install from the Web. Point Navigator to http://www.jasc.com and follow the instructions for downloading and installing the 32-bit version of Paint Shop Pro.

Optionally, to install from the CD-ROM, refer to the instructions for installing Paint Shop Pro in Appendix B.

After you have installed Paint Shop Pro, you can run it as you would any other program. Typically, you just need to click the Start button, select Programs | Paint Shop Pro | Paint Shop Pro-32 Bit. You'll be confronted by a "nag screen" that encourages you to register the product. I hope you'll do so because it's a great program and the author deserves to be paid. Registering the product will rid you of the nag screen and make you eligible for some free future upgrades.

MAKING PAINT SHOP PRO GOLD'S IMAGE EDITOR

After you've installed Paint Shop Pro, you can follow these steps to make it your default image editor while working in Gold:

1. Start Netscape Navigator Gold. (You don't need to be online.)

2. Choose Options | Editor Preferences, and click the General tab.

3. Next to Image under External editors, click the Browse button.

4. Browse to wherever you installed Paint Shop Pro (most likely c:\psp) and double-click on the psp.exe file icon. You should see the path and psp.exe program in the Editor Preference dialog box now, as in Figure 14-1.

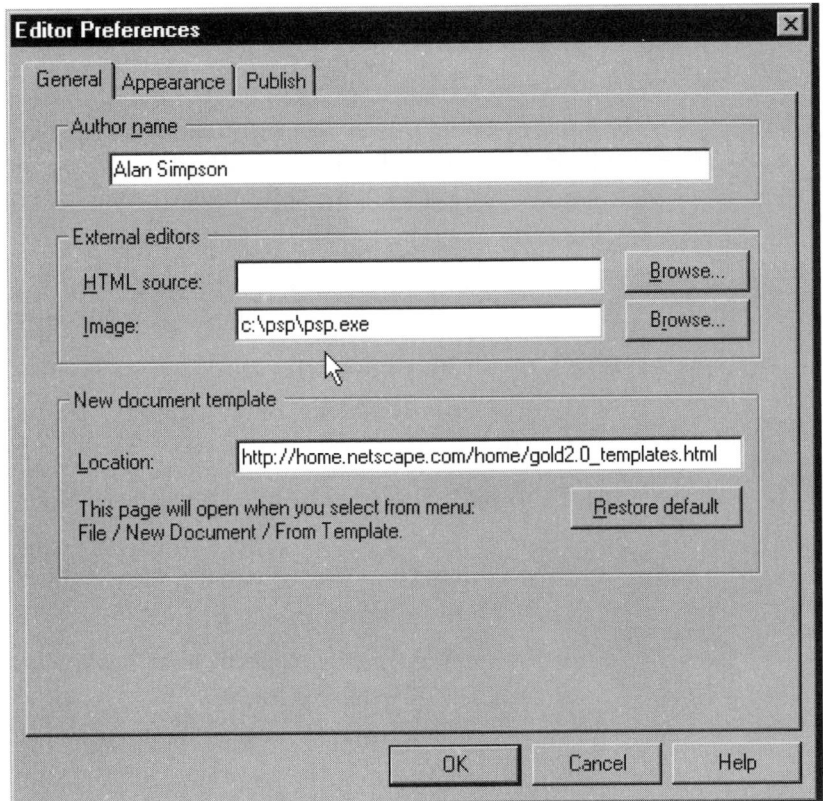

Figure 14-1: *Paint Shop Pro, defined as external editor for images.*

5. Click the OK button.

In the future, you can easily edit any image you've placed in your Web page. Just follow these steps:

1. In Gold's editor, right-click on the image you want to edit.

2. Choose Edit Image from the pop-up menu.

The image appears in Paint Shop Pro, ready for editing.

CREATING A SHORTCUT TO PAINT SHOP PRO

You may want to take a moment to create a shortcut from Windows 95 to Paint Shop Pro. Then, by right-clicking the name of any picture file in My Computer, Find, or Windows Explorer, you can send that picture straight to Paint Shop Pro. To create the shortcut, follow these steps:

1. Starting at the Windows 95 desktop, double-click My Computer and then double-click the icon for your C drive.

2. Open (double-click on) your Windows folder.

3. In the Windows folder, open (double-click on) the SendTo folder.

4. From the SendTo window's menu bar choose File | New | Shortcut.

5. Type **c:\psp\psp.exe**, or use the Browse button to locate the PSP.EXE file. Click the Next button.

6. Type a name for this shortcut icon, such as Paint Shop Pro, and click the Finish button.

You should see a shortcut icon for Paint Shop Pro in the SendTo menu's window. You can now close all the open windows (hold down the Shift key and click the X button in the upper-right corner of the SendTo window).

To verify the procedure, use My Computer, Explorer, or Find to open any file that contains any images, and then right-click the name or icon of any picture file. Point to Send To on the pop-up menu. You should see Paint Shop Pro in your Send To menu, as in Figure 14-2. If you click on that Paint Shop Pro option, Paint Shop Pro will start, automatically loading the selected image file. Very handy!

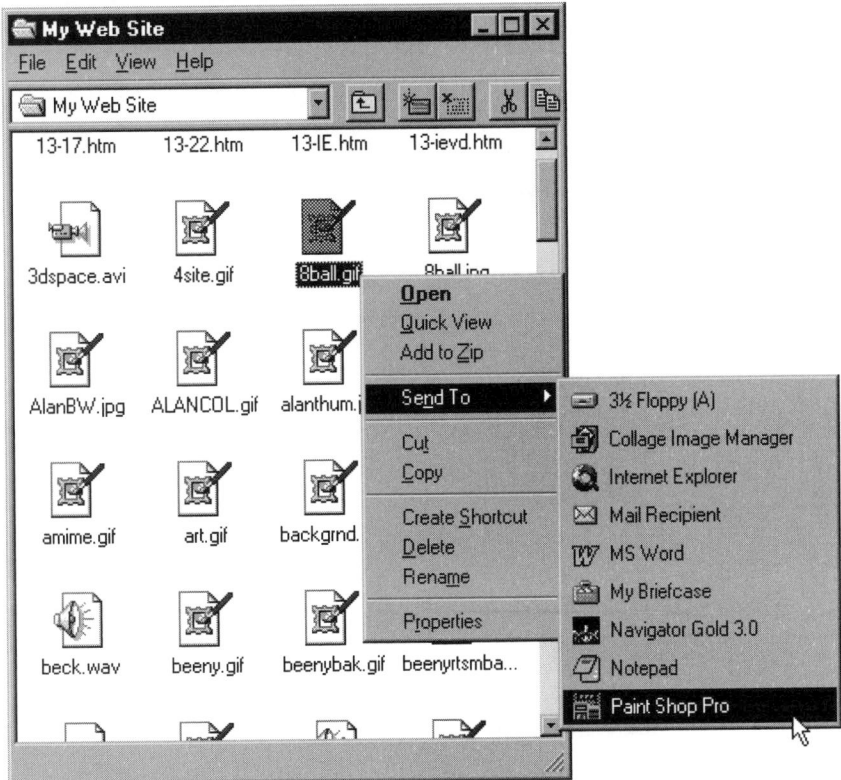

Figure 14-2: *Paint Shop Pro has been added to the Send To menu.*

CONVERTING IMAGES TO GIF OR JPEG

Many clip-art images are delivered to you in a format other than
GIF or JPEG (see Table 14-1).

Format	Extension
Autodesk	.dxf
CompuServe GIF	.gif
Computer Graphics Metafile	.cgm
CorelDRAW!	.cdr
Deluxe Paint	.lbm
Device independent bitmap	.dib
Dr. Halo	.cut
Electronic Arts	.iff
Encapsulated Postscript (image only)	.eps
GEM Paint	.img
Hewlett-Packard Graphics Language	.hgl
Huffman compressed	.jif
Joint Photo Expert Group	.jpg
Kodak Photo CD	.pcd
Lotus/Pixtor/PC Paint	.pic
MacPaint	.mac
Micrografx Draw	.drw
Microsoft Paint	.msp
Photoshop	.psd
Portable Network Graphics	.png
Run-Length Encoded	.rle
Sun Microsystems Type 1	.ras
Tagged Image File Format	.tif
Truevision	.tga
Unencoded pixel data	.raw
UNIX portable bitmap	.pbm
UNIX Portable Graymap	.pgm
UNIX Portable Pixelmap	.ppm
Ventura/GEM	.gem
Windows bitmap	.bmp
Windows Clipboard	.clp
Windows Metafile	.wmf
WordPerfect Graphics File	.wpg
Zsoft Paintbrush	.pcx

Table 14-1: *File formats that Paint Shop Pro can read.*

Making a GIF or JPEG copy (for your Web page) of a clip-art image that's in one of the formats shown in this table is easy. Here's what you do:

> **TIP**
>
> *If you added Paint Shop Pro to your Send To menu, you can skip Steps 1 and 2. Using My Computer, Find, or Windows Explorer, locate the image you want to edit. Then right-click the filename and choose Send To | Paint Shop Pro.*

1. Start Paint Shop Pro in the usual way on your PC.
2. Choose File | Open, and open the picture you want to put in your Web page. The picture appears in Paint Shop Pro's window.
3. Choose File | Save As.
4. Under List Files of Type, choose either GIF-CompuServe or JPG-JPEG-JFIF Compliant.
5. Choose a directory (folder), such as My Web Site, for the converted picture, and enter a filename.
6. Choose OK.

> **TIP**
>
> *GIF files are generally smaller than JPEGs, and give you the option of using a transparent background, but JPEG is the preferred format for photos that look best at 24-bit color.*

A new copy of the picture, with the filename extension of .gif or .jpg, will be added to your My Web Site folder. To insert the picture in a Web page, create or open the Web page with Gold's editor. Then use the Insert Image button, as usual, to insert the GIF or JPEG image.

CUT & PASTE INTO PAINT SHOP PRO

If you can't open a file with Paint Shop Pro, you might still be able to cut and paste the image into that program. For example, some clip-art images are delivered in encapsulated postscript (.eps) formats that Paint Shop Pro can't read directly. But if you can get some other program to display the image, you can cut and paste the image into Paint Shop Pro. The example that follows illustrates how you can open an .eps file with Microsoft Word and then paste it into Paint Shop Pro:

1. Start a program, such as Microsoft Word, that can display the type of image you want to import into Paint Shop Pro.

2. Insert the picture, or open it, using the normal procedure for whatever program you're using. If you're using Microsoft Word, for example, choose Insert | Picture and open the picture you want to convert to GIF or JPEG.

3. Select (click once on) the picture. Depending on the program you're using, the picture will either be displayed in reverse video, or will have sizing handles (see Figure 14-3).

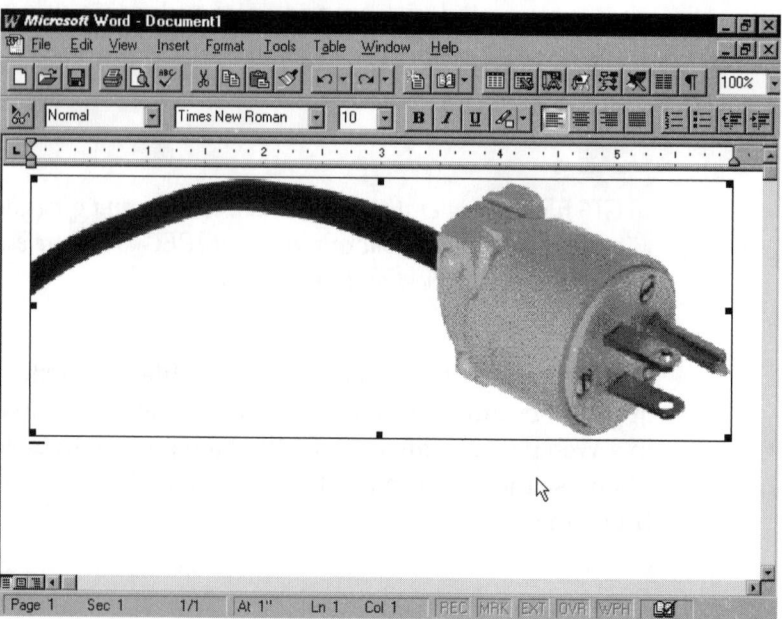

Figure 14-3: *An EPS image displayed in a Word document.*

4. Press Ctrl+C or choose Edit | Copy from the current program's menu bar. This places a copy of the image in the Windows clipboard.

5. Start Paint Shop Pro.

6. Choose Edit | Paste | As New Image from Paint Shop Pro's menu bar. The picture will appear in Paint Shop Pro.

7. Choose File | Save As from Paint Shop Pro's menu bar, then choose GIF-CompuServe or JPG-JPEG-JFIF Compliant under List Files of Type.

8. Choose a folder and filename for the picture, then click on the OK button.

Figure 14-4 shows the sample .eps file after these eight steps are completed. Notice (in the title bar for the picture) that I've saved this copy as a GIF file named plugin.gif.

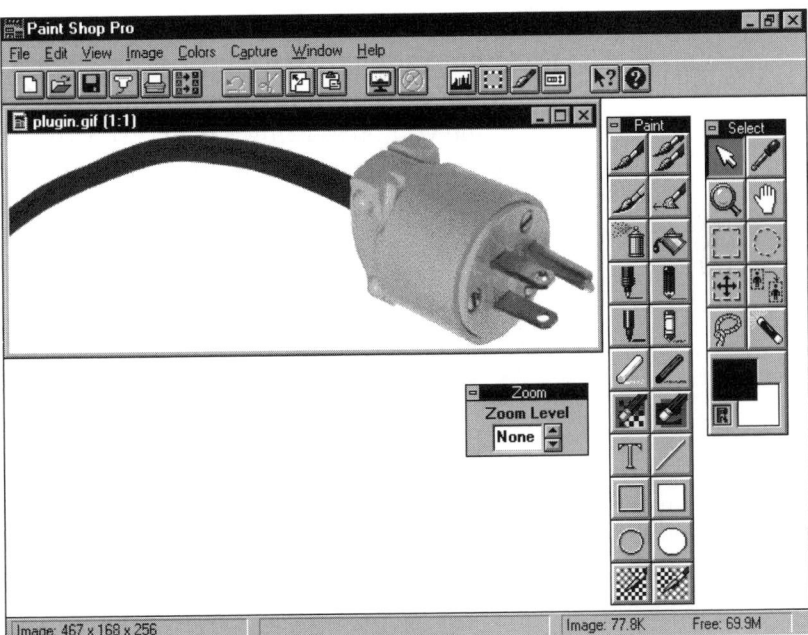

Figure 14-4: *EPS file, saved as a GIF file.*

Now you can exit Paint Shop Pro. Then, when you create or open a page using Gold's editor, you can use the standard Insert Image button in Gold to place the GIF or JPEG image in the page you're editing at the moment.

CAPTURING SCREENS WITH PAINT SHOP PRO

You can use Windows 95 and Paint Shop Pro together to capture anything that's on your screen to a GIF or JPEG file. This can be a handy feature when you want your Web page to show a picture of a dialog box, icon, or other image that appears onscreen. For example, let's suppose I'm writing a little tutorial on how to set up Windows 95 Dial-Up Networking for the Internet and that I want to include a picture of a dialog box in that tutorial. Here are the general steps:

1. Bring to your screen whatever it is you want to show a picture of.

2. To capture the entire screen, press the Print Screen (Prt Scrn) key. To capture just the active window, hold down the Alt key while you press Print Screen (Prt Scrn). To capture the dialog box shown in Figure 14-5, for example, I would press Alt+Print Screen.

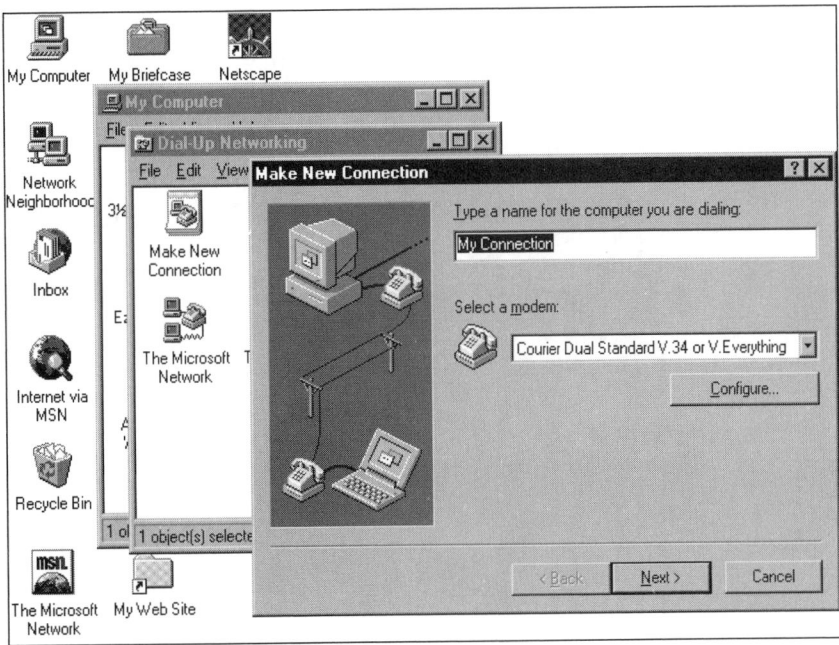

Figure 14-5: *Press Alt+Print Screen to capture the active window only.*

3. Start Paint Shop Pro.

4. Choose Edit | Paste | As New Image from Paint Shop Pro's menu bar. The capture appears in Paint Shop Pro's window.

TIP

If you can't paste the screen shot into Paint Shop Pro, your PC might require that you use the Shift key with Print Screen. Start over at Step 2, but this time hold down the Shift key as you press Print Screen or Alt+Print Screen.

5. If you want to isolate a portion of the screen, such as a single icon (or whatever), use the cropping techniques described later in this chapter to cut out the piece you want. Then close the larger picture without saving it.

6. Choose File | Save As, choose GIF (or JPEG) under List Files of Type, select a folder (e.g., My Web Site), and enter a filename for the image. In Figure 14-6, for example, I named the captured dialog box "dun1.gif."

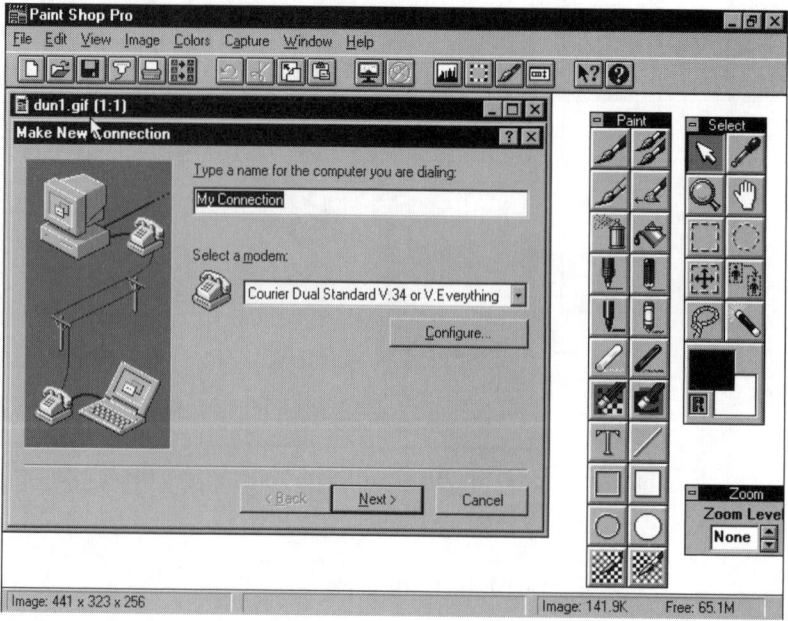

Figure 14-6: *Captured dialog box in Paint Shop Pro, saved as a GIF file.*

Now you can exit Paint Shop Pro. In Gold's editor, you can use the Insert Image button to put the saved GIF or JPEG picture into any Web page.

CONVERTING OBJECTS TO IMAGES

Many of the large software suites offer shared applications (or *applets*) that let you create embedded objects to place in your documents. For example, Microsoft Office includes Word Art, Org Chart, Microsoft Chart, and an Equation Editor. You can include any object that you create with these applets in your Web page (see the examples shown in Figures 14-7 through 14-9).

The basic procedure is to first create the object in the most appropriate program. You might create a business chart in Excel or Microsoft Access, for example, and use Word to create an org chart, an equation, or word art.

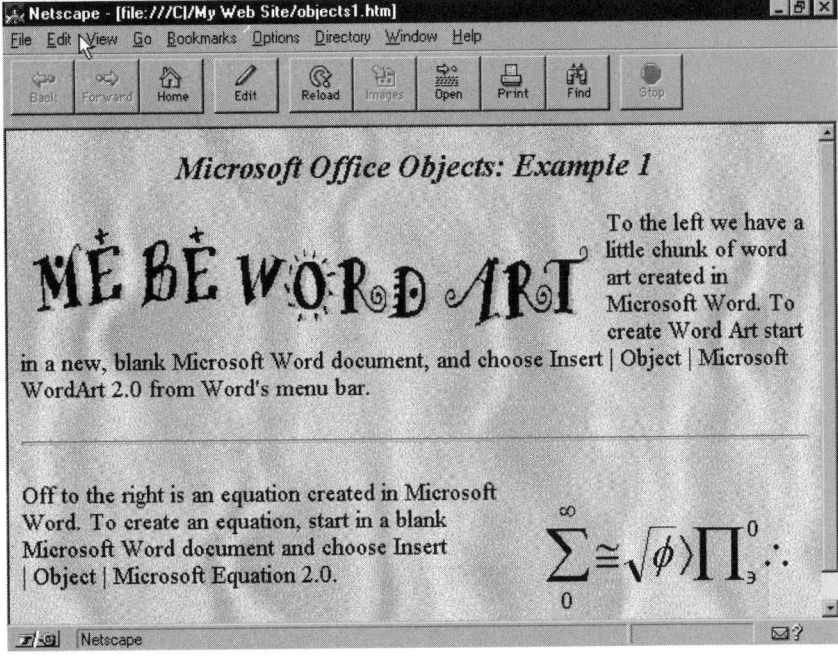

Figure 14-7: *The Word Art and equation in this Web page were created in Microsoft Word.*

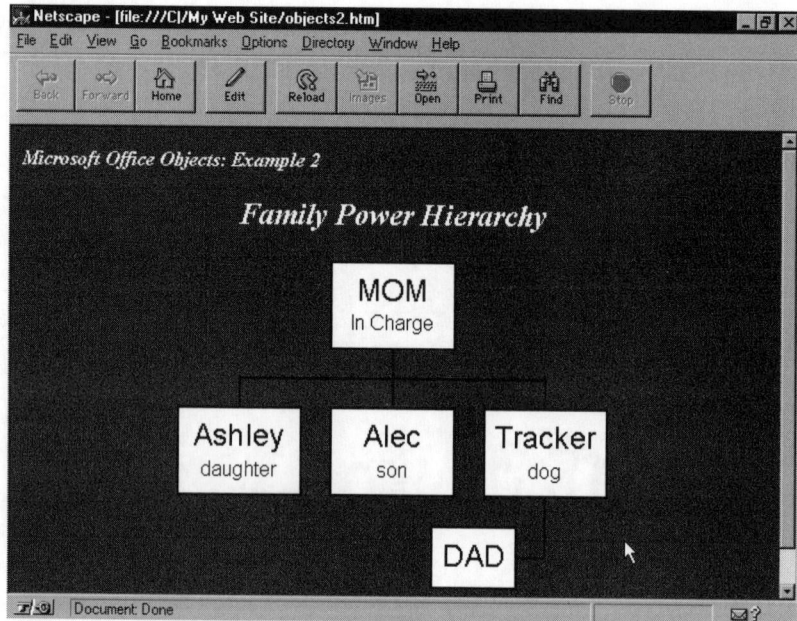

Figure 14-8: *The organization chart in this Web page was created in Microsoft Word.*

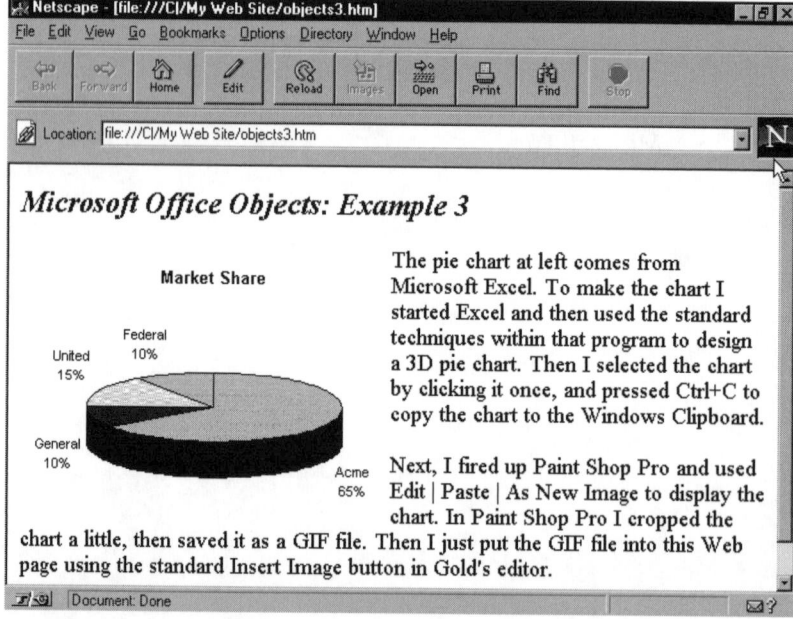

Figure 14-9: *This Web page's chart was created in Microsoft Excel.*

After you've created the object, select it by clicking it once so that it has sizing handles. Copy the object to the clipboard (Ctrl+C). Next, start Paint Shop Pro and choose Edit | Paste | As New Image. Then, choose File | Save As to save the picture as a GIF file for inclusion on your Web page.

Let's work through a step-by-step example by creating a Word Art object in Microsoft Word, and then putting the object into a Web page.

1. Start Microsoft Word and get to a new document.

2. Choose Insert | Object | Microsoft WordArt 2.0, then click OK.

TIP

To create an equation in Step 2, you'd choose Insert | Object | Microsoft Equation 2.0. To create an org chart, you'd choose Insert | Object | MS Organization Chart 2.0. To create a business chart, you'd choose Insert | Object | Microsoft Graph 5.0—or create a chart in Microsoft Excel.

3. Type your text in the Enter Your Text Here box, and apply effects using the buttons across the top of the screen (see Figure 14-10).

Figure 14-10: *Playing with Word Art in Microsoft Word.*

4. To size the object, click outside the object and drag the sizing handles. To make other changes, double-click the object. When you're happy with the object, click outside it. In Figure 14-11, the object appears in the document surrounded by sizing handles, which you can drag to resize the picture further.

Figure 14-11: *Finished Word Art object, still in Microsoft Word.*

5. Press Ctrl+C to copy the object to the Windows clipboard.

6. Start Paint Shop Pro.

7. From Paint Shop Pro's menu bar, choose Edit | Paste | As New Image. Choose OK to keep the suggested size.

8. To save this as a GIF file, choose File | Save As. Under List Files of Type, choose GIF-CompuServe.

9. Under Directories, choose a folder (preferably your My Web Site folder) and enter a filename. Choose OK.

Your GIF file is now on your hard disk. You can exit Paint Shop Pro, and exit Microsoft Word. Then start Netscape Navigator Gold and create (or open) the document into which you want to put this picture. Position the insertion point where you want the picture to appear, and use the Insert Image button to insert the GIF file you created in Step 9.

Note that objects you create in this manner will have a white background. If you want them to have a transparent background, that topic is discussed in this chapter's "Creating Transparent Background GIFs" section.

PAINT SHOP PRO'S EDITING TOOLS

While you have a picture in Paint Shop Pro, there are many things you can do to change that picture. I can't cover *everything* Paint Shop Pro will let you do, but I can focus on the features you're most likely to need. Remember that the version of Paint Shop Pro that came with this book is just an evaluation version. If you order the actual product, you'll get an excellent manual (more than 200 pages) that describes all the features of the program. See Appendix B for ordering information.

Figure 14-12 shows some of Paint Shop Pro's basic tools. To hide or display the Paint Toolbox, Select Toolbox, Tool Control Panel, and Toolbar, just choose the appropriate command from the View pull-down menu. When you point to a tool in the toolbox, the far left edge of the status bar tells you the name of the tool and provides brief instructions.

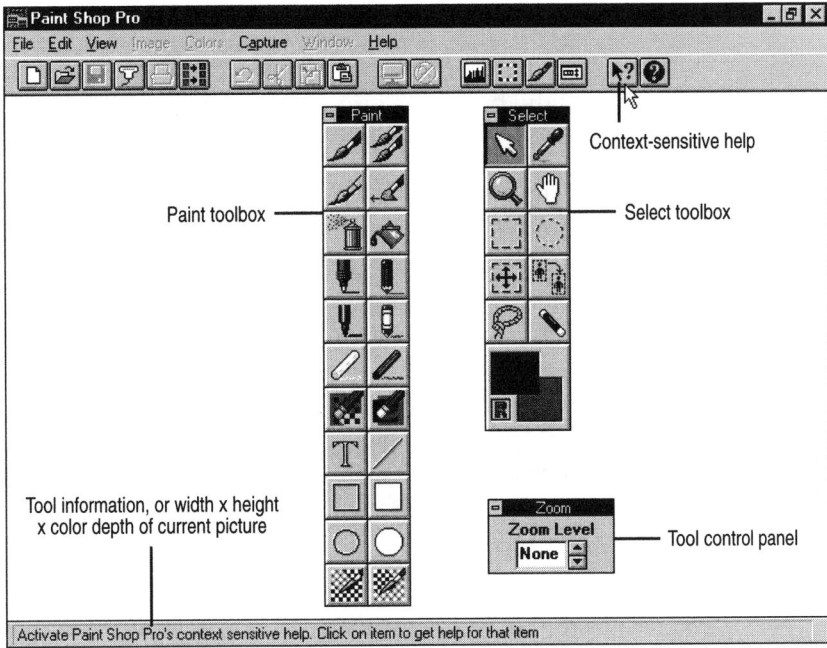

Figure 14-12: *Some of the many editing tools offered by Paint Shop Pro.*

There's also online help. Just click the last button in the toolbar (yellow question mark in a blue circle). For help with a specific tool, click the Context Sensitive Help button, just to the left of the blue help button, and then click on the tool you want help with.

EDITING PICTURES IN PAINT SHOP PRO

You can edit any picture once it's in Paint Shop Pro. And there are many ways to get a picture into Paint Shop, including the following:

- From Windows 95 My Computer, Find, or Explorer, right-click the name of the image file you want to edit, and choose Send To | Paint Shop Pro.

- If you're already working in Paint Shop Pro, use the standard File | Open method to open the file you want to edit.

- Cut and paste, or screen capture the image into Paint Shop Pro, as discussed earlier in this chapter.

- If the picture is already in your Web page, go into Gold's editor and double-click the picture you want to edit.

You can also create a new, empty "canvas" if you want to draw a picture from scratch. First, set the foreground and background colors as discussed under "Setting Foreground & Background Colors" below. Then choose File | New, choose a Width, Height, and Image Type as discussed under "Choosing a Color Depth" below. Then choose OK.

CROPPING AN IMAGE

Because small images download faster than large ones, it's in your best interest to try to keep your images fairly small. One way to do so is to crop out any extraneous background stuff that's not important to the picture. Suppose, for example, that I want to show a picture of the Netscape Navigator icon in my Web page. I take a screen shot of the Windows 95 desktop, and paste it into Paint Shop Pro. To crop such an image, follow these steps:

1. Click the Rectangular Selection or Oval Selection tool in the Select toolbox.

2. Drag a frame around the part of the picture you want to keep. For example, in Figure 14-13 I dragged a frame around the Netscape Navigator icon.

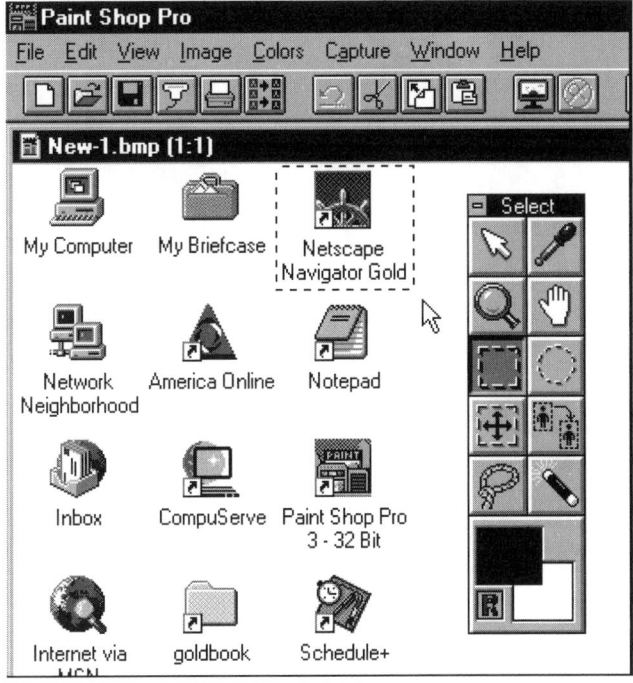

Figure 14-13: *About to crop out the Netscape Navigator Gold icon.*

3. Press Ctrl+C or choose Edit I Copy from Paint Shop's menu bar to copy the selection to the clipboard.

4. Close the larger image without saving it (File I Close I No).

5. Press Ctrl+V or choose Edit I Paste I As New Image to paste in the smaller image.

6. Save this new smaller picture as a GIF or JPEG file, using File I Save As.

Notice that the status bar at the bottom of the screen shows the width x height x color depth of the new, small picture (see Figure 14-14). Now you can exit Paint Shop Pro, fire up Gold's editor, and use the Insert Image button to insert that little graphic image into a Web page.

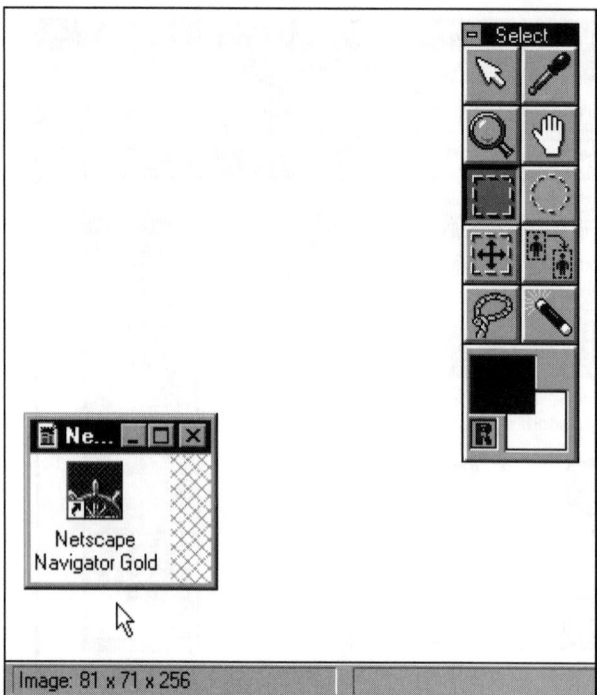

Figure 14-14: *Smaller picture in Paint Shop, with status bar showing its width x height x color depth.*

CHOOSING A COLOR DEPTH

Choosing a color depth for your picture before you start editing is a good idea. In general, you want to use the *smallest* possible color depth, because the fewer the colors in the picture, the smaller the picture file, and the faster it will download. To change the color depth, choose Colors from the pull-down menu. Then choose either Decrease Color Depth or Increase Color Depth, and choose a color depth. Table 14-2 presents some guidelines.

Depth	Use for
2 colors	Black and white
16 colors	Simple logos and filled line art
256 colors	More complex drawings
32K and 64K Colors	Photographs (JPEG files)

Table 14-2: *Color depths for various types of pictures.*

TIP

When you save a file as a GIF, Paint Shop Pro automatically converts it to at least 256 colors. But the resulting file will still be smaller if you set the depth to 2 or 16 colors before you save it.

SETTING FOREGROUND & BACKGROUND COLORS

Paint Shop's Paint tools let you work in color. Before using such a tool you should choose a foreground and background color to work with. Use the boxes at the bottom of the Select toolbox (see Figure 14-15) to choose your colors, as follows:

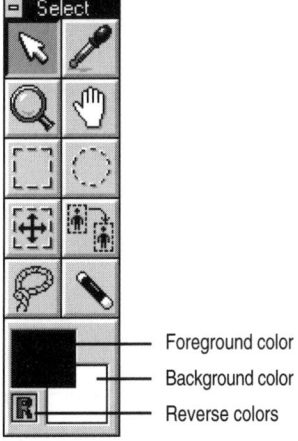

Foreground color
Background color
Reverse colors

Figure 14-15: *The foreground and background colors, and the Reverse button.*

To choose a foreground or background color, double-click the current color. In the palette of colors that appears (see Figure 14-16), click the color you want, then choose OK. If you want to add a new color to the palette, double-click any color that you don't plan to use, then create a new color by using the Color dialog box that appears.

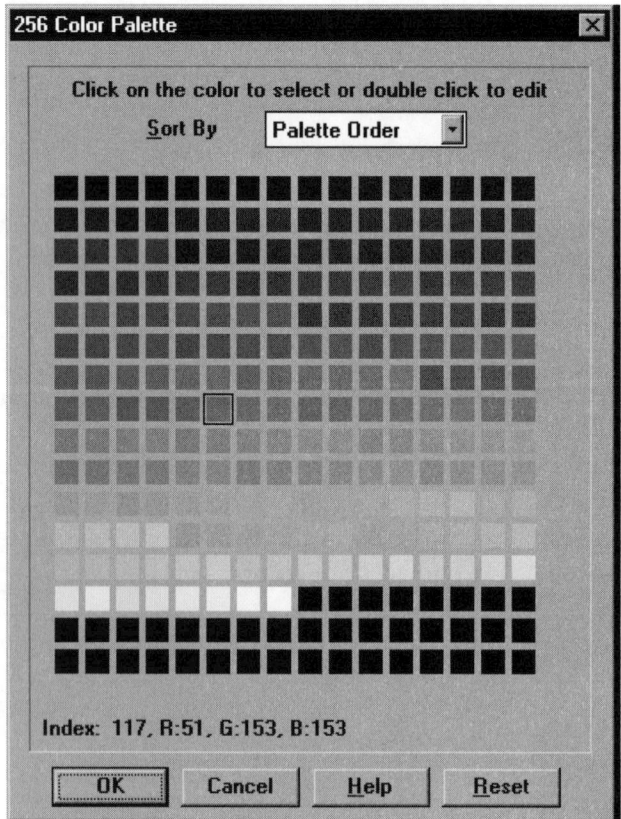

Figure 14-16: *Color palette for 256-color images.*

Coloring Black-&-White Clip Art

Many clip-art images are delivered as simple black-and-white line art. You can easily color these, using Paint Shop Pro. Just open the image, then choose a foreground color for filling in. Click on the

Flood Fill tool in the Paint toolbox, then click in the area you want to color. Repeat this procedure, using different foreground colors. To fill, using the selected background color, right-click the area you want to fill. In the example shown in Figure 14-17, I colored a black-and-white image from Dean Stanton's Hoopla collection (http://www.imageclub.com). You can't see the colors here, but perhaps you can guess from the shades of gray.

Figure 14-17: *A black-and-white image and the colored version.*

TIP

To make an exact duplicate of a picture in Paint Shop Pro, click the picture you want to copy, choose Edit | Copy, then press Ctrl+V or choose Edit | Paste | As New Image.

If, while filling in a color, you find that the color leaks into other areas of the picture, there's a break in the line that encloses the area you want to fill. You can zoom in, find, and fill the break, if you like.

ZOOMING IN

For detail work, you can zoom in on a picture. This is handy when you are working with a very small picture, such as a bullet or one of those tiny little inline images that says "new" or "cool". It's also good for fixing "leaks" that occur when you use the Flood Fill tool and your color fills too large an area.

To zoom in, click the Magnifier in the Select toolbox, then click the area you want to zoom in on. You can keep clicking to keep zooming in. When you get to 10x zoom, you'll see a grid in which each square represents one pixel (see Figure 14-18).

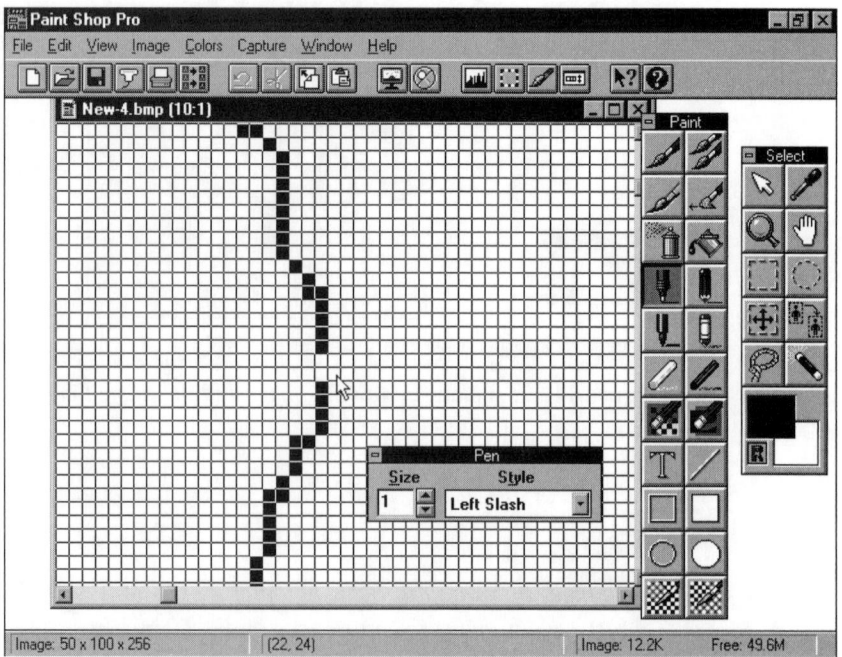

Figure 14-18: *When you zoom in to 10x or higher, each pixel appears as a square in a grid.*

To fill one pixel at a time (to repair a leak, for example), choose the Pen tool from the Paint toolbox. Then, in the Tool control panel, set the Size to 1. Choose a foreground color, and then click in the individual cells that you want to color. You can right-click to fill in with the background color.

To zoom back out to normal size, just choose View | Normal Viewing from Paint Shop Pro's menu bar.

RESIZING AN IMAGE

Resizing an existing image can be tricky business. As I mentioned back in Chapter 10, "Spice It Up With Lines & Pictures," when you scan an image it's best to try to size it during the scan, so that you don't have to resize it later. But in many situations you won't have that choice, and you will need to resize an image.

You can resize an image in either of two ways: by resizing or resampling. The Resample method tries to reduce the "jaggies" caused by resizing an image, but there's no guarantee that a resampled image will look better than a resized image. Your best bet may be to try both. Here's how:

1. In Paint Shop Pro, click the image you want to resize.

2. Press Ctrl+C to copy the image, then press Ctrl+V to make two copies of it.

3. Click one of the copies and choose Image | Resize.

4. Under Custom size, fill in a new width or height (in pixels), and make sure that the Maintain Aspect Ratio check box is checked. (If you don't, the picture may be distorted.) Click OK.

THINKING IN PIXELS

It's not always easy to define how large or small you want a picture to be (in pixels). But you can estimate by thinking of 100 pixels as equal to one inch. Figure the width of the average reader's screen to be about 600 pixels, or 6 inches. In other words, you can think of a 300-pixel-wide picture as being about half the width of the reader's screen.

The height of the reader's screen is a little trickier. At 640 x 480 (the "least-space" scenario that most Web publishers work around), the height, technically, would be about 4.8 inches. But because Navigator's title bar, menu bar, toolbar(s), and status bar take up some of those pixels, it doesn't hurt to round that down to about 400 pixels, or four inches, tall.

Of course, this is all relative. For example, if the reader is browsing at 800 x 600 resolution, then that reader's screen is about 8 inches wide and 6 inches tall (minus the title bar, toolbars, and such).

5. Now click the other copy, the one you didn't resize.

6. Increase its color depth to 16 million colors (required for resampling) by choosing Colors | Increase Color Depth | 16 Million Colors.

7. Choose Image | Resample, keep the same settings you entered in Step 4, and choose OK.

Now you can look at the original, resized, and resampled versions of the picture (see Figure 14-19). Choose (click on) whichever looks the best, and use File | Save as to save that picture as a GIF or JPEG file.

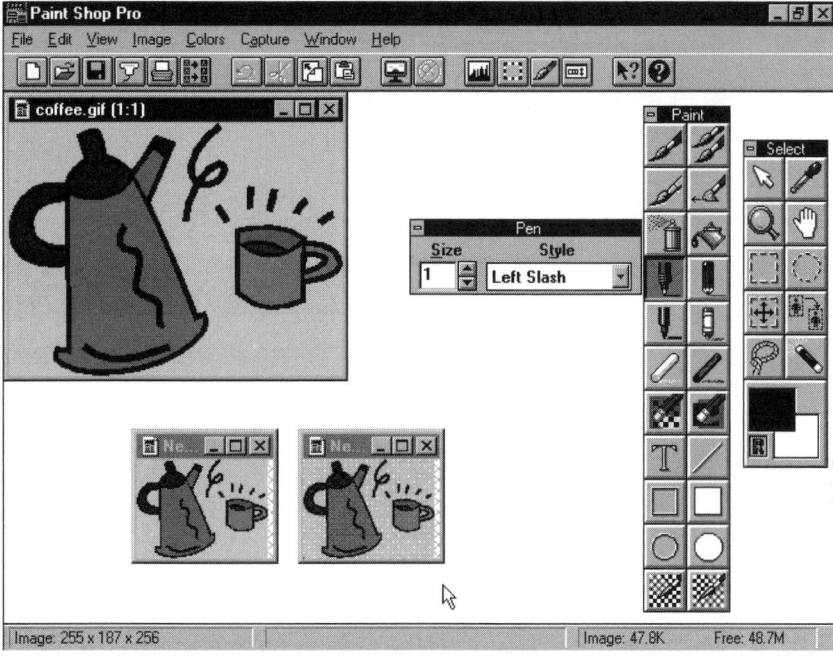

Figure 14-19: *Original, resized, and resampled images in Paint Shop Pro.*

Keep in mind that the smaller your picture is, the faster it will get to your readers. Avoid making any picture larger than it needs to be.

CREATING THUMBNAILS

As you may recall from Chapter 13, "Multimedia Madness," a *thumbnail* is a small representation of a larger picture. To create a thumbnail, you can use Paint Shop Pro to crop out some small representative portion of the larger picture. If the resulting crop is still too large to use as a thumbnail, you can resize or resample it down to whatever dimensions you want.

CREATING INTERLACED "FADE-IN" GIFs

You've probably noticed, as you browse the Web, that some pictures sort of fade into focus when you first open a Web page. Pictures that do that are called *interlaced GIFs*, and they're very easy to create in Paint Shop Pro. Just follow these steps:

1. Open (or create) your picture in Paint Shop Pro.
2. Choose File | Save As from Paint Shop Pro's menu bar.
3. Under List Files of Type, choose GIF-CompuServe.
4. Under File Sub-Format, choose Version 89a-Interlaced.
5. If you haven't already done so, choose a folder (directory) and enter a filename.
6. Click the OK button.

After you place the picture in a Web page, and open that page, you might notice the picture fading in, even on your own PC. But you'll really notice the fade in after you upload the page to your Web server and then visit the page with Navigator.

CREATING TRANSPARENT BACKGROUND GIFs

One of the most unique features of the GIF image format is the capability to define a single color as "transparent." Such images are often called *transparent background GIFs* because people tend to make the background color the transparent color, but you can make any color the transparent color.

In Figure 14-20, for example, you see an image (in a Web page) with no color defined as transparent. To the right of this image are versions of the same photo with white defined as transparent, black defined as transparent, and then a third color added and made transparent. In the last example, the white portions of the picture (eyes, mouths, and so forth) remain opaque white. The checkerboard background pattern shows through the transparent color in each picture.

Figure 14-20: *Original picture, then with white, black, and a new third color defined as transparent.*

It's important to understand that the PC doesn't view "foreground" and "background" as we do. In Figure 14-21 for example, you might think of everything but the person in each photo as being background. But the computer can't see things that way. The actual background for the photo contains thousands, perhaps millions of colors. As you may recall, you can define only one color as transparent in a GIF file. Thus, there is really no way to make the photo's "background" transparent.

Figure 14-21: *Photo "backgrounds" contain millions of colors.*

TIP

I suppose that saying "no way" in the preceding paragraph was a bit harsh. Actually, you could isolate just the face, using the Magic Wand tool in Paint Shop Pro, then flood fill everything outside the face with a single color that you'd then define as transparent. But this process is difficult, time-consuming, and often not worth the effort, because most photos look pretty strange with transparent backgrounds.

Now that you understand that you can define a single color in a GIF file as being transparent, let me show you *how* to do it:

1. Open the picture in Paint Shop Pro.
2. If you want to define as transparent a color that's already in the picture, skip to Step 5.

3. To define a new color for transparency, double-click the background color box at the bottom of the Select toolbox, and choose (or create) a color that doesn't exist anywhere else in the picture. (If the picture is black-and-white, you'll first need to choose Colors | Increase Color Depth | 16 Colors.)

4. Choose the Flood Fill tool, and then right-click any areas of the picture that you want to define as transparent. For example, in Figure 14-22 I've filled with gray the area I want to make transparent.

Figure 14-22: *Gray will be my transparent color in this example.*

5. Click the Eyedropper tool near the top of the Select toolbox.

6. Right-click the color that you want to define as transparent. The background color at the bottom of the Select toolbox will now match the color that you right-clicked.

7. Choose File | Save As, and choose GIF-CompuServe as the file type. Choose Version 89a under File Sub-Format.

8. If you don't want to overwrite the original copy of the image, choose a new filename for this version.

9. Click on the Options button, and choose Set the Transparency Value to the Background Color, as in Figure 14-23. (In this context, "background color" means the color defined as the background color at the bottom of the Select toolbox.)

Figure 14-23: *The background color chosen in the Select toolbox will be treated as transparent in Web pages.*

10. Choose OK to close the transparency options box, then choose OK to save the file.

You won't see any difference in Paint Shop Pro. But when you put the picture in a Web page, the color you defined as transparent will, indeed, be transparent.

DETERMINING THE SIZE OF EMBEDDED OBJECTS

When you insert an image into your Web page by using Gold's Insert Image button, the size of that picture is automatically detected and filled in for you in the dialog box and in the <img> tag that displays the picture. Unfortunately, when you use the <embed> tag to insert an inline video, you have to know, on your own, what size to make the video frame. Your best bet is to use the original frame size. But you may not know, offhand, just how may pixels tall and wide the video should be. Here's a fairly easy solution to this problem:

1. In Windows My Computer, Find, or Explorer, double-click the .avi file that you want to size. The video should start playing on your screen.

2. Click the Stop (square) button to stop the video. Then press the Print Screen key to capture the entire screen.

3. Open Paint Shop Pro, and choose Edit | Paste | As New Image. A copy of the entire screen lands in Paint Shop Pro's window.

4. Use the Rectangular Selection tool to isolate the video frame, and choose Edit | Copy.

5. Choose File | Close | No to close the larger screen capture.

6. Choose Edit | Paste | As New Image to paste in the captured frame.

The status bar will show you the width x length, as in Figure 14-24. Use those measurements while you define the width and height attributes of the <embed...> tag that plays the inline video (refer to Chapter 13, "Multimedia Madness").

Figure 14-24: *Video frame is 163 pixels wide, 119 pixels tall.*

MOVING ON

I hope this chapter has broadened your image making skills for building Web sites. Remember, I've focused here only on the most basic features of Paint Shop Pro. There are other neat things you can try. For example, if you set the color depth to 256 colors or more, you can experiment with special effects by trying the various deformations and filters available on the Image menu. As I said earlier, you can get the Paint Shop Pro manual by ordering the real product after you try out the evaluation copy.

The next chapter takes us away from graphics for a while, and talks about those mysterious little HTML tags that Gold's editor types for you behind the scenes, automatically.

Tuning HTML Tags

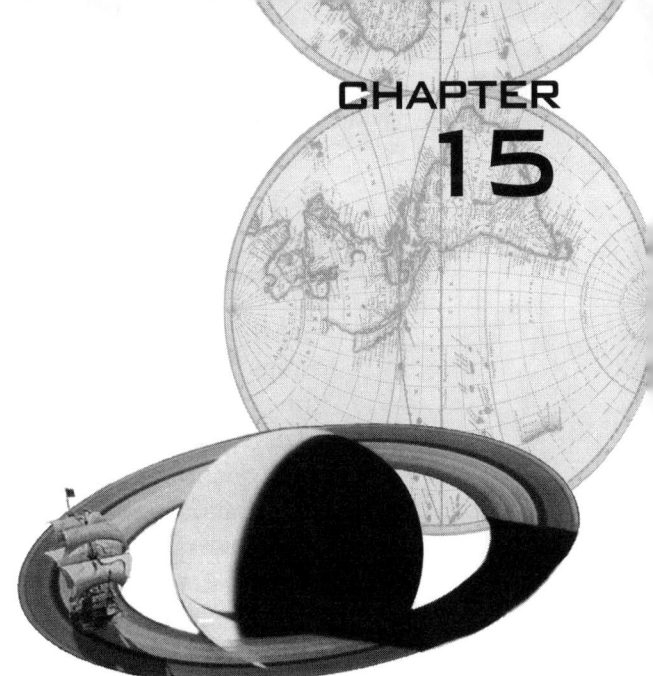

Up to now you've been able to do some pretty fancy stuff in your Web pages without resorting to HTML, the "language" of the World Wide Web. But at some point, you may come across situations in which you want to work directly with the HTML source of your document, to add, change, or delete tags. This chapter is all about HTML and covers the following topics:

- What HTML is all about
- Viewing the HTML source behind every Web page
- Inserting custom HTML tags
- Setting up and using an HTML source editor

In the chapters that follow this one, you'll have ample opportunity to practice the skills and knowledge you glean from this chapter.

WHAT IS HTML?

HTML stands for *HyperText Markup Language*. The *hypertext* part comes from the fact that HTML lets you put hyperlinks and targets into your document. The hyperlinks are "jumping off" spots that take the reader to some other place within a document or to another document. The targets are "landing zones" in a document.

The *markup language* part comes from the fact that you use tags to format the document's appearance—that is, you "mark up" the document with tags to define how the reader will see the page in his or her browser. The total collection of tags available to you is sort of like a programming language, because the tags give the Web browser "instructions" for formatting the text.

When you're browsing the Web or working in Gold's editor, the HTML tags are hidden from you. They clutter up your text, and there's not much reason for you to look at the tags. After all, it's up to the Web browser, not you, to interpret what all the tags mean.

VIEWING THE HTML DOCUMENT SOURCE

You can easily take a look at the HTML tags in any Web page that's on your screen. Just choose View | Document Source from Navigator's menu bar. The pure, unformatted source document, with visible HTML tags, is displayed in its own window. If you want, you can restore this window (by clicking the middle button on the right side of the title bar). Then you can resize that window so you can see both the normal browser/editor view, and the actual underlying document source (complete with HTML tags), as in Figure 15-1.

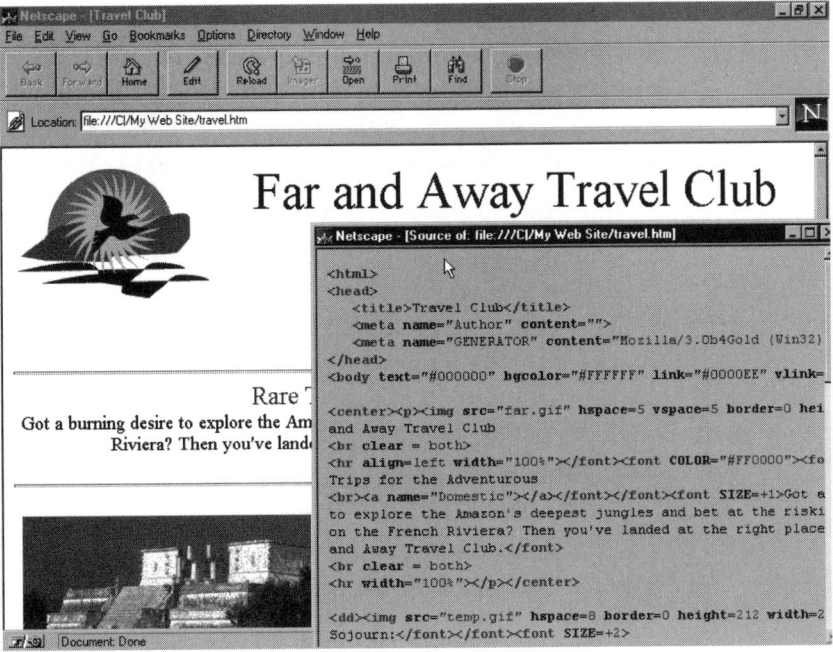

Figure 15-1: *A page and its HTML document source.*

Note that you can't make any changes to the document source in this "look but don't touch" view. It's purely for viewing. When you want to stop viewing the document source, just close its window by clicking the X button near the top right corner of the window that's displaying the document source.

ANATOMY OF AN HTML TAG

All HTML tags are enclosed in angle brackets (<>). A word or abbreviation inside the brackets tells the Web browser what to do. For example, the <br> tag tells the Web browser to "break the line here."

Many tags come in pairs. The opening tag starts some formatting feature, and the ending tag—which starts with a slash (/)—ends that feature. For example, the <h1> tag begins the Heading 1 format, and </h1> ends that format. The <p> tag starts a new paragraph, and the </p> tag ends it.

Some tags have *attributes* that give further instructions to the Web browser. For example, the <img> tag offers several attributes, including src (source), height, and width. The following tag tells the Web browser to display the picture in the file named "mypic.gif", at a width of 50 pixels and a height of 100 pixels:

```
<img src="mypic.gif" width=50 height=100>
```

Remember that you, personally, may never need to deal with HTML tags. If you use Gold's editor, any formatting options you pick are converted automatically to HTML tags, behind the scenes. When you view a page on the Web, the server does send the document source, which is basically the text and tags that define the page. Your Web browser interprets the tags as formatting instructions, however, and hides the tags. All you see is the formatted text. Thus, this little chunk of text and tags . . .

```
<h1>Welcome</h1><p><img src="AlecBW.gif" height=126 width=90
align=left>My name is Alec and I may be the world's youngest
Web author and publisher. What's that? You don't believe I'm
a Web author/publisher? Well, OK, I confess. I did get a lot
of help from grownups to create this page. Well, actually, I
was sound asleep while my Dad created this page for me.</p>
```

. . . looks something like Figure 15-2 in a Web browser, and in Gold's editor.

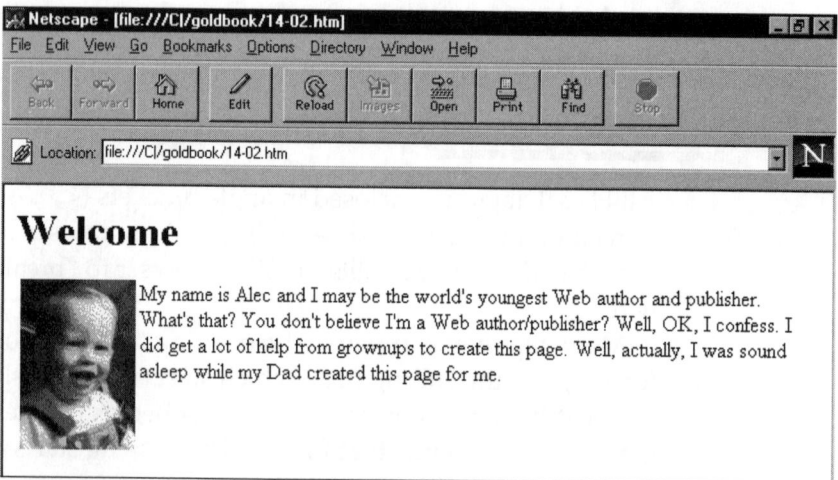

Figure 15-2: *Web browser interprets, then hides, tags.*

So Why Mess With Tags?

Given the fact that HTML tags are pretty "techie," and don't really give you, the author, a WYSIWYG (What-You-See-Is-What-You-Get) view of your document, you might wonder why you would ever want to mess with tags directly. Well, a few of the reasons you might want to get into the document source and add or tweak some tags follow:

- You might want to add tags to accommodate multiple Web browsers. For instance Chapter 13, "Multimedia Madness," presented an example of inserting the <bgsound> and <img dynsrc> tags supported by Microsoft Internet Explorer.

- You might want to use HTML tags that Gold's editor does not support on its own. For example, frames and clickable image maps (discussed in the next two chapters) require some tags and attributes that aren't available from Gold's editor.

- HTML is constantly evolving, and you may want to insert a new tag or attribute that wasn't available when Gold hit the streets.

Inserting HTML Tags

Gold's editor provides a simple means of inserting an HTML tag right into your document:

1. In Gold's editor, click at about where you want to insert the HTML tag.

2. Choose Insert | HTML Tag from Gold's menu bar to get to the dialog box shown in Figure 15-3.

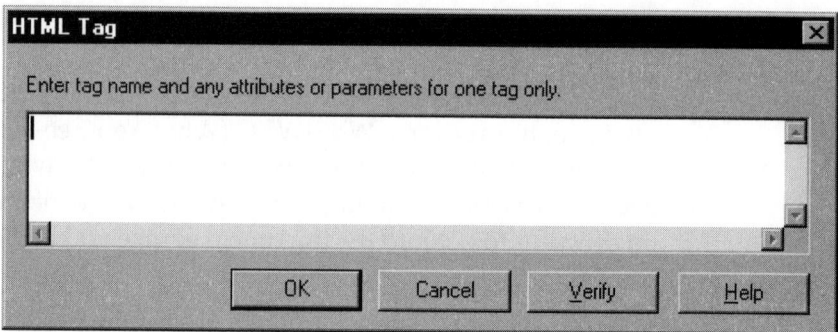

Figure 15-3: *The HTML Tag dialog box.*

3. Type your tag *with* the angle brackets.

4. Optionally, you can click the Verify button to check for obvious errors, such as missing angle brackets. Or click the Help button for help.

5. When you're happy with the tag, click the OK button.

The tag is inserted into your document at the cursor position. Gold's editor displays a little tag icon at that point to indicate that you inserted a custom HTML there. With the tag in place, you can do any of the following:

■ To see how Netscape Navigator interprets the tag, just switch to the browser (click the View in Browser button or choose File | Browse document).

■ To change the tag, return to the editor (click the Edit button), and double-click the tag icon.

■ To delete the tag, return to the editor, click on the tag icon (once) to select it. Then press the Delete (Del) key.

The Insert | HTML Tag commands are fine for inserting individual custom HTML tags in your Web page. But when you really want to get your hands dirty and work right with the entire source document, you need to use some kind of external text editor.

CHOOSING AN HTML SOURCE EDITOR

Navigator's View | View Document Source commands let you see the entire source document, but do not let you make any changes to that document. If you want to be able to view and edit the entire source document, you must first choose a text editor to do the job. As a Windows 95 user, your best bet would probably be to use Notepad.exe, unless you already have some other text editor in mind. Follow these steps to set up Notepad as your document source editor:

> **TIP**
>
> *Do not specify a word processing program (such as Word or WordPerfect) as your HTML editor. Those programs will insert formatting tags that Web browsers cannot interpret.*

1. Choose Options | Editor Preferences from Navigator's menu bar.
2. Click the General tab.
3. Specify **c:\windows\notepad.exe** as your editor, as in Figure 15-4. You can use the Browse button to locate Notepad.exe, if you wish.

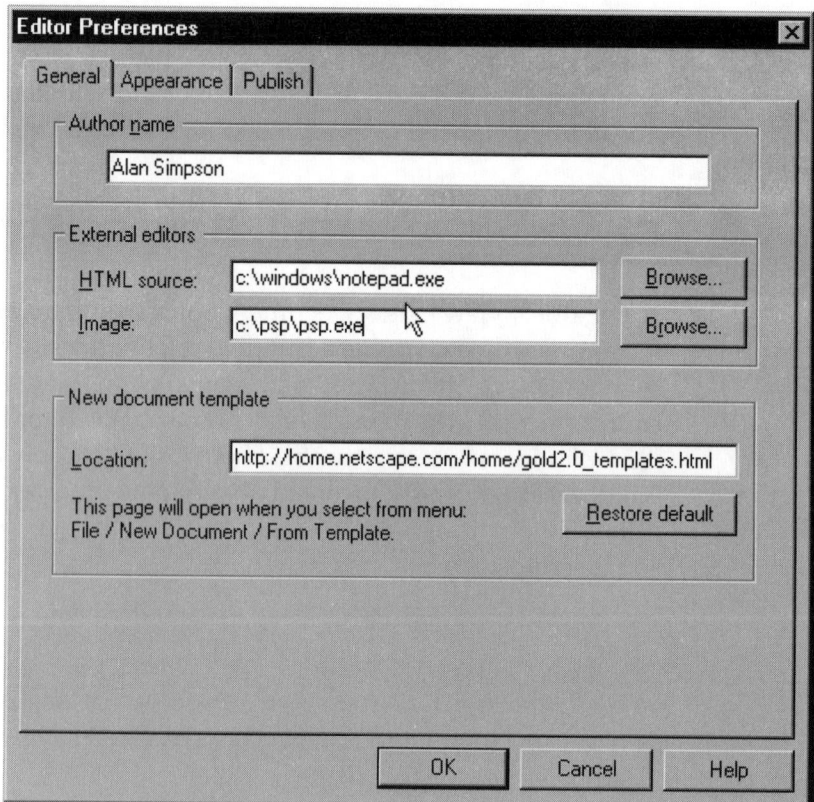

Figure 15-4: *Notepad.exe, set up as HTML source editor.*

    4. Choose OK.

EDITING THE DOCUMENT SOURCE

After you've defined your source editor, you can follow these simple steps to view and edit your source document:

    1. Open, in Gold's editor, the page you want to change (if you haven't already done so).

    2. Choose View I Edit Document Source from the editor's menu bar.

3. If you're prompted to save the document, choose Yes.

The page opens in your text editor, as in the example shown in Figure 15-5. There, you can use all the editing capabilities of the text editor to freely add, change, and delete both text and tags.

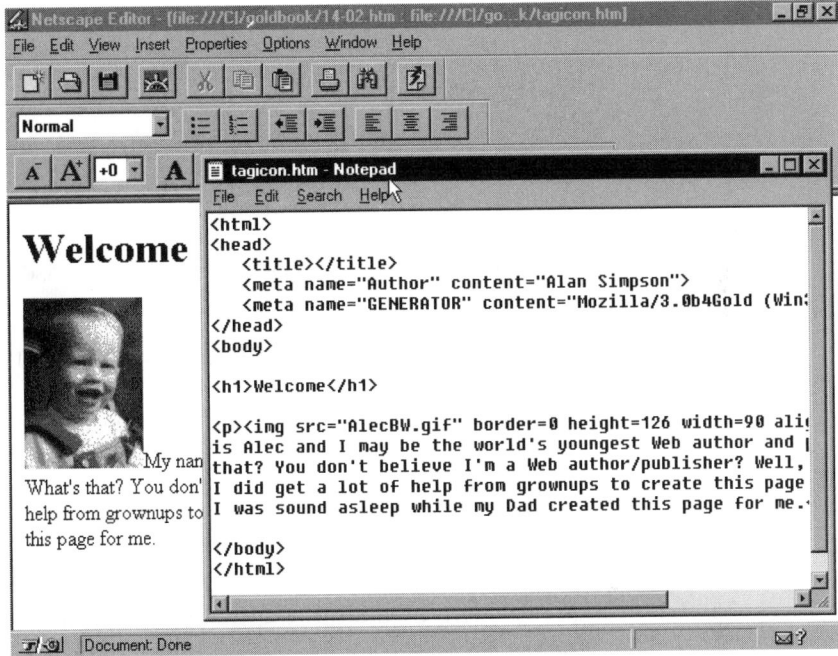

Figure 15-5: *Sample page, opened in Notepad.*

GENERAL STRUCTURE OF AN HTML DOCUMENT

Before you start tearing into your Web page with Notepad, you need to be aware that all HTML documents contain the structural tags <html>, <head>, <body>, </body>, </head>, </html>, in the following order:

```
<html>

<head>
     <more tags here...>
</head>

<body>
     <start of text that reader sees...>
     <with embedded tags...>
</body>

</html>
```

There's no reason to change or delete any of those tags. Instead, you must work within those tags, as follows:

- <html>...</html>: Everything in the document must be typed between these all-encompassing tags. Do not type anything above the <html> tag, nor anything below the </html> tag.

- <head>...<head>: Defines the header information about the page, such as the title that appears in the title bar (between the <title>...</title> tags). In general, only specialized tags go between <head> and </head>. Anything that you want the reader to see should *not* be typed between <head> and </head>.

- <body>...</body>: Marks the beginning and end of the body of the page, the stuff that the reader will see. Changes that you make between these two tags will show up in the Web browser.

With that in mind, let's take a look at the basic editing capabilities offered by Notepad.

EDITING WITH NOTEPAD

When it comes to text editors, Windows 95's Notepad is about as plain-vanilla as they come. Notepad offers basic typing and editing, a simple Find feature (Search | Find), and the usual select, cut, copy, and paste. To select text in Notepad, use the same techniques you'd use in Gold's editor. That is, drag the mouse pointer through the text you want to select. Or hold down the Shift key while you press the arrow keys.

If you need any help in Notepad, choose Help | Help Topics from Notepad's menu bar. Click the Contents tag, double-click the Working with Text book icon, and then read the various topics in that book. What you read in the Help section pretty much sums up everything you can do with Notepad.

It's important to realize that any line breaks or blank lines you type in Notepad will be ignored by Netscape Navigator and all other Web browsers. If you want to end one paragraph and start a new one while you are typing in Notepad, you must type a **<p>** tag between the paragraphs. If you want to break a line without skipping a line, you must type the **
** tag.

SAVING THE EDITED HTML SOURCE

After you've made your changes to the source document, close the text editor and save your changes. To do so, you can click the Close (X) button in the upper right corner of Notepad's window, or choose File | Exit from Notepad's menu bar.

If you made any changes to the document, you'll be asked whether you want to save them. Choose Yes. You'll then see the message shown in Figure 15-6. Choose Yes to update the copy of the page that's in Navigator.

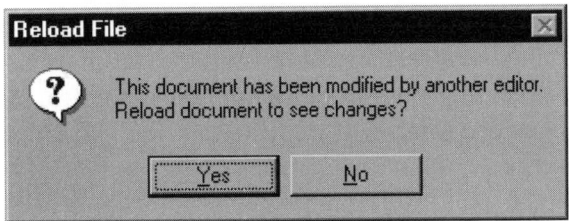

Figure 15-6: *Choosing Yes here will bring Navigator up to date with changes made via an external editor.*

The Notepad window will close and disappear. Now you're back to regular Navigator Gold editing and browsing. To see what the document will look like to readers, click the View in Browser button to switch over to the Navigator Web browser.

EDITING HTML WITH A WORD PROCESSOR

As mentioned earlier, using a word processing program to edit HTML source is risky business. Even if you have an Internet Helper, such as Internet Assistant for Microsoft Word, or Internet Publisher for WordPerfect, you still shouldn't use your word processor to format raw HTML generated by Gold's editor.

> **TIP**
>
> *You can use Word with Internet Assistant and WordPerfect with Internet Publisher to create and edit Web pages, But—like Gold—they are WYSIWYG tools that insert HTML tags behind the scenes, and save the results as a pure text HTML file.*

You can, however, use the nonformatting features of your word processor to edit HTML source. For example, I often use global search and replace (Edit | Replace, in Word) to make global changes to an HTML document. The Speller and Thesaurus also come in handy.

The trick is to get the HTML source into, and out of, the word processor as a pure text file, so that the word processor doesn't have a chance to insert any of its own formatting tags. Let's assume that you're editing your document in Gold's editor, and that you now want to use Microsoft Word to edit the HTML source. Here's what you do:

1. From the menu bar in Gold's editor, choose View | Edit document source. The source document appears in Notepad.

2. In Notepad, press Ctrl+A, or choose Edit | Select All, to select the entire document.

3. Again in Notepad, press Ctrl+C, or choose Edit | Copy, to copy the selection to the Windows clipboard.

4. Create a new, blank document in your word processor. If you're using Word 7, for example, click the Start button, choose New Office Document, then double-click the Blank Document icon.

5. With the blank document onscreen, press Ctrl+V or choose Edit | Paste from the word processor's menu bar.

The raw HTML source document is now in your word processing program (see Figure 15-7). Keep in mind that while the document is in this program (Word, in this example) you should use only the nonformatting features of the program, such as Replace, Spelling, and Thesaurus. Do not save this copy of the document.

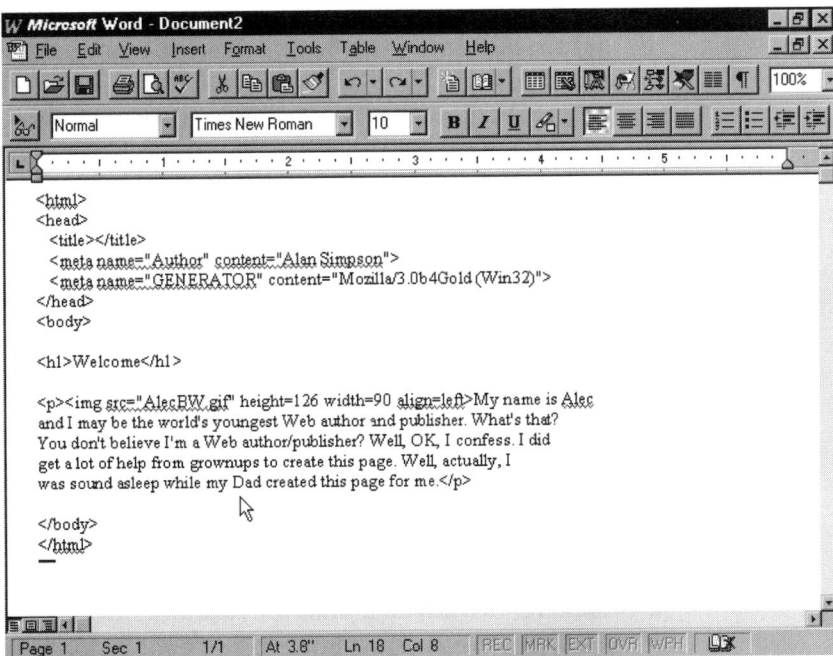

Figure 15-7: *Raw HTML document in Microsoft Word.*

When you've finished making your changes, cut and paste the entire document back into Notepad. Be careful, and follow these steps exactly:

1. In your word processor, press Ctrl+A, or choose Edit I Select All, to select the entire document.

2. Press Ctrl+X, or choose Edit I Cut, to move the entire document into the Windows clipboard. (This copy will replace the copy that Notepad put into the clipboard.)

3. Exit your word processor.

4. Click anywhere inside Notepad's window, then choose Edit I Select All to delete all the text there.

5. Press Ctrl+V, or choose Edit Paste from Notepad's menu bar, to replace that selected text with the text in the Windows clipboard.

That should do it. To view the effects of your changes in Navigator, close Notepad, choose Yes when asked about saving your changes and reloading the document, then click the View in Browser button.

FUSSY, FUSSY, FUSSY

HTML markup language is similar to a programming language in the sense that everything is already defined, and you must use only valid HTML tags, with correct *syntax*. You can't just make up your own tags as you go along. For example, these tags:

```
<bigred>Howdy!</bigred>
```

would have absolutely no effect on the document because <bigred> and </bigred> are not valid HTML tags. And Web browsers ignore any tags that they cannot interpret.

As for the syntax—just be sure that everything is spelled correctly, and that any spaces, commas, or other punctuation marks are typed accurately. For example, this tag is fine:

```
<img src="mypic.gif" height=100 width=50>
```

On the other hand, this tag has numerous problems and won't work:

```
<img src=mypic.gif hieght=100 width=50>
```

The problems are missing quotation marks around mypic.gif, and *height* misspelled as *hieght*. (Yes, it's *that* fussy.)

CASE-SENSITIVE FILE & DIRECTORY NAMES

Although HTML itself is not case-sensitive, directory and filenames on many Unix Web servers *are* case-sensitive. As an example, let's say that on your server you've put all your graphic images in a directory named *images*. One of the files in that directory is named *mypic.gif*. This tag, in a Web page, would show the correct image:

```
<img src="images/mypic.gif">
```

The following series of tags will work on your PC, because Windows 95 isn't case-sensitive about folder and filenames:

```
<img src="Images/MyPic.gif">
```

```
<img src="Images/mypic.gif">
```

```
<img src="images/MyPic.gif">
```

```
<img src="IMAGES/MYPIC.GIF">
```

These tags would *not* work on a Unix server, however, if the upper- and lowercase letters used in the *images/mypic.gif* part don't match the upper- and lowercase letters used to define the directory and filenames on the Unix server.

Getting used to case-sensitive directory and filenames can be very difficult for Windows users. Your best bet is to make up a general rule, and always stick with it. For example, I use *only* lowercase letters when I type directory and filenames.

HTML REFERENCE GUIDES

How do you go about finding what all the valid HTML tags are, and their exact syntax? Where do you find out about new and emerging HTML tags? Well, the problem is a little trickier than you'd think, because the HTML Standard isn't a "standard" at all.

In fact, there are several competing standards. Netscape makes up new tags and attributes for their latest browser. Microsoft makes up new tags and attributes. Even Mosaic, one of the oldest Web browsers, has invented a few.

TIP

Webster's dictionary could use the phrase competing standards *or even* HTML standard *as their definition of the word* oxymoron.

In my opinion (humble as it may be) the best way to keep up with the ever-changing world of HTML is to use an electronic reference guide—either one that's online, or one that you can download and use on your PC while offline. There are many to choose from. You might want to play around with a few to see which works for you. Here are their names, and where to find them:

- HTML Quick Reference (Michael Grobe): Short and sweet, a good online overview: http://www.cc.ukans.edu/info/HTML_quick.html

- HTML Quick Reference (Maran Wilson): Another short, succinct, good online reference: http://sdcc8.ucsd.edu/~m1wilson/htmlref.html

- HTML Style Guide & Test Suite: Good visual examples of the way various tags are translated by the reader's Web browser: http://www.charm.net/~lejeune/styles.html

- HTML Language Spec: An in-depth look at HTML tags through the proposed Version 3.0 standard: http://www.hp.co.uk/people/dsr/html3/CoverPage.html

- Netscape's *Creating Net Sites*: Contains general information for Web authors, and links to *HTML Reference Guides*: http://home.netscape.com/assist/net_sites/index.html

- W³ Writer: HTML, plus general information for aspiring and accomplished Web writers: http://hake.com/gordon/w3-index.html

■   Windows 95 HTML Help: An HTML reference guide that's
    formatted as a Windows 95 Help file. You can use it even
    while you're offline. Point your browser to ftp://
    ftp.swan.ac.uk/pub/ in.coming/htmlib, and download the
    file *htmlib95xx.exe* (where *xx* is the version number, currently
    22). See the 00-index.txt file at this FTP site for additional
    information.

Moving On

This chapter has given you a broad view of what HTML is all
about, as well as some techniques and tools you can use to work
directly with HTML. Chapter 13, Multimedia Madness," showed
you how to insert a single HTML tag. Chapters 16, "Creating
Clickable Image Maps," and 17, "Get Framed," will give you a
chance to edit HTML, using Notepad as your editor.

CHAPTER

16

Creating Clickable Image Maps

Clickable image maps make a presentation fun and give your Web site a professional look and feel. In this chapter you'll learn everything you need to know to create clickable image maps for your own Web pages. The chapter includes:

- Examples of clickable image maps
- What client-side image mapping is all about
- Using Map This! to define an image's hot spots
- Adding appropriate tags to your Web page
- Testing your image map

To make sure that we both know what I'm talking about here, we'll start with a couple of examples that will serve also as food for thought.

EXAMPLES OF CLICKABLE IMAGE MAPS

Clickable image maps are often used as little navigational toolbars on a Web page. They let the reader jump to another page without going back through the home page. For example, the little pictures and words along the bottom of the page in Figure 16-1 are hot spots that, when clicked, take the reader to some other place in CTS's Web site (http://www.cts.com).

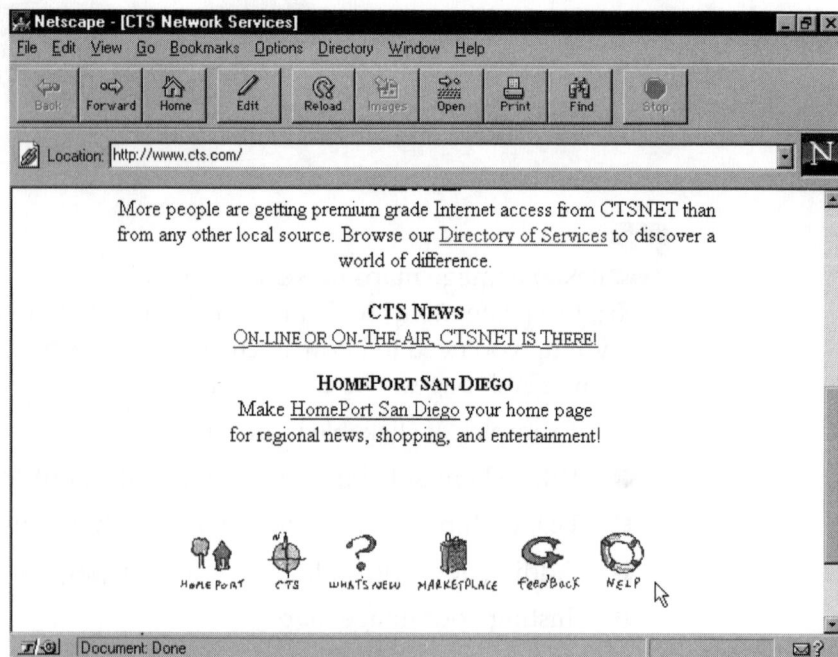

Figure 16-1: *Little pictures and words along the bottom of the page are clickable hot spots.*

You've probably seen many examples of these navigational toolbars, because many popular sites use them. For example, Netscape (http://home.netscape.com), Yahoo (http://www.yahoo.com), and Microsoft (http://www.microsoft.com) all use clickable image maps as on-page navigational toolbars.

MULTIPLE IMAGES VS. IMAGE MAPS

You can actually create a simple navigational toolbar without creating an image map. Just place each "button" in the bar on the screen as a picture, using Gold's standard Insert Image button. Then make each picture a link using Gold's Make Link button.

The one disadvantage to this approach, however, is that most browsers will show each button as a link. That is, each button will be surrounded by a blue or magenta frame, depending on whether or not the reader has already visited the page referred to by the link. In an image map, individual hot spots are not surrounded by the blue/magenta border. And, in general, clickable image maps give you more control over the appearance of the graphic image that contains the hot spots.

You're certainly not limited to the toolbar look. You can create hot spots anywhere on any picture in your site. For example, The Spot's (http://www.thespot.com) opening photo is surrounded by hot spot links to different areas in the site (see Figure 16-2).

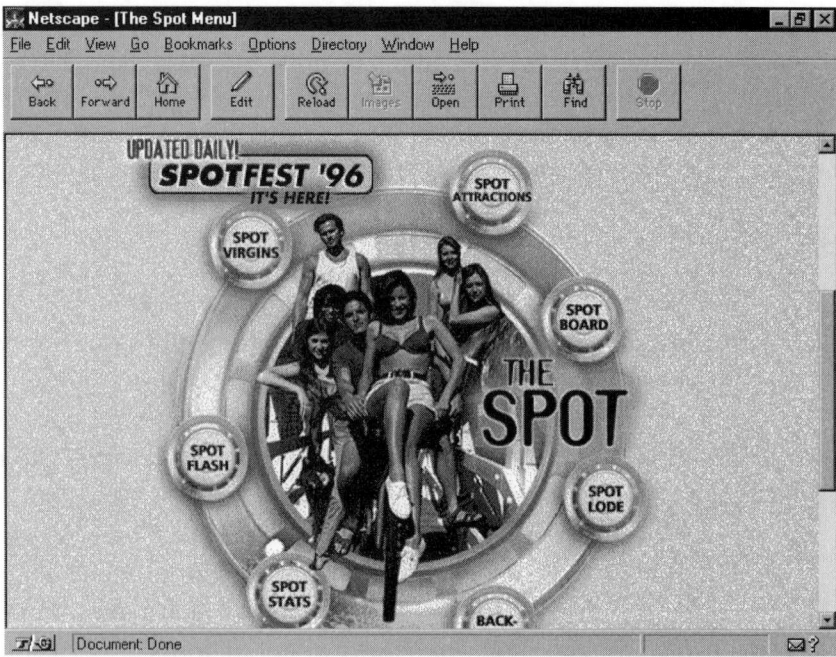

Figure 16-2: *The Spot's opening photo, surrounded by links to specific places in the site.*

A hot spot in a picture is just like any other hyperlink in a page. The link can point to another page in the current Web site, to an entirely different Web site, or to a target in the current page or any other page. But to create a clickable image map (unlike the typical hyperlink that you can create with a simple click of the Make Link button), you need a little outside assistance from third-party programs.

CLIENT-SIDE IMAGE MAPPING

Before you start creating clickable image maps, let me clarify a few buzzwords and acronyms you're bound to run across. In the olden days, all mapping was done through *server-side image mapping* (the Web server computer took care of the mapping). This was a hassle, though, because you either had to write a custom program (called a *cgi script*) to handle the mapping, or you had to hook into your ISP's custom-mapping program.

TIP

The two sets of standards for server-side image mapping were NCSA and CERN.

Most modern Web browsers now support *client-side image mapping* (CSIM). CSIM is much easier for you, the author/publisher, because all the action takes place on the *client machine* (the reader's PC). You just have to create a map identifying the hot spots in a GIF or JPEG file, and then assign a URL to each hot spot. When the reader clicks the hot spot, he or she is sent to the URL, as with any other hyperlink in your document.

MAP THIS! & MAP EDIT

The Companion CD-ROM includes a couple of programs you can use to create client-side image maps for your own Web pages. One is named Map This! and the other is named Map Edit. See Appendix B for installation and startup instructions.

In this chapter I use Map This! as the sample third-party program, rather than Map Edit. Both are excellent programs. But because I have more experience with Map This!, it's the program I picked to demonstrate the basic steps involved in creating a clickable image map.

TIP

If you don't have the CD-ROM handy, you can download Map This! from http://galadriel.ecaetc.ohio-state.edu/tc/mt. You can download an evaluation copy of Map Edit from http://www.boutell.com/mapedit.

OUR GOAL

Image mapping will be easier for me to explain if I can use an example to illustrate the steps involved. In the example we'll develop a Web site for a company named Acme Services. Figure 16-3 shows how the pages in this hypothetical site are organized. There's a home page, index.html, and four separate pages named new.htm, services.htm, guestbk.htm, and contact.htm.

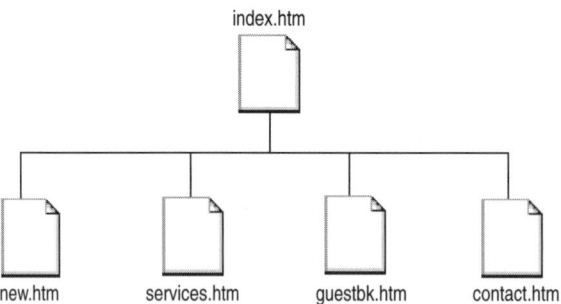

Figure 16-3: *Structure of our hypothetical Web site.*

Our goal is to create a clickable image map for the home page (index.html) like the one near the bottom of Figure 16-4. Note that I created everything in that sample page, *except* the image map, using the standard tools in Gold's editor.

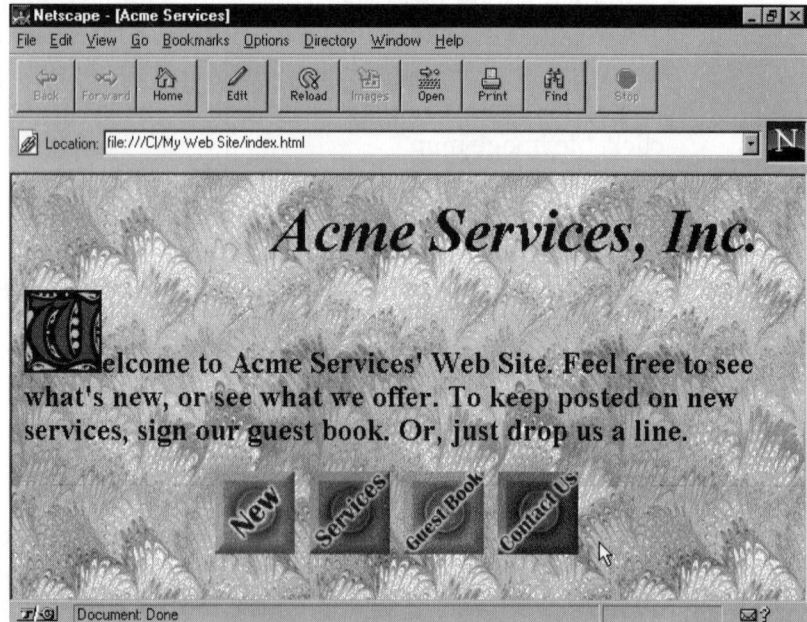

Figure 16-4: *Sample index.html page, with image map across the bottom of the page.*

TIP

The background, large letter W, and buttons in the image map are all from Corel's Web.Gallery. For information on this and related products, point your Web browser to http://www.corel.com.

CREATING THE GIF FILE

Because, initially, every image map is just a GIF or JPEG image, you can use existing clip art, a scanned image—whatever you can get into Paint Shop Pro—as the picture. In the example, I cut and pasted four buttons from Corel's Web.Gallery program into a single Paint Shop Pro picture. I saved the resulting picture, shown in Figure 16-5, to my My Web Site folder with the filename map_pic.gif.

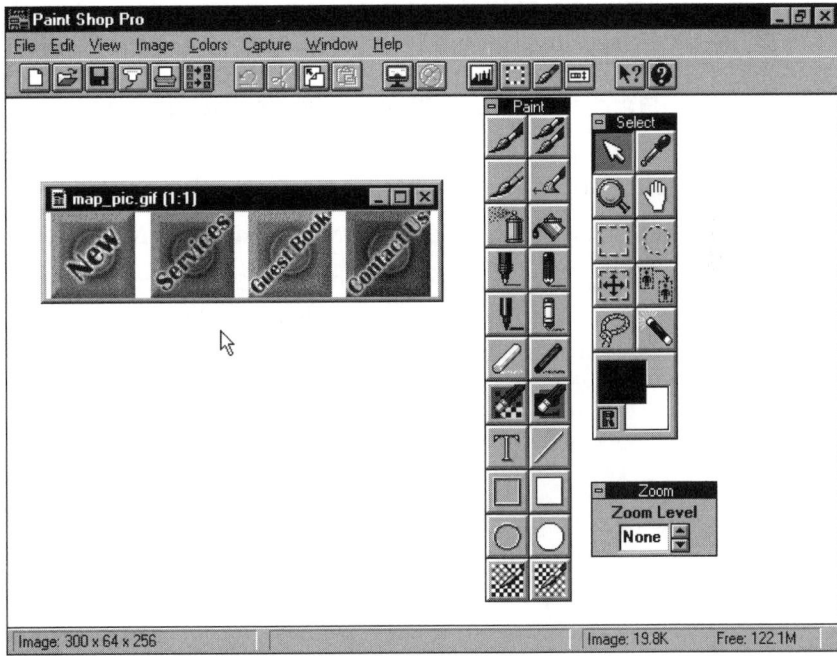

Figure 16-5: *This GIF picture will become the image map.*

TIP

In Paint Shop Pro I used File | New to create a new, blank image with a white background. To get buttons into the picture, I right-clicked whatever button I wanted in Web.Gallery and chose Copy. Then I switched to Paint Shop Pro, clicked my picture, and chose Edit | Paste | As New Selection. A copy of the button landed in the Paint Shop picture, and I positioned it by dragging in the picture's window.

USING MAP THIS! TO DEFINE THE HOT SPOTS

To define the hot spots in an image you need to close and save the image as a GIF or JPEG file, making sure that you put the image in the same file that holds the rest of your Web site materials (My Web Site, in the example). Then, start up Map This! on your PC. (Exactly how you do that depends on how you set up Map This!, as discussed in Appendix B.)

SETTING MAP THIS! PREFERENCES

When you have Map This! open and on your screen, follow these steps to set your initial preferences for the map you're about to create:

1. Choose File | Preferences from the Map This! menu bar.

2. In the dialog box that appears, choose CSIM under Default Map Type. You can also clear the Require default URL check box, as in Figure 16-6.

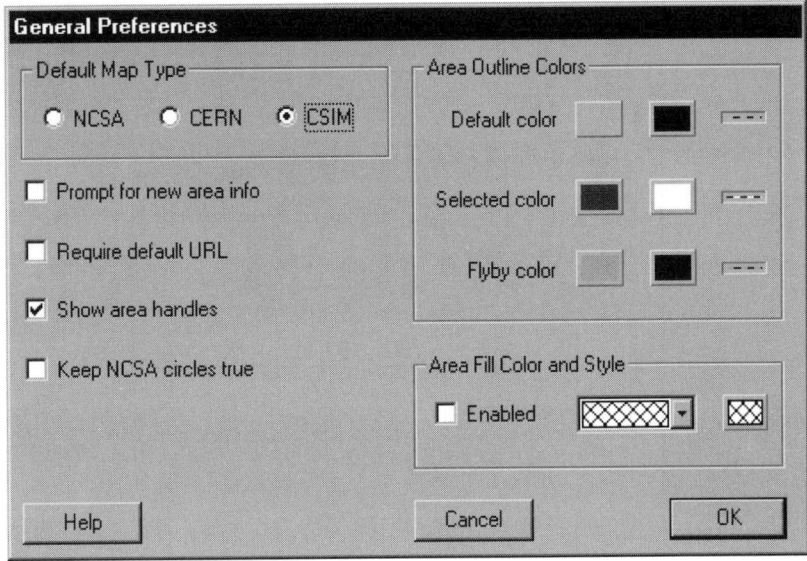

Figure 16-6: *General Preferences dialog box for Map This!*

3. Choose OK to close the dialog box and save your preference.

OPENING YOUR IMAGE MAP

Next, to start creating a new image map, follow these steps:

1. From the Map This! menu bar choose File | New.

2. Click the Let's go find one! button.

3. Next to Look in, work your way to the folder that contains your picture (My Web Site, in the example).

4. Double-click the name of the picture file (map_pic.gif, in the example). The image appears in a document window inside Map This!

If you can't see the entire picture, just drag the sizing pad in the lower right corner of the window to make the window larger, as I've done in the example shown in Figure 16-7.

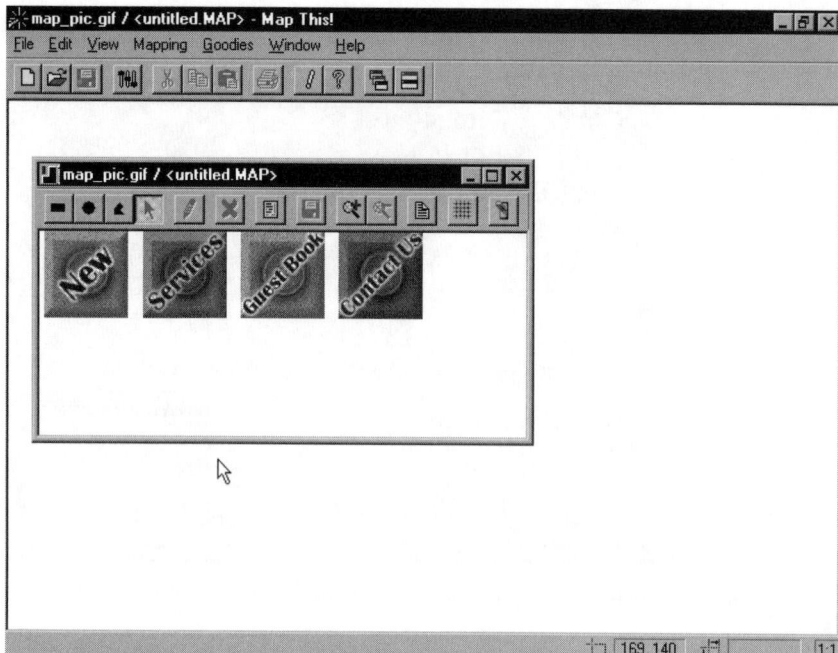

Figure 16-7: *My map_pic.gif picture in Map This!*

TIP

If the hot spots you're defining are small, you can choose Mapping | Zoom In to magnify the picture.

DEFINING THE HOT SPOTS

Now it's time to define the hot spots on your picture. Follow these steps:

1. First, open the Area List (choose View | Area List). Then arrange the windows so that you can see both your picture and the Area List.

2. From the toolbar just above your picture, choose one of the first three buttons to indicate what shape you want the hot spot to be: rectangular, circle/oval, or polygon.

3. Move the mouse pointer to any corner of the area you want to define as a hot spot, then drag the mouse pointer to "frame" the area that will be hot. For example, in Figure 16-8 I've dragged a rectangle around my first hot spot, the New button. Notice that the Area List now has an entry for that hot spot, identified simply as 1:rect.

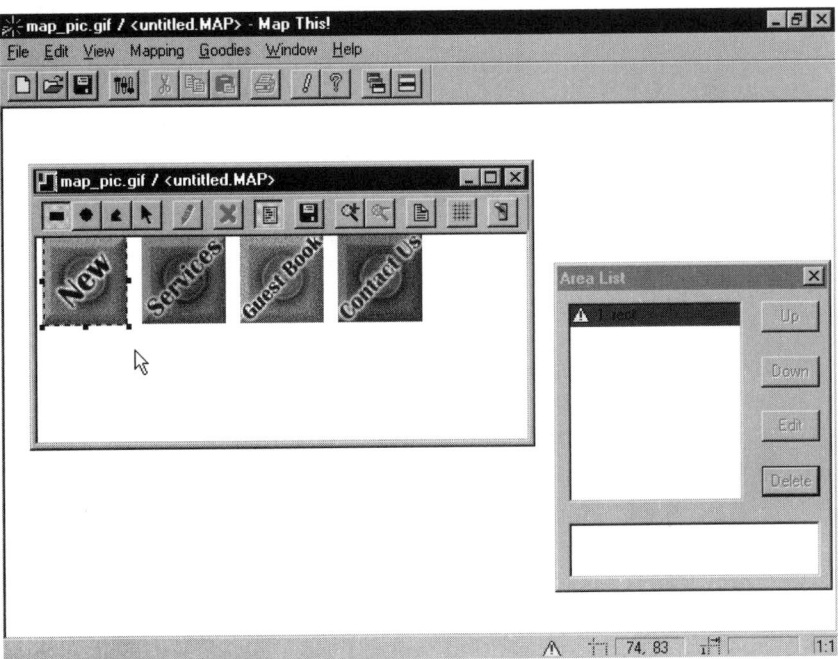

Figure 16-8: *First hot spot defined in my sample image map.*

4. Repeat Steps 2 and 3 until you've identified every hot spot in your picture. In Figure 16-9, for example, I've defined four hot spots, one for each button in the image map.

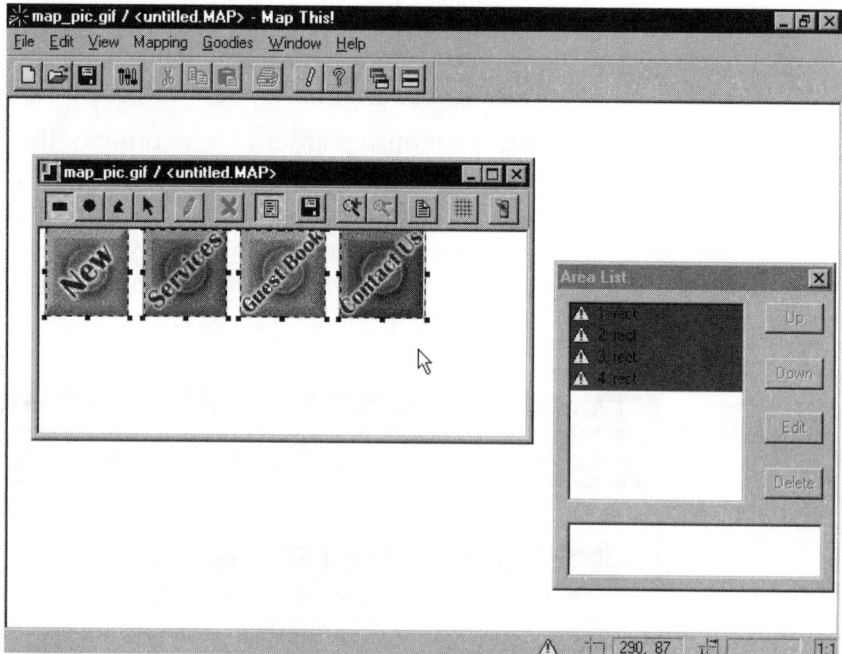

Figure 16-9: *Four hot spots defined in this picture.*

DEFINING THE ACTION FOR EACH HOT SPOT

Next, you need to define the action for each hot spot. In other words, you need to define where readers will be taken when they click the hot spot. To define these destinations, you use the same syntax used to define regular hyperlinks, as summarized in Table 16-1.

Jump to	How Defined
Target (named anchor)	Use #*target* (*target* is the name of the target).
Different page in this site	Use *filename.ext* to specify the filename of the page (e.g., new.htm).
Different Web site	Specify the complete URL of the Web site (e.g., http://www.coolnerds.com).

Table 16-1: *Standard syntax for specifying destinations.*

In the example, each hot spot will take the reader to a different page in my Web site. Because those pages will be in the same directory as the home page, I just need to specify the filename (new.htm, services.htm, guestbk.htm, or contact.htm) when defining my destinations. Here are the steps to follow to define your destinations:

1. In the toolbar above your picture, click the mouse pointer tool (the fourth button from the left).

2. Click anywhere in any hot spot to define its destination. The Area List item for that hot spot will turn blue.

3. In the Area List box, click the Edit button.

4. In the dialog box that appears, define where the hot spot will take the reader. For example, in Figure 16-10 I selected my first hot spot, chose Edit, and defined new.htm as the page to open when the reader clicks that hot spot. The Internal comment is optional, and never visible to the reader, but you can write a note to yourself there if you wish, for future reference.

TIP

I rearranged the windows in Figure 16-10 slightly to give you a better view of all the components.

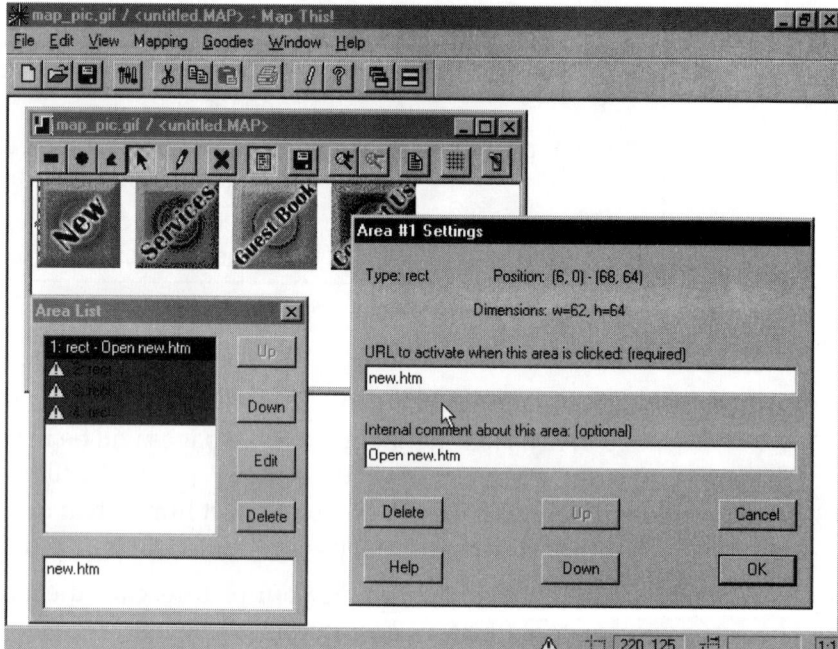

Figure 16-10: *Defined new.htm as the page to open when reader clicks my New button.*

5. Choose OK to save your change. Then start again at Step 2, defining the destination for the next hot spot, until you've defined a destination for every hot spot in the picture.

Figure 16-11 shows my screen after I defined the destinations for all four hot spots. The comments next to each item in the Area List give you a clue as to which rectangular hot spot opens which page.

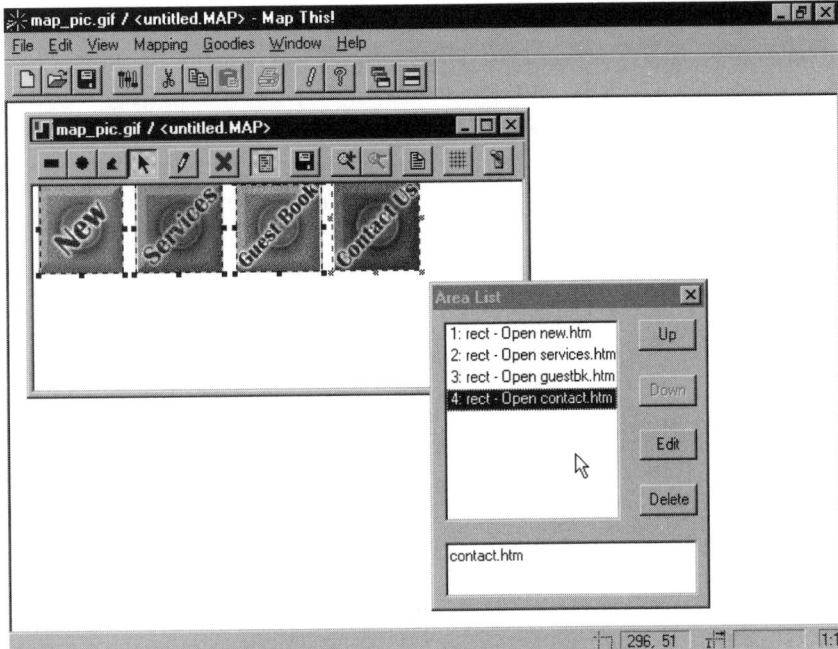

Figure 16-11: *All four hot spots and their actions, defined in my example.*

GENERATE & SAVE THE CODE

The final step in the process is to save all your work and let Map
This! generate the code that the map will need. I use the word *code*
here in the general sense of "instructions for a computer to read."
In this case, those instructions are going to be HTML tags. Here's
the next step:

1. Choose File | Save from the Map This! menu bar.

2. Choose the folder that holds the rest of your Web materials
   (e.g., My Web Site).

3. Type a new name for the generated code. I'll name mine
   map_code.htm.

4. Click the Save button.

5. Now you can close Map This! (Choose File | Exit, or click its Close (X) button.)

THE END RESULT

The end result of all you've done since you started up Map This! is a little file named map_code.htm (or, whatever name you assigned it in Step 3). This file contains the HTML commands that define the client-side image map. If you'd like to take a look at the file, follow these steps:

1. Starting from the Windows 95 desktop, click the Start button and choose Programs | Accessories | Notepad.

2. From Notepad's menu bar, choose File | Open.

3. In the Look in drop-down list, work your way to the folder that contains your map code (c:\My Web Site, in my example).

4. Under List Files of Type, choose All Files (*.*).

5. Scroll to and double-click on the name of the map file you created (map_code.htm, in my example).

Figure 16-12 shows what the map_code.htm file that I created looks like when it's in Notepad. In the next steps, which take place in Gold's editor and Notepad, you do the following:

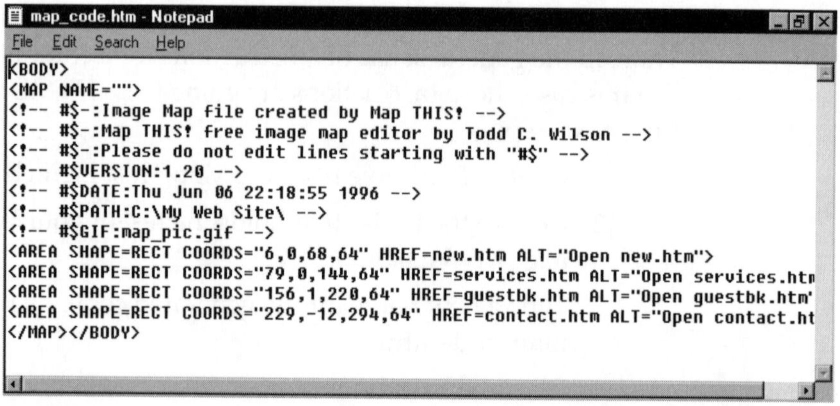

```
map_code.htm - Notepad
File   Edit   Search   Help
<BODY>
<MAP NAME="">
<!-- #$-:Image Map file created by Map THIS! -->
<!-- #$-:Map THIS! free image map editor by Todd C. Wilson -->
<!-- #$-:Please do not edit lines starting with "#$" -->
<!-- #$VERSION:1.20 -->
<!-- #$DATE:Thu Jun 06 22:18:55 1996 -->
<!-- #$PATH:C:\My Web Site\ -->
<!-- #$GIF:map_pic.gif -->
<AREA SHAPE=RECT COORDS="6,0,68,64" HREF=new.htm ALT="Open new.htm">
<AREA SHAPE=RECT COORDS="79,0,144,64" HREF=services.htm ALT="Open services.htm
<AREA SHAPE=RECT COORDS="156,1,220,64" HREF=guestbk.htm ALT="Open guestbk.htm"
<AREA SHAPE=RECT COORDS="229,-12,294,64" HREF=contact.htm ALT="Open contact.ht
</MAP></BODY>
```

Figure 16-12: *The file map_code.htm contains HTML tags generated by Map This!*

1. Put the image map in the Web page (if you haven't already done so).

2. Put the map code into the document source of that page.

3. Change the <img...> tag for the image, so that it "knows" to use the map source code to respond to readers' clicks in the picture.

We'll take it step-by-step in the sections that follow. For now, you can close Notepad if you wish.

PUT THE IMAGE IN THE PAGE

If you have not already done so, your next step is to put the image (map_pic.gif, in my example) into the Web page where it will be displayed (index.html, in my example). You can use the standard Gold techniques to do so:

1. Start up Netscape Navigator Gold (you need not be online).

2. Choose File | Open File in Editor, and use the Look in drop-down list to browse your way to the page's folder (My Web Site, in my example).

3. Open the page that will contain the image map (index.html, in my example).

4. Click about where you want the map to appear, and use the Insert Image button, or Insert | Image menu commands, to put the picture into your page.

In my example, I inserted my map_pic.gif file near the bottom of the page and centered it there, as you can see in Figure 16-13.

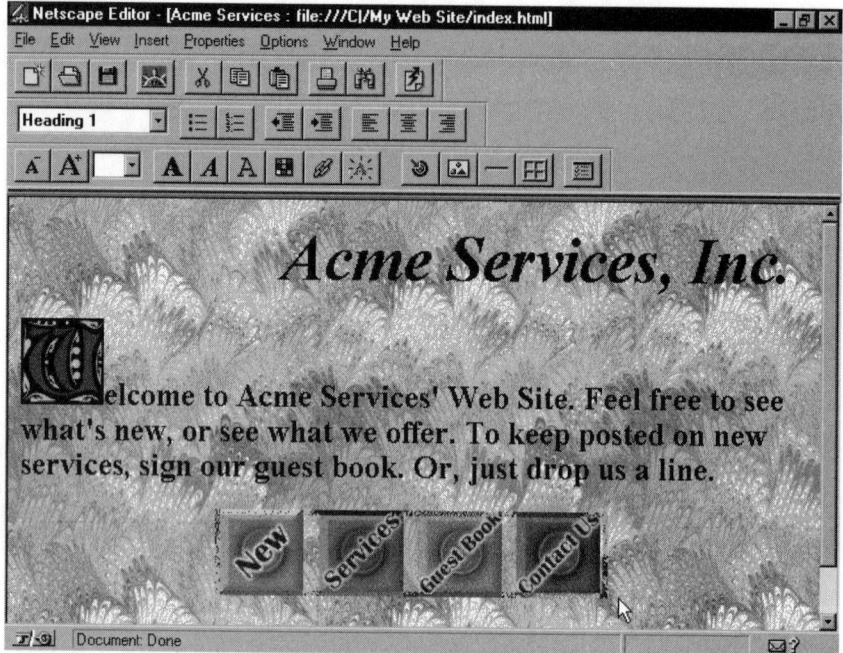

Figure 16-13: *My map_pic.gif file is in index.html.*

Copy the Map Code

Our next step is to copy the map code generated by Map This! to the Windows clipboard, so that we can paste its tags into index.html:

1. Click the Windows 95 Start button, and choose Programs | Accessories | Notepad.

2. In Notepad, choose File | Open, and open the file that contains the map code (c:\My Web Site\map_code.htm, in my example), using the same procedure described in Steps 3-5 in "The End Result" section, earlier in this chapter.

3. Using your mouse or the Shift+arrow keys, select everything between the <BODY>...</BODY> tags, but not the tags themselves, as I've done in Figure 16-14.

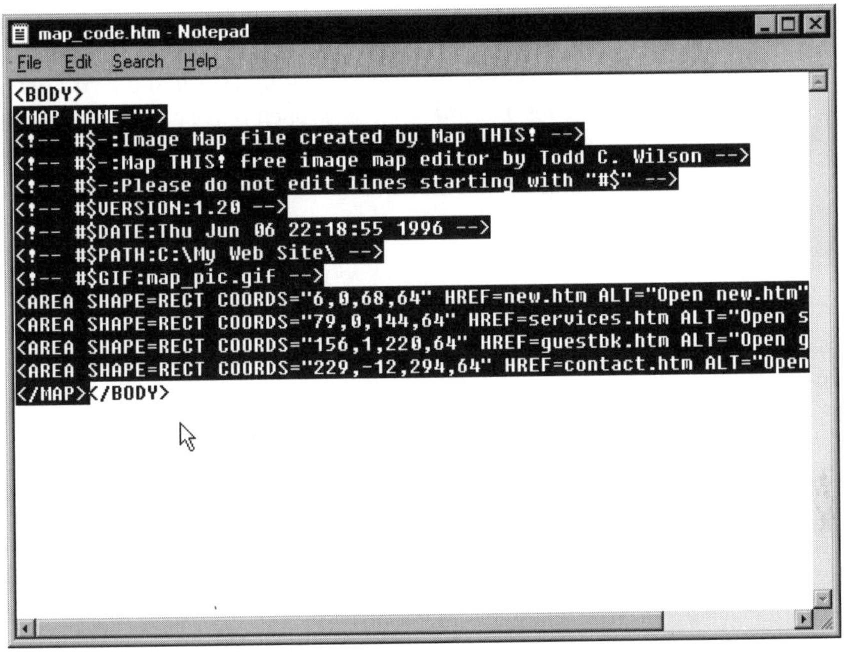

```
map_code.htm - Notepad                                    _ □ ×
File   Edit   Search   Help
<BODY>
<MAP NAME="">
<!-- #$-:Image Map file created by Map THIS! -->
<!-- #$-:Map THIS! free image map editor by Todd C. Wilson -->
<!-- #$-:Please do not edit lines starting with "#$" -->
<!-- #$VERSION:1.20 -->
<!-- #$DATE:Thu Jun 06 22:18:55 1996 -->
<!-- #$PATH:C:\My Web Site\ -->
<!-- #$GIF:map_pic.gif -->
<AREA SHAPE=RECT COORDS="6,0,68,64" HREF=new.htm ALT="Open new.htm"
<AREA SHAPE=RECT COORDS="79,0,144,64" HREF=services.htm ALT="Open s
<AREA SHAPE=RECT COORDS="156,1,220,64" HREF=guestbk.htm ALT="Open g
<AREA SHAPE=RECT COORDS="229,-12,294,64" HREF=contact.htm ALT="Open
</MAP></BODY>
```

Figure 16-14: *Code to be copied is selected in Notepad.*

4. Choose Edit | Copy from Notepad's menu bar (or press Ctrl+C) to copy the selection to the Windows clipboard.

Now you can close Notepad by choosing File | Exit or by clicking its Close (X) button.

PASTE THE MAP CODE INTO YOUR PAGE

Now we need to insert the code that's hidden in the Windows clipboard into the page that contains the map picture. If you've been following along, that page (index.html) is already on your screen in Gold's editor. Follow these steps to get to the source document for that page:

1. From Gold's menu bar, choose View | Edit Document Source.

TRAP

If you get an error message saying that you haven't defined a source editor yet, you must have skipped that part back in Chapter 15, "Tuning HTML Tags." To define an editor now, choose Yes in the message box, and type c:\windows\notepad.exe next to HTML source. Then click the OK button.

2. When a prompt asks whether you want to save recent changes, choose Yes.

3. You might want to enlarge the Notepad window to full-screen (double-click its title bar).

4. Look for the tag that defines the location of the image map. If you like, you can choose Search | Find, type the name of the image map file (**map_pic.gif**, in my example), click Find Next, and then click Cancel to get rid of the Find dialog box.

5. Position the cursor somewhere above the <img src...> tag that defines the picture. Make sure that you *don't* put the cursor in an existing tag. (In other words, the cursor should come after the > character that ends one tag, and before the < character that starts the next tag.)

6. Press Ctrl+V to insert the code you copied earlier from Notepad into the current page at the cursor location.

7. Move the cursor up near the top of the newly inserted code, positioning it right between the quotation marks in the following tag:

```
<MAP NAME="">
```

8. Type a name for this map. (Because this will be an "internal" name, it need not match any filenames.) In my example, I'll type **mapcode**, so that my tag looks like this:

```
<MAP NAME="mapcode">
```

9. Now move the cursor into the <img src...> tag that defines the picture, and place it (the cursor) just before the > in that tag.

10. Press the spacebar. Then type:

   `usemap =#`*`mapname`*

11. For *mapname*, substitute the name you entered in Step 8. In my example, where I named my map *mapcode*, I want the tag to look like this:

   `<img src="map_pic.gif" border=0 height=64 width=300`
   `usemap=#`**`mapcode`**`>`

Figure 16-15 shows the big picture. Notice that the tag <MAP NAME="mapcode"> marks the beginning of the code that Map This! generated for me. That chunk of code ends with </MAP>. The <img src...> tag for map_pic.gif now includes the attribute **usemap=#mapcode,** which is all it takes to make map_pic.gif into a clickable image map, using the information between the <MAP>...</MAP> tags as instructions as to where to take readers (based on where they click in the map).

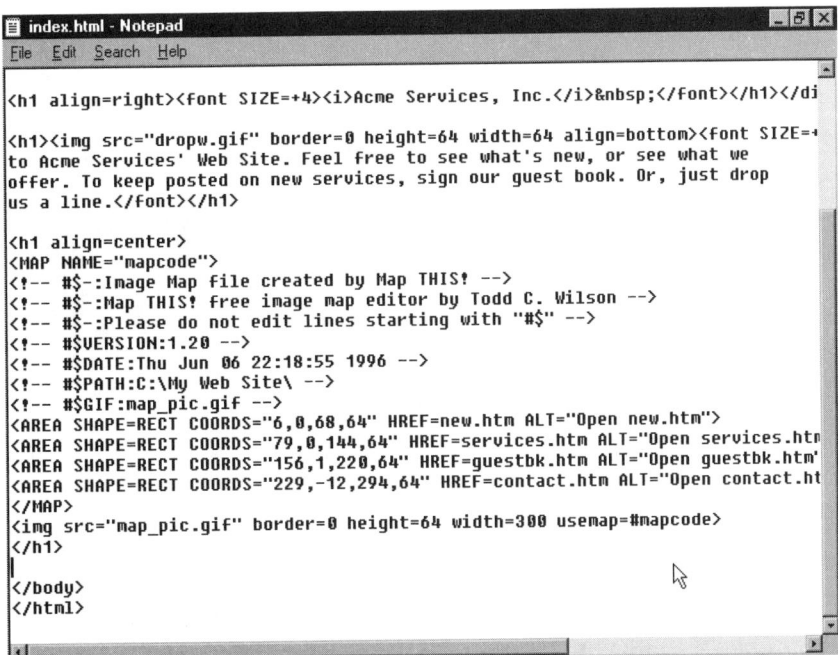

Figure 16-15: *Map code inserted and <img src..> tag for map_pic.gif modified to refer to that map code.*

You may now close Notepad, choose Yes when asked about saving your changes, and choose Yes again when asked about reloading the document.

TESTING THE MAP

When you return to Gold's editor, you'll see a bunch of little tag icons next to your image map. The icons indicate that there are tags behind the scenes that Gold's editor can't display. That's OK—all we care about here is whether the map works in the real browser. To find out, here's what you do:

1. Click the View in Browser button in Navigator's toolbar, or choose File | Browse Document from Navigator's menu bar.

2. Now rest the mouse pointer on one of the hot spots. If all went well, the status bar should show a message indicating where the hot spot will take you, as in Figure 16-16.

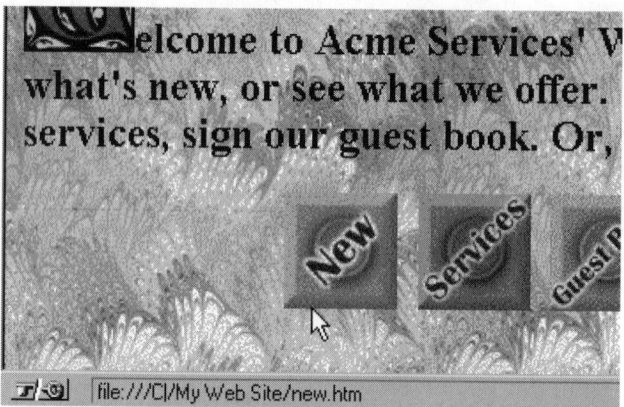

Figure 16-16: *The status bar displays the destination when the mouse pointer is resting on a hot spot.*

When you click the hot spot, the appropriate page should open. Clicking the Back button should take you back to the page that contains the image map. (If you have not yet created the page that the hot spot refers to, you'll get an error message indicating that the page doesn't exist—but at least you know the hot spot *tried* to open the requested page!)

When you upload your pages to your Web server for publication, remember to include the image map (map_pic.gif, in my example). It's not necessary to upload the generated code (map_code.htm, in my example) because that code has already been pasted into the Web page that contains the picture (index.html, in my example).

ALL THAT IN A NUTSHELL

As you've seen, many little steps are involved in creating a clickable image map. If we step back from the trees and take a look at the woods, however, the procedure is not particularly complicated. These are the basic steps:

1. Create a GIF or JPEG file that will act as the image map.

2. Use Map This! to define hot spots on the map, as well as where each hot spot will take the reader.

3. Insert the image map into the Web page that will display the map.

4. Insert into that same Web page the code generated by Map This!

5. Give the map a name in your Web page, then add **usemap =#*mapname*** to the <img src...> tag that displays the GIF or JPEG image.

Here's another way to look at it. The text that follows is the entire index.html file's source code, divided as follows:

■ *Italics*: Code (tags) generated by Map This! and pasted into index.html.

■ **Bold**: Stuff I typed manually.

■ Everything else: already created by Gold's editor.

```
<html>
<head>
   <title>Acme Services</title>
   <meta name="Author" content="Alan Simpson">
   <meta name="GENERATOR" content="Mozilla/3.0b4Gold
     (Win32)">
   <meta name="Description" content="Created on 8/15/96 using
     Netscape Navigator Gold 3.0.
     Copyright (c) 1996 by Alan Simpson.">

</head>
<body text="#000000" bgcolor="#FFFFFF"  link="#0000EE"
     vlink="#551A8B" alink="#FF0000" background=
     "crzylacl.gif">

<h1 align=right><font SIZE=+4><i>Acme Services, Inc.
     </i> </font></h1></div>

<h1><img src="dropw.gif" border=0 height=64 width=64
align=bottom><font SIZE=+2>elcome
to Acme Services' Web Site. Feel free to see what's new, or
see what we
offer. To keep posted on new services, sign our guest book.
Or, just drop
us a line.</font></h1>

<h1 align=center>
<MAP NAME="mapcode">
<!-- #$-:Image Map file created by Map THIS! -->
<!-- #$-:Map THIS! free image map editor by Todd C. Wilson-->
<!-- #$-:Please do not edit lines starting with "#$" -->
<!-- #$VERSION:1.20 -->
<!-- #$DATE:Thu Jun 06 22:18:55 1996 -->
<!-- #$PATH:C:\My Web Site\ -->
<!-- #$GIF:map_pic.gif -->
<AREA SHAPE=RECT COORDS="6,0,68,64" HREF=new.htm ALT="Open
new.htm">
<AREA SHAPE=RECT COORDS="79,0,144,64" HREF=services.htm
ALT="Open services.htm">
```

```
<AREA SHAPE=RECT COORDS="156,1,220,64" HREF=guestbk.htm
ALT="Open guestbk.htm">
<AREA SHAPE=RECT COORDS="229,-12,294,64" HREF=contact.htm
ALT="Open contact.htm">
</MAP>
<img src="map_pic.gif" border=0 height=64 width=300
usemap=#mapcode>
</h1>

</body>
</html>
end
```

TAGS FOR IMAGE MAPS

The tags generated by Map This! are "standard" HTML tags that you'll find in any current HTML Reference. Here's a summary of the tags that Map This! generates:

- <!...>: These are comments, which are ignored by the browser. But don't erase them because the Map This! program uses the information in the comments when you edit the image map. Also, the author of Map This! deserves the credit these tags give him.

- <MAP>...</MAP>: Marks the beginning and end of the actual image map. The NAME= attribute describes the name of this map, and is the name you must specify on the usemap=#*mapname* attribute of the <img> tag that defines the graphic image.

- <AREA...>: Defines a single hot spot area within the image by its shape (SHAPE=... attribute), pixel coordinates (COORDS=...), name of file/URL to jump to (HREF=... attribute), and alternative text for non-graphical browsers (ALT=...).

MODIFYING THE MAP

You can change the image map, the map code, or both at any time. Use Paint Shop Pro to modify the image map (the .gif file). Any changes you make to the picture, however, will *not* automatically be reflected in the code generated by Map This! You'll need to modify the map code as well.

To modify the map code, reopen the code file that you generated with Map This! That is:

1. Start Map This! on your PC.

2. From the Map This! menus, choose File | Open.

3. Get to the folder that contains the code generated by Map This!, and open that file (map_code.htm, in my example).

The map picture will appear in Map This! You can choose View | Area List to see the actions defined for each hot spot. You can now add, delete, and change hot spots and actions, using the same techniques you used to create them all in the first place. If you need any help, just choose Help from the Map This! menu bar.

If you do make changes, be sure to save them. Map This! will generate a new code file to reflect those changes, but the code in your Web page *will not* be updated to reflect those changes. To update the tags in your index.html (or whatever) page, you'll need to reopen that page in Notepad. Delete everything between the <MAP NAME=...> and </MAP> tags. Then copy and paste the new HTML tags from the new code file into the index.html page.

MOVING ON

By adding a clickable image map to your Web page, you definitely add a professional flair to your presentation. Dividing your presentation into *frames*, the topic of the next chapter, is another professional touch.

Get Framed

As you've browsed the Web you've probably come across Web sites that present their pages in frames. In this chapter you'll learn how to add frames to your own site. We'll cover the following topics:

- What are frames?
- Examples of sites that use frames well
- How to plan and implement your own frames
- How to target frames
- Supporting older Web browsers that can't show frames

When taken to extremes, frames, like any formatting feature, can hinder rather than help the reader's experience at your Web site. Before getting into the nitty-gritty details of how to create frames, I'd like to discuss what frames are really all about and then present some examples of sites that, in my opinion, use frames well.

WHAT ARE FRAMES?

In the olden days, Web browsers could show just one page at a time, much as early DOS PC's could display only one program at a time. Newer browsers, including Navigator 3.0, let you divide the reader's screen into separate *frames*. Each frame can show the contents of a different page in your site. Actually, each frame can point to its own individual URL.

The newer browsers work more like Windows. Just as Windows can display several programs at one time, Navigator 3.0 can display several Web pages simultaneously. Windows displays each program in its own *window*. Navigator displays each page in its own *frame*.

Frames give you, as author, tremendous flexibility in the way you present your Web site. You can display a logo that never changes as the reader moves from page to page. You can add navigation tools that make it easier for readers to get around in your site. A couple of examples will help illustrate this flexibility.

EXAMPLES OF FRAMED SITES

The home page for singer Carly Simon (http://www.ziva.com/carly), shown in Figure 17-1, uses frames effectively. The topmost frame displays the site name, *Carly Simon Online*. The leftmost frame acts as a Table of Contents (TOC) to all the different areas in the site. Neither of those frames ever change. For example, when I click Photographs in the left frame, I'm taken to the photos page. Only the larger display window changes (see Figure 17-2). The other two frames remain intact and neither the Carly Simon Online identity nor the Table of Contents is lost.

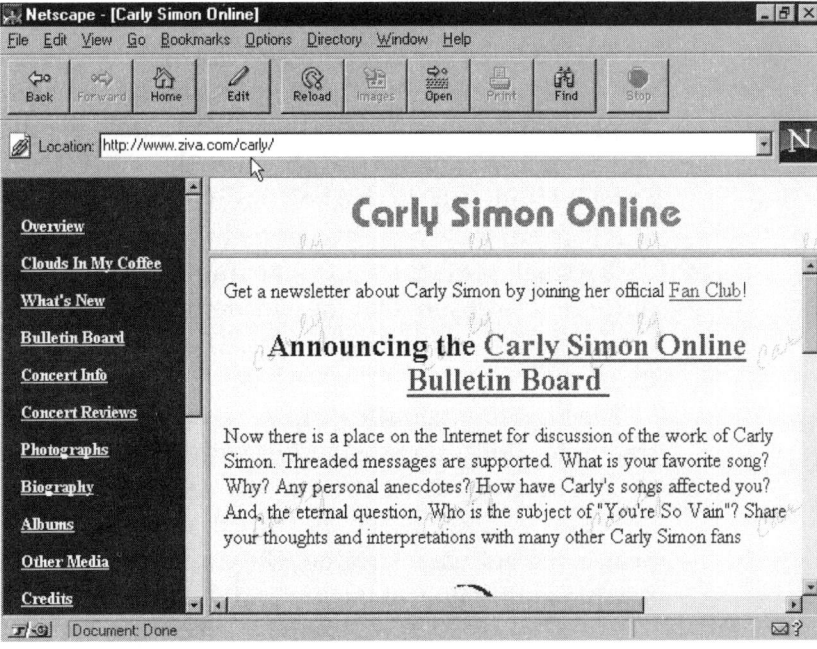

Figure 17-1: *Carly Simon Online uses frames to aid the reader.*

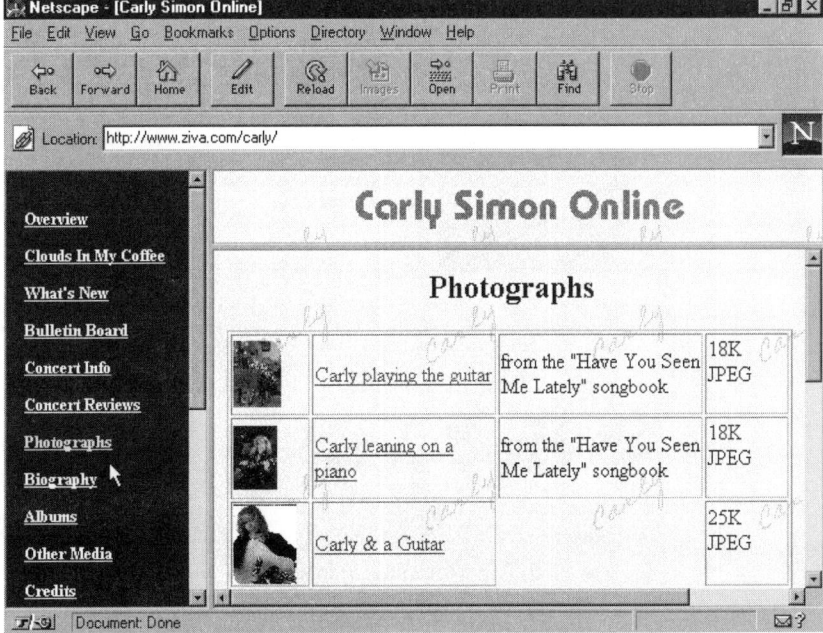

Figure 17-2: *Viewing a different page affects only the largest frame.*

Notice, in Figure 17-2, that the Table of Contents frame has its own scroll bar. I can scroll up and down through the table of contents without disrupting the contents of the other frames. The large display window also has its own scroll bars—a vertical scroll bar and a horizontal one. Again, because these scroll bars are for the current frame only, I can scroll through the Photographs page without disrupting the contents of any other frames.

The small Carly Simon Online frame has no scroll bar because its purpose is to ensure that the site identity, Carly Simon Online, stays on the reader's screen at all times. There is no place to scroll to in that frame.

The Big Mountain site (http://www.bigmtn.com/resort) uses frames to similar advantage, but with a different layout (see Figure 17-3). The main display frame is spread across the top of the window. Navigation tools, in the form of a clickable image map, appear in the bottom left frame. The company logo appears in a ledge (unchanging frame) at the lower right corner of the screen.

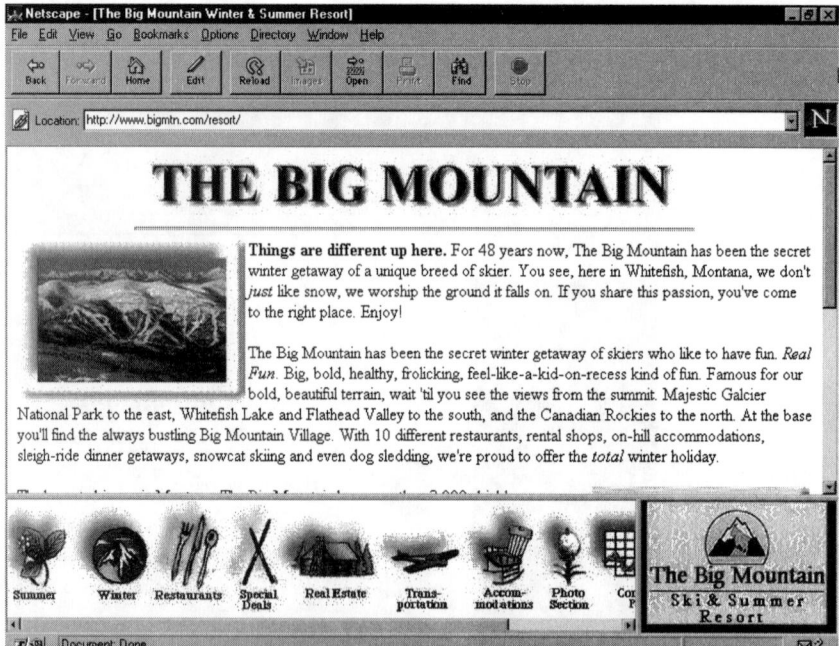

Figure 17-3: *Big Mountain displays page, navigation tools, and logo—each in a separate frame.*

TIP

Netscape uses the term ledge *to refer to an unscrollable frame that always shows the same information.*

An entirely different use of frames might be to set up multiple columns on a Web page, sort of like a newspaper. One frame across the top of the screen could act as a masthead. Two or more frames beneath the headline could act as columns, with each column displaying its own Web page or article, as in Figure 17-4.

Figure 17-4: *Frames used to give a newspaper appearance to a home page.*

These are just a few examples of ways you might use frames. For more examples (and inspiration), point your Web browser to http://home.netscape.com/comprod/products/navigator/ version_2.0/frames and check the demos and the *Companies Using Frames* link.

PLANNING YOUR FRAMES

Unfortunately, there are no simple WYSIWYG tools (that I know of) that let you just "draw" frames on your screen. You need to go right to the HTML source and manually type the appropriate tags. Before you do that, though, you should plan the way you want the site to look to the reader. You can sketch it out in your mind or on a piece of paper.

After you've decided how you want to divvy up the screen, I suggest you make some decisions about each frame. Namely:

- Give each frame a short name, such as TOC (Table of Contents) or Main.

- Decide roughly how much space on the screen each frame will occupy. You can think of this in terms of pixels, or the percent of total width/height of the screen, or in terms of "the rest of the available space."

- Decide which frames will be static (contents never change) and which will be scrollable.

- Decide which page (.HTM file or .GIF/.JEPG image) in your site each frame will display when the reader first opens the page.

When you finish planning, your sketch might look something like Figure 17-5. (My "sketch" is a screen shot of the Navigator window, with notes jotted on it. I wouldn't dare try to draw a "fake" Navigator window because I can't draw worth beans.)

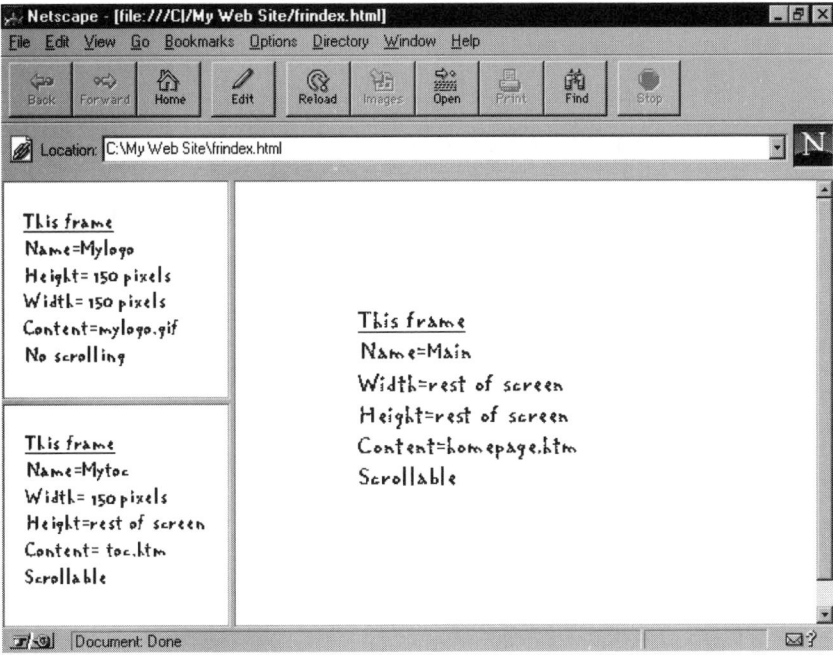

Figure 17-5: *Rough game plan for a framed site that will contain three frames.*

Notice that I've divided the display window into three frames named Mylogo, Mytoc, and Main. I've jotted down how much space each frame will use, which will have scrollbars, and which page each frame will initially display to the reader. This sketch need not be set in concrete. You can change and refine things as you go along. But having *some* idea of how you want to divvy up the screen makes it easier to create the HTML tags that define the frames.

PLANNING THE CONTENTS

Next, you might want to think about what you'll put in each frame. In this chapter, the goal is to create a site, named Daily Dose, that looks something like Figure 17-6. You might want to sketch out the look and feel on paper first. Since I can't draw worth beans, I opted to show the actual logo and table of contents.

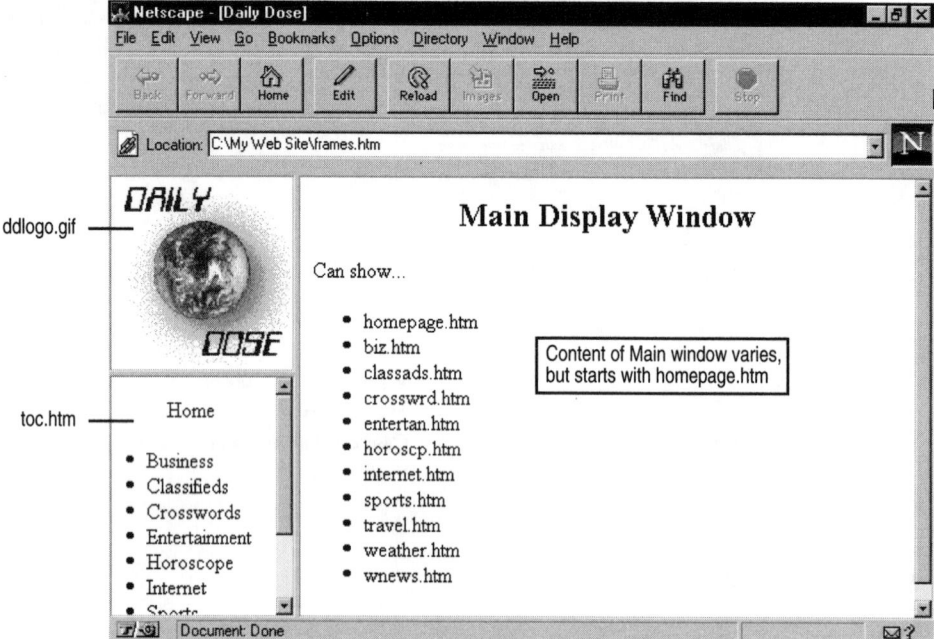

Figure 17-6: *The goal of this chapter.*

CREATING THE PAGES

You don't have to create every page in the Web site before you create the frames, but if you haven't created the pages yet, you should at least create some "dummy" pages. That way, you'll be able to create your table of contents page with real links and test the frames. In the next few sections I create some pages for the Daily Dose site.

THE DDLOGO.GIF IMAGE

The first (upper left) frame in Daily Dose will display the site logo. As you may recall, I've defined that first column as being 150 pixels wide and the first row in that column as 150 pixels tall. Thus, my logo should fit into a 150 x 150 pixel box.

As it turns out, a picture that's about 10 pixels smaller than the box fits best into the box—perhaps because the bars that surround the frames use up pixels. In this case, a logo sized at about 140 x 140 pixels would probably work best. Figure 17-7 shows that picture, which I created in Paint Shop Pro. (The status bar shows 140 x 140 x 256 because the picture has a depth of 256 colors.)

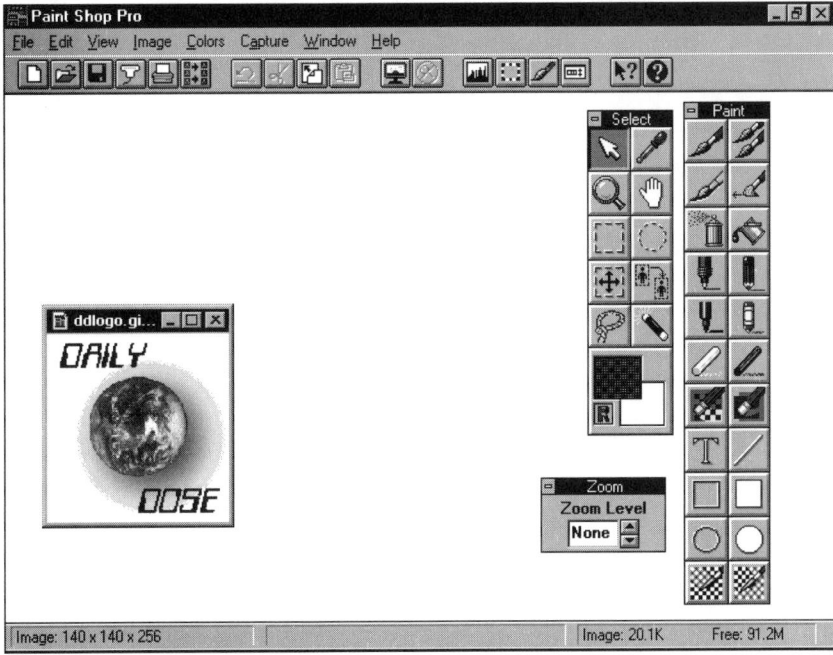

Figure 17-7: *ddlogo.gif in Paint Shop Pro, measuring 140 x 140 pixels.*

I'll name this picture ddlogo.gif and store it in the folder that holds the rest of the materials for this Web site (My Web Site).

THE MAIN DISPLAY PAGES

The main display pages can be created in Netscape Navigator Gold's editor. For the moment, I'll just create dummy pages that show only the name of the page. These will be good for testing purposes, as you'll see. Figure 17-8 shows one of the dummy pages, named homepage.htm in this example.

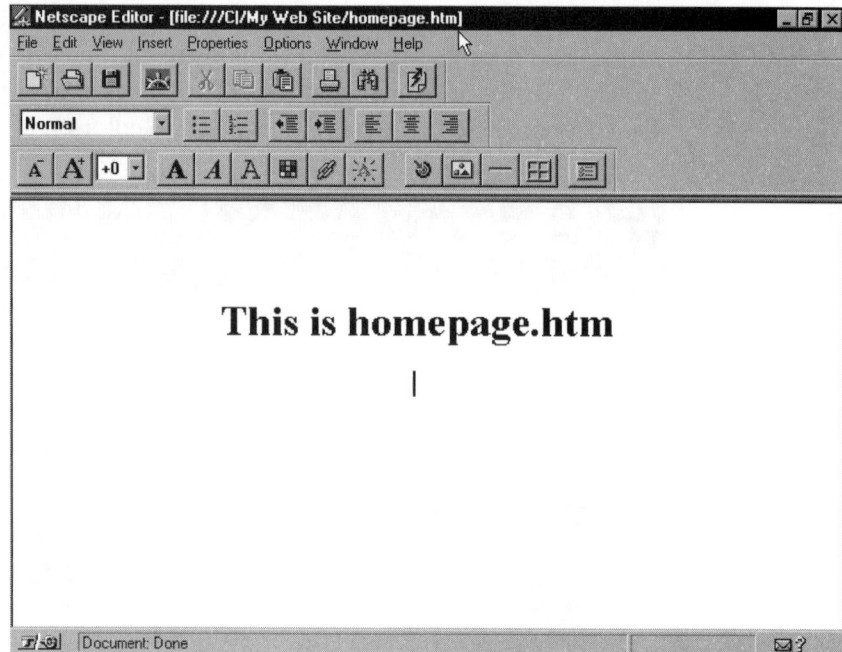

Figure 17-8: *Create several "dummy" pages like this one to test the frames.*

Because my Table of Contents is going to give the reader access to several pages, I'll create a dummy page for each of those pages. The names of those dummy pages follow:

- homepage.htm
- biz.htm
- classads.htm
- crosswrd.htm
- entertan.htm
- horoscp.htm
- internet.htm
- sports.htm
- travel.htm
- weather.htm
- wnews.htm

The easiest way to create these pages is to simply change the filename shown in the page (e.g., change homepage.htm to biz.htm). Then use File | Save As to save the page with that new name (e.g., biz.htm). Don't forget to put all the pages in the same folder that holds the rest of your Web site materials.

THE TABLE OF CONTENTS PAGE

Last but not least comes the Table of Contents page. This is a regular Web page that you can create with Gold and name toc.htm. The one thing to keep in mind is that the frame displaying this page will be only 150 pixels wide. Therefore, you want to keep each line of text short and close to the left margin.

Figure 17-9 shows the toc.htm page I created in this example using Gold's editor. In the figure, I'm just finishing defining the last hyperlink from the Word News entry to the page named wnews.htm. Here are some tips on how I created the toc.htm page:

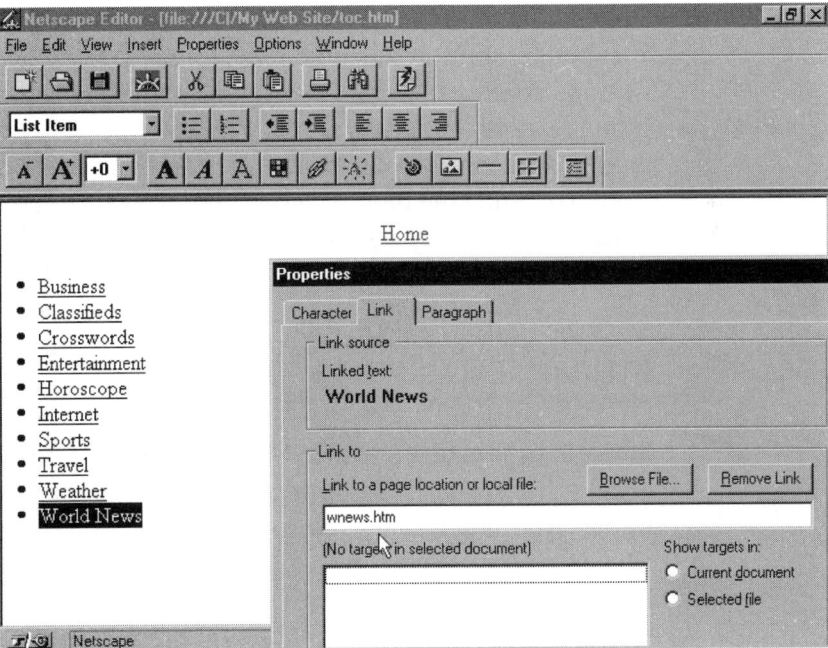

Figure 17-9: *My toc.htm page, with hyperlinks to "dummy" pages.*

- I used the Center button to center the Home title, so that it will also be centered within its narrow frame.

- I typed the list exactly as shown, initially pressing Enter after each item. Then I selected the entire list and clicked the Bullet List button in the toolbar to add the bullets and single-space the list.

- To reduce the level of indentation of the bulleted list, I selected the entire list and clicked the Decrease Indent button in the toolbar.

- To make each entry a hyperlink, I selected the entry, clicked the Make Link button in the toolbar, and specified the name of the file that the link points to.

What I've done here, essentially, is create a normal Web site, in which the "dummy" pages are the standard Web pages used in any site. What makes this effort unique are the small 140 x 140 "stand-alone" graphic image and the narrow Table of Contents, each of which will be displayed in its own frame.

I should mention that if you've already created a standard Web site, you can use its pages instead of creating new "dummy" pages. When readers first visit your site, however, you're going to want the page that sets up the frames to open first. Therefore, you might want to change the name of your home page from index.html (or whatever) to homepage.htm, or some other name that will prevent the Web server from opening that page first.

FRAME TAGS

In Gold there is no built-in WYSIWYG tool that you can use to "draw" frames easily. As far as I know, the only way to set up frames is to *hard code* the appropriate HTML tags the old-fashioned way—by typing them into a simple text editor like Notepad. For this reason, you really need to understand the various tags and attributes required to make frames happen.

Whoops - I spoke too soon. Just as this book was going to press I discovered two programs designed to take some of the drudgery out of creating framed sites. One is called Frame Gang and is available from http://www.sausage.com. The other is called FrameIt for Windows 95 available from http://www.iinet.net.au/~bwk/frame-it1.html.

THE <FRAMESET>...</FRAMESET> TAGS

You define the general layout of the frames in a site by using one or more pairs of <frameset>...</frameset> tags. The <frameset> tag has two attributes: rows and cols. Each attribute is followed by a *value list* that defines the number of frames and the size of each frame in the frameset. The number for these values can be expressed in one of the following three ways:

- Pixels: If you specify a row or column size as a number (such as 100), the browser interprets that as a specific size in pixels.

- Percent: If you specify a row or column size as a percent (such as 50%), the browser calculates the size as a percentage of however many pixels are on the reader's screen.

- * (rest of screen): If you specify a row or column size as an asterisk (*), the browser interprets that as "the rest of the space available on the screen." Multiple asterisks can be used to proportion the available space. For example, "*,*" would create two equal-sized rows or columns.

The first measurement, Pixels, is absolute (fixed). The Percent and "rest of" (*) measurements are relative. Both are very useful because you can't predict exactly how may pixels will be on your reader's screen. Some people browse at 640 x 480 pixels, others at 800 x 600 or 1024 x 768 pixels. The percent and * measurements let you think in terms of relative screen space. Some examples of <frameset> tags should help you understand.

In this first example, the tags divide the screen into two columns: The first column is to be 200 pixels wide and the second column equals "the rest of the pixels on the reader's screen":

```
<frameset cols = "200,*">
...
</frameset>
```

In this example, the tags divide the screen into three rows. The first and last rows are each 25% of the screen height and the row between them is all the rest of the screen space:

```
<frameset rows = "25%,*,25%">
...
</frameset>
```

The first tag *under* a <frameset> tag defines the first frame created by the <frameset> tag. That next tag might be another <frameset>...</frameset> pair of tags that subdivides the first frame. Or it may be a <frame name...> tag the defines the entire frame. Let's look at the <frame name> tag next.

THE <FRAME NAME> TAG

The <frame name...> tag (also referred to as the *frame tag*) defines a single frame within a frameset. The <frame> tag has several optional attributes: name, src, marginwidth, marginheight, scrolling, and noresize. There is no closing </frame> tag.

THE NAME ATTRIBUTE

The name attribute lets you give each frame a unique name to make referring to a specific frame later easier to do. The name must begin with an alphanumeric character.

THE SRC ATTRIBUTE

The src (source) attribute defines what appears first in the frame. The source can be the name of a page in your own Web site, a URL that points to some other site, or even the name of a GIF or JPEG file.

THE MARGINWIDTH ATTRIBUTE

The marginwidth attribute defines the width, in pixels, of the left and right margins in the frame. When this attribute is omitted, the reader's Web browser assigns margins automatically. As a general rule, you'll want to set marginwidth = 0 if the frame will contain a picture (GIF or JPEG) or a clickable image map. If the frame will contain text, omit this attribute or set marginwidth=3 or greater.

THE MARGINHEIGHT ATTRIBUTE

The marginheight attribute defines, in pixels, the height of the top and bottom margins in the frame. As a general rule, you'll want to set marginheight = 0 if the frame will contain a picture (GIF or JPEG) or a clickable image map. If the frame will contain text, omit this attribute or set marginheight=2 or greater.

THE SCROLLING ATTRIBUTE

The scrolling attribute determines whether the frame has its own scroll bar. The options are yes (scroll bars are always visible), no (scroll bars are never visible), and auto (scroll bars are visible only when needed). If you omit this attribute, the auto option is assumed.

THE NORESIZE ATTRIBUTE

By default, frames can be resized by the reader, just by dragging the border that separates a couple frames. If you don't want the reader to resize your frames, add the noresize attribute to the <frame> tag. Be aware that *any* frame adjacent to a nonresizable edge will also be nonresizable after you define the noresize attribute.

CREATING THE FRAMES

Now we need to create a Web page that defines the frames for our site. Because Gold isn't going to help here, we'll use the Windows Notepad program instead. You can close any open programs, including Navigator and Paint Shop Pro, if you wish. Then follow these steps to get started:

1. At the Windows 95 desktop, click the Start button and choose Programs | Accessories | NotePad.

2. Just so that you don't forget to do so later, choose File | Save now and save this new document to the folder that holds your other site materials (e.g., My Web Site), using whatever filename you wish. (I'll use frames.htm.)

3. Because you're starting from scratch, you need to type the mandatory tags that Gold usually puts in for you. Type these *exactly* as shown in Figure 17-10.

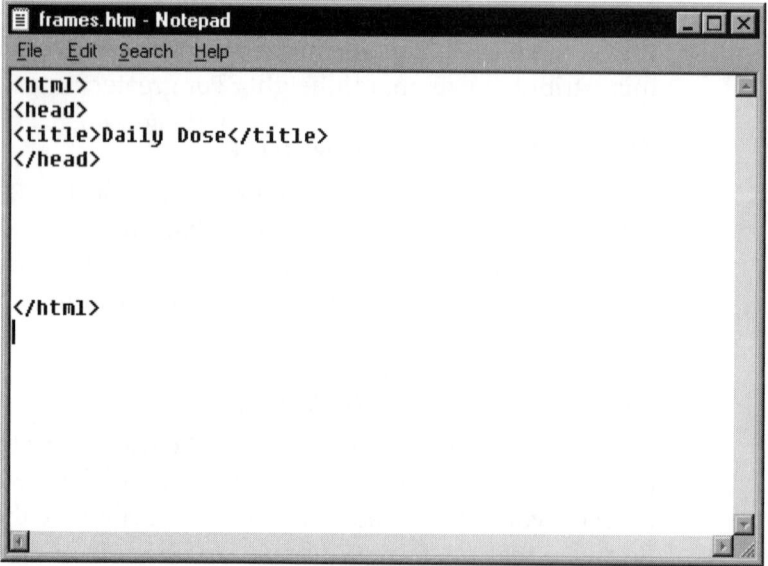

Figure 17-10: *The mandatory tags, typed into frames.htm.*

TRAP

When you're typing tags manually, there is no margin for error. Every angle bracket (<>), quotation mark ("), and so forth must be in place. Otherwise the page will either act weird, or not appear at all, when you attempt to view it later with your Web browser.

Now you can start entering the <frameset>...</frameset> tags to define the frames, as discussed next.

DEFINE THE ROWS & COLUMNS

The next step is to type the <frameset> and <frame> tags to define your frames. These tags start under the head section, just below the </head> tag. I'm going to have you type some *comments* (tags that all browsers will ignore) also. These comment tags start with <! and end with >, and are in the page only for your future reference.

Our first goal is to divide the screen into two columnar frames, the first of which is 150 pixels wide, with the second being the rest of the screen width. Because every <frameset> tag needs a closing </frameset> tag, you might as well type that tag now, too. Type the following tags right under the </head> tag, as shown in Figure 17-11.

```
<!Create two columnwise frames>
<frameset cols="150,*">


</frameset>
```

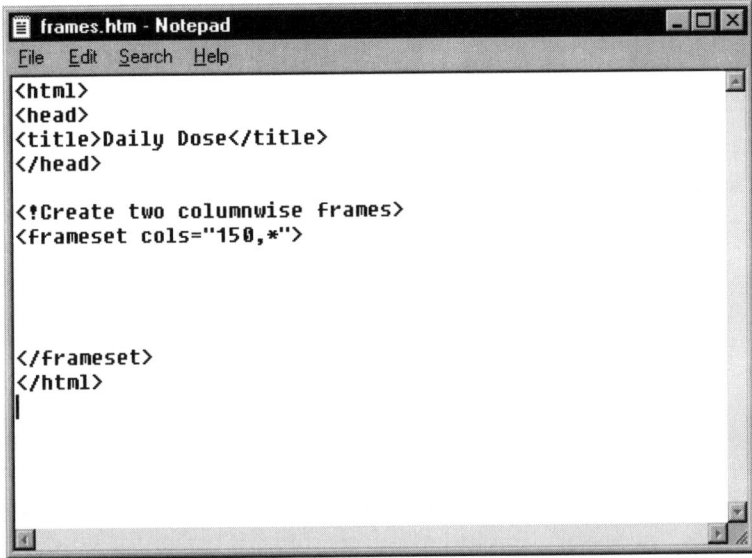

```
frames.htm - Notepad
File   Edit  Search  Help
<html>
<head>
<title>Daily Dose</title>
</head>

<!Create two columnwise frames>
<frameset cols="150,*">




</frameset>
</html>
```

Figure 17-11: *Getting started typing the <frameset> tags.*

The browser will "expect" the first tag under the <frameset> tag to define the first frame in the new frameset. As you may recall, we planned back in Figure 17-5 to break the first column into two rows. The <frameset>...</frameset> tags for the rows must be nested within the tags that defined the columns and should start right after the <frameset> tag for the columns. Therefore, you need to type the following <frameset> tags between the existing frameset tags, as shown in Figure 17-12.

```
<!Split first column into two rows>
<frameset rows="150,*">


</frameset>
```

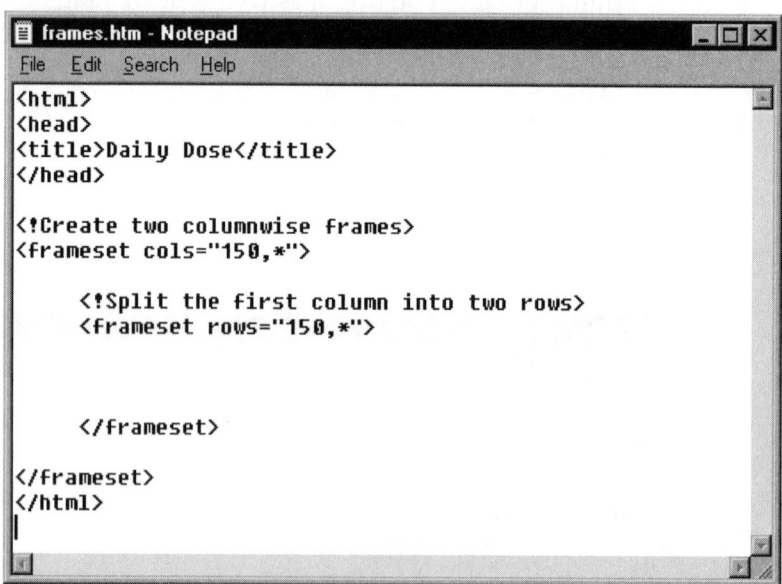

Figure 17-12: *Frameset tags for the rows nested within the frameset tags for the columns.*

You might notice that I've indented this nested pair of <frameset>...</frameset> tags, just by typing a few blank spaces at the start of each line. Although indenting the tags is not technically necessary, the indentations make it easier for you, the "programmer," to see how tags for the rows are nested within the tags for the columns.

DEFINE THE INDIVIDUAL FRAMES

Now that you've laid out the columns and rows, you can define the individual frames and their initial contents. Use the *name=* attribute to name each frame, and the *src=* (source) attribute to define the initial contents. You can also define any optional attributes, such as margins and scrolling, at this time.

The first frame definition under that new <frameset> tag is assigned automatically to the first (top or left) frame in the frameset. As you may recall, we plan to put a logo in that frame. Type the following tags directly under the <frameset rows=...> tag:

```
<!Define the first (top left) frame>
<frame name="Mylogo" src="ddlogo.gif" marginwidth=0
marginheight=0 scrolling="no">

<!Define second (bottom left) frame>
<frame name="Mytoc">
```

When you've finished typing the tags your page should look like Figure 17-13.

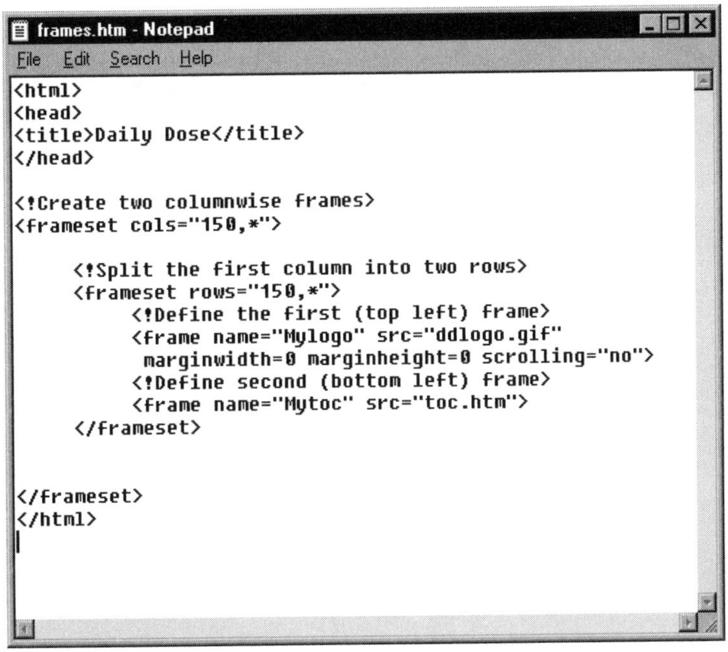

```
frames.htm - Notepad
File  Edit  Search  Help
<html>
<head>
<title>Daily Dose</title>
</head>

<!Create two columnwise frames>
<frameset cols="150,*">

     <!Split the first column into two rows>
     <frameset rows="150,*">
          <!Define the first (top left) frame>
          <frame name="Mylogo" src="ddlogo.gif"
           marginwidth=0 marginheight=0 scrolling="no">
          <!Define second (bottom left) frame>
          <frame name="Mytoc" src="toc.htm">
     </frameset>


</frameset>
</html>
```

Figure 17-13: *The two frames in the left column are defined.*

Next, you want to identify the third frame. Because this third frame is actually the entire second column, it must be defined within the <frameset> tags for the columns. We want this column to appear after (to the right of) the two-row column. Be sure to type these tags *under* the </frameset> tag that ends the row definition, but *above* the </frameset> tag that ends the column definition, as shown in Figure 17-14.

```
<! Define third frame (entire second column)>
<frame name="Main" src="homepage.htm">
```

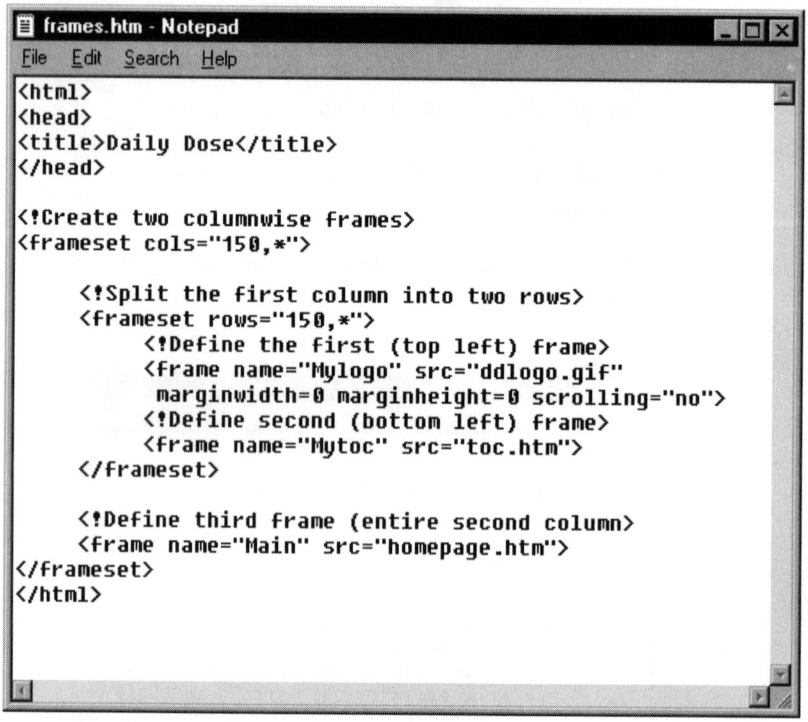

```
frames.htm - Notepad
File  Edit  Search  Help
<html>
<head>
<title>Daily Dose</title>
</head>

<!Create two columnwise frames>
<frameset cols="150,*">

    <!Split the first column into two rows>
    <frameset rows="150,*">
        <!Define the first (top left) frame>
        <frame name="Mylogo" src="ddlogo.gif"
         marginwidth=0 marginheight=0 scrolling="no">
        <!Define second (bottom left) frame>
        <frame name="Mytoc" src="toc.htm">
    </frameset>

    <!Define third frame (entire second column)>
    <frame name="Main" src="homepage.htm">
</frameset>
</html>
```

Figure 17-14: *All frames are defined. All done!*

CHECKING YOUR FRAMES

After you have all the <frameset> and <frame> tags in place, you can take a look at the page in a browser to make sure you've defined them correctly. Follow these steps:

1. Close Notepad and save your changes (choose File | Exit | Yes).

2. Use My Computer, Find, or Explorer in Windows to locate your frames.htm file. Then double-click that filename.

If you typed everything exactly right, you should be able to see the framed site and appropriate contents of each frame, as in Figure 17-15. Success! (Sort of.) We do have one problem to deal with, as you'll see in a moment.

If you click one of the links in the Table of Contents, the new page shows up in the Mytoc frame (see Figure 17-16), *not* in the Main frame (where we want it to appear). To fix that problem, you need to learn about targeting frames, discussed in the next section.

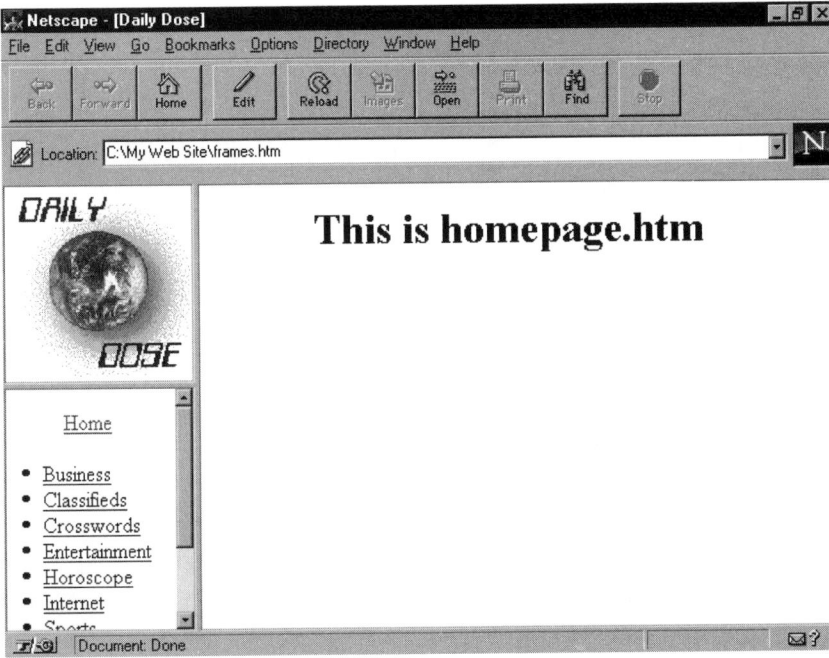

Figure 17-15: *At first glance my framed site looks good.*

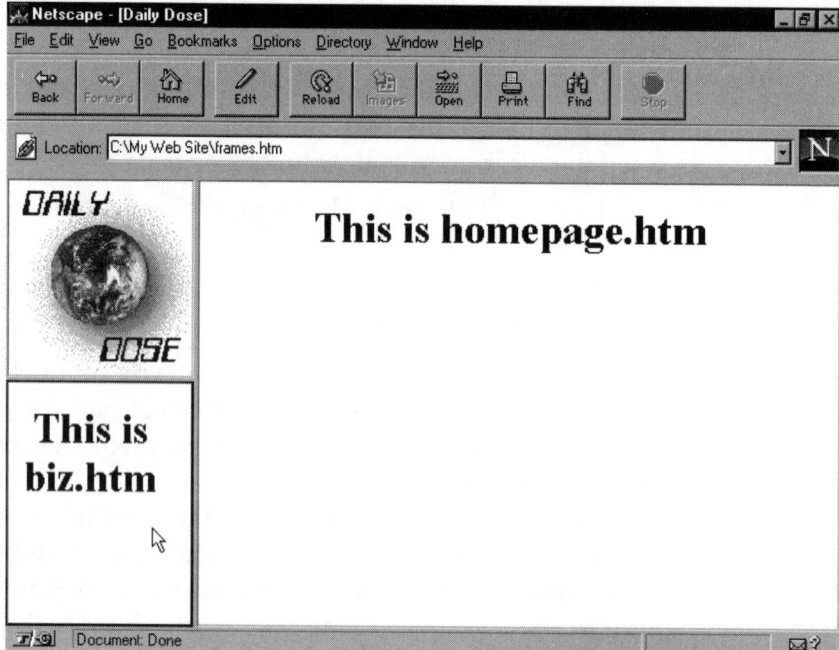

Figure 17-16: *On closer inspection, biz.htm pops up in the wrong frame.*

By the way, to get back to the Table of Contents, you can just right-click the frame in which biz.htm is currently displayed, and choose Back to move back a page in that frame. But we still need to fix this site so that it works correctly.

TARGETING FRAMES

If you got as far as Figure 17-16, you can see we have a problem. When you click a hyperlink in the Mytoc frame, the requested page appears in that Mytoc frame, not in the Main frame where we'd like it to appear. The reason? Well, after you set up frames, simply telling a hyperlink to "display this page" or "go to that URL" is not sufficient. You now need to specify *where* to display the requested page. That is to say, you need to specify which frame the requested page will appear in.

You can use a couple of techniques to define the *target* (the frame) where a requested page will appear. The simplest is to insert a single <base target...> tag that defines a target frame for all the links in the current page. Optionally, you can add a *target=* attribute to each hyperlink tag to specify where that link should display the requested page. Because the <base target...> tag approach is easiest, let's do that now. Follow these steps:

1. From Navigator's menu bar, choose File | Open File in Editor, then open your toc.htm page.

2. Because you need to insert a single tag, choose Insert | HTML Tag.

3. Type the following line:

   ```
   <base target="Main">
   ```

   as shown in Figure 17-17.

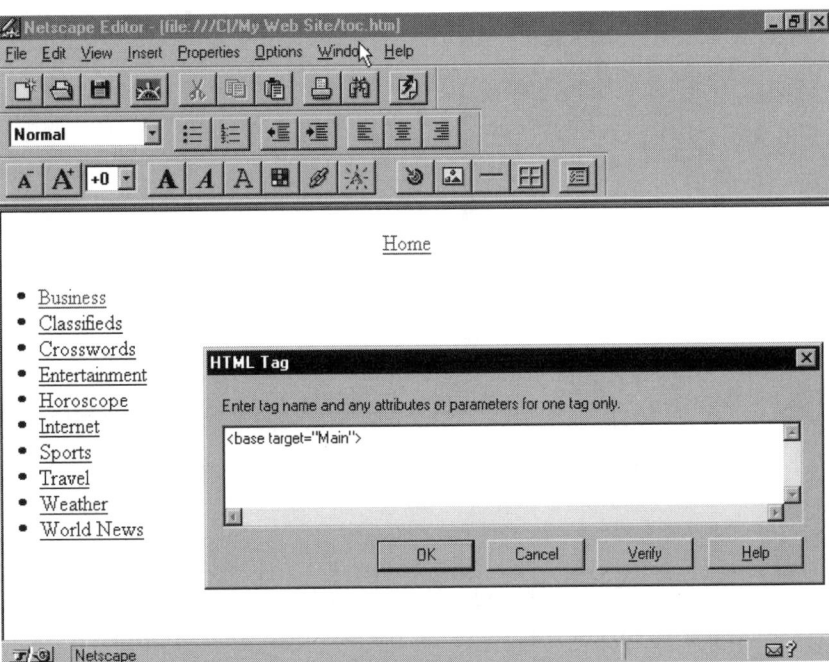

Figure 17-17: *Defining the Main window as target for hyperlinks in toc.htm.*

4. Choose OK. A tag icon appears in your page.

5. Close and save everything. That is, click the Close button in the Netscape editor and choose Yes when asked about saving. Then close down Netscape Navigator as well.

Now we can try again from a clean start. Once again, using Windows's My Computer, Find, or Windows Explorer, locate and double-click your frames.htm file. This time, when you click the Business link in the Table of Contents, the biz.htm page will show up in the Main window, as in Figure 17-18.

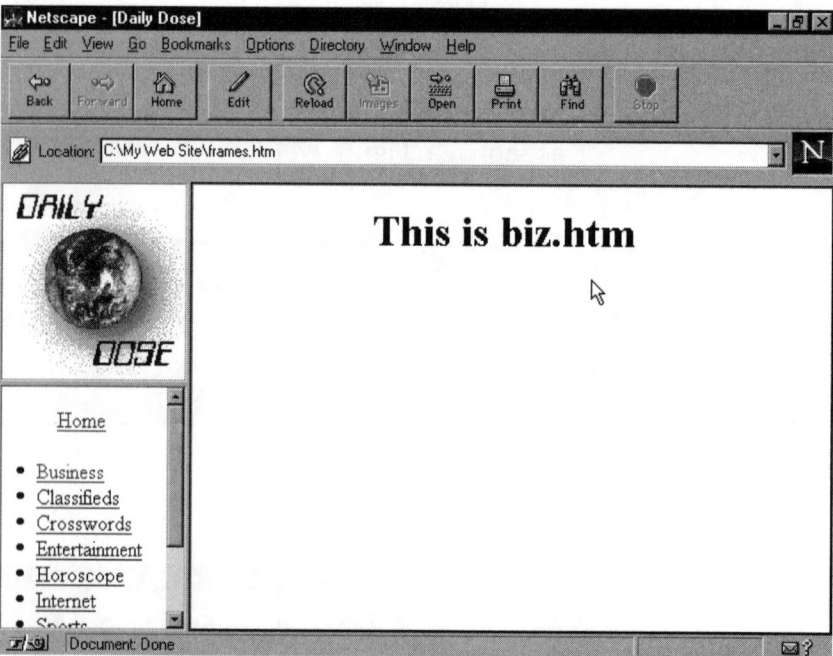

Figure 17-18: *Now clicking on the Business link displays biz.htm in the Main window.*

As mentioned, the <base target=...> tag is just one way to define a target frame for all the hyperlinks in a page. You can also control the target for individual hyperlinks in a page, as described in the next two sections.

TARGETING FROM <A HREF> TAGS

Your typical hyperlink is an <a href=...> tag, in which *href* specifies the filename or URL of the page to load, as in the following example:

```
<a href="biz.htm">Business</a>
```

To change that tag so that the biz.htm page appears in a specific frame, add the target=*"frame name"* attribute to the opening <A> tag. For example, the following tag sends biz.htm to a frame named Main:

```
<a href="biz.htm" target="Main">Business </A>
```

TARGETING FROM <AREA> TAGS

As you may have noticed in the previous chapter, client-side image mapping uses <area> tags to define links from hot spots to specific Web pages. For example, when a reader clicks the hot spot that follows, it displays a page named biz.htm:

```
<area shape=rect coords="81,5,154,26" href="biz.htm">
```

In a frame-aware site, you can add a target= attribute to the <area> tag to define the frame in which the content will appear. For example, if you want to display biz.htm in the frame named Main, you'd need to alter that <area...> tag like this:

```
<area shape=rect coords="81,5,154,26" href=biz.htm
target="Main">
```

MAGIC TARGET NAMES

For future reference, I should also point out that there are four "magic" target names you can specify next to *target=*. You can use one of these magic names in lieu of a specific name. Note that each of these magic names begins with an underscore.

TARGET = "_BLANK"

The _blank target name causes the new page to be displayed in a new, empty Navigator window. This new Netscape Navigator application window replaces the framed window. When the reader clicks the Back button to back out of that page, the Netscape Navigator window that shows the framed site reappears. This is useful for displaying other people's Web sites *outside* your own frames.

TARGET="_SELF"

The _self target name displays the new page in the same window in which the link is located. This name overrides the frame name specified in a <base target=...> tag. For example, the tag <a href="toc2.htm" target="_self"> displays the page named toc2.htm in the current frame, not the frame specified in the <base target...> tag.

TARGET="_PARENT"

The term "parent" in frames refers to the <frameset> tag above the tag that defines the current frame. In deeply nested frames, the _parent target name causes the new content to appear in the immediate frameset parent of the document. This is the same as "_self" when the current frame has no parent.

TARGET="_TOP"

This target causes the new content to be displayed on a full screen, and can be used to break out of deeply nested frames. In other words, "_top" specifies a frame that's above all the parent frames.

For more information on these magic names, refer to any of the electronic references discussed in Chapter 15, "Tuning HTLM Tags."

SUPPORTING FRAME-DEAD BROWSERS

Not all browsers support frames. For people who will visit your Web site with frame-incapable browsers, you can create a regular home page, with your logo and hyperlinks right on that page. For example, in Figure 17-19 I've used Gold's editor to create a home page with the logo, some text, and hyperlinks right on the page, so that browsers that can't see the frame still have access to those elements.

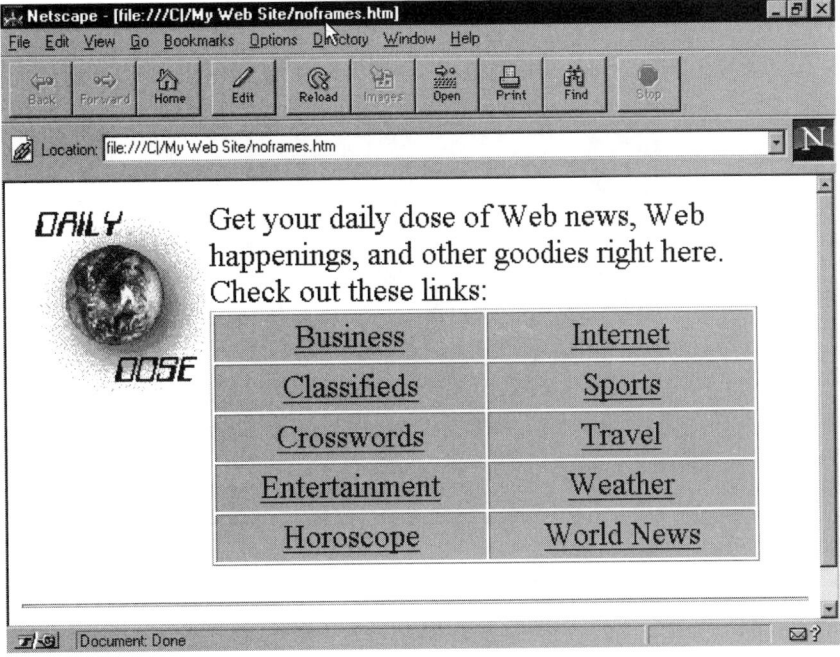

Figure 17-19: *A home page for frame-incapable browsers.*

To display this page to frame-incapable browsers only, you'll need to put everything between the page's <body>...</body> tags (inclusive) between a pair of <noframes>...</noframes> tags in the page that defines the frames (frames.htm, in this example). Here's how to do that:

1. With your no-frames page visible in Navigator, go to Gold's editor (click the Edit button). Then choose View | Edit Document Source.

2. In Notepad, select (by dragging the mouse pointer through) everything below the closing </head> tag down to (but excluding) the closing </html> tag (see Figure 17-20). In other words, you want to select everything from <body> to </body>, inclusive.

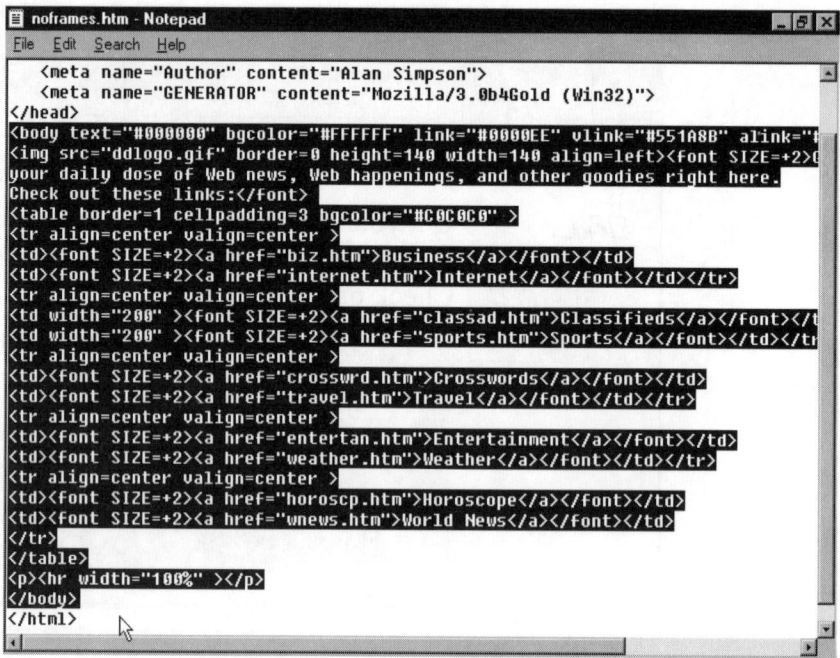

Figure 17-20: *Select everything from the opening <body> tag to the closing </body> tag, inclusive.*

3. Press Ctrl+C to copy the entire selection to the Windows clipboard.

4. Close Notepad and all your Navigator windows.

5. At the Windows 95 desktop, click the Start button and choose Programs I Accessories I Notepad.

6. From Notepad's menu bar, choose File I Open and open the page that defines your site's frames. (That would be frames.htm in the My Web Site folder, using my example.)

7. Now move the cursor just to the right of or below the first <frameset> tag, then type a pair of <noframes>... </noframes> tags, with a blank line between them, as in Figure 17-21.

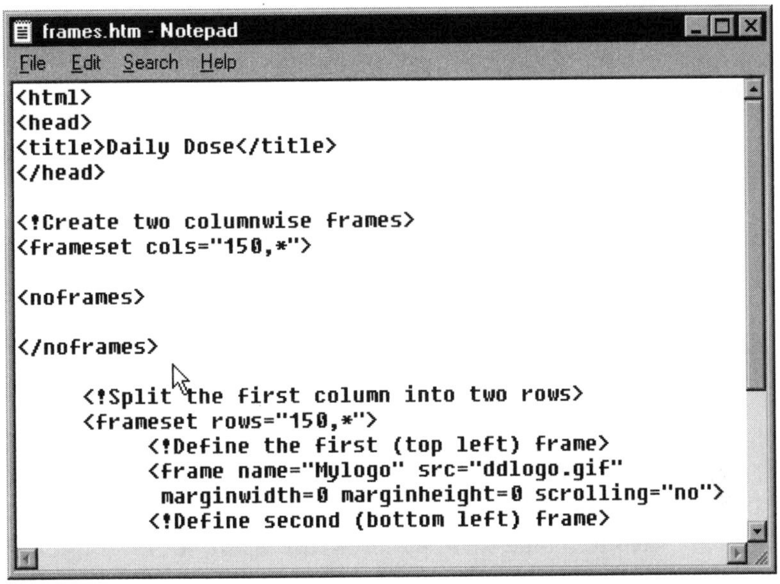
frames.htm - Notepad
File Edit Search Help

```
<html>
<head>
<title>Daily Dose</title>
</head>

<!Create two columnwise frames>
<frameset cols="150,*">

<noframes>

</noframes>

     <!Split the first column into two rows>
     <frameset rows="150,*">
          <!Define the first (top left) frame>
          <frame name="Mylogo" src="ddlogo.gif"
           marginwidth=0 marginheight=0 scrolling="no">
          <!Define second (bottom left) frame>
```

Figure 17-21: *<noframes>...</noframes> tags added to frames.htm.*

8. Put the cursor between the <noframes> and </noframes> tags, then press Ctrl+V to insert between these tags the text you copied to the clipboard.
9. Close Notepad and save your changes.

Now, when you reopen the page with Navigator, you should see your original three-framed site. Navigator, being a frame-capable browser, will simply ignore all the text and tags between the <noframes>...</noframes> tags.

On the other hand, if you can dig up an old frame-incapable browser and open your frames.htm page with *that* browser, you should see just the stand-alone page. The old browser will ignore all the <frameset> and <frame> tags and process only the tags between the <noframes> and </noframes> tags.

UPLOADING TO THE WEB SERVER

Before you upload all these pages to your Web server, you might want to rename frames.htm to whatever home page name your ISP requires. For example, I would rename frames.htm to index.html, because that's the page my ISP displays automatically when a reader points his or her browser to my site.

THE IMPORTANCE OF ORDER

We got bogged down in some details in the latter part of this chapter. Before continuing, I'd like to reinforce what you've learned earlier in the chapter about the order of the <frameset> and <frame> tags in a page. It's important to remember that after you place a <frameset> tag in a page, the first tag under that <frameset> tag defines the first frame in that set. The next tag refers to the second frame in that set, and so forth. The trick to getting your frames laid out correctly is to make sure that you place all the <frameset> and <frame> tags in the correct order.

If you took a peek at the underlying source document, using View | Document Source, for Carly Simon's site (shown way back in Figures 17-1 and 17-2), for example, the tags might look like this (I've made up my own names for the frames):

```
<frameset cols="25%,75%">
    <frame name="Toc">
    <frameset rows="60,*">
        <frame name="Logo" scrolling="no">
        <frame name="Main">
    </frameset>
</frameset>
```

If I were to add comments to explain what each tag does, those tags would look like this:

```
<!Split into two columns, 25% and 75%>
<frameset cols="25%,75%">
    <!Name the first frame (left column) Toc>
    <frame name="Toc">
```

```
<!Divide the second column into two rows>
<frameset rows="60,*">
      <!Name to first row Logo>
      <frame name="Logo" scrolling="no">
      <!Name the second row Main>
      <frame name="Main">
</frameset>
</frameset>
```

TRAP

Remember, the comments inside <!...> are for human consumption only. They are ignored by the browser and have no effect on the real tags. The order in which the <frameset> and <frame> tags are listed determines which frame appears where on the screen. The comments don't influence that at all.

In the Big Mountain site shown back in Figure 17-3, the <frameset> and <frame> tags might look something like this:

```
<frameset rows="*,128">
      <frame name="Body" noresize>
      <frameset cols="*,194">
            <frame name="Toc" noresize>
            <frame name="Logo" scrolling = "no">
      </frameset>
</frameset>
```

If I were to add comments to describe the purpose of each tag, the code would look like this:

```
<!Split the screen into two rows>
<frameset rows="*,128">
      <!Name the entire top frame Main>
      <frame name="Main" noresize>

      <!Split the second row into two columns>
      <frameset cols="*,194">

            <!Name the bottom left frame toc>
            <frame name="Toc" noresize>
```

```
        <!Name the bottom right frame logo>
        <frame name="Logo" scrolling="no">
     </frameset>
 </frameset>
```

In the newspaper example in Figure 17-4, the <frameset> and
<frame> tags that define that newspaperish layout might look like
this:

```
<frameset rows="90,*">
     <frame name="Masthead" src="masthead.htm"
marginheight=0 marginwidth=0      scrolling="no">

     <frameset cols="*,*,*">
           <frame name="Column1" src="story1.htm">
           <frame name="Column2" src="story2.htm">
           <frame name="Column3" src="story3.htm">
     </frameset>
</frameset>
```

With my comments added, this is what you'd see:

```
<!Spit into two rows, top is 90 pixels tall>
<frameset rows="90,*">

<!Top frame will contain masthead.htm>
     <frame name="Masthead" src="masthead.htm"
marginheight=0 marginwidth=0      scrolling="no">

     <!Break bottom row into three columns>
     <frameset cols="*,*,*">
           <frame name="Column1" src="story1.htm">
           <frame name="Column2" src="story2.htm">
           <frame name="Column3" src="story3.htm">
     </frameset>
</frameset>
```

Defining frames is not *the* most intuitive thing you'll ever do.
But, like anything else, after a little practice it becomes pretty easy.

CUTTING-EDGE FRAME DESIGN

A new feature that's currently supported only by Netscape Navigator 3.0 is the ability to control the width and color of frame borders. You can control the borders using these attributes:

- FRAMEBORDER=: Can be set to YES to show frame border, or NO to hide the frame border. Can be used in both <FRAMESET> and <FRAME> tags.

- BORDER=: Sets the width of the border in pixels. Setting BORDER=0 is the same as setting FRAMEBORDER=NO. Can be used only in <FRAMESET> tags.

- BORDERCOLOR=: Specifies the color of the border as either a name or color triplet (see Appendix E). Can be used in <FRAMESET> or <FRAME> tags.

These attributes can be tricky to use because 1) frameset and frame tags are often nested within other frameset and frame tags and 2) every frame shares at least one border with some other frame. Thus conflicts can occur. For example, let's say a frameset tag sets the frame color to red. Then, a frame tag sets the frame color to blue. What color will the frame border be, blue or red? These kinds of conflicts are resolved in the following manner:

- The attributes defined in the top (outermost) <FRAMESET> tag have the lowest priority.

- Attributes defined in the next (deeper) <FRAMESET> tag override the attributes defined in the <FRAMESET> tag that precedes it.

- A BORDERCOLOR attribute defined in a <FRAME> tag overrides all previous <FRAMESET> tags.

- If two or more <FRAME> tags at the same level set different colors, the resulting color is undefined (usually gray).

Whew! It sounds complicated but can be pretty easy. Maybe a couple of examples will illustrate. If you just want all the borders to be the same size and color, specify the color and width in the first frameset tag. For example, referring way back to our Daily Dose site, defining the frames as below displays the page with thick black frame borders as in Figure 17-22.

```
<!Create two columnwise frames>
<frameset cols="150,*" border=15 bordercolor="black">
    <!Split the first column into two rows>
    <frameset rows="150,*">
    <!etc. The rest is same as in original>
```

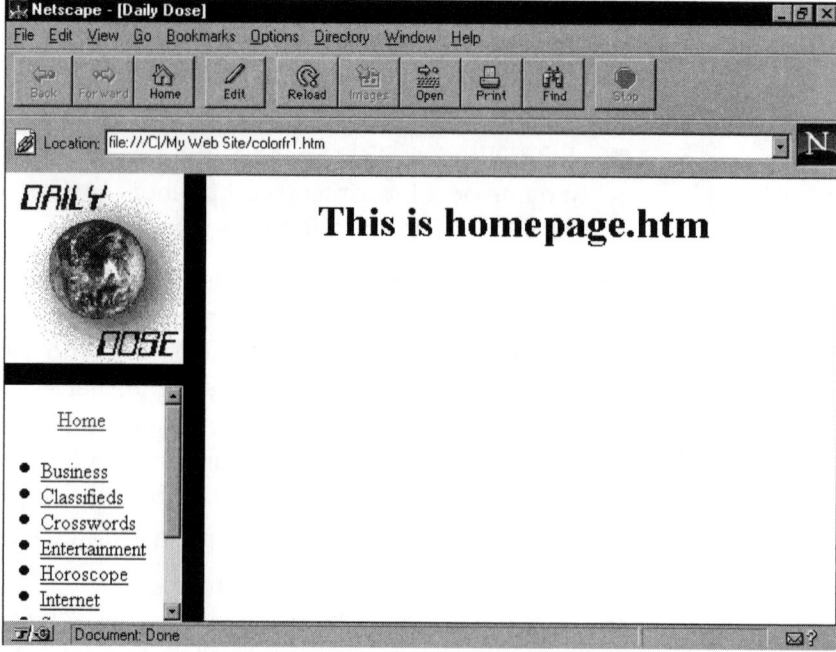

Figure 17-22: *Frames at 15 pixels wide and colored red.*

Going back to our Webhead Examiner example shown back in Figure 17-4, suppose we were to open the document source for that page and change the first <FRAMESET> tag to this:

```
<frameset rows="90,*" frameborder=no>
```

where the only difference is the inclusion of the new frameborder-no attribute. The resulting page would look like the original. However, there would be no borders between the frames. The scrollbars between the stories would act as the visible borders, as in Figure 17-23.

Figure 17-23: *Newspaper example with frame borders removed.*

MOVING ON

Clickable image maps and frames, the topics of these last two chapters, can add a professional polish to your Web site and make the reader's experience richer and more enjoyable. In the next chapter we're going to start looking at another tool you can use to make your pages better—JavaScript.

Introducing JavaScript

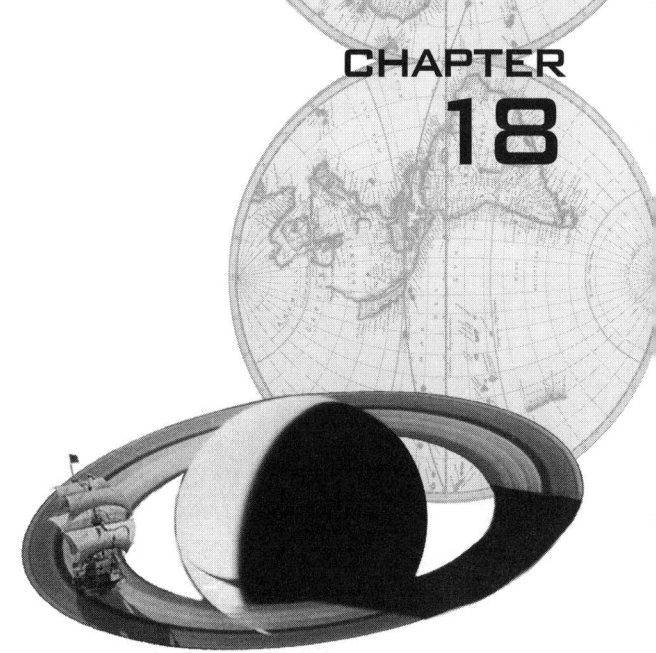

JavaScript is a programming language that can add a whole new level of interactivity to your Web site, giving your readers a more compelling and enjoyable experience. The goal of this chapter is to get you started understanding and using JavaScript in your Web pages. The chapter covers these concepts and techniques:

- What is JavaScript?
- JavaScript objects, properties, methods, and event handlers
- Typing JavaScript code into your page
- Testing and debugging your scripts

When you write JavaScript code, you are actually *programming* the way your page will behave. Thus, after you get into JavaScript, you can stop thinking of yourself as "just" a Web author and publisher, because you will be a Web author, publisher, and programmer. (What a title!)

WHAT IS JAVASCRIPT?

You're already familiar with HyperText Markup Language (HTML), a set of "commands" (tags) that tell the reader's Web browser how to format text and pictures. JavaScript is similar to HTML, except that it's a *programming language* rather than a markup language. So what's the difference?

A markup language can only tell the browser to do specific jobs—"make this a large-lettered heading" or "show image.gif here," for example. JavaScript is much smarter and more interactive than that because it can respond to *events*—things the reader does while viewing your page. Furthermore, JavaScript can make decisions about what to do in response to some event, and then carry out an appropriate action based on that decision.

Let me try to say that more succinctly. Whereas HTML determines the way your page *looks* on the reader's screen, you can use JavaScript to determine the way your page *behaves* on the reader's screen.

Like HTML tags, JavaScript statements are invisible to readers casually browsing your page. You, as author/publisher/programmer, see JavaScript as *code* mixed in with the text and tags of your page. In an external editor, the JavaScript code appears within the angle brackets of an HTML tag, or between a pair of <script>... </script> tags, as in the example shown in Figure 18-1.

TIP

In Figure 18-1, I've boldfaced the JavaScript code for emphasis—it won't be boldfaced on your screen.

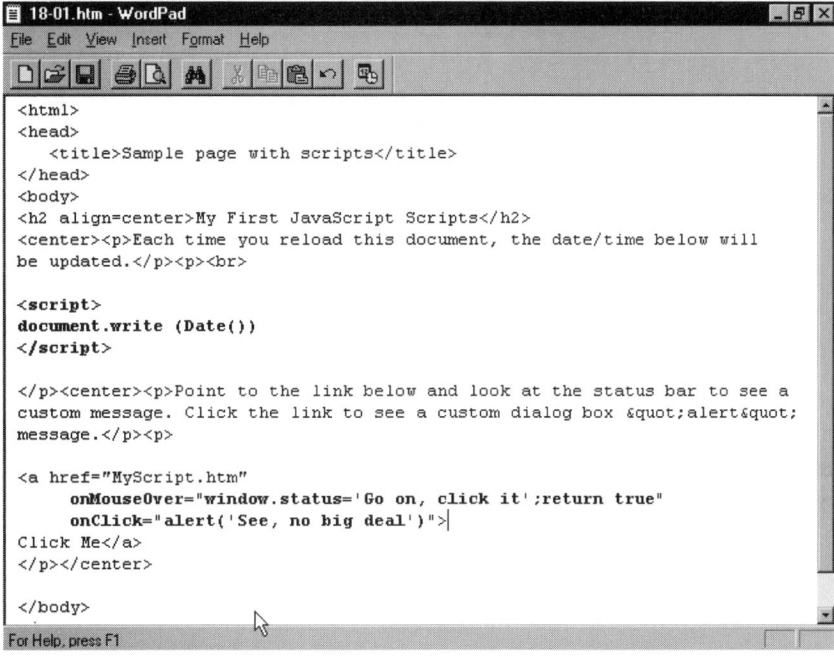

Figure 18-1: *In Notepad, JavaScript statements appear between*
<script...>...</script> tags, or in HTML tags.

In Gold's editor, *scripts* (that is, JavaScript code between
<script>...</script> tags) are displayed in red. You can edit those
statements right there in Gold's editor, but to see and edit all the
JavaScript in a page, you'll need to use your external editor.

JAVASCRIPT LETS YOU MANIPULATE OBJECTS

The idea behind JavaScript is to give you, the programmer, the ability to manipulate *objects* that appear on the readers' screens as they
(the readers) view your Web page. Some of these objects include
the document itself, the current location, the history list, the system
date and time in the reader's PC, hyperlinks, and the entire
browser window. Figure 18-2 points out these objects.

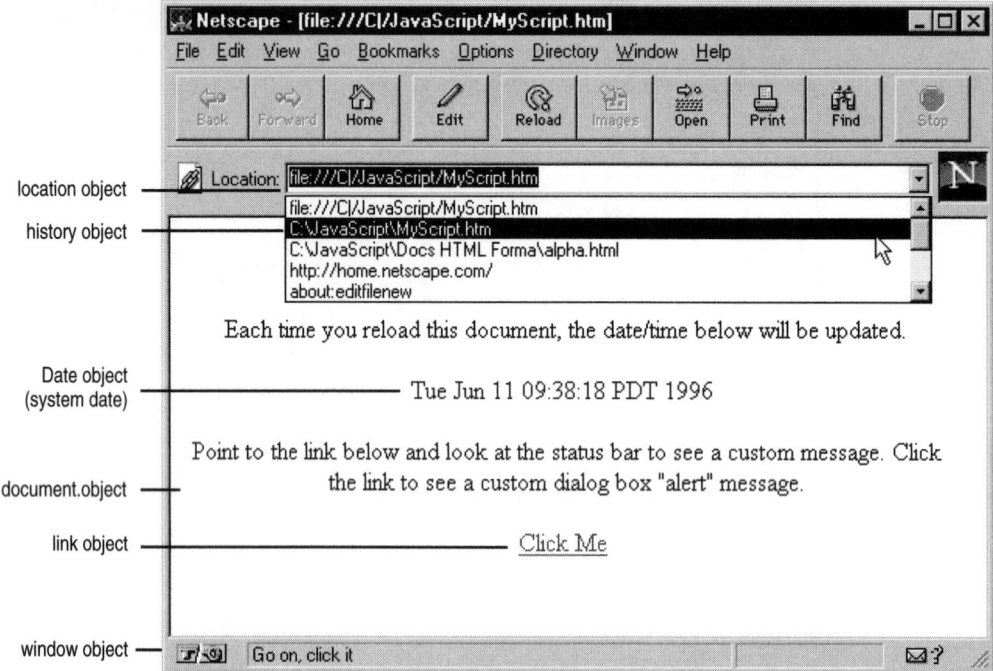

location object

history object

Date object
(system date)

document.object

link object

window object

Figure 18-2: *JavaScript allows you to manipulate these, and other, objects.*

OBJECTS HAVE PROPERTIES

Most objects have *properties* that JavaScript can detect and change. A good way to think of a property is as a characteristic of an object. For example, the document object has properties such as a background color, a text (or foreground) color, a title, and a location (URL). In JavaScript, you always refer to an object's property using the syntax

```
object.property
```

in which *object* is the proper JavaScript name of the object, and *property* is a proper JavaScript property name. Figure 18-3 points out some properties of the document that's currently displayed. In each example I've used the exact syntax that JavaScript would use to refer to the property.

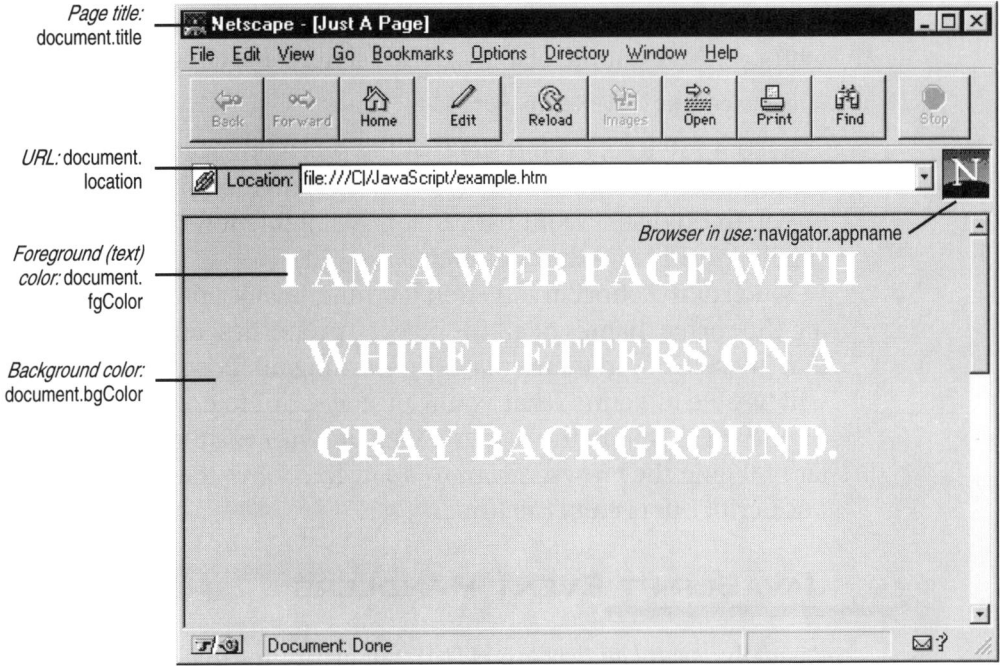

Figure 18-3: *Examples of document properties, as expressed in JavaScript.*

SOME OBJECTS HAVE METHODS

In addition to properties, many objects have *methods*. Think of a method as an action—something JavaScript can *do* to the object. (For example, JavaScript can *write* text into the document.) The syntax for expressing a method is similar to that for expressing a property. Methods, however, are always followed by a pair of parentheses, like this:

```
object.method( )
```

In this syntax, *object* is a valid JavaScript object name, and *method* is a valid JavaScript method for that object. The method's parentheses might contain an *argument* (information that's passed to the method). An example of a JavaScript statement follows:

```
document.write("Hello World")
```

In computerese, I could say that the preceding statement passes the argument "Hello World" to the write() method of the document object. In English, I would say that this statement writes the words "Hello World" into the document.

Much of the effort involved in learning JavaScript is spent learning the correct names of all the objects, properties, and methods that JavaScript can manipulate. By learning all those names, you will be able to define what you want the script to do. But just as important as telling the reader's Web browser *what* to do is the matter of telling the browser *when* to do it. To control the "when," JavaScript offers *event handlers*.

JAVASCRIPT EVENT HANDLERS

Basically, *event handlers* are HTML tag attributes that determine when a JavaScript action happens. For example, you could have a JavaScript script play as soon as the reader opens a document (onLoad), or as soon as the reader closes the document (onUnload). You might have a script play when the reader points to a hyperlink (onMouseOver) or when the reader actually clicks the hyperlink (onClick). Figure 18-4 points out some of the events that JavaScript can respond to.

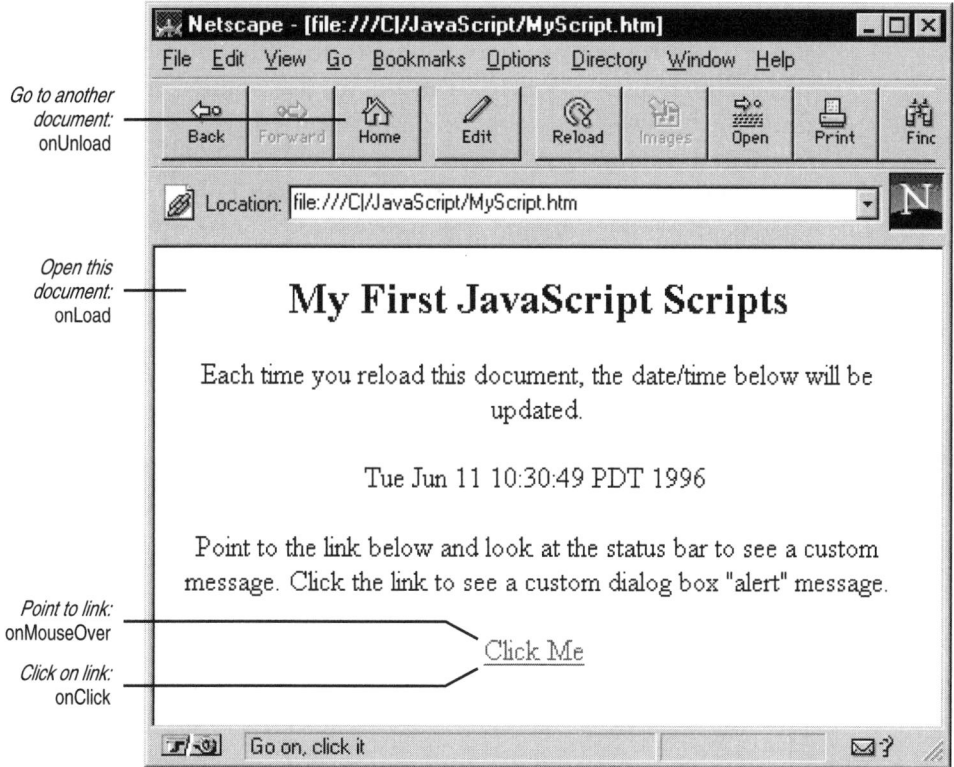

Go to another document: onUnload

Open this document: onLoad

Point to link: onMouseOver

Click on link: onClick

Figure 18-4: *Some sample events that can trigger a JavaScript script.*

Unlike the objects, properties, and methods, which are defined in the script proper (between the <script>...</script> tags), event handlers are defined in HTML tags. Here's an example: Suppose that you're creating a document in Gold's editor, and you add a hyperlink to the URL http://www.coolnerds.com. If you view the source for that document, the hyperlink that Gold created might look something like this:

```
<a href="http://www.coolnerds.com">Go to Coolnerds</a>
```

When the reader is browsing your page, he or she sees the text *Go to Coolnerds* on the page as a hyperlink (blue underlined text). When the reader points to (rests the mouse pointer on) the hyperlink, the browser displays the destination, http://www.coolnerds.com, in the status bar.

As a JavaScript programmer, you could add your own event handler to that tag to make the tag behave differently. For example, in the code that follows I've added an onMouseOver event handler (shown boldfaced) to the tag:

```
<a href="http://www.coolnerds.com"
onMouseOver="window.status='Go for it!';return true")>Go to
Coolnerds</a>
```

The effect of this change is that the custom message *Go for it!* (rather than http://www.coolnerds.com) is displayed in the status bar when the reader points to the hyperlink (see Figure 18-5).

Figure 18-5: *A custom message in the status bar.*

Even though this is a simple (and not particularly exciting) example, it does illustrate the point I made earlier. Whereas HTML lets you format the appearance of the text you display to your readers, JavaScript lets you *customize the behavior* of the reader's Web browser.

There's more to JavaScript than objects, properties, methods, and event handlers. All the elements of classical programming languages, including statements, variables, functions, and operators are there. But before we get into all that, let's turn our attention away from conceptual matters and focus on *how* to create JavaScript scripts in your own Web pages.

YOUR FIRST JAVASCRIPT SCRIPTS

Usually, you'll add JavaScript to an existing Web page to refine the behavior of that page. Before I show you how to create a script, let's create a simple page to work with. Follow these steps:

1. Start up Netscape Navigator in the usual manner on your PC. You need not be online.

2. Choose File | New Document | Blank from Navigator's menu bar to get to Gold's editor.

3. Type the heading and paragraphs shown in Figure 18-6. Press Enter a few times after each line to leave some blank space.

Figure 18-6: *We'll add JavaScript code to this simple page.*

4. Add the little hyperlink near the bottom of the page. That is, select the Click Me text you typed, then click the Make Link button in the toolbar. When asked to save this document, choose Yes, type **MyScript.htm** as the document name, and click the Save button. In the Properties dialog box that appears next, type **MyScript.htm** as the Link to... location (the same name that you gave the document).

TIP

In Step 4 you're creating a link that sends the document "to itself." This would be a strange thing to do in real life—not much point to it. But the purpose of this page is to demonstrate some JavaScript. Don't worry about the seemingly silly "link to myself."

5. To enlarge the first line, apply the Heading 2 style to it.
6. To center all the text, select it (press Ctrl+A), then click the Center button in the paragraph formatting toolbar.
7. Save this page. (Choose File | Save, then choose a folder and enter a filename, such as MyScript.)

Now let's look at how you'd add some JavaScript code to this page, using Gold's editor.

TYPING JAVASCRIPT IN GOLD'S EDITOR

Typing a script into Gold's editor is similar to typing regular text—with some important added rules:

■ Do *not* type the <script>...</script> tags. Those tags will be added automatically later when you apply the JavaScript (Client) style.

■ If you want to indent a line, do so by typing blank spaces at the beginning of the line. The Tab key and Increase Indent button will indent the entire script.

- When you type multiple statements, end each statement with a semicolon (;) or by pressing Shift+Enter. Don't press Enter (even though that's exactly what your hand will want to do!).

- After you've typed the code, select it and choose Properties | Character | JavaScript (Client).

Let's give it a try:

1. With your sample page (the one shown in Figure 18-6) in Gold's editor, put the cursor somewhere under the first paragraph.

2. Type the following small chunk of JavaScript code, *exactly* as shown (same upper- and lowercase letters, spacing, and so forth):

```
document.write (Date())
```

3. Select that line of text (drag the mouse pointer through it), as in Figure 18-7.

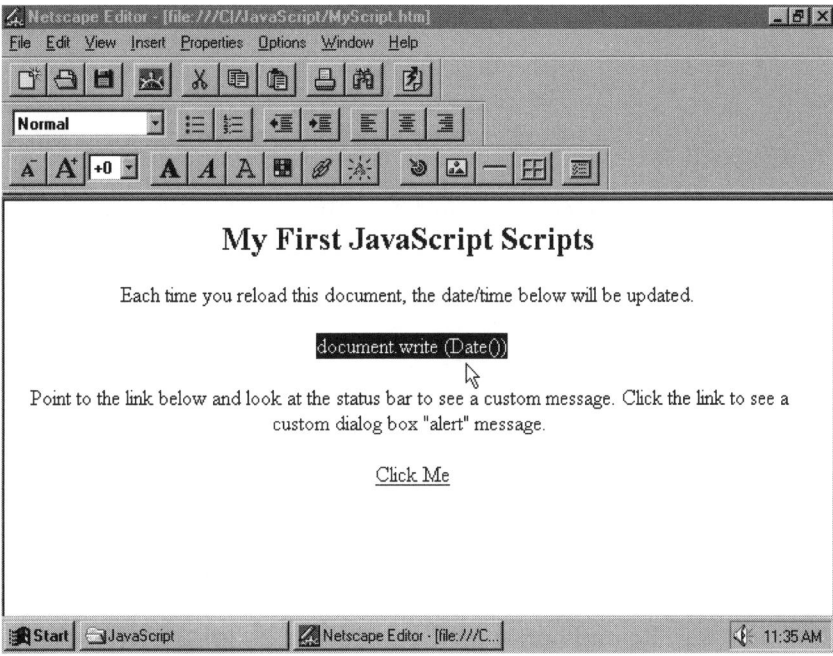

Figure 18-7: *Little chunk of JavaScript code is selected.*

4. From the menu bar choose
Properties | Character | JavaScript (Client).

5. Now click anywhere outside the selected text.

The text you selected turns red, indicating that the Web browser will now treat that line of text as JavaScript code. To test this, switch to browser view (click the View in Browser button or choose File | Browser Document | Yes). The screen will show your computer's current date and time where you placed the code.

If you check out the source document (View | Document Source), you can see where JavaScript automatically entered the <script>...</script> tags around the code, as in Figure 18-8.

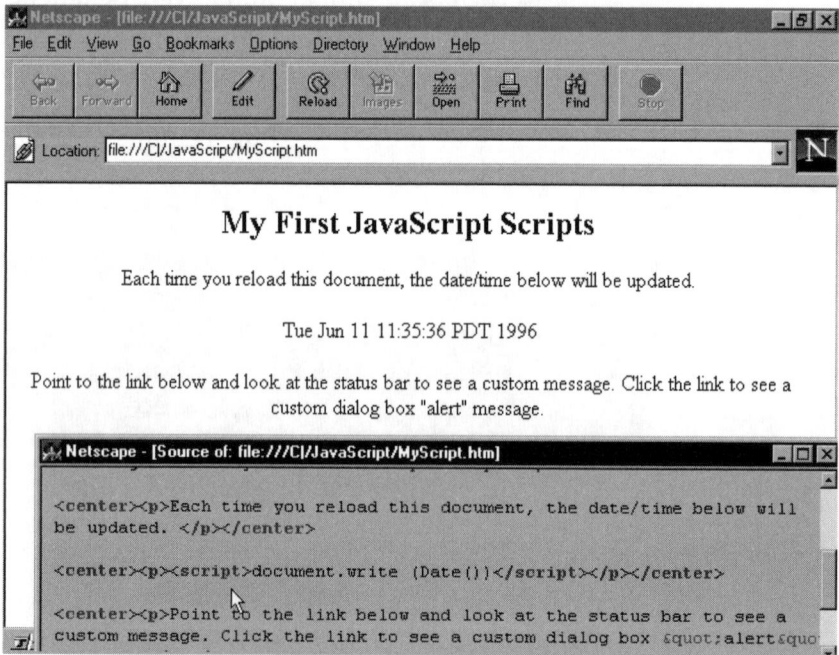

Figure 18-8: *Date and time appear in browser. In the document source you can see the <script>...</script> tags.*

Look closely at the date and time presented on the page. It will be accurate to the second (11:35:36, in my example). If you click the Reload button in the toolbar, the same page will reappear, but the time (at least the seconds portion) will have changed to reflect the current system time—a little "live action" already from JavaScript. You couldn't show the current date and time using just HTML tags. But JavaScript can do the job.

TYPING JAVASCRIPT IN AN EXTERNAL EDITOR

You can manually type JavaScript into a document, using an external editor, just as you would manually type HTML tags. Why would you want to do this? Well, for one thing, because an external editor won't be so fussy about when you press the Enter key, you can end each line by pressing Enter rather than by typing a semicolon or pressing Shift+Enter.

TIP

I find it easier to create all *my scripts in an external editor. If I need to make a slight change to a script, I might do so right in Gold's editor. But, of course, not all JavaScript code will be visible in Gold's editor.*

Another reason to use an external editor to type JavaScript code is that JavaScript event handlers are generally placed inside HTML tags. To type *that* JavaScript code, you need to get to the document source so that you can see the HTML tag to which you want to add JavaScript. Before I show you how to do this, notice a couple of things about your current page before you add any JavaScript to it:

■ When you point to (rest the mouse pointer on) the Click Me link, the status bar displays the name of the file that the link points to (MyScript.htm, in the example).

■ When you click on the link, the page reloads itself (there's a brief flash on the screen, and the system date/time is updated to the current minute/second).

In this example I'll show you how to add a little JavaScript code to the <a href...> tag underlying that link, to customize both its little status bar message and its action at the moment you click it. Follow these steps to enter the tags, using your external Notepad editor:

1. If you're in the browser, click the Edit button to get the document back into Gold's editor.

2. In Gold's editor, choose View | Edit Document Source. The source document for MyScript.htm will open in Notepad. You can maximize that window to better see the entire document.

TIP

If you see a message indicating that you haven't chosen an external editor yet, you can just define c:\windows\notepad.exe as your editor on the spot. Or, if you start feeling overwhelmed by all this, take some time to read about HTML and external editors in Chapter 15, "Tuning HTML Tags."

3. Find the tag that reads:

```
<a href="MyScript.htm">
```

and place the cursor between the closing quotation marks and the > character.

4. Press Enter to break the line right before that closing > tag, then press Tab or type a few spaces to indent. (This is just to give yourself some working room. JavaScript actually ignores your line breaks and spaces.)

5. Now type *exactly* this next snippet of code (same upper- and lowercase letters, same single (') and double (") quotation marks, and the semicolon (;)):

```
onMouseOver="window.status='Go ahead, try it!';
return true"
```

Then press Enter to break to a new line.

TRAP

Remember, when you're typing JavaScript code there is no such thing as a minor typo. It's either correct, or it's not.

6. Press Tab to indent the new line, then type the following
   line, exactly as you see it here:

```
onClick="alert('Easy enough, no?')"
```

If you'd like to tidy up the screen a little so that you can better
see the code you typed between the <a...>...</a> tags, move the
cursor just to the left of the word Click Me, and press Enter to break
the line there. Your screen should look something like Figure 18-9
now.

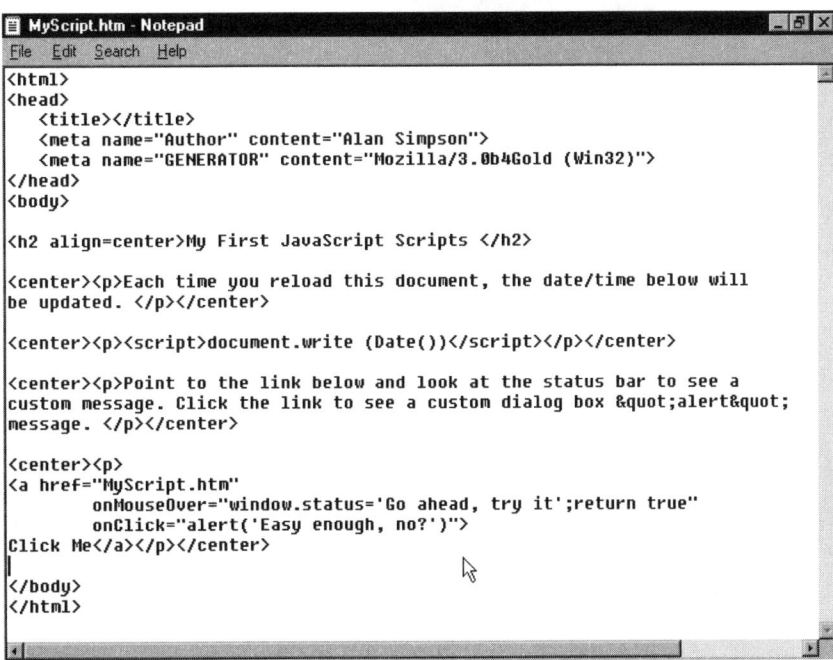

Figure 18-9: *onMouseOver and onClick event handlers added to an
<a href...> tag.*

Now, follow these steps to save this new code and test it:

1. Close Notepad (click its Close button or choose File | Exit)
   and choose Yes when asked about saving your changes.

2. When asked about reloading the document, choose Yes. The
   new event handlers do not appear on the screen because the
   HTML tag that houses the code is invisible in Gold's editor.

3. To test the event handlers, click the View in Browser button or choose File | Browse document.

4. Move the mouse pointer to the Click Me link. The status bar should display your custom "Go ahead, try it" message.

5. Now click the Click Me link. You should see a custom "Alert" dialog box with your message inside, as in Figure 18-10.

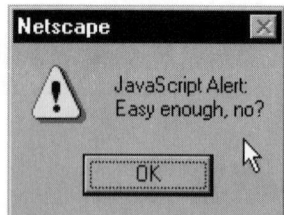

Figure 18-10: *Custom message appears in a dialog box.*

6. Click OK in the Alert box to get rid of the custom message.

That's it! That's all this second custom JavaScript does. It displays a custom status bar message when you point to the link, and displays a custom dialog box message when you click on the link. (And it still reloads the page, too.)

If you get some kind of error message, like the example shown in Figure 18-11, rather than the results you expected, you must have typed something incorrectly. Check your document source code against Figure 18-9, and make sure that every letter, space, and punctuation mark is placed correctly. (See the debugging section later in this chapter as well.)

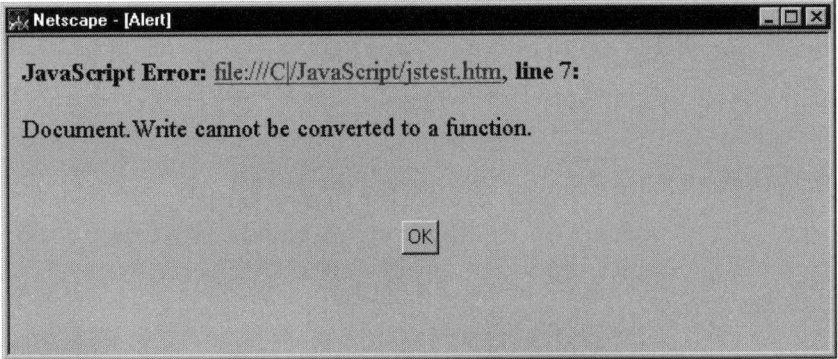

Figure 18-11: *A sample error message.*

JavaScript Rules to Live By

Now you know roughly what JavaScript is about. And you know the mechanics of typing JavaScript code into your Web page. You'll get plenty of practice in the chapters ahead. Before you move on, though, I'd like to point out some especially good things to know about JavaScript.

JavaScript Is Case-Sensitive

It's important to remember that upper- and lowercase letters make a difference in JavaScript. This is just an unpleasant fact that's certain to drive you crazy for the first few months spent learning this language. Just to show you how fussy JavaScript is, take a look at the following sample JavaScript statements:

```
document.write ("Howdy world")

Document.write ("Howdy world")

document.Write ("Howdy world")

Document.Write ("Howdy world")

DOCUMENT.WRITE ("Howdy world")
```

All of the statements say exactly the same thing, but only the first one is correct. And only that one works. All the others generate totally confusing error messages, such as *Document.Write cannot be converted to a function* or *DOCUMENT is not defined.* Yuck.

Appendix F, "JavaScript Reserved Words," lists every word that JavaScript uses, with the proper upper- and lowercase letters. Use that appendix after you've gained some fluency and just need quick reminders about upper- and lowercase.

TIP

When you're first learning JavaScript, you can minimize errors by copying and pasting code directly from an electronic reference. Chapter 19, "Fun With JavaScript," lists several references you can choose from.

COMMENT YOUR CODE

Your JavaScript code can contain programmer *comments*—notes to yourself or other programmers that define what a particular statement or routine does. The following characters are used to define comments:

- //: Defines a single-line comment. All text after the // characters, on the same line, is ignored.

- /*...*/: Defines a multiline comment. All text between the /* and */ characters is ignored.

For example, the following script demonstrates the use of both single-line and multiline comments in a script. The only line between the <script>...</script> tags that JavaScript pays attention to is the *document.write ("Hello World")* statement:

```
<script>
/* This is a mutli-line comment.
JavaScript ignores everything to here */

document.write ("Hello World")
//Line above shows Hello World
</script>
```

HIDE CODE FROM NON-JAVASCRIPT BROWSERS

Many Web browsers do not support JavaScript. When these browsers come across a JavaScript script, they interpret it as text and display it, literally, onscreen. You can avoid this by hiding the JavaScript from non-JavaScript browsers. Use the special comment tags <!-- and //--> to do this.

> **TIP**
>
> *JavaScript event handler code in an HTML tag is ignored by non-JavaScript scripts. You need to hide only complete scripts that are surrounded by <script> and </script> tags.*

Type <!-- beneath, or just to the right of, the opening <script> tag. Type the //--> characters above, or just to the left of, the closing </script> tag. You can type comment text (which JavaScript will ignore) to the right of the <!-- tag, and to the right of the // in the closing comment tag, as in the example shown in Figure 18-12 (Notepad's view of a script).

> **TIP**
>
> *Since you can't predict which Web browser a reader will be using, it's a good idea to always use the <!-- and //--> comment tags to hide the JavaScript code from older JavaScript-incapable Web browsers.*

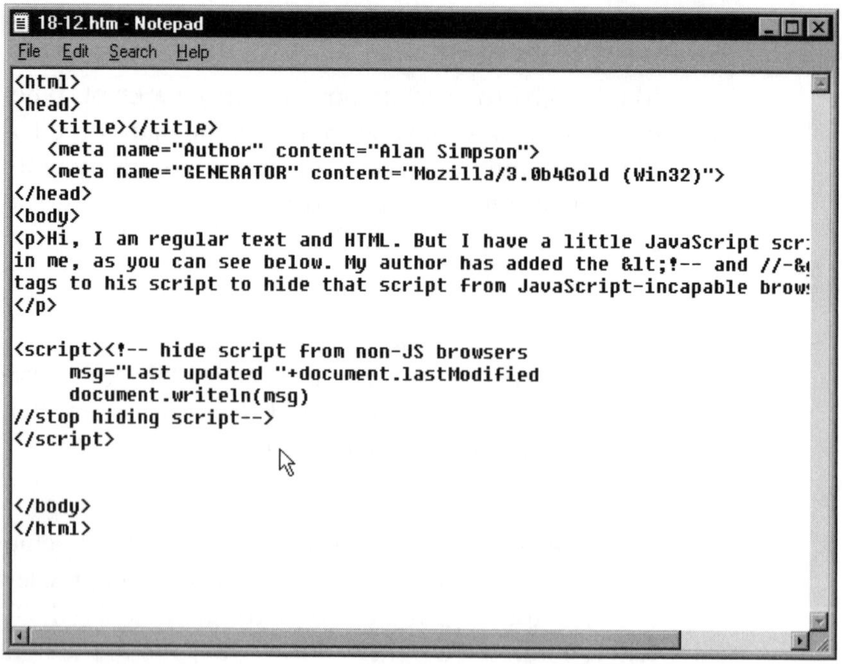

```
📄 18-12.htm - Notepad                                         _□X
File  Edit  Search  Help
<html>
<head>
   <title></title>
   <meta name="Author" content="Alan Simpson">
   <meta name="GENERATOR" content="Mozilla/3.0b4Gold (Win32)">
</head>
<body>
<p>Hi, I am regular text and HTML. But I have a little JavaScript scr
in me, as you can see below. My author has added the &lt;!-- and //-&
tags to his script to hide that script from JavaScript-incapable brow
</p>

<script><!-- hide script from non-JS browsers
     msg="Last updated "+document.lastModified
     document.writeln(msg)
//stop hiding script-->
</script>


</body>
</html>
```

Figure 18-12 : *Comment tags <!-- and //--> added to hide code from non-JavaScript browsers.*

LINKING TO JAVASCRIPT CODE

In some situations you might want to create a hyperlink that, when clicked, executes some JavaScript code instead of taking the reader to another URL. To do that, replace the URL in the href with **javascript:***statements*, where *statements* is one or more JavaScript statement, or (more likely) the name of a JavaScript custom function. For example, this tag:

```
<a href="javascript:alert('Just a test')">Click me</a>
```

presents Click me as a hyperlink on the page. But clicking that link doesn't take the reader anywhere. Instead, it displays an alert box containing the message *Just a test*.

The same approach works if the link is an image. For example, in this tag:

```
<a href="javascript:alert('Just a test')"><img
src="hotpic.gif" height=32 width=32> </a>
```

clicking on the image named hotpic.gif displays the "Just a test" alert box. You can even use the same approach in a clickable image map, as follows:

```
<AREA SHAPE RECT COORDS="6,0,68,64"
HREF="javascript:alert('just a test')">
```

Make sure that you enclose the entire statement in quotation marks (") and start with the word *javascript* and a colon (:), as in all three of the preceding examples.

SIZE YOUR IMAGES!

A strange quirk in early JavaScript centered around something that has nothing to do with JavaScript. If a page that contains JavaScript code also contains any <img src> tags without height and width attributes, the JavaScript code may run incorrectly, or not at all.

This won't be a problem if you always use Gold's editor to insert images into your page, because Gold always adds the height and width attributes to your <img src> tags. But if you're not sure, use the Search | Find commands in Notepad to locate all your <img src...> tags and fix any tags that don't contain the height and width attributes.

PRINTER PROBLEMS

There is a major problem with printing text that's produced by JavaScript in a Web page. You can't do it! That is, when you (or your reader) prints the page that's visible on the screen, the printed output contains only the standard text. Any text that has been placed on the page by JavaScript is not printed. Needless to say, this is a pretty substantial problem. But Netscape has promised to rectify the problem in future versions of JavaScript and Navigator.

JAVASCRIPT DATA: NUMBERS & STRINGS

JavaScript, and computers in general, tend to handle different types of data in different ways. The two main data types are *numbers* and *strings*. A *number* is something you can do basic arithmetic with— add, subtract, multiply, and divide. For example, 543.21 is a number, as is 22.

A *string* is a sequence of letters and perhaps other characters. For example, "Alan" is a string, as is "Jane Doe." So are "P.O. Box 630" and "(619)756-0159." The last example looks like a number. But the acid test is whether it's the kind of thing you'd do arithmetic with. It makes sense to, say, divide two numbers, as in *15/3*, because 15 divided by 3 results in a number, 5. But it makes no sense to attempt to divide a phone "number" by, say, a ZIP code. Mathematically, the expression *(619)756-0159 / 92067-0630* doesn't have a result and doesn't have meaning.

Even though some strings (like telephone numbers and ZIP codes) might look like numbers, they're not. The true numbers are those that contain just numeric characters (0-9), decimal points, and perhaps a leading minus sign (hyphen) for a negative number. To be successful with any programming language, you need to start thinking of data as being either a string or a number.

JAVASCRIPT DATES & TIMES

Yet a third type of data is the "moment in time," which we express as a date and/or time. *Dates* are neither numbers nor strings. They're similar to numbers, because you can do some peculiar arithmetic with them. For example, you can take a date like March 1, 1997, and add 30 days to it to come up with a new date, March 30, 1997.

Technically, there is no Date data type in JavaScript. But there is a Date *object* that gives your JavaScript code some limited capabilities for doing date arithmetic. I won't go into all the gory details right now. Suffice it to say that the Date object includes numerous methods to convert dates to strings and numbers, and vice versa.

In my Coolnerds Web site, I offer up several free custom JavaScript functions that make it much easier to do date arithmetic in JavaScript. Feel free to stop by (www.coolnerds.com) and swipe a few, if you ever need them.

JavaScript Logical (Boolean) Data

Like most programming languages, JavaScript offers a *logical* data type where the data can contain only one of two possible values: **true** or **false**. This data type is generally used to help the JavaScript *if()* statement make a decision about how to behave at a given moment. You'll see examples of using **true** and **false** under "JavaScript Decision Making" a little later in this chapter and under "Detecting Available Plug-Ins " in the next chapter. But before we get there, you need to understand a little bit about JavaScript expressions.

> **TIP**
>
> *The Logical data type is sometimes called the Boolean data type, after George Boole, the mathematician who developed a calculus of symbolic logic used as the basis for modern day computing.*

JavaScript Expressions

Programming involves writing many *expressions*, which are little instructions that tell the computer what to do with data. Most expressions contain some combination of *operators*, *variables*, and *literals*. Let's take a look at what those terms mean.

Operators

Operators are symbols that operate on data. You probably are already familiar with operators from basic arithmetic. In the expression 1+1 = 2, for example, the + sign is the operator. JavaScript uses all the operators that you'll find in any language. Here are some of the more commonly used operators:

+	addition (or string concatenation, discussed in a moment)
-	subtraction
*	multiplication
/	division
=	equals (assign a value to a variable)
>	is greater than
<	is less than
>=	is greater than or equal to
<=	is less than or equal to
==	is equal to (compare two values)
!=	is not equal to
++	increment by one
—	decrement by one

JavaScript uses other operators also, but this list should be enough to get you started. You'll find the full hair-raising set of operators amply documented in any of the electronic reference guides listed at the end of Chapter 19, "Fun With JavaScript."

LITERALS

A *literal* is a chunk of data that the program interprets literally. For example, the number 10 is a literal, as is the string "Hello There." Numeric literals are written as-is. String literals are enclosed in single quotation marks (') or double quotation marks ("). In the JavaScript statements that follow, 0 and -123.45 are numeric literals (numbers), and "Fred" and "Wilma" are string literals:

```
x = 10
y = -123.45
a = "Fred"
b = 'Wilma'
```

VARIABLES

A variable is a *placeholder* that acts as a sort of container, holding a value that is subject to change. A variable looks like a string, but is not enclosed in quotation marks. In the list of statements in the preceding section, x, y, a, and b are all variables. I could use more descriptive names for those variables. For example, I could write the last two lines of the list as:

```
HusbandName = "Fred"
WifeName = "Wilma"
```

When a variable exists and contains some data, it can be used wherever you'd use a literal. For example, after the last line of the following JavaScript code is executed, the variable named GrandTotal would contain the number 108.25:

```
Subtotal = 100
SalesTax = 8.25
GrandTotal = Subtotal + SalesTax
```

Although it is not necessary to do so, you can use the *var* statement to indicate that you are creating a new variable in a script. When you start looking at examples of other people's code, you'll see that it's pretty common practice to type *var* at the beginning of any line that creates a new variable, as in these examples:

```
var qty = 5
var unitprice = 2.00
var subtotal = qty * unitprice
```

VARIABLES ARE CASE-SENSITIVE

Like much of JavaScript, variable names are case-sensitive. Therefore, the variable names MyVar, myVar, MyVAR, and MYVAR *are four different variables*. When you're thinking up a variable name, be sure to think about how you're going to use upper- and lowercase letters in that name.

Do Not Use Reserved Words

Just about any word or phrase (without spaces) will work as a variable name. You cannot use a JavaScript reserved word as a variable name, however. For a list of all the words that are off-limits as variable names, see Appendix F, "JavaScript Reserved Words."

Storing a Date in a Variable

The syntax (rule) for storing a date in a variable is a little different than that for a string or a number, because Date is an object. You must use the *new* keyword to create a new variable that contains a date. For example, the following statement puts the current system date in a variable named *today*:

```
var today = new Date( )
```

Assuming that this statement is executed when the system clock is at 6/15/97 12:30 PM, the variable named *today* would contain a date object. Executing the JavaScript statement *document.write(today)* would display the following line on the reader's screen:

```
Wed Jun 15 12:30:00 PST 1997
```

End-of-Line Semicolons (;)

When you start looking at other people's JavaScript scripts, you may notice that many JavaScript programmers put a semicolon at the end of each line in their scripts. Technically, however, the semicolons are required only when you want to put several statements on a single line. For example, the following line:

```
var a=90; var b= 54; var c= 123
```

could be typed as three lines, like this:

```
var a = 90
var b = 54
var c=123
```

MIXING UP THE DATA TYPES

Sometimes you'll want to store more than one data type in a single variable. For example, you might want to build a custom message, using several data types. To do this, you *concatenate* (chain together) the data types, using a + sign. For example, take a look at this little script:

```
<script>
    var x = 4
    var name = "Alec"
    var msg = name + " is " + x + " years old."
    document.write (msg)
</script>
```

As a result of playing that script, the following message would be displayed on the reader's screen:

```
Alec is 4 years old.
```

You can also mix data types right in a document.write() statement. Use either commas or the plus sign to *delimit* (separate) the literals from the variables. For example, I could have skipped creating the variable named msg in the preceding example, and gotten the same result with this script:

```
<script>
    var x = 4
    var name = "Alec"
    document.write(name + " is " + x + " years old.")
</script>
```

JAVASCRIPT DOES HTML

I've used the document.write() statement for several examples in this chapter. You'll probably use it often in your own scripts, as well. It's important to understand that document.write() types its text to the underlying source document—not directly to the reader's screen. What this means is that JavaScript can add new HTML tags to your document, on the spot, at any time. You just need to treat the tags as string literals. For example, this little script:

```
<script>
document.write ("<p><center>Hello World</center></p>")
</script>
```

Displays *Hello World* as a lone paragraph centered on the screen.
The more complex series of statements:

```
<script>
     var x = 4
     var name = "Alec"
     document.write("<b><i>"+name + " is " + x + " years
     old."+
     </b></i>")
</script>
```

writes this to the underlying source document:

```
<b><i>Alec is 4 years old.</b></i>
```

which, in turn, appears on the reader's screen as boldfaced and
italicized, like this:

Alec is 4 years old.

DOCUMENT.WRITELN()

A slight variation on document.write() is the document.writeln()
method. The latter adds a hidden newline character at the end of
the line it prints. (The newline character being the same as the one
that's entered when you press Enter at the keyboard.) Because that
character is usually ignored, .write() and .writeln() are generally
interchangeable. The one exception is when you use .writeln() to
present text that's formatted within a pair of <pre>...</pre> tags.
Those tags don't ignore newline characters. Instead, they break
the line at the hidden newline character.

VARIABLES CAN HOLD OBJECT PROPERTIES

A variable can also hold the value of an object's property. For example, note the following small script:

```
<script><-- hide script
    var browser = navigator.appName
    document.write ("You are using ",browser)
//stop hiding --></script>
```

In this script, *navigator* is a JavaScript object that refers to the current browser, and *appName* is the name of that browser. If you use Netscape Navigator to browse the page that contains that script, the screen would show:

```
You are using Netscape
```

If you browse that page with Microsoft Internet Explorer 3.0, the page would show:

```
You are using Microsoft Internet Explorer
```

If you open that page with a browser that doesn't support JavaScript, nothing appears on the screen because that browser ignores all the JavaScript code.

TIP

A JavaScript variable can also hold a reader's response to a blank on a fill-in-the-blank form. More on this topic in Chapters 21, "Creating Forms for Business," and 22, "Hyper-Interactive Forms With JavaScript."

WATCH THOSE QUOTATION MARKS

Quotation marks play the important role of identifying literals (as opposed to variables) in a JavaScript expression. Which means that, as in HTML, those quotation marks carry a great deal of "meaning" that they don't carry in the real world. What do you do when you want a script to display a quotation mark, literally, on the reader's screen?

Fortunately, JavaScript makes this pretty easy to do. You just have to alternate between single quotation marks (') and double quotation marks ("). For instance, if you want a string to include double quotation marks, enclose the entire string in single quotation marks, as in the following example:

```
<script>
     var reply = 'Annie said "Happy Birthday"!'
     document.write (reply)
</script>
```

When that little script is played, it displays the following message on the reader's screen:

```
Annie said "Happy Birthday"!
```

If you were to put the double-quotation marks on the outside, and the single quotation marks on the inside, like this:

```
<script>
     var reply = "Annie said 'Happy Birthday'!"
     document.write (reply)
</script>
```

the result would be:

```
Annie said 'Happy Birthday'!
```

Be careful about using apostrophes (as in *Jose's*, *don't*, *can't*, and so forth). That apostrophe character is the same as a single quotation mark and is likely to confuse JavaScript. There's no problem if you use the single quotation mark between a pair of double quotation marks, like this:

```
<script>
     document.write ("Never say <i>I can't</i>.")
</script>
```

the result, on the screen, of running this script would be:

```
Never say I can't.
```

However, the script below would just generate an error message because JavaScript wouldn't know what to make of the three apostrophes:

```
<script>
document.write ('Never say <i>I can't</i>.')
</script>
```

JavaScript Decision Making

One of the best capabilities that JavaScript offers is the capability to make decisions. The *if* statement provides this power and uses the syntax:

```
if (condition) {
     do these statements
}
```

in which *condition* is an expression that results in a "true" or "false" result, and *do these statements* is one of any number of JavaScript statements that are executed only if *condition* proves true. If the *condition* proves false, the statements within the curly braces ({}) are passed over and ignored.

Figure 18-13 shows an example in which the condition *navigator.appname=="Netscape"* checks to see if the appname property of the navigator object is Netscape. If so, the script places an <embed...> tag in the current page. If the condition *navigator.appname=="Netscape"* proves false, the <embed> tag is not written to the page. Thus, only people browsing with a JavaScript-cable version of Netscape Navigator would be exposed to the inline video that the <embed> tag offers.

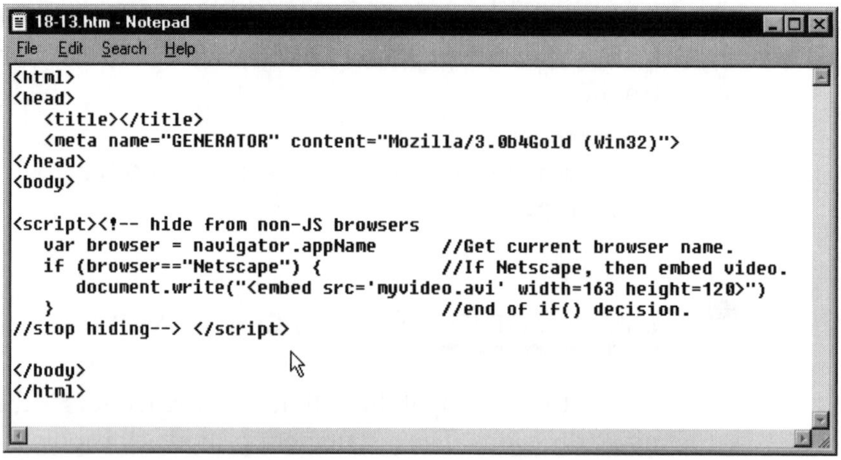

```
18-13.htm - Notepad                                          _ □ X
File  Edit  Search  Help
<html>
<head>
   <title></title>
   <meta name="GENERATOR" content="Mozilla/3.0b4Gold (Win32)">
</head>
<body>

<script><!-- hide from non-JS browsers
    var browser = navigator.appName        //Get current browser name.
    if (browser=="Netscape") {             //If Netscape, then embed video.
       document.write("<embed src='myvideo.avi' width=163 height=120>")
    }                                       //end of if() decision.
//stop hiding--> </script>

</body>
</html>
```

Figure 18-13: *Sample script, using an* if *statement.*

You can use an optional *else* clause in an *if* statement. The *else* clause defines a set of statements to be executed if the condition proves false. The syntax of the if...else statements looks like this:

```
if (condition) {
     do these statements
} else {
     do these instead
}
```

Figure 18-14 shows an example of an if...else statement. In that example, the condition checks to see if the reader is browsing our page with a JavaScript-capable version of Microsoft Internet Explorer. If so, the document.write() statement puts an <img dynsrc...> tag into the page (this is the tag that Internet Explorer uses to display inline video). If the reader is *not* using Internet Explorer, then the *else* statements kick in, inserting the Netscape <embed> tag into the page to display the inline video.

```
18-14.htm - Notepad                                              _ 8 X
File  Edit  Search  Help
<html>
<head>
    <title></title>
    <meta name="GENERATOR" content="Mozilla/3.0b4Gold (Win32)">
</head>
<body>

<script><!-- hide from non-JS browsers
    var browser = navigator.appName     //check browser name

    if (browser=="Microsoft Internet Explorer") {
       document.write ("<img dynsrc='myvideo.avi' start='fileopen'>")

    } else {
       document.write("<embed src='myvideo.avi' width=163 height=120 autostart
       //Note - the <embed> tag above ends with autostart=true>")
    }                                      //end of if...else.
//stop hiding--> </script>

</body>
</html>
```

Figure 18-14: *Sample JavaScript if...else statement.*

IMMEDIATE IF

JavaScript offers a shortcut operator for performing an "if" decision in a single small statement. The syntax looks like this:

var *x* = (*condition*) ? *this* : *otherwise this*

For example, the statement:

var ampm = (hours<12) ? "AM" : "PM"

sets the variable named *ampm* to AM if the variable *hours* is less than 12. If the variable named *hours* is greater than or equal to 12, the variable named *ampm* receives the value PM.

JAVASCRIPT ARRAYS

Like most programming languages, JavaScript supports arrays. An *array* is a list of variables that all have the same name, but a different subscript number. Use the new Array() object type to define an array. For example, this little script defines an array of five color names:

```
<script>
     var color = new Array(5)
     color[0]="darkblue"
     color[1]="darkcyan"
     color[2]="darkgoldenrod"
     color[3]="darkgreen"
     color[4]="darkkhaki"
</script>
```

Note that the first *array element* (item) in the list is always numbered zero. Regular parentheses are used to define the number of elements in the array within the new Array(*x*) statement. But square brackets are always used for defining names. Programmers regularly use the word *sub* when speaking about array elements. For example, in the colors array I would say "color sub zero is dark blue, color sub one is dark cyan," and so forth.

TIP

The Array() object is new to Netscape Navigator version 3.0.

One of the beauties of an array is that you can reference data in the list by its position in the list—i.e., by its subscript. Thus, you can set up a loop to search through the array and/or to process all the items in the array.

JavaScript Loops

A *loop* is a pair of JavaScript statements that repeat a set of instructions over and over again. JavaScript supports the common *for* loop, as well as *while* loops. The syntax of a *for* loop looks like this:

```
for (start,condition,increment)  {
     statements
}
```

start is an expression that defines the starting value of the variable that will serve as the loop counter, *condition* is an expression that results in true or false, and *increment* is an expression that indicates how much to increment the counter with each pass through the loop. And *statements* are one or more JavaScript statements that are executed with each pass through the loop.

Here is an example. Assuming that the color array script described in the preceding section exists, this small loop would print the names of the items in the list:

```
<script>
     for (i=0; i<=4; i++) {
     document.writeln(color[i])
}
</script>
```

The for statement says something like: "For the variable *i* starting at zero and continuing as long as *i* is less than or equal to four and incrementing *i* by one (i++) with each pass through the loop, write the contents of the variable color[*i*]." In the first pass through the loop the script prints color[0], which is "darkblue." On the second pass, the script prints color[1], which is "darkcyan," and so forth, until *i* is no longer less than or equal to 4. The result is a list of the color names on the screen, as follows:

```
darkblue
darkcyan
darkgoldenrod
darkgreen
darkkhaki
```

A more interesting application of the array and loop might be to print the color name *in its color*. To do that, you could use the color name as an attribute of the <font> tag. You'd need to have the loop print the appropriate tag and color name with each pass through the loop.

Figure 18-15 shows the entire Web page required to print the little color list in color. Figure 18-16 shows the results of running that script. To see the actual colors, however, you'd need to run the script on a color monitor.

```
18-15.htm - Notepad                                              _ 8 X
File   Edit   Search   Help
<html><head>
<title>Sample Array</title>
<script>        //define and fill an array named color, here in the head.
    var color = new Array(10)
    color[0]="darkblue"
    color[1]="darkcyan"
    color[2]="darkgoldenrod"
    color[3]="darkgreen"
    color[4]="darkkhaki"
    color[5]="darkmagenta"
    color[6]="darkolivegreen"
    color[7]="darkorange"
    color[8]="darkviolet"
    color[9]="deeppink"
</script>
</head>          <! head ends here>
<body>           <! body starts here>
<h1><center>
<script>                  //Now use the color array to print names in color.
    for (i=0;i<=9;i++) {
        document.write("<font color='"+color[i]+"'>")
        document.write(color[i])
        document.write("</font><br>")
    }
</script>
</center><h1>
</body>
</html>
```

Figure 18-15: *A script to define an array and another script to print it.*

Figure 18-16: *The results of running the scripts shown in Figure 18-15. The actual colors do not show in this black-and-white reproduction.*

The full set of Navigator color names and triplets is listed in Appendix E, "Color Names & Triplets." The Color Schemer script in the JavaScript section of my Web site (www.coolnerds.com) provides one-click access to all the colors.

JAVASCRIPT CUSTOM MESSAGES

JavaScript can display custom messages on your reader's screen. The messages can be displayed in any one of three custom dialog box types:

- alert(): Displays an alert (!) box with your message, an OK button, and an audible beep.

- confirm(): Displays your message, OK and Cancel buttons, and an audible beep.

- prompt(): Displays your message, a prompt for user input, and OK and Cancel buttons.

Figure 18-17 shows an example of each type of box. To see each dialog box live on your screen, type and run the script shown in Figure 18-18. Note that when you run the script, you need to click a button in each box that appears, so that you can view the next dialog box.

Figure 18-17: *Examples of three JavaScript dialog boxes.*

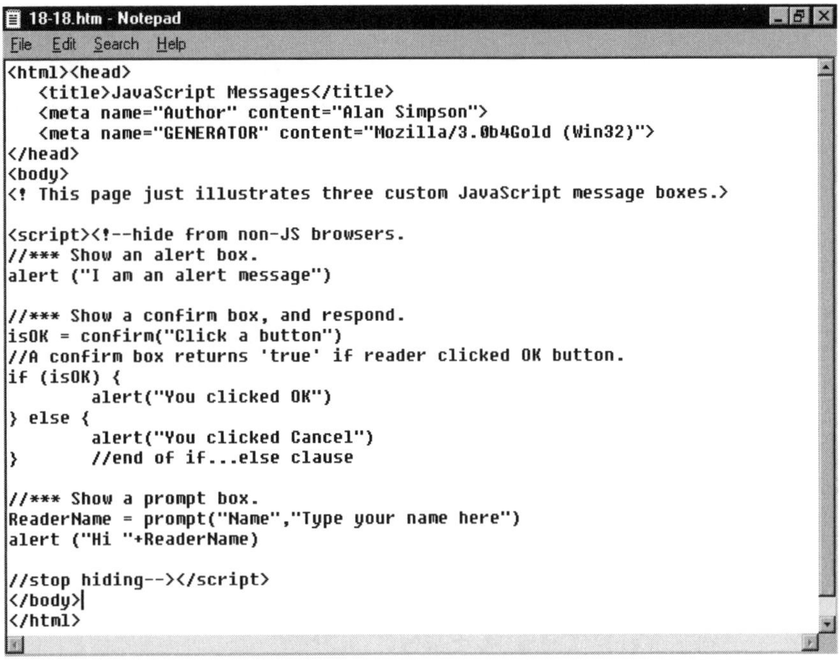

```
18-18.htm - Notepad                                        _ 8 X
File  Edit  Search  Help
<html><head>
    <title>JavaScript Messages</title>
    <meta name="Author" content="Alan Simpson">
    <meta name="GENERATOR" content="Mozilla/3.0b4Gold (Win32)">
</head>
<body>
<! This page just illustrates three custom JavaScript message boxes.>

<script><!--hide from non-JS browsers.
//*** Show an alert box.
alert ("I am an alert message")

//*** Show a confirm box, and respond.
isOK = confirm("Click a button")
//A confirm box returns 'true' if reader clicked OK button.
if (isOK) {
        alert("You clicked OK")
} else {
        alert("You clicked Cancel")
}       //end of if...else clause

//*** Show a prompt box.
ReaderName = prompt("Name","Type your name here")
alert ("Hi "+ReaderName)

//stop hiding--></script>
</body>
</html>
```

Figure 18-18: *Create and run this script to see sample messages on your screen.*

CREATING CUSTOM JAVASCRIPT FUNCTIONS

When you start exploring other people's scripts, the first thing you'll discover is that virtually all programmers organize their code into *functions*. The functions are generally defined between the <head>...</head> tags and then are called upon by scripts within the <body>...</body> section of the Web page.

There are many advantages to organizing JavaScript code into functions. First, after you create a function, you can easily cut and paste it into whatever page you're working on, so you don't have to reinvent the wheel every time you need a script to do some job. Second, you can test and debug the function once. After you are confident that it works, you just call it when you need it. You don't have to retype and debug the script every time you use it. Finally, the whole approach enables you to build up your own collection of user-defined functions (UDFs, or *custom functions*) relevant to your own work. It's almost as though you get to create your own programming language, with capabilities and syntax *you* design.

WHAT IS A FUNCTION?

Now that I've given you a sales pitch on custom functions, I'd better explain what they are. A *function* is a little routine, written in JavaScript, that has a name (which you give it) and a purpose (which you write into it). For example, you might create a function called calctax() that calculates the sales tax for any number.

All function names are followed by parentheses, as in calctax(). You can pass values to the function simply by putting the value (or a variable that represents the value) inside the parentheses. For example, you can design you calctax() function so that it can accept a single number. Then, let's say that you have a variable named TotalSale in the body of your Web page. If you created a custom calctax() function capable of accepting a number, you could calculate the sales tax on a total sale by using this relatively simple command:

```
var SalesTax = calctax(TotalSale)
```

It helps to think of the parentheses as standing for the word *of*. For example, the preceding statement reads as *SalesTax equals calctax of TotalSale.*

All functions *return* some value. Thus, when you enter a statement such as

```
var SalesTax = calctax(TotalSale)
```

you assume that the calctax() function will calculate the sales tax and *return* that number. That returned number is what gets stored in the SalesTax variable in the preceding example.

CREATING A CUSTOM FUNCTION

A custom function is a script. It's good practice to define all your custom functions in the <head>...</head> portion of your Web page, to ensure that JavaScript "knows" that the custom function exists before you call upon that function from within the body of the Web page. Because you'll be typing the script into the page's head, you'll need to use an external editor—not Gold's editor—to do the job.

Each custom function that you create must start with the *function {* statement and end with a *}* character. The exact syntax is

```
function name(parameters) {
      statements
}
```

name is the name you want to give the function, *parameters* are names assigned to any data that gets passed to the function and *statements* are normal JavaScript statements that define what the function does.

We need an example. Suppose that I want to create the aforementioned calctax() function, such that it calculates 8.25% of whatever number is passed to it. (In JavaScript, 8.25% is expressed as a decimal, 0.0825. That is, the number, divided by a hundred, with the percent sign removed.) Because this is a custom function, I'd define it in the <head> of the page. That section of page would look something like this:

```
<html>
<head>
<title>First function demo</title>
<script>
    function calctax(anynumber) {
            return (0.0825 * anynumber)
    }
</script>
</head>
```

In the body of this page I could enter the following JavaScript statement to calculate the sales tax on the value currently stored in a variable named TotalSale:

```
<script>
    TotalSale = 100.00
    SalesTax = calctax(TotalSale)
</script>
```

When JavaScript executes the SalesTax = calctax(TotalSale) statement, it substitutes the value for TotalSale (100.00, in this example). For a split second, the function looks something like SalesTax=calctax(100). Then it passes the 100.00 to the calctax() function, which multiplies 100 by 0.0825, resulting in 8.25. The calctax() function then returns that value (8.25), and for a split second, the statement looks something like SalesTax = 8.25. That statement is the one that JavaScript actually executes. By the time the execution cycle reaches the next line in the script, the variable SalesTax contains the number 8.25.

You'll see hundreds of examples of custom functions when you start browsing the Web and peeking at other people's scripts. In fact, there are dozens in the JavaScript section of my Web site at www.coolnerds.com. You're welcome to view, swipe, and use any of my custom functions that might be useful in your own work.

DEBUGGING JAVASCRIPT CODE

Chances are, you'll encounter many error messages during your JavaScript apprenticeship—just one of those unpleasant facts of life. The error message, though always a bummer to encounter, is there for some good reasons:

- To inform you that there is an instruction in your script that the computer doesn't understand.

- To give you some clue as to where it stopped understanding the script.

- To give you some hints about what might be wrong with the script.

Therefore, you want to be sure to read the message before you click the OK button to get rid of it. If more errors exist in the script, you may see more error messages. Just keep reading and clicking OK until no more error messages appear.

Then, you have to get back to Gold's editor or your external editor, figure out what's wrong, and fix it. Then save all your changes and browse the document again. It may take several tries to get all the kinks worked out. We call this process *debugging* and believe me, all programmers spend *lots* of time doing it.

The following sections explain three of the most common error messages you're likely to come across and some possible solutions to each error.

<WHATEVER> CANNOT BE CONVERTED TO A FUNCTION

In English, this means "I don't understand what you're trying to do here." These are the most likely causes for such a message:

- You used the incorrect upper- or lowercase letters.

- You misspelled some part of the JavaScript statement.

- You've called on a custom function that's not defined in the <head> section of the current document.

Back in Figure 18-11, the error message is displayed because my code contains the statement *Document.Write("whatever")* instead of *document.write("whatever")* with a lowercase *d* and lowercase *w*. The fix in this example is to return to Gold's editor and type the line with proper upper- and lowercase letters.

UNTERMINATED STRING LITERAL

In English, this means "a chunk of text that starts with a quotation mark (either " or '), is missing the closing quotation mark. For example, in Figure 18-19 the error message points to the opening quotation mark for the string literal "Hello World!" As you can see, however, there is no closing quotation mark. The fix is to go back to Gold's editor and insert the missing quotation mark, as follows.

```
document.write("Hello World!")
```

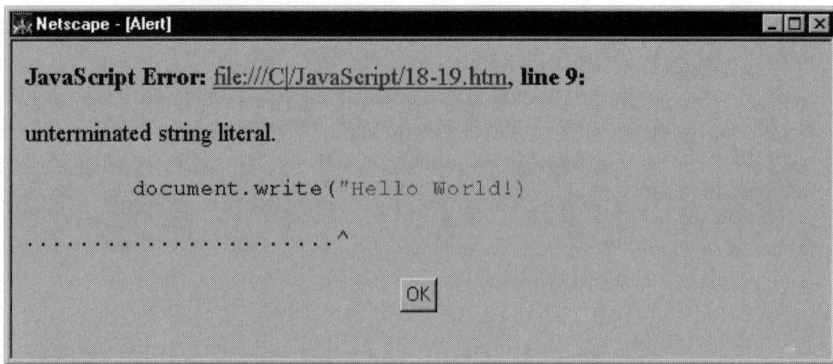

Figure 18-19: *Sample Unterminated String Literal error message.*

MISSING <WHATEVER>...

If a line of JavaScript code is missing some important element, such as a closing parenthesis or quotation mark, the Missing *<whatever>* message will appear and point to the line in which the character is missing. You'll need to figure out what's missing and then go back to the editor and type the missing character.

The Browser Just Shows the Code

If you switch to your Netscape Navigator browser and see your raw JavaScript code rather than the *results* of that code, then Navigator "thinks" the code is regular text (most likely because the script is not surrounded by <script>...</script> tags).

To fix the problem, go back to Gold's editor and select all the JavaScript code by dragging the mouse pointer though it. Then choose Properties|Character|JavaScript (Client). Click anywhere in the page. The code should now be displayed in red, because Gold has inserted the <script>...</script> tags, behind the scenes. This time when you switch to the browser, the code will be executed.

JavaScript Versus Java

Many people are confused about the various Java products —Java, Hot Java, and JavaScript—that are getting so much hype these days. No, these are not just different names for one product. They are, indeed, three separate products.

Hot Java is a Web browser, like Navigator. It was the first Web browser to support Java programs (called *applets*). That is far from a unique feature these days. Many Web browsers, including your trusty Netscape Navigator Gold, support Java now.

Java is a complete stand-alone programming language for professionals, similar to the C and C++ languages used to create most high-end products, such as spreadsheets, word processing programs, even operating systems like Windows. A big weakness of the current C and C++ languages is that you need to use a version that's geared to a particular operating system. For example, suppose that a company creates a program to sell to PC users. If they want to extend their market to the Mac, they need to create a new Mac version of that program, largely from scratch. A huge task!

Unlike C and C++, Java is a *cross-platform language.* Using Java, a company can create a program once and rest assured that the program will work on PCs, Macs, and Unix machines. This cross-platform capability makes Java ideal for creating programs that will be distributed over the Internet.

JavaScript, the subject of this chapter, is a *scripting language* or *extension language* that allows you to extend the capabilities of Netscape Navigator. Unlike Java, JavaScript does not allow you to create stand-alone programs that can run outside of a browser. But it has many advantages:

- JavaScript is *much* easier to learn and to use than Java.

- JavaScript is more than sufficient for the level of interactivity that most Web authors/publishers/programmers are trying to accomplish in their Web sites.

- Unlike Java, which requires third-party software (compiler, Java Development Kit), JavaScript requires no additional software.

If you're tempted to learn both JavaScript and Java, do yourself a huge favor. Learn JavaScript first. The early stages of the learning curve will be much easier and more productive. And, you may discover that JavaScript offers all the power you need. Should you decide to move on to Java, no big deal. Everything you learned about JavaScript will carry right over to Java, and make *that* new learning curve a bit more palatable.

MOVING ON

Whew! I called this chapter "Introducing JavaScript." But that was more like an intense, quick ramp-up crash course! As intense as it may seem, you're off to a good start because when you start looking at other people's scripts, they'll make some sense to you now. And that's exactly what you want to do after you get a rough feel for the language—explore other people's scripts to get a feel for the way experienced programmers get things accomplished with JavaScript code. The next chapter presents some examples, as well as pointers to Web sites that offer hundreds of additional sample scripts you can experiment with live online.

Fun With JavaScript

In this chapter I present some sample JavaScript scripts to illustrate and reinforce what we covered in the preceding chapter. Some small easy scripts, fun scripts, and useful scripts including the following:

- Scripts to show the date of the page's last update
- On-page Back and Forward buttons
- Scripts to detect available plug-ins
- Fun script to change the background color

After that, you should easily be able to set forth on the Web and take a look at the hundreds of additional ready-made scripts available to you. I end this chapter by pointing out all the best sites to visit.

SHOW THE MOST RECENT MODIFICATION DATE

We got into some pretty heavy stuff at the end of Chapter 18, "Introducing JavaScript." Now let's lighten up and make the first script here an easy one. This script shows the date on which the current page was last modified. It uses the lastModified property of the document object to do this.

To create this script, open any page in Gold's editor. Switch to the external editor (View I Edit Document Source) and move the cursor to about where you want the modification date to appear. Then type the script as shown here. Make sure that you put the script somewhere between the <body>...</body> tags, and that you type the document.write() statement as one long line, as shown in Notepad's editor in Figure 19-1.

TIP

Remember, if you type the script in Gold's editor, omit the <script>... </script> tags, press Shift+Enter to break lines, and apply the JavaScript (Client) character property to the JavaScript statement. If you use an external editor, go ahead and type the <script>...</script> tags.

```
<script><!-- hide from non-JS browsers
     var modiDate = document.lastModified
     document.write ("This page last updated on " + modiDate)
//stop hiding--></script>
```

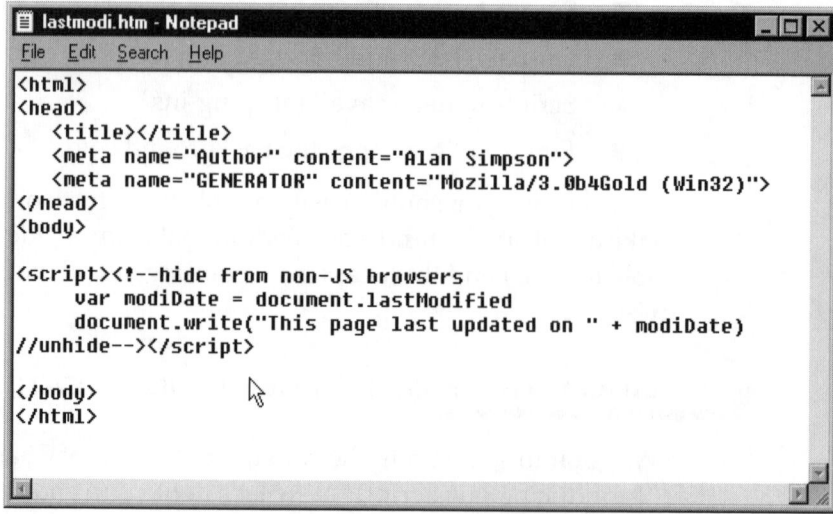

Figure 19-1: *Script to show the date of the most recent update.*

To see the script played out, exit your external editor and save your work. Reload the document if asked to do so, and then switch to the browser (click the View in Browser button). The line will resemble this, but will show the date and time that you created (or most recently changed) the page:

```
This page last updated on 06/16/97 12:00:00 PM
```

Figure 19-2 shows what the script looks like in Gold's editor, near the bottom of a sample page. Gold's editor, of course, hides all the HTML tags, including the <script>...</script> tags. But you can see the actual JavaScript code that's between those tags.

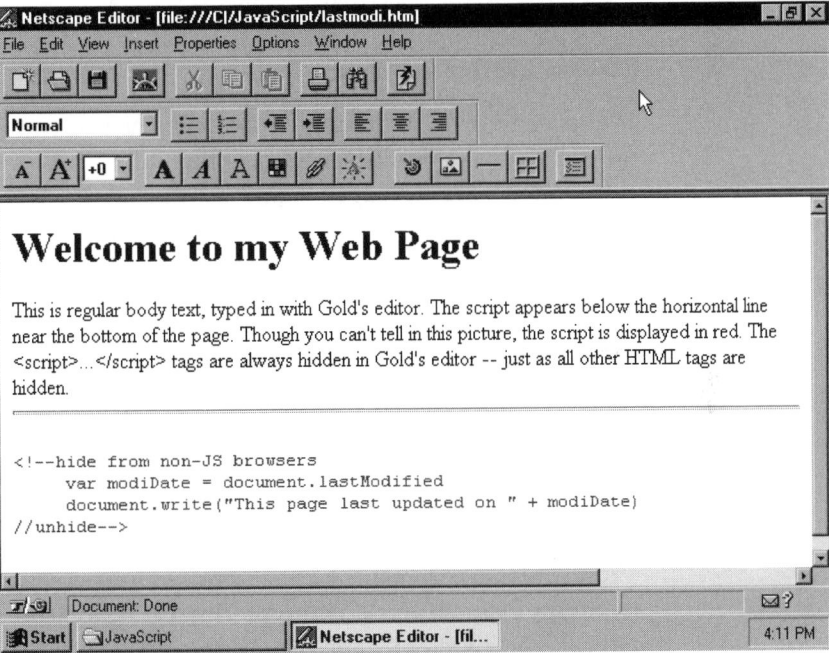

Figure 19-2: *The Last Modification Date script as it would look in Gold's editor.*

Variations on the Last Modification Date Theme

I can show you some little JavaScript tricks for changing the appearance of that date. You could make these changes right in Gold's editor, or in an external editor—it doesn't matter which.

The first example illustrates how to use the substring method of JavaScript's String object to remove the time from the last modification date. That variation would look like this:

```
<script><!-- hide from non-JS browsers
    var modiDate = document.lastModified
    modiDate = modiDate.substring(0,8)
    document.write ("This page last updated on " + modiDate)
//stop hiding--></script>
```

When you browse the page that contains this script, the last modification date looks something like this:

```
This page last updated on 06/16/97
```

Why does this work? Well, the value returned by document.lastModified is a string in the format mm/dd/yy hh:mm:ss. The substring (*start,end*) method of the String object returns a substring, starting at position *start* and ending at position *end*, in which the first character in the string is position 0. Because the character at position *end* is not included—only characters up to that point are included—modiDate.substring(0,8) returns just the first eight characters in modiDate, which is the mm/dd/yy portion in this example.

You can also convert the modification date from a string to a JavaScript Date object. That gives you a couple of other alternative methods for displaying the date. For example, this rendition of the script

```
<script><!-- hide from non-JS browsers
    modiDate = new Date(document.lastModified)
document.write ("This page last updated on " + modiDate)
//stop hiding--></script>
```

displays its output in the following format, where PDT stands for Pacific Daylight Time, which happens to be my time zone:

```
This page last updated on Mon Jun 16 12:00:00 PDT 1997
```

This version of the script uses the toGMTString() method of JavaScript's date object to display the date in the Internet's Greenwich Meridian Time:

```
<script><!-- hide from non-JS browsers
      tempDate = new Date(document.lastModified)
   modiDate = tempDate.toGMTString()
document.write ("This page last updated on " + modiDate)
//stop hiding--></script>
```

This last version of the script displays its output in this format:

```
This page last updated on Mon, 16 Jun 1996 12:00:00 GMT
```

If you want to format the line displayed by this little script, you can insert the appropriate HTML tags—outside the <script>... </script> tags—using an external editor. For example, this version shows the message in small italicized letters centered on the screen beneath a horizontal line:

```
<hr><small><i><center>
<script><!-- hide from non-JS browsers
      var modiDate = document.lastModified
      modiDate = modiDate.substring(0,9)
document.write ("This page last updated on " + modiDate)
//stop hiding--></script>
</small></i></center>
```

ONSCREEN NAVIGATION BUTTONS

Chapter 16, "Creating Clickable Image Maps," showed how to create clickable image maps that allow readers to scroll to specific areas in your site. With JavaScript you can extend that onscreen navigation ability to include Back and Forward buttons. To accomplish this feat you need to use JavaScript's history object, as follows:

- history.back(): Takes the reader to the previous page in the history list (if any).

- history.forward(): Takes the reader to the next page in the history list (if any).

The simple way to create onscreen Back and Forward controls would be as hyperlinks. Just type the word *Back* and the word *Forward* right onto the page, in Gold's editor, wherever you want the links to appear. You can separate them with the | character as I did, if you wish. Then use the Center button in the toolbar to center the text.

To convert the word *Back* to a hyperlink, select that word, click the Make Link button, and specify **javascript:history.back()** as the "Link to" file, as shown in Figure 19-3.

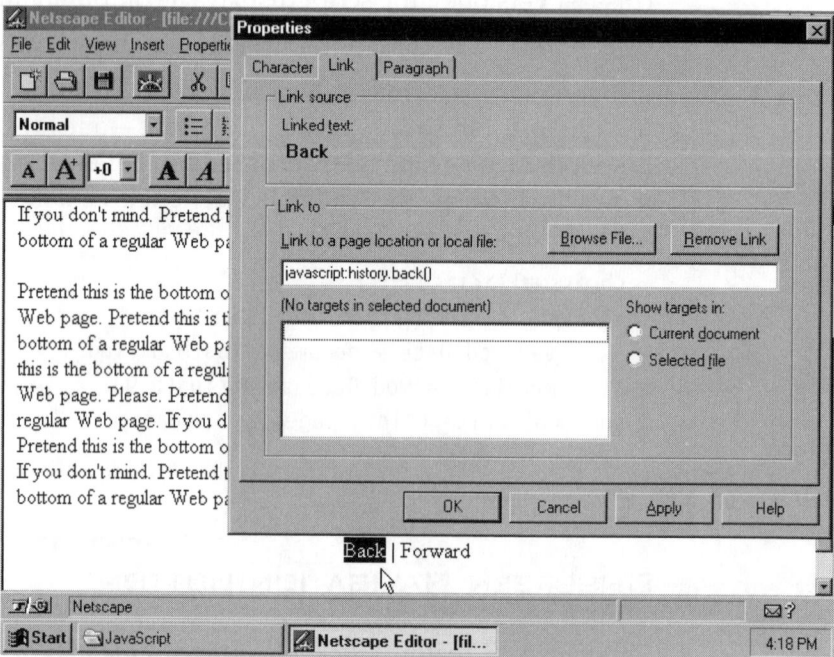

Figure 19-3: *Creating a simple onscreen Back link.*

Then select the Forward link and specify **javascript:history.forward()** as its "Link to" file.

When you view the document source you'll see that the javascript:history... entry has been placed in the <a href...> tag for each link, as follows:

```
<a href="javascript:history.back()">Back</a>
<a href="javascript:history.forward()"> Forward</a>
```

TESTING THE BACK & FORWARD BUTTONS

The onscreen Back and Forward buttons won't really work until you have a history list in the current session to work with. To properly test these buttons, you should go online and visit a few sites. Then, from Navigator's menu bar, choose File | Open File in Browser, and open the file that contains your onscreen Back and Forward buttons.

TIP

Unlike the Back and Forward buttons in Navigator's toolbar, these links won't be dimmed when there is no page to scroll to. If the reader clicks the link when there is no page to go to, nothing happens.

Visit a couple of sites from your Bookmarks menu to put some sites ahead of the page you just opened, then use the Back button in the toolbar to go back to the page that contains your onscreen buttons. *Then* you can test the Back and Forward buttons on that page.

VARIATIONS ON THE BACK & FORWARD BUTTONS THEME

Specifying *javascript:history...* as the HREF for a link works just as well when you want to use graphic images, rather than words, as the hot link. For instance, if you use two graphic images named backbtn.gif and fwrdbtn.gif as the links, the tags would look something like this:

```
<a href="javascript:history.back()"><img src="backbtn.gif"
height=40 width=40></a>
<a href="javascript:history.forward()"><img src="fwrdbtn.gif"
height=40 width=40></a>
```

If you use a single picture with two buttons, you can create a clickable image map as described in Chapter 16. In the map code, use javascript:history.back() and javascript:history.forward() as the HREFs for the areas that act as the Back and Forward buttons, like this:

```
<AREA SHAPE=RECT COORDS="6,0,68,64"
HREF="javascript:history.back()"ALT="Back">
<AREA SHAPE=RECT COORDS="79,0,144,64"
HREF="javascript:history.forward()" ALT="Forward">
```

Optionally, you can use JavaScript's form object to draw the buttons on the page. We'll talk more about forms in Chapter 21, "Creating Forms for Business." Now, however, suffice it to say that if you put these tags in a Web page you'll end up with two functional Back and Forward buttons on that page:

```
<! Create onscreen Back and Forward buttons>
<center>
<form>
<input type="button" value="Back"
    onMouseOver="Back"
    onClick="history.back()">

<input type="button" value="Forward"
    onMouseOver="Forward"
    onClick="history.forward()">

</form>
</center>
```

Notice that there are no <script> and </script> tags in the above "script." The tiny JavaScript actions are defined right next to the onClick event handler. The text at the top inside the <!...> tags are regular HTML comments, not JavaScript comments, because the form itself is defined by HTML tags.

Figure 19-4 shows what the buttons look like when you browse the page. The Notepad window covering the page shows the tags in the underlying source document. No <script> tags are required because the JavaScript statements are expressed in the onClick and onMouseOver attributes of the <input> tags.

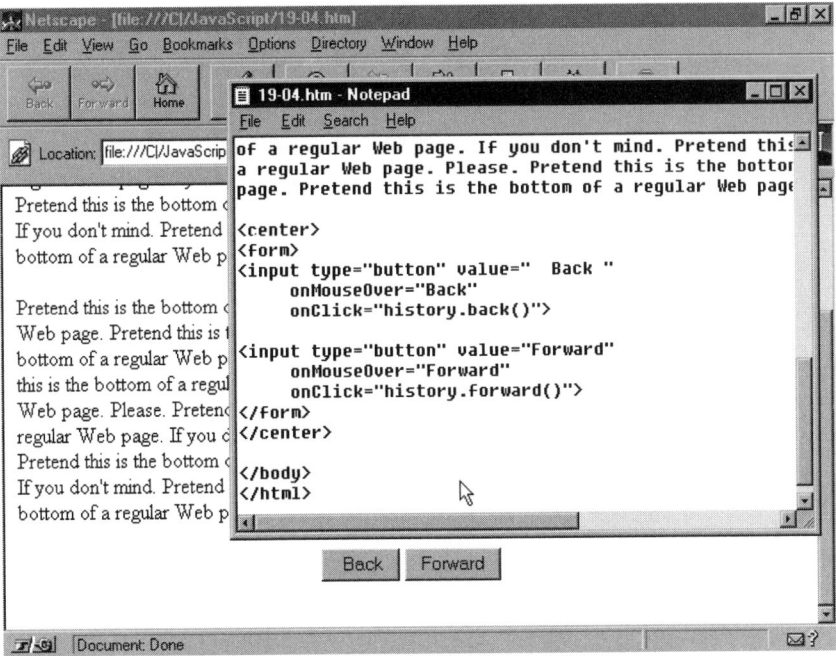

Figure 19-4: *Onscreen Back and Forward buttons created with JavaScript's form object.*

In a multiframe site you can put the Back and Forward links in some frame other than the main frame that's displaying the page. You can't use just history.back() and history.forward() as the HREFs for those links, however, because they would affect the *current* frame rather than the main frame. To make the links act upon some other frame, you need to specify parent.*framename*.history.*whatever*() in the HREF. For example, the following link tags move the reader back and forward through a frame named Main:

```
<a href= "javascript:parent.Main.history.back()">
<a href= "javascript:parent.Main.history.forward()">
```

Notice, in Figure 19-5, the small set of navigation buttons at the bottom of the left frame. The Notepad window for navbttns.htm—the page displayed in that bottom left frame—shows the <AREA...> tags that control the left and right buttons on that little

graphic. The leftmost area uses "javascript:parent.Main.
history.back()> as its HREF, the rightmost area uses "javascript:
parent.Main.history.forward()> as its HREF.

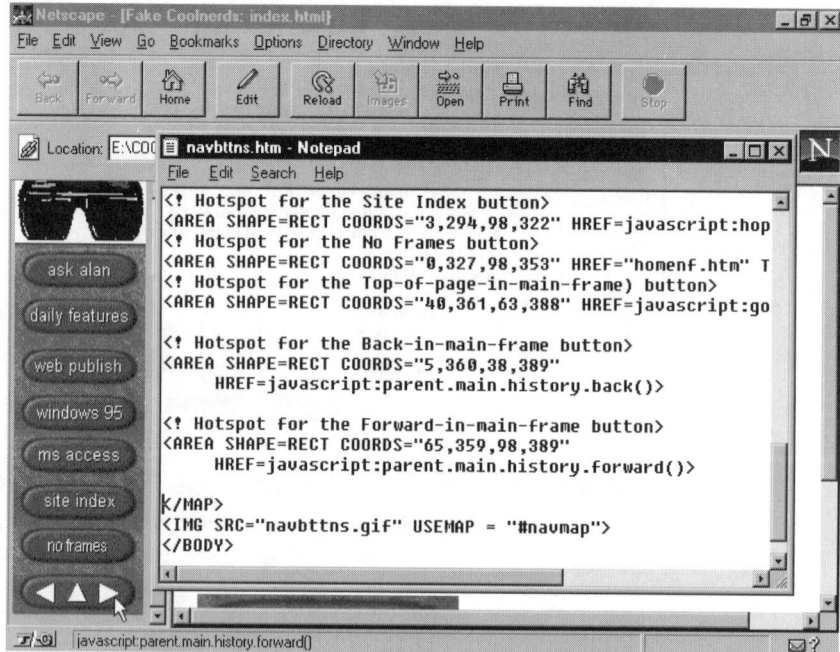

Figure 19-5: *The Notepad window shows <AREA...> tags for the little button bar at the bottom of the leftmost frame.*

DETECTING AVAILABLE PLUG-INS

JavaScript's navigator object has two properties capable of determining what plug-ins are available for, and what external file types are supported by, your reader's Web browser. The syntax for using these properties follows:

- navigator.plugins["*name*"]: Returns true if the reader has the plug-in specified in *name*. Otherwise, returns false.

■ navigator.mimeTypes["*mimetype*"]: Returns true if the reader's browser supports the specified *mimetype*, otherwise returns false.

TIP

The plugins and mimeTypes properties are new to Netscape Navigator 3.0. They may not be supported by all JavaScript-capable browsers.

Let's suppose that you have a Shockwave movie you want to display to your readers, and that you want to tell readers who don't have Shockwave where they can get a copy. The JavaScript shown in Figure 19-6 (Notepad view) will do the trick.

```
19-06.htm - Notepad
File  Edit  Search  Help
<html><head>
   <title>Plug-in Test</title>
   <meta name="Author" content="Alan Simpson">
   <meta name="GENERATOR" content="Mozilla/3.0b4Gold (Win32)">
</head>
<body>

<script>
    //Test for Shockwave plugin.
    var plugin = navigator.plugins["Shockwave"]

    //If plugin found, embed tag for Shockwave movie.
    if (plugin) {
        document.writeln("<embed src='MyMovie.dir' height=75 width=75>")
    }
    //If no Shockwave plug-in, show message and hyperlink.
    else {
        document.writeln("Sorry, I cannot show you my movie because you d(
    }
</script>

</body></html>
```

Figure 19-6: *Script tests for Shockwave before attempting to show a movie.*

The lengthy message in the "else" condition is too wide to show in its entirety. That entire line actually looks like this:

```
document.writeln("Sorry, I cannot show you my movie because
you do not have Shockwave installed. If you would like to
install Shockwave right now, go to <a href='http://
www.macromedia.com'>Macromedia</a> and follow their download
and installation instructions.")
```

The logic for determining whether or not the reader has the Shockwave plug-in starts with the line *var plugin = navigator.plugins["Shockwave"]* which automatically checks all the available plug-ins. If the Shockwave plug-in is available, the variable named *plugin* receives a value of **true**. If the Shockwave plug-in isn't found, the variable *plugin* receives a value of **false**. The clause starting with *if (plugin) {* then determines how to behave based on whether the variable *plugin* contains **true** or **false**.

As an alternative to checking for a specific plug-in, JavaScript can check for a support file (mime) type. For example, the script in Figure 19-7 tests to see whether the reader's browser supports the video/quicktime mime type. If so, the script embeds a hyperlink to the movie. If not, the script presents a message to the reader, including a link to a spot that offers QuickTime players.

```
19-07.htm - Notepad                                              _ |&| X
File  Edit  Search  Help
<html><head>
    <title>Mime type Test</title>
    <meta name="Author" content="Alan Simpson">
    <meta name="GENERATOR" content="Mozilla/3.0b4Gold (Win32)">
</head>
<body>

<script>
//See if this browser supports Quicktime.
var mimetype = navigator.mimeTypes["xxxvideo/quicktime"]

//If this browser supports quicktime, insert a link to movie.
if (mimetype) {
    document.writeln("Click <A HREF='MyMovie.qt'>here</A> to see movie")

} else {          //If no Quicktime, no movie.
    document.writeln("Sorry, you don't have a plug-in for Quicktime movies. If
}

</script>

</body></html>
```

Figure 19-7: *Script tests for QuickTime support before attempting to show a movie.*

Once again, the message in the "else" portion of the script is too wide to fit on the screen. Here's the entire content of the line:

```
document.writeln("Sorry, you don't have a plug-in for
Quicktime movies. If you want to get one check out <a
href='http://www2.cybernex.net/~mps/VideoLinks/Quicktime-
Downloading'> this site</a>.")
```

RESPOND TO A SPECIFIC BROWSER

You can use the appName property of the navigator object to detect which browser the reader is using to view your site. Use that property in an *if* clause to determine which tags to embed in a page. To see an example, please refer to "JavaScript Decision Making" in Chapter 18.

FUN WITH BACKGROUND COLORS

You can use the bgColor property of JavaScript's document object to change the background color of the screen at any time. Figure 19-8 shows a sample page, named colors.htm, that lets the reader choose any one of nine background colors, just by clicking a radio button.

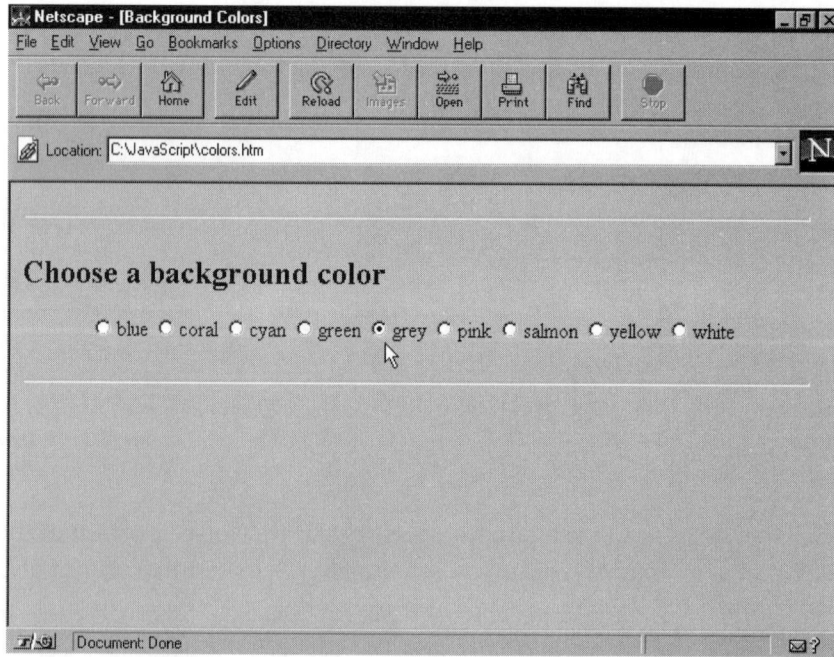

Figure 19-8: *Readers can click a radio button to choose a background color.*

Let's take a look behind the scenes to see what makes colors.htm tick. Figure 19-9 shows the document source for the entire page. I've boldfaced the JavaScript components of this page because it illustrates a "typical" Web page that contains JavaScript. A custom JavaScript function is defined in the head. Then, event procedures down in the body of the page call upon that function in response to readers' mouse clicks.

```
<html>
<head>
<title>Background Colors</title>

<script>
  // Custom function to change background color.
  function bcolor(anycolor) {
     document.bgColor=anycolor
  }
</script>

</head>
<body>
<hr><h2>Choose a background color</h2>
<center><form>
<input type="radio" name="bkclr" onclick="bcolor('lightblue')">blue
<input type="radio" name="bkclr" onclick="bcolor('lightcoral')">coral
<input type="radio" name="bkclr" onclick="bcolor('lightcyan')">cyan
<input type="radio" name="bkclr" onclick="bcolor('lightgreen')">green
<input type="radio" name="bkclr" onclick="bcolor('lightgrey')">grey
<input type="radio" name="bkclr" onclick="bcolor('lightpink')">pink
<input type="radio" name="bkclr" onclick="bcolor('lightsalmon')">salmon
<input type="radio" name="bkclr" onclick="bcolor('lightyellow')">yellow
<input type="radio" name="bkclr" onclick="bcolor('white')">white
</form></center><hr>
</body>
</html>
```

Figure 19-9: *Source document for colors.htm.*

Let's look more closely at the code. The custom function named
bcolor() accepts one parameter, named *anycolor*. It passes that value to
the JavaScript statement *document.bgColor=anycolor*, in which bgColor
is a property of the document object. As you may have guessed, it's
the property that defines the document's background color:

```
<script>
// Custom function to change background color.
function bcolor(anycolor) {
     document.bgColor=anycolor
}
</script>
```

Down in the body of the page, the <form> and <input> tags present the radio buttons to the reader. For example, the tag

```
<input type="radio" name="bkclr"
onclick="bcolor('lightblue')">blue
```

displays a radio button that, when clicked, calls upon the bcolor() custom function, passing the color name *lightblue* to it. The word *blue* at the end of the tag is just the word *blue* that appears next to the radio button on the reader's screen.

TRAP

The <input...> tags will not work unless placed between the <form>...</form> tags. We'll examine forms in depth in Chapters 21 and 22.

The series of <input> tags is pretty easy to type because you need to type only the first one. Then you can copy and paste that one and change color name—from *blue* to *coral,* for example—in the second line. I used the "light" version of each color, because we're coloring the document background here. The color names come from Appendix E, "Color Names & Triplets."

TRAP

The beta version of Microsoft Internet Explorer 3.0 wasn't supporting the color names listed in Appendix E. But that may change when the final product is released. If in doubt, you can always use the color triplet rather than the color name.

ON BECOMING A JAVASCRIPT GURU

JavaScript is a huge topic, and complete mastery takes time. Your best bet, at this juncture, is to get a good online electronic reference to the entire language and then expose yourself to as many live JavaScript examples as you can find. The beauty of exploring live is that you can *see* what the script does, right on your screen. Then just choose View | View Document Source to take a peek at the underlying JavaScript code—to see what makes the page tick.

> **TIP**
>
> *I'm sure that if you swing by your local bookstore, you'll find plenty of books devoted entirely to JavaScript! The* Official Netscape JavaScript Book *by Netscape Press is a great resource.*

Of course, you can also make a copy of any page that contains JavaScript. Just choose File | Edit document and copy everything to a folder on your hard disk. Then you can explore to your heart's content, offline. Many sites will even let you swipe JavaScript code. For example, you're more than welcome to explore (pilfer, modify, or criticize) any of the custom JavaScript functions from my site (www.coolnerds.com). You can help yourself to entire pages, such as my Calculator, Clocks, Color Schemer, Conversion Table, Banner, and "HyperInteractive" business form if you like.

ELECTRONIC REFERENCE GUIDES

Originally, Netscape offered a great online JavaScript reference that you could download as zipped files and use offline. Recently, however, it has disappeared from their site. The rumor is that they plan to sell it, rather than give it away, in the future. Bummer.

Some of the sites listed here offered slightly modified versions of those original Netscape docs. Whether they will still be able to give away their versions remains to be seen. But stop by and see for yourself. I'll keep an eye out for some good electronic documentation and post any findings in my own Web site at www.coolnerds.com.

- ■ JavaScript docs in PDF: The most current set of documentation from Netscape, in Adobe Acrobat PDF format: http://www.ipst.com/docs.htm

- Learn JavaScript via Windows Help: Downloadable JavaScript documentation in handy Windows Help file format: http://www.jchelp.com/javahelp/javahelp.htm

- Netscape's JavaScript Authoring Guide: http://home.netscape.com/eng/mozilla/2.0/handbook/javascript/index.html

- Thomas Winzig's Personal Space: Zipped JavaScript docs in HTML format. Download the tar.gz file and unzip with WinZip95 (Appendix B). http://www.webcom.com/phantasm

OTHER ONLINE JAVASCRIPT RESOURCES

In addition to electronic documentation, there are many JavaScript tutorials, demos, chat rooms, and such all over the Web. Just point your Web browser to any of the sites that follow. If you don't want to type all those lengthy URLs, just point your Web browser to my www.coolnerds.com site. My JavaScript links there give you one-click access to all of these sites, and perhaps others:

- Ask the JavaScript Pro: Lots of JavaScript information, from Basics to Advanced, in question-and-answer format: http://www.inquiry.com/techtips/js_pro

- Coolnerds: Stop by the JavaScript section (see Figure 19-10) on my Web site at http:www.coolnerds.com.

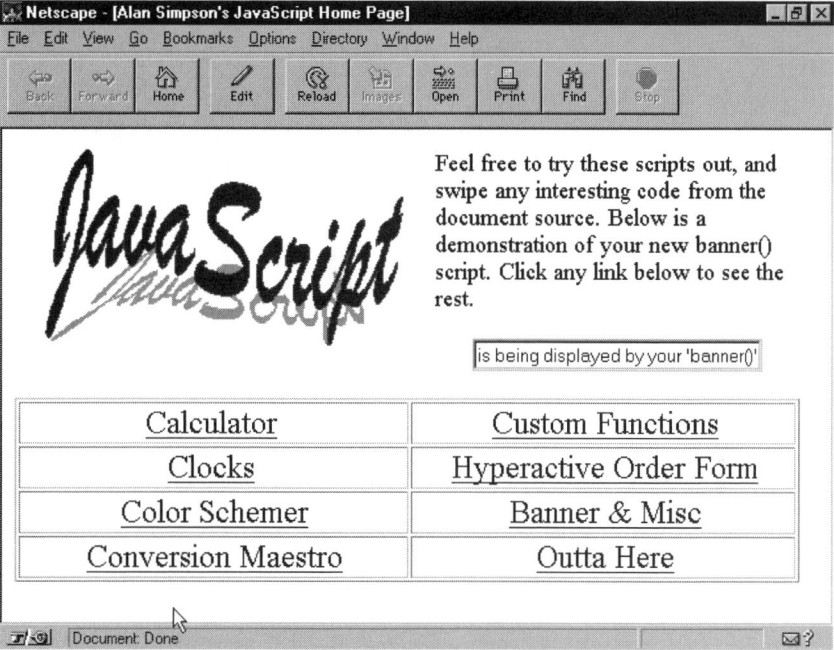

Figure 19-10: *JavaScript code to explore and swipe at www.coolnerds.com.*

■ Denise's JavaScript Page: Fun and casual Web page from a JavaScript enthusiast: http://www.loginet.com/users/d/denise/javascript.html

■ Experiments in JavaScript: Gordon McComb—scripting guru, author, and practically my next-door neighbor—shows what JavaScript can really do, and gives you lots of code to "steal": http:/www.gmccomb.com/javascript

■ JavaScript 1040 EZ: Example of using JavaScript to present an interactive tax form: http://www.homepages.com/fun/1040EZ.html

■ JavaScript 411: Tutorials, examples, and FAQs on JavaScript: http://www.freqgrafx.com/411

- JavaScript Examples: Lots of cool scripts to play around with: http://www.geocities.com/SiliconValley/9000

- JavaScript Index: News, JavaScript in Action examples, Learning about JavaScript, and Talk about JavaScript. A must-see: http://www.c2.org/~andreww/javascript

- Live Software: A Java and JavaScript resource center featuring code samples, newsgroups, discussions, chat rooms, and documentation: http://jrc.livesoftware.com

- Netscape's My First JavaScript and JavaScript Authoring Guide: Right from the source (see Figure 19-11) at http://home.netscape.com/assist/net_sites/starter/samples/java1.html

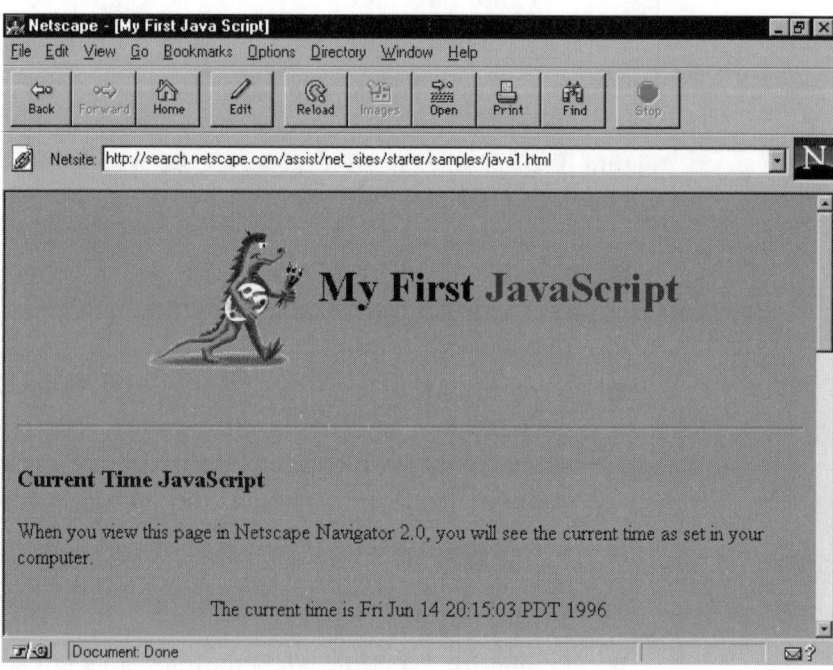

Figure 19-11: *Netscape's launch pad into JavaScript.*

- Simple Little Things to Add to Your Web Pages: A great JavaScript starter site. Cool scripts written by a guy who claims he can't even program his VCR: http://tanega.com/java/java.html

- Unofficial JavaScript Resource Center: All kinds of fun stuff, including Stupid JavaScript Tricks. Stop by: http://www.intercom.net/user/mecha/java.html

MOVING ON

I hope that those of you who are interested in pursuing JavaScript further will explore some of the sites I've listed here. On the other hand, I suspect that many of you would like to dispense with the technical programming stuff and "get down to business"—talk about ways of generating some income from your Web site. That's exactly where we'll turn our attention, starting in the next chapter.

PART IV

Getting Down
to Business

Doing Money on the Internet

Today, almost everyone is trying to figure out how to make money over the Internet. Which means that they're also trying to figure out how to get other people to spend money over the Internet. In Chapter 4, "Golden Opportunities (or, Why Create a Web Site?)," we looked at some possible scenarios for earning money from a Web site. In this chapter, I want to look specifically at actually doing financial transactions on the Internet. Which brings us right to the topic of *security*. Whether you're buying or selling, it's important to understand what security is all about. In this chapter we'll look at the following topics:

- How to protect money on the Internet
- How secure servers and browsers work
- How to use Netscape Navigator's security features
- How to know when you're visiting a secure or nonsecure site
- Where to learn more about security

HOW TO PROTECT MONEY ON THE INTERNET

In the past, worries about security on the Internet slowed the growth of online commerce. Why? Because virtually anything you sent from your computer to another computer could be grabbed by every computer in between and possibly intercepted by resourceful crooks. Figure 20-1 shows this unnerving scenario.

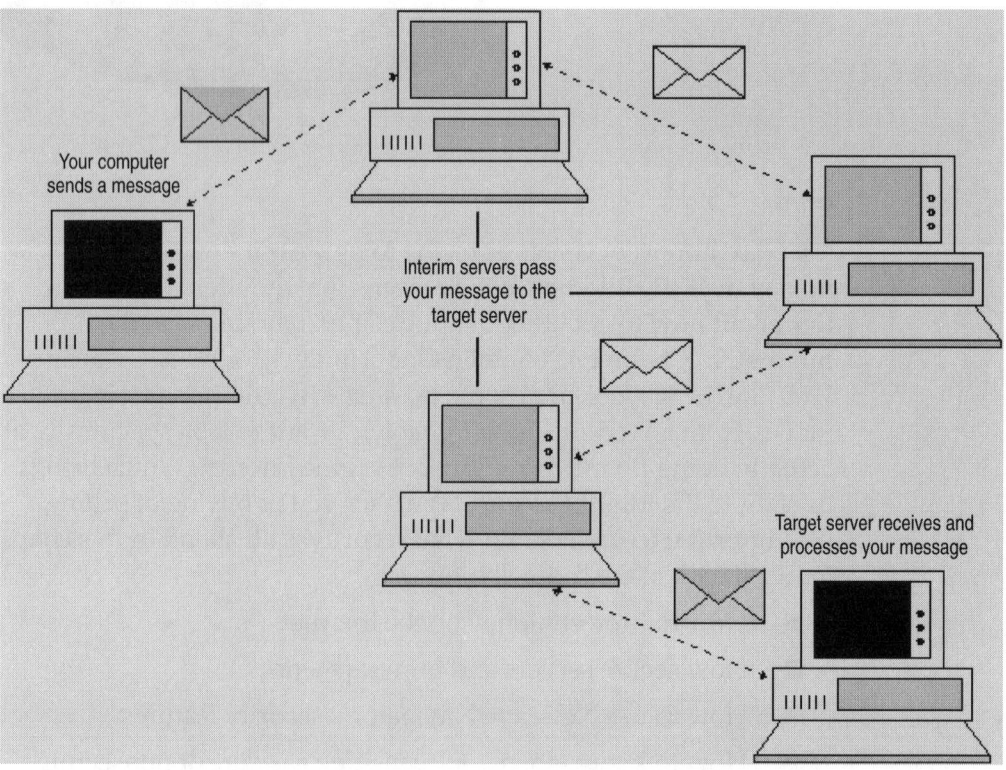

Your computer sends a message

Interim servers pass your message to the target server

Target server receives and processes your message

Figure 20-1: *Messages sent through the Internet can be intercepted by intermediate computers.*

With the advent of sophisticated security technology, online commerce is picking up. Today, many companies doing business on the Internet offer *secure sites*, which prevent unauthorized people from snatching financial and personal information as it's transmitted over the Internet.

SECURITY ISN'T THE ONLY ISSUE

Although much of this chapter focuses on security, I don't want to imply that lack of security is the *only* thing preventing people from spending money via the Web. Many other factors keep people from doing business online.

One reason is that people are accustomed to everything on the Web—everything on the Internet—being free, because it has been that way for many years. Another is that experienced users know that there are *tons* of freebies out there. When they come across a site that asks for money, it's very easy for them to skip it and move on to another site. Also, consumers like to be able to see and feel a product—inspect it—before they buy. And they like to see the product and money exchange hands at the same time, as at a cash register.

Despite that last issue, catalog sales and mail-order houses can do a thriving business after they've built up a level of trust in their consumers. Perhaps the *real* obstacle to selling products online is just the fact that the Internet is new to many people and has not had time to build up that level of trust. Security can *help* build up that trust. But that other ingredient, *time*, is still a factor and there are no quick-and-easy shortcuts around that one.

For online security to succeed, both the Web site's server software and the Web browser must work together to enforce the security measures. Moreover, the secure server must be placed in a secure physical environment (such as a locked room), and the employees who handle the secure information must themselves be honest. Shortly, we'll look at how secure sites work; but first we'll explore some common ways for buyers to pay for purchases on the Internet.

Low-Tech Solutions for Paying Outside the Internet

As a seller (or buyer) on the Internet, you might want to stick with low-tech payment solutions. For example, you should consider the traditional option of billing or being billed for purchases. For example, if you sell personalized children's books over the Internet, when you send the product you simply mail the customer an invoice for the purchase price. The customer pays you according to the payment methods you offer (cash, credit card, check), without sending any sensitive information over the Internet.

Another low-tech option includes calling in or faxing orders to charge purchases to credit cards. The telephone company's network is a reasonably safe way to transmit credit card information because it's almost impossible to eavesdrop on conversations that travel through the telephone company wires. Phoning in or faxing credit card information does pose some minor security risks. But the risks are remote and, perhaps more important, many people are already comfortable with transmitting account numbers through phone and fax lines.

TRAP

It's not *to use a cellular phone or cordless phone to send or receive credit card information, because cellular phone and cordless phone transmissions spend some time traveling through the air (like radio signals). Crooks with the right eavesdropping equipment can intercept your messages rather easily.*

High-Tech Solutions for Online Payments

Increasingly, people are using the Internet to purchase and pay for many products and services online. Several high-tech online payment methods are in use today. Of course, many of these are still in their infancy and the coming years are sure to bring refinements and new options.

TRAP

All the high-tech approaches discussed here can only guarantee secure connections between the server and the client. They cannot control the security of information after the client or server machine has it, nor can they prevent physical access to the machine or to its directories and files. Humans must take the final responsibility for guarding the sensitive information they receive.

NONSECURE ONLINE PAYMENTS

If you've ever bought anything online, you've probably submitted your credit card numbers and expiration dates in an e-mail message or by filling in an online form. In many cases, this information is transmitted to nonsecure servers, which poses a slight risk of intercepted messages and stolen credit card information.

As you might imagine, stealing your financial information as it flies through cyberspace takes a lot of work. Still, people remain justifiably suspicious. For example, they might be perfectly happy to cruise the Internet to find a product, but unwilling to trust the Internet with their money. Therefore, even if you offer electronic payment methods via the Internet (whether they're secure or not), your online forms should also give customers the option to call, fax, or mail in their credit card numbers, or to have you call them for the information.

SECURE ONLINE PAYMENTS

A security-enabled browser or e-mail program is a high-tech solution to the security issue. When a person sends online forms or e-mail messages to a secure server, it's nearly impossible for anyone between the client and the server to steal information. (More about this later.)

If your Web pages will reside on an Internet Service Provider's server—rather than your own secure server—find out whether your ISP offers secure servers. If the answer is "Yes," find out which secure browsers and e-mail programs will work with the secure servers offered. You'll certainly want support for the two most popular browsers—Netscape Navigator and Internet Explorer—so that you can offer secure payment options to the majority of your online customers.

If your Internet Service Provider can't provide transaction security, you should be sure to offer the low-tech payment methods discussed earlier.

TIP

Netscape Commerce Server (from Netscape) and Internet Information Server (from Microsoft) both offer built-in security and both support the security features in Netscape Navigator and Internet Explorer. Secure e-mail systems include Lotus Notes (http://www.lotus.com/home/notes.htm), *Microsoft Exchange Server* (http://www.microsoft.com/Exchange/exchdata.htm), *and Netscape Mail Server* (http://home.netscape.com/comprod/server_central/product/mail/index.html).

SENDING PAYMENTS THROUGH A THIRD PARTY

Credit card companies have long offered a convenient way to collect money from buyers on behalf of sellers worldwide. But as you know, thieves often use both high-tech and low-tech methods to steal credit card numbers and expiration dates. Then they make purchases by telephone, using the stolen information. They don't even need to have the credit card in their possession!

First Virtual has one solution to this credit card security problem. This company issues buyers a Personal Identification Number (PIN), called a VirtualPIN, that's an alias for a real MasterCard or Visa credit card number. Only the buyer and First Virtual know the connection between the VirtualPIN and the real credit card.

When you buy from a seller that's part of the First Virtual system, you send your VirtualPIN to the seller. First Virtual sends you e-mail asking you to verify each purchase made via the VirtualPIN. If you confirm the sale, your real credit card is charged (completely off the Internet) and payments go into the vendor's checking account. This method requires no special hardware, software, or encryption, and it's simple, secure, and safe. To learn more about First Virtual, visit *http://www.fv.com*.

TRAP

Third-party payment methods such as First Virtual's put yet another middleman into the payment pie. This can add to the cost of buying and selling on the Internet, especially for low-priced items. For example, a product costing $1 typically yields the seller $.69 after First Virtual's fees are deducted; a product costing $10 yields $9.51; and a product costing $100 yields $97.71. The seller incurs some other fees as well.

PAYING WITH ELECTRONIC CASH (ECASH)

Some exciting new stuff has begun floating through the Internet. It's called *electronic cash*, or *ecash*, a digital equivalent of cash that lets you make online payments anonymously. The ecash concept was developed by a Dutch company named Digicash. With ecash, you can withdraw digital coins from your Internet bank account and store them on your hard disk or in "smart cards" that you can carry with you. When you want to buy something, you pay for it with these coins. Security features are included to protect your ecash as it travels through the Internet and to prevent other users from accessing your ecash.

TIP

You can learn more about Digicash by visiting their home page at http://www.digicash.com. *To further explore electronic money on the Internet, fire up your favorite search engine and look for* digicash, ecash, *or* electronic money.

HOW SECURE SERVERS & BROWSERS WORK

If you're just planning to buy stuff on the Internet, you don't need to know much about the way security is implemented, provided that you're assured that good security features exist. On the other hand, if you're planning to sell online and want to offer the latest security features to your customers, it's probably worth learning some buzzwords and concepts.

THE SECURE SOCKETS LAYER PROTOCOL

Most security-enabled browser and server software uses *Secure Sockets Layer* (SSL), a standard protocol that provides advanced security features for data communications on the Internet. SSL incorporates three main features—authentication, encryption, and data integrity.

AUTHENTICATION

Authentication thwarts impostors by preventing any computer from impersonating the real server or attempting to appear secure when it isn't. Authentication ensures that the server you're connecting with is the *real* server. Here are the basic authentication steps (I've simplified them a bit):

1. The client asks to connect to the secure server.

2. The server sends a *signed digital certificate* to the client. (See "About Security Certificates," later in this chapter.)

3. The client decrypts the digital signature and matches it against the certificate information. If the certificate doesn't match, the client suspects that another server is masquerading as the real server and ends the connection with the server. If the certificate does match, the client assumes that the server is who it says it is.

4. The client generates a *session key* and encrypts it, using the server's public key from the certificate. The session key is used to encrypt and decrypt data and ensure data integrity. (See "About Public & Private Keys," later in this chapter.)

5. The client sends the encrypted session key to the server. Only the server's private key can decrypt the session key.

Thus, impostors are prevented from getting involved in the transaction.

ENCRYPTION

Encryption thwarts eavesdroppers by using advanced crypto-graphic means to scramble the transferred data. Data is scrambled so that only someone with a specific *key* can unscramble (or decrypt) the message to a readable form. You might think of the key as being sort of a "decoder ring" that explains how to decode the secret message. The keys used in SSL encryption are long (either 40 bits or 128 bits) and the effort required to break any given message is too huge to be worthwhile. Even if eavesdroppers can snatch your messages from the Internet, the stolen encrypted messages will be unintelligible and will do the crooks no good.

DATA INTEGRITY

Data integrity defeats vandals seeking to damage your messages. You're immediately alerted if any person or computer along the public route has altered your data in any way.

TRAP

The entire communication will be secure only if both the browser and the server use the same security protocol. For example, both Netscape Navigator and Internet Explorer are SSL-enabled browsers. However, unless you're connecting to an SSL-enabled server, such as Netscape Commerce Server or Internet Information Server, your sensitive information may not be completely secure.

ABOUT SECURE COMMERCIAL SERVERS

You can build your own secure server by installing the Netscape Commerce Server (NCS) software from Netscape Communications. NCS supports the standard SSL security protocol as well as SSL-enabled browsers, including Netscape Navigator (of course) and Internet Explorer. Netscape Commerce Server runs on many Unix and Windows NT hardware platforms. As Chapter 5, "Finding a Home for Your Page," mentioned, the build-your-own-server approach involves a serious investment in time, money, hardware, and expertise, but for large businesses it can be the best approach.

Perhaps the best place to learn more about setting up your own Netscape server is at *http://home.netscape.com/comprod/server_central/index.html*. Here you'll find a fun page with animated graphics and a great overview of all the servers Netscape offers—including SuiteSpot, an integrated package of Internet server software.

TIP

Microsoft Corporation also offers Internet Information Server (IIS), a Windows NT-based server that supports SSL and SSL-enabled browers. For general information about IIS, visit http://www.microsoft.com/infoserve *and explore the links from there. You can take a product tour and find links to more detailed information at* http://www.microsoft.com/infoserve/tourstart.htm.

ABOUT PUBLIC & PRIVATE KEYS

A secure communication involves two types of keys: *public keys* (which are publicly known) and *private keys* (which are known only to the key's user).

- Public keys are used to exchange session keys, to verify the authenticity of digital signatures, and to encrypt data.

- Private keys are used to decrypt session keys that were encrypted, using the matching public key, and to create a digital signature when setting up a digital certificate.

TIP

You need to know about public and private keys only if you're administering a secure Web site. If you're simply using a security-enabled browser to exchange data with a secure Web site, you can ignore the details because all the public key and private key transactions take place invisibly and automatically.

ABOUT SECURITY CERTIFICATES

Security certificates unmistakably identify a secure server, much as your signed driver's license, Social Security card, and photo-ID cards identify you. Certificates are sent along with messages so that your security-enabled browser can verify the server's identity.

A server must have a digital certificate before it can use SSL protocol. Only authorized Certification Authority (CA) companies, such as VeriSign (a spin-off of RSA Data Security, Inc.), can issue digital certificates.

Each signed security certificate contains two groups of security information:

■ The certificate information itself, along with the certificate issuer's name, the server's name, the server's public key, and some time stamps that indicate how long the certificate is valid.

■ A secret digital signature that cannot be forged.

For more about what digital certificates are and how to buy them for your Web site, see your secure server's manual or check out Netscape's excellent documentation about security at the following URLs:

■ *http://www.netscape.com/comprod/server_central/config/ secure.html* provides a great launching pad for exploring security, especially if you're setting up (or planning to set up) security on your own server.

■ *http://www.netscape.com/newsref/ref/internet-security.html* offers good general reference material about Internet security.

OTHER SECURITY SCHEMES

Some companies use additional security measures to protect servers against Internet cyberthugs and vandals. These techniques involve using special computers to guard against electronic assaults:

- Firewalls stand between the server or local area network you want to protect and the outside world. All outside communications are made to the firewall, rather than to the "real" computer. The firewall then lets valid communications through to the real computer.

- Proxy servers answer requests intended for the machine you want to protect from direct contact with the outside world. The proxy, which presumably can be trusted, routes network packets to the "real" destination.

- Filtering routers verify the source and destination network address of each network *packet* (message) and determine whether to let each packet through. Filtering routers prevent vandals on an Internet machine from masquerading as an internal network machine. They also can prevent attacks that deluge various services on a machine with meaningless traffic.

USING NETSCAPE NAVIGATOR BROWSER SECURITY

Now that you have some security theory under your belt, let's take a look at how to set Netscape Navigator's security preferences and how to know whether a transaction will be secure or nonsecure, from the buyer's perspective.

TIP

For more information about setting any of the security options discussed next, open the appropriate Preferences dialog box (by choosing Options | Security Preferences or Options | Network), choose the tab that contains the options you're curious about, and then click the Help button at the bottom of the dialog box.

SETTING GENERAL SECURITY OPTIONS

As a buyer, you can use Netscape's general security preferences to choose which alerts you'll see as you cruise the Internet. Here's how to set the security alerts:

1. Choose Options | Security Preferences from the Netscape Navigator menu bar and select the General tab, as shown in Figure 20-2.

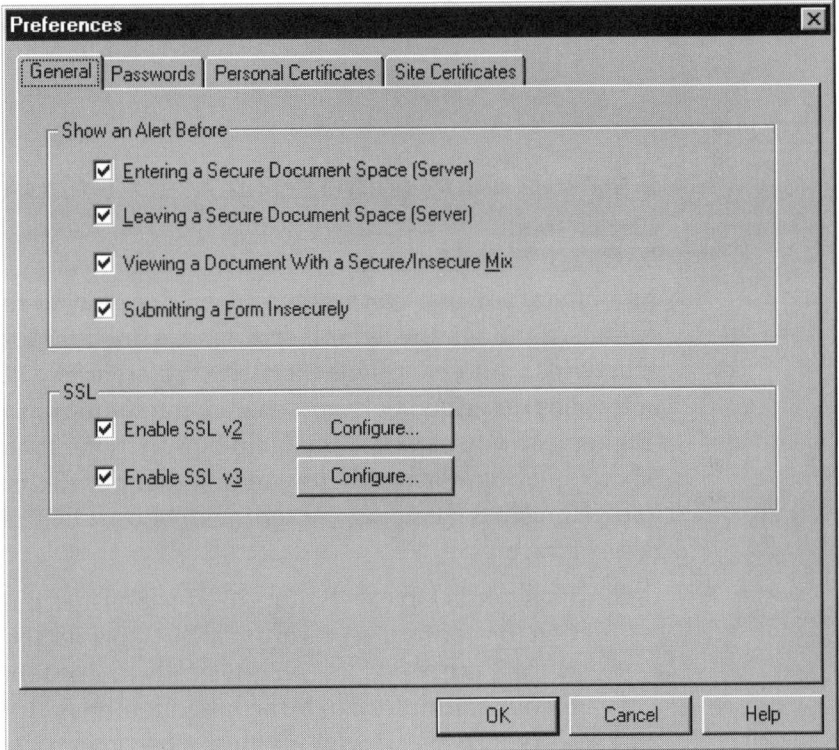

Figure 20-2: *The Preferences dialog box for general security.*

2. In the Show an Alert Before area, select (check) the boxes next to alerts you want to display and deselect (clear) the boxes next to alerts you don't want to display.

3. In the SSL area, check or clear the boxes that enable or disable the SSL version 2 and version 3 security. (Advanced users also might want to configure each version of SSL by clicking on the appropriate Configure button in the dialog box.)

4. Choose OK to save your settings.

TIP

For maximum security, select (check) all the boxes on the General tab.

SETTING CERTIFICATE-RELATED SECURITY OPTIONS

As a buyer, you also can set a number of certificate-related security options, although the default settings are fine for most people. To get started, choose Options | Security Preferences. Then, choose one of the tabs described here and change the settings as necessary. (Remember, you can click the Help button in the Preferences dialog box to find out more about any option that puzzles you.) When you've finished changing the settings, choose OK. Here are descriptions of the tabs:

■ Passwords tab (see Figure 20-3) establishes password protection for your security certificates. Consider using a password if other people can physically access your computer or if your computer can be accessed remotely through a network. (The Set Password button becomes a Change Password button after you've set a password.)

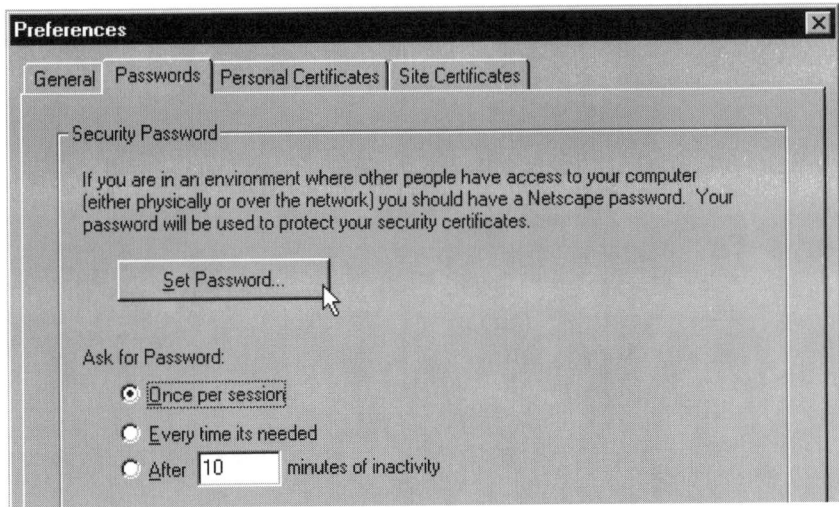

Figure 20-3: *The Passwords tab of Netscape's Security Preferences dialog box.*

■ Personal Certificates tab (see Figure 20-4) establishes the personal certificates that identify you to others on the Internet. You'll rarely need to set up a personal certificate, but if you do, the More Info button and the Help button offer some guidelines to follow.

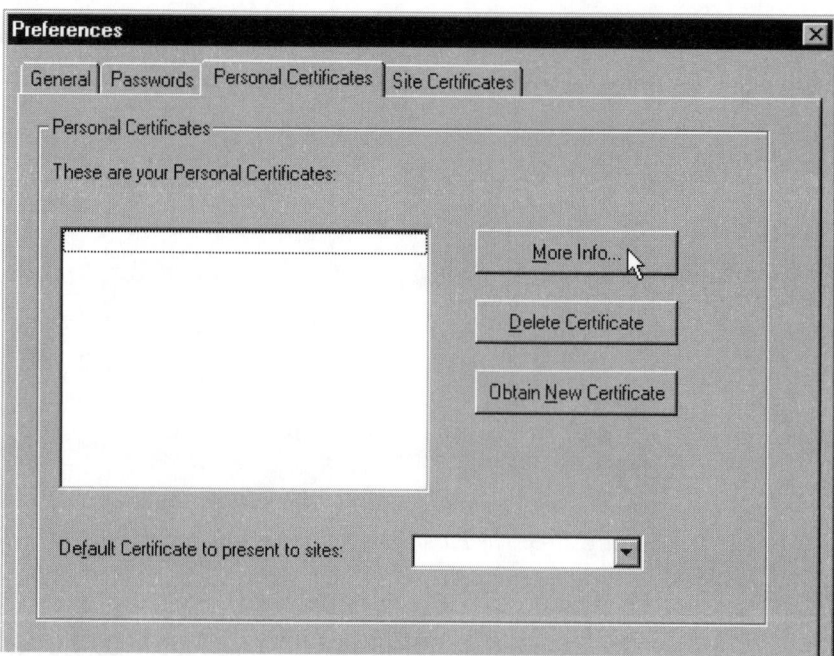

Figure 20-4: *The Personal Certificates tab of Netscape's Security Preferences dialog box.*

■ Site Certificates tab (see Figure 20-5) lets you edit or delete the site certificates issued to your server. Just as personal certificates identify you to others on the Internet, site certificates identify others on the Internet to you. Netscape Navigator comes with the capability to recognize several types of site certificates, and you'll rarely need to change the options on the Site Certificates tab.

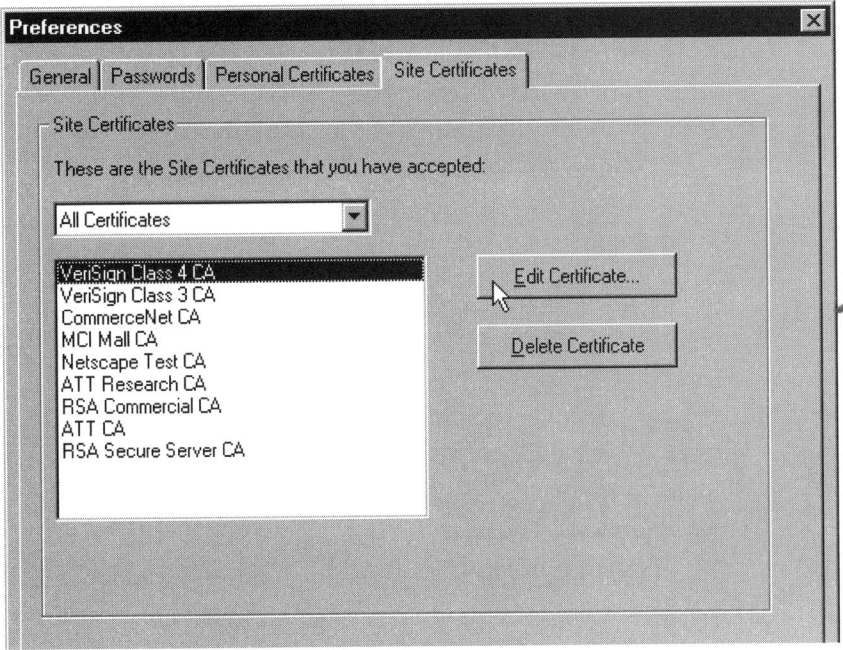

Figure 20-5: *The Site Certificates tab of Netscape's Security Preferences dialog box.*

CONNECTING TO A SECURE SERVER

As a buyer, connecting to a secure server is easy: You simply use a URL access method called *https*, instead of the usual *http*. For example, to connect to the secure site for ordering exotic Hawaiian flowers, type **https://www.branch.com/hawaii/ordhawai.html** in the Location box of your Netscape browser, and press Enter. (The nonsecure version of the flower order form is at *http://branch.com/hawaii/ordhawai.html*.)

Both of these Hawaiian flower sites are part of the Branch Mall, one of the first storefronts on the Web. Many other stores in the Branch Mall also offer secure online ordering and encryption of credit information. You can shop these stores by visiting the Branch Mall at *https://www.branch.com*.

TIP

To learn more about the https protocol, go to the Alta Vista search engine (http://www.altavista.digital.com/), type **https +security** *in the text box, and click the Submit button.*

IS THIS SITE SECURE?

How do you know, as a buyer, whether you're visiting a secure site? First, if you've requested security alerts, a Security Information dialog box will alert you when you're about to enter or leave a secure space, submit a nonsecure form, or view a secure document that contains nonsecure information. Figure 20-6 shows a typical alert message.

TIP

If you clear the Show This Alert Next Time check box in the Security Information dialog box, Netscape will not display the security alert in the future. To enable the security alert again, simply choose Options | Security Preferences or (Options | Network Preferences), click the appropriate tab in the dialog box, and check the box next to the alert you want to enable.

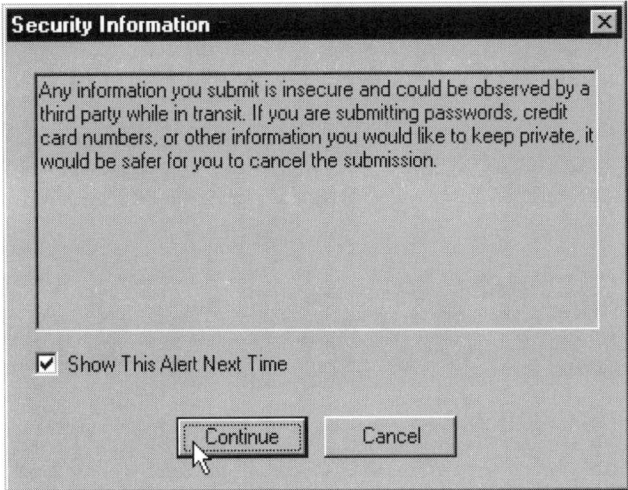

Figure 20-6: *This Security Information message appears when you're about to submit nonsecure information.*

Second, a "security colorbar" will appear near the top of each Netscape Navigator window, just above the scrolling document area. Secure documents have a blue color bar, and nonsecure documents have a gray (invisible) color bar. The icon in the lower-left corner of each Netscape Navigator window indicates the same thing as the security colorbar. A broken doorkey icon with a gray background indicates a nonsecure document (see the left side of Figure 20-7). A solid doorkey icon over a dark blue background indicates a secure document (see the right side of Figure 20-7).

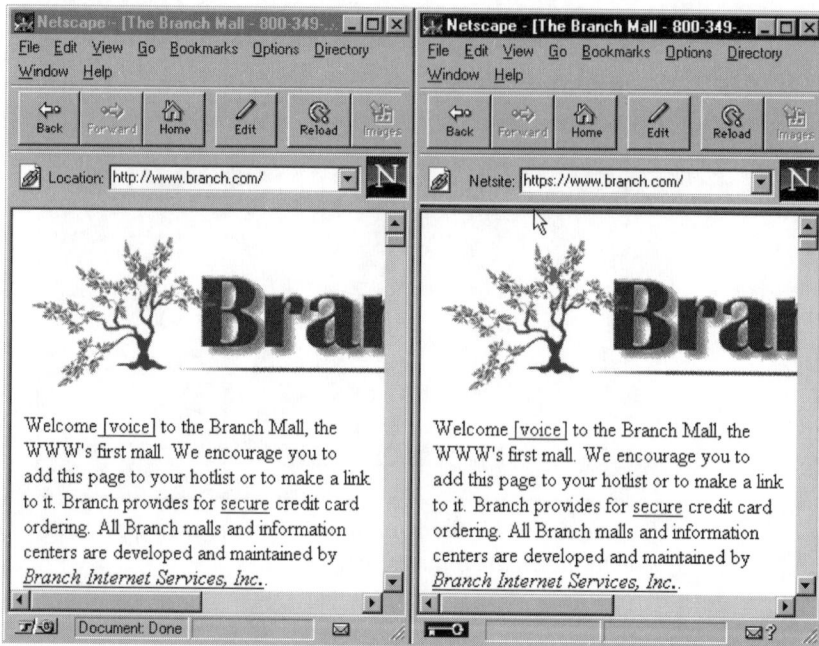

Figure 20-7: *The colorbar and doorkey icon for a nonsecure Web page (at left), and the colorbar and doorkey icon for a secure Web page (at right).*

You can display the security details for the current Web page by choosing View | Document Info. A new window will open, as shown in Figure 20-8. The top portion of the window describes the structure of the Web page; the bottom portion displays additional information, including the page's security status. When you're ready to close the Document Info window, press Alt+F4 or click the window's Close button.

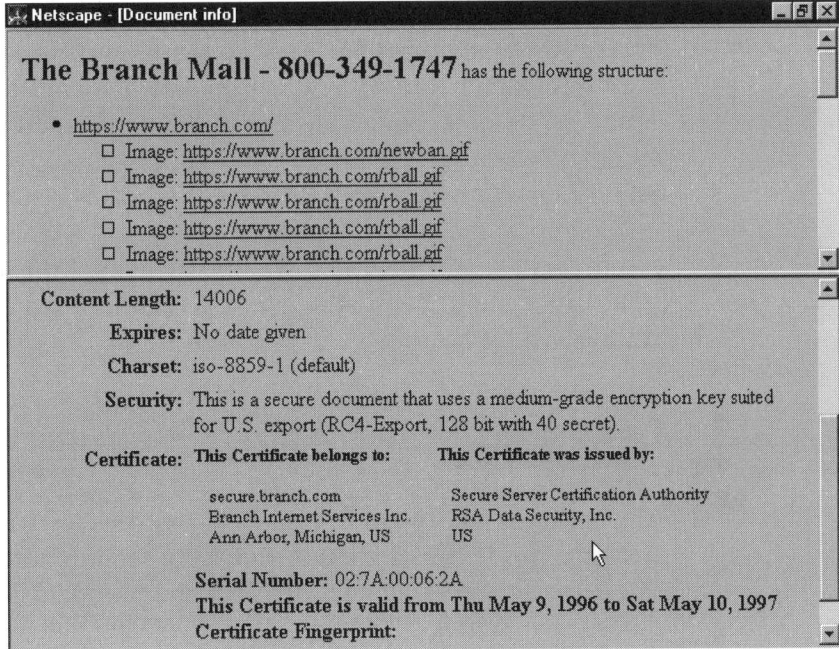

Figure 20-8: *Netscape Navigator's Document info page for a secure page.*

EXPLORING OTHER SECURITY OPTIONS

Netscape offers still other security options. If you'd like to explore them, choose Options I Network Preferences from the menu bar. You'll see a Preferences dialog box with several tabs.

Use the Proxies tab to configure proxy servers and port numbers for FTP, Gopher, HTTP, SSL, WAIS, and SOCKS protocols—something that's usually necessary *only* if you're running Netscape from behind a firewall. Your company's Network Administrator can help you fill in the options on this tab.

Use the Protocols tab to choose whether to send your e-mail address as an anonymous FTP password and to choose whether to display an alert before accepting a cookie or submitting a form by e-mail. (A *cookie* is a small piece of internal information that's transmitted between server software and your Netscape application. Servers sometimes use cookies to track who has visited the server.)

Use the Languages tab to choose whether to enable automatic execution of Java applets and whether to allow the execution of JavaScript code embedded in a page's HTML source. These options are checked by default.

LEARNING MORE ABOUT SECURITY

An enormous amount of information about security is available. Netscape itself offers a great starter set of security information specific to Netscape Navigator and Netscape products. To find it, choose Help | On Security from Netscape Navigator's menu bar. Or, choose Help | Frequently Asked Questions from the menu bar, and click the *Netscape Communications and Commerce Servers FAQ* link or the *Netscape Proxy Server FAQ* link. Another approach is to choose Help | Handbook, scroll all the way down to the Index, click the letter *S*, and look up topics under *Security*.

You also can find general information about security by searching for topics such as *credit card*, *encryption*, and *security* in your favorite Internet search engine. Also check out the *alt.privacy*, *alt.security*, *comp.society.privacy*, *comp.security.misc*, and *talk.politics.crypto* newsgroups.

Want even more security information right from the Internet? Try these URLs:

- *http://www.alw.nih.gov/Security/security.html* is a handy index with links to general information about computer security.

- *http://www-genome.wi.mit.edu/WWW/faqs/www-security-faq.html* is a lengthy FAQ document about security on the World Wide Web. Many of the questions and answers are Unix-oriented.

■ *http://www.rsa.com/faq/* offers FAQs about cryptography. This page is sponsored by RSA Laboratories, a division of RSA Data Security, Inc., the company that developed the standard technologies for public-key encryption and digital signatures. For general information about RSA Data Security, visit RSA's home page at *http://www.rsa.com/*.

■ *http://www.verisign.com/* is the home page for VeriSign, a company that provides digital authentication services and products for electronic commerce and other forms of secure communications. VeriSign was founded in 1995 as a spin-off of RSA Data Security and is probably the company you'll deal with if you implement Netscape Commerce Server.

MOVING ON

In this chapter you've learned about many security options, both low-tech and high-tech, for handling money and payments on the Internet. We've looked at the matter from the perspective of the seller and of the buyer. In the next chapter, you'll learn how to create Web pages that include online forms. These forms can make it easy for people to order your company's products and services over the Internet.

Creating Forms for Business

Forms give you the power to interact with your readers through your Web site. You can create forms that let your readers give you feedback, make suggestions, publish tips, and ask questions. If you're in business on the Web, forms can make your site more profitable by allowing people to join your mailing list, or even order products. In this chapter you'll learn almost everything you need to know about forms, including:

- Sample Web forms
- How to use fields and controls to design forms
- How to create forms
- How form data gets from the reader to you
- HTML tags for forms
- Formatting forms

TRAP

Be forewarned! Some Web servers do not allow forms at all. Many ISPs support forms in their commercial accounts, but not their personal accounts. So before you start doing anything with forms, check with your ISP to make sure that they will allow you to use forms in your site!

SAMPLE WEB FORMS

A form on the Web is identical to any fill-in-the-blank form on paper. I'm sure you've dealt with thousands of paper forms in your life: order forms, tax forms, you name it. You've probably seen a few forms on the Web, as well. For example, Figure 21-1 shows a form from Netscape's site that lets you download one of their products. The drop-down lists in the form lets you choose which product you want to download, what operating system you use, your preferred language, and your location.

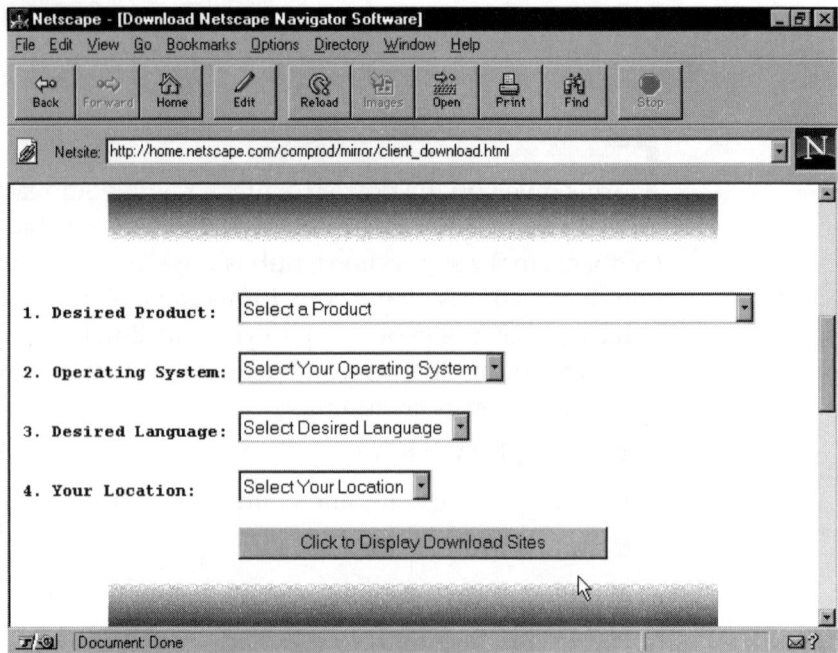

Figure 21-1: *Form for downloading software from Netscape's site.*

Figure 21-2 shows a simple "Guest Book" form that lets readers sign in and join a mailing list—a great way to meet people with similar interests, or to generate leads for a business.

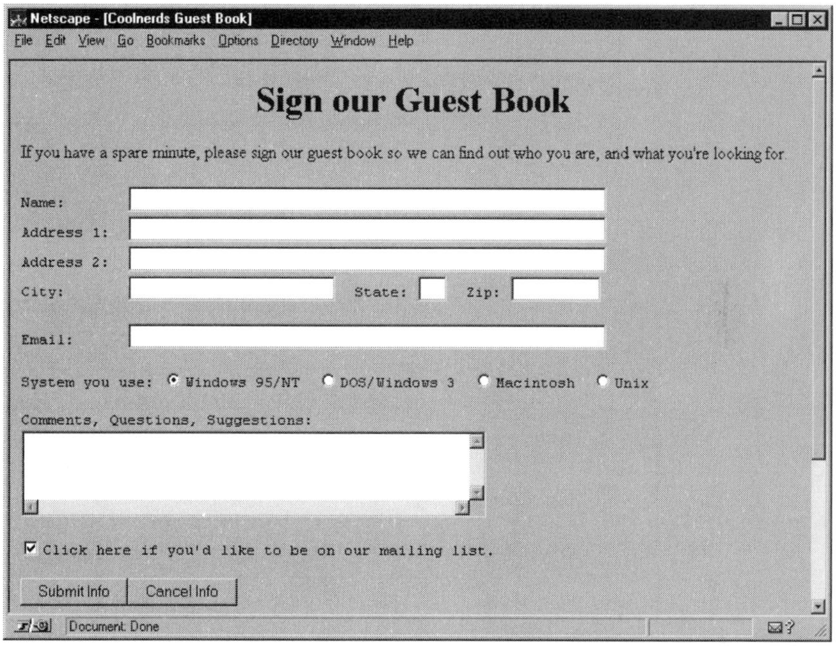

Figure 21-2: *A Guest Book can help you meet people or generate sales leads.*

Mix in some tables and JavaScript and you can create a very fancy online order form that closely resembles the paper order forms people are accustomed to. For example, Figure 21-3 shows the top of a sample order form, in which the reader can type a billing address and shipping address. (Note the button that lets the reader copy the "Bill To" info right to the "Ship To" info).

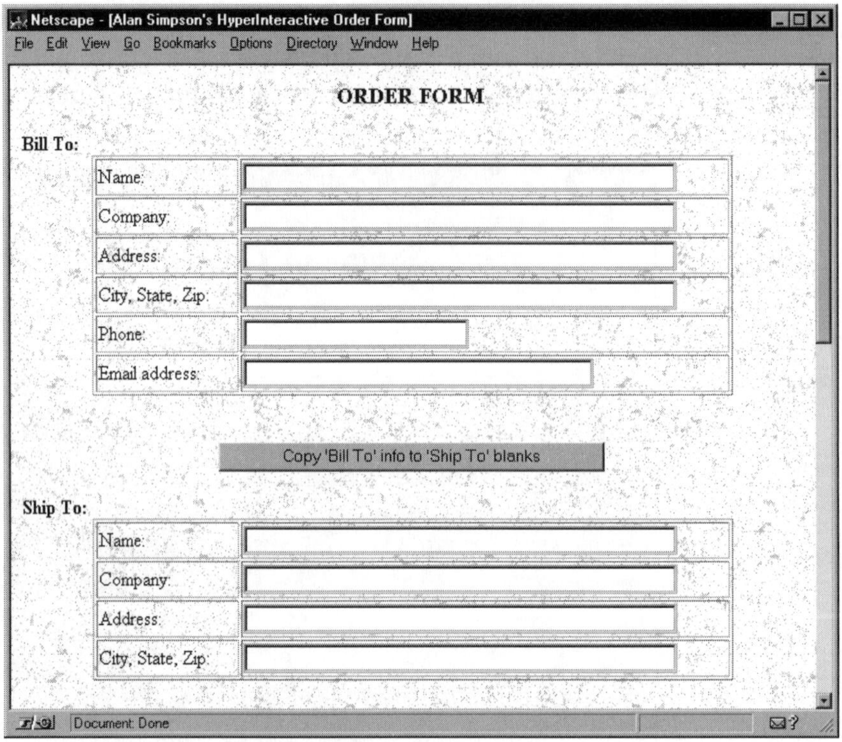

Figure 21-3: *Bill to and Ship To portions of sample form.*

After the reader scrolls down to the actual ordering section of the form, selects a product from the drop-down list, and types a quantity, the form automatically calculates the extended price, subtotal, sales tax, and grand total (see Figure 21-4).

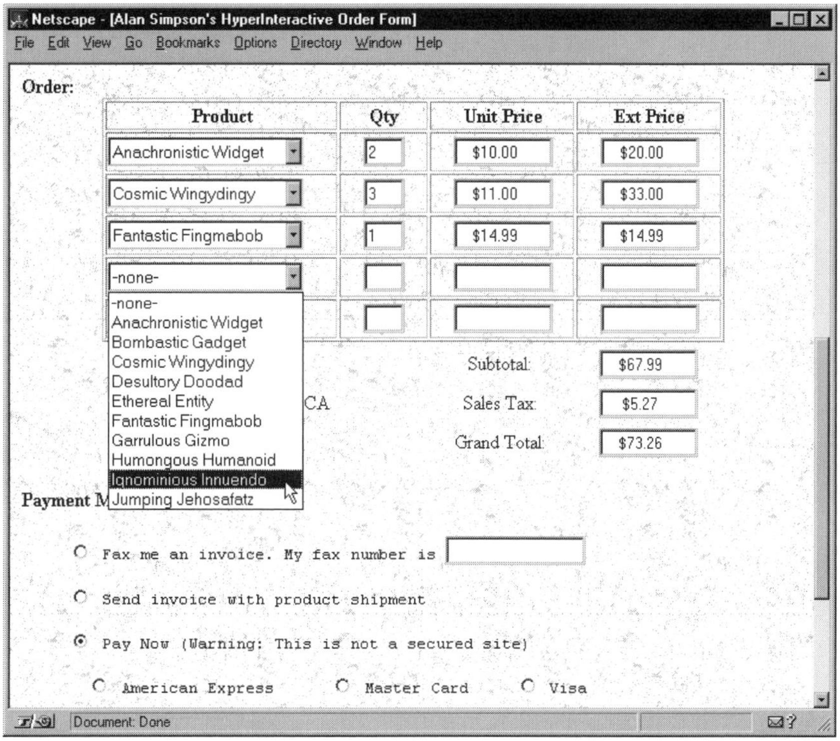

Figure 21-4: *This fancy form offers drop-down lists and automatically calculated totals.*

The bottom of the form lets the reader select a payment method. That is also where the Submit and Reset buttons for this form appear (see Figure 21-5).

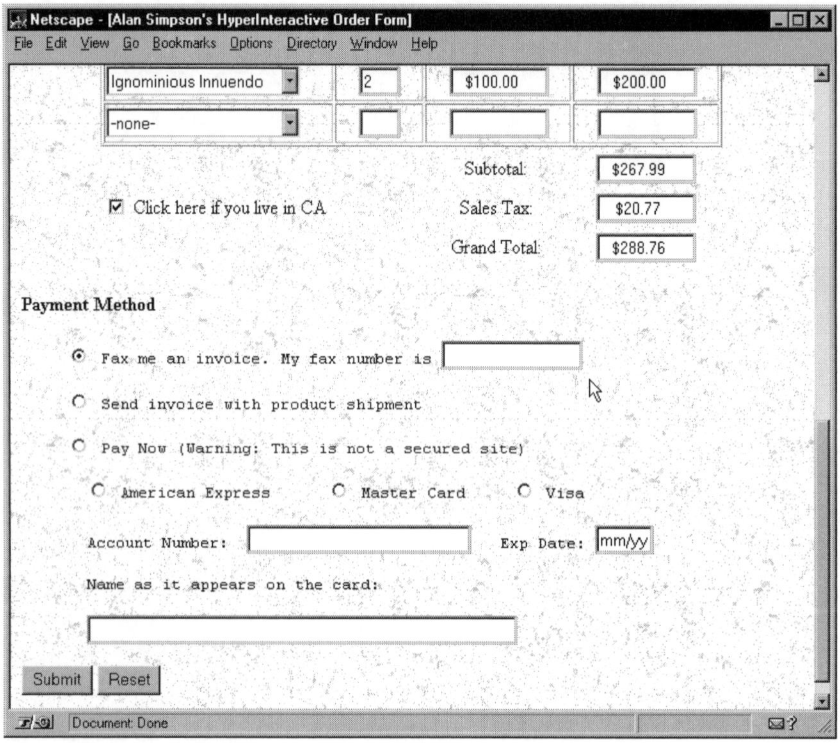

Figure 21-5: *Bottom portion of sample order form.*

I don't want to mislead you. This sample form was not easy to create. There are all kinds of fancy things with tables and JavaScript going on behind the scenes in that form. But you're more than welcome to lift a copy from the JavaScript section of my Web site (www.coolnerds.com) and modify it to your own business needs, if you like.

Anyway, looking at some of the possibilities is getting me way ahead of myself here. Let me slow down and talk about how you go about designing and creating forms.

FORM FIELDS

As you can see from the preceding examples, a form contains "blanks" for the reader to fill in. The "official" name for those blanks is *fields,* or *controls.* You can add several kinds of fields to your own forms. Each field type is designed to handle a specific type of response from the reader.

TEXT FIELDS

The reader can type (enter) text in *text fields*. There are two types of text fields: a small, single-line *text box* (like the e-mail address shown in Figure 21-6) and the larger *text area* or *comment field* (like the Comments, Questions, Snide Remarks box in Figure 21-6).

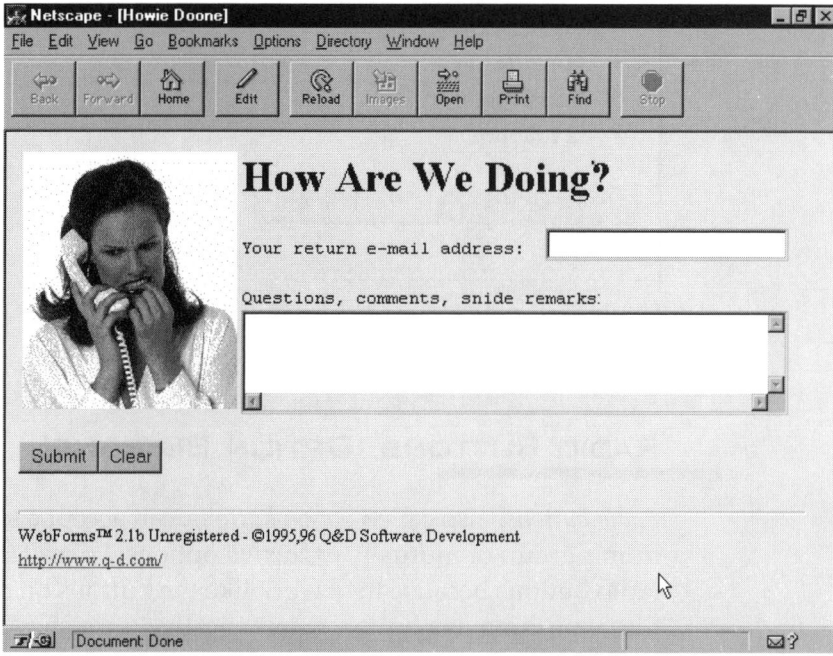

Figure 21-6: *Examples of a single-line text box and larger comment field.*

CHECK BOX

You use a *check box* to accept a yes or no answer or to let the customer make several selections from a list. In the example shown in Figure 21-7, a customer can choose toppings for a pizza.

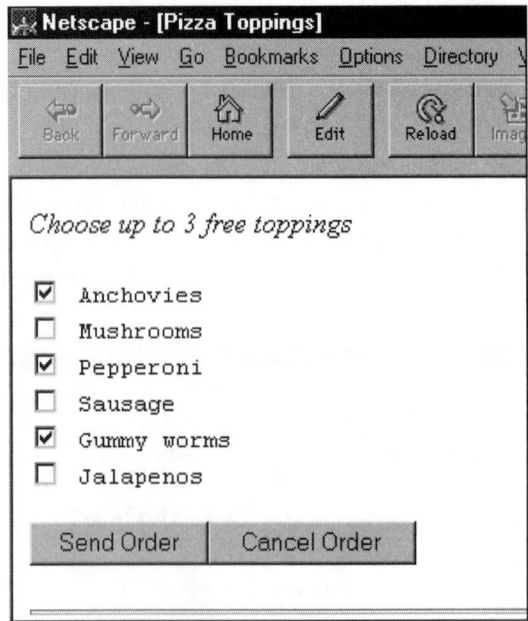

Figure 21-7: *Examples of check boxes.*

RADIO BUTTONS (OPTION BUTTONS)

Radio buttons, also called *option buttons*, can accept a single choice from a group of mutually exclusive options. We call these buttons radio buttons because they work like the buttons on older car radios—pushing in a button automatically "unpushes" whatever button happens to be pushed in. Thus, only one button can be selected at a time. Figure 21-8 shows examples of radio buttons.

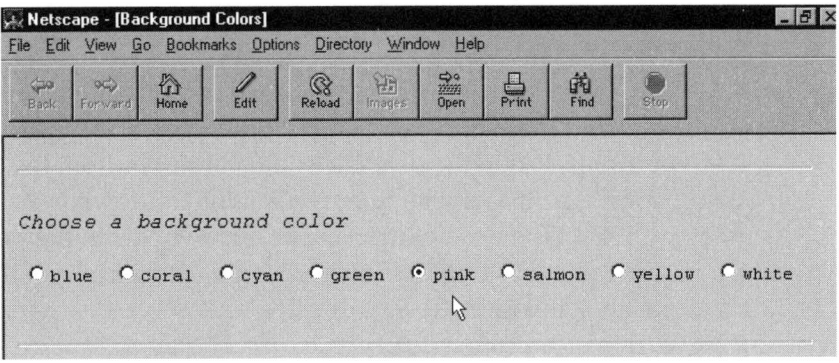

Figure 21-8: *Examples of radio-button form fields.*

DROP-DOWN LIST (SELECT LIST)

A *drop-down list* is another way to present a list of mutually exclusive options. This type of field takes up less room than a set of radio buttons, because the options stay hidden until the reader clicks on the drop-down list button. Figure 21-9 shows an example of a drop-down list on a Web form, with the list already open.

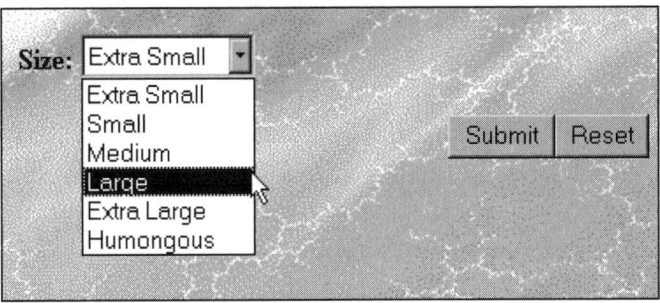

Figure 21-9: *A drop-down list (a.k.a. select list) on a form.*

COMMAND BUTTONS

A Web form typically contains two command buttons labeled Submit and Reset. But you can put whatever labels you want on those buttons. When the user clicks the Submit button, the completed form is sent to the recipient—usually your own e-mail address. Clicking the Reset button clears all the fields in the form. You can see sample Submit and Reset buttons to the right of the drop-down list box in Figure 21-9.

FORMS BEHIND THE SCENES

Forms are defined by HTML tags in your Web page. In general, a form is enclosed in one pair of <form>...</form> tags. And each field—including buttons—is defined by an <input> tag within those form tags. General text on the form is outside the <input> tags. For example, take a look at the simple form shown in Figure 21-10. It contains a text box, larger text area box, and two buttons labeled Submit and Clear.

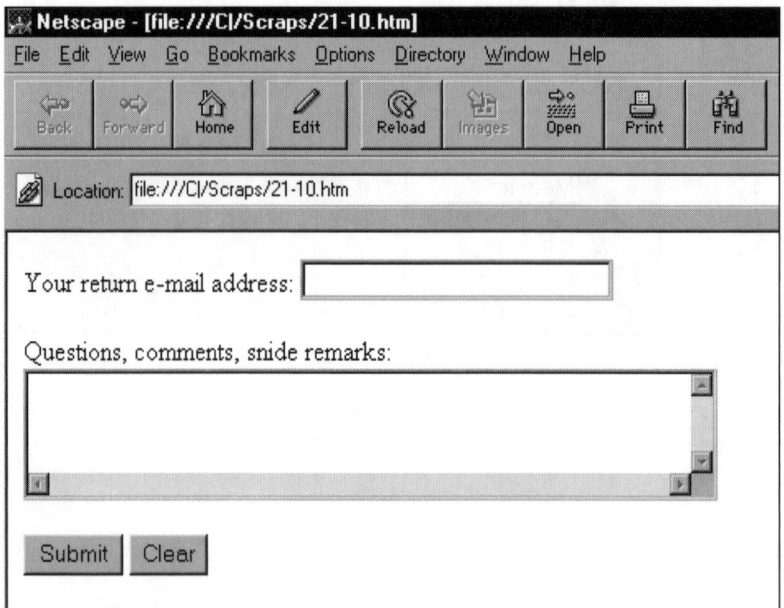

Figure 21-10: *A very simple form, in the Web browser.*

Figure 21-11 shows the document source code for the simple form. Here's a quick summary of the text and tags that define the form.

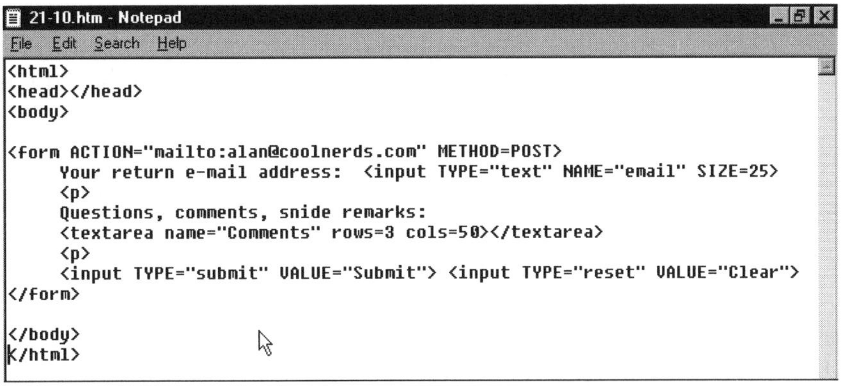

```
21-10.htm - Notepad                                    _ 8 X
File  Edit  Search  Help
<html>
<head></head>
<body>

<form ACTION="mailto:alan@coolnerds.com" METHOD=POST>
    Your return e-mail address:  <input TYPE="text" NAME="email" SIZE=25>
    <p>
    Questions, comments, snide remarks:
    <textarea name="Comments" rows=3 cols=50></textarea>
    <p>
    <input TYPE="submit" VALUE="Submit"> <input TYPE="reset" VALUE="Clear">
</form>

</body>
</html>
```

Figure 21-11: *The document source for the page shown in Figure 21-10.*

The tag <form ACTION="mailto:alan@coolnerds.com" METHOD=POST> defines the start of the form, as well as the ACTION and METHOD used to submit the form when the reader clicks the Submit button. (I'll talk about ACTION and METHOD in more detail in a moment.)

The Your return e-mail address: line is just regular text. The <input TYPE="text" NAME="email" SIZE=25> defines the text box field that follows that text. The type is *text* (for text box), the name is *email*, which is just a name I assigned, and the *size* is 25 characters (not pixels) wide. The <p> that follows the <input> tag marks the start of a new paragraph (i.e., inserts a blank line).

Below all of that, the words *Questions, comments, snide remarks:* are just regular text. The tags <textarea name="Comments" rows=3 cols=50></textarea> define the large text typing area. In this example, I've named that field *Comments,* and made the box three lines tall and 50 characters wide. The <p> that follows inserts another blank line.

The <input TYPE="submit" VALUE="Submit"> and <input TYPE="reset" VALUE="Clear"> tags define the Submit and Reset (labeled "Clear," in this example) buttons. And </form> marks the end of the form.

THE METHOD & POST ATTRIBUTES

The ACTION and METHOD attributes of the <form> tag that starts the form play an important role in the way you, the Web publisher, receive data that the reader types into your form. The ACTION attribute defines what happens when the reader clicks the Submit button and the METHOD attribute defines the method used in that action.

Unfortunately, I can offer only a little assistance defining your ACTION and METHOD attributes in your own forms, because it's really up to your Internet Service Provider to determine how form submissions are handled. In the following simple and commonly supported action:

```
ACTION="mailto:emailaddress"
```

emailaddress is your own e-mail address, or whatever e-mail address you want the reader's responses sent to.

The two most common METHODs are POST and GET. The POST method—used primarily for mailing data from forms—is by far your most likely candidate in this situation. The GET method is generally used when you're sending information to some program that sends information back. For example, some sites offer a text box in which you fill in a word or phrase to search for. When you click a button, that word or phrase is sent to some search engine, such as Yahoo.

HOW THE DATA ARRIVES

The appearance of the data when it arrives in your e-mail box depends on 1) how you define your ACTION and METHOD attributes, and 2) how your ISP handles them. Let me show you two simple examples. First, let's say the reader fills in my simple form, as shown in Figure 21-12, and then clicks the Submit button.

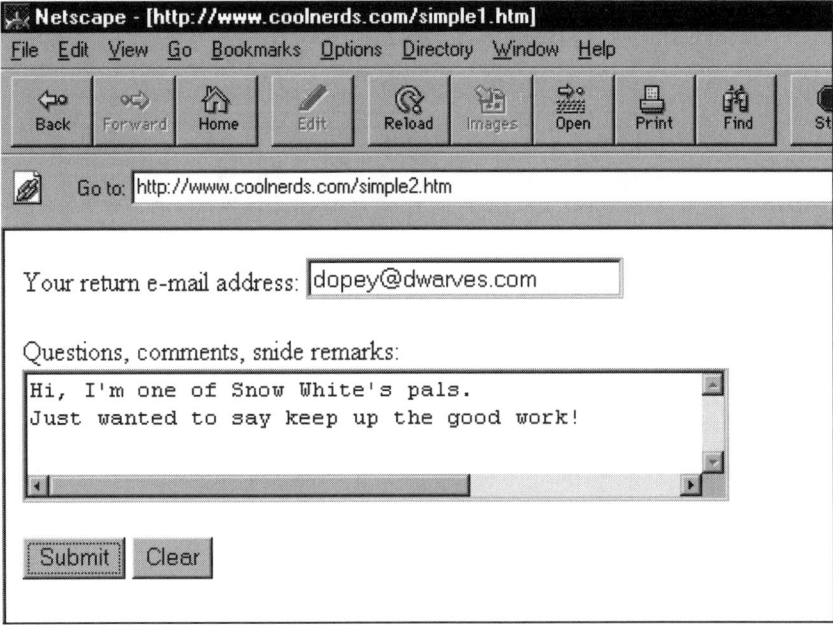

Figure 21-12: *Reader has responded to my form.*

Within a few seconds, an e-mail message arrives in my message box. If I set up the <form> tag, using the simple mailto: method that follows:

```
<form ACTION="mailto:alan@coolnerds.com" METHOD=POST>
```

the contents of the e-mail message look like Figure 21-13. Remember, this is just how *my* ISP sends the data. Yours may be different.

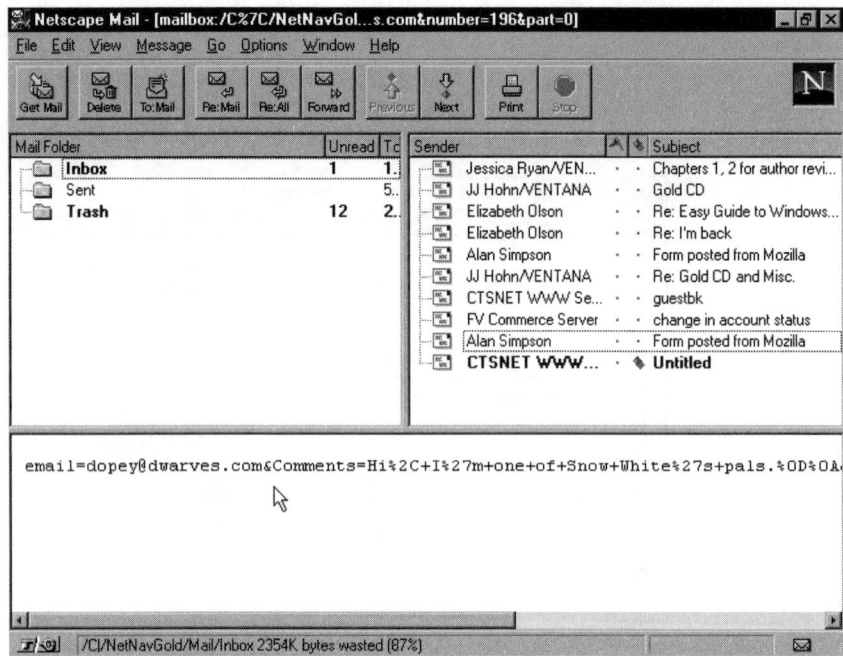

Figure 21-13: *Data as sent by a simple mailto action.*

Note that only the form *data*—the names of the fields and what the reader typed into those fields—are sent in the e-mail message. In this first example, the data looks pretty weird because it's "Unix-ized," with ampersands (&) representing blank spaces, and hex codes representing punctuation characters (e.g., &27 represents an apostrophe). This format is difficult for humans to read, but if you were shipping the form data off to some other program on your PC, the format might be fine.

My ISP offers an alternative to the simple mailto—one that sends form data to me in a format that's easier to read. To use their custom alternative, I need to set up my <form> tag as follows:

```
<form ACTION= "/cgi-bin/mailto?alan@coolnerds.com"
METHOD=POST>
```

When I use this custom action in my form, the data from the form arrives in my e-mail box looking like that shown in Figure 21-14.

My ISP's custom mailto action places each field name and its contents on a separate line—a format that's more palatable for us humans. They also alphabetize the data by field name, which is why the Comments field is listed before the email field.

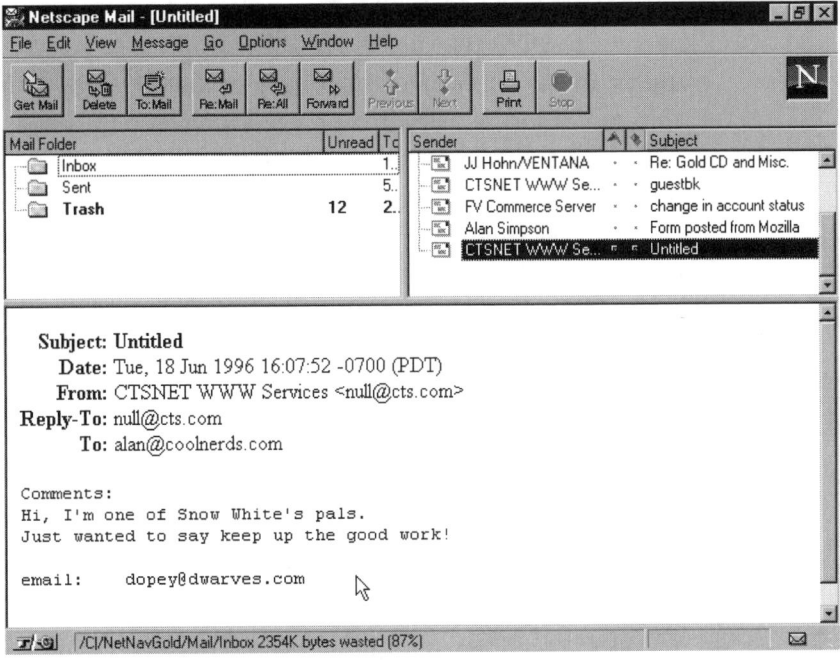

Figure 21-14: *Data, as sent by my ISP's custom mailto? action.*

The moral of the story is that, when setting up a form, you should contact your ISP for instructions on how best to set up the ACTION attribute in your own <form> tag.

HTML TAGS FOR FORMS

As you can see, forms are controlled by HTML tags. As you'll learn in this chapter and the next, forms are also tied in closely with JavaScript. I think the best way to fully understand all the things you can do with a form is to take a look at the HTML tags used to define your forms.

EASIER WAYS TO CREATE FORMS

Gold has no built-in editor for easily creating forms. You are pretty much stuck with typing the tags manually (using an external text editor). Other tools are available to you, however.

WebForms is one such tool. An evaluation copy of WebForms is on the CD-ROM that came with this book (see Appendix B). After you've installed WebForms, you can just start it up and check its Help menu for instructions on how to create forms.

If you have Microsoft Word version 6 or 7, you might want to look into Microsoft Word Internet Assistant (Word IA), available free from Microsoft at http://www.microsoft.com. A true WYSIWYG forms capability is built right in to Word IA.

In their current versions, neither of these tools lets you add JavaScript event handlers to your tags, but both produce HTML files that you can open and edit with Gold or any external editor. Thus, you can define custom JavaScript actions, if you wish, by adding attributes to the <form> and <input> tags that these tools produce.

In the sections that follow I show the exact syntax for the various <form> and <input> tags. Note that any attribute displayed in square brackets ([]) is *optional* (you can omit it if you like). If you do include the attribute, do *not* type the square brackets. Square brackets are never part of the tag syntax.

THE <FORM>...</FORM> TAGS

A single <form> tag marks the beginning of a form in your page. A </form> tag marks the end of the form. The complete syntax for the <form> tag follows:

```
<FORM
    [NAME="formName"]
    [TARGET="frameName"]
    ACTION="whatToDo"
    METHOD=GET or POST
    [ENCTYPE="encodingType"]
    [onSubmit="JavaScript"]>
</FORM>
```

where NAME gives the form a name, which can be used to refer to the form from within JavaScript code.

After the reader clicks the Submit button, most servers send him or her a feedback message. In a multiframe Web site you can use the TARGET="*frameName*" attribute to specify which frame displays that feedback message. Omitting this attribute sends that feedback message to the main display window.

The ACTION and METHOD attributes were discussed earlier in this chapter. The ACTION attribute defines "what to do" when the reader clicks on the form's Submit button. Typically the ACTION is the word *mailto:* followed by an e-mail address, all enclosed in a pair of quotation marks. The METHOD attribute can be POST, for e-mailing, or GET, for sending information to a Web search engine. For example a typical <form...> tag might look something like:

```
<form ACTION="mailto:alan@wherever.com" METHOD=POST>
```

The optional ENCTYPE="*encodingType*" specifies the MIME encoding of the data sent. Omitting this attribute sends the data in the default format for the server involved, as in the examples shown back in Figures 21-13 and 21-14.

The onSubmit="*JavaScript*" is an event handler where *JavaScript* is JavaScript code, or the name of a custom function, to be executed when the reader clicks the Submit button. The ACTION defined in the form tag is also carried out in the usual manner.

TAG FOR TEXT FIELDS

The tag for a text field on a form can contain all of these attributes:

```
<INPUT
  TYPE="text"
  NAME="fieldName"
  VALUE="initialValue"
  SIZE=integer
  [MAXLENGTH=integer]
  [onBlur="JavaScript"]
  [onChange="JavaScript"]
  [onFocus="JavaScript"]
  [onSelect="JavaScript"]>
```

where:

- *fieldname* gives the field a name.

- *intitalValue* specifies the *default value* of the field; text that automatically appears in the box. If you omit the VALUE attribute, the text box initially appears empty on the screen.

- The SIZE attribute specifies the width of the box, in characters, on the screen.

- The MAXLENGTH integer specifies the maximum number of characters that can be typed into the field. If MAXLENGTH is greater than SIZE, the text scrolls within the field. If MAXLENGTH is omitted, no maximum length is assigned to the field's contents.

The event handlers trigger JavaScript code in response to the reader doing something to the field. You can be very specific about "what happens when" with these four event handlers. Here's when each is triggered:

- onBlur: The cursor leaves the text box field.

- onChange: The cursor leaves the text box field *and* the reader has changed that field while the cursor was in the field.

- onFocus: The cursor lands in the field.

- onSelect: The user selects text within the field.

As an example, the lead-in prompt (*Name:*) and text box in the top half of Figure 21-15 are displayed by this text and tags:

```
<b>Name:</b> <input TYPE="text" NAME="fullname" VALUE="Type
your name here" SIZE=65>
```

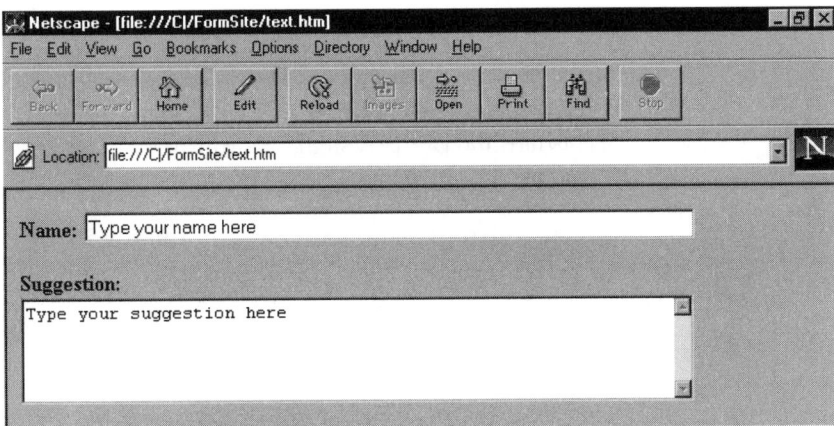

Figure 21-15: *Sample text and text area fields.*

TAG FOR THE TEXT AREA FIELD

The HTML tag for defining a text area field uses the following syntax:

```
<TEXTAREA
    NAME="fieldname"
    ROWS="integer"
    COLS="integer"
    WRAP="off" or "virtual" or "physical"
    [onBlur="JavaScript"]
    [onChange="JavaScript"]
    [onFocus="JavaScript"]
    [onSelect="JavaScript"]>
    defaultText
</TEXTAREA>
```

where:

- *fieldname* is a name you assign the field.
- The ROWS attribute defines how many lines tall the field is.
- The COLS attribute defines how wide the field is, in characters.
- The WRAP attribute controls word wrapping inside the field and in the data that's sent to you, the publisher. To specify the wrapping behavior, you can use the word "off," "virtual," or "physical," as follows:
  - off: Sends (the default) lines exactly as they are typed.
  - virtual: Wraps text within the field, but are sent exactly as typed.
  - physical: Wraps text within the field and sends text with newline characters (line breaks) embedded at the wrapping points within the field.
- The event handlers onBlur, onChange, onFocus, and onSelect play the same roles in a text area field that they play in a text field.
- The *defaultText* specifies the text that initially appears in the text area field. If you omit defaultText, the text area field is initially displayed as empty.

For example, the following text and tags display the lead-in prompt and text area field in the lower half of Figure 21-15:

```
<b>Suggestion:</b><br>
<textarea NAME="suggestion" ROWS="4" COLS="62"
WRAP="virtual">
```

```
Type your suggestion here
```

```
</textarea>
```

TAG FOR CHECK BOXES

The tag for a check box on a form uses this syntax:

```
<INPUT
    TYPE="checkbox"
    NAME="fieldname"
    VALUE="checkedvalue"
    [CHECKED]
    [onClick="JavaScript"]>
    textToDisplay
```

where

■ *fieldname* specifies the name of the check box field.

■ *checkedvalue* specifies a value that is returned to the server when the check box is selected and the form is submitted. If omitted, the field returns the word "on" if the reader selects (checks) the box before submitting the form.

■ The CHECKED attribute specifies that the check box is initially displayed with a check mark already in the box.

■ The *textToDisplay* specifies the label to display beside the check box.

■ The onClick event handler is triggered when the reader clicks the check box.

The sample check box at the top of Figure 21-16 is displayed by this tag and text:

```
<input type="CHECKBOX" NAME="MailingList" VALUE="True"
CHECKED>Put me on your mailing list
```

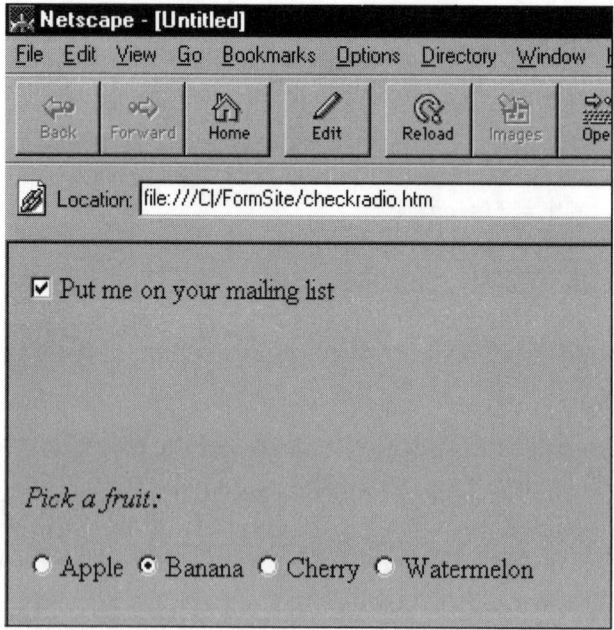

Figure 21-16: *Sample check box and radio buttons.*

TAG FOR RADIO BUTTONS

Radio button controls always appear in a group, because the purpose of the buttons is to allow the reader to select one item from a group of options. Multiple buttons within the same group all share the same NAME= attribute. The tag for a single button uses the following syntax:

```
<INPUT
    TYPE="radio"
    NAME="fieldname"
    VALUE="buttonValue"
    [CHECKED]
    [onClick="JavaScript"]>
    textToDisplay
```

where:

- *fieldname* is the name of the group to which this button belongs.
- *buttonValue* specifies the value that is returned to the server when the radio button is selected and the form is submitted. The default setting is "on."
- The optional CHECKED attribute specifies that the button is initially displayed as selected. (Only one button in a group can have the CHECKED attribute.)
- The *textToDisplay* specifies the label to display beside the radio button.

For example, the group of radio buttons shown in the lower half of Figure 21-16 is displayed by this text and series of tags:

```
Pick a fruit:<BR>

<INPUT TYPE="RADIO" NAME="fruits" VALUE="Apple">Apple

<INPUT TYPE="RADIO" NAME="fruits" VALUE="Banana"
CHECKED>Banana

<INPUT TYPE="RADIO" NAME="fruits" VALUE="Cherry">Cherry

<INPUT TYPE="RADIO" NAME="fruits"
VALUE="Watermelon">Watermelon
```

TAG FOR DROP-DOWN LIST

The drop-down list box, also called a *select box*, hides its options until the reader clicks the drop-down list button in the control. Here is the syntax for defining a drop-down list control:

```
<SELECT
   NAME="fieldname"
   [SIZE="integer"]
   [MULTIPLE]
   [onBlur="JavaScript"]
   [onChange="JavaScript"]
   [onFocus="JavaScript"]>
   <OPTION VALUE="optionValue" [SELECTED]>
   optionText [ ... <OPTION> optionText]
</SELECT>
```

where:

- *fieldname* is a name you assign to the field.

- The optional SIZE parameter specifies how many options are visible in the list box. If omitted, a normal drop-down list control appears. If specified and greater than one, the control is displayed as a list box rather than a drop-down list. (I'll show you an example in a moment.)

- The optional MULTIPLE attribute allows the reader to select multiple items from the list by holding down the Ctrl key while clicking items.

- The OPTION attribute specifies one item in the list. The VALUE="*optionValue*" attribute specifies a value that is returned to the server when the option is selected and the form is submitted. The *optionText* specifies how the item looks, to the reader, in the list.

- The SELECTED attribute specifies that the option is selected by default. (Only one option in the list can be defined as the SELECTED option.)

The control at the left of Figure 21-17 shows a standard drop-down list control, without the list open. The following tag defines that control:

```
<select NAME="sport">
   <option VALUE="baseball">Baseball
   <option VALUE="football">Football
   <option SELECTED VALUE="golf">Golf
   <option VALUE="hockey">Hockey
   <option VALUE="skiing">Skiing
   <option VALUE="skating">Skating
   <option VALUE="tennis">Tennis
</select>
```

The right half of the page shown in Figure 21-17 contains a list box. The tag that displays that box is shown next. (Note that this tag is identical to the tag for the drop-down list, except that this one contains the SIZE=7 attribute, which makes it display all seven items in the list.)

```
<select NAME="sport" SIZE=7>
   <option VALUE="baseball">Baseball
   <option VALUE="football">Football
   <option SELECTED VALUE="golf">Golf
   <option VALUE="hockey">Hockey
   <option VALUE="skiing">Skiing
   <option VALUE="skating">Skating
   <option VALUE="tennis">Tennis
</select>
```

If this <select> tag contained both SIZE=7 and MULTIPLE, the reader could pick multiple sports by clicking one, then Ctrl+clicking others.

TAGS FOR THE SUBMIT & RESET BUTTONS

The tag for the Submit button uses the following syntax:

```
<INPUT
   TYPE="submit"
   NAME="fieldname"
   VALUE="buttonlabel"
   [onClick="JavaScript"]>
```

The syntax for the Reset button is as follows:

```
<INPUT
    TYPE="reset"
    NAME="fieldname"
    VALUE="buttonlabel"
    [onClick="JavaScript"]>
```

where:

- *fieldname* is a name you give the button
- *buttonlabel* is the text that actually appears on the button face.
- The onClick event occurs when the reader clicks the button.

The Submit and Reset actions are still carried out, even if onClick calls JavaScript. Thus, you can't use onClick to *replace* the standard Submit and Reset button actions. But you could use onClick to run a procedure that does something *in addition to* the standard Submit and Reset buttons. If you want to create custom buttons that don't submit or reset the form or if you want to create custom Submit and Reset buttons, use the syntax defined in the next section.

TAG FOR CUSTOM BUTTONS

You can create a custom button that just activates JavaScript code without submitting or resetting a form. Use this syntax:

```
<INPUT
    TYPE="button"
    NAME="fieldname"
    VALUE="buttonlabel"
    [onClick="JavaScript"]>
```

Again,

- *fieldname* is a name you give to the button.
- *buttonlabel* is the text that appears on the button face.
- The onClick event occurs when the reader clicks the button.

Figure 21-17 shows examples of three buttons: a custom button labeled "Click Me," a Submit button, and a Reset button. The tags defining each of those buttons follow:

```
<!Tag for the custom button>
<INPUT TYPE = "BUTTON" Value = "Click Me" NAME =
"CustomButton" onClick="alert('Howdy Howdy Howdy')">
<p>

<!Tag for the Submit button>
<INPUT TYPE=SUBMIT VALUE="Submit" NAME="SubmitButton">

<!Tag for the Reset button>
<INPUT TYPE=RESET VALUE="Reset">
```

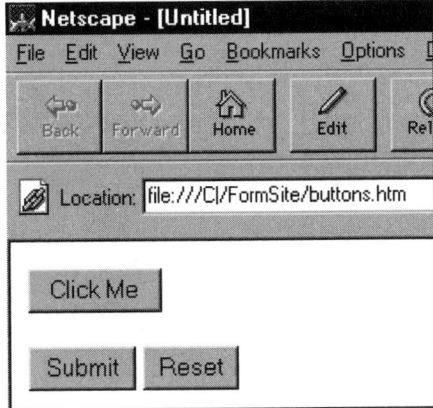

Figure 21-17: *A custom button and Submit and Reset buttons.*

TRAP

An input tag must be enclosed in a pair of <form>...</form> tags. Even if you're just displaying a single custom button on your page, its <input> tags must be within <form>...</form> tags.

TAG FOR HIDDEN FIELDS

A form can also contain one or more hidden fields. The reader never sees these fields, but their values are returned with the rest of the data when the reader submits a form. This is handy when you have several forms in your site. You can use a hidden field in each form to return the name of the form that the data came from. This is the syntax for the hidden control:

```
<INPUT
    TYPE="hidden"
    NAME="fieldname"
    [VALUE="textValue"]>
```

where:

- *fieldname* is a name you give the field
- *textValue* is the word or phrase that the field always returns when the reader submits the form.

There are no event handlers for hidden fields because nothing is visible onscreen for the reader to click on.

TAG FOR PASSWORD FIELDS

A special version of the text field displays whatever the user types as asterisks. This is handy when you want to treat the reader's entry as a password. The syntax for defining a password text field is as follows:

```
<INPUT
    TYPE="password"
    NAME="fieldname"
    [VALUE="textValue"]
    SIZE=integer>
```

where:

- *fieldname* is a name you give to the field.
- *textValue* is the default text that initially appears in the field (though each letter is displayed as an asterisk). The *integer* value specifies the width of the field in characters.

THE BIG PICTURE

Let's look at a completed form from the three possible angles: the browser view, the "Gold's editor" view, and the raw document source. Figure 21-18 shows a sample form in the browser view, with the Platform drop-down list open.

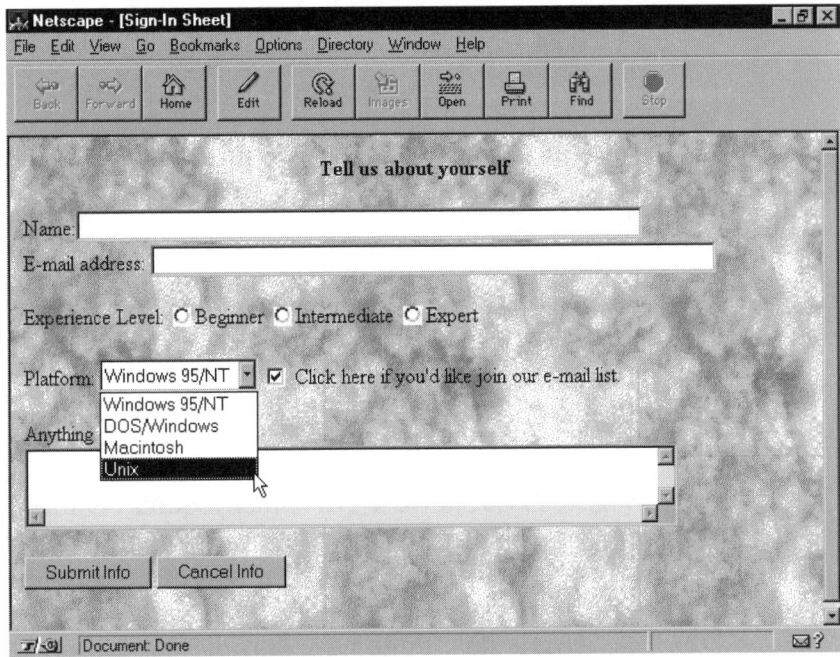

Figure 21-18: *Browser view of a sample form.*

Figure 21-19 shows that same page in Gold's editor. Because Gold has no built-in capability for editing forms, the <form> and <input> tags are displayed as "custom tag" icons. In this view, you can double-click any one of those tag icons to view (and, optionally, modify) the underlying tag.

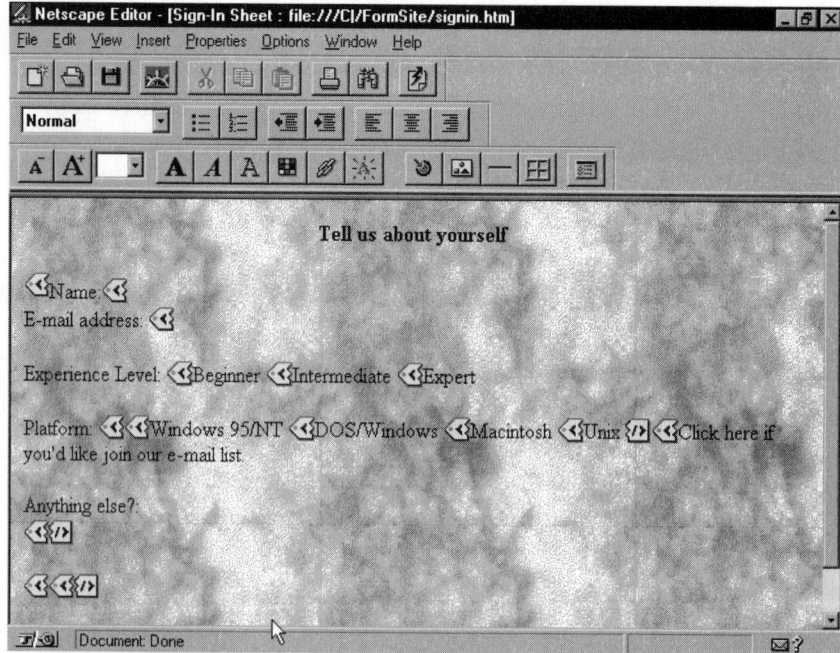

Figure 21-19: *Gold editor's view of the page shown in Figure 21-18.*

Figure 21-20 shows the document source behind the scenes, in Notepad. I had to increase the screen resolution to 800 x 600 to get it all on the screen. But as you can see, this page is like any other, in the sense that it contains a head, a body, standard text, and HTML tags. What makes it unique are the various <form> and <input> tags that define the form within the page.

```
signin.htm - Notepad
File  Edit  Search  Help
<html>
<head>
    <title>Sign-In Sheet</title>
    <meta name="GENERATOR" content="Mozilla/3.0b4Gold (Win32)">
</head>
<body text="#000000" background="marbl021.gif">

<h4 align=center>Tell us about yourself </h4>

<p><form METHOD=POST ACTION="/cgi-bin/mailto?alan@coolnerds.com:signin">
Name:<input NAME="Name" VALUE="" SIZE=60><br>
E-mail address: <input NAME="Email" VALUE="" SIZE=60></p>

<p>Experience Level:
<input TYPE="RADIO" NAME="Experience" VALUE="Beginner">Beginner
<input TYPE="RADIO" NAME="Experience" VALUE="Intermediate">Intermediate
<input TYPE="RADIO" NAME="Experience" VALUE="Expert">Expert </p>

<p>Platform: <select NAME="Platform">
    <option VALUE="Win32">Windows 95/NT
    <option VALUE="DOSWin">DOS/Windows
    <option VALUE="Mac">Macintosh
    <option VALUE="Unix">Unix
</select>

<input TYPE="CHECKBOX" NAME="MailingList" VALUE="MailingList" CHECKED>
Click here if you'd like join our e-mail list. </p>

<p>Anything else?:
<br><textarea NAME="Comments" ROWS=2 COLS=60></textarea></p><p>

<input TYPE="submit" VALUE="Submit Info">
<input TYPE="reset" VALUE="Cancel Info"></form></p>

</body>
</html>
```

Figure 21-20: *Notepad's view of the sample page shown in Figures 21-18 and 21-19.*

TIPS ON FORMATTING FORMS

As with all regular text and tags, Navigator ignores any indents, spaces, and line breaks in the document source, which can make the process of getting everything lined up neatly in your form a little tricky. You can line things up better, however, simply by applying the Formatted style to the text. For example, in Figure 21-21 I've selected everything in the form and am about to apply the Formatted style to it all. I'll also apply Boldface to this selection, to darken the prompts.

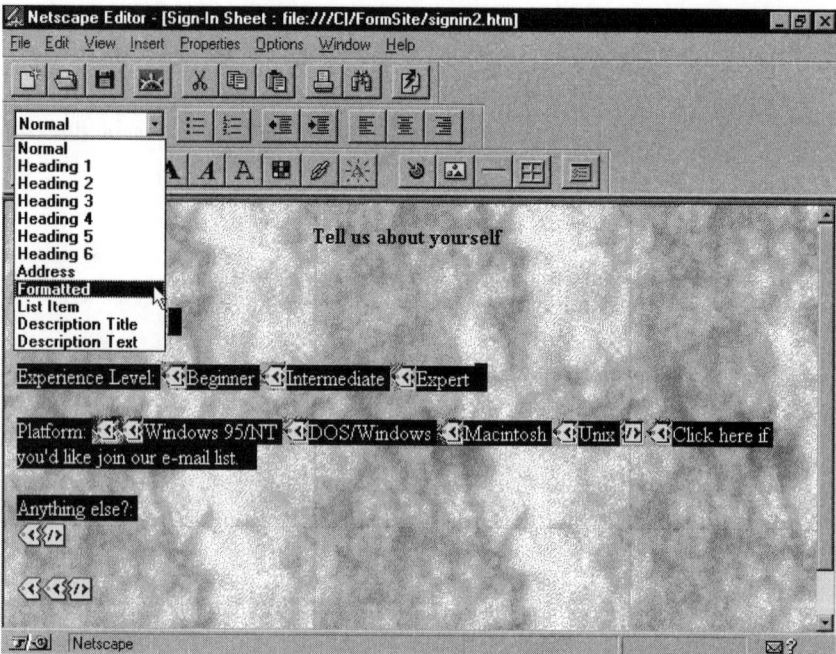

Figure 21-21: *About to apply the Formatted style to my form.*

Applying the Formatted style converts all the text to a fixed-width font. Now, any spaces that I type in the page will be honored, rather than ignored. In Figure 21-22, you can see that I've taken advantage of this fact by aligning the colons and input tag icons in the Name and E-Mail address prompts. I've put some blank space between the Beginner, Intermediate, and Expert radio buttons, and in front of the Click here.... prompt (after Unix) to indent that a little, and I've also shortened the prompt. (Most of that prompt is scrolled off the screen in this view, but won't be in the browser view.) I've indented the tag for the text area tag under *Anything else?* and, just for the heck of it, I selected the tag icons for the Submit and Reset buttons at the bottom of the form and centered them, using the Center button in Gold's toolbar.

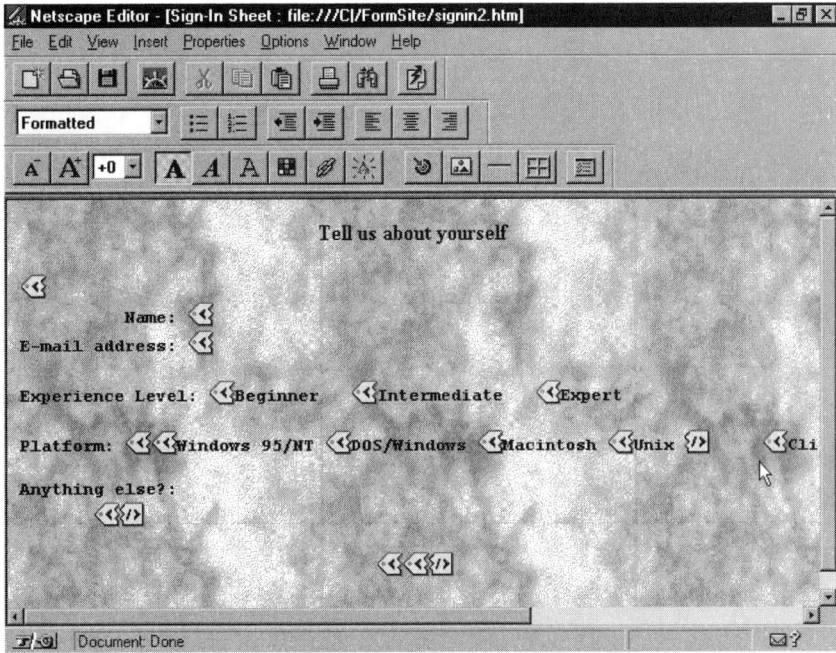

Figure 21-22: *My sample form, with some blank spaces added to better line things up.*

Figure 21-23 shows the results. It's still the same form, but things look a little tidier and better aligned.

TIP

In the document source view (not shown here), text to which you've applied the Formatted style is enclosed in <pre>...</pre> tags.

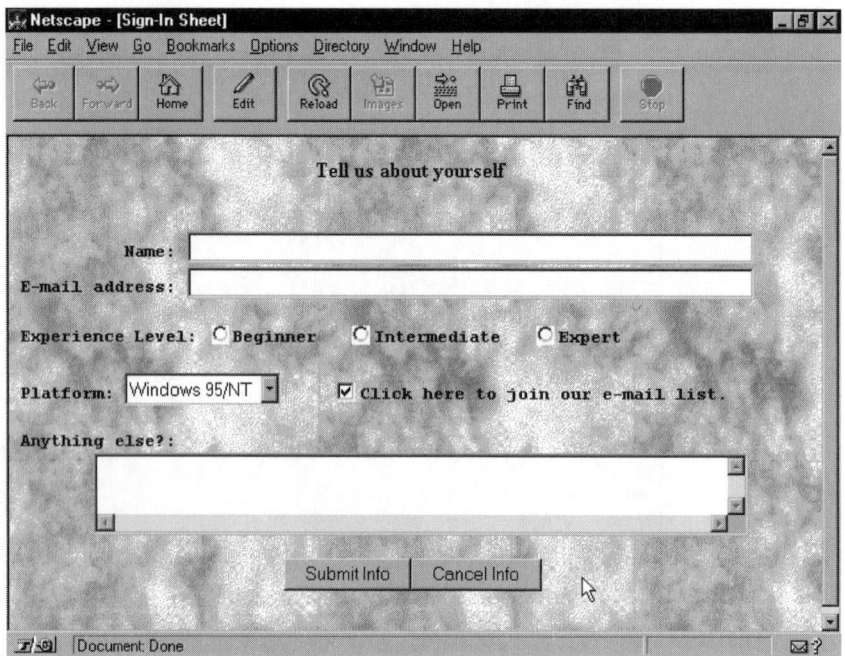

Figure 21-23: *Browser view of the page shown in Figure 21-22.*

You can also put text and <input> tags in Table cells to line things up. For example, the Bill To and Ship To fields in the sample form shown way back in Figure 21-3 are in two separate tables. To arrange fields within tables, just be sure to put the <table>...</table> tags within the <form>...</form> tags. Then any cell in the table can contain either text or an <input> tag. Figure 21-24 shows the Bill To: portion of the sample form in Gold's editor. The tag icons in the second column represent the various <input> tags.

TRAP

If you do want to put form fields in a table, make sure that you put the <table>...</table> tags that define the table inside the <form>... </form> tags that define the form. Otherwise things might act strangely!

If you were to take a peek at the document source behind the Bill To section of the form, you'd see that a <form> tag starts the form normally. The Bill To: text is just regular text. Then a <table> tag starts the table. The text prompts and <input> tags appear within individual table cells and hence are enclosed in <td>...</td> (table data) tags, each of which defines one cell in the table.

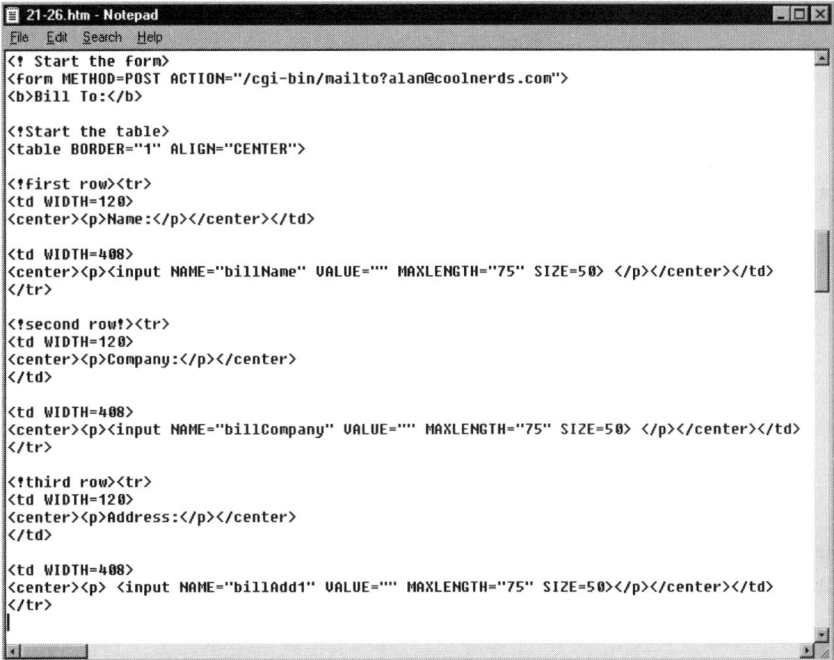

```
21-26.htm - Notepad
File  Edit  Search  Help
<! Start the form>
<form METHOD=POST ACTION="/cgi-bin/mailto?alan@coolnerds.com">
<b>Bill To:</b>

<!Start the table>
<table BORDER="1" ALIGN="CENTER">

<!first row><tr>
<td WIDTH=120>
<center><p>Name:</p></center></td>

<td WIDTH=408>
<center><p><input NAME="billName" VALUE="" MAXLENGTH="75" SIZE=50> </p></center></td>
</tr>

<!second row!><tr>
<td WIDTH=120>
<center><p>Company:</p></center>
</td>

<td WIDTH=408>
<center><p><input NAME="billCompany" VALUE="" MAXLENGTH="75" SIZE=50> </p></center></td>
</tr>

<!third row><tr>
<td WIDTH=120>
<center><p>Address:</p></center>
</td>

<td WIDTH=408>
<center><p> <input NAME="billAdd1" VALUE="" MAXLENGTH="75" SIZE=50></p></center></td>
</tr>
```

Figure 21-24: *The <table> is defined under the <form> tag.*

A slight variation on the use of a table would be to right-align the prompts in the left column and left-align the prompts in the second column. Then remove the table borders. Also, remove any <p>...</p> tags in the table to minimize the space between rows. The result is a neat little form with right-aligned text prompts next to left-aligned fields (see Figure 21-25). The little Notepad window gives you a peek at part of the underlying HTML tags.

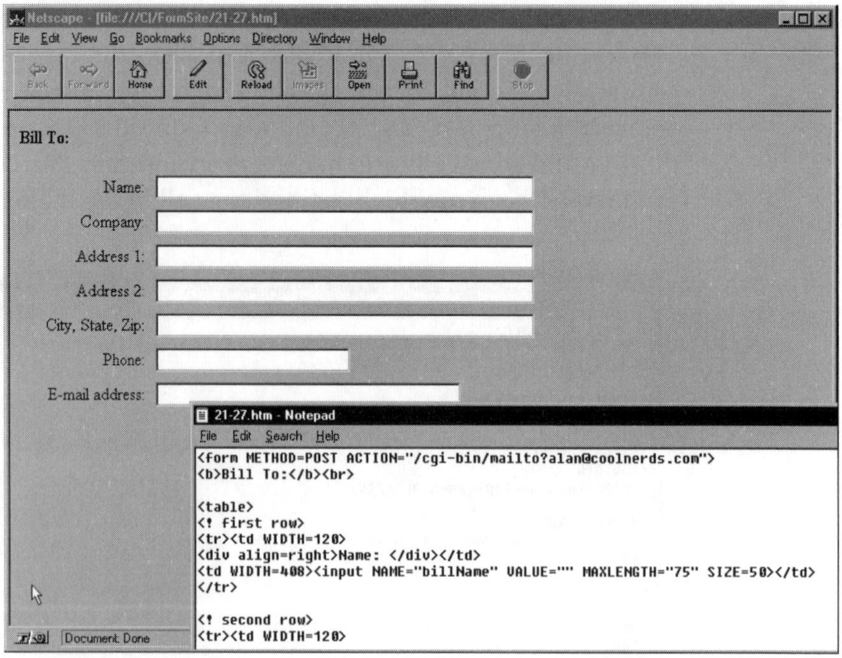

Figure 21-25: *Prompt text and fields in a borderless table.*

MOVING ON

We've covered a lot of ground in this chapter. You now know everything you need to know to create any form that you can imagine. Of course, practice makes perfect, and much of the knowledge you've gained here will solidify as you start building your own forms. In fact, I recommend that you start building some forms on your own right now. In the next chapter we'll go beyond creating and formatting forms to customizing the *behavior* of your completed forms, using JavaScript. Some very cool stuff, comin' right up.

Hyper-Interactive Forms With JavaScript

The forms discussed in the preceding chapter are often called *interactive forms* by experienced Webbies. By adding a little JavaScript to your forms, however, you can make them much more interactive. I suppose the correct term would be *hyper-interactive*. In this chapter you'll learn about using JavaScript to make your forms more interactive. Let me explain what I mean by "more interactive."

Normally when a reader fills in a form, the form is passive in that it does not respond to the reader's entries. The reader just fills in the blanks and then presses the Submit button. With JavaScript, you can create small routines that respond to the reader while he or she is actually filling in the blanks. For example, you might have the form reject a blank entry, or present some message in response to a particular form entry. In this chapter you'll learn:

- How JavaScript views a form
- Providing immediate feedback
- Detecting the contents and status for form fields
- Changing the contents of a field
- Disallowing blank fields

How JavaScript Views a Form

Back in Chapter 18, "Introducing JavaScript," I talked about the way JavaScript views the different things on the reader's screen as *objects*. In addition to the various objects I pointed out in that chapter, JavaScript also views a form as an object. Furthermore, each individual control in the form is an object also. Figure 22-1 shows a sample form and the objects you can manipulate with JavaScript.

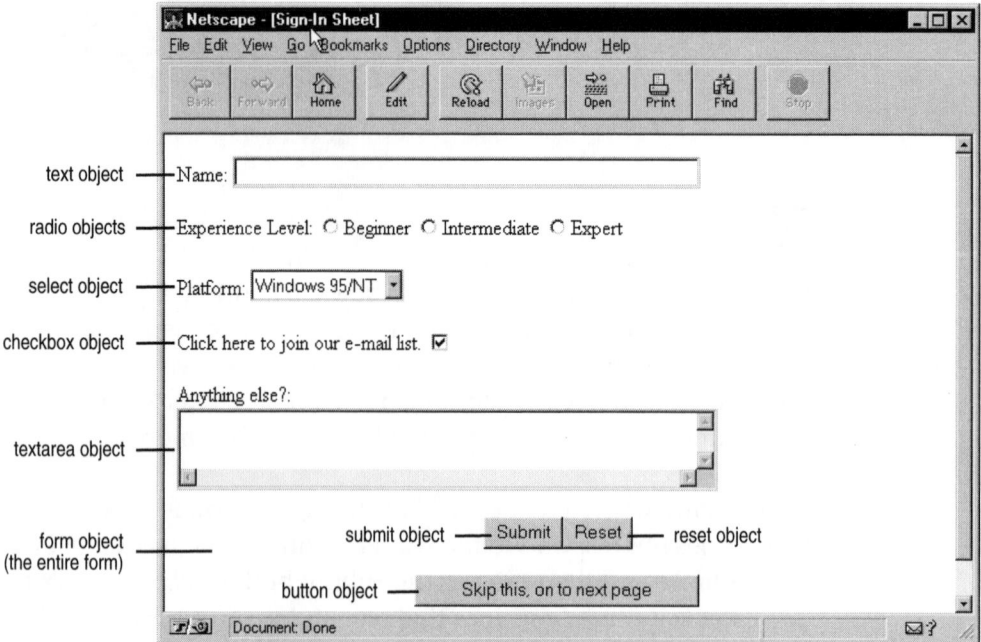

Figure 22-1: *The form object and objects within the form.*

As with all the other JavaScript objects we've discussed, each of the objects shown in Figure 22-1 has its own unique set of properties and methods that you can detect and manipulate with JavaScript code. The *object.property* and *object.method()* syntaxes described in Chapter 18 don't exactly work the same with forms and controls, however. Here's why.

Even though a form is an object, it is also a *property* of the overall document. Which is to say, a document can have many objects and one or more of those objects can be a form. Therefore, the syntax for referring to a form looks like this:

document.*formname.property*

or

document.*formname.method()*

Furthermore, even though each control on a form is an object in its own right, it's also a property of the larger form that encompasses that control. That is, a form can contain many objects (controls). The syntax for referring to a specific control on a Web page takes the syntax:

document.*formname.controlname.property*

or

document.*formname.controlname.method()*

I realize that this is confusing at first, but notice that there is a progression from the larger "general" object down to a specific object. That is, document.*formname.controlname.property* says, in English, "In this document, there's a form named *formname*. And in that form there's a control named *controlname*. And I want to detect/change the *property* of that specific control."

WHERE DO THE NAMES COME FROM?

In the preceding examples, I used the terms *formname* and *controlname* as sort of generic names. When you write JavaScript code, you'll want to refer to your forms and controls by their real names. Where do those names come from? They come from the NAME= attribute defined within the <form> or <input> tag.

Here's an example. If you were to look at the document source "behind the scenes" in Figure 22-1, looking at *just* the relevant parts of the <form> and <input> tags, you'd be able to see the names I gave to the form and to each of its controls, as follows (because some attributes within the tags are not relevant to this particular discussion, I've used ellipses (...) to replace them):

```
<form NAME="myForm" METHOD...>
Name:
<input NAME="readerName" VALUE="" SIZE=50>
Experience Level:
     <input TYPE="RADIO" NAME="experience"...>
     <input TYPE="RADIO" NAME="experience"...>
     <input TYPE="RADIO" NAME="experience"...>

Platform:
<select NAME="platform">
     <option VALUE="Win32">Windows 95/NT
     <option VALUE="DOSWin">DOS/Windows
     <option VALUE="Mac">Macintosh
     <option VALUE="Unix">Unix
</select>

Click here to join our e-mail list.
<input TYPE="CHECKBOX" NAME="mailingList"...>

Anything else?:
<textarea NAME="comments"...></textarea>

<!Buttons at bottom of form>
<input TYPE="submit" NAME="subBttn" VALUE="Submit">
<input TYPE="reset" NAME="rstBttn" VALUE="Reset">
<input TYPE="button" NAME="skip"...>
```

Notice the various NAME= attributes I've assigned to each control in Figure 22-1. Given the fact that a form is a property of the document and a control is a property of the form it belongs to, the correct way to address the form and its controls, from within JavaScript code, would be as shown in Figure 22-2.

TIP

JavaScript lets you refer to the current object using the this. *keyword, which can be a great alternative to typing out those long names. I'll show you some examples of this a little later in this chapter.*

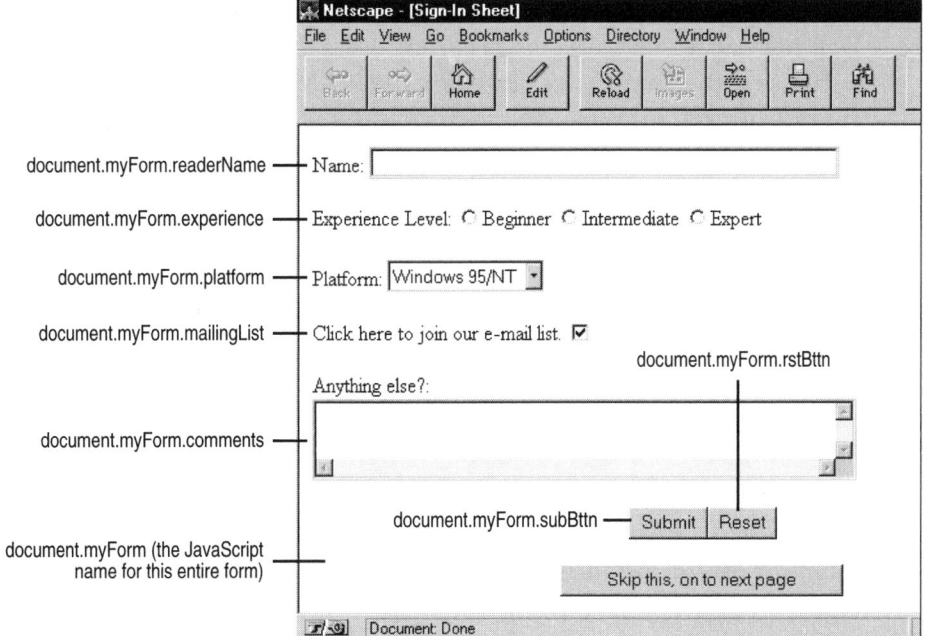

Figure 22-2: *JavaScript names of the sample form and its controls.*

TRAP

JavaScript object names are case-sensitive. Hence, the obsessive attention to detail applies here. The names shown in Figure 22-2 exactly match the names given in each control's NAME= attribute.

Are you with me here? (Are you still awake?) Just to recap—when referring to a form from within JavaScript code, you have to use the syntax document.*formname*, where *formname* is the name of the form as defined by the NAME= attribute of the <form> tag that defines the form. Thus when you're writing JavaScript code and want to refer to the form named myForm, you must use the complete syntax *document.myForm.*

When referring to a control within a form, you need to use the syntax document.*formname.controlname,* where *controlname* is the name of the control as defined by the NAME= attribute of the control's <input> tag. And *formname* is still the name of the form that contains the control, as defined in the NAME= attribute of the <form> tag. Thus, if you're writing JavaScript code and want to refer to the field named readerName on the form named myForm, the correct syntax would be *document.myForm.readerName.*

OBJECT-ORIENTED PROGRAMMING LANGUAGES (OOPs)

This whole business of things being defined as objects, with some objects acting as properties of some larger container object, is called the *object hierarchy.* This is not something that's unique to JavaScript. All modern *object-oriented programming languages* (OOPs) use some kind of object hierarchy, where each object has properties and/or methods.

You'll be happy to know that everything you learn about JavaScript in this book will carry over quite nicely to any future object-oriented languages you care to learn, including Java, C++, and Visual Basic for Applications (VBA), the programming language that let's you control the entire Microsoft Office for Windows 95 suite of applications!

A SIMPLE EXAMPLE

Now I'd like to show you a sample Web page that contains a form and a couple of custom JavaScript functions that can interact with that form. I'll try to keep the example fairly simple, because this is our first shot at it. Even though this example isn't terribly practical, it does illustrate the basic techniques used in mixing forms and JavaScript in a page. Figure 22-3 shows the sample page I'll be talking about here. If you like, you can type it into Notepad *exactly* as shown in the figure.

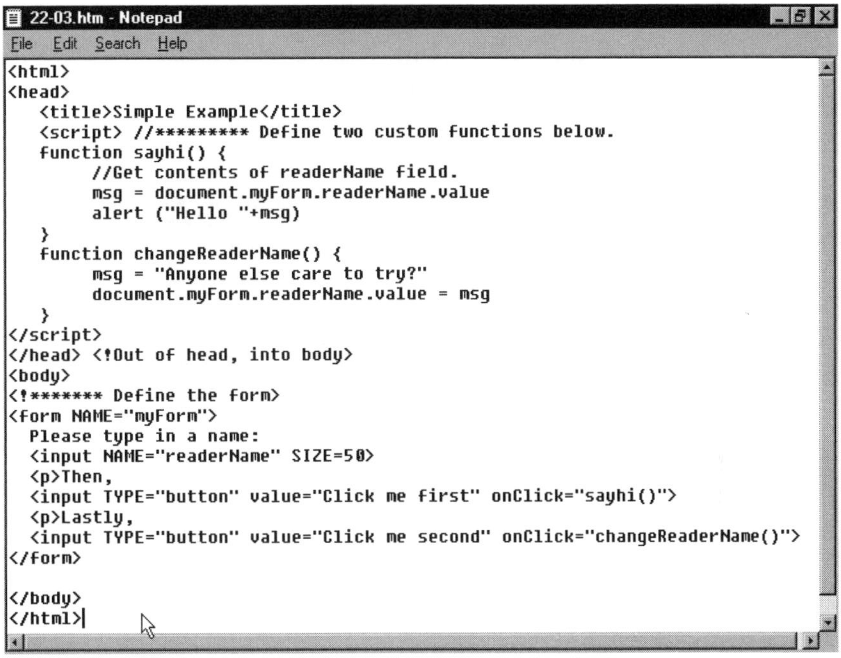

```
22-03.htm - Notepad
File  Edit  Search  Help
<html>
<head>
    <title>Simple Example</title>
    <script> //********* Define two custom functions below.
    function sayhi() {
        //Get contents of readerName field.
        msg = document.myForm.readerName.value
        alert ("Hello "+msg)
    }
    function changeReaderName() {
        msg = "Anyone else care to try?"
        document.myForm.readerName.value = msg
    }
</script>
</head> <!Out of head, into body>
<body>
<!******* Define the form>
<form NAME="myForm">
  Please type in a name:
  <input NAME="readerName" SIZE=50>
  <p>Then,
  <input TYPE="button" value="Click me first" onClick="sayhi()">
  <p>Lastly,
  <input TYPE="button" value="Click me second" onClick="changeReaderName()">
</form>

</body>
</html>
```

Figure 22-3: *Custom JavaScript functions will get/change form data.*

Let's say you do type the page shown in the figure and then open it with your Web browser. Initially, the screen looks like Figure 22-4.

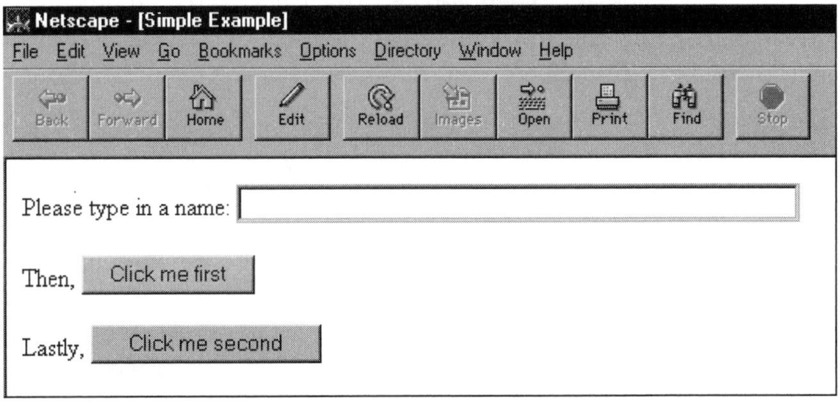

Figure 22-4: *The page from Figure 22-3, in the Web browser.*

Suppose that you type a name, such as Alan, in the text box and then you click the button labeled *Click me first*. You'll see a small alert message that says "Hello," followed by whatever name you typed into the text box (see Figure 22-5).

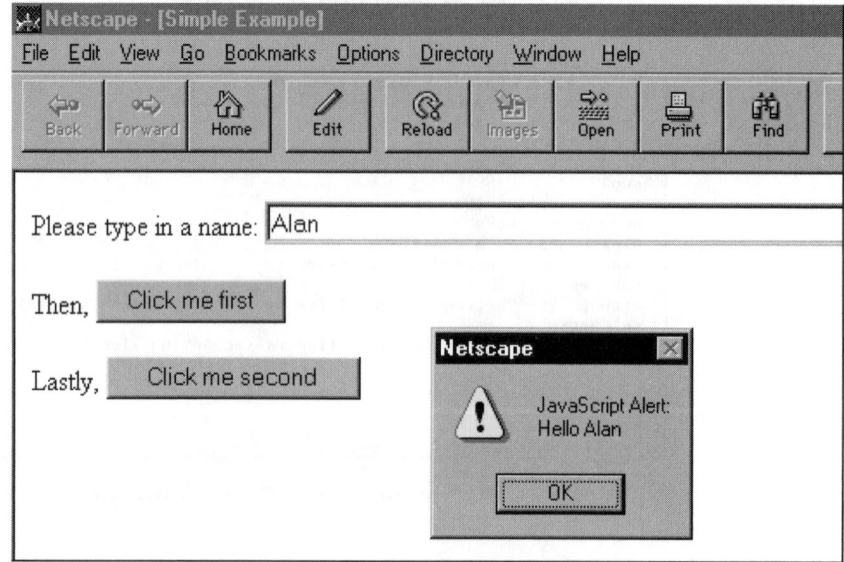

Figure 22-5: *Message that appears after you click the Click me first button.*

Now, let's say you click the OK button to get rid of the "Hello..." message. Then you click the *Click me second* button. That button changes the contents of the text box to *Anybody else care to try?*, as in Figure 22-6.

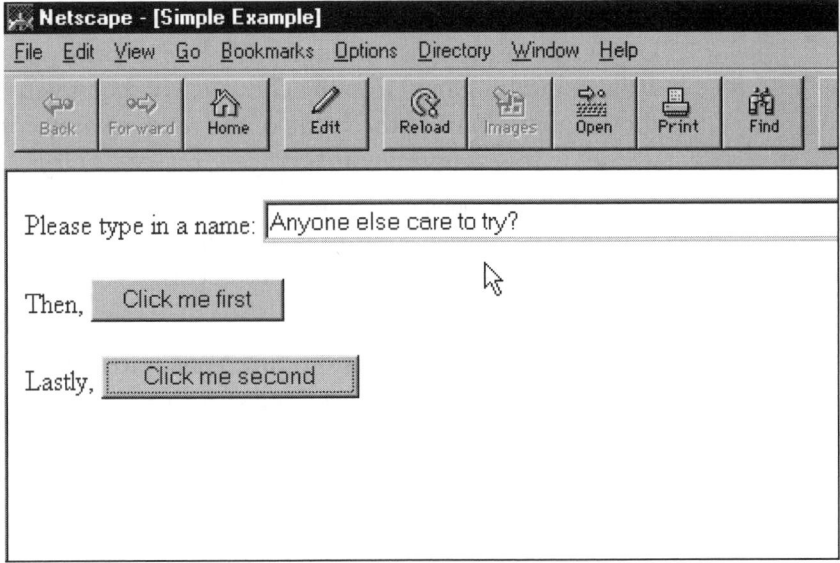

Figure 22-6: *Clicking the second button changes the contents of the text field.*

Where do these two buttons get their power to read and change the contents of the text field? The secrets lie within the two custom functions defined in the page's head. The first function looks like this:

```
function sayhi() {
//Get contents of readerName field.
    msg = document.myForm.readerName.value
    alert ("Hello "+msg)
}
```

The important line here is the one that reads *msg = document.myForm.readerName.value,* because it gets the *value* (contents) of the readerName control (the text box), and puts a copy of that value into a variable named msg. Then, the line *alert ("Hello "+msg)* displays an alert box containing the word *Hello,* followed by a space and the contents of that text box.

The value property of a control often works both ways. That is, JavaScript can read what's currently in the control and can also write something new into the control. My second custom function, shown next, changes the value of the readerName control from whatever it was to the words *Anyone else care to try?*

```
function changeReaderName() {
    msg = "Anyone else care to try?"
        document.myForm.readerName.value = msg
}
```

What triggers these custom functions into action? The onClick() event procedures in the input tags for the two custom buttons do, as shown here:

```
<input TYPE="button" value="Click me first"
onClick="sayhi()">
```

```
<input TYPE="button" value="Click me second"
onClick="changeReaderName()">
```

And that, in a nutshell, is pretty much how all interactions between forms and JavaScript take place. You define custom JavaScript functions that detect and/or modify the contents of form fields. And you use event handlers in <input> tags to determine *when* the custom function is executed.

IMMEDIATE FEEDBACK ON CLICK

One very cool thing you can do with JavaScript in a form is provide immediate feedback to the reader, based on a selection he or she makes. For example, Figure 22-7 shows a series of radio buttons that let the reader pick a payment method. If the reader picks the first option, Pay now, a warning appears on the screen telling the reader that this is not a secure site. (Better to tell them now, rather than wait until *after* they've filled out the entire form and clicked the Submit button.)

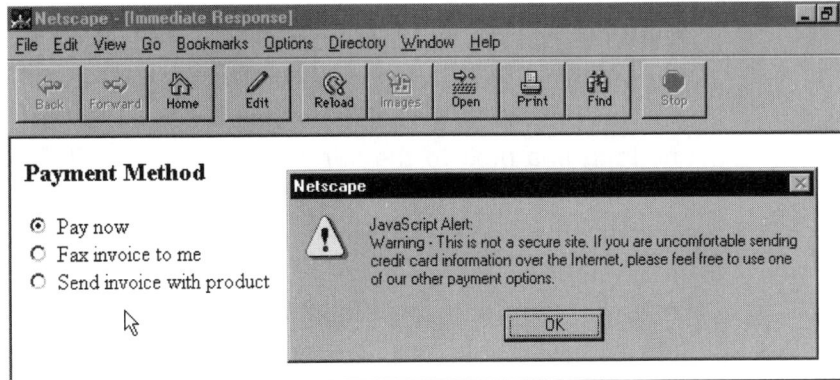

Figure 22-7: *Choosing the* Pay now *radio button sends up an immediate message.*

Figure 22-8 shows the document source for the example shown in Figure 22-7. Note the custom JavaScript function, named warning():

```
<script>     //****** Custom function to show warning message.
function warning() {
     var msg="Warning - This is not a secure site. If you "
     msg+="are uncomfortable sending credit card information"
     msg+="over the Internet, please feel free to use one "
     msg+="of our other payment options."
     alert(msg)
}
</script>
```

The function creates a message and stores it in a variable named msg. Then, the *alert(msg)* statement displays the message on the screen.

WHAT'S WITH THE MSG+=?

You might be wondering about all those msg+= lines in the custom function. Well, I could have just typed the whole message as one long line next to the *var msg=* statement. But then it would have scrolled off the screen and you wouldn't be able to see it. I broke the message into smaller chunks just so you could see it on the screen.

The += operator in JavaScript means *"equals itself plus..."* Thus, initially the variable msg just contains the text next to the *var msg=* statement. But it grows with each subsequent *msg+=* statement. The *alert(msg)* statement then displays the entire message.

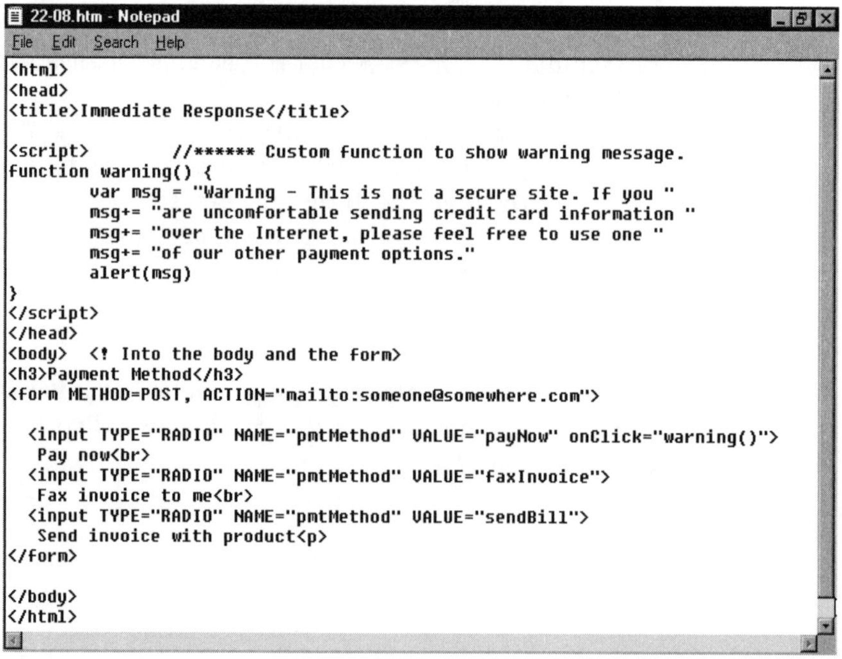

```
22-08.htm - Notepad                                    _ 8 X
File  Edit  Search  Help
<html>
<head>
<title>Immediate Response</title>

<script>        //****** Custom function to show warning message.
function warning() {
        var msg = "Warning - This is not a secure site. If you "
        msg+= "are uncomfortable sending credit card information "
        msg+= "over the Internet, please feel free to use one "
        msg+= "of our other payment options."
        alert(msg)
}
</script>
</head>
<body>  <! Into the body and the form>
<h3>Payment Method</h3>
<form METHOD=POST, ACTION="mailto:someone@somewhere.com">

  <input TYPE="RADIO" NAME="pmtMethod" VALUE="payNow" onClick="warning()">
  Pay now<br>
  <input TYPE="RADIO" NAME="pmtMethod" VALUE="faxInvoice">
  Fax invoice to me<br>
  <input TYPE="RADIO" NAME="pmtMethod" VALUE="sendBill">
  Send invoice with product<p>
</form>

</body>
</html>
```

Figure 22-8: *Document source for the page shown in Figure 22-7.*

Of course, here we've just defined *what* the function does. We also have to decide *when* the function does its thing. In this situation, because we want the custom warning() message to display its message when (and if) the reader chooses the Pay now radio button, we put the event handler in that field's <input> tag, as follows:

```
<input TYPE="RADIO" NAME="pmtMethod"
    VALUE="payNow" onClick="warning()">
    Pay now<br>
```

DETERMINING THE CONTENTS OF VARIOUS FIELD TYPES

In many situations you'll want to present immediate information to the reader, based on the specific selection he or she makes in a field. For example, you might want to display a message if the reader checks, or unchecks, a check box. Or, you might want to display a message based on a selection from a drop-down list. In the sections that follow, I'll show you how to set up custom functions that are sensitive to the contents of fields. I'll have each function show some generic message, but you can easily type the custom function into your own page and customize the message to your own needs. (Don't forget to include the event handler in the <input> tag when defining the field.)

DETECT THE STATUS OF A CHECK BOX

Let's suppose that you want to send your reader a message as soon as she (or he) checks or clears, a check box. First, in the head of your document, you need to set up a custom JavaScript function like this one:

```
<head>
<!other head tags here...>

<script>
function showMe(isChecked) {
      if (isChecked) {
              msg="Check box is checked"
      } else {
              msg="Check box is empty"
      }
      alert (msg)
}
</script>
</head>
```

Down in the body of your document, within a pair of <form>...</form> tags, you could use a simple onClick event handler to determine the contents of any check box. For example, you could use something like this:

```
<body>
<form NAME="myForm">
<input TYPE="CHECKBOX" NAME="myCheckBox"
   onClick="showMe(this.checked)">
<!...other text and input tags...>
</form>
</body>
```

The *checked* property of a check box is true if the check box is checked. If the check box is empty, the *checked* property is false. When your reader clicks on the check box defined by this <input> tag, the current status of the *checked* property is sent immediately to the custom function named showMe(). That function, in turn, makes a decision about which message to display, based on whether *checked* is true or false at the moment.

If you care to type the entire page and try this example for yourself, use Notepad to create the page exactly as shown in Figure 22-9.

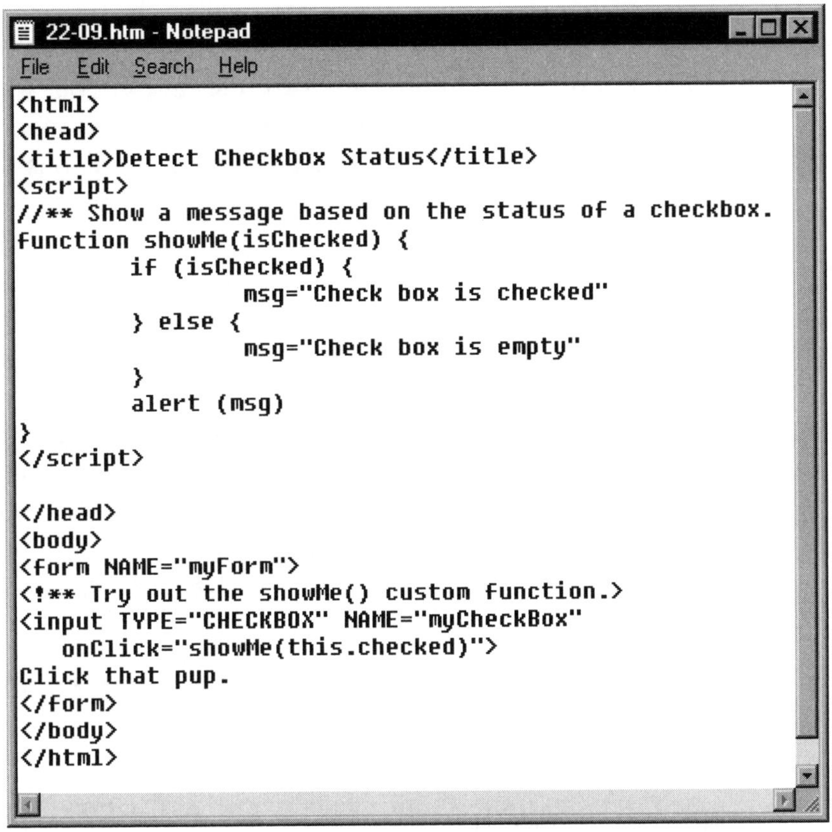

```
22-09.htm - Notepad                                    _ □ ×
File  Edit  Search  Help
<html>
<head>
<title>Detect Checkbox Status</title>
<script>
//** Show a message based on the status of a checkbox.
function showMe(isChecked) {
        if (isChecked) {
                msg="Check box is checked"
        } else {
                msg="Check box is empty"
        }
        alert (msg)
}
</script>

</head>
<body>
<form NAME="myForm">
<!** Try out the showMe() custom function.>
<input TYPE="CHECKBOX" NAME="myCheckBox"
   onClick="showMe(this.checked)">
Click that pup.
</form>
</body>
</html>
```

Figure 22-9: *This page demonstrates status-checking of a check box.*

TIP

It's not necessary to use the expression if (isChecked==true) *in the showMe() function, because the* condition *is "solved" as soon as the parentheses contain a true or false value. In this example, because* this.checked *is sending true or false,* if(isChecked) *is a sufficient test.*

THE THIS. KEYWORD

Earlier I pointed out how you can refer to a property of a form or specific control by using the general syntax document.*formname.controlname.property*. Typing all those long names can become pretty tedious. As an alternative, JavaScript offers the keyword *this*. Technically, *this.* refers to the current object. For example, *this.form* refers to the form in which JavaScript code is being executed. The term *this.value* (used within an <input> tag) refers to the value that the reader typed in the field defined by *this* <input> tag.

The most common use of the *this.* keyword is to pass the current contents of a field to a custom JavaScript function. For example, function *xyz(frm,cntrl)* accepts two parameters, a reference to a specific form (*frm*), and a reference to a specific control (*cntrl*). An event handler might call that function using xyz(this.form,this.name) so that the function "knows" which form is being referred to and which specific control is being referred to.

DETERMINE CONTENTS OF A DROP-DOWN LIST

As you probably know, a Select List (or *drop-down list*) contains several mutually exclusive options to the reader. For example, the list might present three shipping options: US Mail; UPS Ground, and Federal Express. Now, let's say that if the reader selects Federal Express from the list, you want to display a message, perhaps telling the reader that there's an extra shipping charge for that method. Which is to say, as soon as the reader makes a selection you want JavaScript to take a look at the reader's choice and, if the choice is "Federal Express," you want to show a custom message.

JavaScript can determine what the user has selected from a drop-down list (select box) in two ways: as a number indicating the selected option's position in the list, or as text, indicating the actual text of the selection. For example, take a look at this select box definition:

```
<select NAME="prize">
     <option>Dream House
     <option>Ferrari
     <option>Money - $50,000
     <option>Motor Yacht
     <option>Porsche
     <option>Sailing Yacht
</select>
```

From JavaScript's view, the first option, Dream House, is option[0]. The next one, Ferrari, is option[1], and so forth, down to option[5], the Sailing Yacht. After the user makes a selection from the select box, the selectedIndex property of the box contains the subscript number. For example, if the reader chooses Motor Yacht from the list, then the selectedIndex property of this *prize* control would be 3.

The text of any given option is the *text* property of the specific option. In this example, the expression *option[0].text* would equal "Dream House." We can pass these properties to a JavaScript function. Allow me to illustrate, using a sample page (see Figure 22-10) that contains a select box and a custom function that displays the contents of that select box (both as a number and as text).

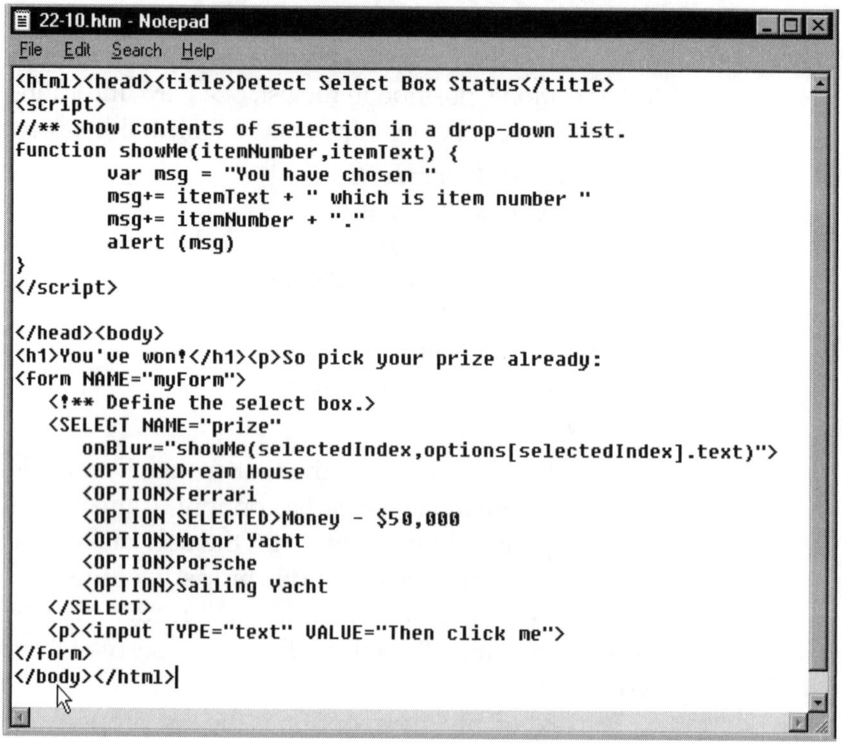

```
22-10.htm - Notepad
File  Edit  Search  Help

<html><head><title>Detect Select Box Status</title>
<script>
//** Show contents of selection in a drop-down list.
function showMe(itemNumber,itemText) {
        var msg = "You have chosen "
        msg+= itemText + " which is item number "
        msg+= itemNumber + "."
        alert (msg)
}
</script>

</head><body>
<h1>You've won!</h1><p>So pick your prize already:
<form NAME="myForm">
    <!** Define the select box.>
    <SELECT NAME="prize"
        onBlur="showMe(selectedIndex,options[selectedIndex].text)">
        <OPTION>Dream House
        <OPTION>Ferrari
        <OPTION SELECTED>Money - $50,000
        <OPTION>Motor Yacht
        <OPTION>Porsche
        <OPTION>Sailing Yacht
    </SELECT>
    <p><input TYPE="text" VALUE="Then click me">
</form>
</body></html>
```

Figure 22-10: *A Select box and new showMe() custom function.*

Let's look first at the <input> tag. Notice in the <select>tag below that when the onBlur event occurs, control is to pass *selectedIndex* and *options[selectedIndex].text* to the function named showMe. Remember that the selectedIndex property contains the number of the item selected (thus, *options[selectedIndex].text* contains the text of that selection).

```
<select NAME="prize"
  onBlur="showMe(selectedIndex,
  options[selectedIndex].text)">
      <option>Dream House
      <option>Ferrari
      <option>Money - $50,000
      <option>Motor Yacht
      <option>Porsche
      <option>Sailing Yacht
  </select>
```

TIP

The onBlur event, like the onChange event, occurs after the reader moves the cursor out of the field and into another field. Two fields are needed to test this example because we need to move the cursor out of the select box and into another field in order to trigger the onBlur event. The event handlers (onClick, onBlur) that a field type supports are shown with the syntax of the various <input> tags in Chapter 21, "Creating Forms for Business."

When the reader clicks outside the select box, the showMe() custom function, shown here, displays the selectedIndex and text of the option:

```
function showMe(itemNumber,itemText) {
      var msg = "You have chosen "
      msg+= itemText + " which is item number "
      msg+= itemNumber + "."
      alert (msg)
}
```

Of course, we could make a custom function that makes some kind of intelligent decision based on the reader's selection. For example, the following prizeComment() custom function accepts just the item number and then displays a (semi-)intelligent message based upon that number:

```
<script>
//** Decide on a message based on reader's selection.
function prizeComment(itemNumber) {
    if (itemNumber == 0) {
        msg="Hope your dream house costs less than $50K"}

    if (itemNumber == 1 || itemNumber == 4) {
        msg="Insurance on those cars is murder!"}

    if (itemNumber == 3 || itemNumber == 5) {
        msg="You better be able to swim!"}

    if (itemNumber == 2) {
        msg="Whew, we were hoping you'd pick the money."}

    alert (msg)
}
</script>
```

The Select box that calls this function need only pass the item number, as follows:

```
onBlur="prizeComment(selectedIndex)"
```

TIP

In JavaScript, the characters | | mean "or." Also, like the items in the select box, virtually every list in JavaScript starts at zero, rather than one. Because we humans usually think of the first item in a list as being number 1, not 0, these "zero-based" lists can take some time to get accustomed to.

When this event occurs, the prizeComment() function displays *Hope your dream house costs less than $50K* if the reader chose the first item in the list, Dream House. If the reader chose one of the cars— item 1 or 4 in the list—the function displays the message *Insurance on those cars is murder!* and so forth.

DETERMINE WHICH RADIO BUTTON IS SELECTED

Radio buttons are an alternative to the drop-down list as a means of showing several mutually exclusive options. Just as you can use JavaScript to determine which option a reader chose from a Select list, you can also use JavaScript to determine which button a reader selected from a group of radio buttons.

From the Web publisher's perspective a radio button group is a series of <input TYPE="radio" NAME="*groupname*"...> tags in which all the buttons in a single group share the same *groupname*. From JavaScript's perspective, the radio buttons within the group can be referenced as *groupname*[0] for the first button in the group, *groupname*[1] for the second button and so forth where *groupname* is the name of the radio button group.

TRAP

In Netscape Navigator 2.0, the radio buttons were numbered backwards. That is, the last button was numbered 0, the second-to-last was numbered 1, and so forth. To fix this bug in version 2.0, you need to add onClick=0 to every <input TYPE="radio"...> tag on the page. Since you don't know what browser your reader will be using, consider adding onClick=0 to every <input TYPE="radio"...> tag in your page.

Each button has properties. For example the *.value* property returns the value assigned in the VALUE= attribute of a specific button. The *.checked* property returns true if the radio button is selected. There's also a *.length* property that tells how many buttons are in the group. We can use these properties to set up a loop that checks the *.checked* property of each button in a group to determine which button, if any, the user has selected. In fact, we can build a generic custom function that will work with any group of radio buttons in any form. Here's what that function looks like:

```
<script>
//Determine which radio button is selected.
//In calling event handler pass this.form.radiogroup.
function whichBttn(group) {
     msg="Nothing"
     for (var i=0;i<group.length;i++) {
          if (group[i].checked) {
               msg=group[i].value
               msg+=" which is item number "+i+"."
               break
          }
     }
     msg="You have selected "+(msg)
     alert (msg)
}
</script>
```

The logic of the function is as follows. The (group) parameter passes to the function a reference to the radio button group we want the function to analyze. It creates a variable named msg, which contains just the word *Nothing*, under the assumption that perhaps nothing has been selected from the radio button group.

Then a for() loop, which will count from 0 to however many items are in the radio button group (group.length), kicks in. This if() statement checks the current button to see if it is selected (group.checked). When it finds the button that is selected, it sets the msg variable to the value of that radio button (as defined in the VALUE= attribute for the radio button's <input> tag), and also tacks on the value of *i*, the loop counter. When it has found the checked button, it stops looking (break) and displays the value and number of the selected button in an alert box.

Figure 21-11 shows this custom function applied in an actual Web page. The call to the custom function takes place in the tag *<input TYPE="button"... onClick="whichBttn(this.form.prizes)">*, which passes to the function the radio group named "prizes" in the current form (this.form.prizes). What makes the function so generic is that it could be used to analyze a group of buttons. For example, if this page also contained a radio button group called

VacationDestinations, the only change that would be required to analyze that radio button group would be the name of the group, as follows:

```
onClick="whichBttn(this.form.VacationDestinations)"
```

```
22-11.htm - Notepad
File  Edit  Search  Help
<html><head><title>Detect Selected Radio Button</title>
<script>
//Determine which radio button is selected.
function whichBttn(group) {
        msg="Nothing"
        for (var i=0;i<group.length;i++) {
                if (group[i].checked) {
                        msg=group[i].value
                        msg+=" which is item number "+i+"."
                        break
                }
        }
        msg="You have selected "+(msg)
        alert (msg)
}
</script>
</head><body>
You've won again! Choose another prize...
<form>
<input TYPE="radio"  NAME="prizes"  VALUE="Dream House">Dream House<br>
<input TYPE="radio"  NAME="prizes"  VALUE="Ferrari">Ferrari<br>
<input TYPE="radio"  NAME="prizes"  VALUE="Money - $50,000">Money- $50,000<br>
<input TYPE="radio"  NAME="prizes"  VALUE="Motor Yacht">Motor Yacht<br>
<input TYPE="radio"  NAME="prizes"  VALUE="Porsche">Porsche<p>
<input TYPE="button"  VALUE="Then click here"
        onClick="whichBttn(this.form.prizes)">
</form>
</body></html>
```

Figure 22-11: *The whichBttn() custom function, used in a sample page.*

DETERMINE THE CONTENTS OF A TEXTAREA CONTROL

Back in the "A Simple Example" section, we used the *.value* property to get the contents of a text box, as well as to change the contents of a text box. The same principle works with textarea boxes, as well. As an example, I'll show you a sample function named capText() that takes whatever a reader typed in a text or textarea box and displays that in a Confirm dialog box message that looks something like Figure 22-12.

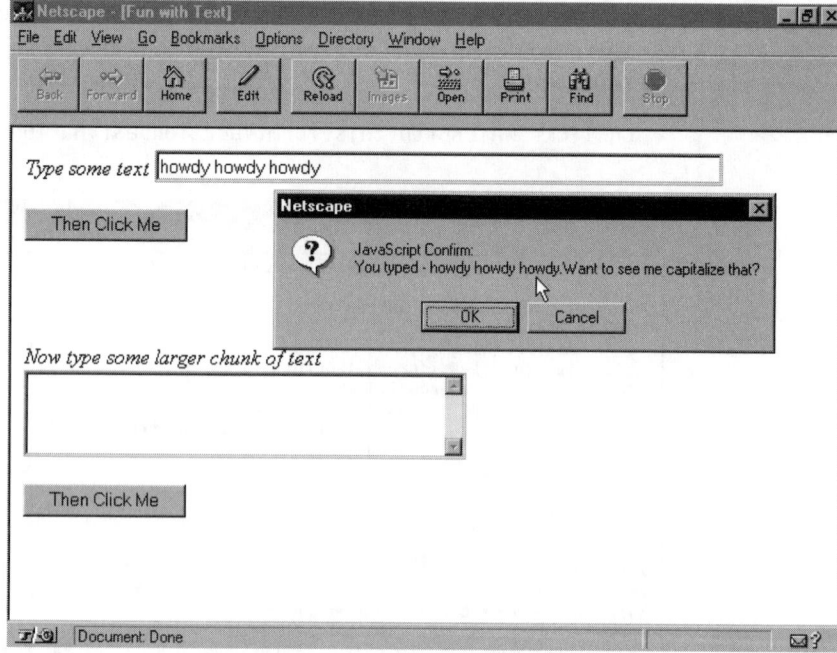

Figure 22-12: *Custom function displays text and asks for permission to capitalize it.*

If the reader clicks the Cancel button, the text in the box remains unchanged. If the reader clicks the OK button, the text in the box is converted to uppercase letters. Perhaps this isn't the most practical function in the world, but it does demonstrate how you can use the .value property to read, as well as to change, the contents of a text or textarea box. Here is the custom function:

```
<script>
//Play with text and textarea boxes
function capText(ctrl) {
    msg="You typed - " + ctrl.value +"."
    msg+="Want to see me capitalize that?"
    pleaseChange=confirm(msg)
    if (pleaseChange) {
        ctrl.value=ctrl.value.toUpperCase()
    }

}
</script>
```

The function accepts a reference to a particular control on a form (ctrl) as its parameter. Then the next lines display the contents of that control (ctrl.value) in a Confirm dialog box. If the reader clicks the OK button in the Confirm box, the contents of the field are converted to uppercase letters, using JavaScript's built-in toUpperCase() method, in this statement: *ctrl.value=ctrl.value.toUpperCase()*. Figure 22-13 shows the document source for the entire Web page, in Notepad, that demonstrates the function.

```
22-13.htm - Notepad
File  Edit  Search  Help
<html><head>
<title>Fun with Text</title>
<script>
//Play with text and textarea boxes
Function capText(ctrl) {
        msg="You typed - " + ctrl.value +"."
        msg+="Want to see me capitalize that?"
        pleaseChange=confirm(msg)
        if (pleaseChange) {
                ctrl.value=ctrl.value.toUpperCase()
        }

}
</script>

</head>
<body>
<form NAME="myForm">
    <i>Type some text</i> <input NAME="shortText" SIZE=60><p>
    <input TYPE="button" value="Then Click Me"
        onClick="capText(this.form.shortText)"><p><br><p>

    <i>Now type some larger chunk of text</i><br>
    <textarea NAME="longText" ROWS=3 COLS=40 WRAP="virtual"></textarea><p>
    <input TYPE="button" value="Then Click Me"
        onClick="capText(this.form.longText)">
</form>
</body></html>
```

Figure 22-13: *The document source behind the page shown in Figure 22-12.*

DISALLOWING BLANK ENTRIES

You can create a custom function that checks whether a reader left a field blank on your form. If the function determines that the field is blank, it immediately displays a message like the one in Figure 22-14 and puts the cursor back into the field that needs to be filled.

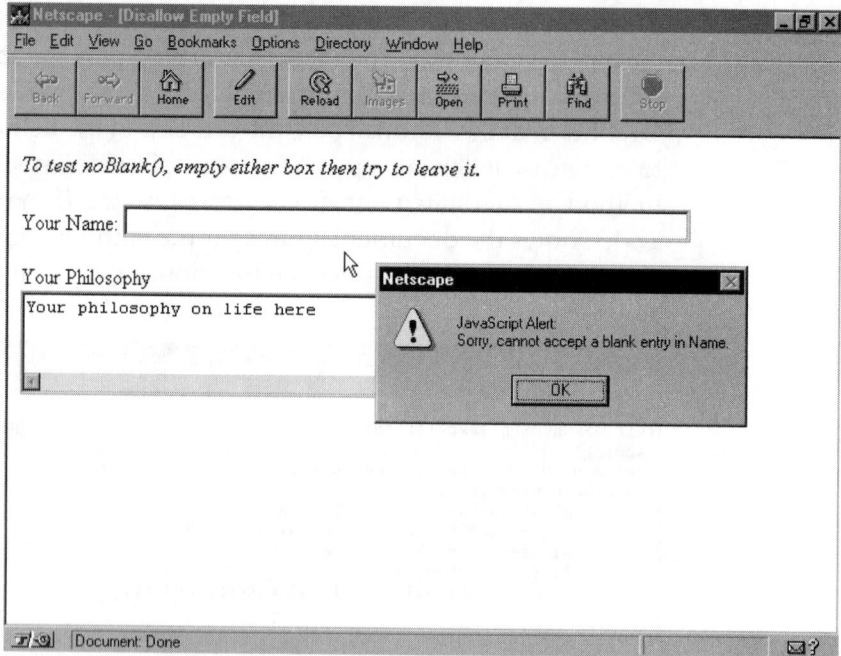

Figure 22-14: *Message disallowing blank Your Name field.*

The custom function, which I've named noBlank(), follows:

```
<script>
function noBlank(anyText) {
    if (anyText.value == "") {
        anyText.focus() //Move focus back to blank field.
        msg="Sorry, cannot accept a blank "
        msg+="entry in "+anyText.name+"."
        alert (msg)
    }
}
</script>
```

To use the function, add the attribute *onBlur="noBlank(This)"* to the <input> tag of a text field, or to a <textarea> tag. Be forewarned that the function is *very* insistent. If you initially present the form with two or more fields that call upon noBlank(), you may get the "Sorry..." message for two fields at a time—once for the field you left blank, and again for the field you clicked. The reason this happens is that when noBlank() detects the blank in the field you just left, it moves the cursor out of the field you're in, which in turn triggers *that* field's onBlur() event. (This is something that, I think, should be changed in the very definition of the JavaScript language.) Displaying each field with some initial text in the field makes for a slightly kinder, gentler noBlank() function. If you'd like to test it out, type the script shown in Figure 22-15.

```
22-15.htm - Notepad
File  Edit  Search  Help
<html><head>
<title>Disallow Empty Field</title>

<script>
function noBlank(anyText) {
        if (anyText.value == "") {
                anyText.focus() //Move focus back to blank field.
                msg="Sorry, cannot accept a blank "
                msg+="entry in "+anyText.name+"."
                alert (msg)
        }
}
</script>
</head>

<body>
<form NAME="myForm">
   <i>To test noBlank(), empty either box then try to leave it.</i><p>
   Your Name:
   <input NAME="Name" SIZE=60 VALUE="Your name here"
     onBlur = "noBlank(this)"><p>
   Your Philosophy<br>
   <textarea NAME="Philosophy" ROWS = 3 COLS=60 onBlur="noBlank(this)">
Your philosophy on life here</textarea>
</form>

</body>
</html>
```

Figure 22-15: *The noBlank() function in a sample Web page.*

MOVING ON

I could yak about JavaScript and forms for another 500 pages. But, alas, this is a book about Netscape Navigator, not JavaScript per se, and I don't have 500 pages to spare. I do, however, have more JavaScript examples on my Web site at http://www.coolnerds.com. And you're welcome to use, pilfer, explore, or abuse whatever you find there. Also, remember that you can get lots more detail on form tags and JavaScript statements from any of the electronic references mentioned near the ends of Chapters 15, "Tuning HTML Tags," and 19, "Fun With JavaScript." In the meantime, let's take a break from the technical stuff and talk about something *really* important—promoting your Web site.

CHAPTER
23

Promoting Your New Web Site

How many pages are on the World Wide Web? No one knows for sure, but the answer is in the tens of millions. Given those figures, how can you be sure that your Web site will get noticed? In a word, *promotion*. In this chapter, you'll learn about many easy and (mostly) free ways to promote your Web site so that people will see it. Topics in this chapter include:

- How to plan keywords, categories, and descriptions for your Web site
- Where to find promotion guides online
- How and where to publicize your site on the World Wide Web
- How to measure the results of your online promotion efforts
- Low-tech promotion methods you should consider

PLANNING AHEAD

Before you dive into promoting your Web site, you need to plan ahead. First and foremost, make sure that your Web site is working perfectly before you tell the world about it. Few experiences are more embarrassing than sending people to a broken Web site. And few mistakes are as likely to keep would-be visitors from coming back to your site.

Once you're sure your Web site is working correctly, the next step is to choose some keywords, categories, and descriptions that will make your site easy to find.

CHOOSING KEYWORDS, CATEGORIES & DESCRIPTIONS

When you search for information on the Web, you typically do so by specifying keywords and phrases or by choosing categories in an Internet search engine or directory. For example, to learn about llama ranching, you'd fire up your favorite search engine and search for the keyword *llama,* or perhaps the phrase *llama ranch.*

Because searching is such a popular way to find things on the Web, you'll want to choose keywords and categories that describe your Web site accurately. To get started, write down as many relevant words and phrases as you can. You might even want to use a thesaurus to help you come up with keywords. As an example, I might choose the keywords and phrases *Web publishing, JavaScript, Windows 95,* and *MS Access* for my own Coolnerds Web site at *http://www.coolnerds.com.*

> **TIP**
>
> *You can find a handy online thesaurus at the Gopher site* gopher://odie.niaid.nih.gov/77/.thesaurus/index. *(See Chapter 29, "FTP, Gopher & Telnet," for more about Gopher.) Simply go to this site, type the word you want to look up in the thesaurus, and press Enter.*

Also jot down some broad categories that describe your Web site. If you're unsure about which categories to use, pay a visit to some of the following search engines and either search for Web pages, using the keywords you jotted down earlier, or click on various categories until you find categories that fit your own site.

- Infoseek at *http://www2.infoseek.com*

- Lycos at *http://www.lycos.com*

- Yahoo! at *http://www.yahoo.com*

Figure 23-1 shows the screen after I searched for *llama ranch* in Yahoo! Notice that each set of Web site links is preceded by a descriptive category (*Business and Economy:Companies:Animals:Alpacas* and *Business and Economy:Companies:Animals:Llamas* in this example).

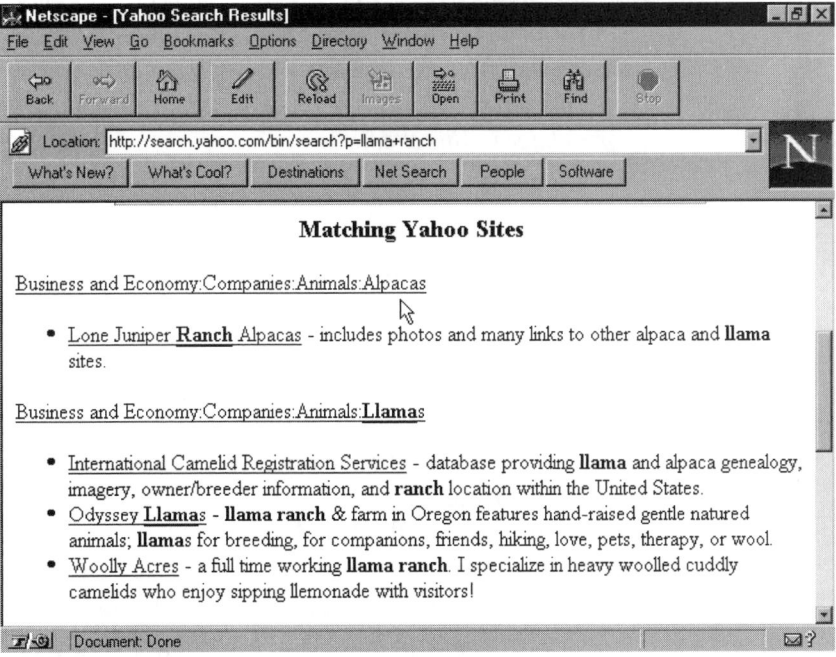

Figure 23-1: *A search for* llama ranch *in Yahoo! yields listings in several related categories.*

After you've developed your keywords and categories, try using them with several different search engines to find Web sites that are similar to yours. If your searches always come up empty or they find sites that seem completely unrelated to yours, the keywords and categories might need some tweaking. (Of course, it's also possible that your site is truly unique.)

Keywords and categories are just part of the picture. You'll also want to write a description that will entice readers to visit your Web site. For best results, avoid any hints of advertising or hype, write concisely and with a clear focus, be specific but leave the reader wanting a little bit more, and for heaven's sake, be sure you've checked the description for grammar and spelling errors.

TIP

To save yourself some time, compose your description in Notepad and store it in a text file on disk. Later, you can copy and paste the prepared description from the text file into whatever form you're using to submit information about your Web site. You'll learn more about submission forms later in this chapter.

SETTING THE DOCUMENT PROPERTIES FOR YOUR WEB PAGE

Lycos, Inktomi, and Web Crawler are examples of *robots,* or *spiders,* which traverse the Web's hypertext structure and retrieve and index all the documents they find. You can help the robots index your Web site accurately by including keywords and other descriptive information right in the HTML code at the top of your Web pages. Adding this information is easy in Netscape's Editor and doesn't require you to know HTML. Here's what you do:

1. Open your document in the Gold's editor.

2. Choose Properties | Document from the menu bar and click the General tab in the Document Properties dialog box that appears.

3. Fill in the Title, Author, Description, Keywords, and Classification text boxes, using Figure 23-2 as a guide. (For details about these text boxes, click the Help button at the lower-right corner of the Document Properties dialog box.)

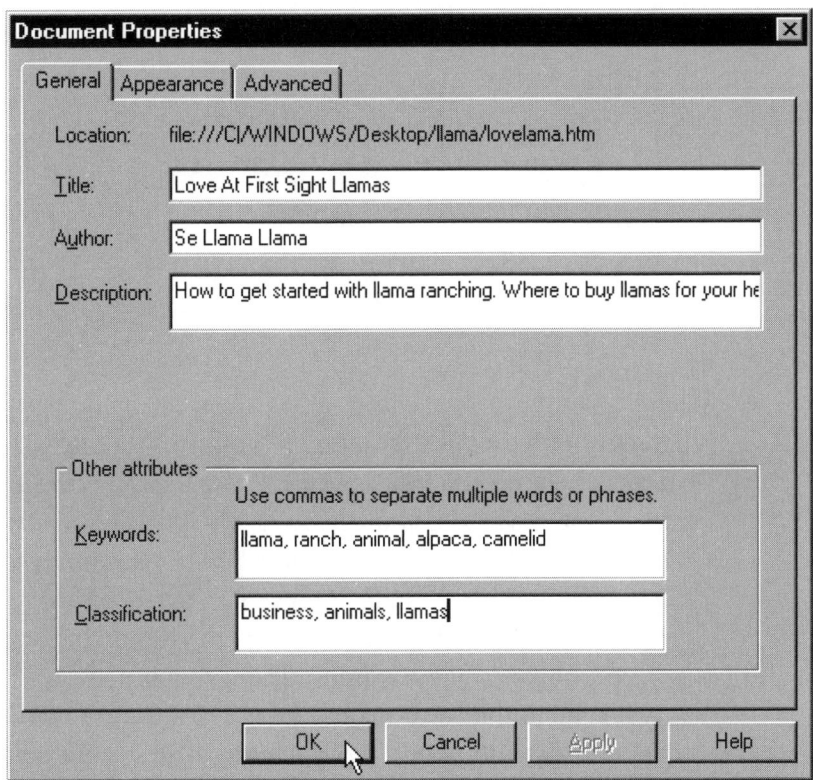

Figure 23-2: *The completed General tab of the Document Properties dialog box for a sample Web site on llama ranching.*

4. Choose OK to save your changes.

Netscape will insert the information you supplied in Step 3 into appropriate <meta...> tags between the <head> and </head> tags in your Web page, as shown in Figure 23-3. (To view the HTML code for any Web page, choose View | Document Source from the Netscape menu bar.)

TIP

> *The information you supply in the Document Information dialog box doesn't appear when you display the Web page in your browser. It is part of the document, however, and is available to any robot that wants to index it.*

```
Netscape - [View Document Source]                                    _ □ ×
<html>
<head>
   <title>Love At First Sight Llamas</title>
   <meta name="GENERATOR" content="Mozilla/3.0b4Gold (Win32)">
   <meta name="Author" content="Se Llama Llama">
   <meta name="Classification" content="business, animals, llamas">
   <meta name="Description" content="How to get started with llama ranching
</head>
<body vlink="#COCOCO">
```

Figure 23-3: *Document source for the Web page shown in Figure 23-2.*

LEARNING MORE ABOUT YOUR AUDIENCE

Many people on the Web participate in user surveys that ask such nosy questions as *Are you willing to pay for Web site accesses?, How old are you?, What is your income?,* and *How many years of school did you attend?* The results of these surveys can help you better understand how to pitch your Web page to your online audience.

If you'd like to view some survey results or participate in the surveys, go to the Yahoo! search engine at *http://www.yahoo.com,* click the *Computers and Internet* category, scroll down to the bottom of the page and click the *WorldWide Web@* category, and then scroll down to and click the *Statistics and Demographics* category. Now explore the survey links from here.

To find some other user surveys, search for *survey web* in InfoSeek (*http://www2.infoseek.com*), Yahoo!, Alta Vista (*http://www.altavista.digital.com*), and other popular search engines.

ONLINE PROMOTION GUIDES

Several thoughtful citizens on the Web have compiled online guides to help you figure out how to publicize your Web site. These guides include many hyperlinks that take you right to a spot where you can publicize your site. In fact, I used the following three online guides to find many of the resources discussed in this chapter:

- How do I publicize my work? at *http://www.boutell.com/faq/pub.htm* offers some top-notch suggestions for publicizing your new site.

- FAQ: How to announce your new Web site at *http://ep.com/faq/webannounce.html* is another treasure trove of information about announcing new sites.

- Promoting your page at *http://www.orst.edu/aw/stygui/propag.htm* offers still more suggestions for increasing traffic on your site.

To find other resources for announcing your Web site online, start the Yahoo! search engine at *http://www.yahoo.com*, click the *Computers and Internet* category, scroll down to and click *WorldWide Web@*, and then click the *Announcement Services* category and explore the links you find.

You can get some good ideas about free publicity—both online and in the traditional media— also by checking out the tips in "Six Steps to Free Publicity," by Marcia Yudkin. Look for these tips at *http://www.obs-us.com/obs/english/books/penguin/sixsteps*.

ONLINE PROMOTION

Now that you've prepared the keywords, categories, and descriptions for your Web site, and explored some of the online guides, you're ready to publicize your site on the World Wide Web. We'll start by looking at two scenarios—the one-step "submit it to a bunch of places at once" approach and the targeted "submit it to one place at a time" approach.

Keep in mind that the exact methods you use for publicizing your site online will depend on where you're submitting the information. For instance, a one-step submission form works a bit differently than the form for submitting information to a specific search engine. But after you've seen the two hands-on examples that follow, you should have little trouble figuring out what to do.

ONE-STEP SUBMISSION EXAMPLE

One-step submission services submit information about your page to many search engines, directories, What's New pages, and other resources in one fell swoop. A submission service is a great time-saver and is often the best approach if you're in a hurry to get the word out about your site. Some submission services are free and some are not, but they all work in similar ways. Here's how to publicize your site using the free Submit It! service:

1. Point Navigator to *http://www.submit-it.com*.

2. Scroll down to the Submit It! Submission Form and read the paragraph of instructions. Then scroll down further so that you can see the part of the form shown in Figure 23-4.

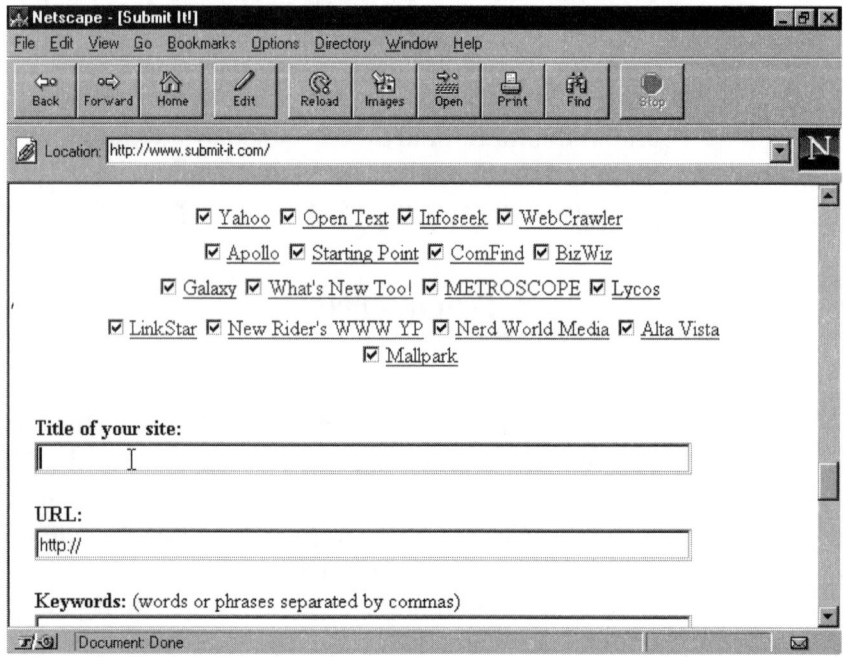

Figure 23-4: *Submit-It! will publicize your Web site in many places at once—free!*

3. Select (check) the places where you want to publicize your Web site. Initially, all the available boxes are checked.

4. Fill in the remaining information on the form, pressing the Tab key or clicking your mouse to move to each text box. You'll need to fill in the Title of your site, its URL, a list of keywords or phrases (separated by commas), the name of your organization or business, your city, your state or province, your country, a contact name, a contact e-mail address, and a brief paragraph (25 words or less) that describes your site.

TIP

When typing the description paragraph, you can press Enter at the end of each line, and you can use standard text editing methods to insert and delete text and to select, copy, cut, and paste text. Be sure that your final description is concise, accurate, and typo-free.

5. When you've finished filling in the boxes, click the *OK, move on to the submitting area* button at the bottom of the form.

6. If a Security Information dialog box appears, click the Continue button.

7. You'll be taken to the submitting area. Scroll down to the description for your Web page (see Figure 23-5) and read all the instructions *carefully.* If your description is okay, continue with Step 8. If it isn't, click the Back button in Netscape's toolbar, return to Step 3 or 4, and make any changes you want.

TIP

It's a good idea to bookmark the Submitting Area page so that you can return to it quickly if you do any browsing before you've sent in all your submissions. To set the bookmark, go to the appropriate page and choose Bookmarks | Add Bookmark from Navigator's menu bar.

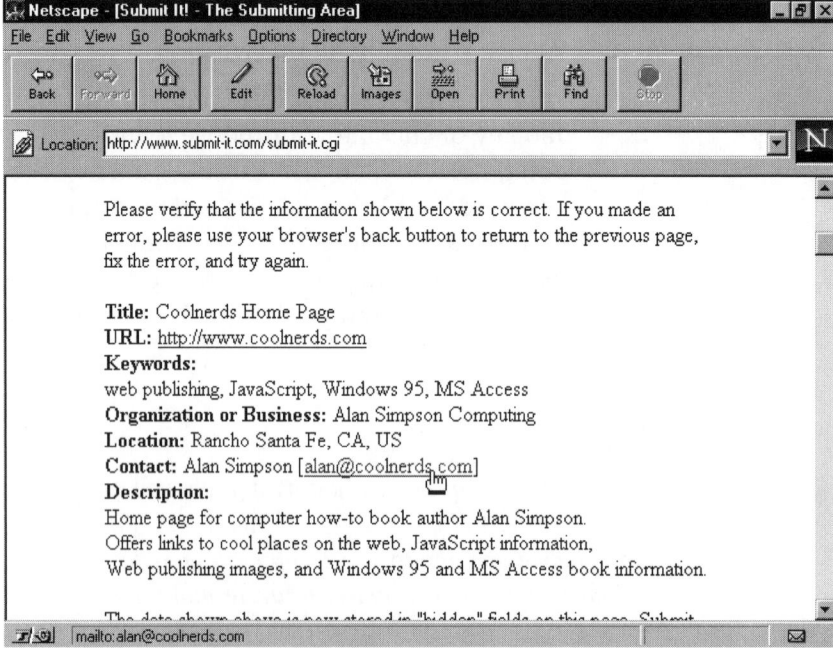

Figure 23-5: *Review your submission on the Submission Area page.*

8. To submit your information, scroll down until you see the search engine name and Submit It! button for the engine that should "know" about your site. Then complete any additional information required for the search engine (see Figure 23-6 for an example) and click the Submit It! button. Respond to any additional prompts that appear.

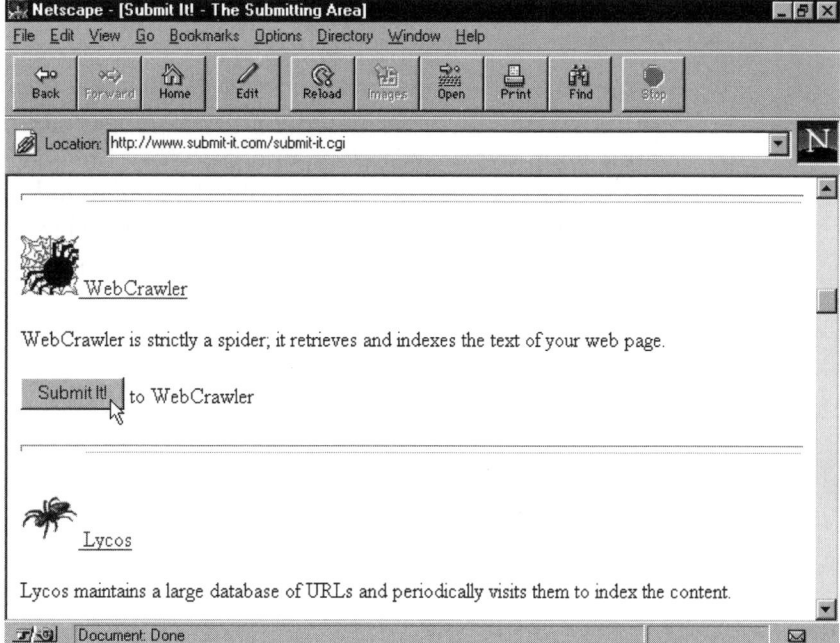

Figure 23-6: *Scroll down to a search engine and click Submit It! to submit your Web site information.*

TRAP

Choosing categories for the Yahoo! search engine is a bit tricky, but don't let that worry you. The next section explains how to pick an appropriate category in Yahoo! The basic techniques described there apply also when you're using the one-step Submit It! service.

9. Repeat Step 8 until you've submitted your Web site information to as many places as you want.

That's it. You're done! Now just sit back and wait for people to visit your site.

INDIVIDUAL DIRECTORY EXAMPLE

Sometimes, it's handy to submit your Web site information to individual databases, especially if your one-step service doesn't include your favorite search engine, directory, or What's New page. To do this, you typically click an *Add Site*, *Add*, *Add URL*, *Submit*, or a similarly named hypertext link or button (see Figure 23-7 for an example) and follow any instructions that appear.

TIP

Typically, the robot engines (such as Lycos, InfoSeek, and WebCrawler) only need to know your site's URL in order to visit your site and index it automatically. For other types of resources (such as some directories mentioned in this chapter), you'll probably need to complete a form similar to the one shown in Figure 23-4.

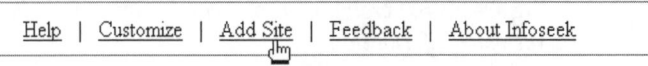

Help | Customize | Add Site | Feedback | About Infoseek

Figure 23-7: *Most search engines, directories, and What's New pages offer a way to add your Web site to their listings.*

Yahoo! is one of the oldest, most widely used directories around. Although publicizing your Web site there is a little tricky, the publicity is free and well worth your time. (The tricky part is that you first must browse to the perfect category for classifying your Web site.) Here's how to tell Yahoo! about your Web site:

1. Go to the Yahoo! search engine at *http://www.yahoo.com*, and use standard searching methods to see whether your Web page is already listed in Yahoo! If it's not, continue with Step 2. If it is, you're done.

2. Go to the category where you want your Web site to appear. For example, if you've composed a Web site describing your experiences as a llama rancher, you'd click the categories in the sequence given here: *Business and Economy*, then *Companies*, then *Animals*, then *Llamas*.

TIP

You also can use keyword searching to find Web sites that are similar to yours. When the list of matching sites appears, click the category that best describes your own Web site (see Figure 23-1) and then continue with Step 3.

3. After you've selected a category, click the Add URL icon at the top of the page, as shown in Figure 23-8. (If you get a message telling you that the category is too generic, return to Step 2 and dig a little deeper into the category list.)

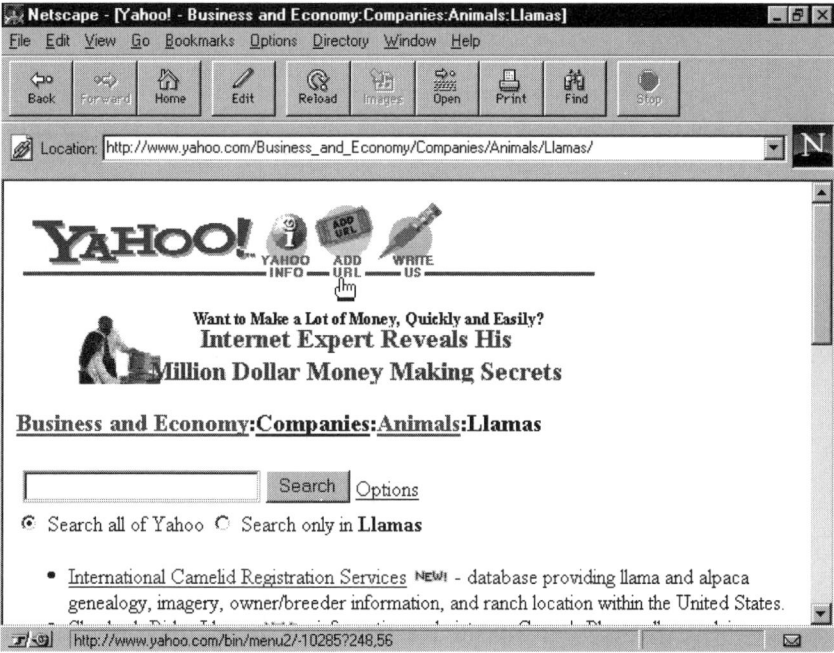

Figure 23-8: *Click the Add URL hot spot in Yahoo! to start adding your Web site to Yahoo's database.*

4. Carefully read the instructions on the Add To Yahoo page and then scroll down to the form shown in Figure 23-9. Notice that the Category text box is filled in automatically.

TRAP

Do not *try to fill in the category box by typing text into it. For the submission to work properly, you must use the automatic fill-in technique described in Step 2.*

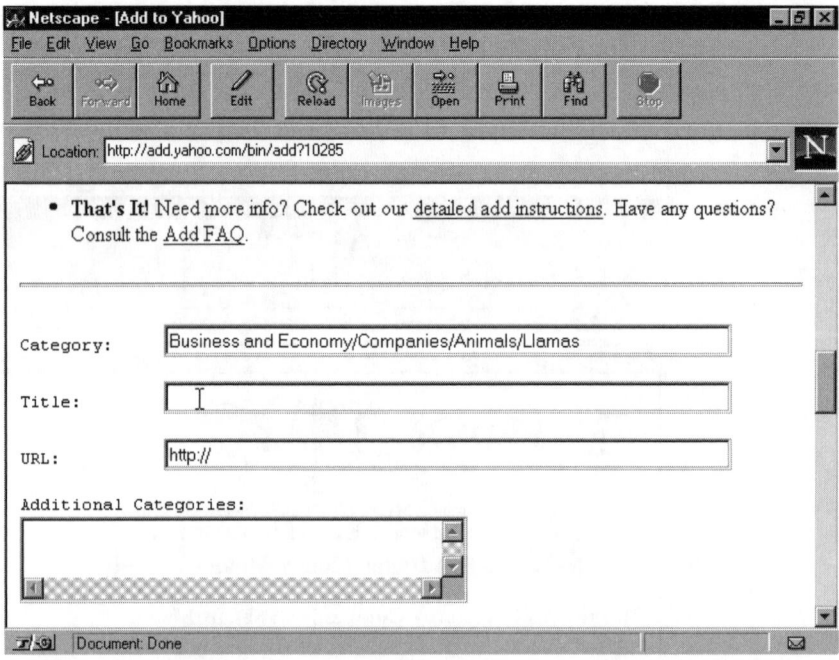

Figure 23-9: *The beginning of the Yahoo! form for submitting information about your Web site.*

5. Complete the boxes on the form, using the same techniques described earlier for Submit It!

6. When you've completed the boxes, click the Submit button at the bottom of the page.

TIP

The bottom of the Yahoo! submission page offers links to many other places where you can submit information about your Web site. By all means, click the hyperlinks and explore what's available. You'll be astounded at just how many places are willing to publicize your new site!

Now that you've seen some hands-on examples of submitting information to a one-step submission service and to Yahoo!, let's look at some other submission services and online resources that will gladly accept information about your Web site.

FREE ONE-STEP SUBMISSION SERVICES

One-step submission services such as Submit It! offer a time-saving, no-cost way to submit information about your Web site to several places at once. Here are some free one-step submission services you should consider using:

- onLine Business at *http://online-biz.com/promote* lists free places to promote your WWW site. It also offers one-step submission, reciprocal linking arrangements, and guides to other promotional services on the Web.

TIP

In a reciprocal link *arrangement, another Web site includes a link to your Web site if you return the favor by including a link to their Web site on your page. It's the high-tech version of "I'll scratch your back if you'll scratch mine." See "Other Online Possibilities," later in this chapter, for more information about linking to other Web sites.*

- Promote Assist at *http://online-biz.com/cgi-bin/cgiwrap/online/assist.cgi* submits your Web site information to some of the more popular indexes, catalogs, spiders, and What's New lists on the Internet. The opening page provides instructions for using this service.

- Submit It! (described earlier) at *http://www.submit-it.com* lets you register your site in these places: Alta Vista, Apollo, BizWiz, ComFind, Galaxy, Infoseek, LinkStar, Lycos, Mallpark, METROSCOPE, Nerd World Media, New Rider's WWW Yellow Pages, Open Text, Starting Point, WebCrawler, What's New Too!, and Yahoo!

- wURLd Presence at *http://www.ogi.com/wurld* provides one-stop registration of your Web site with popular search engines, catalogs, and What's New pages. It'll register you in these spider-based catalogs: Alta Vista, excite Netsearch, Infoseek, Inktomi, Lycos, Open Text, WebCrawler, and World Wide Web Worm; in these list-based catalogs: EINet Galaxy and GNN's Whole Internet Catalog; in these What's New pages: NCSA, Netscape, and What's New Too!; and in these miscellaneous sites: Starting Point and URouLette. Yahoo! isn't supported here.

FOR-A-FEE ONE-STEP SUBMISSION SERVICES, PROMOTION, & MEDIA PLACEMENT

Free one-step submission services probably will do the trick for publicizing most Web sites to folk on the Net, but you might prefer the additional time savings, targeted marketing, and extra publicity that the following for-a-fee submission services offer:

- Postmaster at *http://www.netcreations.com/postmaster* announces your Web site in more than 350 places. The service costs $500 for a single use, or $1000 for four uses. Other plans are available, including a try-before-you-buy test that posts to about two dozen popular sites.

- SponsorNet Media Market at *http://www.sponsor.net* offers a realtime online auction for purchasing advertising banners on popular Web pages. Definitely a place to consider if you plan to advertise on the Web.

- TheYellowpages at *http://theyellowpages.com/services.com* offers a one-line link to your existing home page, listed in the category of your choice ($19.95 for a 6-month listing, and $29.95 for a 1-year listing). From this URL, you also can learn about the DIGITAL SALESROOM autoresponder service, which automatically sends a prearranged response when people send messages to your special autoresponder e-mail address. Prices for the autoresponder service start at $9.50 per month for multiple sites.

■ WebConnect at *http://www.worldata.com/wcover.htm* will place advertising for you on high-traffic Web sites. Prices start at $200 per link per month, plus setup charges of $50 per link per site, and a $750 minimum link charge per month.

■ WebPromote at *http://www.webpromote.com* provides Web announcement services for your initial announcement needs, as well as targeted marketing for your ongoing promotion needs. They offer a variety of plans, starting at $175. Their WebPromote 100 announcement plan, for example, submits your announcement to 15 major directories, 15 search engines, 19 yellow pages, 7 What's New sites, 21 minor directories, and 23 general submission sites.

■ Yahoo Web Launch at *http://www.yahoo.com/docs/pr/ launchform.html* gives you a screenshot or logo thumbnail sketch, a two-line description, and a link to your site from a highly trafficked page on Yahoo! The current price of $1000 for one week is expected to rise. To see a sample launch page, visit *http://www.yahoo.com/weblaunch.html*.

In the following sections, you'll discover many individual places where you can look for information and be found on the Web. Remember, however, that the one-step submission services automatically cover many of these same resources and you'll rarely need to duplicate the efforts of the one-step services unless you want to customize your listing in some way.

WHAT'S NEW WEB PAGES & CLASSIFIEDS

What's New pages and classifieds offer a great way to publicize your Web site and to buy or sell stuff on the Web. Figure 23-10 shows the top portion of NCSA's What's New page, which lists new or changed sites on the Web, and the top five sites of the day. The *Submit an Entry* button makes it easy for you to submit your own site to the What's New page.

TIP

Many of the What's New pages will not include sites that are blatant advertisements, distasteful, or uninteresting.

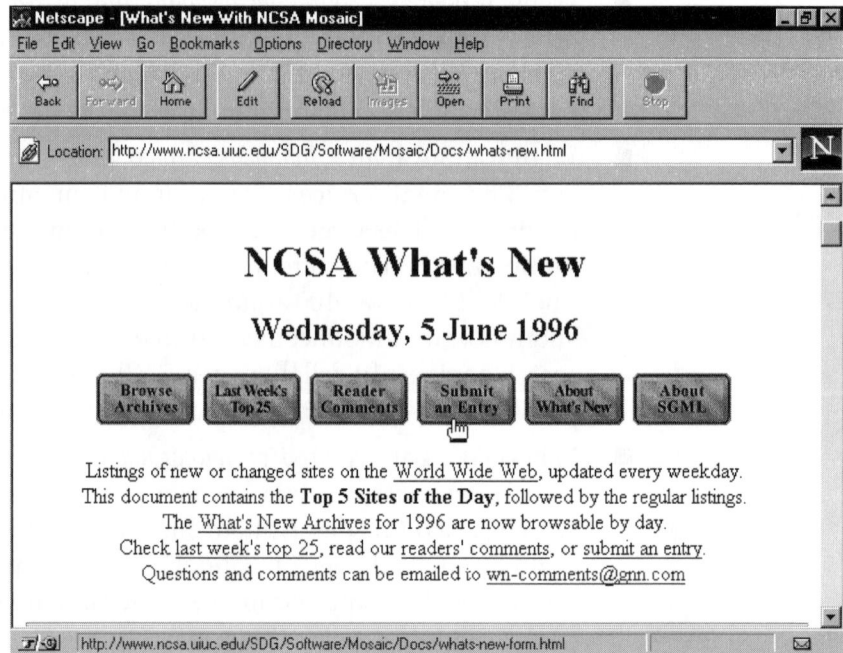

Figure 23-10: *The NCSA What's New page announces new and changed sites.*

Here are some of the most popular What's New pages and online classifieds:

■ Epage Classifieds at *http://ep.com* offers a place for you to post a seven-day classified ad (free). From this Web site, you can search for classified ads by region or subject, and post and delete your classified ads.

■ NCSA What's New page at *http://www.ncsa.uiuc.edu/SDG/ Software/Mosaic/Docs/whats-new.html* lists new and changed sites on the Web (see Figure 23-10). Your submission will take about three weeks to appear.

- Netscape What's New at *http://www.netscape.home/home/ whats-new.html* publishes information about pages that provide unique content or are good examples of Web publishing. Visit this site to find links to some of the best Web sites in the business.

- Open Market at *http://www.directory.net* provides a directory of commercial services, products, and information on the Internet. Its fast one-day turnaround on submissions makes it a great place to submit listings about your commercial Web site.

WEB CATALOGS & DIRECTORIES

People often search for companies, products, and services in the many catalogs and directories available on the Web. Certainly, you won't want *your* Web site to be overlooked. Here are some of the catalogs and directories to consider for your own listings:

- Galaxy at *http://galaxy.einet.net/galaxy.html* is a guide to worldwide information and services, organized by topic. To submit your own Web site for consideration, first find the category and subcategory in which information about your site should appear (much as you locate a category in Yahoo! before adding your URL). Then, click the *Add* hyperlink and fill in the form that appears.

- ISP Internet YellowPages at *http://yp.gte.net* and Business Web Pages at *http://wp.gte.net* are brought to you by GTE, a major publisher of Yellow Pages directories. A basic business listing is free, and you can purchase other advertising services, as necessary.

- Starting Point at *http://www.stpt.com* offers an extensive database of news, reference, weather, sports, business, online magazines, investing, travel, education, computing, entertainment, and shopping information. It's a great place to submit information about your Web site.

For quick access to a bunch of online magazines, visit the electronic newsstand at http://www.enews.com. *You can purchase advertising in many of these magazines.*

■ Submit All at *http://www.hometeam.com* is a perfect location in which to find real estate information or to list your real estate Web site.

■ The Virtual Tourist at *http://www.vtourist.com/webmap/na.htm* is a unique geographical guide to products, services, and servers on the Net.

■ WWW Virtual Library at *http://www.w3.org/hypertext/DataSources/bySubject/Overview.html* is a distributed public catalog, with listings in categories from Aeronomy to Zoos. The WWW Virtual Library Project was started at CERN in 1991 by Tim Berners-Lee, the inventor of the World Wide Web.

■ WWWLib at *http://www.scit.wlv.ac.uk/wwlib* is the place to go if you're looking for Web sites in the United Kingdom or if you want to list your Web site in the United Kingdom. This interesting directory uses the Dewey Decimal classification scheme to organize information.

■ Yahoo! at *http://www.yahoo.com* is the famous Yahoo! directory described earlier (see Figures 23-1 and 23-8). Like the search engines in the next section, Yahoo! expands its knowledge automatically. It also allows you to submit your own listings, either by clicking the Add URL icon in Yahoo! or by using a one-step submission service.

SEARCH ENGINES

Search engines offer a popular way to find information on the Net. You simply fire up the search engine, type a keyword or phrase, and click a Search button to begin the search. All the search engines listed here update their databases automatically; they also allow you to submit information about your Web site.

TIP

If you'd like to work with many different search engines from one central place, you can go to an all-in-one search page. To view Netscape's all-in-one page, choose Directory | Internet Search from the Netscape menu bar. Another great all-in-one tool is c | net's search.com engine, which you'll find at http://www.search.com.

These are some of the most popular search engines:

- Alta Vista at *http://www.altavista.digital.com* claims the largest index on the Web—30 million pages, found on 235,000 servers; three million articles from 14,000 Usenet newsgroups; and over 12 million access every weekday. All that, and lightning-fast, too!

- Infoseek at *http://www2.infoseek.com* allows searches by category or keyword, and lets you choose to search the World Wide Web, Infoseek select sites, Usenet newsgroups, a company directory, e-mail addresses, timely news, and Web FAQs.

- Lycos at *http://www.lycos.com* is another popular search engine that lets you search by keyword or category. Its searches return links to Web pages, with each link rated for relevance to your search.

- WebCrawler at *http://webcrawler.com* offers keyword and category searches and gives you the option of showing titles or summaries for each Web site it retrieves.

TIP

Be sure that your Web site is included in your own favorite search engine! Chances are that if you especially like a particular search engine, other people will, too.

NEWSGROUPS

Although Usenet newsgroups do not accept or welcome any kind of blatant advertising, you can post noncommercial announcements to the *comp.infosystems.www.announce* newsgroup. Before posting your announcement to this moderated newsgroup, be sure to lurk in the newsgroup for a while, and by all means read the charter posting at *http://boutell.com/%7Egrant/charter.html*.

TIP

> *To quickly access a newsgroup from your browser, click in the Location box of your browser, type* **news:** *followed by the newsgroup name, and press Enter. For example, type* **news:comp.infosystems.www. announce** *to reach the announcement newsgroup. See Chapter 28, "Cruising the Newsgroups With Gold," for more about newsgroups.*

NEWSLETTERS & MAILING LISTS

You might want to consider announcing your Web site in some of the following online newsletters and mailing lists:

- Net Surfer Digest at *http://www.netsurf.com/nsd/index.html* presents an overview of new and interesting Web sites, and accepts brief articles.

- Net-Happenings at *http://www.mid.net:80/NET* is a service of InterNIC Directory & Database Services. It's a moderated list aimed at network staff and end users.

- Scout Report at *http://rs.internic.net/scout_report-index.html* is a weekly service provided by InterNIC. Its filtered and summarized articles are of special interest to researchers and educators.

MISCELLANEOUS LISTS OF LISTS

If all the resources listed so far aren't enough to satisfy your craving for attention on the Web, here are several other places to get your Web site noticed:

- A1 Index of Free WWW URL Submission & Search Sites at *http://www.vir.com/~wyatt/index.html* lists more than 600 online directories and magazines that will take your announcement (free). The list is comprehensive but doesn't include any descriptions. Still, it's a great place to get some ideas.

- Nexor List of Web Robots at *http://web.nexor.co.uk/mak/doc/robots/active.html* provides hyperlinks to all the known Web robots, including WebCrawler, Lycos, and Inktomi. (To learn more about the way WWW robots, wanderers, and spiders work, point your browser to *http://info.webcrawler.com/mak/projects/robots/robots.html*.)

OTHER ONLINE POSSIBILITIES

Well, believe it or not, there are still other online methods for publicizing your site. First, you can consider your own Internet Service Provider (ISP). With all the competition among ISPs, many ISPs offer free publicity for customers who publish on their sites. Check with your own ISP to see what kind of promotional services you can get.

Here's another suggestion. As you're cruising the Web, look for sites that are similar to your own. You may be able to set up a *reciprocal link* arrangement, in which you agree to link to their site if they'll link to yours. Many sites welcome reciprocal links, and many offer instructions, cool graphics, and HTML code to make linking easier. Figure 23-11, for example, shows the instructions page for linking to WinZip, one of the most popular file-compress and decompress programs around.

TIP

> *You can copy the sample HTML tags from a page like the one shown in Figure 23-11 to your own Web site. Use your mouse to select the HTML tags (see Figure 23-11), and press Ctrl+C to copy the code to the Windows clipboard. Then, open your Web page in Gold's editor, choose View | Edit Document Source from the menu bar, position the insertion point where the tags should appear in your Web page, and press Ctrl+V to paste.*

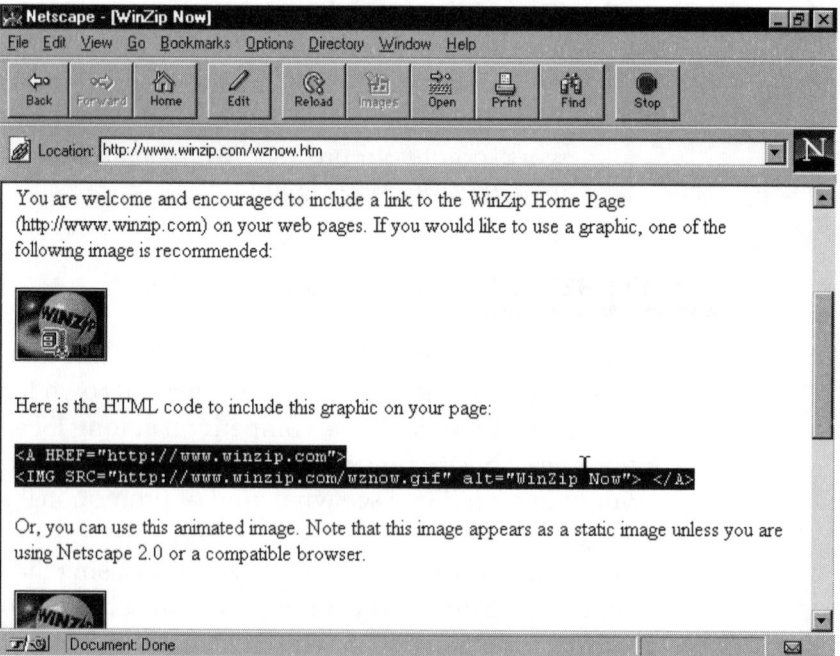

Figure 23-11: *The page at* http://www.winzip.com/wznow.htm *explains how to link to WinZip's home page.*

Still another option is to sponsor a Web page, or to add your own advertising banner to a popular Web page. Figure 23-12 shows a sample ad and a link inviting you to advertise on the excite search engine's Web page. (Of course, *you* can invite others to advertise on or sponsor your own Web site. If your site is popular, people just might shell out the extra bucks to be seen on your page.)

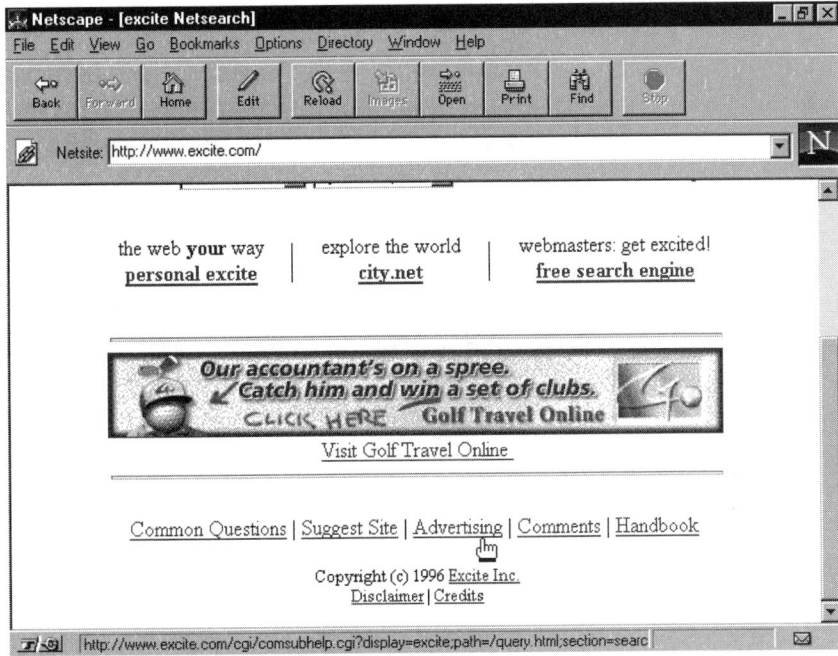

Figure 23-12: *Many sites on the Web welcome advertisements and sponsorship.*

MEASURING YOUR PROMOTION EFFORTS

Clearly, promotion is worthwhile only if it results in increased awareness of your Web site and increased sales of your products. How can you find out whether your online promotion efforts are working?

For standard business accounts, most ISPs provide daily reports on the World Wide Web activity for the site (see Figure 23-13). Many of the for-a-fee promotion services, such as WebPromote, also provide reports summarizing the promotional accomplishments. When you review the reports, be sure to focus on the accesses (or *hits*) for your index.html or default.html page, because these hits are the best measures of activity on your Web site.

TIP

The total number of hits on your Web site does not accurately reflect the number of visitors, because a "hit" occurs every time a file is opened. One visitor might open several dozen files. For this reason, the number of hits on just your opening home page is probably the most accurate measure of how many people actually visited the site.

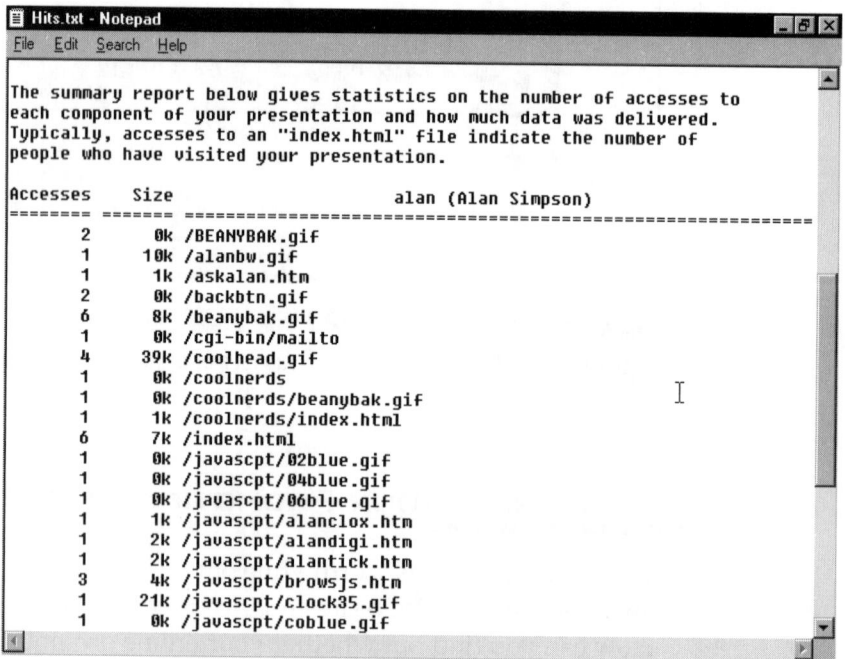

Figure 23-13: *An activity report for a Web site.*

Of course, the hits on your Web site are an important part of the story. But for people trying to make money on the Net, what really matters is how those hits translate into increased sales of products and services.

PRINT MEDIA & OTHER "LOW-TECH" PROMOTION IDEAS

Even as you're considering the many possibilities for publicizing your Web site online, don't underestimate the power of traditional low-tech media—especially for reaching your local market. For example, always include your Web site URL on your letterhead and business cards. And don't forget to put your URL in print ads (billboards, magazines, newspapers) and radio and television spots. You might even want to mention your Web site in your company's "on hold" telephone blurbs—you know, the ones in which a smooth voice discusses your products, accompanied by soothing background music. Also consider listing your URL on community calendars, flyers, and circulars.

MOVING ON

After reading this chapter, I'll bet you're no longer worried about finding enough places to promote your Web site. (Believe it or not, I've only skimmed the surface of what's available.) As you've seen, there are tons of places to announce your presence on the Web, and most of them are free and easy to use. Combine these high-tech methods with the traditional low-tech methods and you're sure to get your site noticed on the Web.

In the next section, we'll switch gears and discuss ways to use Netscape with various services on the Internet, including additional Web browsing, e-mail, newsgroups, file transfer, and more.

More Golden Internet Services

Web Browsing Mastery

We discussed the basics of browsing the World Wide Web way back in the Part I of this book. There we also covered 3.0's new multimedia capabilities. In this chapter I want to round out your Web browsing skills to include:

- Using search engines like Yahoo to look up specific information on the World Wide Web

- Organizing your favorite Web sites into your own personal categories

- Scanning all your favorite Web sites for new information, with just a few mouse clicks

- Creating instant shortcuts to your favorite Web sites

- Printing and saving Web pages

Those of you with prior Web-browsing experience might consider much of this material to be old stuff. This chapter is really for Web newbies. You'll want to read Part I of this book first. Then use this chapter to beef up your Web browsing skills.

ABOUT SEARCH ENGINES

A *search engine* is a program on the World Wide Web that lets you search for sites that deal with a particular topic. If you think of the World Wide Web as a huge electronic book containing all the information known to human beings, a search engine is sort of like the electronic index to that book.

There are dozens of search engines for the Web. In this chapter, I've chosen one, named Yahoo, as an example. I chose Yahoo because it's one of the more popular search engines and because it's really good at finding information. (I don't intend to discredit any of the other fine search engines out there.) After you learn to use Yahoo, I hope you'll try some of the other engines listed near the end of this chapter, to broaden your searches and to find which engine(s) work best for you.

SEARCHING WITH YAHOO

The first step in using Yahoo is to point your browser to Yahoo's Web site:

1. Make sure you're online.

2. Fire up Netscape Navigator.

3. Type **http://www.yahoo.com** in the Location box, and press Enter.

You'll come to the home page for Yahoo, which will look something like Figure 24-1. (The advertisement might be different when you get there.) There are several ways you can use Yahoo, as you'll see in the sections that follow.

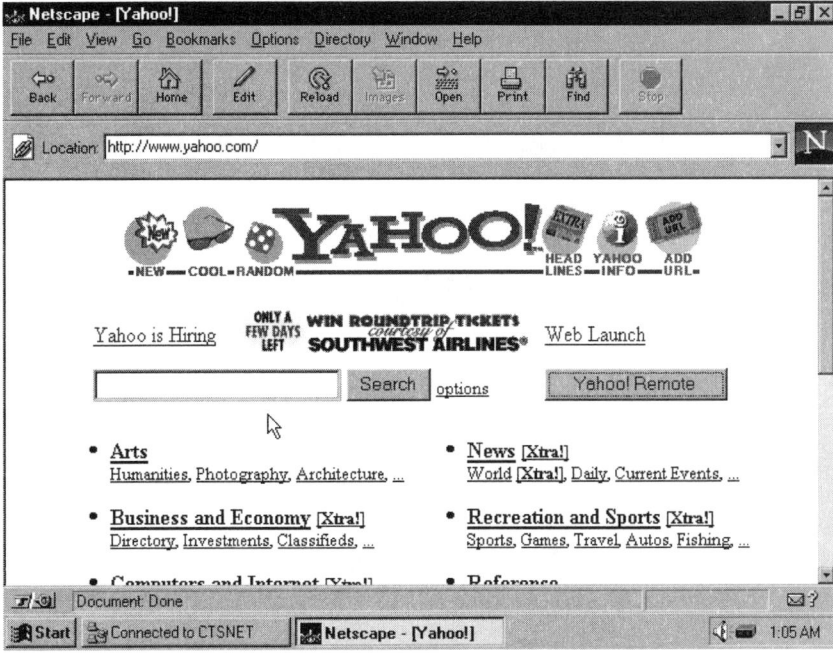

Figure 24-1: *Yahoo's home page.*

SEARCHING BY CATEGORY

When you're in Yahoo you can start searching by simply choosing some broad category and following links down to more specific types of information. If you scroll down a little, using the scroll bar to the right of the Navigator window, you can see the categories and subcategories more clearly, as in Figure 24-2.

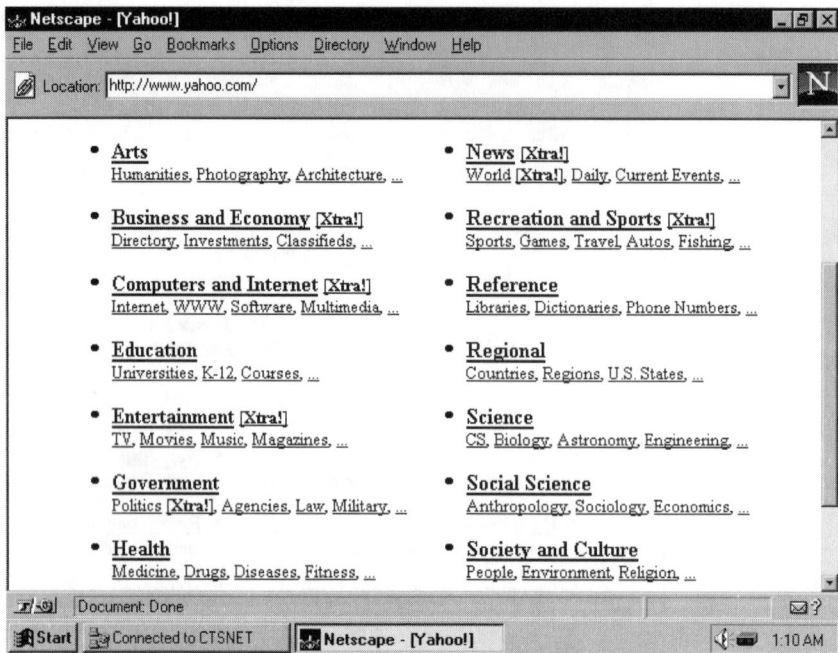

Figure 24-2: *Categories and subcategories in Yahoo.*

For example, you can click Recreation and Sports, which is shown in large letters, to view that large category. Or you can click the [Xtra!] that appears next to some categories to view just the current headline news within that category. You can also search a subcategory within the larger category. Under Recreation and Sports, for example, you can click on Sports, Games, Travel, Autos, or Fishing to go straight to the subcategory that interests you. As an example, let's say you click on Games.

You're taken to a new screen where you can type a word or phrase to search for. Or, if you scroll down a bit, you can see subcategories under Games, as in Figure 24-3.

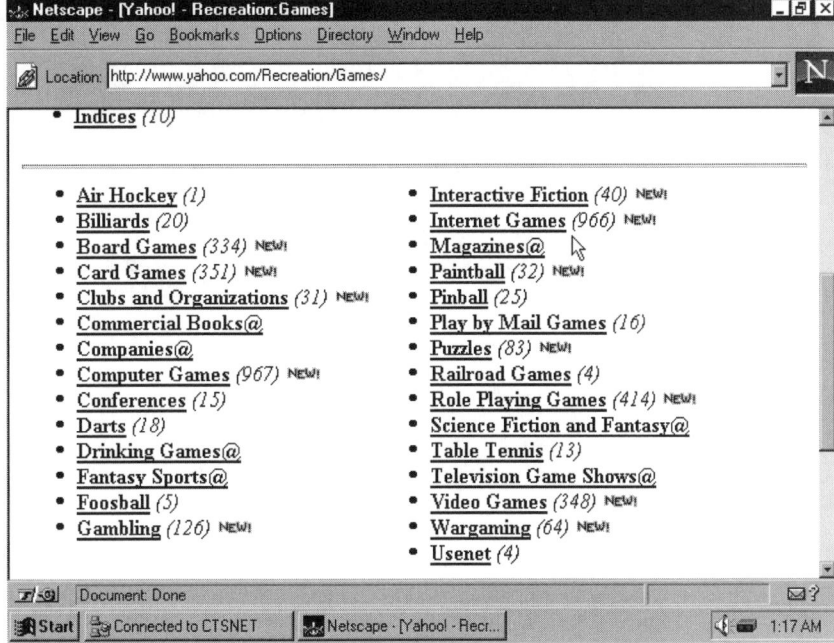

Figure 24-3: *The search has been narrowed down to Games.*

In the new set of categories, you can narrow the search by clicking on any subcategory. For example, if you click on Internet Games, you come to yet another screen. You can just keep going this way, always narrowing your previous selection to a more specific category.

When you feel you've narrowed your search enough, scroll down and start looking for individual sites. Links to individual sites start with the site name, followed by a brief description of the site. For example, in the lower half of the screen shown in Figure 24-4, you can see some links to individual sites in the Internet Games subcategory. The upper half of the screen shows a list of subcategories you can explore within Internet Games.

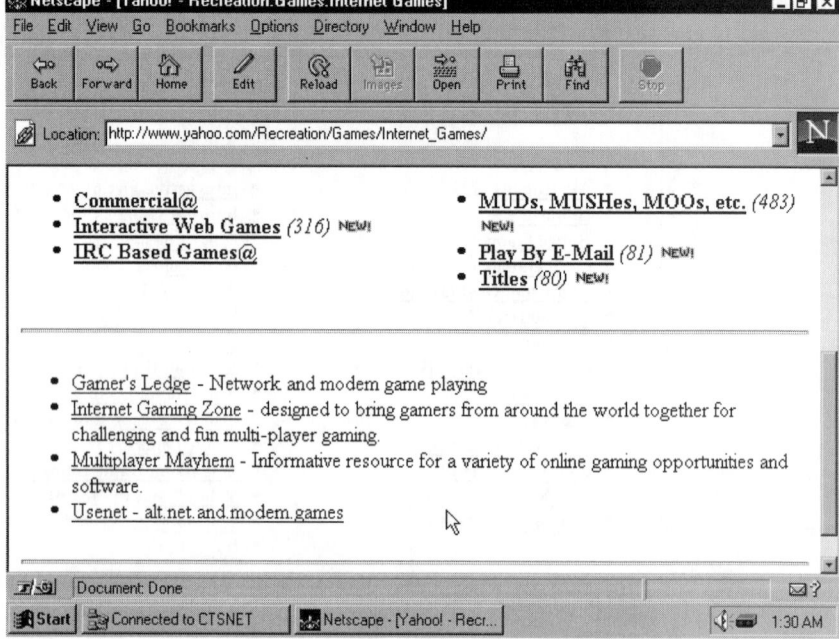

Figure 24-4: *More subcategories and links to individual sites in the Internet Games subcategory.*

And so it goes. Just continue narrowing down your choices until you find individual sites that you like. When you find a site that you really like, you might want to *bookmark* it. Just choose Bookmarks | Add Bookmark from Navigator's menu bar. That way, you'll be able to return to this site in the future simply by choosing its name from the Bookmarks menu.

TIP

Later in this chapter I'll show you ways to organize a large collection of bookmarks.

If you turn off Navigator's toolbar to make the display area larger, you can choose Go | Back from the menu bar to go back to the previous page.

SEARCHING BY TOPIC

Searching by increasingly specific categories and subcategories is just one way to use Yahoo. A more direct approach is to ignore the categories and just type a word or phrase that describes the topic you're interested in. Let's take it from the top. Suppose that you point your Web browser to http://www.yahoo.com to get back to Yahoo's home page. Near the top of that page, in the text box next to the Search button, you type the word or phrase that best describes your interest. In Figure 24-5, for example, I'm about to ask Yahoo to search for sites that deal with ice hockey.

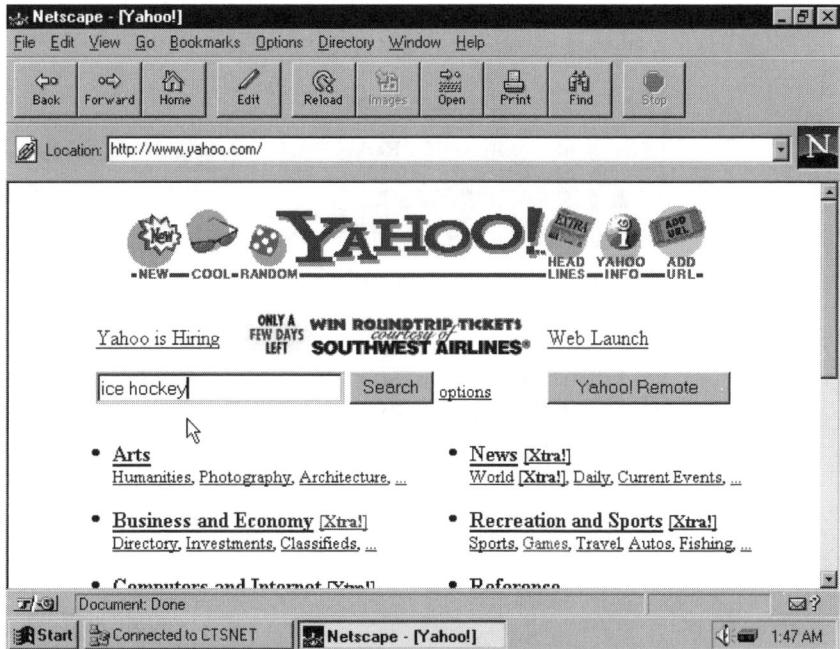

Figure 24-5: *A direct search for information about ice hockey.*

Clicking the Search button takes me to a new screen, where Yahoo informs me that it has found 249 items that contain the words *ice hockey*. As you can see in Figure 24-6, this search transcends the initial set of categories. For instance, the first matching site is in the Business and Economy category. The next two are from the Recreation category.

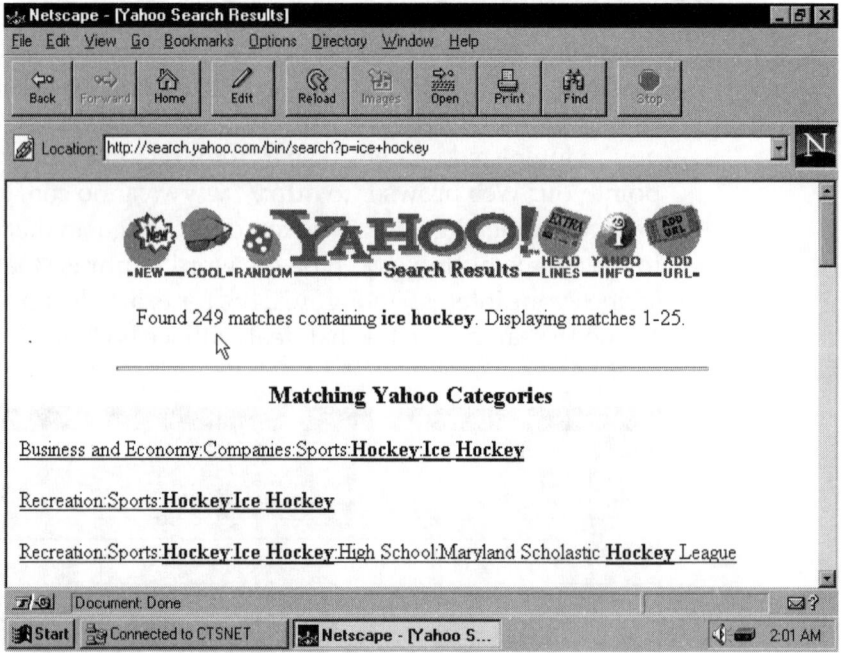

Figure 24-6: *Results of the search for ice hockey.*

At this point, I can start clicking on links to explore categories and sites that deal with ice hockey. Notice that, near the top of Figure 24-6, Yahoo informs me that it is currently displaying matches 1 through 25. When I scroll to the bottom of the current page, I'll see a link that takes me to the next 25 matches (see Figure 24-7).

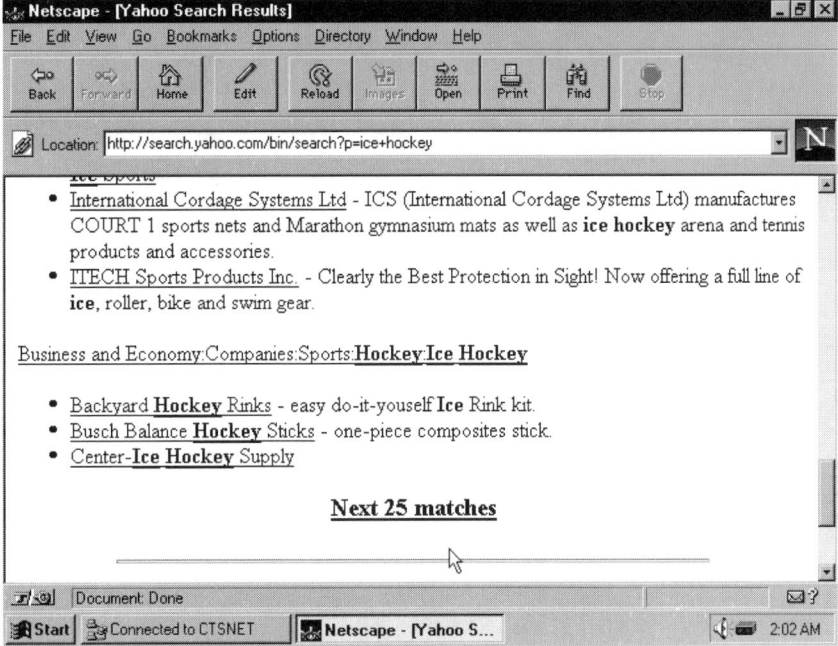

Figure 24-7: *Click the link to explore the next 25 matches.*

The whole process is generally quick and easy. I can usually find exactly the information I'm looking for within a few minutes of starting the initial search.

MORE REFINED SEARCHING

There's yet another way to search Yahoo. If you look back at Figure 24-5, you'll notice a small link, named *options*, next to the Search button. If you click that link, Yahoo takes you to a form that you can fill in to tell Yahoo exactly how to conduct your search (see Figure 24-8).

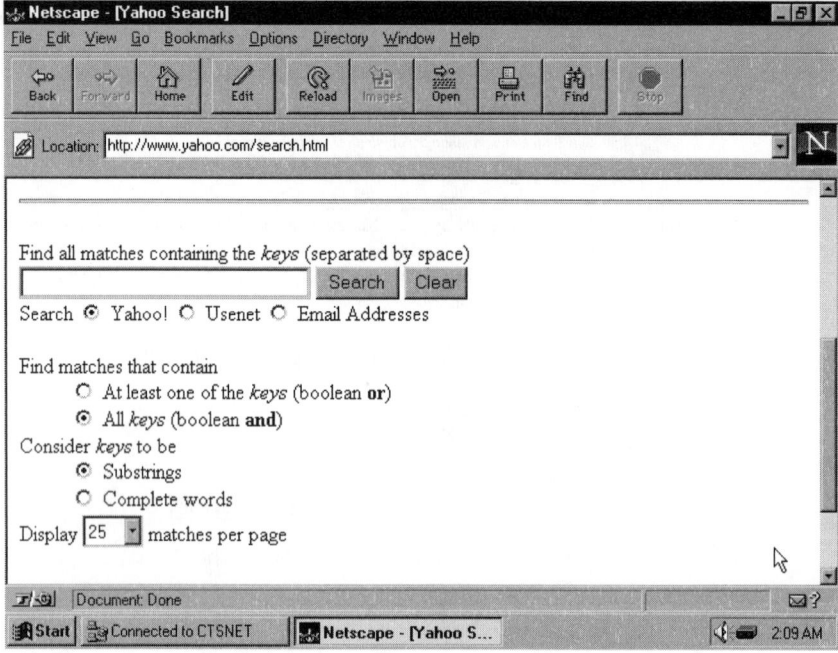

Figure 24-8: *Yahoo's search options form.*

You can start by typing a word or phrase in the text box. Then, before you click the Search button, you can make selections from the options below the text box. Next to Search, you can choose Yahoo, Usenet newsgroups (discussed in Chapter 28), or E-mail addresses (see Chapter 27).

FIND MATCHES THAT CONTAIN...

You can search for references that contain *any* word in your phrase, or *all* the words in your phrase. For example, let's say you opt to search for Windows 95. If you tell Yahoo to search for *At least one of the keys*, you'll get a whole lot of matches—including sites that contain just the word *windows* (some will contain information about "real" glass windows; others, information about all versions of Microsoft Windows, programs that run on Windows, and so forth). You'll also find sites that contain just the number *95*—maybe one with all the lyrics to the song "95 Bottles of Beer on the Wall." (Wouldn't that be a thrill?)

The alternative selection—*All keys*—narrows your search considerably by matching only sites that contain both words (*windows* and *95*).

CONSIDER KEYS TO BE...

The Consider keys to be... option lets you decide whether the words you're searching for must be matched exactly. Say, for example, that I decide to search for the word *fish*. If I set the Consider keys to be option to Substrings, I'll get many matches, including words that start with the word *fish*, such as *fishing, fisheries, fishnet, fishy, fishbowl,* and so on.

If, on the other hand, I set Consider keys to be... to Complete words, I'll get far fewer matches. Only sites that contain the exact word *fish* will appear.

The last item on the page—Display...matches per page—lets you decide how many matching items you want displayed at one time.

YAHOO HELP

If you want more information about Yahoo, just go to its home page (http://www.yahoo.com) and choose Yahoo Info from the options at the top of that page. You'll come to the Yahoo Information Center, where you can scroll through a variety of Yahoo-related topics (see Figure 24-9).

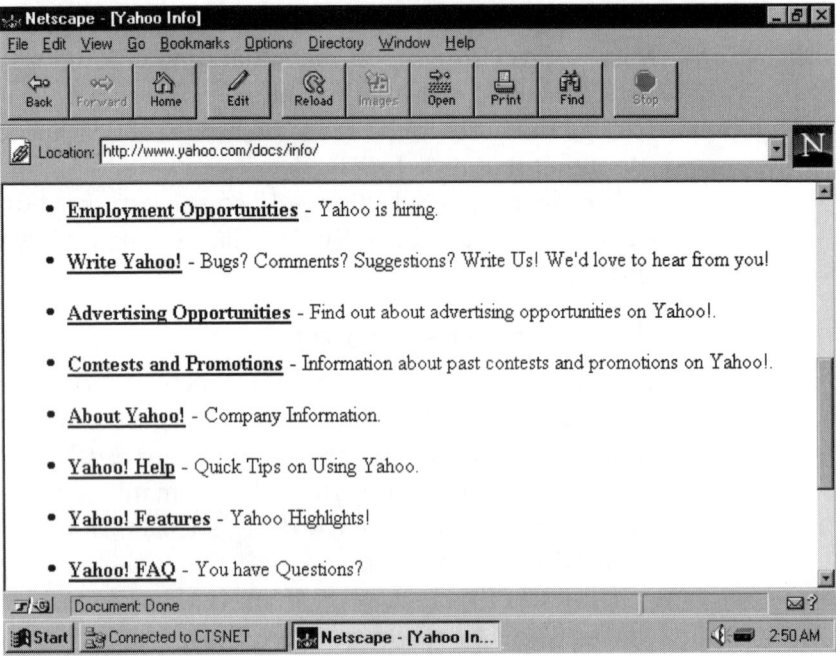

Figure 24-9: *A section of Yahoo's Information Center.*

TIP

Chapter 23, "Promoting Your New Web Site," explains how you can add your Web site to Yahoo and other search engines.

OTHER SEARCH ENGINES

Remember, Yahoo is just one of many search engines available on the World Wide Web. Be sure to try out some of the other engines (listed in the "Site Seeing" section near the end of this chapter) to broaden your search skills and your horizons.

SEARCHING THE CURRENT PAGE

When you get to a Web page, you don't always have to read the entire page to find what you're looking for. Instead, you can search the current page for a word or phrase. The technique is identical to the one used to search a word processing document:

1. Choose Edit | Find from Navigator's menu bar.

2. Next to Find What, type the word or phrase you're looking for.

3. Optionally, choose Match Case if you want to find words or phrases that exactly match your request (i.e., the same use of upper- and lowercase letters).

4. Optionally, choose the direction in which you want to search, either Up or Down, from the current position in the page.

5. Click the Find Next button.

Navigator will look for your word or phrase, highlighting it if it finds it. The Find dialog box might cover the found text, but you can drag the dialog box (by its title bar) to a different position on the screen. To search for additional occurrences of the word or phrase, click on Find Next.

If Navigator can't find the word or phrase, it displays a Search String Not Found message. (Click on OK to clear that message.)

To end the search, click on the Cancel button to remove the Find dialog box from the screen.

USING BOOKMARKS TO RECORD FAVORITE SITES

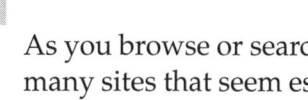

As you browse or search the World Wide Web you'll come across many sites that seem especially useful or fun and you may want to visit them often. You can easily keep a list of favorite sites by *bookmarking* them. The procedure is simple:

- When you're viewing a site that you'd like to revisit, select Bookmarks | Add Bookmark from Navigator's menu (or press Ctrl+D).

- Or right-click a neutral area of the page (text or white space—not a link) and choose Add Bookmark from the pop-up menu.

TIP

The latter (right-click) technique is preferable when you want to bookmark a specific page in a framed site. Use the menu technique to bookmark the entire framed site.

The name of the site will be added to your collection of bookmarks and will be visible when you select Bookmarks from the menu bar. For example, Figure 24-10 shows the sites I've added to my bookmark collection. To go to any one of those sites, I just click on the site name.

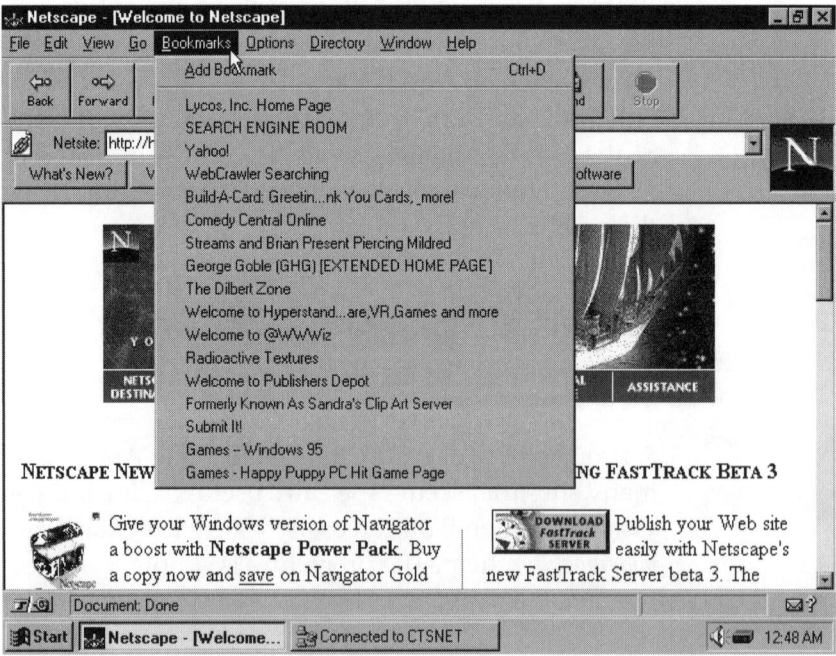

Figure 24-10: *The Bookmarks menu with some bookmarks in place.*

ORGANIZING YOUR BOOKMARKS

As your collection of bookmarks grows, you may want to start organizing them into categories. Here is the basic procedure:

1. Choose Window | Bookmarks (or press Ctrl+B) to get to the Bookmarks window (see Figure 24-11).

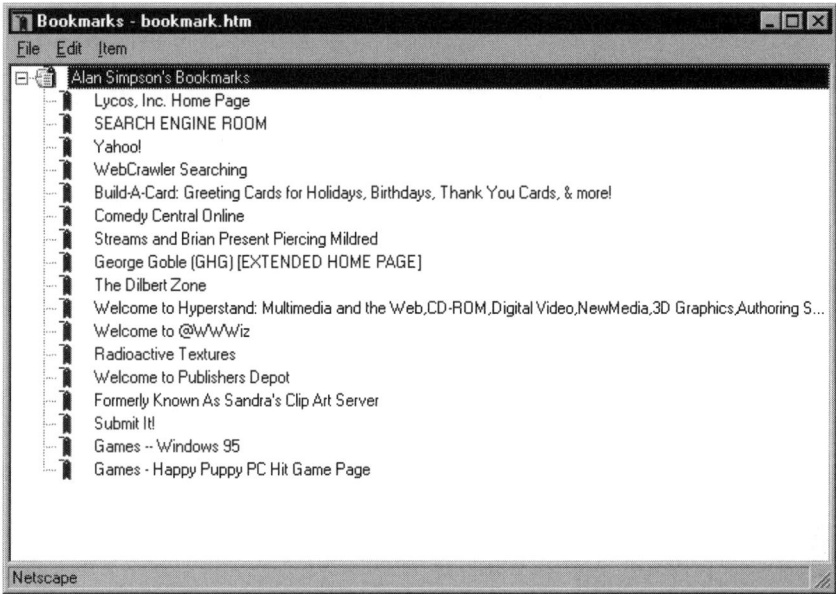

Figure 24-11: *The Bookmarks window.*

2. To create a category of bookmarks, first create a bookmark folder. To do so, choose Item | Insert Folder from the menu bar in the Bookmarks window.

TIP

To create a folder within a folder, first open the containing folder. Put the highlighter in that new, open folder. Then choose Item | Insert Folder to insert a folder inside the current folder.

3. Type a name and description for the bookmark. In Figure 24-12, for example, I'm creating a new folder named Fun Stuff.

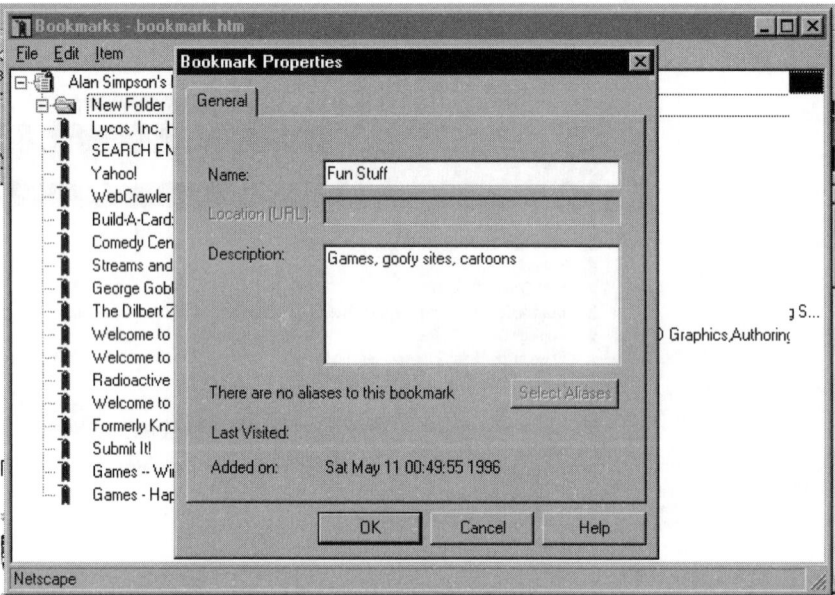

Figure 24-12: *Creating a new folder named Fun Stuff.*

4. Choose OK. An open folder appears in your bookmark list.

5. To move an item out of the general list and into the new folder, just drag the item to the folder. For example, Figure 24-13 shows how I've dragged seven bookmarks from my general list of bookmarks into my new Fun Stuff folder.

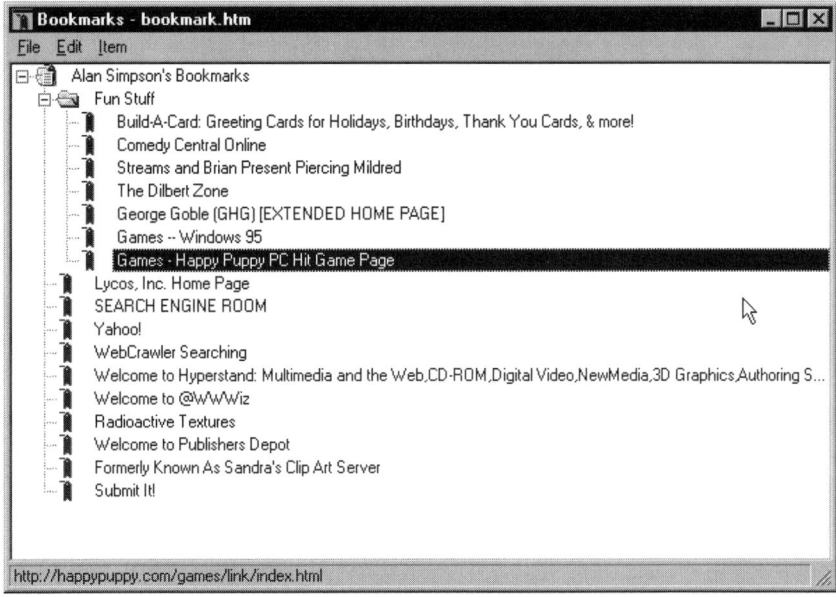

Figure 24-13: *Seven bookmarks moved into the Fun Stuff folder.*

6. From now on, you can open and close the folder just by clicking the + or – sign next to the folder (where – means that the folder is open, and + means it's closed). In Figure 24-14, the Fun Stuff folder is closed and now the items in that folder are hidden.

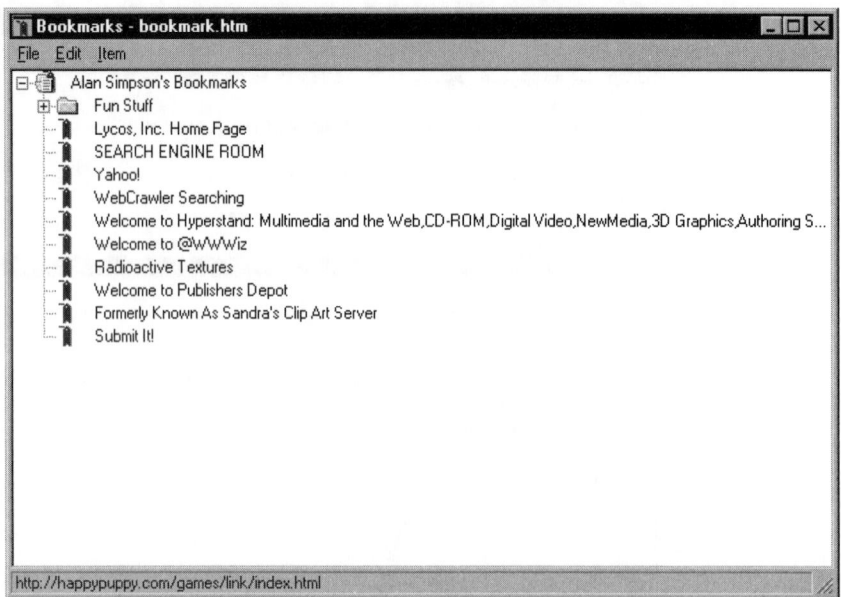

Figure 24-14: *Closing the Fun Stuff folder hides its contents.*

So what's the big deal? Well, if you create lots of folders, you can have a very nicely organized collection of bookmarks. When you're looking for a particular site or topic, you can open the one folder that interests you without having to slog through the whole collection of bookmarks.

For example, in Figure 24-15 I've organized all my bookmarks into folders. Currently, I'm looking at the contents of the Web Publishing folder. Notice how uncluttered the list is now.

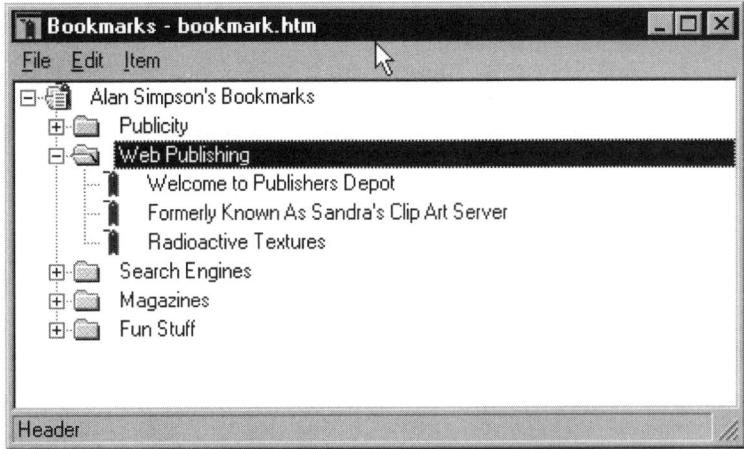

Figure 24-15: *Bookmarks, neatly organized into folders.*

The way you organize sites and folders in the Bookmarks window carries right over to the Bookmarks menu. Figure 24-16 shows how my Bookmarks menu reflects the organization on the screen shown in the previous figure.

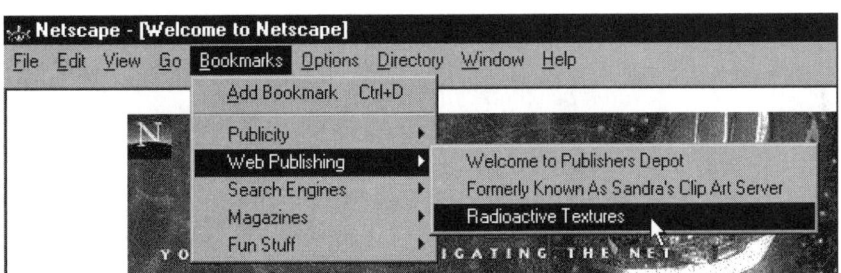

Figure 24-16: *Organization carries over to the Bookmarks menu.*

MANAGING YOUR BOOKMARKS

Navigator offers many tools and techniques for managing your personal bookmarks. To get to these tools, choose Window | Bookmarks to display the Bookmarks window. Then choose the appropriate options for managing your bookmark collection. The following list summarizes the available options.

- File | Open: Lets you select a different bookmark file—previously created by using File | Save As—as your current bookmark file.

- File | Import: Lets you add a different bookmark file—previously created by using File | Save As—to your current bookmark file.

- File | Save As: Saves the current bookmark file with a new name. The saved file can be opened and imported by other Netscape users.

TIP

The Open, Import, and Save As commands let people share bookmark files. For example, you can save your bookmarks to a file, then e-mail that file to a friend, who can then import your bookmarks into his or her own bookmark file.

- File | What's New?: Lets you quickly scan bookmarked files for new information. (See "Checking for New Information in Favorite Sites," later in this chapter.)
- File | Close: Saves and closes the current bookmark file.
- Edit | Undo: Cancels the previous action.
- Edit | Redo: Reverses the previous Undo.
- Edit | Cut: Removes the current selection and places it in the Windows clipboard, where it can be pasted elsewhere.
- Edit | Copy: Copies the current selection to the Windows clipboard.
- Edit | Paste: Places the text in the Windows clipboard into the bookmark file at the current selection position.

TIP

You can use the Edit | Cut and Edit | Paste options to move bookmarks into new folders. You can also cut an entire folder and paste it into a new folder, making the current folder a subfolder of the larger folder.

- Edit | Delete: Deletes the selected bookmark(s).
- Edit | Select All: Selects all the bookmarks in the dialog box.

HOW TO SELECT BOOKMARKS

From the Bookmarks window, you can use the standard Windows selection techniques to select bookmarks. For example, to select a single bookmark, just click it. To select additional bookmarks, hold down the Ctrl key while you click on the bookmarks you want to add to the selection.

To select a range of bookmarks, click (or Ctrl+Click) the first bookmark in the range. Then hold down the Shift key (or Ctrl+Shift keys) to extend the selection to the bookmark that the mouse pointer is touching.

- Edit | Find: Lets you search for a bookmark by title or URL.
- Edit | Find Again: Repeats the previous Find, looking for the next match.
- Item | Properties: Displays detailed information about the currently highlighted bookmark.
- Item | Go to Bookmark: Activates the currently highlighted bookmark, taking you to the Web site or page to which the bookmark refers.
- Item | Sort Bookmarks: Puts bookmarks into alphabetical order. This item will be greyed out unless a bookmark is highlighted.
- Item | Insert Bookmark: Lets you add a new bookmark to the list.

- Item | Insert Folder: Lets you create a folder for organizing bookmarks, as discussed earlier in this chapter.

- Item | Insert Separator: Creates a separator line below the currently highlighted bookmark. In the Bookmarks window, the word *separator* actually appears, but in the Bookmarks menu, the separator is just a line across the menu.

NAMING & ALPHABETIZING BOOKMARKS

The name that's automatically assigned to a bookmark might not always be ideal. To change the name of a bookmark, just right-click the bookmark name, choose Properties, and enter the new name in the Name textbox. Then choose OK.

To alphabetize all the folders and bookmarks in your collection, choose Edit|Select All from the Bookmarks window's menu bar. Then choose Item|Sort Bookmarks from that same menu bar.

- Item | Make Alias: Creates a bookmark (identical to the currently selected bookmark) that you can put into another folder. Unlike a copied bookmark created with Edit | Copy, an alias bookmark is updated automatically as you change the original bookmark.

- Item | Set to New Bookmarks Folder: Lets you choose which folder automatically receives new bookmarks that you create with Add Bookmark. By default new bookmarks don't go into any folder at all—they're just listed right on the Bookmarks menu. To choose a folder for new bookmarks, first click on the folder that you want to use for the new bookmarks then choose Item | Set to New Bookmarks Folder.

- Item | Set to Bookmark Menu Folder: Limits the folders and bookmarks displayed in the Bookmarks drop-down menu to those beginning at the highlight's current position in the list.

CHECKING FOR NEW INFORMATION IN FAVORITE SITES

In addition to helping you keep track of favorite sites, bookmarks provide a way to quickly scan those sites to see which ones have changed since you last viewed them. The procedure is simple:

1. Choose Window | Bookmarks from Navigator's menu bar.

2. To check on all your bookmarks, skip this step and proceed to Step 3 now. To check on only some of your bookmarks, select the ones you want to check.

3. From the Bookmarks window's menu bar choose File | What's New?

4. To search all your bookmarks, leave the All Bookmarks option selected. To check on only the bookmarks you selected in Step 2, choose the Selected Bookmarks option.

5. Click the Start Checking button.

You'll see a new dialog box that keeps you posted on the search's progress. When the search is complete, a new dialog box appears, telling you how many bookmarks were searched, how many were reached, and how many have changed since you last visited. Choose OK to leave that dialog box.

You'll be taken back to the Bookmarks window, where you'll see that...

■ Sites that have been changed are marked with accentuating lines.

■ Sites that have not changed are not accentuated.

■ Any sites that could not be reached or could not be verified are identified with a question mark.

In Figure 24-17, five of my bookmarks—Yahoo, Build-A-Card, Comedy Central, The Dilbert Zone, and Games - Happy Puppy— have all changed since my last visit.

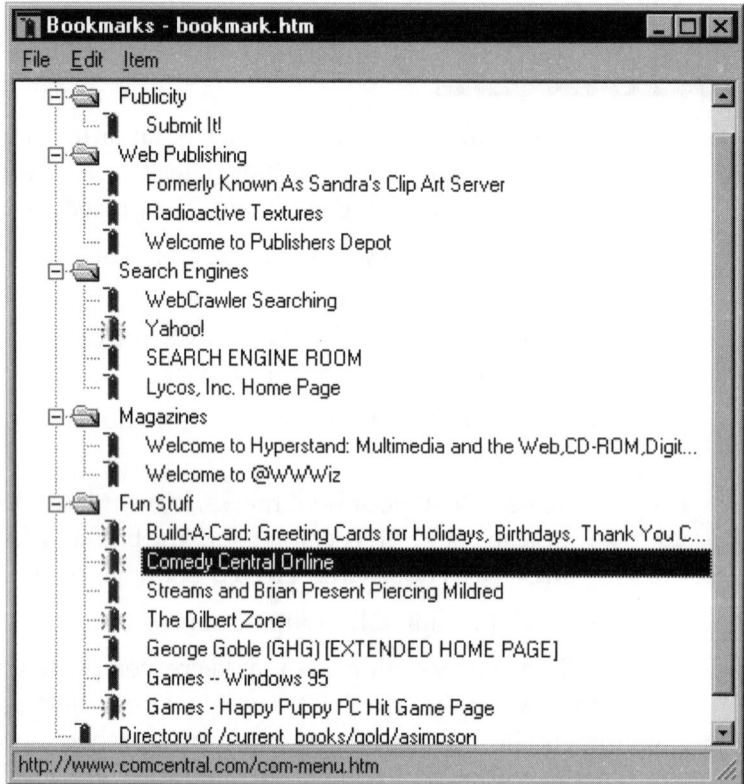

Figure 24-17: *Five sites have changed since my last visit.*

DESKTOP INTERNET SHORTCUTS

For *really* easy access to favorite sites, consider creating a Windows 95 desktop shortcut to the site. Here's how:

1. While viewing a site to which you'd like to create a shortcut, reduce the size of Navigator's window so that you can see part of the Windows 95 desktop in the background.

2. Move the mouse pointer to the little chain-link icon just to the left of the Location box.

3. Drag the little chain icon out to the Windows 95 desktop, and release the mouse button.

That's all there is to it. In the example shown in Figure 24-18, I've pointed my Web browser to Microsoft's online technical support page at http://www.microsoft.com/support.

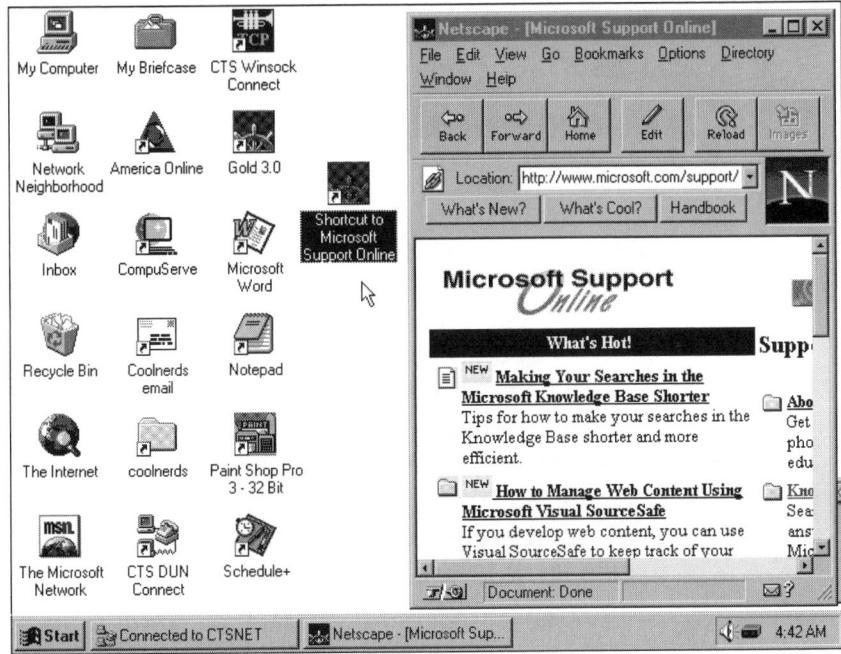

Figure 24-18: *A quick desktop shortcut to Microsoft's online tech support site.*

In the future, whenever I need some quick technical support for a Microsoft product, I just have to double-click that new shortcut icon. (Believe me—it's worth its weight in diamonds!) My Web browser will automatically kick in and take me right to that site.

USING INTERNET SHORTCUT ICONS

The exact way an Internet shortcut behaves depends on the way your system is set up. If you're set up to autodial whenever a program requests Internet access, then you'll be taken online and to the site automatically. (You control autodial via the Internet icon in the Windows 95 Control Panel.)

If you're not set up to autodial, you'll need to get online first, using whatever procedure you normally use to connect to the Internet. After you're connected, you just double-click the shortcut icon to start your Web browser and go to the requested site.

CHANGING YOUR STARTUP PAGE

Normally, when you first start up Navigator, you need to wait while your PC loads Netscape's home page. Then you can go to some other destination from that page. But here's a little tidbit of information that few people know about. You can make *any* site on the Web your startup page. If, for example, you're more interested in the weather or the stock market than you are in Netscape's current products, you can change your browser so that you go straight to your favorite Web site. Here's how:

1. Choose Options | General Preferences from Netscape Navigator's menu bar.
2. Click on the Appearance tab (if you're not already viewing the Appearance tab).
3. Under Startup, select the Home Page Location option button.
4. In the text box below the option button, type the complete URL of the Web site you want to act as your startup page. In Figure 24-19, for example, I've changed my default Startup page to my own Web site at http://www.coolnerds.com.
5. Click on the OK button.

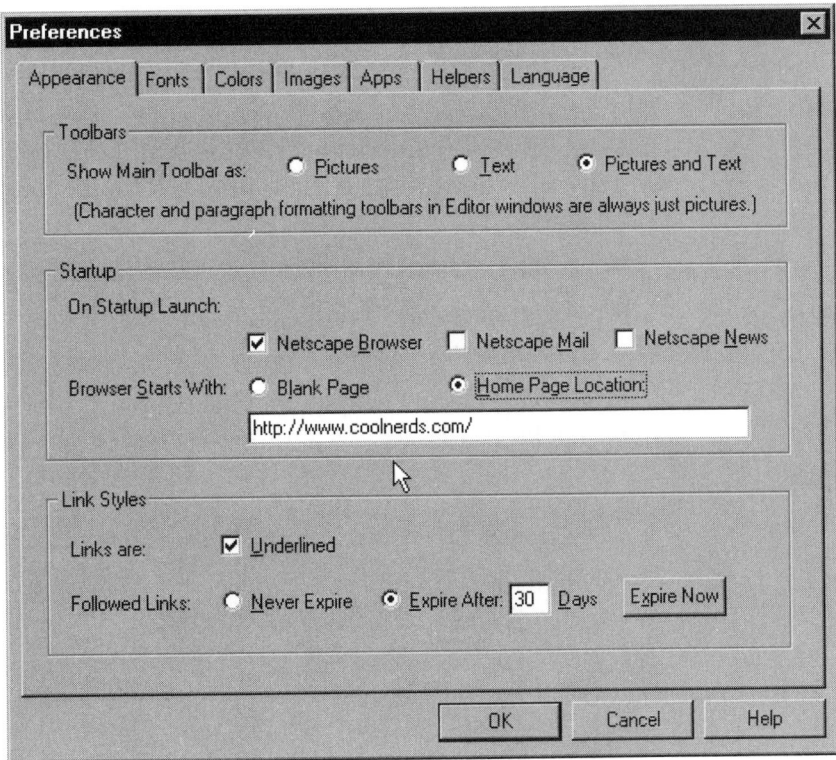

Figure 24-19: *Use the Appearance tab in the Preferences dialog box to change your default startup page.*

You won't be taken to that new site right away. The next time you start Netscape Navigator from scratch, however, you'll be taken directly to your chosen home page, rather than to Netscape's home page.

Notice too that in the Preferences dialog box there's an option to start the browser with a Blank Page. Choosing that option makes Navigator start up without pointing to any page at all. This option is handy if you often work offline because you won't see that "Netscape is unable to locate the server..." message every time you start Netscape Navigator offline.

PRINTING WEB PAGES

You can print any Web page that's on your screen. In a framed site, you can print the contents of any single frame. Just click first somewhere within the frame to indicate which frame you want to print. Then do either of the following:

- Click the Print button in Navigator's toolbar.
- Or, choose File | Print | OK (or File | Print Frame | OK) from Navigator's toolbar.

Either way, you'll be taken to Navigator's Print dialog box, shown in Figure 24-20.

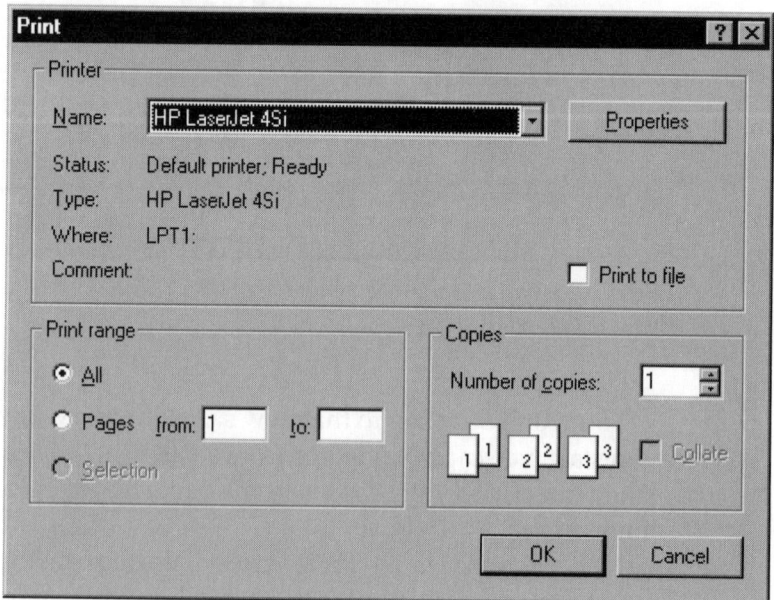

Figure 24-20: *Navigator's Print dialog box.*

As with all Windows applications, you can use options in the Print dialog box to choose a printer if you have multiple printers attached to your computer. Just click the drop-down list button to the right of the current printer name, then choose your printer from the list that appears.

You can also choose a range of pages to print, the number of copies to print, and how to collate the pages. When you're ready to start printing, click the OK button.

PREVIEWING A PAGE

You can see a preview of a printed page by following these simple steps:

1. Choose Print | Preview from Navigator's menu bar. You'll come to a window like the one shown in Figure 24-21.

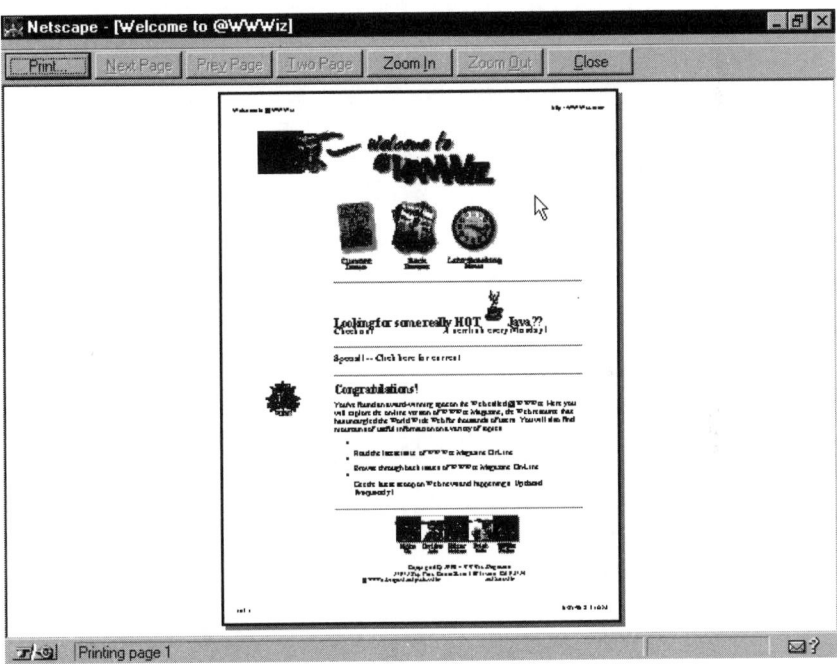

Figure 24-21: *A sample Web page in Print Preview.*

2. Optionally, use the Print, Next Page, Prev(ious) Page, Two Page, Zoom In, and Zoom Out buttons to change your view to your liking. (You can also zoom in and out of a particular area on the page by clicking that area.)

3. When you've finished previewing, click the Close button.

PAGE SETUP

You can set margins and other options for printed pages by choosing File | Page Setup from Navigator's menu bar, which takes you to the Page Setup dialog box shown in Figure 24-22. Make your selections and then choose OK. To print the page, click the Print button in the toolbar, or choose File | Print from the menus.

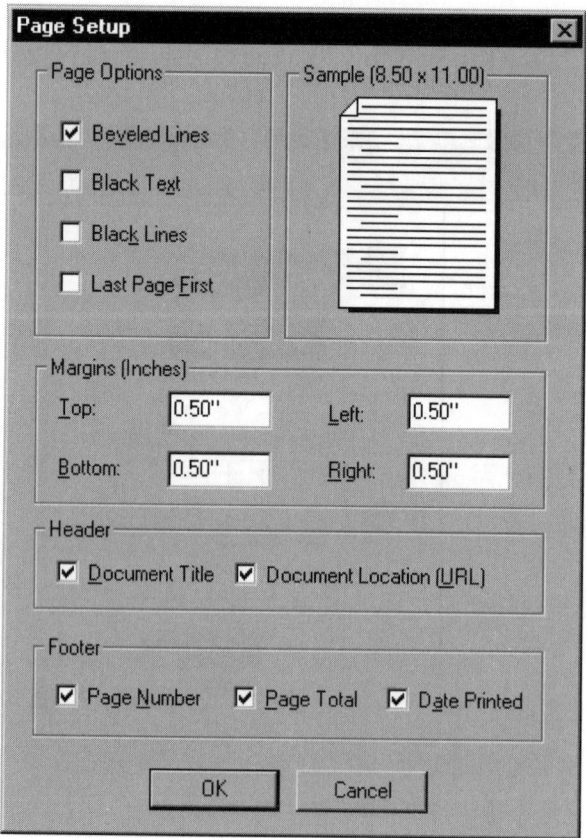

Figure 24-22: *Navigator's Page Setup dialog box.*

SAVING WEB PAGES

You can save (to your hard disk) a copy of any Web page you see. This is handy when you want to spend a little time offline with the page, instead of racking up connect-time costs as you view the page. The procedure is simple:

1. When you get to a Web page that you want to save, choose File | Save As from Navigator's menu bar. You'll come to the Save As dialog box.

2. In the Save in drop-down list, choose the folder in which you want to save the page.

3. In the File name text box, type the name of the file as you want it called on your PC. For example, in Figure 24-23 I'm about to save a page named Whitehouse.htm in my My Documents folder.

4. Click the Save button.

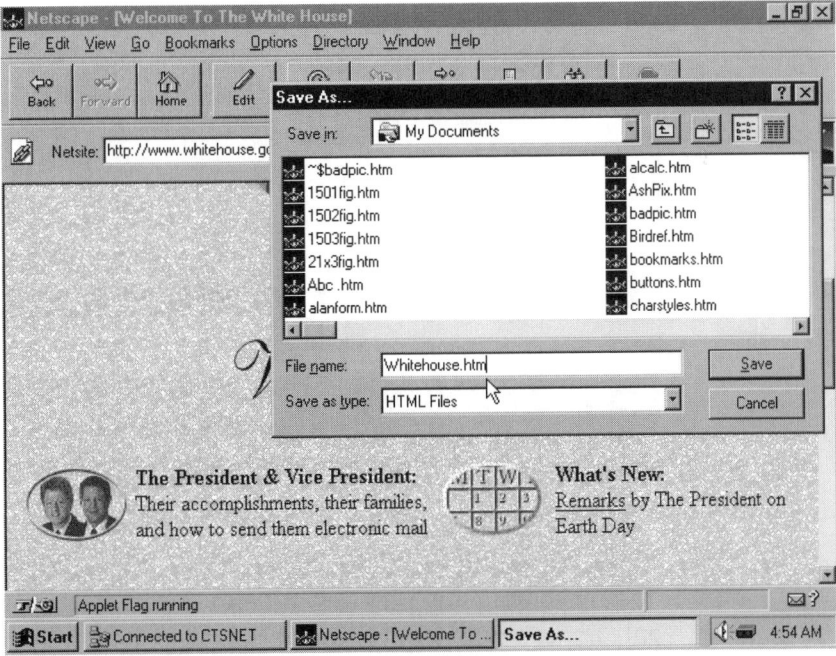

Figure 24-23: *About to save Whitehouse.htm in my My Documents folder.*

You might briefly see a little progress odometer, then the Save As dialog box will disappear and you'll be right back where you started—online and viewing the page.

Now let's see how you might look at the saved page later, offline. As an example, suppose that I close Netscape Navigator, disconnect from the Internet, and then want to view the copy of the saved Web page on my own PC.

First, you need to find the saved file. In this example I'd need to use My Computer or Windows Explorer to open my My Documents folder. Then, I'd double-click the Whitehouse.htm file in that folder, automatically opening that saved Web page in Navigator, as in Figure 24-24.

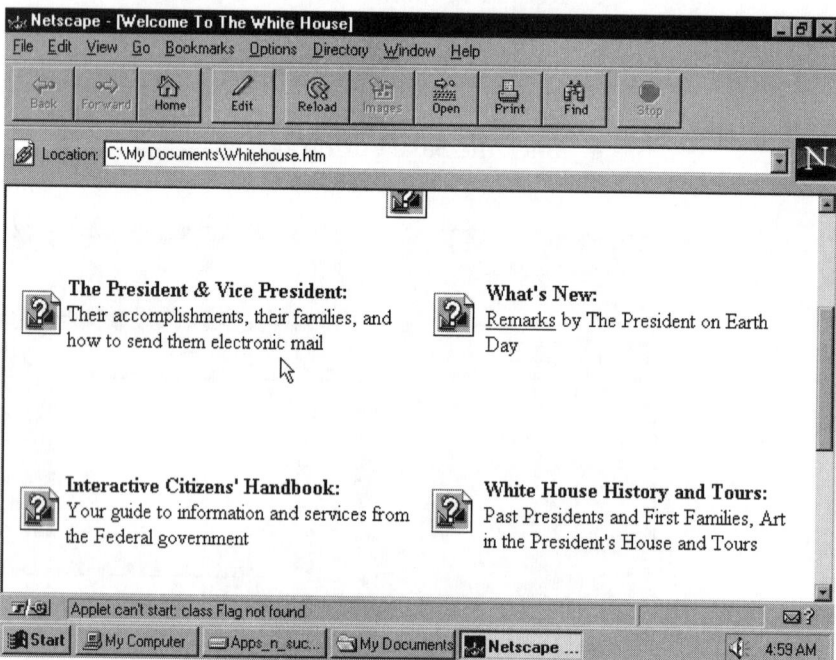

Figure 24-24: *Local saved copy of a Web page.*

The first thing you'll notice about this saved page is that it doesn't contain any pictures. Wherever you saw a picture online, only an icon with a question mark is displayed here on my local copy. Why? Because when you save a Web page, you actually save only the *HTML source* for that page. Which is to say, you save the text and the *HTML tags* that tell the browser how to format the page, but you don't save any pictures or multimedia files.

Even though you lose the pictures when you save a Web page, the technique can still be useful. For example, you might come across a lengthy article, with few or no pictures in it. When you save a copy of the article, you still get all the text, which may be sufficient if you're just looking to print and read the text of the article.

Optionally, you can save both the text and pictures for a site. But in order to view the text and pictures offline, you need to make sure that the pictures are where the text page "expects" them to be. You can accomplish that by requesting to edit the document (choose File | Edit Document from the menus) and saving the document locally.

TIP

The section titled "Using a Template to Create Your First Page" in Chapter 6 presents a practical example of how to download a page and all its pictures to use as a template in creating your own custom page.

By the way, I should also point out that the message "Applet can't start..." in the status bar is also a symptom of viewing the page locally. An applet is a small program that's embedded in the page. But it can't play here because like the pictures, it wasn't saved locally.

SITE SEEING

As I've mentioned, tons of search engines, and some interesting sites that give you quick access to multiple engines, are out there on the Internet. When you get a chance, check out some of these Web sites:

■   100 Hot Sites: http://www.100hot.com

■   AccuFind: http:/nln.com

- AltaVista: http://www.altavista.digital.com
- Deja News: http://www.dejanews.com
- Electric Library: http://www.elibrary.com
- Excite: http://www.excite.com
- IBM InfoMarket: http://www.infomarket.ibm.com
- InfoMarket Products and Services: http://www.infomarket.ibm.com
- InfoSeek: http://www.infoseek.com
- Lycos: http://www.lycos.com
- Magellan: http://www.mckinley.com
- Microsoft All-In-One Search: http://www.msn.com/access/allinone.asp
- Microsoft Technical Support: http://www.microsoft.com/support
- Netscape Local Search: http://home.netscape.com/search/index.html
- Netscape Multi-Search: http://home.netscape.com/home/internet-search.html
- Open Text Index: http://www.opentext.com
- Point: http://www.pointcom.com
- Shareware.com: http://www.shareware.com
- WebCrawler: http://www.webcrawler.com

If you're interested in creating your own custom startup page, or adding more power and flexibility to your bookmark collection, you might want to look at these pages:

- Netscape's "My Page": http://home.netscape.com/custom/index.html
- Netscape SmartMarks: http://home.netscape.com/comprod/smartmarks.html
- Netscape Power Pack: http://home.netscape.com/comprod/power_pack.html

MOVING ON

What you've learned here has taken you from a "good" Web-browsing skill level to an "expert" Web-browsing skill level. In the next chapter we'll look at some more advanced Web browsing concepts, including techniques to soup-up your browser with plug-ins. By the time you finish that chapter, you'll be a Web-browsing guru.

Plug-ins, Java & LiveConnect

After reading Chapter 13, "Multimedia Madness," you might think that Netscape Navigator has every capability in the world built right into it. But that's not exactly true. There are dozens of "things" out there on the World Wide Web that Netscape can't read on its own. Fortunately, however, there are also *inline plug-ins* for most of those things. These plug-ins easily and seamlessly extend the capabilities of Navigator to include those other things.

In this chapter we'll discuss plug-ins and a couple of other built-in capabilities of Navigator. To summarize what we'll cover, here you'll learn:

- How to find and install Navigator plug-ins
- What kinds of plug-ins are available
- The roles played by LiveConnect and Java
- Sources for finding plug-ins and other handy Internet-related programs

WHAT IS A PLUG-IN?

An *inline plug-in* (often called simply a *plug-in*) is a special type of program that extends the capabilities of Netscape Navigator. Typically, you use a plug-in to access data that Navigator can't read on its own.

PLUG-INS VERSUS HELPER APPS

If you're familiar with earlier versions of Netscape Navigator, you might remember *helper apps*. They, too, are programs that allow you to access data on the Internet that Navigator can't handle on its own. But plug-ins offer one very big advantage that will soon make helper apps a thing of the past—plug-ins are seamlessly integrated into Netscape Navigator.

What, exactly, does that mean? Well, when you access data via a plug-in, you stay within the familiar Navigator window. You don't have to go out to some new program with an entirely different set of menu commands and quirks. Also, plug-ins can create data that Navigator or other plug-ins can use. In short, whereas a helper app is sort of a separate program that you use while browsing the Web, a plug-in is more like a means of beefing up your browser, so that it can do more than it could before you installed the plug-in.

An example will best illustrate the concept. In the sections that follow I'll show an example of discovering a need for a plug-in, finding, installing, and then using that plug-in.

AN EXAMPLE OF ADDING A PLUG-IN

If you're now thinking, "How do I know what plug-ins I need?," the answer is, "You don't." But as you explore the Web, you'll come across sites that require a particular plug-in for maximum effect.

For example, let's say that as you're cruising the World Wide Web, you come across a link to an MPEG movie, as in Figure 25-1. When you click on that link, you don't get a movie. Instead, you get a dialog box like the one shown in Figure 25-2.

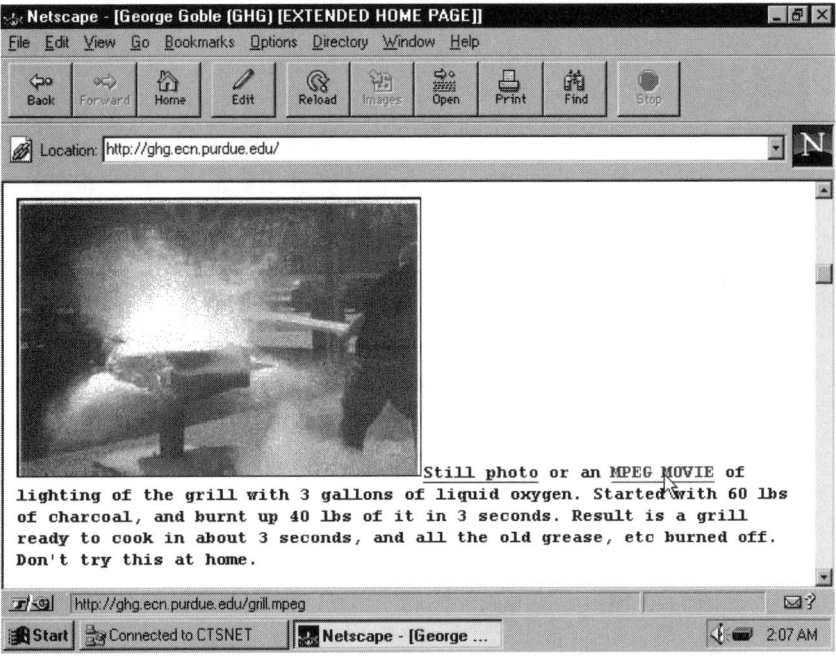

Figure 25-1: *I'm about to click a link that promises to show me an MPEG movie.*

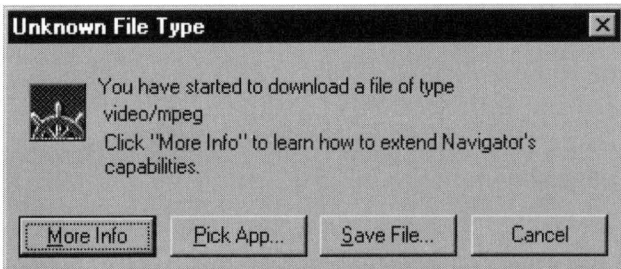

Figure 25-2: *Message telling me that I'm about to download a movie that Navigator can't play.*

The dialog box is telling you that Navigator, by itself, won't be able to play the movie that you're about to *download* (copy to your computer.) It then gives you the following choices:

- More Info: Takes you to a site that describes plug-ins and includes a link to Netscape's Plug-Ins resource.

- Pick App: Lets you choose a program that's already on your computer to open the incoming file. For example, if you're downloading a Microsoft Word .doc file, you might pick Microsoft Word as the program to view this incoming file.

- Save File: Lets you save the incoming file to your hard disk without opening it. This is the option you choose when downloading a program (.exe file) or compressed zip file (.zip) that you want to work with later.

- Cancel: Terminates the download.

If you look closely at Figure 25-2, you'll see that Navigator is trying to download a file of the type video/mpeg. And, as you may recall, I started this process by requesting an MPEG movie. Let's say that you decide that now is as good a time as any to find an MPEG plug-in and download it to your computer. You click on the More Info button, which takes you to a page that tells you a bit about plug-ins.

TIP

In many cases you'll come across a site that provides a button or link that lets you download the appropriate plug-in, right on the spot. In that situation, you just need to click the button or link and then follow whatever instructions appear onscreen.

Down near the bottom of that page, you come to a link to Netscape's Plug-In Registry. Clicking that link, in turn, takes you to the page shown in Figure 25-3.

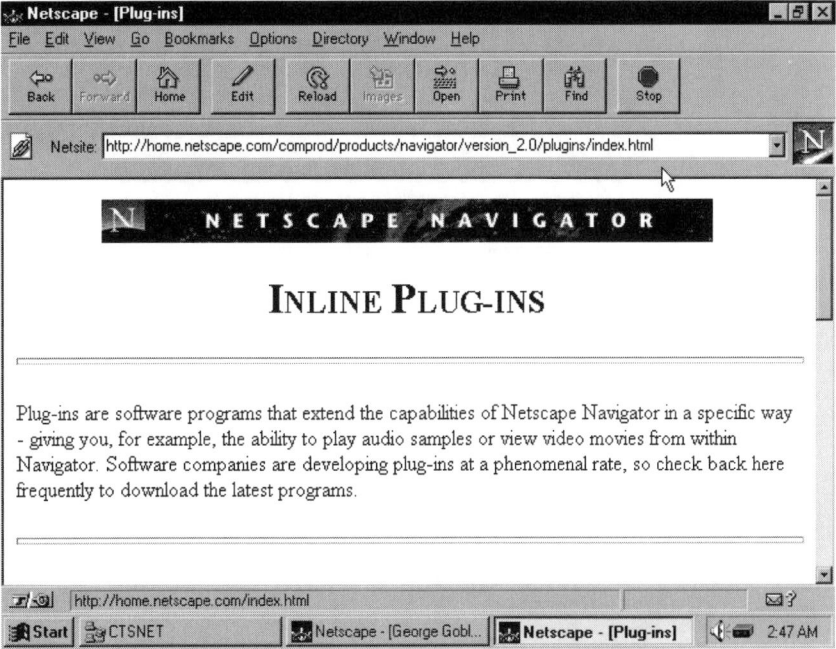

Figure 25-3: *Netscape's Plug-Ins Registry.*

In the Plug-Ins Registry, you can look around for MPEG plug-ins. Carefully read each plug-in's description to make sure that you're getting a Windows version.

TIP

If you get to a lengthy list of plug-ins, you can use Edit | Find to locate a particular word. For instance, in this example you might want to look for the word MPEG.

Let's say that you find a plug-in that looks as though it might do the trick, as in Figure 25-4. Clicking on the Download PreVU link will take you to a site where you can do just that (download preVU.) Just follow the links and any instructions on the screen to download and (if necessary) install the plug-in.

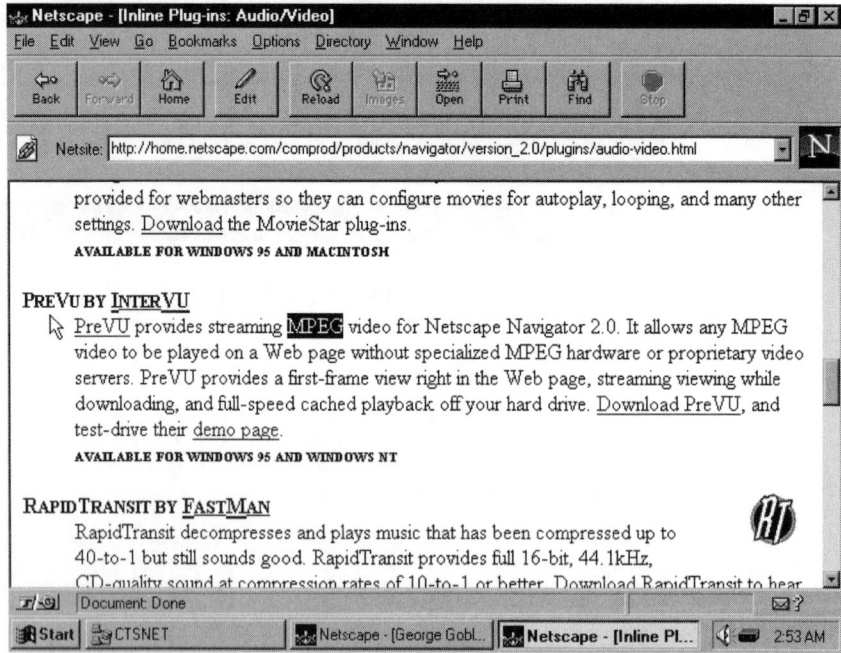

Figure 25-4: *I found a plug-in for viewing MPEG movies.*

When you've finished, you'll be able to download and play the MPEG movie. Also, because you've installed the plug-in, you'll be able to play *any* MPEG movie you find, without having to go through that Unknown File Type dialog box shown back in Figure 25-2.

HELP WITH PLUG-INS

Even though the preceding scenario is just one example of using a plug-in, most plug-ins will work the same way. The basic procedure is similar in just about every case. That is, you:

1. Discover the need for a plug-in.

2. Go to Netscape's Plug-In Registry and find an appropriate plug-in.

3. Follow the plug-in manufacturer's instructions for downloading, installing, and using the plug-in.

If you have any problems downloading, installing, or using a plug-in, your best bet is to go to the Web site you downloaded the plug-in from, and look for some kind of technical support, feedback link, or e-mail address to contact the manufacturer. Send them a note explaining the problem and I'm sure they'll be happy to help you out.

OTHER WAYS TO GET PLUG-INS

As I said, the preceding scenario is just an example. Often, acquiring a plug-in is much simpler. For example, you might come to a site that not only recommends a plug-in, but also includes a link to get the plug-in right there, on the spot. Or, you might come to a dialog box that provides a simple button to get a plug-in, as in the example shown in Figure 25-5.

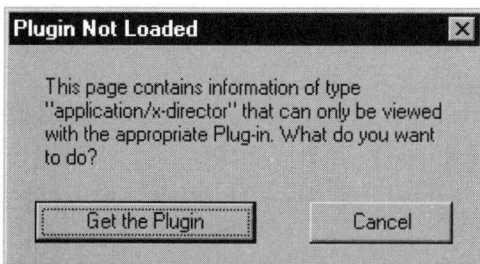

Figure 25-5: *This dialog box lets you download a plug-in with a simple button click.*

You can also go to any site that offers plug-ins and download and install any that look interesting. See "Resources for Plug-Ins," later in this chapter, for some sites to visit. Do keep in mind, however, that Netscape Navigator 3.0 already has the capability to read files in many formats, as summarized in Table 25-1. You won't need to install any plug-ins to read those types of files.

Built-In Capability	Types of Files Supported
Graphics	GIF, JPEG, animated GIF
Java	All Java applets and all JavaScript code.
Sound	AIFF, AU, MIDI, WAV
Text	HTML, HTTP, FTP, NNTP, SMTP, MIME
Video	AVI, QuickTime
Virtual Reality, 3D	VRML

TYPES OF PLUGS-INS

Despite the many built-in file types that Navigator can read, there are plenty others out there that require plug-ins. Just to give you a feel for what's available, the next sections will cover some of the different categories and types available. Remember, this is only a sampling. The number of available plug-ins increases almost daily!

3D & ANIMATION PLUG-INS

Navigator can read Virtual 3D worlds based on VRML (Virtual Reality Markup Language) and it can read animations based on Java, as well as animated GIFs. But you'll find lots of plug-ins for cruising 3D worlds and playing animations created with other programs. Here are just a few examples:

- FutureSplash: Plays FutureWave vector-based animations.
- MBED: Plays embedded multimedia mbedlets created with mBED software.
- Play3D: Has limited authoring capabilities including the ability to attach behaviors to 3D objects and 2D sprites.
- Shockwave: Interacts with courses created with Multimedia's AuthorWare and Director presentations.
- Sizzler: Allows streaming animation to play while you're viewing and interacting with Web pages.

- Topper: Explores 3D world created with 3D Studio.
- Viscape: Provides true interactive 3D with the ability to grab objects and does walkthroughs.
- Web-Active: Views and manipulates 3D images.
- WebXpresso: Views 2D and 3D drawings, graphs, and controls.

AUDIO/VIDEO PLUG-INS

Here are plug-ins that can enhance your multimedia browsing experience:

- ACTION: Plays MPEG movies with synchronized sound.
- CoolFusion: Plays streaming inline AVI video.
- Crescendo: Plays streaming MIDI music with simple "CD-player" controls.
- EchoSpeech: Plays recorded, compressed speech files.
- Koan: Plays music files created with the Koan Pro program.
- RealAudio: Lets you experience and deliver audio from your Web site.

BUSINESS & UTILITIES

Be sure to look into some of these commonly used plug-ins for accessing popular business data formats and for adding functionality to your browser.

- Acrobat Amber: Views, navigates, and prints Portable Document Format (PDF) files without leaving your browser.
- ActiveX: Lets you view Active Documents like Microsoft's Word, Excel, and PowerPoint.
- Carbon Copy/Net: Lets you remotely control a PC over the Internet.
- Chemscape Chime: Scientists can display chemically significant 2D and 3D structures with this plug-in.

- Concerto: Provides powerful data-entry capabilities to Web-based forms.

- EarthTime: Tells the time anywhere in the world at a glance.

- Envoy: Views rich Envoy documents with flexible fonts and layouts.

- Formula One/Net: An online Excel-compatible spreadsheet.

- Isys Hindsite: Keeps better track of where you've been on the Web and makes return trips easier.

- Look@Me: Lets two Look@Me users with cameras talk face-to-face over the Internet!

- PointCast Network: Views live, up-to-the-minute news, weather, financial news, sports, and more.

- StockWatcher: Views live stock quotes.

- Word Viewer: Views any Microsoft Word 6.0/7.0 document from inside Netscape Navigator.

IMAGE VIEWERS

After spending time on the Web, you might start to think that GIF and JPEG are the only graphics formats in the world. Not true! Look at what some of these viewers let you see:

- ABC QuickSilver: Places, views, and interacts with Micro-Grafx objects inside Web pages.

- CMX Viewer: Views Corel CMX vector graphics.

- Fractal Viewer: Supports inline fractal images.

- InterCAP Inline: Views, zooms, pans, and magnifies Computer Graphics Metafile (CGM) vector graphics.

- TMSSequoia ViewDirector: Views graphics in TIFF, PCX/DCX. BMP, and other formats.

- WHIP!: Views and navigates AutoCAD 2D vector graphics.

ABOUT JAVA

If you've been involved with the Internet at all recently, you've no doubt heard of Java—the programming language that's going to revolutionize the (already revolutionary) World Wide Web. Sites that use Java can offer you a richer browsing experience with a higher level of interactivity and great live action.

Netscape Navigator 3.0 already has Java and JavaScript support built right in. You don't need to do anything to start enjoying sites that offer Java programs. Just point Navigator to any site that offers Java, or click a link to a Java applet, and Navigator will play the applet for you. To get a feel for what's possible, you might want to visit some of the sites listed under "Java, JavaScript, and LiveConnect " in the "Site Seeing" section near the end of this chapter.

ABOUT LIVECONNECT

LiveConnect lets you interact with the super-interactive Web sites of tomorrow, starting today. In a nutshell, LiveConnect can coordinate the actions of three key technologies—Navigator Plug-Ins, Java Applets, and JavaScript. Which means that Web developers can bring you an even richer experience than Java alone.

You don't have to install anything to use LiveConnect, it's already built in. When you visit a Web site that uses any combination of those three technologies, LiveConnect will kick in automatically and present the site as its author intended.

Nothing I show you on paper can adequately convey the richness of a Web site that uses LiveConnect. But Navigator certainly can. Check out Netscape's Media Showcase to start exploring the possibilities. Point Navigator to http://home.netscape.com and look around for information on LiveConnect or Media Showcase. Or work your way to http://home.netscape.com/comprod/products/navigator/version_3.0/showcase/index.html.

■ Site Seeing

Here are some sites you can cruise to explore available plug-ins, experience Java, and much more.

Plug-ins & Other Software

- Netscape's Plug-In Resources: A good first-stop for keeping up with the latest plug-ins: http://home.netscape.com/comprod/products/navigator/version_2.0/plugins/index.html

- Netscape Tech-Demo: Demonstrate or view plug-ins at http://sager-bell.com/techdemo

- Plug-In Plaza: Another great resource for Navigator plug-ins: http://www.browserwatch.com/plug-in.html

- Shareware.com: All kinds of shareware for all kinds of platforms: http://www.shareware.com

- The Ultimate Collection of Windows Software: Plug-ins and all kinds of other Internet-related shareware: http://www.env.com/tucows

- Windows 95 Internet Software Collection: The name says it all: http://omni.cc.purdue.edu/~xniu/winsock/win95.htm

- WinSite: Tons of cool Windows 95 stuff: http://www.winsite.com

Java, JavaScript & LiveConnect

- Coolnerds: For some JavaScript examples (including clocks, calculators, color schemer, hyperinteractive online order form, and more), see the JavaScript area, under Web Publishing, in my own Web site: http://www.coolnerds.com

- Earthweb's Gamelan-The Java Directory: Lots of applets: http://www.gamelan.com

- JARS—Java Applet Rating Service: Top 1 percent of Java Applets for your viewing pleasure: http://www.jars.com

- Java Centre: A showcase for cool Java applets and more: http://www.java.co.uk

- JavaScript Index: Tons of sample JavaScript goodies to play with: http://www.c2.org/~andreww/javascript

- Spotted Antelope: An experiment in advanced multimedia that uses LiveConnect: http://www.spottedantelope.com/wander.html

MOVING ON

The topics covered in this chapter represent very new and cutting-edge World Wide Web capabilities. And you will see more and more sites that embrace those capabilities to give you a more rewarding Web experience. Starting in the next chapter I'd like to introduce you to non-Web Internet services. We'll start with CoolTalk, the online telephone that lets you talk to anyone in the world virtually toll free!

CoolTalk: Talking on the Net

Imagine holding a conference with people anywhere in the world, all for the price of a local call (or free—if you have a toll-free connection to your Internet Service Provider). Well guess what? Imagine no more, because with CoolTalk you can yak to your heart's content. And that's just the start of it. In this chapter you'll learn how to:

- Talk long distance without long distance charges
- Type notes "chat" style with anyone in the world
- Share photos and drawings "live" with anyone
- Use your PC as a CoolTalk answering machine

Just to whet your whistle, Figure 26-1 shows a sample conference call in action, using the whole shebang: White Board, Chat Tool, and microphones and speakers for voice.

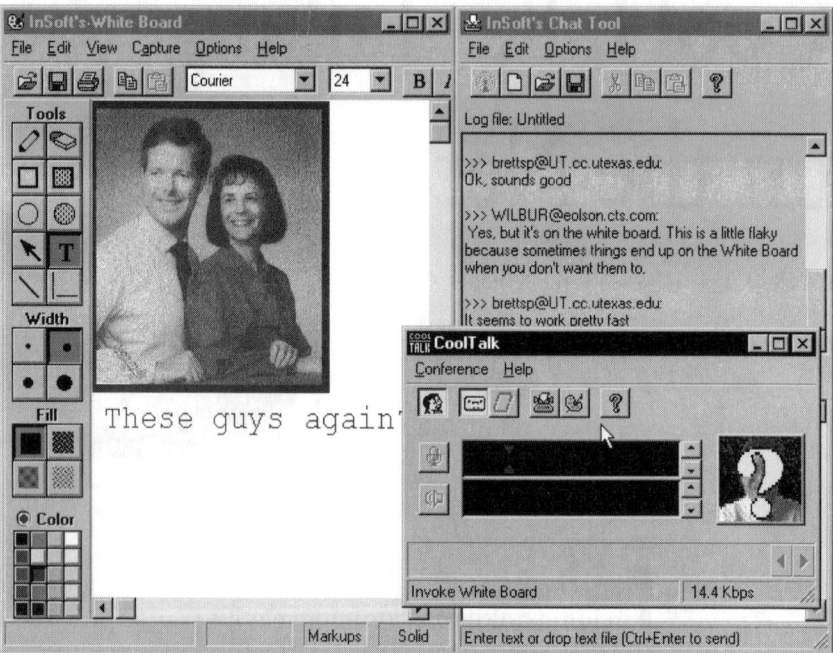

Figure 26-1: *A sample CoolTalk conference in progress.*

CoolTalk, including its White Board and Chat Tool, are part of your Netscape Navigator Gold (version 3.0) package. When you installed Navigator Gold, you also installed CoolTalk automatically.

CoolTalk Hardware & Software Requirements

If you have a connection to the Internet and you're using a multimedia computer that's running Windows 95, you probably have all the hardware and software you need to run CoolTalk. Here's the least you'll need to get started:

- PC 486 50 MHz machine with 8MB of RAM
- 14,400 bps or 28,800 bps modem
- MS Windows-compatible sound card

- Microphone and speakers, if you want to talk to and hear people over the Internet

- A SLIP or PPP Internet account, or any Winsock 1.1-compatible TCP/IP connection to the Internet

- Windows 95 multimedia device drivers (especially the GSM audio compression device driver)

CoolTalk also works with Windows 3.1, Windows NT, and several flavors of Unix.

TIP

*A codec is a driver that **compresses** and **dec**ompresses audio data. To find out which multimedia codecs are installed on your computer, start CoolTalk (as explained later) and choose Help | System Info; or choose Start | Settings | Control Panel, double-click the Multimedia Icon, and choose the Advanced tab in the Multimedia Properties dialog box. Finally, double-click Audio Compression Manager or Audio Compression Codecs to see a list of the installed multimedia device drivers.*

INSTALLING COOLTALK

You probably installed CoolTalk when you installed Netscape Navigator Gold 3.0, but if you haven't installed CoolTalk yet, you can follow these steps to do so:

1. Start the Netscape Navigator Gold 3.0 installation program, setup.exe.

2. When asked if you want to install CoolTalk, choose Yes.

3. When asked if you want to install the CoolTalk Watchdog in your Startup group, choose Yes if you want the Watchdog (described in a moment) to start automatically when you start your computer.

4. Follow the instructions that appear on the screen.

When you're done, you can hop right down to "Starting CoolTalk," later in this chapter. Or, if you'd like more information about CoolTalk and Watchdog, read on.

WHAT'S THAT COOLTALK WATCHDOG?

The CoolTalk Watchdog is a program that continuously checks your Internet connection to see whether anyone is trying to call you, and lets your computer accept CoolTalk calls even when CoolTalk isn't loaded in memory. When someone does invite you to join a CoolTalk conference, the Watchdog starts CoolTalk so that you don't miss the invitation.

Remember, when someone invites you in for a CoolTalk session, you'll get the call *only* if you're connected to the Internet, and *only* if Watchdog is active. If you have any problems or concerns with Watchdog, please see the "Some Notes on Watchdog" section near the end of this chapter.

STARTING COOLTALK

Starting CoolTalk is pretty easy. Here's how:

1. Connect to the Internet in the usual manner for your PC.
2. Start CoolTalk by choosing Start | Programs | Netscape, and then double-clicking the CoolTalk icon in the Netscape Navigator window.

> **TIP**
>
> *If you plan to use CoolTalk often, why not put a CoolTalk icon on your desktop? Right-click an empty place on the desktop and choose New | Shortcut. Click the Browse button, locate the CoolTalk program, and double-click the CoolTalk program icon. Click Next, and then click Finish.*

3. If a Connect To dialog box asks you to connect to your
   Internet Service Provider, click the Connect button.

You'll see the CoolTalk window, shown in Figure 26-2.

Figure 26-2: *The CoolTalk window.*

USING THE COOLTALK SETUP WIZARD

After installing CoolTalk and starting it for the first time, you
should set up CoolTalk. You need to set up CoolTalk only once.
Here are the setup steps:

1. Choose Help | Setup Wizard from CoolTalk's menu bar, and
   follow the instructions presented by the Setup Wizard.

2. When you see the Setup Wizard dialog box that resembles
   Figure 26-3, fill in the text boxes with as much information
   as you care to provide. (Most of the choices are optional.)

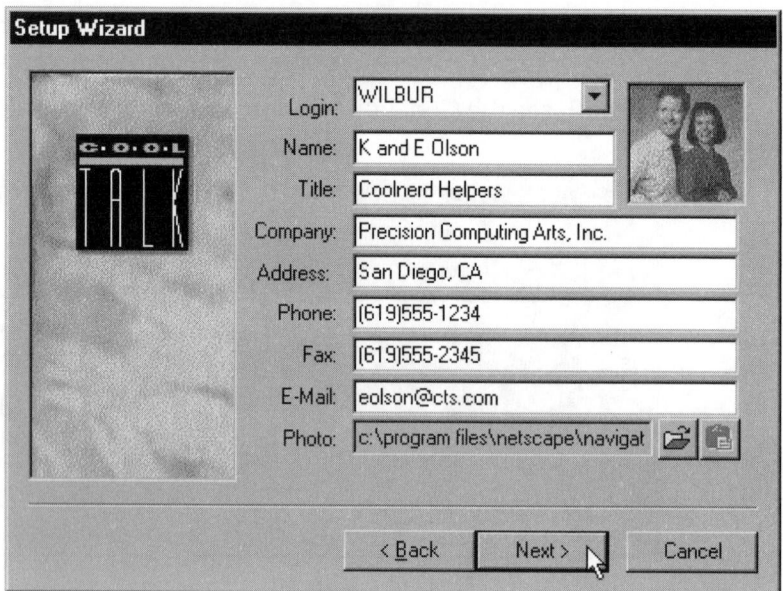

Figure 26-3: *The Setup Wizard asks for your personal information and lets you insert a picture.*

3. Click the Next button, and then click Finish to finish setting up CoolTalk.

The Setup Wizard sets up the most important options for using CoolTalk effectively. If you'd like to tweak the options further, re-run the Setup Wizard or choose Conference | Options and adjust the settings in the Options dialog box. For more about setting CoolTalk options, see "Customizing the CoolTalk Options," later in this chapter.

GETTING HELP

Like all self-respecting Windows applications, CoolTalk offers lots of online Help, both in a table of contents form and in an index form. To get started with the online Help, click the big ? button on any CoolTalk toolbar, or choose Help | Help Topics.

Anytime you're using a dialog box that offers a small ? button at the upper-right corner, you can click that button and then click the option you're curious about. A brief pop-up help description will appear. Click on or just outside the pop-up description to clear it from the dialog box.

If a dialog box offers a Help button, you can click it to open a standard CoolTalk Help window.

MENU & BUTTON HELP

To see the name of a button, rest the mouse pointer on that button until the tooltip appears.

To learn more about any option on a CoolTalk menu, open the menu you want to use and move the mouse pointer to the option you're curious about. A brief explanation of the option appears on the status bar. If you need more information about the highlighted option, open a Help window by pressing the F1 key.

HELP FROM THE NET

Not surprisingly, you can find some help with CoolTalk on the Internet, as well. Here are two URLs you'll want to know about:

- To view a list of frequently asked questions, point your browser to http://www.insoft.com/TechSupport/CTfaq.html

- To get support from humans, point your browser to http://ice.insoft.com, or send electronic mail to ice-support@insoft.com

Don't forget that when you're typing a URL, you want to use the exact upper- and lowercase letters shown here.

LET'S TALK

Chatting over a CoolTalk line is as simple as starting a conference or joining a conference you've been invited to, and then talking on your microphone, sharing and updating images on the White Board, and typing messages in the Chat Tool.

STARTING A CONFERENCE

You can start a new conference by following the steps below:

1. Click the Start Conference button in CoolTalk, or choose Conference | Start from the CoolTalk menu bar. You'll see the Open Conference dialog box.

2. Choose the Address Book tab (see Figure 26-4) or the IS411 Directory tab (see Figure 26-5) to view a list of conference participants you can choose. The Address Book tab contains a list of all the CoolTalk users you've talked with in the past. The IS411 Directory tab shows all the users who are registered with the default IS411 server.

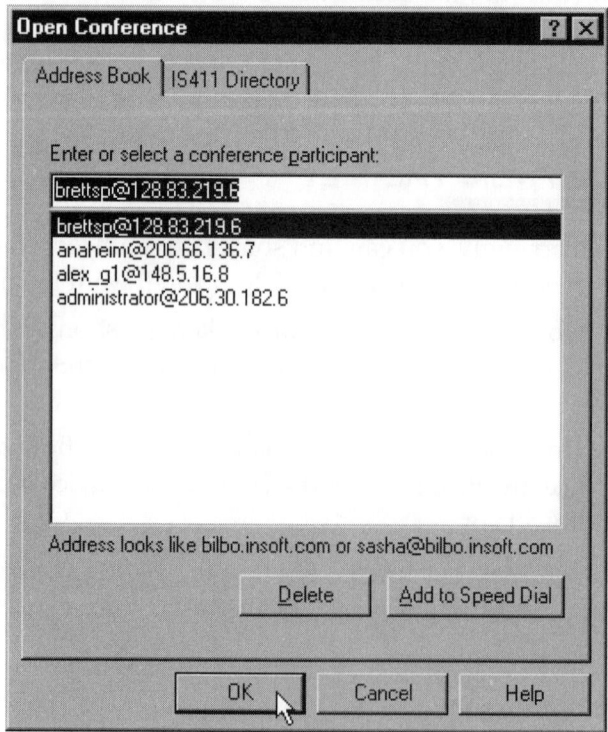

Figure 26-4: *Example of an Address Book tab in the Open Conference dialog box.*

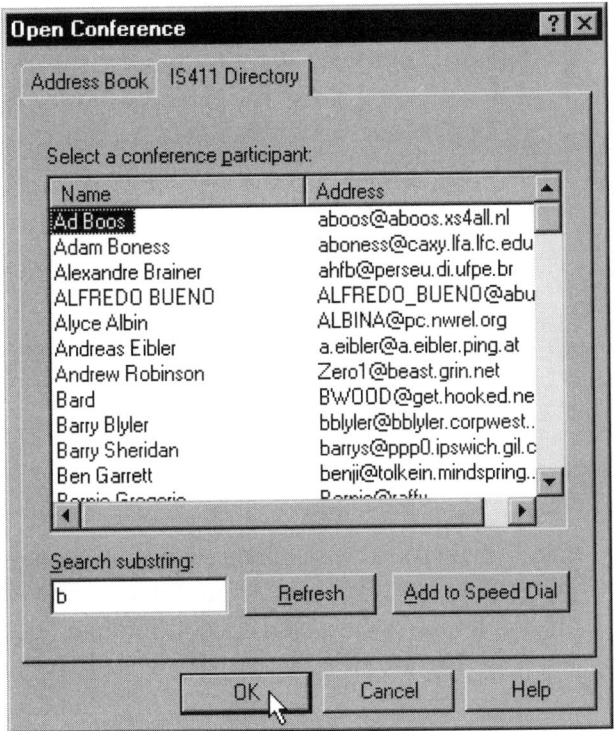

Figure 26-5: *Example of the IS411 Directory tab in the Open Conference dialog box.*

ABOUT THE IS411 SERVER

Initially, you will be connected to the default IS411 server, which has the host name *live.netscape.com*. If you want to connect to a different IS411 server, choose Conference|Options from the CoolTalk menu bar, select the Conference tab, and type the IS411 host name you want in the Host Name text box. To make yourself available to other CoolTalk users on the IS411 server, select (check) the Make Me Available Through Server box on the Conference tab. When you've finished making changes, choose OK. See "Customizing the CoolTalk Options," later in this chapter, for more details.

3. If you chose the Address Book tab in Step 2, click the name of the participant you want to invite to your conference, or type the person's name and the host name of the participant in the box below "Enter Or Select A Conference Participant." You should type the user name and host in the form *user@host*, as in WILBUR@eolson.cts.com.

> **TIP**
>
> *You can delete an entry from your Address Book by clicking the name of the participant you want to delete and then clicking the Delete button on the Address Book tab of the Options dialog box.*

4. If you chose the IS411 Directory tab in Step 2, click a conference participant's name in the list that appears. Or, type any part of the name of a participant you want to search for in the Search Substring box, click the Refresh button, and then click the name of the person you want to invite.

> **TIP**
>
> *You can sort participants by name or by address by clicking on the Name or Address heading buttons above the participant list.*

5. Choose OK to invite the selected participant to your conference.

CoolTalk will attempt to connect to the person you selected. If the connection is successful, you'll see that person's photo on the CoolTalk window. If CoolTalk cannot connect, it will let you know and may ask whether you want to leave a message on that person's CoolTalk answering machine.

> **TIP**
>
> *You can make a CoolTalk connection also by visiting the CoolTalk Phonebook Web page. Simply fire up Netscape, point the browser to http://live.netscape.com, and follow the instructions that appear on your screen.*

JOINING A CONFERENCE

When someone invites you to join a CoolTalk conference, a message will appear on your screen (you'll need to respond rather quickly, or the connection will fail). If you want to join the conference, click the Accept button. After you accept the invitation, you'll see the other person's photo on your CoolTalk window, and you can begin the conference.

To find out information about your own computer when you're not involved in a conference, or to find out more about the person you're conversing with, click on the big Cool Talk button near the right side of the CoolTalk window (or choose Conference | Participant Info, and choose the name of a participant from the CoolTalk menu bar).

CARRYING ON A CONFERENCE

When you're connected to a call or conference, use your computer's microphone and speakers to carry on your conversation. When you talk over your mike, be sure the microphone and speaker switches are in the On position. Then, put your mouth near the microphone and speak normally, just as you would over the telephone. If you can't hear the person you're talking with, you may need to adjust your recording volume or speakers. If you use CoolTalk frequently for voice calls, consider getting a headset for your PC. (Headsets are available at many computer stores.)

TIP

To use the Windows volume controls, double-click the Volume icon in the taskbar, or choose Start | Settings | Control Panel and double-click the Multimedia icon. For more information on using the Windows volume controls, refer to Chapter 13, "Multimedia Madness."

As you'll learn in a moment, you can also use CoolTalk's White Board and Chat Tool during your telephone call or conference.

LEAVING A CONFERENCE

When you've finished talking with someone, you can leave the conference by choosing Conference | Leave from the CoolTalk menu bar and clicking Yes when asked for confirmation. Your connection to the other conference member will be closed, though you'll still be connected to the Internet.

EXITING COOLTALK

When you finish using CoolTalk, you should exit CoolTalk. Also, if you're using a dial-up account and are done with the Internet for the time being, you might want to disconnect from the Net. You can exit CoolTalk through the usual File | Exit commands. If applicable, you can then close your Internet connection in the usual manner.

USING THE CHAT TOOL

The Chat Tool lets you hold your CoolTalk conversation by using your keyboard (rather than speakers and microphone). This might be handy when you specifically want to send text information to other conferees, keep a written record of a conference, or communicate with people who don't have a microphone and speakers.

To use the Chat Tool, just click the Chat Tool button in CoolTalk's toolbar (while you're in a conference). The Chat Tool opens in its own window, as in Figure 26-6.

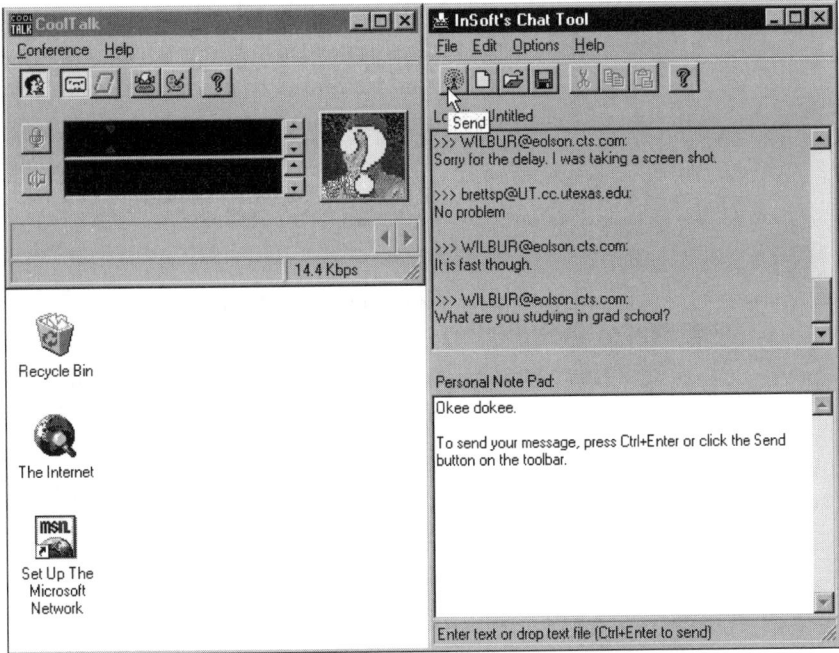

Figure 26-6: *The Chat Tool window, opened and tiled vertically on the desktop.*

SENDING A MESSAGE

Using the Chat Tool to send a message is easy. Just follow these steps:

1. Position the insertion point in the Personal Note Pad area (lower pane) of the Chat Tool window.

2. Type the message text, or insert it from an existing text file (as explained at the end of this section).

3. To send the message, press Ctrl+Enter, or click the Send button on the toolbar.

The conference participants will see your message in the window's Log File (upper pane).

When you work with the Chat Tool, you can use standard word processing techniques to position the insertion point and select text; to copy, cut, and paste text; and to insert and delete text. If you'd like to insert text from an existing text file at the insertion point position, click the Include button on the toolbar (or press Ctrl+I, or choose File | Include) and locate and double-click the text file you want to include.

SAVING THE MESSAGE LOG

You can save the current message log to a text file on your disk, a handy feature when you need to preserve an online record of your conference. To save the log file, click the Save button on the toolbar (or press Ctrl+S, or choose File | Save). If you're prompted for a filename, type the filename, choose a disk and folder location, then choose Save.

TIP

To save a copy of the current log file to a different file, *choose File | Save As instead of File | Save or its shortcuts.*

PRINTING THE MESSAGE LOG

You can print the contents of the message log any time during your conference. To choose a printer, choose File | Print Setup, choose options in the Print Setup dialog box that appears, and choose OK. Then, when you're ready to print, choose File | Print from the Chat Tool menu bar.

CLOSING THE CHAT TOOL

When you've finished using the Chat Tool window, close it as you'd close any standard window. That is, click the window's Close (X) button, or press Alt+F4, or choose File | Close from the Chat Tool menu bar.

USING THE WHITE BOARD

The White Board, shown in Figure 26-7 is the perfect tool for showing pictures and other information during your conference. Anyone can draw on or erase the White Board at any time, so be prepared for a bit of a free-for-all. To open the White Board window during your call, just click the White Board button on the CoolTalk window's toolbar.

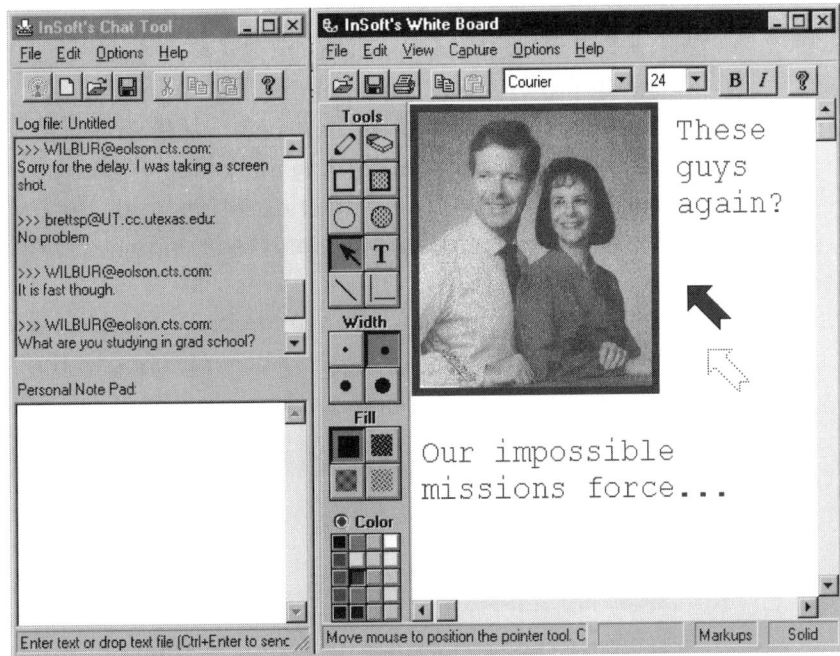

Figure 26-7: *The CoolTalk White Board window and the Chat Tool window, opened and tiled vertically on the desktop.*

WINDOWS-A-POPPIN!

After you get two or more CoolTalk tool windows open, CoolTalk windows will pop up automatically whenever a conferee uses that tool to send you information. For example, if you're typing in the Chat Tool window while someone is updating the White Board, the White Board will pop up on top of your Chat Tool window and you may end up typing on the White Board instead! Things can become pretty confusing! There are some solutions, however.

One is to turn off the automatic pop-up behavior (or turn it on) by choosing Options|Pop Up On Receive from the Chat Tool or White Board window menu bars.

Also, you can tile the windows so that they don't overlap. Minimize any windows you *don't* want to see. Then right-click on an empty area of the taskbar and choose Tile Vertically from the shortcut menu. You can then resize and rearrange the windows to your liking.

If a window "disappears" while you're working with it, simply click its button on the taskbar to bring it back to the forefront on your screen.

WHITE BOARD TOOLS

If you're already familiar with any painting or drawing program, you'll have no trouble using the CoolTalk White Board. Feel free to practice with the tools and experiment with the White Board features (even when you're not in a conference). Figure 26-8 shows the tools you can use for drawing on the White Board. To draw on the White Board canvas, follow these steps:

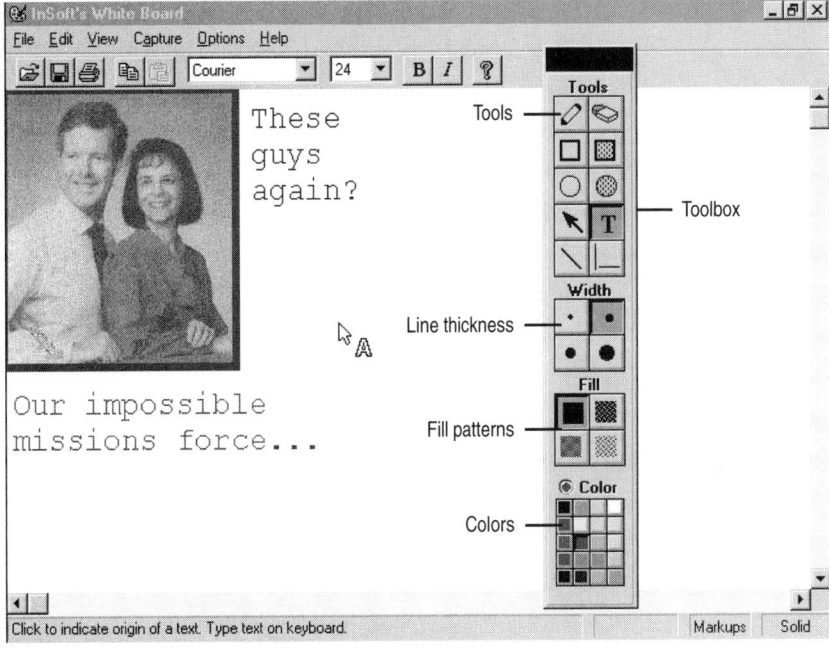

Figure 26-8: *The White Board offers many handy drawing tools.*

1. Choose the tool you want to use by clicking it in the Tools area of the toolbox.

2. Choose a width, fill, and color from the Line Thickness, Fill Pattern, and Color areas of the toolbox.

TIP

You can press Ctrl+T or choose Options | Floating Toolbox to switch between a docked and a floating toolbox.

3. If you chose the Text tool in Step 1, choose a font name, font size, and font attributes from the toolbar.

4. Move the mouse pointer to the place on the canvas where you want to draw. The status bar will provide a tip on how to use the selected tool.

5. Click on the White Board canvas, or click and drag on the White Board canvas, to draw with the selected tool. If you're using the Text tool, just click and then type your text.

TRAP

There's no Undo command on the White Board! If you draw something accidentally, you can erase your mistake with the Eraser tool. For bigger cleanups, choose Edit | Clear Markups (which erases all markups while leaving the bitmap images intact), or choose Edit | Clear White Board (which erases the entire White Board).

PUTTING PICTURES ON THE WHITE BOARD

As the next sections explain, there are several ways to put pictures (also called *bitmap images*) on the White Board.

ADDING A PICTURE TO THE WHITE BOARD

Here's how to copy a picture from a file to the White Board:

1. Click the Open File button on the White Board toolbar (or press Ctrl+O, or choose File | Open). You'll see the Open dialog box, shown in Figure 26-9.

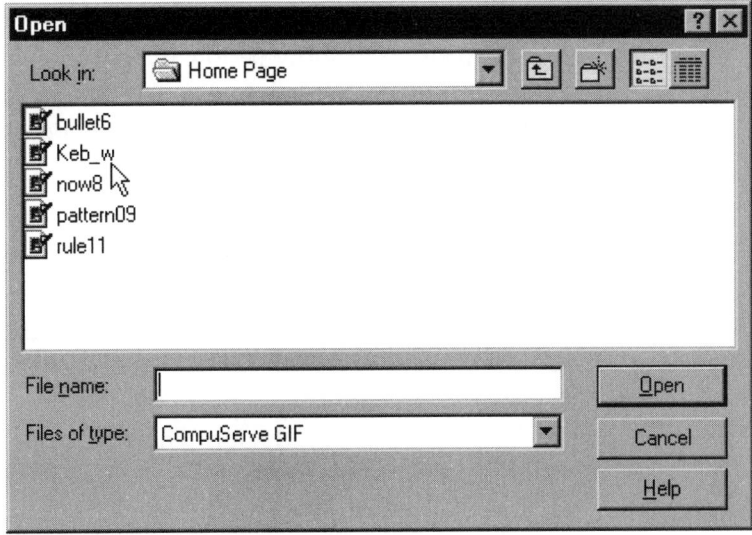

Figure 26-9: *Use the Open dialog box to locate a bitmap image stored on disk.*

2. Choose an image type from the Files Of Type drop-down list near the bottom of the Open dialog box.

3. Use standard browsing techniques to choose the disk and folder location of the file you want to copy to the White Board.

4. Double-click the filename you want to copy. You'll be returned to the White Board, and the mouse pointer will change to a cross-hair and selection marquee.

5. Position the cross-hair where the upper-left corner of the image should appear, and click your mouse button. The image appears on the White Board.

CAPTURING IMAGES TO THE WHITE BOARD

Have you ever wanted to show people the current status of a program or your desktop? CoolTalk makes this easy. Simply capture a picture of the screen and place it on your White Board for all to see. Here are the steps to follow:

1. Minimize the White Board window (if you wish), open the programs and arrange the windows you want to capture, and then return to the White Board window.

2. Open the Capture menu on the White Board menu bar, and choose the option that describes the area you want to capture—you can choose to capture the Window, the entire Desktop, or a selected Region. The White Board window will disappear temporarily.

3. If you chose Capture | Window, click on the window you want to capture. If you chose Capture | Region, draw a rectangle selection marquee around the area you want to capture. CoolTalk will copy the entire screen, the window, or the region (as appropriate) and return you to the White Board window.

4. Position the cross-hair mouse pointer where the upper-left corner of the captured image should appear, and click the mouse button. The image appears on the White Board.

COPYING & PASTING BITMAPS

You can copy material from the White Board to the Windows clipboard, and then paste it elsewhere. Here's how:

1. Click the Copy Bitmap button on the White Board toolbar, or press Ctrl+C, or choose Edit | Copy.

2. Drag a rectangle selection marquee around the material you want to copy from the White Board.

3. Click the Paste Bitmap button on the White Board toolbar (or press Ctrl+V, or choose Edit | Paste).

4. Position the cross-hair mouse pointer where the upper-left corner of the bitmap should appear, and click the mouse button. The image appears on the White Board.

Whenever you've copied material to the Windows clipboard, you can paste it onto the White Board or into any other Windows program. For example, you can copy material from the White Board, switch to another program, and choose Edit | Paste (or press Ctrl+V) to paste that material. Likewise, you can copy material from another program, switch to the White Board, and choose Paste options from the Edit menu (or use equivalent shortcuts) to place that material on the White Board.

ERASING THE WHITE BOARD

The CoolTalk White Board consists of two layers:

- The *markup layer*, which consists of drawings you've made with tools from the toolbox, as well as any material you've pasted onto the White Board from the Windows clipboard.

- The *image layer*, which consists of images you've placed on the White Board via the Capture menu or the Open File commands.

The Eraser tool will erase either the markup layer or the image layer. To choose which layer is erased by the Eraser tool, open the Options menu and then click either Erase Markups or Erase Image. (The default is Options | Erase Markups.)

If you want to erase the entire markup layer with one quick command, choose Edit | Clear Markups. Should you wish to erase the entire White Board (both the markup and the image layers), choose Edit | Clear White Board.

SAVING THE WHITE BOARD

Suppose that you've created a masterpiece on your White Board, and you want to save it for later use. Saving the White Board is easy enough to do:

1. Click the Save button on the White Board, or choose File | Save As. The Save As dialog box will open.

2. Choose an image type from the Save As Type drop-down list near the bottom of the Save As dialog box.

3. Use standard browsing techniques to choose the disk and folder location of the file you want to save.

4. In the File Name box, type the filename and extension of the file you want to save. For example, type **Ad Plan.gif** if you want to save an advertising plan and you've selected CompuServe's GIF format in the Save As Type drop-down list.

5. Click the Save button.

The White Board will be saved as a file on disk, and the title bar of the White Board window will reflect the filename and extension you typed in Step 4. The next time you open the White Board window during the current CoolTalk session, the most recently saved White Board file will open automatically.

PRINTING THE WHITE BOARD

You can print your White Board image at any time, by clicking the Print button on the White Board toolbar or choosing File | Print from the menu bar. When the Print dialog box appears (see Figure 26-10), choose the options you want, and then click OK. (If you need help with the Print options, click the Help button in the dialog box.)

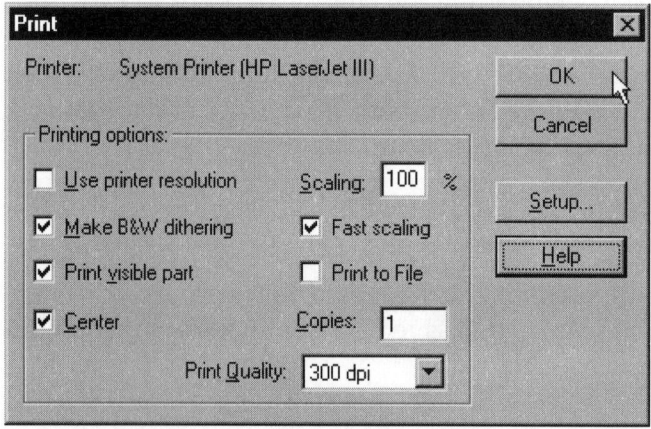

Figure 26-10: *The White Board's Print dialog box offers many printing options.*

CUSTOMIZING THE WHITE BOARD'S APPEARANCE & BEHAVIOR

The White Board's View and Options menus offer oodles of options for viewing the White Board and customizing its behavior. The View menu options let you zoom in and out on the White Board, and redraw the screen if it becomes garbled. The Options menu lets you control whether to use solid or transparent paint for fill patterns, whether to erase markups or images, whether the toolbox floats on the window, whether to hide the White Board window when you're doing a capture, and more.

CLOSING THE WHITE BOARD

When you've finished using the White Board window, you can close it. Click the White Board window's Close (X) button, or press Alt+F4, or choose File | Close from its menu bar.

USING THE ANSWERING MACHINE

CoolTalk's answering machine works much like a standard telephone answering machine, except that it works only with CoolTalk calls. If you've turned on the answering machine and you're not available to receive a CoolTalk call, the answering machine kicks in after three rings and lets the caller record a message. When you return to your computer, you can open the answering machine and listen to any message you wish. You can also call the person back, save the message to a .wav file on disk, or delete the message.

TURNING THE ANSWERING MACHINE ON OR OFF

If you want people to be able to leave messages for you when you're not available to take your CoolTalk calls, you must turn on the answering machine. To turn the answering machine on or off, click the Answering Machine button on the CoolTalk toolbar. When the button is "pushed in," the answering machine is on and will pick up your messages.

WORKING WITH YOUR MESSAGES

When someone has left you messages, the Read Messages button to the right of the Answering Machine button on the CoolTalk toolbar will display the number of messages you have. To pick up your messages, click the Read Messages button (or choose Conference | Options and click the Answering Machine tab in the Options dialog box). Figure 26-11 shows the screen after I chose Conference | Options and clicked the Answering Machine tab.

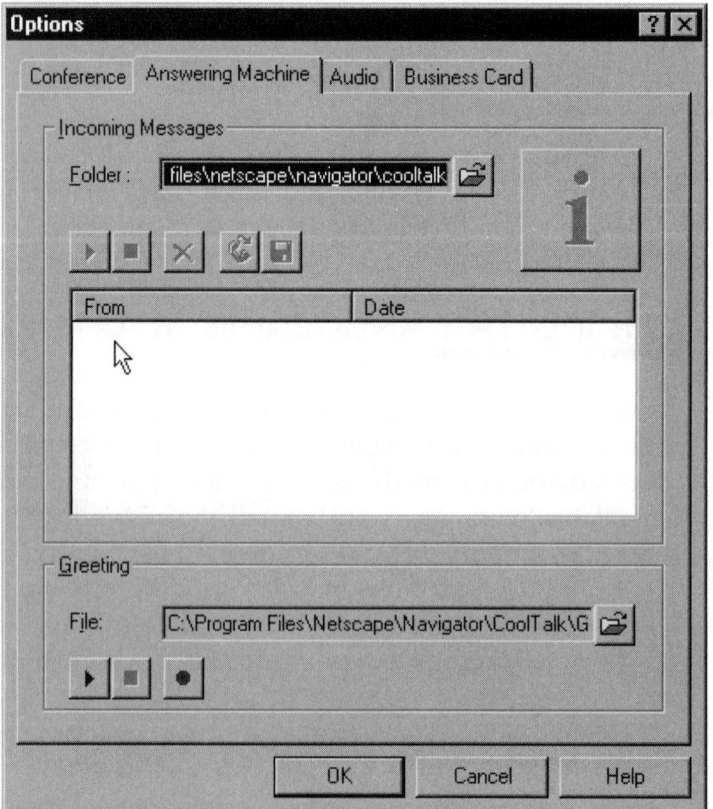

Figure 26-11: *The Answering Machine window, after choosing Conference | Options and clicking the Answering Machine tab.*

To work with a message in the Answering Machine window, click the message in the Incoming Messages list. The message will be highlighted, and the business card photo of the caller will appear in the Sender Info area of the dialog box. Now, do any of the following:

- To play the highlighted message, click the Play Message button in the dialog box.

- To stop message playback, click the Stop Playing button.

- To delete the highlighted message, click the Delete Message button.

- To call the person back, click the Call Back button.

- To save the highlighted message to a .wav file, click the Save WAVE File button and complete the Save As dialog box that appears.

- To see detailed information about the highlighted caller, click the Sender Info button.

TIP

To sort the messages by caller or by date, click the From or Date headings in the Incoming Messages list. To choose a different folder in which to store incoming messages, click the Browse button next to the Folder box, choose a new folder in the dialog box that appears, and choose OK.

LEAVING A MESSAGE FOR SOMEONE

When you call someone and an answering machine picks up the call, a dialog box will ask you to leave a message. To leave a message, speak into your microphone. When you've finished recording your message, click the Hangup button in the dialog box.

RECORDING A NEW OUTGOING MESSAGE

CoolTalk's answering machine comes with a standard greeting that does the standard job of asking callers to leave a message at the tone. If you'd prefer to greet callers with a custom message, you can record a new outgoing message at any time. Here's how:

1. Choose Conference | Options, and click the Answering Machine tab.

2. Click the Record Greeting button, and speak your outgoing message.

3. When you've finished recording, click the Stop Playing button. CoolTalk stores your message in the Greeting file in the CoolTalk installation folder.

4. To test your outgoing message, click the Play Greeting button. If you like it, you're done. If you don't like it, you can return to Step 2 and record a new message.

CUSTOMIZING THE COOLTALK OPTIONS

You can customize many CoolTalk options by choosing Conference | Options from the CoolTalk window's menu bar. When the Options dialog box opens, choose the tab that contains the options you want to customize. Here's a summary of each tab:

- The Conference tab, shown in Figure 26-12, lets you change the default IS411 Server options, select a bandwidth (14,400 bps, 28,800 bps, or higher), and choose when you'll accept CoolTalk invitations (never, when asked, or always).

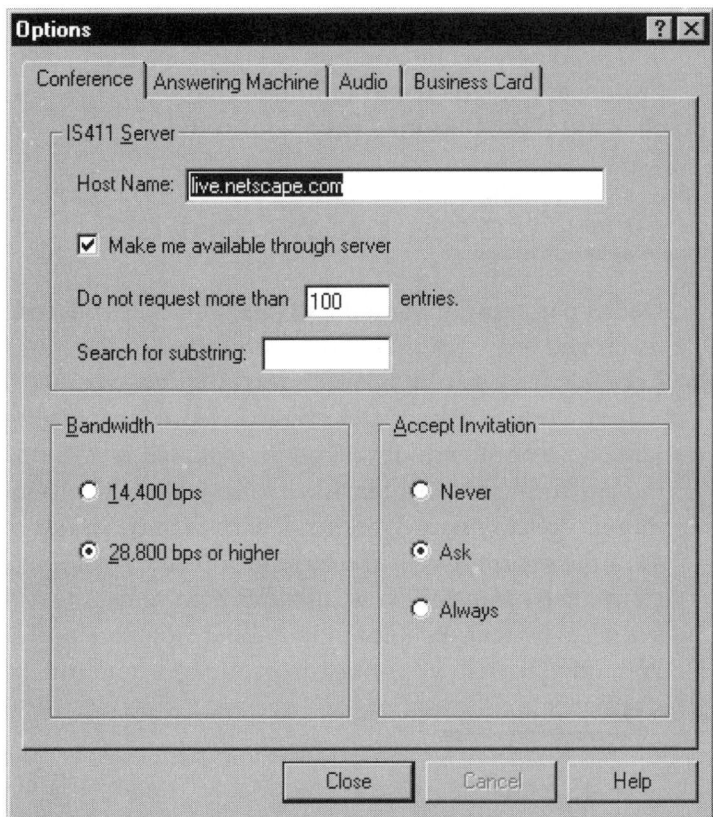

Figure 26-12: *The Conference tab of the Options dialog box.*

■ The Answering Machine tab (refer to Figure 26-11) lets you pick up messages from your answering machine and record new outgoing messages.

■ The Audio tab lets you choose whether to switch automatically between recording and playback, and allows you to select the proper recording and playback devices. You probably won't need to change the options on the Audio tab.

■ The Business Card tab lets you identify yourself to other conference members. Information on this tab is put there automatically when you use CoolTalk's Setup Wizard.

You can adjust as many options on as many tabs as you want. If you need help while you're working, click the Help button or the ? button, as explained earlier in this chapter. When you've finished, click the Close button to save your settings.

 ## SOME NOTES ON WATCHDOG

Do keep in mind that all those folks out there using CoolTalk can reach you only when 1) you're connected to the Internet, and 2) CoolTalk is open or the Watchdog is active.

If you remove the Watchdog icon from your Startup group, or you chose not to add it when you installed Netscape, you can add the Watchdog to your Startup group later. Unfortunately, there's more to getting your Watchdog to bark at the Internet than adding a simple shortcut to the Startup group. To add the icon, you must completely uninstall Netscape and then reinstall it (be sure to answer Yes when asked about installing CoolTalk and adding the Watchdog icon to your Startup group). Or you must follow these steps:

1. Right-click the Start button on the taskbar, and choose Open.

2. Double-click the Programs icon.

3. Double-click the StartUp icon.

4. Choose File | New | Shortcut from the Startup window menu bar. The Create Shortcut dialog box will open.

5. In the Command Line text box, type the following (all on one line with a space between the quoted path names):

    ```
    "C:\CoolTalk-path\wdog.exe"  "C:\CoolTalk-path\
    cooltalk.exe"
    ```

    Note that *CoolTalk-path* is the full path to your CoolTalk program. Here's a completed example in which *CoolTalk-path* is C:\Program Files\Netscape\Navigator\CoolTalk:

    ```
    "C:\Program Files\Netscape\Navigator\CoolTalk\wdog.exe"
    "C:\Program Files\Netscape\Navigator\CoolTalk\
    cooltalk.exe"
    ```

6. Click the Next button.

7. In the Select A Name For the Shortcut text box, type **CoolTalk Watchdog,** and click the Finish button.

PUTTING THE WATCHDOG TO SLEEP

You can temporarily suspend the Watchdog so that it won't monitor your system for incoming conference invitations. To do this, right-click the Watchdog icon in the Windows 95 taskbar and choose Suspend (or simply double-click the Watchdog icon in the taskbar). The same steps will reactivate the doggy. When the Watchdog is suspended, a universal "No" symbol will appear atop the Watchdog icon in the system tray; when the Watchdog is active, the Watchdog icon appears in the taskbar without the universal "No" symbol.

To turn off the Watchdog altogether, right-click its icon in the taskbar, choose Exit, and click the Yes button when asked for confirmation. You can always restart the Watchdog by choosing Start|Programs|StartUp|CoolTalk Watchdog, or by restarting your computer.

MOVING ON

Well, you've seen just how cool CoolTalk can be for sharing conversations and information with almost anyone on the planet who has CoolTalk installed—all for the price of a local call (or less). After you've set up CoolTalk, you can start a conference, converse using your microphone and speakers, share pictures and text via the White Board, and type messages via the text-based Chat Tool. It's fun, it's easy, and it's definitely cool.

In the next chapter we'll look at Netscape's built-in electronic mail features, which let you send and receive e-mail without ever leaving the comfort of your browser.

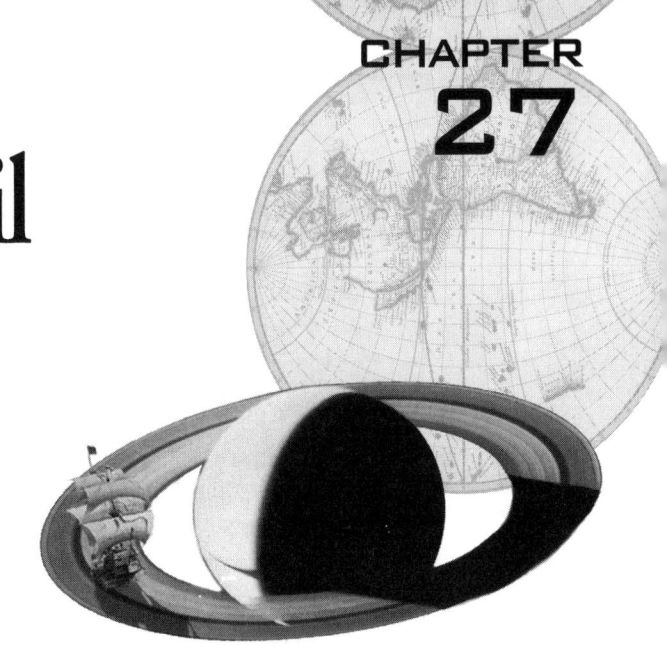

Doing E-Mail
With Gold

If you haven't already used e-mail, you've probably at least heard
of it. Everybody's doing it and for good reason. Your mail gets delivered instantly, it's free (or as close to "free" as you can get), and
you can use it to send virtually anything from your computer to
any other computer on the Internet.

Netscape Navigator makes e-mail so easy and so much fun that
you may never send a traditional letter again. In this chapter, you'll
learn about the many ways to use e-mail, including:

- How to specify an e-mail address
- How to set up Netscape to connect to your mail server
- How to get around Netscape's mail window
- How to compose and send e-mail messages
- How to read, reply to, and forward messages
- How to manage your e-mail messages and folders
- How to manage an electronic address book

With this chapter under your belt, you'll be able to communicate
electronically with anyone on the planet. And you'll have a founda-
tion of basic knowledge necessary for working with newsgroups
and mailing lists—topics discussed in Chapter 28.

UNDERSTANDING E-MAIL ADDRESSES

Before you send your first e-mail message, you must understand how to address the message. Every e-mail address has the following general form:

```
user@domain
```

In this address, *user* is the user ID of your intended recipient (for example, *alan*) and the *domain* identifies the computer on which the recipient's electronic post office is located (for example, *coolnerds.com*). Thus, the e-mail address for the user named *alan* at the domain *coolnerds.com* is *alan@coolnerds.com*.

When you type an e-mail address, you must be *exact*. No part can be misspelled, no blank spaces are allowed, and you must specify the correct upper- and lowercase letters.

FINDING PEOPLE ON THE NET

There are many ways to find out someone's e-mail address. For example, someone can give the address to you personally; the address might appear in a book, newspaper, or magazine, or on television or radio; or the address might appear automatically when you reply via e-mail to someone's message.

You can find e-mail addresses and other information about people right on the Internet, also. One of the best starting points is Netscape's "People on the Net" Web page, which takes you to a number of online directories that let you search for people and companies. To reach this handy Web site, choose Directory‖Internet White Pages from the Netscape menu bar, or point your browser to http://home.netscape.com/home/internet-white-pages.html. Then, click on the hyperlink for the directory you want to use. Some of my favorite hyperlinks on this page include Bigfoot, Four11 Directory Service, OKRA, and Who Where.

TRAP

If the e-mail address you specify is invalid or unreachable, the electronic post office will "bounce" the e-mail message back to you, along with an explanation of what went wrong.

E-MAIL ADDRESSES FOR ONLINE SERVICES

Many people use online services such as America Online (AOL), CompuServe, and MCI Mail, rather than plain old Internet PPP or SLIP accounts. You can exchange e-mail with these people, no sweat. You must do a little translation, however, to convert their user ID numbers into valid Internet e-mail addresses. Table 27-1 explains how to translate sample user IDs from the most popular online services into valid Internet e-mail addresses, in the form *user@domain*.

Service	Online Service User ID	Internet E-Mail Address	Comments
America Online	joe cool	joecool@aol.com	Remove any spaces from the AOL user's screen name and append *@aol.com*.
AT&T Mail	joecool	joecool@attmail.com	Append *@attmail*.com to the AT&T username.
CompuServe	72420,2236	72420.2236@ compuserve.com	Change the comma in the CompuServe user ID to a period and append *@compuserve.com*.
MCI Mail	123-4747	1234747@ mcimail.com	Remove the hyphen in the MCI Mail address and append *@mcimail.com*.

Service	Online Service User ID	Internet E-Mail Address	Comments
MCI Mail	jcool	jcool@mcimail.com	Append *@mcimail*.com to the MCI "handle" or abbreviated name.
	Joe Cool	joe_cool@ mcimail.com	Change the space in the MCI Mail full name to an underscore and append *@mcimail.com*.
Prodigy	joe123 cool	joe123@prodigy.com	Remove any spaces from the Prodigy user ID and append *@prodigy.com*.

Table 27-1: *User IDs on various online services and their equivalent Internet e-mail addresses.*

If you are using the *same* online service as your intended recipients, you can send e-mail directly to their user IDs on the service. Suppose, for example, that you're on CompuServe, and you want to send a message to the CompuServe user whose ID is 72420,2236. In this case, you can use CompuServe's Mail | Create/Send Mail command to address the message directly to 72420,2236. By contrast, if you're using a PPP or SLIP account on my Internet provider (rather than CompuServe), you must address the message to 72420.2236@compuserve.com.

GETTING SET UP

Before you can send or receive e-mail through Netscape, you need to complete the following setup steps:

1. From any Netscape window, choose Options | Mail And News Preferences, and click the Servers tab. Figure 27-1 shows a completed Servers tab. (Of course, you should provide information for *your* account, not for the account shown in the example.)

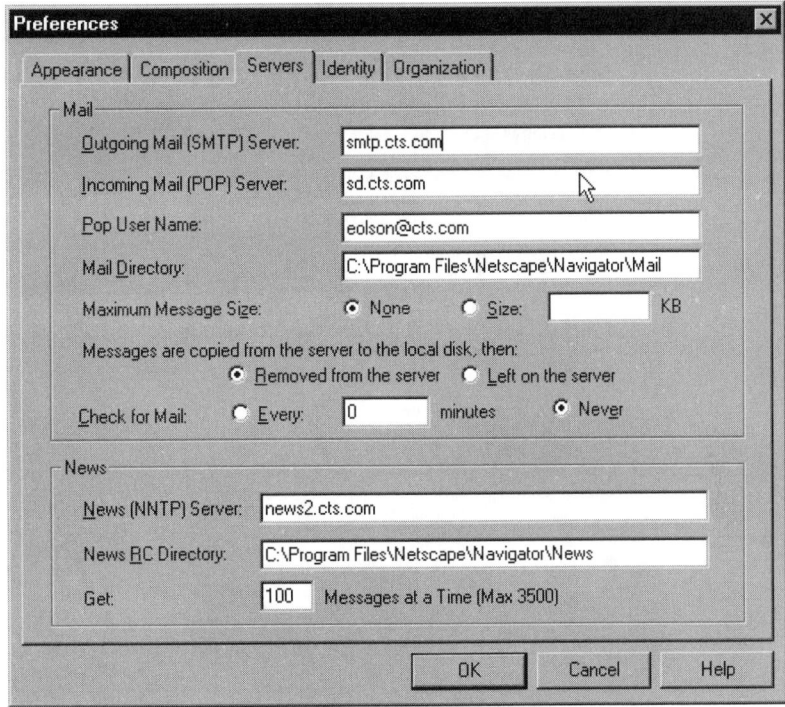

Figure 27-1: *The Servers tab of the Preferences dialog box, with some sample information filled in.*

2. On the Servers tab, specify the correct Outgoing Mail (SMTP) Server, Incoming Mail (POP) Server, and Pop User Name (usually your e-mail address) for your account. Ask your Internet Service Provider for this information if you don't know it already. You can change the other settings on the Servers tab if you want, though it's not necessary.

3. Click the Identity tab. Figure 27-2 shows an example of a completed Identity tab. (Again, be sure to provide your own information rather than using my example.)

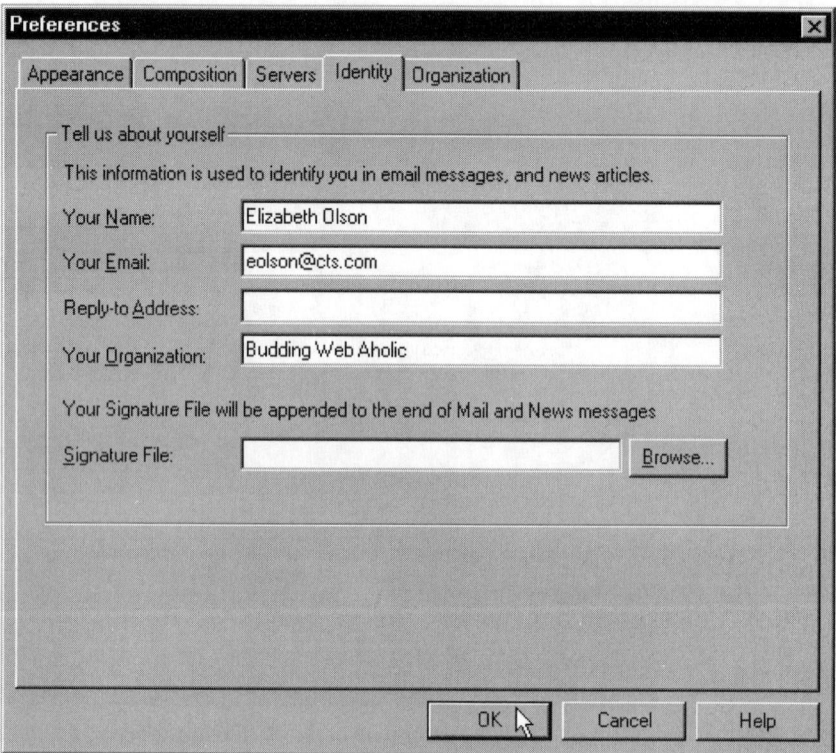

Figure 27-2: *The Identity tab of the Preferences dialog box, with some sample information filled in.*

4. On the Identity tab, specify Your Name and Your Email address. If you want people to send replies to a different electronic mailbox than the one you're using to send messages, specify the alternative mailbox name in the Reply-To-Address text box. The other items on this tab are optional.

5. Choose OK to save your changes.

With just the few exceptions mentioned in Steps 2 and 4, you can stick with the default settings on the Preferences tabs. Should you need more information about any Preferences option, simply click on the appropriate tab in the Preferences dialog box, and then click the Help button.

TIP

If you're a dyed-in-the-wool Microsoft Exchange user, you can force Netscape to use Exchange rather than Netscape's own e-mail system. To do this, choose Options | Mail And News Preferences from the Netscape menu bar, click the Appearance tab, choose Use Exchange Client For Mail And News, and choose OK. Then skip the rest of this chapter.

ABOUT SIGNATURE FILES

When you create an e-mail message, Netscape can automatically "sign" the message for you. For example, you might want to sign your messages automatically with the text:

Best regards,

Hanley Strappman

strappman@rnaa47.com

To set up Netscape so that it will sign your messages automatically, use a text editor such as Notepad to type and store the signature text in a file named *sig.txt* (or a similar filename). Then, return to Netscape, choose Options|Mail And News Preferences from the menu bar, click the Identity tab, click the Browse button, locate and double-click the signature filename, and choose OK.

GETTING AROUND

After you've finished the setup steps, you're ready to use Netscape to send and receive e-mail messages. The first step is to open the Netscape Mail window, using any of the following methods:

- Choose Window | Netscape Mail from any Netscape menu bar.

- Click the envelope icon at the right edge of the Netscape status bar.

■   Click a "mailto:" hyperlink on any Web page.

Figure 27-3 shows an example of the Netscape Mail window after clicking the Inbox folder in the top-left pane of the window and then clicking on the message from Mozilla in the top-right pane of the window. The selected message from Mozilla appears in the gray pane at the bottom of the window. (The first time you open the Netscape Mail window, you'll be greeted by a message from Mozilla, Netscape's dragon mascot.)

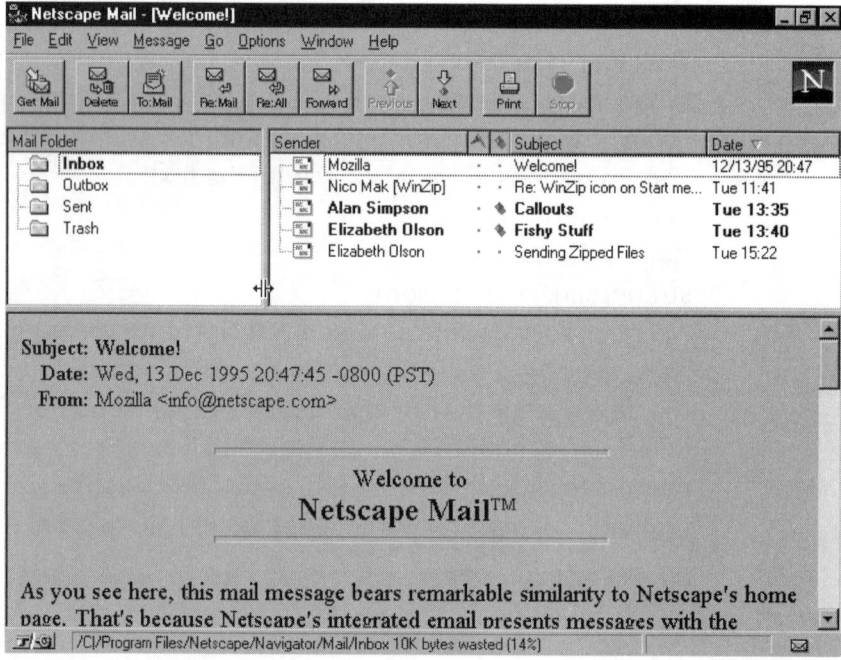

Figure 27-3: *The Netscape Mail window after choosing a folder (Inbox) and a message (from Mozilla).*

You can leave the Netscape Mail window and return to the Netscape browser window by clicking the browser's button in the Windows 95 taskbar, or by choosing the appropriate window from the bottom of any Netscape Window menu. If no browser window is open, you can open a new one by choosing File | New Web Browser, or pressing Ctrl+N in the Netscape Mail window.

Using the Netscape Mail Window

Figure 27-3 shows the three panes of the Netscape Mail window. The top-left pane shows your message folders, the number of unread messages, and the total number of messages in each folder. If a folder contains unread messages, its folder name will appear in **boldface**.

Descriptions of the standard folders (you'll learn how to create folders of your own, later in this chapter) follow:

- Inbox folder stores incoming messages.

- Outbox folder stores messages you're in the process of sending. Netscape automatically moves messages from the Outbox folder to the Sent folder after sending them. (If the Outbox folder isn't displayed in your Netscape Mail window, it will appear as soon as you create and send a message.)

- Sent folder stores messages you've sent.

- Trash folder stores messages you've deleted. (If this folder isn't shown in your Netscape Mail window, it will appear as soon as you delete a message.)

The top-right pane shows messages in the current folder. Information about unread messages appears in boldface; information about messages you've already read appears in normal (nonbold) text.

The bottom pane shows the contents of the current message.

TIP

If you want to adjust the layout of the Netscape Mail window panes, choose Options | Mail And News Preferences, and click the Appearance tab. Then, choose the layout you want in the Pane Layout area of the dialog box. Your options are Split Horizontal (the default arrangement described in this chapter), Split Vertical, and Stack.

SELECTING & VIEWING A MESSAGE

Viewing a message is a snap. In the top-left pane, click the folder that contains the message you want to view. Then, in the top-right pane, click the message you want to see. The message will be highlighted in the top-right pane, and the text of the message will appear in the bottom pane. You can use the vertical and horizontal scroll bars, as needed, to view the message in the bottom pane.

ADJUSTING THE NETSCAPE MAIL WINDOW PANES

Adjusting the Netscape Mail window panes and columns is no pain at all. Here are some ways to do it:

- To resize the upper panes, move the mouse pointer to the vertical border between the panes. When the mouse pointer changes to a two-headed arrow with cross hair, drag the border to the left or right.

- To resize the bottom pane, move the mouse pointer to the horizontal border above the bottom pane. When the mouse pointer changes to a two-headed arrow with cross hair, drag the border up or down.

- To resize the columns shown in the upper panes, move the mouse pointer to the vertical line just to the right of the column heading "button" for the column you want to adjust. When the mouse pointer changes to a two-headed arrow with cross hair, drag the line to the left or right.

- To rearrange the columns shown in the upper panes, move the mouse pointer inside the column heading button for the column you want to adjust. When the mouse pointer changes to a hollow arrow, drag the column heading to the left or right.

- To sort the messages in the top-right pane according to text in a particular column, click the column heading button for the column you want to sort. For example, click the Subject column heading button to sort messages by subject. (Note that Netscape ignores Re: and Fwd: text in the Subject line when sorting. For other sorting alternatives, choose View I Sort, and then choose the option you want.)

TIP

To change the default sort order, choose Options | Mail And News Preferences, click the Organization tab, pick a Sort Mail By option in the Sorting area of the Preferences dialog box, and choose OK.

EXPLORING THE NETSCAPE MAIL COMMANDS

The buttons on the Netscape Mail window's toolbar offer some of the handiest ways to work with Netscape e-mail. From left to right, here's what each button on the toolbar will do, along with each button's equivalent menu bar options and shortcut keys:

- Get Mail checks your electronic post office for new e-mail. (Same as choosing File | Get New Mail from the menu bar, or pressing Ctrl+T in the Netscape Mail window, or clicking the envelope icon at the right edge of the status bar in any Netscape window.)

- Delete deletes the current message. (Same as choosing Edit | Delete Message from the menu bar, or pressing Delete.)

- To: Mail lets you compose a new message. (Same as choosing File | New Mail Message from the menu bar, or pressing Ctrl+M.)

- Re: Mail lets you reply to the sender of the current message. (Same as choosing Message | Reply from the menu bar, or pressing Ctrl+R.)

- Re: All lets you reply to the sender and all other recipients of the current message. (Same as choosing Message | Reply To All from the menu bar, or pressing Ctrl+Shift+R.)

- Forward lets you forward the current message, as an attachment, to anyone you want. (Same as choosing Message | Forward from the menu bar, or pressing Ctrl+L.)

- Previous displays the previous unread message. (Same as choosing Go | Previous Unread from the menu bar.)

- Next displays the next unread message. (Same as choosing Go | Next Unread from the menu bar.)

- Print prints the current message. (Same as choosing File | Print from the menu bar, or pressing Ctrl+P.)

- Stop interrupts the current transfer. (Same as choosing Go | Stop Loading from the menu bar, or pressing Esc.)

In addition to using the buttons, menu options, and shortcut keys to choose commands, you can right-click an item on the screen and choose options from the shortcut menu that appears, just as you can in many places throughout Windows 95.

GETTING HELP

There are several ways to get help while you're using the Netscape Mail system, including the following:

- Pull down a menu, point to an option, and read the help message that appears on the status bar.

- Point to a button on the toolbar, and then read the pop-up ToolTip and the help message on the status bar.

- Click the Help button if it's available in a dialog box. A standard Help window will provide information about using the dialog box.

COMPOSING & SENDING E-MAIL MESSAGES

Most of your e-mail activities will consist of composing and sending e-mail messages, reading messages, and replying to them. We'll look first at the steps for composing and sending an e-mail message.

TIP

When you're first learning to use e-mail, it's best to compose and send messages to your own e-mail address, a technique that gives you immediate feedback about what other people might see when you send them a message.

To compose and send an e-mail message, follow these steps:

1. Starting from the Netscape Mail window, click the To: Mail button on the toolbar, or press Ctrl+M, or choose File | New Mail Message. A message composition window will open. Figure 27-4 shows the message composition window after I filled out the most important items for the message.

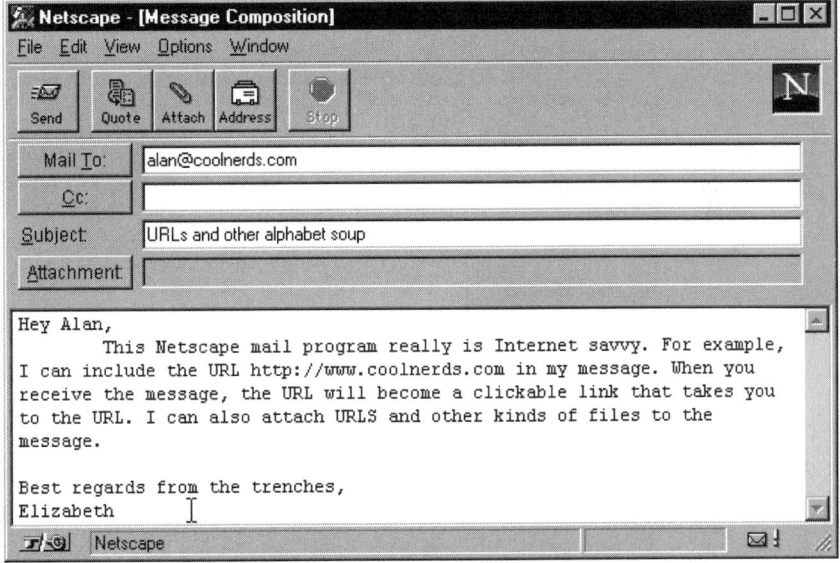

Figure 27-4: *A new message that's ready to send.*

2. In the box next to the Mail To: button, specify the e-mail address or the nickname of your main recipient(s). Use either of these methods to fill in an e-mail address:

   ■ To enter the address or nickname manually, type the address or nickname into the text box. If you want to include more than one recipient, use a comma (,) to separate each recipient name.

   ■ To select names or address lists from the electronic address book, click the Mail To: button or the Address toolbar button. The Select Addresses dialog box will open (see Figure 27-5 for an example). Now, either double-click an address in the Select Addresses dialog box or click an address and then click the To:, Cc, or Bcc button to add the selection to the appropriate box in the message composition window (repeat this step as needed). When you've finished adding addresses, choose OK.

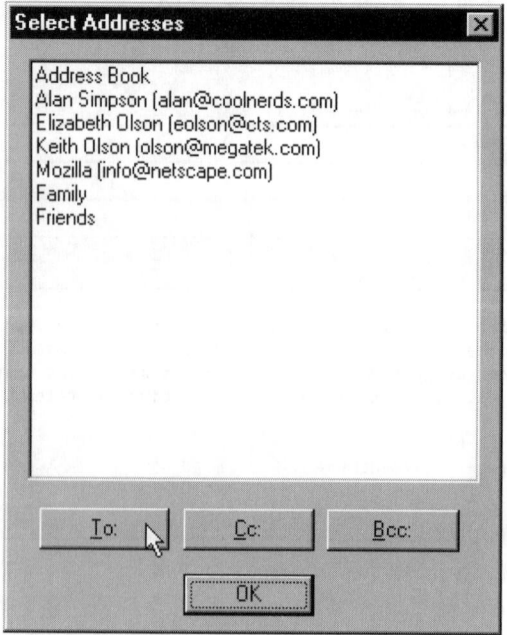

Figure 27-5: *The Select Addresses dialog box.*

The Netscape address book stores individual e-mail addresses and nick-names as well as address lists that automatically send the same mes-sage simultaneously to several e-mail addresses. You'll learn how to set up the address book later in this chapter.

3. In the box next to the Cc: button, specify the e-mail address or the nickname of anyone who should receive a copy of your message. You can either type the address or nickname into the text box or click the Cc: button or Address toolbar button to select an address from the address book. This step is optional.

BLIND CARBON COPIES

To send a blind carbon copy of your message, choose View|Mail Bcc from the message composition window's menu bar, and enter the appropriate e-mail address in the box next to the Blind Cc: button that appears. The names of the Mail To: and Cc: recipients are visible to all message recipients. The names of the Blind Cc: recipients, however, are hidden from other recipients. Other options on the View menu display let you fill in additional fields at the top of your message.

4. In the Subject box, type a descriptive subject for your message.

5. If you want to include attachments in your message, click the Attachment: button below the Subject line, or click the Attach button on the toolbar. Then, complete the Attachments dialog box that appears, and choose OK. There's more about attachments later in this chapter.

6. In the white message editing area below the Attachment: line, type the message text as you would in any text editor, such as Notepad. You can position the insertion point, select text, insert and delete text, and copy, cut, and paste text, using standard Windows techniques. If you include a standard URL or a mailto: tag in your message—for example, *http://www.coolnerds.com* or *mailto:alan@coolnerds.com*—that text will become a clickable hypertext link when the recipient opens your message.

TIP

To paste a URL from the browser into your e-mail message, switch to the Netscape browser window, browse to the URL you want to copy, and double-click the chainlink icon next to the Location: box. Then, return to the message composition window, position the insertion point where the URL should appear, and press Ctrl+V to paste it in.

7. When you're ready to send the message, click the Send button in the message composition window's toolbar, or choose File | Send Now, or press Ctrl+Enter.

If you aren't connected to your ISP at the moment you finish typing your e-mail message, you can defer delivery until you are connected. Choose Options | Deferred Delivery from the message composition menu bar *before* you send the message. Your messages will remain in the Outbox until you reconnect to your ISP and choose File | Send Mail In Outbox, or press Ctrl+H, to send them on their way. To resume immediate delivery of messages after choosing a deferred delivery method, choose Options | Immediate Delivery from the message composition menu bar.

E-MAIL ETIQUETTE

Citizens of the Internet (also called *netizens*) will appreciate it if you follow certain rules of etiquette when composing and replying to e-mail messages. Here are the most important rules you'll need to know:

■ *Watch your tone,* and be as polite as you can. If necessary, use emoticons—tiny pictures drawn with punctuation characters—to convey your mood. The most commonly used emoticons are the smiley face :-) and the frown :-(.

■ *Don't flame.* That is, don't write anything in anger and never write anything you would be afraid to see in a court of law.

➡

- *Don't SHOUT by writing everything in CAPITAL LETTERS.* Shouting annoys people to no end and may cause them to flame *you*. If necessary, use *asterisks* around words you want to emphasize.

- *Specify e-mail addresses carefully,* and double-check your address lists before you send e-mail that's sensitive in nature.

- *Use short paragraphs* and an informal writing style.

- *Make the subject line informative.* Your Subject line appears in the Subject column of the Mailbox window and helps recipients decide when (or whether) to read your messages.

- *When replying to a message,* delete quoted material from the original message that isn't relevant to your response. Indicate edited material with ellipses (...) or some other text to indicate that information is missing.

- *Check for mistakes* in spelling and punctuation to avoid appearing careless.

CREATING ATTACHMENTS

You can attach entire files to your messages. The attachments will appear at the bottom of the message when your recipient reads it. To create an attachment while you're composing a message, follow these steps:

1. In the message composition window, click the Attachment: button below the Subject: line, or click the Attach toolbar button, or choose File | Attach File. The Attachments dialog box will appear. Figure 27-6 shows a completed Attachments dialog box, after I chose to attach a URL and a file.

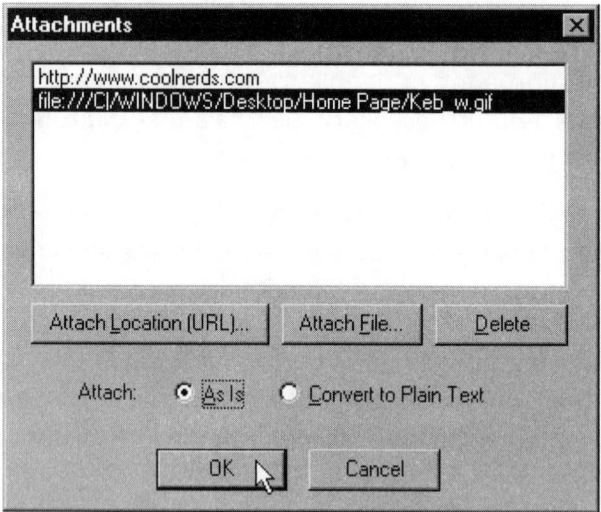

Figure 27-6: *An Attachments dialog box after choosing to attach a URL and a file to the message.*

2. Do either of the following:

   ■ To attach a URL (for example, an entire HTML Web page) to the message, click the Attach Location (URL) button, type the URL into the dialog box that appears, and choose OK.

   ■ To attach a file to the message, click the Attach File button. Then, locate and double-click the file you want to attach. You can attach any kind of file you want.

3. If you want to attach the URL or file as-is (without conversion), choose the As Is option. If you prefer to convert the URL or file to plain text, choose the Convert To Plain Text option. Use the Convert To Plain Text option when you don't know if the recipient has the appropriate software for interpretting your formatted text.

4. You can repeat Steps 2 and 3 as necessary. If you've attached a URL or file by mistake, click on it in the list of attachments, and then click the Delete button.

5. When you've finished choosing the attachments for your message, click OK to return to the message composition window.

SOME TECHNICAL MIME STUFF

By default, Netscape sends messages in an 8-bit format that accommodates the widest range of e-mail servers in the United States and Europe. If your message recipients complain that your attachments look garbled or are corrupted in some way, you may need to choose a MIME-compliant format to prevent non-ASCII characters from being misinterpreted. MIME, which stands for Multipurpose Internet Mail Extensions, is the Internet standard for sending messages across multiple platforms (i.e., Windows, Mac, Unix.) Non-ASCII characters are the formatting characters you normally don't see, such as line breaks, paragraph breaks, and so forth.

To select the format used when composing mail and news messages, choose Options|Mail And News Preferences from any Netscape menu bar, and click the Composition tab. Then choose either Allow 8-Bit to use the default 8-bit format, or choose Mime Compliant (Quoted Printable) to use the format required by MIME mail readers. Choose OK to save your settings.

PICKING UP YOUR MAIL

Messages that others have sent to you are stored on your Internet Service Provider's mail server computer until you pick them up and transfer them to your own computer. When you first open the Netscape Mail window, Netscape will contact your incoming POP mail server automatically and transfer any new mail to you. You can ask for delivery of new mail at any time, however, by connecting to your ISP (if you haven't done so already) and doing any of the following:

- Choose File I Get New Mail from the Netscape Mail window menu bar.
- Click the Get Mail button on the Netscape Mail window toolbar.
- Press Ctrl+T in the Netscape Mail window.
- Click the envelope icon at the right edge of any Netscape window status bar.

TIP

A question mark (?) next to the envelope icon means that Netscape can't automatically check your mail server. So there may, or may not, be new mail waiting for you. An exclamation point (!) next to the envelope icon means that you have new messages.

If you're prompted for your POP3 user password, type your password (it'll appear as a series of asterisks, for privacy) and choose OK or press Enter. If you have any new mail, Netscape will open the Inbox folder and display the newest message in the bottom pane of the window.

TIP

To make Netscape remember your password so that you won't be prompted for it again during this or any other Netscape session, choose Options I Mail And News Preferences, click the Organization tab, select (check) Remember Mail Password, and choose OK.

READING A MESSAGE

Reading your messages is an effortless job. Simply click the folder you want to work with (usually the Inbox folder) and then click the message you want to read. The message appears in the gray pane at the bottom of the window (refer to Figure 27-3). You can scroll through the message and click any hyperlinks it contains.

By default, the header at the top of the message includes basic information such as the Subject, Date, From, Reply-To, Organization, and To lines. To get more control over how much header information is displayed, choose Options | Show Headers, and then choose All (lots of stuff), Normal (the default information), or Brief (the concise *Cliff's Notes* version).

MARKING MESSAGES AS READ OR UNREAD

In the top-right pane of the Netscape Mail window, the information lines for unread messages appear in boldface and have a small green icon just to the left of the Subject information. The lines for messages you've read appear in normal type and have a little dot next to the Subject information. Figure 27-7 shows some examples.

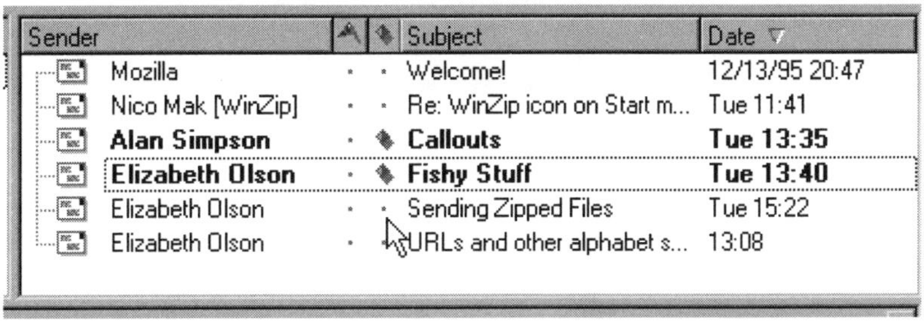

Figure 27-7: *In the top-right pane, unread messages are in boldface, with little "unread" icons next to the Subject line.*

If you want to display only unread messages in the top-right pane, choose Options | Show Only Unread Messages from the Netscape Mail menu bar. To display all the messages again, choose Options | Show All Messages.

Sometimes it's handy to toggle messages between their "read" and "unread" status. For example, if you've read a message but aren't ready to respond to it, you can mark it as unread as a reminder to attend to it later. To toggle a message between its read and unread status, click the icon or dot that's just to the left of the message's Subject information in the top-right pane. Alternatively; click on the message you want to change, and choose Message | Mark As Read or Message | Mark As Unread from the menu bar.

WORKING WITH ATTACHMENTS

The appearance of an attachment at the bottom of a message will depend on the type of data in the attachment and whether you're viewing attachments inline or as links. Figure 27-8 shows a .gif file, viewed as an inline item. Figure 27-9 shows the same file, viewed as a link. To tell Netscape how to display e-mail attachments, choose either View | Attachments Inline or View | Attachments As Links from the Netscape Mail menu bar.

Figure 27-8: *A .gif file displayed inline.*

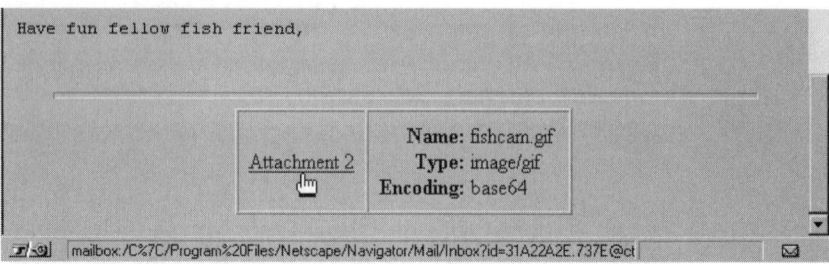

Figure 27-9: *The same .gif file displayed as a link.*

To display an attachment that appears as a link, simply click its colored hyperlink (in Figure 27-9, for example, I clicked the *Attachment 2* hyperlink, to view the attachment). You may see the attachment itself, or you might see a dialog box that requires you to take some action in order to view or work with the attachment. For instance, a Save As dialog box might prompt you to save the attachment as a file on your hard disk. An Unknown File Type dialog box might prompt you to ask Netscape for more information, to pick an application to associate with the type of file in the attachment, to save the file to disk, or to cancel the operation.

TRAP

If the attachment hides the original message in the bottom pane of the Netscape Mail window, you can redisplay the message by clicking the appropriate message line in the top-right pane of the window.

 ## REPLYING TO OR FORWARDING A MESSAGE

You can reply to the sender of a message, or to the sender and all recipients of a message. You also can forward any message to another person who can be reached via e-mail. Here are the steps to follow:

1. Select the folder that contains the message you want to reply to or forward, if it isn't selected already. Then, select the message you want to reply to or forward (again, if it isn't selected already).

2. Do one of the following:

   ■ To reply to the sender of the message, click the Re: Mail button on the Netscape Mail toolbar (or choose Message | Reply, or press Ctrl+R).

   ■ To reply to the sender of the message and anyone who received the original message, click the Re: All button on the Netscape Mail toolbar (or choose Message | Reply To All, or press Ctrl+Shift+R). Before choosing this option, be sure you *really* want everyone who received the original message to receive your reply also.

   ■ To forward the message to anyone in cyberspace, click the Forward button on the Netscape Mail toolbar (or choose Message | Forward, or press Ctrl+L).

3. A new message composition window (which resembles Figure 27-4) will open. In this window, you can fill in the message form as you would when composing a new message. Here are some points to ponder about replies and forwards:

■ Replies: The Mail To line is filled in automatically and you cannot change it. The Subject: line shows the original subject, preceded by *Re:* to indicate a reply (you can change this). The original message appears in the message editing area; each line of the original message is preceded by a greater than symbol (>), as shown in Figure 27-10. The insertion point appears at the bottom of the original message, but you can place it anywhere in the message editing area before you type your reply.

■ Forwards: The insertion point appears in the Mail To line, so that you can address the message. The Subject line shows the original subject, enclosed in square brackets and preceded by *Fwd:* to indicate a forward (you can change this). A reference to the original message appears in the gray Attachment: box. (You can click the Attachment: button to attach additional items, if you want.)

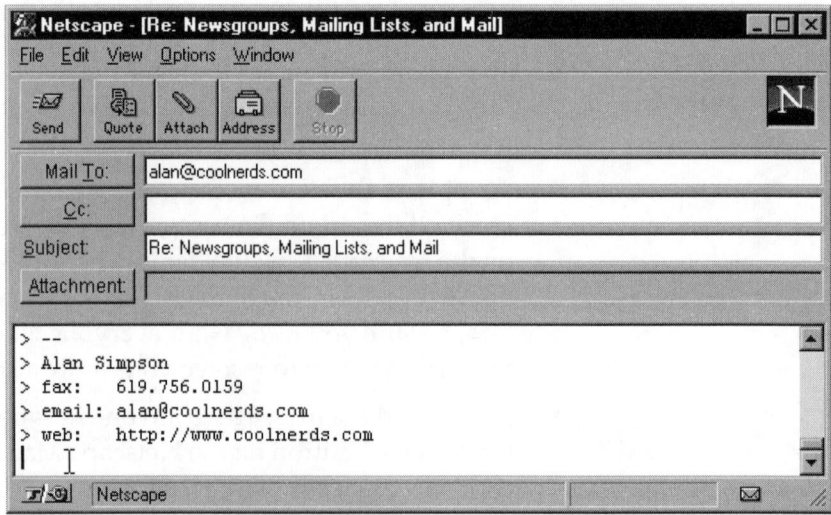

Figure 27-10: *The message composition window for a sample reply to a message.*

4. When you've finished editing your reply or forwarded message, click the Send button on the toolbar, press Ctrl+Enter, or choose File | Send Now.

MANAGING YOUR MESSAGES & FOLDERS

You now know the basics of working with electronic mail. The following sections offer some tips that'll help you push the envelope of your knowledge about e-mail. Let's start with a couple of tips for saving and printing your messages:

■ To save the current message to a disk file, choose File | Save As, or press Ctrl+S. Then, type a valid filename, locate the drive and directory where you want to store the message, and click Save or press Enter.

■ To print the current message, click the Print button on the toolbar, choose File | Print, or press Ctrl+P. Then, complete the Print dialog box and choose OK.

SELECTING MESSAGES

After you've sent and received a number of messages, you'll probably want to organize them so that you can find them easily. You'll also want to delete unnecessary messages so that they don't waste space on your hard disk.

To work with messages, you first select (highlight) the folder that contains the messages by clicking on the folder in the top-left pane. Next, you select the message or messages you want to move, copy, or delete. Finally, you move, copy, or delete the selected message(s).

Here's how to select one or more messages in the current folder:

■ To select one message, click it in the top-right pane.

■ To select several adjacent messages, click the first message you want to select. Then, hold down the Shift key and click the last message you want to select (that is, *Shift-click* the last message you want to select).

■ To select several nonadjacent messages, click the first message you want to select. Then, hold down the Ctrl key and click each additional message you want to select (that is, *Ctrl-click* each entry). If you select a message accidentally, Ctrl-click it again to deselect the message.

The selected messages are highlighted in the top-right pane.

MOVING, COPYING & DELETING MESSAGES

After you've highlighted the message(s) you want to work with, you can move, copy, or delete them as follows:

■ To move the selected messages to a different folder, move the mouse pointer to any of the highlighted messages, hold down the left mouse button, and drag the selected messages to another folder. The messages will be moved to the folder you chose.

■ To copy (duplicate) the selected messages to another folder, move the mouse pointer to any of the highlighted messages, hold down the left mouse button *and* the Ctrl key, and drag the selected messages to another folder. The messages will be copied to the folder you chose.

■ To delete the selected messages, press the Delete key (or click the Delete button on the toolbar, or choose Edit | Delete Message). The messages will be moved to the Trash folder.

Deleted messages remain in the Trash folder until you empty the trash. To permanently delete individual messages in the Trash, click the Trash folder, select the messages you want to delete, and press Delete. To completely empty the Trash folder in one fell swoop, choose File | Empty Trash Folder.

FINDING A MESSAGE

Suppose that you have many messages in your Netscape Mail window and you want to find a specific message, or you want to find specific information in the current message. No problem! Simply use the Find command to locate the message or text. Here's how:

1. Click the folder you want to search in or click the message you want to search.

2. Choose Edit | Find or press Ctrl+F. You'll see the Find dialog box, shown in Figure 27-11.

Figure 27-11: *Use Find to locate messages in the current folder or to find specific text in the current message.*

3. In the Find text box, type the text you want to find.

4. In the Find In area, choose whether to search Message Headers in This Folder or to search the Body of This Message.

5. Optionally, choose Up or Down to pick a search direction, and select (check) or deselect (clear) Match Case to choose whether to match the exact upper- and lowercase letters you typed into the Find box.

6. Click Find Next to start the search.

Depending on your choice in Step 5, Find highlights the next message header that matches your search text, or the next matching text in the current message. If Find doesn't find a match, a "Search String Not Found!" message appears. (Choose OK to remove it from the screen.) To repeat the search, choose Edit | Find Again, or press F3.

MANAGING YOUR FOLDERS

Netscape comes with an Inbox and Sent folder and creates the
Outbox and Trash folders as necessary. But just as you can create
new folders in Windows 95 to organize your files more efficiently,
you can create new folders also in Netscape Mail to organize your
messages. Creating a folder is easy:

1. From the Netscape Mail menu bar, choose File | Add Folder.

2. When prompted for a folder name, type the name for your
   new folder.

3. Choose OK or press Enter.

The new folder will appear in the top-left pane of the Netscape
Mail window. (Folder names that you create are listed in alphabetical
order below the standard Inbox, Outbox, Sent, and Trash folders.)

After you've created a folder, you can move and copy messages
to the folder and delete messages from the folder, as explained earlier. If you want to delete a folder, first delete all the messages in the
folder. Then, click the folder in the top-left pane of the Netscape
Mail window, and press the Delete key (or choose Edit | Delete
Folder from the menu bar).

COMPRESSING FOLDERS

As you add and remove messages in folders, space may be wasted
in the folder and on your hard disk. To compress a folder and re-
cover the wasted space, choose File | Compress Folder, or press
Ctrl+K. (Sometimes Netscape will warn you that a folder contains
wasted space and will give you a chance to compress the folder if
you want.)

TIP

To find out how much space is being wasted in a folder, click the folder in the top-left pane and look at the status bar. You'll see a message indicating the current folder name and the number of bytes wasted.

MANAGING YOUR ADDRESS BOOK

You can use the Netscape address book to store frequently used e-mail addresses and nicknames. While composing or forwarding messages, you can specify message recipients by choosing names from the address book or by typing a nickname (rather than a complete e-mail address).

ADDING ADDRESSES AUTOMATICALLY

Suppose that one of your folders contains a message sent by someone whose e-mail address you want to add to your address book. Here's a quick way to put that person's e-mail address in the address book:

1. In the top-left pane of the Netscape Mail window, select the folder that contains the message. Then, in the top-right pane, click the message that contains the e-mail address you want to copy to your address book.

2. Choose Message | Add To Address Book from the menu bar. You'll see an Address Book dialog box that resembles Figure 27-12.

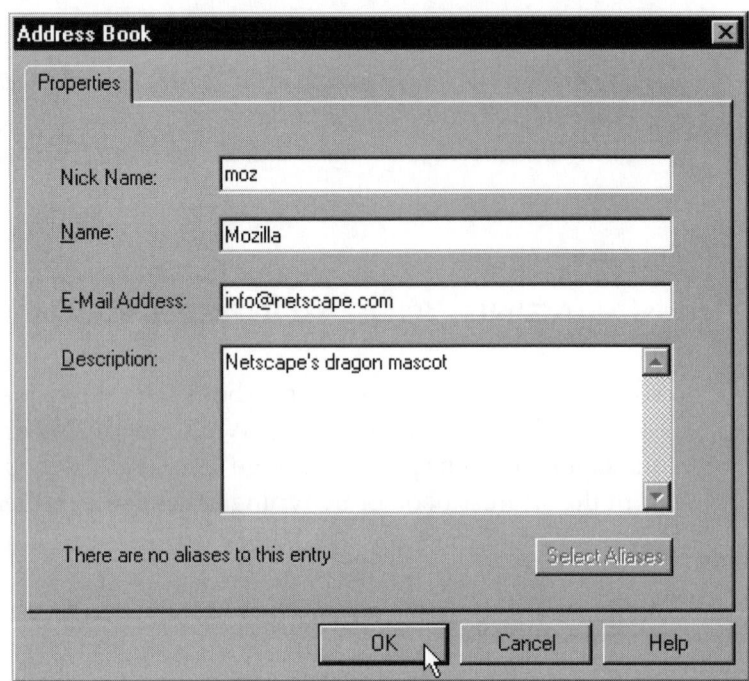

Figure 27-12: *Use the Address Book dialog box to quickly add an address to the address book.*

3. If you want to be able to type a short nickname in the Mail To:, Cc:, and Blind Cc: boxes when you're sending a message, type the nickname in the Nick Name text box. The nickname must contain only lowercase letters and numbers (no uppercase letters or spaces are allowed).

4. Edit or fill in the Name, E-Mail Address, and Description boxes, as necessary.

5. Choose OK to add the address to your address book.

UPDATING THE ADDRESS BOOK MANUALLY

If you need to update the address book manually (for example, to add or delete addresses or to create address lists), choose Window | Address Book from any Netscape window. Figure 27-13 shows an address book that contains four e-mail addresses (Alan Simpson, Elizabeth Olson, Keith Olson, and Mozilla) and two address lists (Family and Friends).

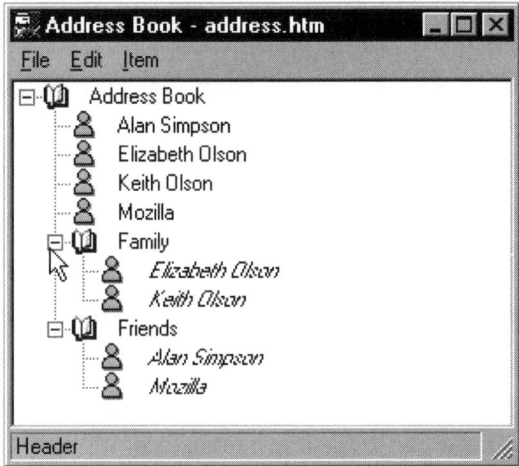

Figure 27-13: *This Address Book window contains several e-mail addresses and two address lists.*

The Address Book window is arranged hierarchically, and it works very much like the Windows Explorer window. For example, you can double-click any book icon to expand (view) or collapse (hide) the entries below the icon. You can also click an item to select it; and then Ctrl-click items to select nonadjacent items, or Shift-click items to select adjacent items.

ADDING A NEW USER

Adding a new e-mail address to the Address Book window is easy. Simply choose Item | Add User from the Address Book window's menu bar, and complete the Address Book dialog box (refer to Figure 27-12), as explained in the previous section.

CREATING ADDRESS LISTS

You can set up address lists (also called *distribution lists* or *mailing lists*) that contain the e-mail addresses of several people you'll want to mail to as a group. For example, if I send a message to the

Friends address list shown in Figure 27-13, Netscape will send the same message to everyone on that list (namely, Alan Simpson and Mozilla). Here's how to set up an address list:

1. Choose Item | Add List from the Address Book window menu bar. An Address Book dialog box similar to the one shown in Figure 27-12 will appear (the e-mail Address box is unavailable, but everything else is the same as what's shown in Figure 27-12).

2. Type a Nick Name, a Name, and a Description for the address list (the Description and Nick Name are optional, but including a Nick Name makes the address list more convenient to use).

3. Choose OK to return to the Address Book window.

4. In the list below Address Book, select the users you want to add to the address list. Then, drag the selected names to the appropriate address list. The user names are copied to the address list you chose. (User names that appear in an address list are called *aliases*.)

> **TIP**
>
> *To send a message quickly to any user name in the Address Book window, double-click on the user name. For more cool stuff you can do in the Address Book window, check out the options on the File and Edit menus.*

CHANGING ADDRESSES IN THE ADDRESS BOOK

If necessary, you can return to the Address Book dialog box and fix the nickname, name, e-mail address, or description for any entry in the Address Book window. To do this, right-click the item you want to change, and choose Properties from the shortcut menu; or, click the item and choose Item | Properties from the menu bar. Make whatever changes you want, and choose OK.

DELETING ADDRESSES & ADDRESS LISTS

If you no longer want an address or address list to appear in your address book, select the item(s) you want to delete, and press the Delete key or choose Edit | Delete. Answer any prompts that appear.

When you've finished using the Address Book window, close it by clicking its Close (X) button or pressing Ctrl+W.

MOVING ON

Sending and receiving electronic mail is quick and convenient in Netscape. You simply open the Netscape Mail window (for example, by choosing Window | Netscape Mail from any Netscape menu bar). Then, choose buttons on the toolbar to get your mail from the server, to delete the current message, to send new mail, to reply to the sender of the current message, to reply to the sender and all recipients of the current message, to forward the current message, to view the previous or next unread message, or to print the current message.

In the next chapter, we'll explore two other Internet services that you can access right from Netscape Navigator: Newsgroups and Mailing Lists. As you'll see, both of those features work much like e-mail. With what you've learned in this chapter, you have a head start in learning those new features.

Cruising the Newsgroups With Gold

Are you looking for a good, cheap place to stay in Amsterdam? Do you need the name of an inexpensive treadmill to use at home? Would you like to receive automatic information about the latest developments at Microsoft? If so, you can join a *newsgroup* or subscribe to a *mailing list.* This chapter explains:

■ What newsgroups are

■ How to set up Netscape to access newsgroups offered by your ISP

■ How to find and join a newsgroup

■ How to read, reply to, and post newsgroup articles

■ What mailing lists are and how to find them

■ How to get on (and off) mailing lists

USING NEWSGROUPS

Before explaining how to use newsgroups, I'd like to give you a little background information about them. Newsgroups are electronic discussion groups carried via Usenet, a global network of cooperating computers that are interconnected via the Internet. A newsgroup consists of messages written by its members.

TIP

Be sure to read Chapter 27, "Doing E-Mail With Gold," before you dive into newsgroups and mailing lists. Why? Because the basic techniques for using e-mail in Netscape apply also to working with newsgroups and mailing lists.

Unlike e-mail messages, which go to specific electronic mailboxes, Usenet messages are sent to specific newsgroups. Anyone with access to the newsgroup can read its messages. Each newsgroup discusses topics in a specific category. For example, one newsgroup might discuss chocolate in all its delectable forms, another might discuss the latest antics of royal families, and still another might exchange humorous anecdotes and jokes.

There are thousands of newsgroups in which people exchange ideas, ask questions, express opinions, and relate their experiences. Some newsgroups are *moderated* by people who screen the articles for appropriate content before posting them for all to see, but most are *unmoderated*, which means that anyone can post anything, at any time.

The messages in a newsgroup are called *articles* and the individual discussions posted to a particular newsgroup are called *threads*. Suppose that I write a newsgroup article with the Subject line *Most Fattening Chocolate*, in which I ask people in the chocolate newsgroup (*rec.food.chocolate*) which brand of chocolate candy has the most calories per pound. I've now started a *Most Fattening Chocolate* thread. If someone replies to my article and then someone else replies to that reply, all these articles will appear in the same *Most Fattening Chocolate* thread. If I then post a new article that asks which company sells the best chocolate in Hershey, Pennsylvania, I've started a new thread.

TRAP

Do not post articles to a newsgroup until you've spent some time reading the articles that are there already (a process called lurking*). If you post articles before you thoroughly understand the culture of a newsgroup, other newsgroup members may send you insulting messages in return (we call this behavior* flaming*).*

Because there's so much Usenet traffic, few newsgroups retain their messages forever. When an article has *expired* (by exceeding the time limit the newsgroup allows), it is removed from the newsgroup. (Fortunately, some long-standing newsgroups keep archives of expired articles.)

E-MAIL VERSUS NEWSGROUPS

E-mail and newsgroups are similar in many ways. For example, both e-mail and newsgroups let you send messages electronically via networked computers. Moreover, the techniques for composing, reading, and replying to messages are nearly identical for both e-mail and newsgroups.

The main differences between e-mail messages and newsgroup articles are 1) only designated recipients can read and respond to the e-mail messages you send, whereas anyone in the newsgroup can read and respond to your newsgroup articles; 2) e-mail messages are copied automatically to your computer's hard disk, but newsgroup articles usually remain on the news host (although you can ask Netscape to save your newsgroup articles, if you wish).

NEWSGROUP CATEGORIES

As mentioned earlier, newsgroups focus on specific categories. Within each category there can be many subcategories, sub-subcategories, and so forth. Newsgroup names reflect this hierarchy (reading from left-to-right), starting with the least specific category and ending with the most specific one. Each category in the newsgroup name is separated from the next by a period.

Consider, for example, the newsgroup *rec.food.chocolate* (in which people discuss edible chocolate). This newsgroup's name goes from the broad category, *rec,* to the more specific category, *food,* to the most specific category, *chocolate.* Table 28-1 lists the main categories of newsgroups and provides a brief description and a sample newsgroup name within each category.

Top-Level Category	Description	Sample Newsgroup Name
alt	Alternative topics and lifestyles. Watch out! The alt newsgroups often contain offensive material.	alt.humor.puns
bionet	Biology topics	bionet.molbio.molluscs
bit	Bitnet, redistribution for the more popular BitNet LISTSERV mailing lists	bit.listserv.allmusic
biz	Business topics	biz.books.technical
comp	Computer-related topics	comp.client-server
humanities	Arts and humanities topics	humanities.music.composers.wagner
misc	Miscellaneous topics that don't fall into other categories	misc.books.technical
news	Usenet news network and software topics	news.answers
rec	Arts, hobbies, and recreational activities	rec.food.chocolate
sci	Scientific topics	sci.med.nutrition
soc	Social issues and socializing	soc.culture.latin-america
talk	Debates, opinions, and general yakking	talk.politics.medicine

Table 28-1: *Sample newsgroup categories, descriptions, and names.*

TRAP

Newsgroups come and go. Don't worry if some of the newsgroups listed in Table 28-1 are gone by the time you read this book. Also, note that your service provider may block some newsgroups, especially those in the alt *category, which often contain controversial or objectionable material. Parents beware! You should not let your children participate unsupervised in a newsgroup. There are software services available, such as SurfWatch, that help parents control what their children can go to on the Net.*

ADVICE FOR NEWSGROUP NEWBIES

The online world of newsgroups is a rough-and-tumble one, with little supervision. Some people on newsgroups are civilized and helpful; others are downright rude, strange, stupid, insulting, crazy, or some combination thereof. To make your newsgroup experience as enjoyable as possible, consider the following advice:

- *First*, learn to use your newsreader software (this chapter will help) and read the newsgroups *news.newusers.questions* and *news.announce.newusers* to learn how newsgroups work.

- *Next*, before you post any real messages to a newsgroup, post test messages to *alt.test* or *misc.test*, as explained later in this chapter.

- *Finally*, learn about network etiquette (*netiquette*), join different newsgroups, and study their frequently asked questions (FAQs). If you still have questions about how to use newsgroups, post them in *news.newusers.questions*.

Before you post articles to newsgroups other than *alt.test* or *misc.test*, you should lurk in the newsgroups that interest you, simply reading articles without replying to them and without posting new articles. When posting an article, follow these netiquette rules and conventions:

- Post only to the most appropriate newsgroup.

- Be sure that your article doesn't repeat one of the frequently asked questions (FAQ) for the newsgroup. Repeating FAQs annoys people, and it can entice people to flame you.

- Make the Subject line short but descriptive.

- Make the article text short, but be sure to include adequate details. Don't assume that everyone already knows what you're talking about or what kind of computer and software you're using.

- Do not post to the entire newsgroup when it's more appropriate to send e-mail to the author of an article.

- Do not send flames, silly jokes (unless you're writing for a humor newsgroup), commercial or political advertising, chain letters, offensive material, or anything illegal. Never follow up or respond to such postings. If you must react, do so via private e-mail to the author or to his or her system administrator.

TIP

For more newsgroup do's and don'ts, take a look at http://home.netscape.com/eng/mozilla/1.1/news/news.html *and the* news.announce.newusers *newsgroup.*

GETTING SET UP

Now that you know the rules of the road, you're ready to set up Netscape to use newsgroups. Here are the steps to follow:

1. From any Netscape window, choose Options I Mail And News Preferences, and specify the correct e-mail settings on the Servers and Identity tabs of the Preferences dialog box, as explained in Chapter 27, "Doing E-Mail With Gold."

2. Click the Servers tab in the Preferences dialog box and specify the name of your News (NNTP) Server in the News area at the bottom of the dialog box. Your Internet Service Provider can provide this information if you don't know it already. Figure 28-1 shows a completed Servers tab (be sure to provide information for *your* account, not for the account shown in the example).

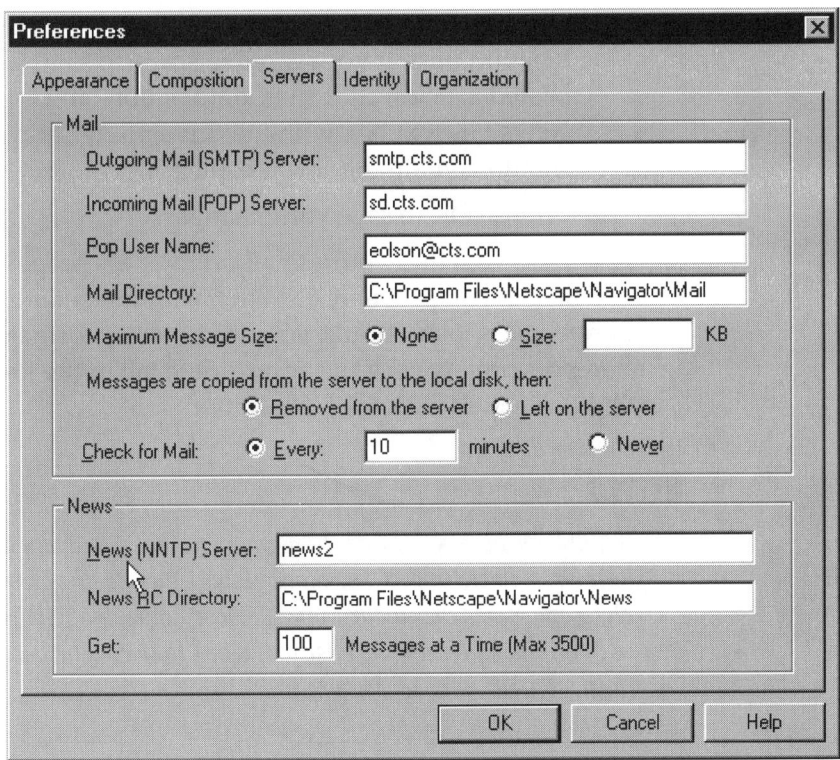

Figure 28-1: *The Servers tab of the Preferences dialog box, with some sample information filled in.*

3. Optionally, change the News RC directory and the number of messages to Get at one time.

TIP

NNTP stands for Network News Transfer Protocol, *the method news hosts use to communicate with your browser. The News RC Directory specifies the location for your newsgroup subscription files (.rc) and newsgroup information files (.rcg). Netscape maintains a news RC file for each news host you connect to.*

4. Netscape doesn't usually save a copy of newsgroup articles that you post. If you want Netscape to save copies of your posted articles, click the Composition tab and fill in the News File text box with the drive, folder, and filename that should contain the saved copies.

5. Choose OK to save your changes.

After you've set up your e-mail preferences properly and completed Step 2, you probably can stick with the default settings on the Preferences tabs. Should you need more information about any Preferences option, click the appropriate tab in the Preferences dialog box, and then click the Help button.

TIP

If you have access to more than one news host, you can choose an alternate news host. To do this, choose File | Open News Host from the Netscape News menu bar, type the host name, and choose OK. Then click on the folder for the host you want to use. (The host folder appears in the top-left pane of the window.)

GETTING AROUND & GETTING HELP

After you've finished the setup steps, you're ready to use Netscape with newsgroups. Here's how:

1. Get online and start up Netscape Navigator, using the standard procedure for your PC.

2. Open the Netscape News window by choosing Window | Netscape News from any Netscape menu bar.

3. If you just see folder icons in the left window, click on the little plus (+) sign next to a folder to open the folder. Names of individual newsgroups will appear beneath the folder.

In the example shown in Figure 28-2, I've opened the Netscape News window, then opened the news2 (default news host) folder. In that folder I clicked on the *news.announce.newusers* group and then, over to the right, I clicked on the article titled *Welcome To Usenet!* The selected article appears in the gray message pane at the bottom of the window.

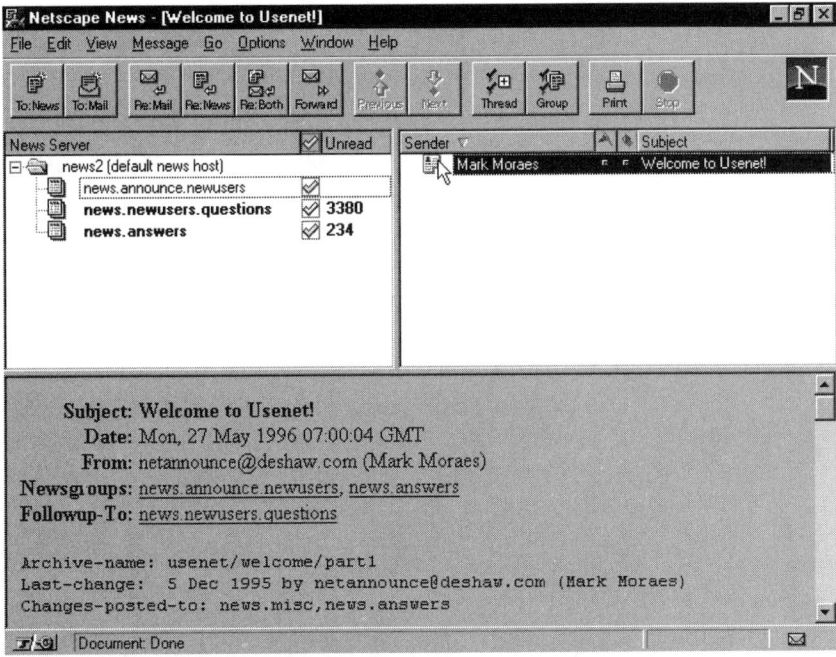

Figure 28-2: *The Netscape News window after a newsgroup and an article have been chosen.*

USING THE NETSCAPE NEWS WINDOW

Figure 28-2 illustrates the three panes of the Netscape News window. The *newsgroup list pane* (top-left pane) shows available news hosts and newsgroups, which newsgroups you've subscribed to (indicated by checkmarks after the newsgroup name), the number of unread messages, and the total number of messages in each newsgroup (the total number of messages may be hidden, unless you've resized the panes or the column headings). If a newsgroup contains unread messages, its newsgroup name appears in **boldface**.

TIP

To change the layout of the Netscape News window panes, choose Options | Mail And News Preferences, and click the Appearance tab. Then, choose an option from the Pane Layout area selections near the bottom of the dialog box.

The *message heading pane* (top-right pane) shows headings for articles in the current newsgroup. Information about unread articles appears in **boldface**; information about articles you've already read appears in normal (nonbold) text. The columns in the message heading pane display the name of the message sender, whether the message is flagged or read, the subject, and the date the message was posted (the date may be hidden unless you've resized the panes or the column headings).

The *message pane* (bottom pane) shows the contents of the current article. At the top of the article, you'll typically see information such as the subject, date, author's e-mail address and name, and the names of newsgroups to which the article was posted. Other information at the top of the article may vary. That's followed by the text of the article. (Scroll down to see the article text.)

VIEWING AN ARTICLE: THE BASICS

The steps for viewing an article in a newsgroup are almost identical to those for viewing an e-mail message in a folder:

1. In the newsgroup list pane, be sure that you can see the newsgroup that contains the articles you want to view. If it's not there, add it to the newsgroup list (as explained later in this chapter).

2. In the newsgroup list pane, click the newsgroup that contains the articles you want to view. Netscape will refresh the list of articles in the message heading pane.

TIP

The newsgroup list pane automatically includes the three default newsgroups news.announce.newusers, news.newusers.questions, *and* news.answers. News.announce.newusers *contains announcements of interest to newsgroup newbies.* News.newusers.questions *provides answers to questions commonly asked by newsgroup newbies. And* news.answers *is a repository for periodic Usenet articles. (This newsgroup is moderated.)*

3. In the message pane, click the article you want to read.

The article will be highlighted in the message heading pane and the text of the article will appear in the message pane at the bottom. You can use the vertical and horizontal scroll bars, as necessary, to view the message in the bottom pane. For practice, why not open some articles in the default newsgroups on your news host?

You can adjust the panes in the Netscape News window the same way you adjust the panes in the Netscape Mail window (refer to Chapter 27, "Doing E-Mail With Gold"). For example, you can resize the panes, resize the columns in the upper panes, rearrange the columns in the upper panes, and sort the messages in the message heading pane.

EXPLORING THE NETSCAPE NEWS COMMANDS

The buttons on the Netscape News toolbar make it easy to work with newsgroup articles. From left to right, here's what each button on the toolbar will do, along with each button's equivalent menu bar options and shortcut keys:

- To: News lets you post a new article in the current newsgroup. (Same as choosing File | New News Message from the menu bar.)

- To: Mail lets you send a new e- mail message to someone. (Same as choosing File | New Mail Message or pressing Ctrl+M.)

- Re: Mail lets you send a reply to the author of the current article via e-mail. Your reply goes only to the author's electronic mailbox, not to the newsgroup members. (Same as choosing Message | Mail Reply or pressing Ctrl+R.)

- Re: News lets you post a reply to the author of the current article in the current newsgroup. Your reply goes to the newsgroup itself. (Same as choosing Message | Post Reply from the menu bar.)

- Re: Both lets you reply to the author of the current article. The reply goes both to the newsgroup and to the author's electronic mailbox. (Same as choosing Message | Post And Mail Reply.)

- Forward lets you forward the current article, as an attachment, to anyone you want, just as though you were forwarding normal e-mail. The forward goes to the recipient's electronic mailbox, not to the newsgroup. (Same as choosing Message | Forward or pressing Ctrl+L.)

- Previous displays the previous unread article. (Same as choosing Go | Previous Unread from the menu bar.)

- Next displays the next unread article. (Same as choosing Go | Next Unread from the menu bar.)

- Thread marks all messages in the current thread as read. (Same as choosing Message | Mark Thread Read.)

- Group marks all articles in the current newsgroup as read. (Same as choosing Message | Mark Newsgroup Read.)

- Print lets you print the current message. (Same as choosing File | Print Message(s) or pressing Ctrl+P.)

- Stop interrupts the current transfer. (Same as choosing Go | Stop Loading or pressing Esc.)

You can also right-click an item on the screen and choose options from the shortcut menu that appears, just as you can in the Netscape Mail window and in many places throughout Windows 95.

Getting Help

Getting help in the Netscape News window is basically the same as getting help in the Netscape Mail window. Simply highlight a menu option or point to a toolbar button, then read the help message on the status bar and the pop-up ToolTip message near the mouse pointer (if you pointed to a button). You can also click the Help button, if it's available in a dialog box.

Returning to Your Browser

To return to the Netscape browser window at any time, click the browser's button in the Windows 95 taskbar. If no browser window is open, you can open a new one by choosing File | New Web Browser, or by pressing Ctrl+N in the Netscape News window. To return to the Netscape News window from the browser, click the Netscape News button on the taskbar, or choose Window | Netscape News from any Netscape menu bar.

Adding a Newsgroup to the Newsgroup List Pane

Although Usenet offers thousands of newsgroups, you probably won't see many of them in the newsgroup list pane, especially if you've opened the Netscape News window for the first time. But it's easy to add newsgroups to the newsgroup list pane at any time. Here are several ways to do so:

- To add a newsgroup when you know its name, choose File | Add Newsgroup, type the exact name of the newsgroup you want to add, and press Enter or click OK. The newsgroup will appear in the newsgroup list pane.

- To show only the newsgroups you've subscribed to, choose Options | Show Subscribed Newsgroups.

- To show only the newsgroups that contain unread articles, choose Options | Show Active Newsgroups.

- To show all the newsgroups available on your news host, choose Options | Show All Newsgroups, and wait patiently. Figure 28-3 shows the newsgroup list pane after I chose Options | Show All Newsgroups and double-clicked the *biz.** *(55 groups)* folder.

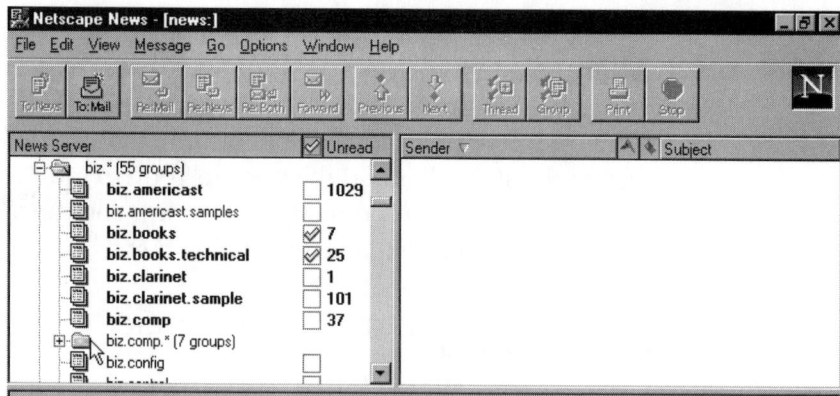

Figure 28-3: *The newsgroup list pane, with the biz.* folder expanded to reveal newsgroups in the biz category.*

■ To show newsgroups that have been added to your news host since the last time you checked, choose Options | Show New Newsgroups.

■ To add a newsgroup whose name appears as a hyperlink on a Web page, e-mail message, or newsgroup article, click the hyperlink.

TIP

To add a news hyperlink to your Web pages, e-mail messages, or newsgroup postings, or to jump to a newsgroup from your browser, simply type news: *followed by the newsgroup name. For example, type* news:biz.books *to access the biz.books newsgroup.*

Notice in Figure 28-3 that some newsgroup items in the newsgroup list pane are preceded by folder icons that have + or – symbols next to them; others have newspaper icons (without + or – symbols) instead. The folder icons indicate categories that contain additional newsgroups and or subcategories. The newspaper icons indicate an actual newsgroup. To expand a folder icon so that you can see the newsgroups below it, simply double-click the folder icon or click its + symbol. To collapse a folder icon and hide the newsgroups below it, double-click the folder icon again or click its – symbol.

FINDING THE PERFECT NEWSGROUP

Scrolling through the entire list of newsgroups can be a slow way to locate newsgroups you're interested in. Fortunately, it's easy to find the right newsgroup for you. Perhaps one of the best places to look is Sunsite's Usenet Info Center Launch Pad, located at *http://sunsite.unc.edu/usenet-i/home.html*. There you can click hyperlinks that let you get help with Usenet, browse or search for a Usenet group, display Usenet FAQs, search in Deja News for Usenet topics, and search other Usenet indexes and services.

When you want to locate Usenet articles on particular topics, you definitely should try out the Deja News search engine at *http://www.dejanews.com* or the Alta Vista search engine at *http://altavista.digital.com*.

SUBSCRIBING TO & "UNSUBSCRIBING" FROM A NEWSGROUP

You can *subscribe* to a favorite newsgroup so that it always appears in the newsgroup list pane when you open the Netscape News window. To subscribe, first add the newsgroup to the newsgroup list pane (as explained earlier). Then click the check box next to the newsgroup name in the newsgroup list pane (a checkmark will appear in the box).

If you no longer want the newsgroup to appear automatically when you open the Netscape News window, you can *unsubscribe* from the newsgroup. To do this, click the check box next to the newsgroup you want to unsubscribe from. The checkmark will disappear and the newsgroup won't appear in the newsgroup list pane the next time you open the Netscape News window. (The newsgroup list pane in Figure 28-3 shows both subscribed and unsubscribed newsgroups.)

Remember that you don't have to subscribe to a newsgroup in order to read its messages. Subscribing is necessary only if you always want the newsgroup to appear when you open the Netscape News window.

TIP

To immediately refresh the newsgroup list pane without closing and reopening the Netscape News window, choose either Options | Show Subscribed Newsgroups or Options | Show Active Newsgroups, if you haven't done so already. Then, in the newsgroup list pane, double-click the folder for your news host a couple of times.

READING AN ARTICLE

Reading an article is as simple as clicking the newsgroup that contains the article (in the newsgroup list pane) and then clicking the article in the message heading pane. After you've selected an article, you can proceed quickly through the unread messages in the current newsgroup by clicking the Next and Previous buttons on the toolbar.

SAVING INFORMATION FROM AN ARTICLE

You can save various pieces of information from the current article, using these techniques:

- To save a picture in the current article to your hard disk, right-click the picture in the message pane, choose Save Image As, type a filename and extension for the image, choose the drive and folder in which you want to store the picture, and click Save.

- To add the author's e-mail address to your online address book, right-click in the message pane, choose Add To Address Book, type a Nick Name if you want, and choose OK. (See Chapter 27, "Doing E-Mail With Gold," for more information about using the address book.)

- To copy text from the current article to the Windows clipboard, use your mouse to select the text in the message pane, and choose Edit | Copy, or press Ctrl+C. To paste the copied text into your e-mail messages, article responses, or other files, position the insertion point and choose Edit | Paste, or press Ctrl+V.

CHOOSING WHICH MESSAGES APPEAR IN THE MESSAGE HEADING PANE

Just as you can control which newsgroups appear in the newsgroup list pane, you can control which messages appear in the message heading pane:

- To show all messages in the current newsgroup, choose Options | Show All Messages from the Netscape News menu bar.

- To show only unread messages in the current newsgroup, choose Options | Show Only Unread Messages from the menu bar.

- To force Netscape to update the list of articles in the current newsgroup, click the newsgroup name again in the newsgroup list pane, or choose File | Get More Messages from the menu bar.

TIP

If you'd like more control over the amount of header information that appears at the top of each article shown in the message pane, choose Options | Show Headers, then choose All, Normal (the default setting), or Brief.

REPLYING TO AN ARTICLE

You can reply to the author of the current article in any of several ways:

- To reply via e-mail, so that only the author can read your response, click the Re: Mail toolbar button. Use this technique when you're not sure whether your answer would interest anyone else in the group.

- To reply via the newsgroup, so that all newsgroup members can read your response, click the Re: News toolbar button. Use this technique when you're sure that your answer will interest most people in the group.

- To reply via e-mail as well as to the newsgroup, click the Re: Both toolbar button.

- To forward the article as an e-mail message to anyone you choose, click the Forward toolbar button.

Depending on which toolbar button you chose, a new window will open and you can address and compose your reply or forward, much as you would address and compose an e-mail message. Figure 28-4 shows the form for sending a reply to the entire newsgroup. (By the way, the author of the article shown in Figure 28-4 was having trouble with a beta test version of CoolTalk, *not* the released version.) When you've finished addressing and composing your response, click the Send button on the toolbar.

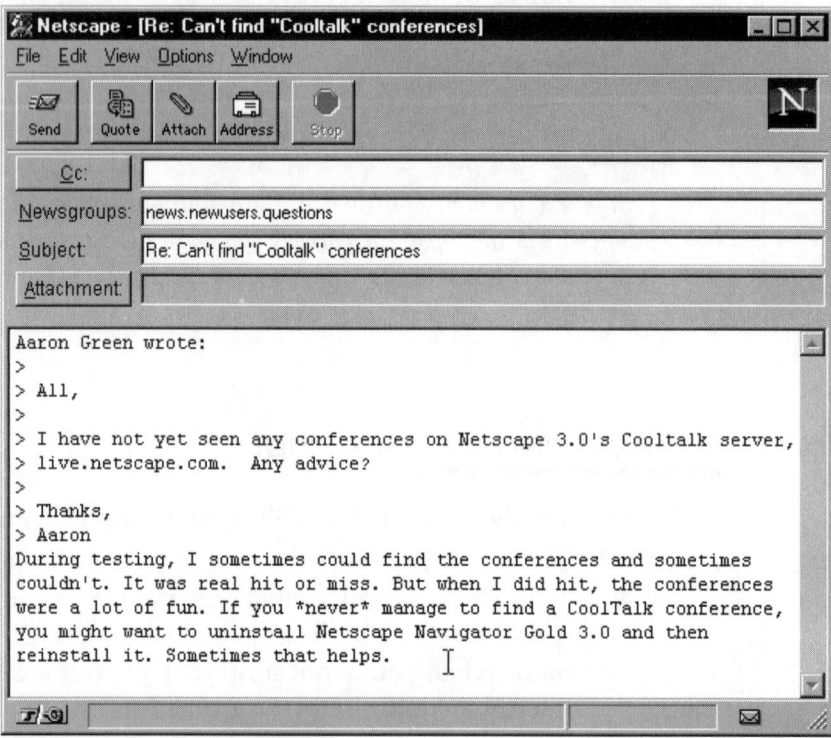

Figure 28-4: *Replying to a newsgroup article.*

POSTING A NEW ARTICLE

Posting a new article to a newsgroup is easy. Just click the To: News button on the Netscape News toolbar, fill in the window that appears (it resembles Figure 28-4), and click the Send button on the toolbar. Your article will take some time to propagate to various news hosts and even your own news host might not show the article for half an hour or more.

The best way to practice your skills is to post and reply to some practice articles in the test newsgroups *alt.test* and *misc.test.* When you post to these newsgroups, be sure to include the words *ignore* or *no reply* in your Subject line. If you omit those words, many automatic messages will appear in your electronic mailbox to illustrate how your article was propagated to various newsgroup hosts.

MANAGING NEWSGROUP ARTICLES

You can work with one article at a time or several at once. The first step is to select the messages you want. You can use the same click, Shift-click, and Ctrl-click methods that work for selecting e-mail messages (refer to Chapter 27), as well as these additional selection techniques:

- To select all the messages in a specific thread, click any message in the thread, then press Ctrl+Shift+A or choose Edit | Select Thread.

- To select all messages in the newsgroup, click any message in the newsgroup, then press Ctrl+A or choose Edit | Select All Messages.

The selected articles are highlighted in the message heading pane. After you've selected the articles, you can do any of the following:

- To print the current article (assuming you've selected only one), click the Print toolbar button or press Ctrl+P.

- To mark the selected articles as read or unread, choose Message from the menu bar, and then choose either Mark As Read or Mark As Unread.

> **TIP**
>
> *As a shortcut, you can quickly mark an entire thread or newsgroup as read by clicking the Thread or Group buttons on the toolbar. And you can mark a single article as read or unread by clicking the "read" column in the heading for the article you want to change. (A green icon appears next to an unread article and the heading for an unread article is shown in boldface.)*

■ To flag or unflag the selected articles for later processing, choose Message from the menu bar, and then choose either Flag Message or Unflag Message. As a shortcut, you can flag and unflag articles by clicking the "flag" column in the heading for the article you want to change. (A flag icon appears next to flagged articles.)

After you've flagged some articles, you can read through them quickly by choosing Go from the menu bar, followed by First Flagged, Next Flagged, or Previous Flagged. To read quickly through unread messages, click the Previous and Next toolbar buttons, or choose appropriate options on the Go menu (First Unread, Next Unread, or Previous Unread).

USING MAILING LISTS

Mailing lists allow you to receive one or more e-mail updates dealing with a specific topic. When you've *subscribed* to a mailing list—usually at no cost—the messages automatically come to your electronic mailbox. The messages continue coming to your electronic mailbox until you *unsubscribe* from the list, unless you've chosen a one-time-only mailing list. Like subscribers to newsletters and magazines, all subscribers to mailing lists receive the same information.

> **TIP**
>
> *Many mailing list addresses begin with* listserv, majordomo, *or* listproc *(the names of the automated programs that process subscription requests).*

Most mailing lists have two e-mail addresses. The *administrative address* is used for subscribing and unsubscribing. The *list address*, or *group address*, is used to send e-mail to other mailing list members. You'll get the list address when you subscribe.

SUBSCRIBING TO A MAILING LIST

Subscribing to a mailing list is easy: Simply use your e-mail program to send a message in the format required by the mailing list. Table 28-2 shows how to subscribe to several mailing lists. When you subscribe to the lists shown in that table, leave the Subject: line blank, except where noted.

What	Subject: Line	Message Area
*Accessing Internet by E-Mail	mail-server@rtfm.mit.edu	send usenet/ news.answers/ internet-services/ access-via-email
*Calendar of online classes	calendar@horizons.org	
*Internet Roadmap	LISTSERV@UA1VM.UA.EDU	GET NEWUSER PACKAGE F=MAIL
*Yanoff list of Internet services	inetlist@aug3.augsburg.edu	
Internet Tourbus (cool sites)	listserv@listserv.aol.com	subscribe Tourbus firstname lastname
Internet newsletter	LISTSERV@PEACH.EASE. LSOFT.COM	SUBSCRIBE ONLINE-L FIRSTNAME LASTNAME
Microsoft Windows News	admin@winnews. microsoft.com	subscribe winnews
Newbie News	Majordomo@Newbie.NET	subscribe newbienewz
World events (daily summary)!	incinc@tiac.net	subscribe db

Table 28-2: *Sample mailing lists and how to subscribe to them.*

After you subscribe to a mailing list, you'll receive, via e-mail, a confirmation message that usually explains how to *unsubscribe* from the mailing list. Unsubscribing stops the flow of e-mail messages from the mailing list to your electronic mailbox. The confirmation message might include other information also (such as the purpose of the mailing list and the mailing list rules of etiquette). *Keep this confirmation information handy!*

TRAP

Be forewarned that some mailing lists will flood your inbox with tons of messages!

UNSUBSCRIBING FROM A MAILING LIST

To unsubscribe from a mailing list, follow the instructions that come in the confirmation e-mail message. Because each mailing list has its own procedures, be sure to follow the steps carefully. You'll usually receive a confirmation message that your unsubscribe command worked.

FINDING THE PERFECT MAILING LIST

Finding the perfect mailing list can take some research. To get started, pay a visit to *http://www.webcom.com/impulse/list.html.* If you'd like to see text-only information about available lists, type *ftp://rtfm.mit.edu/pub/usenet-by-group/news.lists* in the Location box of your browser, press Enter, and click on the name of the list you want to view. (The next chapter explains how to use FTP to download or view information.) Another way to look up information about mailing lists is to search Yahoo or any other Internet search engine for *mailing lists.*

Moving On

If you've seen references to newsgroups and mailing lists while browsing the Web, you now know what they're about and how to use them. Congratulations! In the next chapter, we'll switch gears and look at some other widely used Internet services: FTP, Gopher, and Telnet.

FTP, Gopher & Telnet

In this chapter, we're going to step back in time to discuss three of the granddaddy applications for the Internet: the File Transfer Protocol (FTP); Gopher, an Internet search tool; and Telnet, used for connecting directly to other computers on the Internet. Because these applications were developed during the early days of the Internet, they don't present the glitzy face that Web pages do, but they're useful, nonetheless. Here's what you'll learn about in this chapter:

- How to download files from FTP servers to your computer
- How to upload your own files to an FTP server
- How to use Gopher to find information on the Internet
- How to use Telnet to connect directly to other computers

Because FTP is perhaps the most-used application of the bunch, we'll start with it and spend the most time on it.

WHAT IS FTP?

The Internet offers thousands of files—programs, program bug fixes (called *patches*), text, graphics, sounds, animations, movies, magazines, and more—for you to copy onto your own computer, if you want. Many of these files are free (*freeware*, or *public domain*). Others are in the "try before you buy," or *shareware*, category. How do you get the files from a computer on the Internet to your own computer? Well, in some cases, you just click a hyperlink in a Web page and the FTP download starts automatically. But in many other situations you'll need to go to the FTP site directly before you can download the file.

FREE OR NOT FREE?

Public domain files are not copyrighted and there are no restrictions on their use. Public domain files might include Shakespeare plays and sonnets or software that people have written and altruistically released to the public.

Freeware files are copyrighted, but you can use them free of charge. Freeware authors usually require you to acknowledge them as the source of the freeware and usually forbid you from reselling the file (though it's usually okay to redistribute the file, free, to others).

Shareware files are copyrighted and distributed for you to use on a trial basis. If you like and use the files, you're expected to either pay the author a fee (usually very reasonable) or delete the file from your machine. Often, the shareware author will allow you to redistribute the software (free), but anyone using your copy is expected to adhere to the standard shareware rules of "try, then buy or delete."

File Transfer Protocol (FTP) is a standard set of rules that allow many different types of computers to send and receive data over networks. Each computer that offers files for you to download to your own computer or allows you to upload files from your computer is called an *FTP site* or *FTP server*. There are two main types of FTP sites: anonymous and nonanonymous.

- Anonymous FTP sites let you transfer files without having to be a registered user of the computer. When you log on, the FTP site will usually accept anonymous as your user name and your e-mail address as a password. Because Netscape handles this type of logon automatically, you don't have to worry about it.

- Nonanonymous FTP sites do require you to be a registered user. You'll have to specify a valid user name and password to use them. Ordinarily, these sites are not open to the general public. Rather they are used to transfer files to and from some corporate computer.

Netscape can handle both anonymous and nonanonymous FTP, and you'll learn how to do both in this chapter.

WHAT KIND OF FILE IS IT?

All downloadable files reside in folders or directories on some computer, somewhere. FTP itself doesn't describe the files or tell you much about them—other than their name, size, time, date, and data type. Typically, you need to know the exact name of the file you're looking for when you visit an FTP site.

In some cases, you'll find a description, and perhaps a filename, on a Web page. Figure 29-1 shows an example for the popular WinZip program, which can compress and decompress files for you (more about this topic later). When you're ready to download, you click a link to start FTP. This link will either start the download process right away or take you to an FTP site.

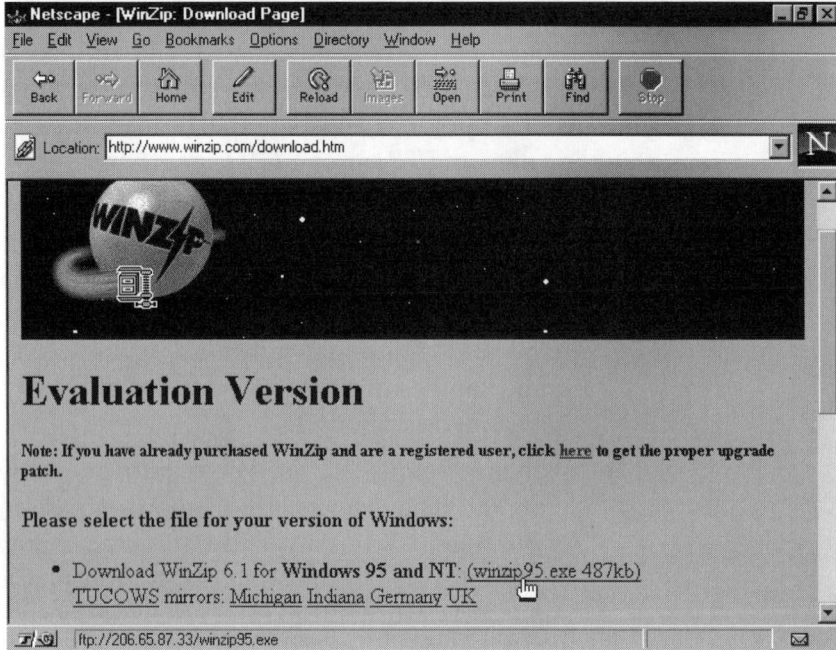

Figure 29-1: *Getting ready to download by clicking a hyperlink on a Web page.*

Figure 29-2 shows, generally, what your screen will look like when you arrive at an FTP site. Notice the first characters (*ftp://*) in the Navigator's Location box. The main part of the screen is a list of directory names and file names, which is typical of most FTP sites.

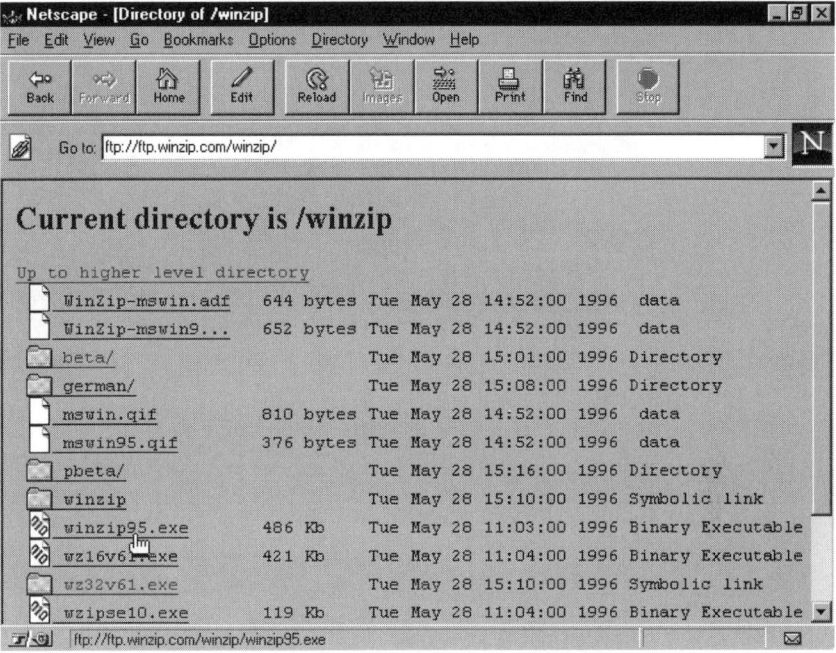

Figure 29-2: *A sample FTP site.*

Some FTP sites include information that describes the rest of the files in a directory. Typically, these files are named README or INDEX (sometimes in lowercase letters and sometimes preceded by numbers or a period to ensure that their names appear at the top of the list). You simply click the filename to read the text in the file, as I'm about to do in Figure 29-3. When you've finished reading, click the Back button in Netscape's toolbar.

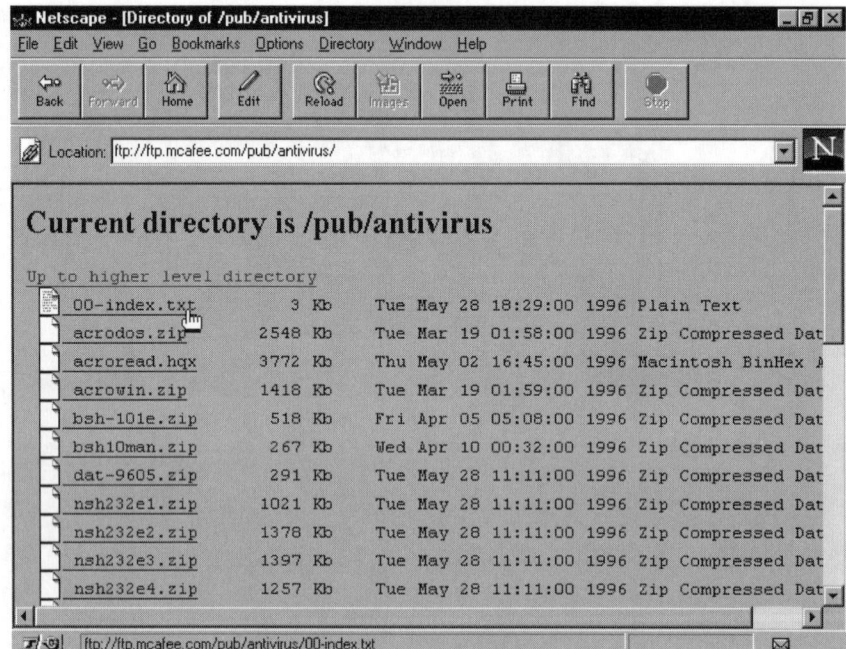

Figure 29-3: *The 00-index.txt file provides details about other files in this directory.*

While viewing the README file, you can search it for specific text. To do this, click the Find button on the Netscape toolbar, or choose Edit | Find, or press Ctrl+F. Then type the text you're looking for and click Find Next. When you've finished searching, click Cancel.

NAVIGATING IN AN FTP SITE

Don't be daunted by the unfriendly appearance of an FTP site. Navigating an FTP site is easy as long as you keep the following points in mind:

- The title shown just below the Location or Go To box always indicates the name of the current directory (for example, */winzip* or */pub/antivirus*).

- Folder icons indicate subdirectories. Simply click on a folder icon or the text next to the folder icon to go to that directory.

- You can bounce up to a higher-level directory by clicking the *Up to higher level directory* hyperlink that usually appears above the list of files and folders.

- You can go to higher-level directories also by deleting the directory name or names in the URL shown in the Location or Go To box. For example, deleting */pub/antivirus/* in the URL shown in Figure 29-3 and pressing Enter takes you to the top-level directory of the mcafee.com FTP site (*ftp:// ftp.mcafee.com*).

"DELETE FROM END" NAVIGATION

The "delete from end" style of navigation is also useful when you get a message saying that Netscape is unable to find a file or directory. For example, if you typed **ftp://ftp.somewhere.com/pub/ games** into Netscape's Location box and you got a dialog box saying 'Netscape is unable to find the file or directory named ftp:// ftp.somewhere.com/pub/games', the directory name might have changed. Try deleting */games* from the end of the URL and pressing Enter. Then see if you can find another directory name.

- The last column of the directory list indicates the type of data each item contains. For example, *Directory* tells you that an item preceded by a folder icon is a directory (something you knew already); *Binary Executable* indicates a program, possibly one you'll want to download.

- When you've found the file you want to download, simply click its name to start the download process.

TIP

When you click the link for a text file, Netscape displays the text on your screen rather than saving the file to your disk. You can change this default action, as explained later in the chapter.

ABOUT FILENAME EXTENSIONS

A file's *extension* can tell you a lot about what kind of information the file contains. For example, the .TXT extension in a filename, such as README.TXT, indicates an ASCII text file that any simple text-viewing program (including Netscape) can read. Table 29-1 describes the file extensions you're most likely to encounter when using FTP.

Extension	Description
.ARC	See .ARJ.
.ARJ	Compressed file that you can decompress with a program such as WinZip or Drag And Zip.
.ASC	Usually the same as .TXT.
.DOC	Text file or a Microsoft Word document.
.EXE	Executable program. Some .EXE files are self-extracting archives that are decompressed into several files when you run them.
.GZ	Compressed Unix GNU Zip file that you can decompress with a program such as GZIP, WinZip, or Drag And Zip.
.HQX	Compressed file that you can decompress with BinHex (usually designed for use on a Macintosh).
.LHA	See .ARJ.
.SIT	Compressed or "stuffed" Macintosh file. The Net offers several PC unstuff programs if you need to decompress a .SIT file.

Extension	Description
.TAR	Compressed Unix file that you can decompress with a PC version of tar, or with a program such as WinZip or Drag And Zip.
.TXT	Simple text file that's readable by Notepad, WordPad, most word processors, and Netscape.
.Z	Compressed Unix Zip file that you can decompress with a program such as GZIP, WinZip, or Drag And Zip.
.ZIP	Compressed file that you can decompress with a program such as PKUNZIP or WinZip.
.ZOO	See .ARJ.

Table 29-1: *Common filename extensions and descriptions.*

ABOUT COMPRESSED FILES

Many of the notes in Table 29-1 include the terms *compress* and *decompress*. *Compression* is a technique that squeezes large files into smaller ones without damaging the files. Compressing the files helps to speed their transfer over the Internet. After a compressed file reaches its destination (your computer, for example), it must be decompressed before you can use it. *Decompressing* restores the files to their original form.

WinZip, by Niko Mak Computing, is one of the most popular programs around for compressing and decompressing files in many common formats. I've included an evaluation copy of WinZip on the CD-ROM that accompanies this book. You can also get more information, and download the latest evaluation version from WinZip's home page at *http://www.winzip.com.*

PROTECTING YOUR COMPUTER FROM VIRUSES

Before we get into the nitty-gritty of downloading files from the Internet, a word about viruses. *Computer viruses* are small programs that can get into your computer and damage or destroy your files or disable your computer in other ways. Unlike the viruses humans catch, computer viruses are not created by nature. They're created by vandals who want to make life unpleasant for the rest of us.

Viruses are not as common as people think, but they are a pain and some can do serious damage to your hard disk. Here are some steps you can take—*before* you download any files from the Internet—to safeguard your computer from viruses:

- Make a complete backup of your system, if you have a fast backup device. At the very least, back up any files you've created and can't afford to lose. Be sure to do this *before* you download any files from the Internet.

- Get a good *antivirus* program that can search for and clean out any viruses it detects. Many excellent antivirus programs are available, including McAfee VirusScan and Norton Anti-Virus. You can download many antivirus programs (including VirusScan) from the Internet, or buy them at your favorite software store.

- After downloading programs or other files, and before running or opening the downloaded files for the first time, use your antivirus program to find and remove any viruses in the downloaded file. (Or better yet, delete any infected files.)

To learn more about how to protect your system from computer viruses, visit one of the following Web sites (many of which offer links for downloading antivirus programs):

- *http://www.mcafee.com*—McAfee's home page, where you can learn more about viruses and download evaluation copies of McAfee software

- *http://www.cis.ohio-state.edu/hypertext/faq/usenet/ computer-virus-faq/faq.html*—Basic information about viruses and what to do if your system becomes infected

- *http://csrc.ncsl.nist.gov/virus/*—Links to additional virus-related sites and reviews of antivirus software

- *http://cws.wilmington.net/95virus.html*—Ratings, reviews, and links for downloading several Windows 95 antivirus programs

FTP Downloading in a Nutshell

Enough yakking about compression and viruses. Let's get back to the task at hand–using FTP to download files to your PC. Here we'll look at the steps involved when you know the URL of the FTP site that contains the file you want to download. (If you get to an FTP site automatically from a Web page, then Steps 1 and 2 have already been completed for you.) This is what to do:

1. Get online and start Netscape Navigator in the usual manner for your PC.

Tip

To save a text file (rather than view its text), Shift-click the file's hyperlink.

2. If you're not already in an FTP site, type an *ftp://* URL in the Location box of your browser, and press Enter.

3. Click on the name of the file you want to download.

4. If you see the Unknown File Type dialog box shown in Figure 29-4, click the Save File button. This message box just means that you don't have a plug-in or helper app for the type of file you selected. But when you're downloading from an FTP site, that's fine. You *do* just want to save the file to your hard disk.

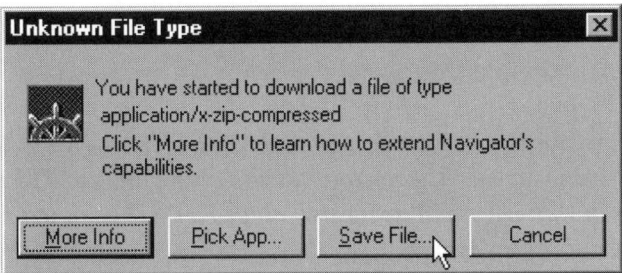

Figure 29-4: *The Unknown File Type dialog box.*

5. If the Save As dialog box appears (see Figure 29-5), type a filename into the File Name box, or accept the suggested filename. Then use standard browsing techniques to choose the drive and folder to which Netscape should copy the downloaded file. Click the Save button and wait. Patiently, if the file is large.

Figure 29-5: *Use the Save As dialog box to tell Netscape where to download the selected file.*

If you clicked the link for a text file (.TXT or .ASC), the text will appear on your screen. To save the text file, choose File | Save As, or press Ctrl+S, and skip to Step 6. To close the text file, click the Back button on Netscape's toolbar—you're done.

TIP

You can set a bookmark to jump to an FTP site. This is handy if you want to revisit the site. You can also create links to FTP sites on your own Web pages and you can include FTP URLs in your e-mail and newsgroup messages.

If you copied files to your hard disk in Step 5, you can exit Netscape Navigator when the download is complete. Optionally, if you want to scan the downloaded file for viruses, now might be a good time to do so.

If the downloaded file is compressed (has a .zip or .exe extension, for example), decompress the file. In Figure 29-6, for example, I double-clicked v95i203e to start WinZip, which I had installed previously. (Because v95i203e has a .zip extension, double-clicking it launches WinZip automatically.) The next step is to click the Extract button on WinZip's toolbar and follow the prompts.

TIP

If the downloaded file has a .exe extension, double-clicking it will either start the program or decompress the .exe file into a bunch of component files. (Most likely it'll decompress the file.)

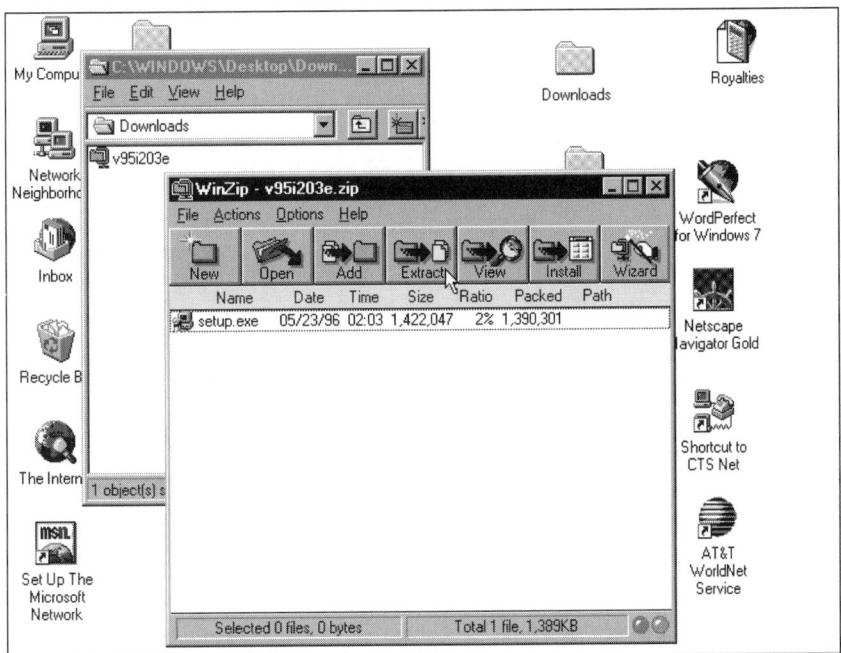

Figure 29-6: *Getting ready to decompress a compressed file in WinZip.*

If the downloaded files include an installation or setup program—typically named *INSTALL.EXE* or *SETUP.EXE*—you'll need to complete the installation by double-clicking that setup program's filename. For example, after decompressing the setup.exe file shown in Figure 29-6, I double-clicked the setup.exe icon in my Downloads folder to install an evaluation version of the McAfee antivirus program.

Because the setup program usually copies all the necessary files to their proper locations automatically, you don't need to bother with that. You'll rarely need to move or copy the setup program itself.

USING NONANONYMOUS FTP

Not every FTP site offers anonymous access. For example, some sites require that you specify a user name and password if you want to upload files (as explained later). Others require a user name and password for downloading private files.

If the site requires a user name and password, but you haven't supplied them, you may get an error message when you try to open that site, or you may be prompted for a user name and password. Figure 29-7 shows a typical Password Entry dialog box for an FTP site that requires a password (the asterisks appear when you type your password into the box).

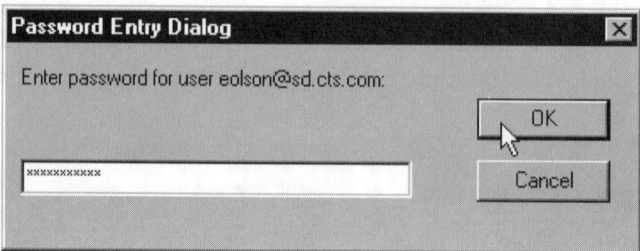

Figure 29-7: *You may be prompted to enter a password for the FTP site you want to access.*

You can specify your user name and, optionally, your password when you type the FTP URL into Navigator's Location box. To specify just the user name, type the URL in this form:

```
ftp://username@ftpsite
```

In this form, *username* is your valid user name and *ftpsite* is the URL you're trying to access. Here's an example:

```
ftp://eolson@sd.cts.com/uw/e/eolson/
```

With the *ftp://username@ftpsite* form, you'll be prompted to supply the password, as shown in Figure 29-7. If you want to supply both the user name and the password in the URL, use this form instead:

```
ftp://username:password@ftpsite
```

In this form, *username* and *ftpsite* have their usual meaning and *password* is your password for accessing the site. The following example shows an FTP URL with both a user name (eolson) and a password (yeahright):

```
ftp://eolson:yeahright@sd.cts.com/uw/e/eolson/
```

TROUBLESHOOTING FTP PROBLEMS

If you're having trouble getting into an FTP site, the site may be busy. Many FTP sites limit the number of users allowed to upload or download files at one time. You might get a message that the site is busy, or you might get Netscape's "Error -57" message box. Simply clear the message box from the screen. Then try again during a less busy time, or use a mirror site.

Mirror sites are alternative FTP sites that mirror (or duplicate) other anonymous FTP sites. For example, the mirror site at *ftp:// ftp.adelaide.edu.au/pub/WWW/Netscape/pub/navigator/gold*, in Australia, offers an alternative location for downloading Netscape Navigator Gold software. If you're choosing an FTP site from a Web page, you'll often be given a list of main sites and mirror sites to use. Try to pick a location near you (if you're not working during the peak hours for your local time), or choose a location for which the local time is the wee hours of the morning or late at night.

What else can go wrong with a download? Well, two things. First, if the download isn't finishing properly, your network connection, your modem, or the FTP server may be suffering from a temporary glitch. Your best bet is to cancel the download procedure (click the Cancel button), delete any remnants of the downloaded file from your hard disk, and try again later. If the problem persists, contact your local system administrators or your ISP.

A second problem might occur if the download finished properly but you can't run or view the file. Chances are, the glitch gremlin caused a temporary hiccup on the communications line and the file became corrupted. Again, the solution is to delete the damaged file and try the download again.

TIP

Occasionally, a file might not download properly if the file's extension isn't listed (or is not listed properly) on the Helper tab of Netscape's general preferences. There's more about helper applications later in this chapter and you can visit http://home.netscape.com/assist/support/client/tn *and scroll down to the* FTP issues *section to learn more about FTP troubleshooting.*

SEARCHING FOR FTP TREASURE

As you've probably guessed by now, thousands, perhaps millions, of files are available for downloading. How are you supposed to know where they are? Perhaps the easiest way to find them is to click the appropriate hyperlink on a Web page, e-mail message, newsgroup article, or FTP directory listing.

TIP

To quickly determine whether a hyperlink will take you to an FTP site, point to the link with your mouse, and read the URL shown in the Netscape browser's status bar. An FTP URL always starts with ftp://.

If you've read about a downloadable file in some print or online medium, you can simply type the described URL into the Location or Go To box of your browser. (If the *ftp://* portion of the URL isn't written down, be sure to supply it when you type the URL.)

To locate some great Internet-related software, try Stroud's terrific Web site at *http://cws.wilmington.net/win95.html*. The main menu, shown in Figure 29-8, is organized into convenient categories. Simply click the category you want, read the reviews (if you want), and then click the FTP address provided.

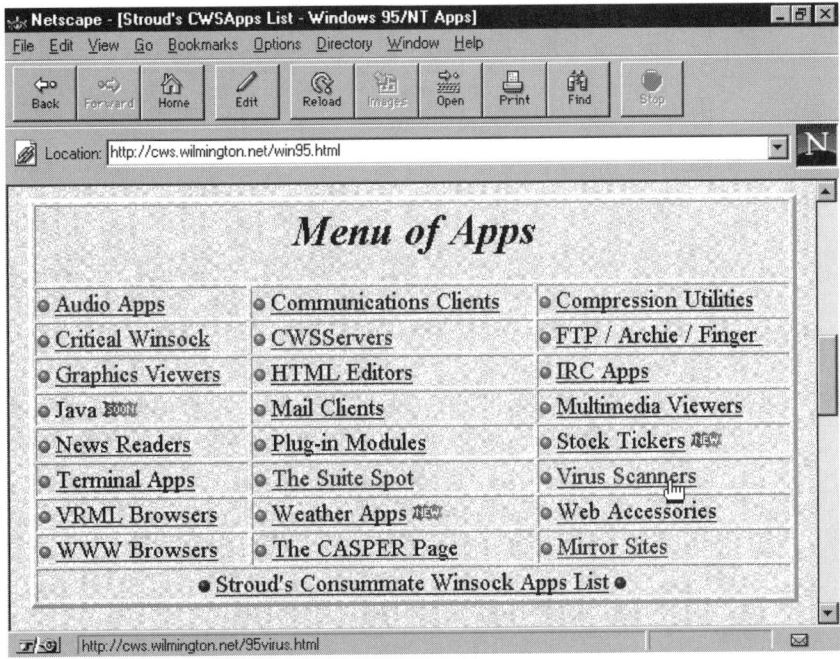

Figure 29-8: *Stroud's main menu for Internet-related Windows 95 applications.*

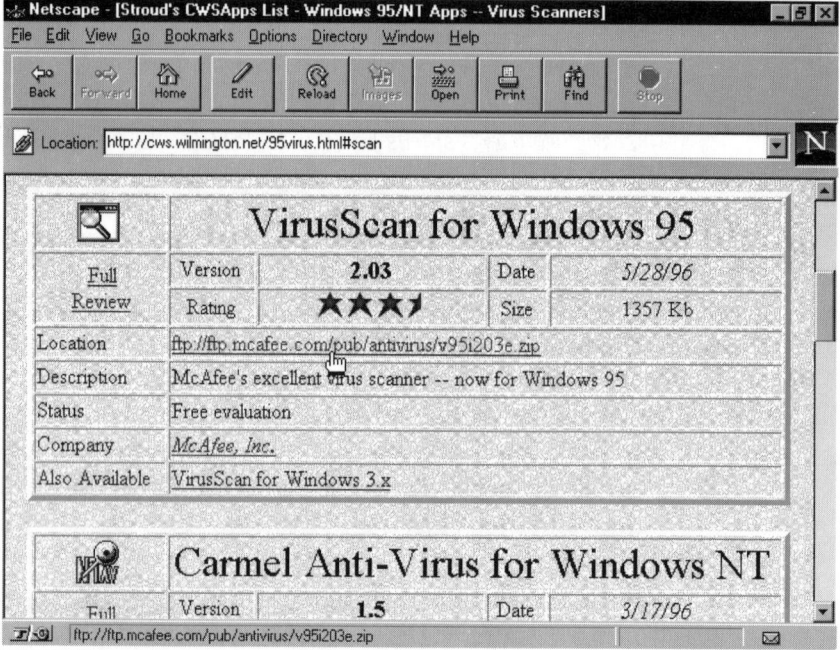

Figure 29-9: *Stroud's page on virus scanners.*

GENERAL SEARCH ENGINES

Search engines offer another great way to find files to download. Simply go to the search engine you prefer, and type the name or keywords for the file. To reach a variety of search engines all shown on the same page, visit *http://www.search.com*. If you're looking for shareware programs, try c l net's shareware.com search engine at *http://www.shareware.com*. Also check out WinSite, which claims to be "The Planet's Largest Software Archive for Windows." You'll find WinSite's home page at *http://www.winsite.com* and its search engine at *http://www.winsite.com/cgi-bin/supersearch*.

THE ARCHIE SEARCH ENGINE

Archie is a database service that's specially designed to help users locate specific files and directories on anonymous FTP servers anywhere on the Internet. With Archie, you only need to know a few characters that appear anywhere in the name of the file you're looking for.

Rutgers University hosts one popular Archie server at *http://
www-ns.rutgers.edu/htbin/archie.* After you enter this URL into your
browser, an Archie Request Form appears. The top of the form explains how to do the Archie search; the middle half of the form has
places you fill in, as shown in Figure 29-10.

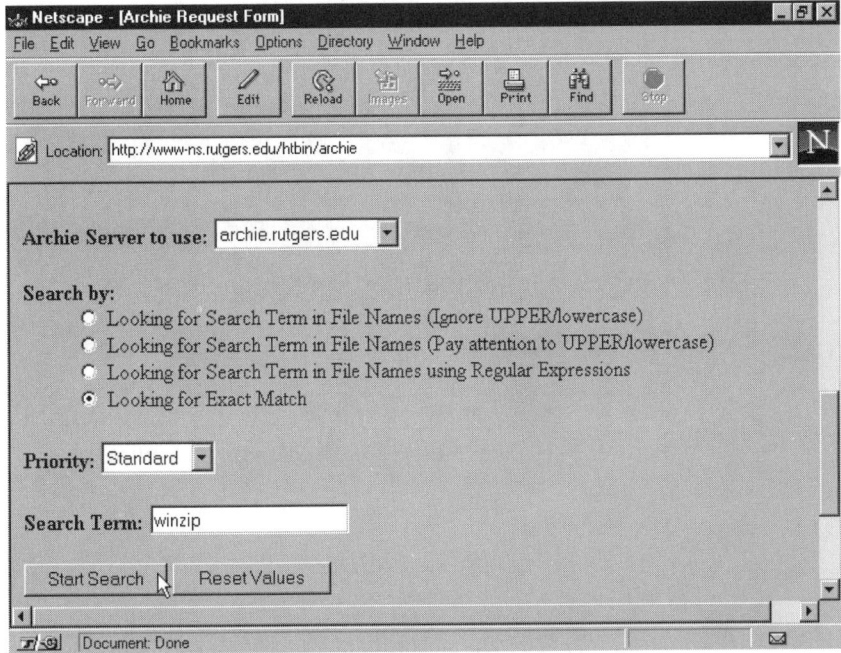

Figure 29-10: *Filling in the form at Rutgers University's Archie site.*

To fill in this form, choose an Archie server, choose a Search By
method, choose a Priority (lower priorities take longer but have a
less adverse effect on other people), type your Search Term, and
click Start Search. Now wait. When the search is complete, you'll
see a list of hypertext links you can click to jump to the appropriate
FTP server, as shown in Figure 29-11.

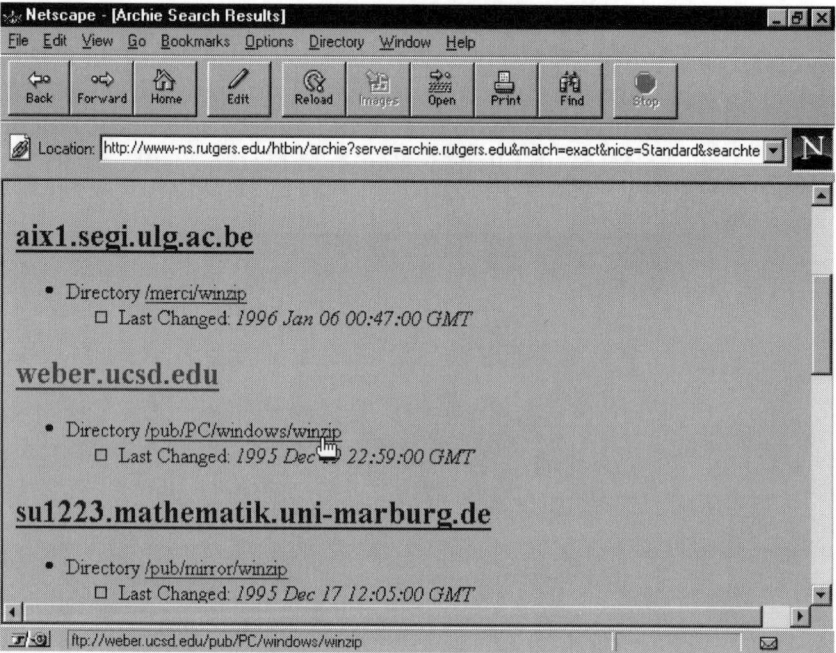

Figure 29-11: *The results of an Archie search for* winzip.

TRAP

Archie looks for specific file and directory names, not for general categories of software. If you need to search by keywords or concepts, use one of the other search engines mentioned earlier. Also, be aware that Archie searches can be very slow!

To locate other Archie servers, look up *archie* in your favorite search engine (for example, the all-in-one search page at *http://www.search.com*). Note that some Archie-related links take you to a Telnet site rather than to an FTP site.

FTP & HELPER APPLICATIONS

You already know that when you click a text filename (.TXT) at an
FTP site, Netscape automatically displays the text in the file. Similarly, when you click an HTML filename (.HTM or .HTML), Netscape serves up a Web page. And when you click an executable
filename (.EXE), Netscape prompts you to save the file. Helper applications (or *helpers*) make all this automation possible in Netscape.

It's easy to choose or change the way helpers handle each type of
file. Be careful not to assign the wrong action to a particular type of
file, however. When this happens, the results are very strange. To get
started, choose Options | General Preferences from any Netscape
window, and click the Helpers tab in the Preferences dialog box that
appears. (You needn't be connected to your ISP for this command to
work.) Figure 29-12 shows an example of the Helpers tab.

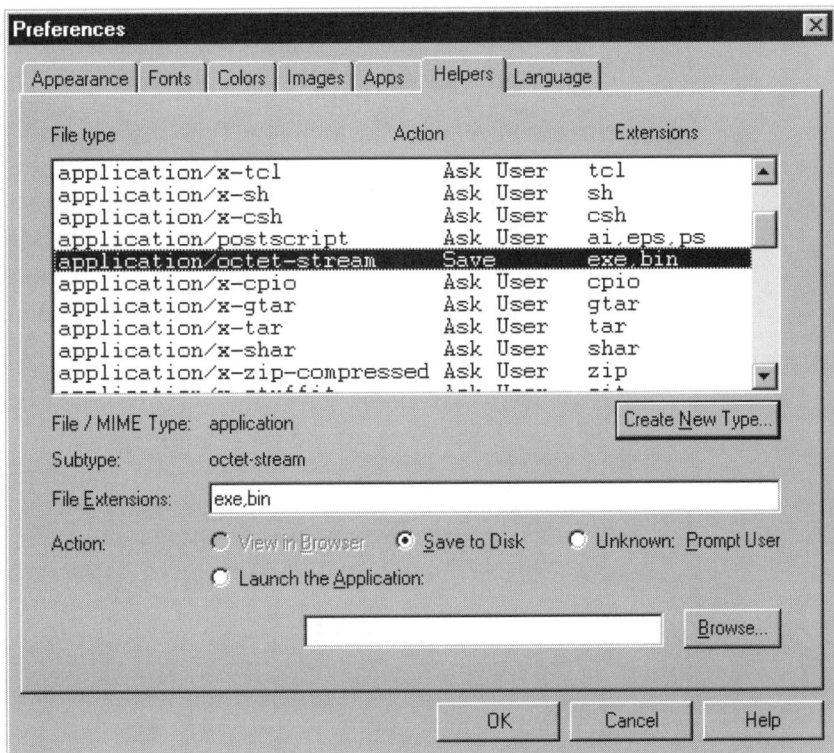

Figure 29-12: *The Helpers tab of the Preferences dialog box.*

This Preferences dialog box is a little tricky, but perhaps I can demystify it for you. The scrollable list in the dialog box shows all the types of files Netscape knows about, with information displayed in the three columns described here:

- File Type: The file type and subtype, according to the Multipurpose Internet Mail Extensions (MIME) naming standard. In the MIME nomenclature, for example, files with a .exe or .bin extension have a file type of application and a subtype of octet-stream. You don't need to worry much about the file type, unless you're creating new file types for Netscape to recognize.

- Action: The default action Netscape should take when it encounters the file type. For example, if you scroll down to the .exe and .bin extensions shown in Figure 29-12, you'll see that the default action for the associated application/octet-stream file type is to Save the file to disk.

- Extensions: The file extensions associated with the file type. For instance, the extensions .exe and .bin are associated with the application/octet-stream file type.

Below the list is the Create New Type button, which lets you configure a new MIME type and subtype. I won't trouble you here with this feature, which is mainly for experts and propeller-heads. Also shown below the scrollable list is the File/MIME Type for the currently highlighted item in the list, along with the Subtype, the associated File Extensions, and the Action to take when Netscape encounters the file.

MORE WAYS TO HOOK UP HELPERS

You can download (via FTP, of course) many helper applications for processing movie clips, sound files, and more. A good place to find these helpers is Netscape's Windows Helper Applications Web page at *http://home.netscape.com/assist/helper_apps/windowhelper.html*.

If a helper application is already installed on your machine, you can set up the helper association without opening the Preferences dialog box. During an FTP download that encounters an unknown file type, simply click the Pick App button in the Unknown File Type dialog box (refer to Figure 29-4), and locate and double-click the program that should process the unknown file type. (Be sure to choose the correct program for the file type!) Netscape will add the association to the Helpers tab of the Preferences dialog box, and immediately process the downloaded file with whatever program you chose.

RECONFIGURING AN EXISTING HELPER APPLICATION

Here's how to reconfigure the file extensions and action for any existing Netscape helper:

1. Choose Options | General Preferences and click the Helpers tab.

2. In the scrollable list, click the application you want to change.

3. If necessary, type or change the file extension(s) associated with the file format. For example, type **txt** for a text file. You needn't include the period before the extension. To list several extensions, use a comma (,) to separate each extension from the next.

TRAP

Be careful not to add an extension that's more commonly associated with another file type. For instance, a .DOC file can either be a plain text file or a Microsoft Word file. If you add the DOC extension to the text/plain file type, however, Netscape will display strange hieroglyphics on your browser screen when you click on the hyperlink for a Microsoft Word file.

4. From the following options, choose the action Netscape should execute when it encounters the file:

- View In Browser: Opens the file in the content area of the browser (if Netscape supports the file type). The Action column will display Browser for items with this action assigned.

- Save To Disk: Saves the file to disk. The Action column will display *Save* for items with this action assigned.

TIP

Any time your mouse is poised over a hyperlink, you can save the associated file (rather than taking the default action assigned for the file type) by holding down the Shift key while you click the hyperlink.

- Unknown: Prompt User: Displays the Unknown File Type dialog box (refer to Figure 29-4) so that you can decide how to handle the file type on a case-by-case basis. The Action column will display Ask User for items with this action assigned.

- Launch The Application: Opens the file with an application. Specify the application name in the text box below the Launch The Application box, or click the Browse button to locate the application and fill in the text box automatically. The Action column will display the application name. For example, to download and

automatically unzip .zip files, specify the path to the
WinZip program in the Launch The Application text
box. Of course, the helper application must be installed
for this to work.

TRAP

*If you leave blank the text box below Launch The Application, Netscape
will try to launch the associated file as an application. Because this is a
pretty dangerous practice, avoid leaving the text box blank. For example, if you choose Launch The Application for a .exe file type, but
leave the box empty, Netscape will launch the .exe file right from the
Net. Unfortunately, viruses can lurk in a .exe or .bin file! Therefore, it's
best to save such files to disk, run your antivirus program against the
executable files, and then install and run them.*

5. Click OK to save your changes.

UPLOADING FILES

In addition to downloading files from FTP servers to your computer, you can go the other way—from your computer to an FTP
server—if you have the proper permissions. For example, whenever I finished writing a few chapters of this book, I uploaded those
chapters to the publisher's FTP site—no need to ship disks and
such.

Many ISPs offer free storage for e-mail, files, Web pages, programs, and so forth. Some also offer FTP dropboxes so that others
can upload files from their PCs to you. For example, after the publisher reviewed the first submission of one of my chapters, they
could send the chapter back to *my* FTP dropbox, with their editorial
questions, comments, and snide remarks. (Just kidding on the
snide remarks, gang.)

TIP

Actually, the publisher compressed the edited chapter files and then sent them back to me as e-mail attachments (refer to Chapter 27, "Doing E-Mail With Gold"). They could have used my FTP dropbox. But e-mail works fine for sending a single chapter or two, now and then.

Anyway, when you do want to upload a file to an FTP site, follow these steps:

1. In Navigator's Location box, type the nonanonymous URL for your upload directory.

2. If you're prompted for a password, type the password and choose OK.

When you've connected successfully to the upload directory, you can use drag and drop or Netscape's File | Upload File command to upload the files.

ALTERNATIVE FTPING

Netscape's file upload features are modest. You can upload files to the remote server, but you cannot move, delete, or rename them. For those jobs, you'll need a stand-alone FTP program, such as WS_FTP32.EXE from Ipswitch, Inc. To learn more about WS_FTP32, or to download a free evaluation copy, visit *http://www.ipswitch.com.*

DRAG-AND-DROP UPLOADING

To drag and drop files to the current FTP directory, follow these steps:

1. Tile the Windows 95 desktop so that you can see (in the browser) the FTP upload directory and the file(s) you want to drag and drop.

2. Use standard click, Shift-click, and Ctrl-click techniques to select the files you want to upload, as shown in Figure 29-13.

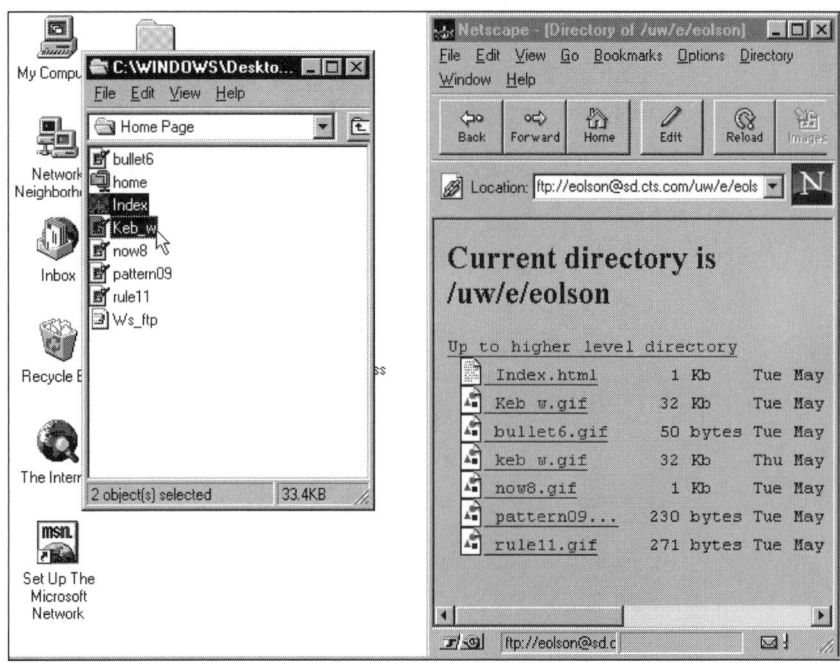

Figure 29-13: *Getting ready to drag and drop some files to an FTP upload directory.*

3. Drag the selected files to the Netscape browser window, and release the mouse button.

4. When asked whether you want to upload the dragged files to the FTP server, choose OK. (If you change your mind about uploading, choose Cancel. The dragged files will appear in your browser. Simply click the Back button until you reach your FTP directory.)

5. If you're asked to confirm security information, click the Continue button. The upload will begin.

The files you dragged and dropped will appear in the FTP up-load directory. No muss, no fuss. If you've set up one-button pub-lishing (as described in Chapter 7, "Presenting Your Page to the World"), you may see a message asking whether you want to browse to your default publishing location. Choose No unless, say, you've just uploaded a bunch of files to your Web server directory and now want to see how they'll look to the rest of the world.

Using Menu Commands to Upload Files

Here's another way to upload a file to a nonanonymous FTP site:

1. When you're at the FTP site, open the directory to which you want to write the file(s).

2. Choose File | Upload File from Navigator's menu bar. You'll see a File Upload dialog box, similar to the one shown in Figure 29-14.

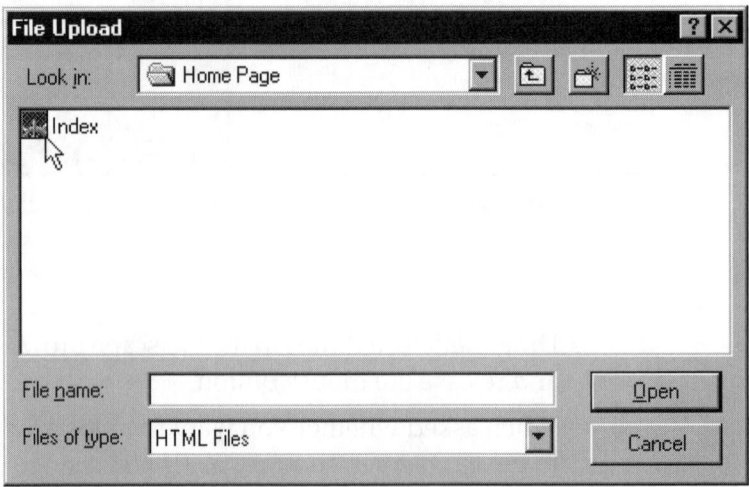

Figure 29-14: *Use the File Upload dialog box to locate the file you want to upload.*

3. From the Files Of Type drop-down list at the bottom of the dialog box, select the type of file you want to upload.

4. Use standard browsing techniques to locate the disk drive and folder that contains the file you want to upload.

5. Click on the filename you want to upload and choose Open or double-click the filename.

The file you uploaded will appear in the FTP upload directory. Again, if asked whether you want to browse to your default publishing location now, choose No.

FINDING STUFF WITH GOPHER

The Internet has been around for nearly 30 years. During the first 20 of those years, there was no World Wide Web with pictures and multimedia. Most of the information on the Internet was in simple text-based documents stored by universities, research institutions, and government agencies. Much of that information is still out there, having never been groomed and glamorized for the highly commercial World Wide Web. To find this non-Webified information, you may want to try *Gopher*.

With Gopher, you find information by clicking on hierarchical menus and submenus or by typing search text into a form. Eventually, you end up at a text screen that displays the information you seek. For example, Figure 29-15 shows the main menu for the popular Whole Earth 'Lectronic Link (WELL) archive at *gopher://gopher.well.com/*. Figure 29-16 shows the screen after I clicked the first folder, *About this gopherspace...*, on the Gopher menu.

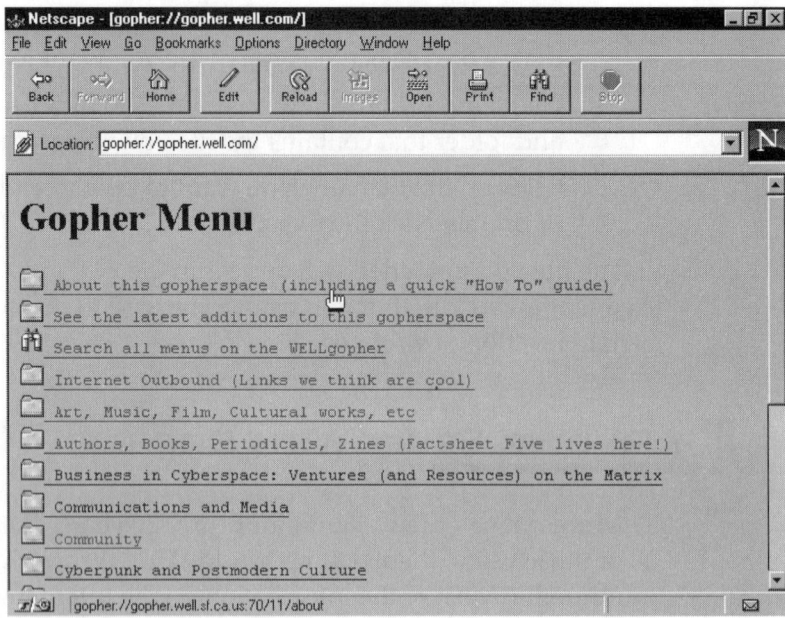

Figure 29-15: *Like all Gopher sites, the WELL site is organized hierarchically.*

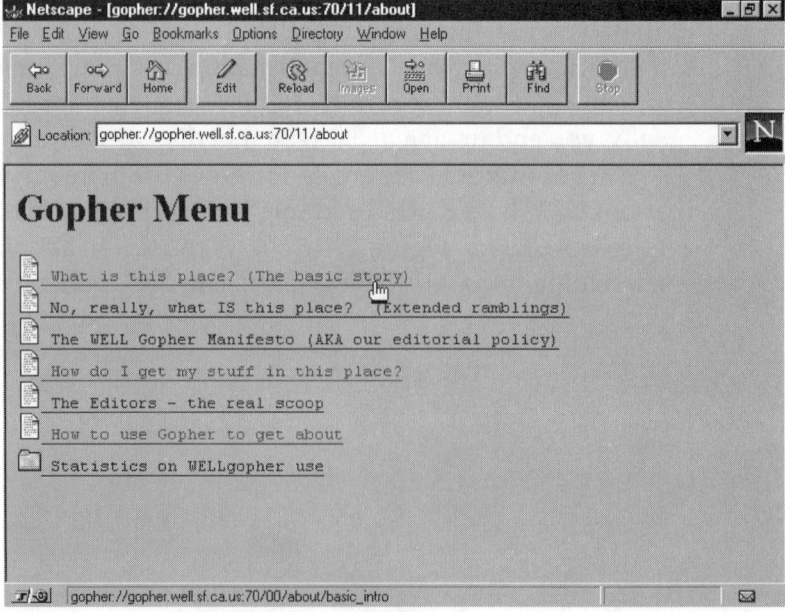

Figure 29-16: *Clicking the first folder shown in Figure 29-15 brought me here.*

Figure 29-17 shows the screen after I clicked the folder named *What is this place? (The basic story).*

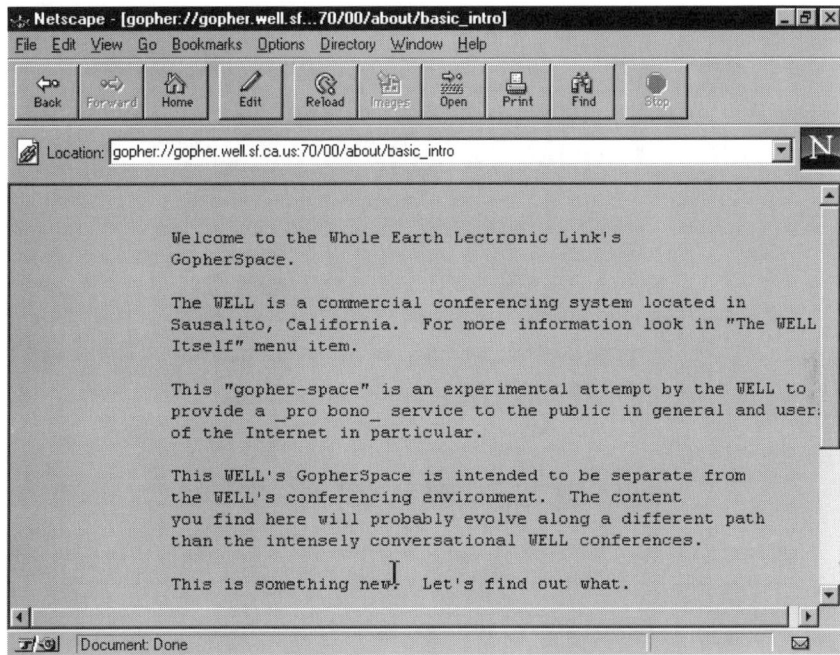

Figure 29-17: *Clicking the first item in Figure 29-16 displayed this text.*

Many Gopher sites, including the WELL, offer search features. Simply click on a binoculars icon (like the one shown in Figure 29-15) or the text next to the binoculars icon to start searching the Gopher site. For instance, after clicking the binoculars icon shown in Figure 29-15, the search form shown in Figure 29-18 appeared on my screen. The next step is to click the text box, type the keyword or keywords I want to find, and press Enter to start the search. The search results for the *music* keyword appear in Figure 29-19.

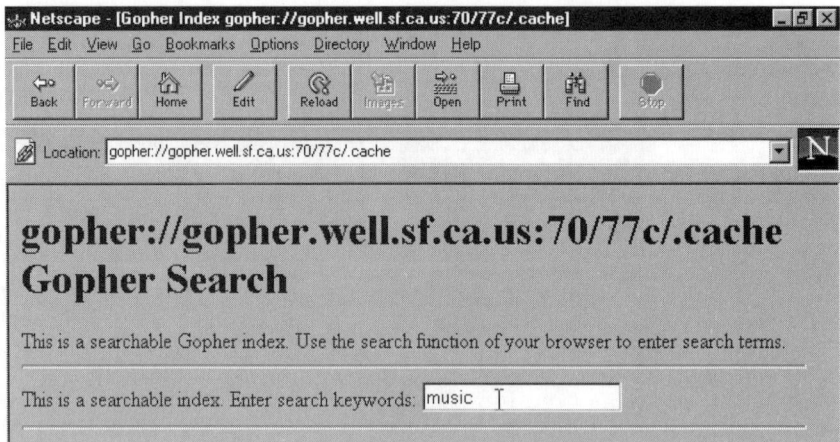

Figure 29-18: *Searching for* music *at the WELL Gopher site.*

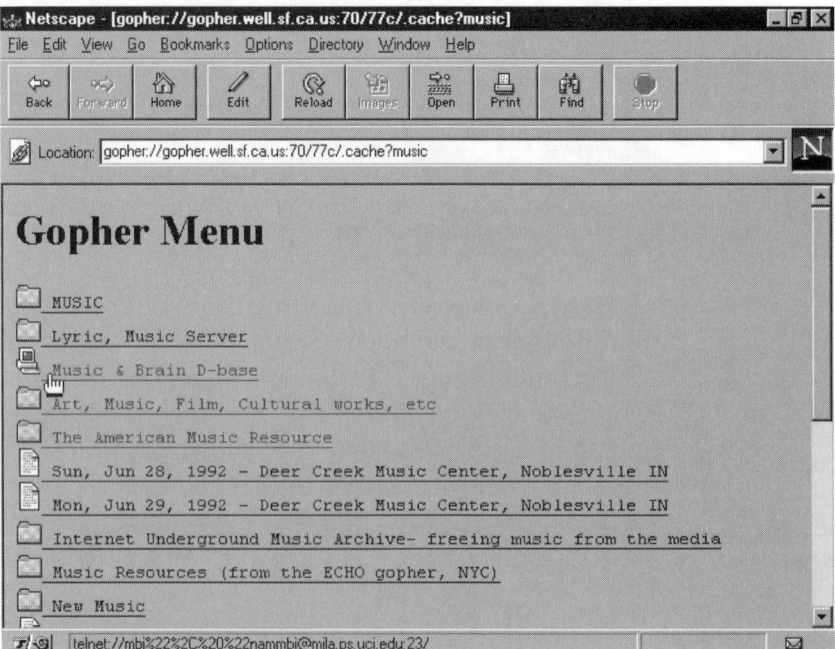

Figure 29-19: *The search results from Figure 29-18.*

WHAT DO THOSE ICONS MEAN?

The icons next to items on the Gopher menus can give you clues about what will happen when you click the icon or the text next to the icon. Here's a summary of the icons you're most likely to see:

- Folder icon takes you to the next lower level in the information hierarchy.

- Paper icon displays plain text information.

- Binoculars icon lets you search for a topic or an item.

- Computer icon takes you to a Telnet site.

To get to a Gopher site, click the Location box of your browser, type *gopher://* followed by the Gopher's URL, and press Enter. Table 29-2 describes URLs for several cool Gopher sites, including the InterNIC site (which offers a great way to find people, companies, and domain names). To find other Gophers, search for *gopher* in your favorite search engine.

TIP

If you think up a great custom domain name and want to find out whether it's available, search the InterNIC Gopher site for that name. Read through the resulting list of names and addresses to see whether somebody has already taken the domain name you want.

Description	URL
Internet Wiretap archive (includes government and San Francisco Bay area information)	gopher://wiretap.spies.com
InterNIC directory of people, companies, products, and services	gopher://rs.internic.net: 70/11/.ds
Library of Congress	gopher://marvel.loc.gov
University of Michigan archive	gopher://gopher.uis.itd.umich.edu
University of Minnesota archive	gopher://ashpool.micro.umn.edu
WELL site gopher, described in this chapter	gopher://gopher.well.com

Table 29-2: *Some cool Gopher sites.*

TIP

You can save, print, copy, and bookmark Gopher menus, just as you can any other pages that you view in Netscape.

CONNECTING TO COMPUTERS WITH TELNET

Prior to the days of PCs and graphical user interfaces, people used dumb terminals to connect remotely to some big computer somewhere, and then typed text commands to tell that computer what to do. In return, the big computer spit back screens full of text. Those big computers are still out there and accessible through an Internet service known as Telnet.

Figure 29-20 shows a typical Telnet session. In this example, I'm logged into Baker Library at Dartmouth College in Hanover, New Hampshire. Notice that the session takes place in a separate window, is interactive, and is completely text-based.

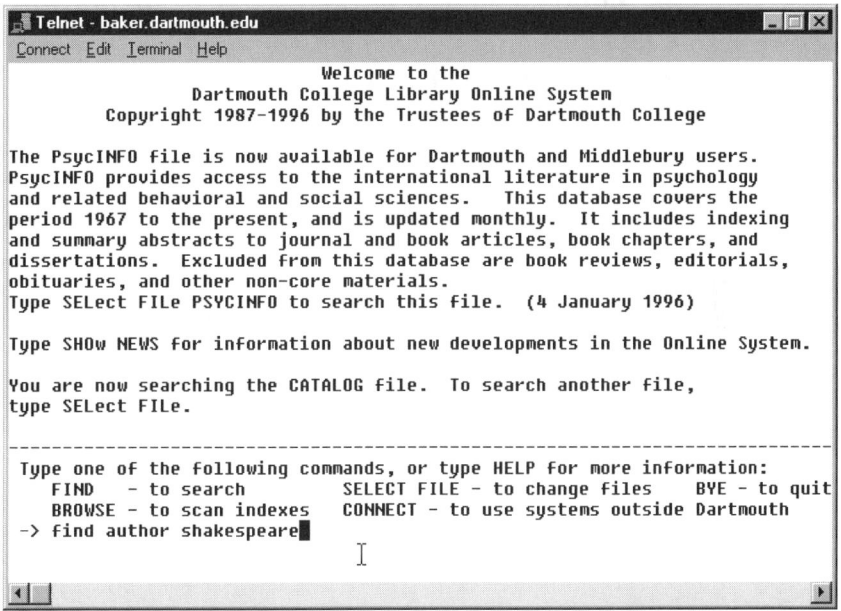

Figure 29-20: *An interactive session, using Telnet to connect to Baker Library at Dartmouth College.*

WHAT ELSE CAN YOU DO WITH TELNET?

Telnet is often used to browse card catalogs at libraries around the world. But it has many other uses.

For example, I sometimes use Telnet to pick up my CompuServe e-mail when it's inconvenient to use the friendlier graphical software and connection methods. To pick up my mail, I simply enter *telnet://gateway.compuserve.com* in my browser's Location box, enter my host name, user name, and password, and enter *GO MAIL.*

Some people use Telnet to engage in interactive role-playing fantasy games—called MUDs, MOOs, MUCKS, MUSHes, and MUSEs—with other Internet gamers. If you'd like to explore fictional worlds in real-time (and don't mind paying the telephone and connect-time charges), check out the links at *http://jefferson.village.virginia.edu/iath/treport/mud.html* and *http://www.oise.on.ca/~jnolan/mud.html* for more information.

To find other interesting Telnet sites, look up *telnet site* in Yahoo or your favorite search engine.

SETTING UP YOUR BROWSER TO USE TELNET

A Telnet program comes with Windows 95. To tell Netscape where to find this program, follow these steps:

1. Choose Options | General Preferences from Navigator's menu bar and click the Apps tab. Figure 29-21 shows the top portion of a completed Preferences dialog box.

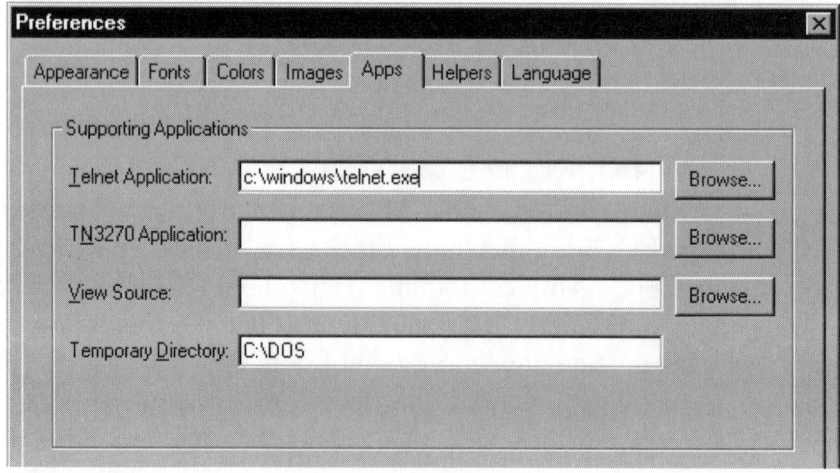

Figure 29-21: *Setting up Netscape to use Telnet.*

2. In the Telnet Application text box, specify the path to your Telnet program. Or click the Browse button next to the Telnet Application text box and locate and double-click the Telnet filename.

3. If you need to connect to an IBM mainframe and have your PC behave like an IBM 3270 terminal instead of the standard DEC VT100 supported by most Telnet sites, specify the path to your TN3270 program in the TN3270 Application text box (or click the Browse button next to the TN3270 Application text box to fill in this path by browsing).

TIP

Most plain Telnet programs do not have TN3270 capabilities, but you can download TN3270 programs by using FTP. To find a TN3270 program, look up TN3270 in your favorite search engine.

4. Choose OK to save your settings.

Now you're ready to roll with Telnet.

USING TELNET

Using Telnet is as easy as following these steps:

1. Open your Internet connection and start Netscape Navigator in the usual manner for your PC. Then, do one of the following:

   ■ Click a Telnet link in a Web document or at a Gopher site.

   ■ Type a Telnet URL in the Location box of your browser, and press Enter. Telnet URLs begin with *telnet://*. For example, enter *telnet://baker.dartmouth.edu*.

   ■ Launch the Telnet program window by typing *telnet://* and pressing Enter. You'll see the Connect dialog box shown in Figure 29-22. To connect to a remote system, choose Connect | Remote system, type a host name,

such as *baker.dartmouth. edu,* in the Host Name text box
(or use the drop-down list next to Host Name to select
a previously visited host), and click the Connect button.

TIP

*The menu bar in the standard Windows 95 Telnet application offers
some other interesting options. Feel free to explore the Connect, Edit,
Terminal, and Help menus to learn more about making your Telnet
sessions more productive.*

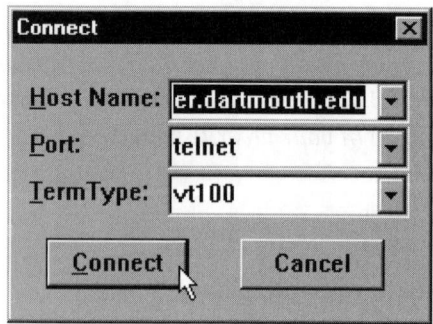

Figure 29-22: *The Connect dialog box in Telnet.*

2. If prompted to do so, supply your login name and press
   Enter. Again if prompted, supply your password and press
   Enter. Some Telnet services will let you in without a pass-
   word, others will not.

TIP

*If a small message box telling you how to log on to the site pops up,
click the OK button in the box, and do what the box says. If you don't
see the message box and you're still not sure how to log on, try moving
or minimizing the Telnet window to see whether the message is hiding
somewhere. If all else fails, try using the login name* guest.

From this point on, you're pretty much on your own. Carefully follow the instructions on the screens that appear. Depending on the system you're using, you may need to press Enter after each command you type. If you're unsure about whether to press Enter, type your command and wait a moment. If nothing happens after a decent interval, press Enter.

When you've finished using the remote system, be sure to log off the remote computer and disconnect. Usually, the remote system will explain how to log off. In Figure 29-20, for example, you can see that the logoff command for Baker Library is BYE. Logging off tells the remote site that you've finished using it and frees the connection so that others can use it. If you simply can't find a way to log off gracefully, choose Connect | Disconnect from the Telnet window's menu bar.

After you type the log off command and press Enter, you may see a message telling you that the connection to the host was lost. Click OK to clear the message. When you've finished using the Telnet window, close it.

MOVING ON

This chapter explored some oldie-but-goodie applications on the Internet—namely, FTP, Gopher, and Telnet. Combine those with the World Wide Web, e-mail, newsgroups, CoolTalk, and all the other features discussed in this book, and you can say you've seen it all. We've certainly covered every Internet service to which Netscape Navigator will give you access.

In the next part of the book we switch to reference materials. Most of the upcoming chapters contain fairly technical trouble-shooting and tweaking techniques that many of you will never even have to bother with. But if you do have to get your hands dirty and change some settings to get past a glitch, hopefully you'll find the information you need somewhere in those chapters.

PART VI:

This 'n' That, Technical Stuff

Getting Online (for Newbies)

If you haven't actually dipped your feet into cyberspace yet, then the first thing you need to do is get some kind of Internet access. As you'll learn in this chapter, there are many, many ways to jack into cyberspace. You'll also need a copy of Netscape Navigator Gold 3.0 (if you don't already have one). This chapter, which looks at different ways to accomplish those two goals, discusses the following topics:

- How to access the Internet from America Online, CompuServe, or the Microsoft Network
- How to access the Internet through a local or national Internet Service Provider (ISP)
- How to connect to the Internet from an organization's permanent Local Area Network (LAN) connection
- Where to get a copy of Netscape Navigator Gold 3.0

By the time you finish this chapter, you'll have—or be well on your way to having—all the resources of the Internet at your fingertips and a copy of one of the coolest Internet browsers—Netscape Navigator Gold.

WHAT YOU NEED TO USE NETSCAPE NAVIGATOR GOLD 3.0

To use Netscape Navigator Gold 3.0, you'll need at least the following:

- A PC or compatible with a 486 or Pentium Processor
- At least 6MB RAM (preferably 8MB)
- A hard disk with at least 5MB of disk space available
- Windows 95 installed
- A connection to the Internet—either a dial-up account (if you're an individual) or permanent LAN connection (if you work for a large organization)
- If you'll be connecting online via a dial-up account, you'll also need a modem

WHAT YOU NEED TO GET ONLINE

If you work for a company or organization that has a full-time connection to the Internet, you probably won't need any special equipment to get online. Just ask your *network administrator* (the person in charge of your company network) to get your PC connected to the Internet.

If you want to get your own PC connected to the Internet and don't work for a company with full-time Internet access, you need a *modem*, a simple device that connects your PC to a wall jack for a telephone line.

CHOOSING A MODEM

If your computer came with a built-in modem, you don't need to buy anything special. Just follow the computer manufacturer's instructions to connect your modem to a telephone jack and, optionally, to your telephone.

If your computer doesn't have a built-in modem, you'll need to buy one. Modems are available at all computer stores and by mail order. You can choose from the following three basic types:

- Internal modem: one that you install inside your PC. You might choose this type of modem if you're comfortable taking your PC apart and installing new hardware inside the case.

- External modem: connects to your PC from the outside. An external modem might take up a little desk space and will take up one of your COM ports. Also, you'll need to plug it in to (yet another) wall outlet. To install it, however, you won't need to fiddle with the "guts" of your PC.

- PC Card modem: A PC Card (or PCMCIA) modem is one that slides into the PCMCIA slot on a portable computer.

Perhaps the most important factor in choosing a modem is speed. Internet connections, by nature, are painfully slow. But the faster your modem, the faster things will move along. The speed of a modem is measured in *baud, bits per second* (bps), or *kilobits per second* (kbps).

You can spend from $50 to $350 on a modem. If you were to buy a modem right now, you'd probably find two speeds available—14.4kbps and 28.8kbps—with 28.8kbps being the faster (and hence more expensive) of the two. I strongly recommend that you not settle for anything less than 28.8kbps.

WHAT ABOUT ISDN?

As an alternative to connecting to the Internet through "regular" modems, you can get a special high-speed ISDN line to connect to the Internet. If you go that route, you'll need a special modem— sometimes called a *terminal adapter*—to connect your PC to the ISDN line.

An ISDN line is about twice as fast as a 28.8 modem line, but it's also much more trouble to set up and more expensive. You need to call your local telephone company and have an ISDN line installed. Then you need to find an Internet Service Provider that offers ISDN access. I talk more about setting up ISDN in Chapter 31, "Windows 95 Tweaking & Troubleshooting."

INSTALLING A MODEM

When you have a modem in hand, you need to follow the manufacturer's instructions to connect the modem to your PC and your telephone line. You'll need to shut down *everything* (PC, monitor, printer) first and follow the manufacturer's instructions to a tee. After the modem is hooked up, you can turn everything back on.

Because you're using Windows 95, chances are you won't need to install any of the software that came with the modem. Windows 95 automatically detects the modem and installs all the necessary software. You can probably ignore the manufacturer's instructions for installing DOS and Windows 3.x drivers.

SETTING UP THE MODEM

After you've installed the modem, you'll need to make sure that Windows 95 "knows" the modem is there. Here's how to do that:

1. Click on the Start button in the Windows 95 taskbar.
2. Choose Settings | Control Panel.

3. Double-click the Modems icon to get to the dialog box shown in Figure 30-1.

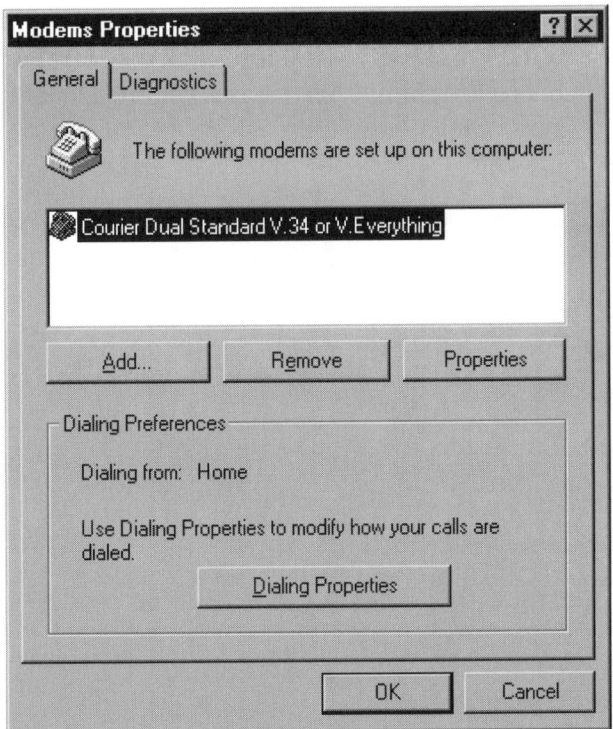

Figure 30-1: *Use the Modems Properties dialog box to install and tweak modems.*

If you see your modem listed under "The following modems are set up on this computer," you're halfway to modem nirvana. If you have not already done so, you should indicate your area code and dialing preferences by clicking the Dialing Properties button and filling in the blanks in the dialog box that appears.

If you don't see your modem listed in the Modems Properties dialog box, first make sure that the modem is properly connected to a telephone line. If it's an external modem, make sure it's plugged in and turned on. Then click the Add button and follow the instructions on the screen to set up the modem.

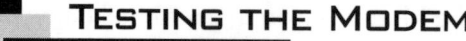

TESTING THE MODEM

When you're sure that your modem is set up, you need to test the connection to the telephone line. Here's a simple way to do so:

1. At the Windows 95 desktop, click the Start button and choose Programs I Accessories I Phone Dialer to get to the Phone Dialer (see Figure 30-2).

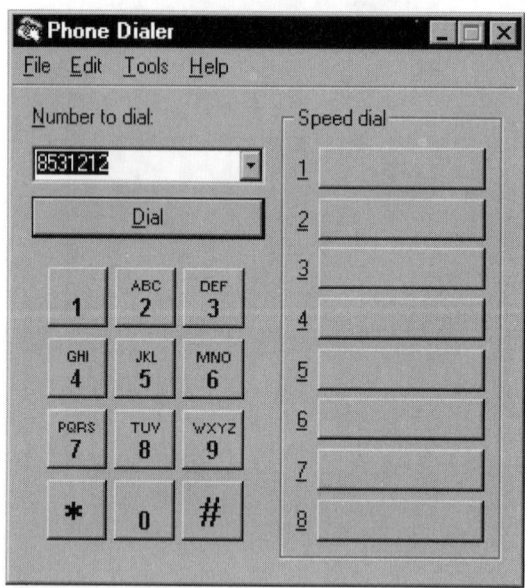

Figure 30-2: *The Windows 95 Phone Dialer.*

2. Click or type in any telephone number (your own will do) and then click on the Dial button.

Chances are, you'll hear a dial tone and hear the modem dialing the number. Even if you don't hear any noise, you'll see a message telling you to Lift the Receiver and then talk. If you see that message, you're in good shape. You can just click the Hang Up button, confident that your modem is working.

If Phone Dialer isn't an option on your Accessories menu, that option just hasn't been installed. If you'd like to install the phone dialer, click the Windows 95 Start button and choose Settings | Control Panel, Add/ Remove Programs. Click the Windows Setup tab, then click Communications | Details. Select (check) the Phone Dialer check box, choose OK (twice) and follow the instructions on the screen.

If instead you see a message that there is no dial tone, or that the line is in use, the modem probably isn't connected correctly to the telephone jack. Make sure that the "Line" (*not* the "Phone") jack on the modem is connected to the wall jack for the telephone, then try again.

If you still have problems, try the Windows 95 troubleshooter:

1. Click the Start button on the Windows 95 taskbar.

2. Choose Help and click the Contents tab.

3. Double-click the Troubleshooting book icon.

4. Double-click *If you have trouble using your modem* and follow the instructions on the screen.

If you still have problems, you'll need to check the modem manufacturer's instructions for other troubleshooting tips. Or (worst-case scenario), contact the modem manufacturer and explain that you're having trouble getting their modem to work on your PC.

With your modem installed and able to dial the telephone, you can begin the next phase—finding a way to access the Internet.

PATHS TO CYBERSPACE

As I've said, there are many ways to get connected to the Internet. But we can boil all the alternatives down to three main categories:

- A commercial online service, such as America Online (AOL), CompuServe (CIS), or the Microsoft Network (MSN).

- A national or local Internet Service Provider (ISP).
- Your organization or company's permanent LAN connection.

The rest of this chapter explores all the options and takes you through the necessary steps to being online and using the Internet.

TIP

*Windows 95's online help also offers lots of information about connecting to the Internet. At the Windows 95 desktop click the Start button and then click on Help. Click the Index tab and then type **Internet**.*

CONNECTING THROUGH YOUR PC SOFTWARE

If your brand-new PC came with some kind of built-in Internet connectivity, all you need to do is find the appropriate instructions in the manuals that came with the PC. This built-in connectivity is actually a program that sets you up with some Internet Service Provider—perhaps NetCOM or IBMConnect. Before you set up that service, you should be aware of a couple of alternatives.

The built-in connection is probably not a free connection. After you make that connection, you may be billed monthly. If you have (or plan to have) an online account with America Online, CompuServe, Wow!, Prodigy, the Microsoft Network, or any other large commercial online service, you might prefer to use that service rather than your PC's built-in connection and just pay the monthly charge for that service.

CONNECTING THROUGH AMERICA ONLINE

If you're an America Online member, the Internet is just a few mouse clicks away. Here's all you need to do:

1. Sign onto America Online in the usual manner.

2. After you're connected, you'll probably come to the In The Spotlight window. Click on Go To Main Menu to get to the main menu shown in Figure 30-3.

Figure 30-3: *America Online's main menu.*

3. Click on Internet Connection to get to the screen shown in Figure 30-4.

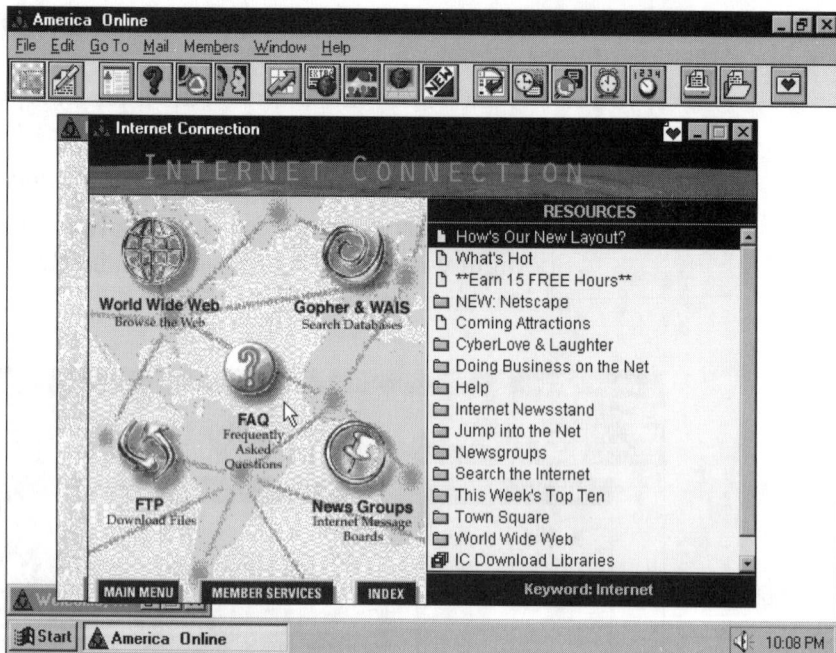

Figure 30-4: *America Online's Internet Connection.*

You are now on the Internet! If you're new to the Internet, you might want to start by clicking on the Frequently Asked Questions (FAQ) button or any other topic that looks interesting. You might also want to check out the World Wide Web, the hottest feature of the Internet these days and the main topic of this book.

CAN I USE NETSCAPE NAVIGATOR WITH AOL?

When you first start browsing the World Wide Web via America Online, you'll be using their Web browser. Because the focus of this book is the Netscape Navigator Gold Web browser, you'll probably want to use Navigator to browse the Web, even though you're connected to the Internet via AOL.

This isn't a problem, but you do have to jump through a few hoops to use Netscape Navigator as your AOL Web browser. To get started, check out the Netscape and Winsock sections on AOL. If you don't see a direct route to either section, follow these steps:

1. From the Internet Connection screen (refer to Figure 30-4), choose Go To | Keyword.

2. Type **netscape** as your keyword and then click Go.

This will bring you to a page similar to the one shown in Figure 30-5, where you can learn about Navigator. If you don't already have a copy of Netscape Navigator, click the Download Netscape! button to download a copy to your PC, so that you can learn how to use it as your Web browser in America Online.

TIP

The term download *means to copy a program from some other computer on the Internet "down" to your own PC.*

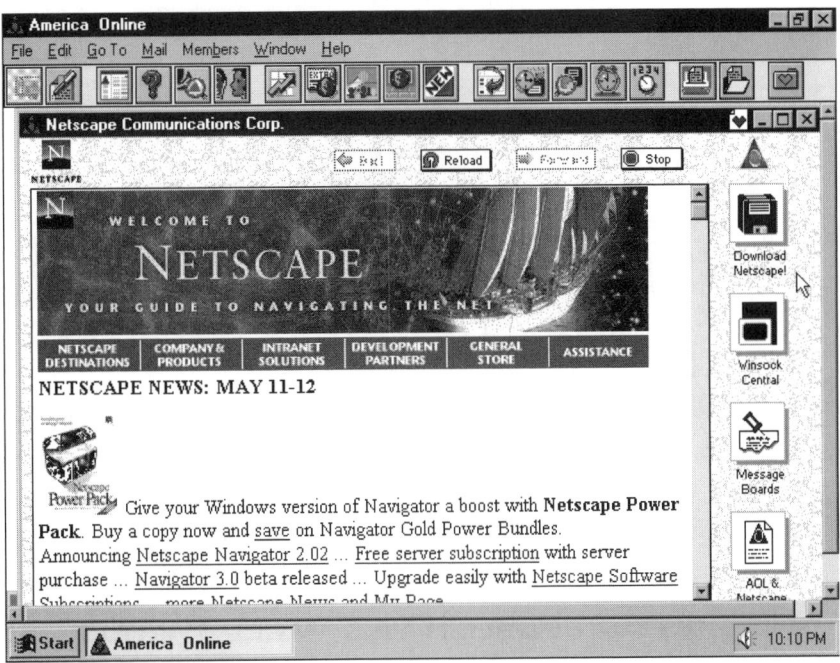

Figure 30-5: *Netscape's area on America Online.*

You'll also need to download and install a program named Winsock. To get started, click the Winsock Central button on your screen. Or, if you don't see that button, repeat Step 1 from the preceding list of steps, this time typing **winsock** (rather than *netscape*) as your keyword. You'll come to the screen shown in Figure 30-6.

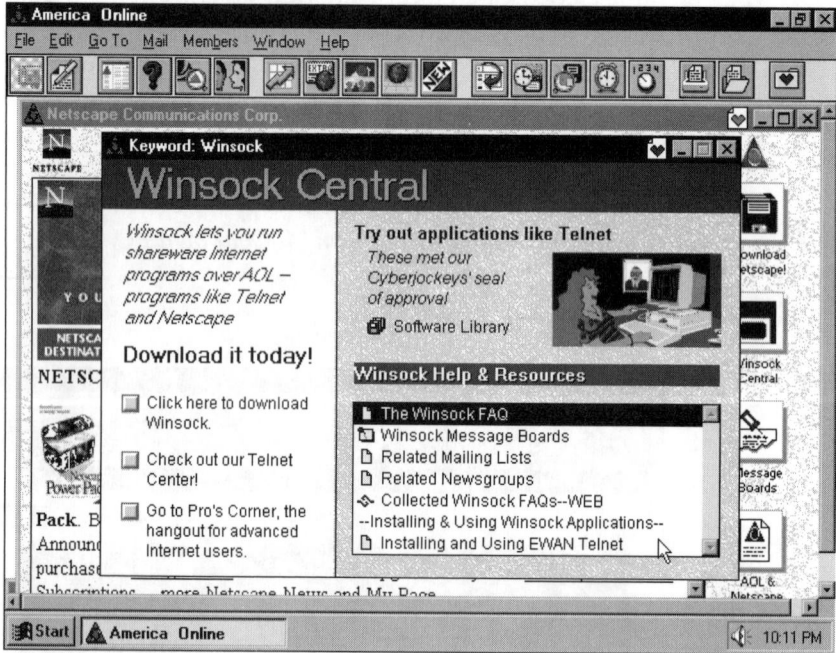

Figure 30-6: *Winsock Central at America Online.*

If you have any problems or need assistance, the people at America Online are your best bet for help. You can check out some of the Winsock- and Web-related message boards and FAQs. There you'll find many people who've been there, done that, and will be more than willing to lend a helping hand.

CAN I PUBLISH WEB PAGES THROUGH AOL?

You can use America Online to browse the World Wide Web (as a spectator), as well as to publish on the Web (as a business or publisher). You're limited to one megabyte of free space, which is enough for a few pages and a few graphic images.

You can find out more about publishing on America Online by visiting their Personal Publisher area. Assuming that you're connected to America Online and at one of their screens, just follow these steps:

1. Click the Go To button in the menu bar, and choose Keyword.

2. Type **personal publisher** and click the Go button to get to the screen shown in Figure 30-7.

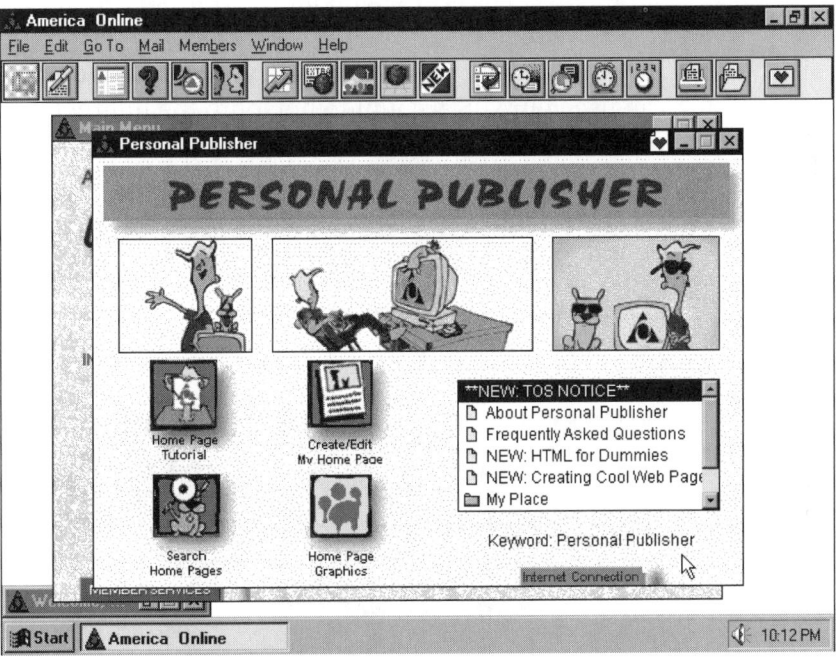

Figure 30-7: *How to publish your Web page via AOL.*

I suspect that many of you will want to do more than publish a personal home page on America Online (and believe me, this book gets into other alternatives quite deeply), but creating a personal home page through AOL is a good way to get your feet wet. When you have some spare time, you might want to give AOL's personal publisher a try.

How to Disconnect From AOL

Remember that while you're connected to the Internet through America Online, you are racking up AOL connect-time charges. Be sure to log off when you're not actively using the Internet. This is simple to do. Just choose File | Exit from AOL's menu bar, or click the Close (X) button in its upper right corner. When you see the "Are you sure....?" message, click the Exit Application button to disconnect. You'll be returned to your Windows 95 desktop.

CONNECTING THROUGH COMPUSERVE

If you're a member of CompuServe Information Service (CIS), you can use your CIS account to hop onto the Internet. Just follow these steps:

1. Start up your WinCim program in the usual manner, as though you were just going to connect to your regular CompuServe account.

2. In the Explore Services box (see Figure 30-8), click the Internet option.

Figure 30-8: *You can get on the Internet from CompuServe's Explore window.*

3. You'll come to the initial Internet screen. As a Netscape Navigator fan, your main interest is in the Web Central area. To get there, choose Services I Go from WinCim's menu bar, type **webcentral**, and then click the OK button.

The Web Central screen (shown in Figure 30-9) is the place to learn more about your Internet connection via CompuServe. To start browsing the World Wide Web, just click the Hot Destinations button, and then choose a Web Site to view.

Figure 30-9: *CompuServe's WebCentral.*

If instead of getting to a Web page, you see a message that you need to install WinSock, just follow the instructions on the screen. CompuServe will help you download and configure the appropriate software.

When you're able to connect to the World Wide Web from your CompuServe account, you can download a copy of Netscape Navigator Gold from Netscape's Web site. Just click the large Enter a Web Site button anywhere in Web Central and enter this URL:

```
http://home.netscape.com
```

When you get to Netscape's home page, click any Netscape Now! button. Or click their General Store or Company & Products button and follow the instructions to purchase and download Netscape Navigator Gold 3.0.

CAN I PUBLISH WEB PAGES THROUGH COMPUSERVE?

Yes, you can publish a personal Web page (up to one megabyte in size) on CompuServe's "Our World" area. The site will be accessible worldwide to everybody on the World Wide Web. To learn more about publishing a Web page via CompuServe, choose Services | Go, type **ourworld** (as one word), and choose OK. You'll come to the window shown in Figure 30-10.

Figure 30-10: *CompuServe's home page wizard.*

If you have a CompuServe account, you might want to give the home page wizard a try. It might not give you the Web site you're dreaming of, but it's a good way to get your feet wet. And you'll have a home page on the World Wide Web that anyone in the world can visit.

CAN I USE NETSCAPE NAVIGATOR WITH COMPUSERVE?

You can use any Web browser, including Netscape Navigator, to browse the World Wide Web via CompuServe. To learn more, check out the All Aboard and Software Express areas on Web Central. For some really great support and help, hop over to the Netscape Users (NSUERS) forum on CompuServe. To do so:

1. Choose Services | Go from WinCim's menu bar.

2. Type **nsuser** and click the OK button.

In the Netscape User's forum, you can find lots of information about setting up Netscape Navigator as your CompuServe Web browser. Choose Library | Browse Library and double-click the Windows 95/NT section. If you have any problems or questions, the Netscape User's Forum is your best resource for answers and solutions.

DISCONNECTING FROM COMPUSERVE

Remember that when you connect to the Internet via CompuServe, you're still paying for your CompuServe connect time and you'll want to log off when you finish exploring the Web. To log off from CompuServe and the Web, just click the Exit button in WinCim's toolbar. Or choose File | Exit from WinCim's menu bar.

CONNECTING THROUGH MSN

The Microsoft Network (MSN) also offers Internet Access to its members. If you're already a member, you just need to run the Internet JumpStart kit to get started on the Internet. The JumpStart kit comes with the Microsoft Plus! Program and is also available with Microsoft's Windows 95 Internet Kit, available at many computer stores, book stores, and directly through Microsoft (call 1-800-MSPRESS). To get connected without buying anything, just follow these steps:

1. Log in to MSN in the usual manner.

2. Go to MSN Central. (If you don't get there automatically, right-click the little MSN icon in your Windows 95 taskbar, then click Go to MSN Central.)

3. Click Categories.

4. Double-click the Internet Center icon to get to the screen shown in Figure 30-11.

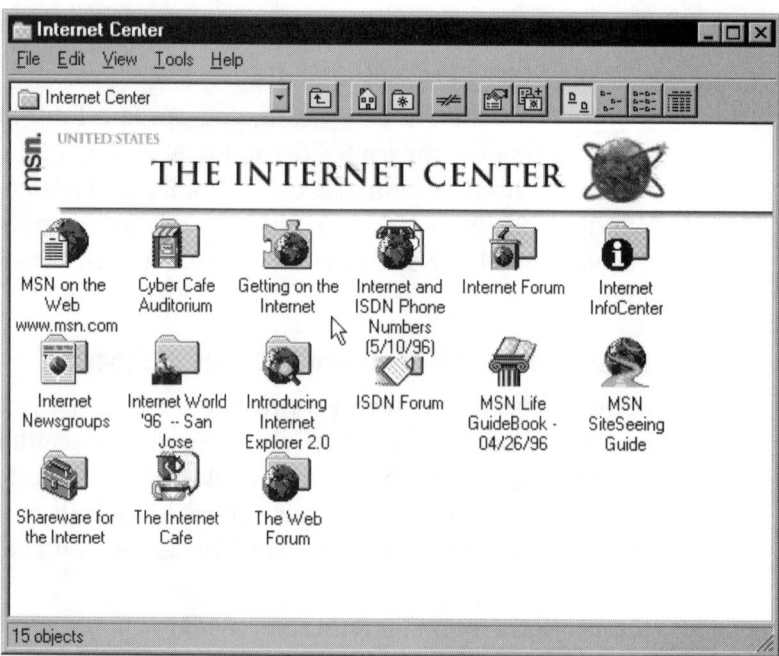

Figure 30-11: *The Microsoft Network's Internet Center.*

Start by double-clicking the Getting on the Internet icon and then just follow instructions as they're presented on the screen.

After you've converted your MSN access to Internet and MSN access, you can connect to both simply by going through the usual

MSN log on procedure. Say, for example, that you've just logged on to MSN through the Windows 95 desktop's The Microsoft Network icon and that you're looking at MSN Central or MSN Today.

If you fire up your Web browser, chances are the browser will see that you're hooked into MSN and the Internet and will take you wherever you want to go. In Figure 30-12, for example, I fired up Netscape Navigator Gold and, lo and behold, it took me straight to Netscape's Web site on the Internet.

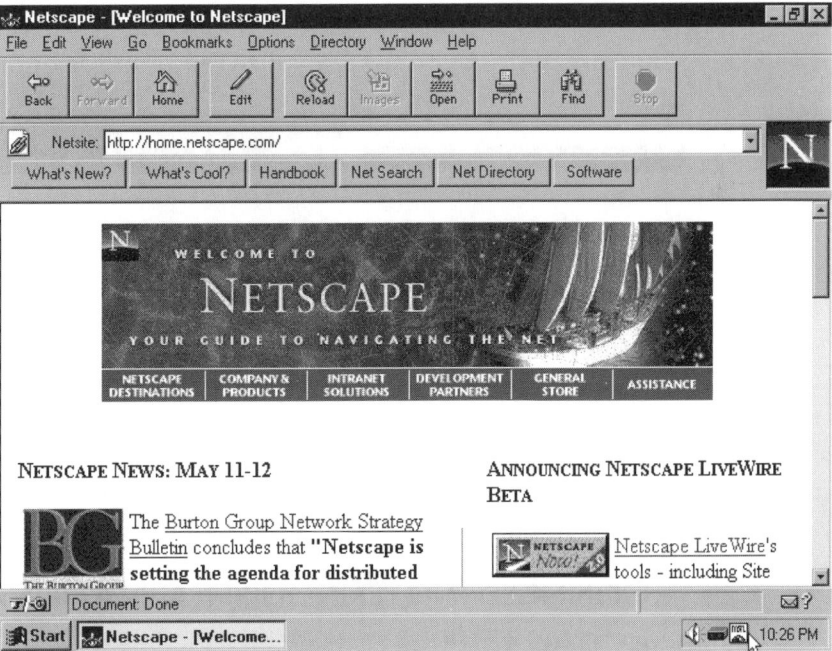

Figure 30-12: *Netscape Navigator works fine with MSN as your Internet Service Provider.*

If you don't already have a copy of Netscape Navigator Gold, you can download a copy from the World Wide Web, via your Microsoft Internet Connection. Point whatever Web browser you have available (e.g., Internet Explorer) to http://home.netscape.com and follow the instructions at Netscape's site to download a copy of Navigator. If you need help downloading, see "Purchasing Netscape Navigator Gold," later in this chapter.

But I Don't Want to Log in to MSN!

After you set up an Internet/MSN account, any request for Internet services will automatically prompt you to log in to MSN. If you have multiple Internet on-ramps installed on your PC, this little fact can drive you crazy. Fortunately, it's also easy to fix.

Just click the Windows 95 Start button and choose Settings|Control Panel. Double-click the Internet icon, clear the Use AutoDial check box, then choose OK. From this point on, you'll need to connect your PC to the Internet, using whatever on-ramp you want, before you fire up your Web browser or other Internet program.

Can I Publish Web Pages Through MSN?

As I write this chapter, Microsoft does not offer Web publishing to its members (but some MSN staffers have told me that they are working on such a service). If you're an MSN member, you might want to see whether that service is available now. Just go to the aforementioned Internet Center and poke around the Web Forum to see what's new.

Connecting Through a National or Local ISP

As an alternative to hooking up to the Internet via some large commercial online service, you can set up an account with a local or national Internet Service Provider (ISP). Typically, a *local* ISP is a company that provides Internet access to people in a particular community or with a certain area code. *National* ISPs provide Internet access to people all over the world. Some even have (800) access for toll-free connections (although the 800 access costs more than regular access). Some of the many ways to find out about national ISPs serving your area and about your local ISPs follow:

■ Contact some of the ISPs listed in Table 30-1 by voice phone, and ask them to mail you information about the services they offer.

Internet Service Provider	Voice Phone
AT&T WorldNet Service	(800)WORLDNET
CERFnet, Inc.	(800)876-2373
Concentric Network Corporation	(800)939-4262
Earthlink Network	(800)395-8425
GTE Intelligent Network Services	(800)927-3000
Internet & Web Services Corporation	(800)701-6NET
Pacific Bell Internet Services	(800)708-4638
PSINet's PSIWeb	(800)827-7482
Web Communications	(408)457-9671
You Tools/FASTNET	(610)954-5910

Table 30-1: *Some of the ISPs supporting Netscape's One-Button Web Publishing.*

■ Check your local Yellow Pages under Internet, or Computer Networking.

■ Look for local circulars at computer stores. Many ISPs advertise in them. Also, check out Internet-related magazines at your local bookstore or newsstand.

■ If someone you know already has Internet access in your area, ask that person for recommendations.

■ If you know anyone in the country who has Internet access, ask them to send you a list of ISPs in your area code. Tell them to look under *http://www.thelist.com*. (They'll know what that means.)

WHAT TO LOOK FOR IN AN ISP

All ISPs are not created equal. When you select an ISP, ask, specifically, whether they can provide the following services:

- Flat-fee service: Will the ISP charge you a flat monthly fee for your Internet access. Or will they also tack on connect-time charges? Generally, a flat fee is better, because you know exactly what the cost will be.

- PPP access: As a Windows 95 user, you'll most likely want to get a PPP dial-up account. If you're given a choice between SLIP and PPP, choose PPP.

- 28.8 kbps access: Can the potential ISP support 28.8 kbps access? This is important, because you really don't want to access the Internet at a lower speed.

- ISDN access: If you're looking for faster Internet access, you might want to set up an ISDN account. Ask your potential ISP whether they can provide one and what it will cost. Does that cost include the $40 per month (or so) that the local telephone company will charge?

- E-mail: Does this ISP offer you an e-mail address and, if so, does it cost extra?

- FTP site/drop box: If you plan to offer your customers many files to download at no cost, you might want to get an FTP site. If you want customers to be able to upload files to you, you'll need an FTP drop box. (See Chapter 29, "FTP, Gopher & Telnet," for more information and examples.)

- Newsgroups: Can this ISP give you full access to the Usenet newsgroups and, if so, does it cost extra?

- Web publishing: Can this ISP give you space for publishing your own Web site? If so, how much does it cost?

- One-button publishing: Netscape Navigator Gold offers one-button publishing to selected ISPs. If you plan to create your own Web page, your ISP shopping list should include those vendors. Table 30-1 lists their names and voice phone numbers. (See Chapters 5, "Finding a Home for Your Page," and 7, "Presenting Your Page to the World," for more information.)

TIP

If you already have Internet access and just want to find an ISP that supports Netscape's one-button publishing, see One-Click Publishers in Chapter 5, "Finding a Home for Your Page."

■   What kind of connection do you have?: The faster your ISP's connection to the Internet, the better. The three basic types of connections that ISPs can have to the Internet are T3 (the fastest), T1 (pretty fast), and fractional T1 (not so great, but usually adequate).

■   Custom domain name: Can this ISP give you a custom domain name and e-mail address? *Be very specific about the name(s) you want.* For example, if you'd like your e-mail address to be *betty@boop.com*, and your Web site address to be *www.boop.com*, ask whether you can have those exact names and, if so, what the cost will be.

■   Toll-free access: The Internet itself is "free," in the sense that there are no long-distance charges. But you will have to pay telephone charges for the connection between your own PC and your ISP. If you can find an ISP in your toll-free dialing area, you can avoid even those charges.

■   Technical support: Getting, and maintaining, a connection can have its difficulties. And the only people who can help you with some of those difficulties will be those at your ISP. Try to find an ISP that offers free technical support, preferably by e-mail, phone, and fax.

Figure 30-13 summarizes the features you'll want to consider, and includes some blanks for you to fill in. I suggest that you make a few photocopies of the figure—one for each ISP you're considering. Talk to these ISPs to find out who offers what (or fax each potential ISP a copy of the form and let *them* fill it in). Then you can easily compare the features and costs of each ISP.

Internet Service Provider

Name:	
Address:	
City, State Zip:	
Voice:	Fax:
Email:	URL:

Service	Offered (Yes/No)	Cost	Comments
Flat-fee service			*Please send rate card*
PPP access			
28.8 kbps			
ISDN access			*Does cost include phone company charges?*
E-mail			*What will my e-mail address be?*
Newsgroups			
Web Publishing			*What will my Web site's URL be?*
Your connection?			*i.e., T3, T1, fractional T1?*
Custom domain name?			*Can I get a simple, custom name for my e-mail address and Web site?**
Free Technical Support?			
Toll free access from my location?			

* For example, can you give my Web site a simple http://www.*mybizname*.com name, and a matching e-mail address such as *myname*@*mybizname*.com?

Feel free to send me any promotional material you have. Send to me at:

_____

_____

Figure 30-13: *Have potential ISPs fill out this form, so that you can compare them.*

The Value of a Custom Domain Name

The last item on the form, custom domain names, is especially important if you want people to remember your domain name. What makes a domain name easy to remember? Here are a couple of examples: a large mall in San Diego—University Towne Centre (UTC)—has a Web site whose address is www.shoputc.com. Pretty easy to remember. Our local news station, KGTV, also has an easy-to-remember Web site address: www.kgtv.com.

Compare those addresses to some of the not-so-custom Web site addresses you'll see, such as www.someplace.users~alan/index.html or http://193.65.230.1/mp/rec/santa/santa.html. There's no way anybody is going to memorize such complicated addresses.

One major catch here is that no two Web sites can have the same address and many address names are already taken. You need to come up with a list of several possible names that might work for you, then ask your ISP whether they can give you any of those names. Your ISP will need to check the database of taken names (at InterNIC) and then let you know which, if any, they can give you.

Remember, not all ISPs can give you a specific e-mail address and domain name. If you can't get a custom domain name, you should find out what names the ISP is likely to give you. If I were you, I'd avoid ISPs that plan to give you some extremely complicated domain name.

My Custom Names

When I first set out to get an e-mail address, I wanted it to be alan@simpson.com. But simpson.com was already taken and I had to come up with something else. I figured most of my e-mail would come from people in the computer book industry, so I tried to think of a name that would be easy for those people to remember.

At that time, the words *cool* and *nerd* were used heavily in computer literature (as they still are, I suppose). I combined the two into *coolnerds*, then made my e-mail address alan@coolnerds.com, and my Web site's address www.coolnerds.com. Both addresses work, in the sense that nobody ever forgets how to get in touch with me online!

After You Select an ISP

After you select a local ISP and set up an account, you'll need to get some very specific information from them in order to set up Netscape Navigator as your Web browser. Chances are, they'll send you all the appropriate information automatically. To make sure that you're getting everything you need, however, you can send them the form shown in Figure 30-14, and have them fill in the blanks.

Please send me the following information about my new account:

My local access number:
My user ID:
My account password:
My IP address (if any):
My subnet mask (if any):
My primary DNS (if any):
My secondary DNS address (if any):
Address of my mail server:
My e-mail address:
My mail server:
My e-mail account address:
My e-mail password:
My news server (if any):
My Web site's address (if any):
My ftp address (if any):
My ftp dropbox address (if any):

Please send me the following checked items:

- ❏ Instructions for connecting to my account using Windows 95 Dial-Up Networking.
- ❏ Complete instructions for setting up Netscape Navigator Gold 3.0 as my Web browser.
- ❏ Complete instructions for uploading Web pages to my Web site.
- ❏ Complete instructions for uploading files to my ftp site.

Plus any additional materials I'll need to get online. Send to:

_____

_____

Thank you!

Figure 30-14: *Information you'll need from your ISP after you set up an account.*

Your Internet Service Provider will probably provide you with complete instructions for setting up the Windows 95 Dial-Up Networking (DUN) feature to make your connection to the Internet. If you have any problems configuring DUN, see "Setting Up Dial-Up Networking" in Chapter 31, "Windows 95 Tweaking & Troubleshooting."

CONNECTING THROUGH A PERMANENT LAN CONNECTION

As mentioned earlier, if the company or organization you work for has a full-time, permanent connection to the Internet, you don't even need a modem to get online. Chances are, you can just install Netscape Navigator, fire it up, and—bingo—you're on the Internet.

If you try it, and it doesn't work that way, then your best bet is to meet with your network administrator—the person in charge of the LAN—and explain that you're trying to get on the Internet via Netscape Navigator. Chances are, the administrator will know exactly what to do. He or she should be able to get you set up and show you exactly how to get online from your own terminal or PC.

If you are the network administrator and you don't know how to set up a Windows 95 workstation for access to the Internet, you'll need to set up TCP/IP as a network protocol on the user's PC, enter your IP address, and so forth. For more information, see "Setting Up a Permanent LAN Connection," in Chapter 31.

PURCHASING NETSCAPE NAVIGATOR

At one time, software companies were so eager to get market share on Internet software they would give away their software. In fact, they would let us put copies of those programs on the CD that accompanies a book like this one. Unfortunately, those days are coming to an end. Netscape no longer gives away the Gold product through CD-ROMs in books.

But there are plenty of convenient ways to purchase a copy of Netscape Navigator Gold 3.0. You can download it from Netscape's Web site, or purchase it in a computer store or through a mail-order catalog.

BUYING NAVIGATOR ONLINE

If you already have Internet access and a Web browser and you know how to use that browser, you can purchase Netscape Navigator Gold 3.0 from Netscape's Web site. To do so, follow these steps:

1. Point your Web browser to http://home.netscape.com.

2. Click on the General Store button. You'll come to a screen that looks something like Figure 30-15.

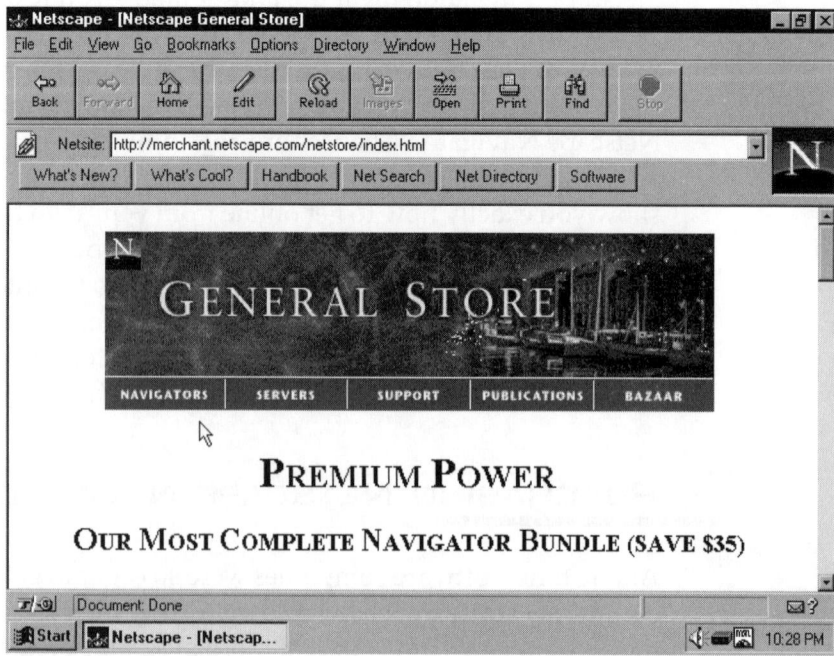

Figure 30-15: *Netscape's General Store.*

3. Locate the Netscape Navigator Gold 3.0 product, click that link, and follow the instructions on the screen.

Buying Navigator From a Store or by Mail Order

If you don't already have access to World Wide Web, you can purchase Netscape Navigator Gold 3.0 from any computer store. Or pick up any computer or Internet magazine, where you'll no doubt find many mail-order houses from which you can order by mail, phone, or fax. Optionally, you can call Netscape directly at (415) 937-3777.

> **TIP**
>
> *If you work for a company with a permanent LAN connection to the Internet, you might ask your network administrator to install Netscape Navigator for you.*

You're Ready to Roll

At this point, you have, or are well on your way to getting, some kind of Internet access. You either have a copy of Netscape Navigator Gold 3.0 installed on your PC, or you're well on your way to getting a copy.

Now I realize that much of this chapter is rather vague. I wish I could tell you specifically, step-by-step, *exactly* how to get connected to the Internet, and exactly how to install your copy of Netscape Navigator Gold. Unfortunately, because every service provider has its own set of steps to follow, the only place you can get the exact step-by-step instructions you need is from that Internet Service Provider (including America Online, CompuServe, and MSN).

As far as installing Navigator Gold goes—the exact procedure will depend on how you purchase the product: whether you download it, purchase a CD-ROM or floppy disks, or get it free with your PC or some service provider. But I'm confident that whichever route you take, you'll get some easy instructions for setting up Navigator on your PC.

I should warn you that the whole procedure can be complicated and confusing, especially if your service provider doesn't offer adequate support. But keep in mind that tens of millions of people, just like you, have "made it" to the Internet. It definitely can be done.

MOVING ON

Where you go from here depends on what you accomplish in this chapter:

- If you get an Internet account, but have trouble getting online, see the next chapter for information on getting Windows 95 and your Internet account in sync.

- When you can get online, you can go skim Chapter 1 and then go on to Chapter 2.

- If you can't get Internet access right away, but want to start learning about the World Wide Web and Netscape Navigator Gold while you're waiting, go on ahead and back to Chapter 1, "Go for the Gold."

Windows 95 Tweaking & Troubleshooting

Perhaps the toughest part of using the Internet is getting set up and getting connected. With that done, the rest is a piece of cake. This chapter takes the mystery and pain out of Internet setup, so that you can get on and start cruising. Here are some of the topics you'll be learning about:

- Setting up a permanent LAN connection to the Internet
- Setting up dial-up networking and connecting to the Internet with your modem
- Setting up a dial-up script to speed up modem connections to the Internet
- Setting up Windows 95 to use ISDN

WHO NEEDS THIS CHAPTER?

Not everyone will need to read this chapter. In fact, before you even look at this chapter you should set up some kind of account with an Internet Service Provider (ISP), as discussed in Chapters 5, "Finding a Home for Your Page," and 30, "Getting Online (for

Newbies)." Follow that ISP's instructions to set up your PC. If you *still* have problems connecting to the Internet, even after following your ISP's instructions, then maybe you need to do a little tweaking in Windows 95, as discussed in this chapter.

By the way, be sure that your modem can dial out (as discussed in Chapter 30), before you tackle the procedures listed in this chapter. Also, feel free to use the Windows 95 online help for further support while reading this chapter. At the Windows 95 desktop, click the Start button and choose Help. Then click the Index tab and type **internet**. Double-click the *connecting to* index entry.

If you work for an organization that will be giving you access to the Internet through the organization's LAN, then you really should contact that organization's network administrator for Internet access. Once again, do so before you try any of the procedures described in this chapter.

If you're still reading, then you must be looking for a solution to a specific problem in getting connected to the Internet. Even so, you may not have to read this entire chapter. Just dip into the sections that apply to your own situation:

- If your computer will be connected directly to the Internet through a local area network (LAN) rather than through a modem, read "Setting Up TCP/IP for a Permanent LAN Connection."

- If you'll be dialing into the Internet with a modem, read "Setting Up Dial-Up Networking."

- If you'd like to explore ISDN, the fast alternative to using modems for connecting to the Internet, read "Setting Up Windows 95 to Use ISDN."

TCP/IP, PPP, SLIP, ISDN & OTHER ALPHABET SOUP

Your desire to communicate with the Internet will expose you to all sorts of weird terms and technical mumbo jumbo. It's not important to understand all the underlying details of how information gets from one place to another on the Internet, but it is useful to know a little jargon so that you don't drown in the alphabet soup of cyberspace. Here's a quick list of terms you're likely to encounter when setting up your Internet connection for the first time:

ISDN (*Integrated Services Digital Network*) is a high-speed, fully digital telephone service that can operate at speeds of up to 128Kbs—up to five times faster than today's fastest analog modems. ISDN is still pretty expensive and it's not available everywhere.

PPP (*Point-to-Point Protocol*) is a communications standard that lets your computer dial into the Internet, using a modem and a standard telephone line. Windows 95 has built-in support for PPP. Most Internet Service Providers (ISPs) support either PPP or SLIP, but PPP is preferable.

SLIP (*Serial Line Internet Protocol*) is a communications standard that (like PPP) lets your computer dial into the Internet, using a modem and a standard telephone line. SLIP works with Windows 95 only if you've installed the Internet components available in Microsoft Plus!, on the CD-ROM version of Windows 95, or available for free downloading from Microsoft's Web site (more about this later).

TCP/IP (*Transmission Control Protocol/Internet Protocol*) is the standard technique used on the Internet to package and unpackage Internet information so that everything gets to the right destination.

Setting Up TCP/IP for a Permanent LAN Connection

Many businesses and research institutions share information within their organization by using *local area networks* (LANs). Some of these office LANs are wired directly to the Internet via high-speed communications lines. If you're lucky enough to work for an organization that's hardwired to the Internet, you can just fire up Netscape Navigator and start cruising the Internet. Whenever Netscape Navigator is running, you'll be connected automatically to the Internet. And when you exit the program, you'll be disconnected automatically from the Internet.

Trap

> *If you'll be connecting to the Internet through a modem, skip all the way down to "Setting Up Dial-Up Networking" now.*

Your network administrator already may have configured the necessary TCP/IP software on your local machine and adjusted the settings for your network account. If that's the case, you're home free and can start cruising cyberspace without any preliminaries. If the configuration has not yet been done, here's what you'll need to do:

1. Gather your setup information from your network administrator and jot it down on Table 31-1 or on a copy of that table. (By the way, if you're on a Novell network, you may be able to find your IP address and your gateway IP address in the file NET.CFG, which usually is located in the root directory of your hard drive (C:\).)

Your IP address:
Your subnet mask:
WINS configuration (usually not necessary):
Primary WINS Server
Secondary WINS Server
Scope ID:
Use DHCP for WINS Resolution (Yes/No):
Your gateway IP address:
Bindings (in addition to Client for Microsoft Networks):
Your user name (computer's host name):
Your company's domain name:
Your company's main DNS server IP address:
Your company's alternate DNS server IP address (if any):
Your company's domain suffix:
Manufacturer and model of your network adapter:
Type of network driver to use:
Protocols that are necessary on your LAN:

Table 31-1: *What you'll need to know to set up a permanent LAN connection.*

TRAP

Always get permission from your network administrator before making changes to your network or TCP/IP settings. Network administrators are known to get cranky when "users" start messing with network settings.

2. Install the TCP/IP software, as explained in "Installing TCP/IP."

3. Configure the TCP/IP software for a permanent connection, as explained in "Configuring TCP/IP for a Permanent Connection."

4. Install and configure the network adapter software, as explained in "Installing and Configuring the Network Adapter Software."

INSTALLING TCP/IP

Follow these steps to install the TCP/IP protocol:

1. Double-click My Computer on the Windows 95 desktop, then double-click Control Panel (or choose Start | Settings | Control Panel). The Control Panel window will open.

2. Double-click the Network icon. You'll see a Configuration dialog box that resembles Figure 31-1. (Don't worry if the components listed on your screen don't match my example.)

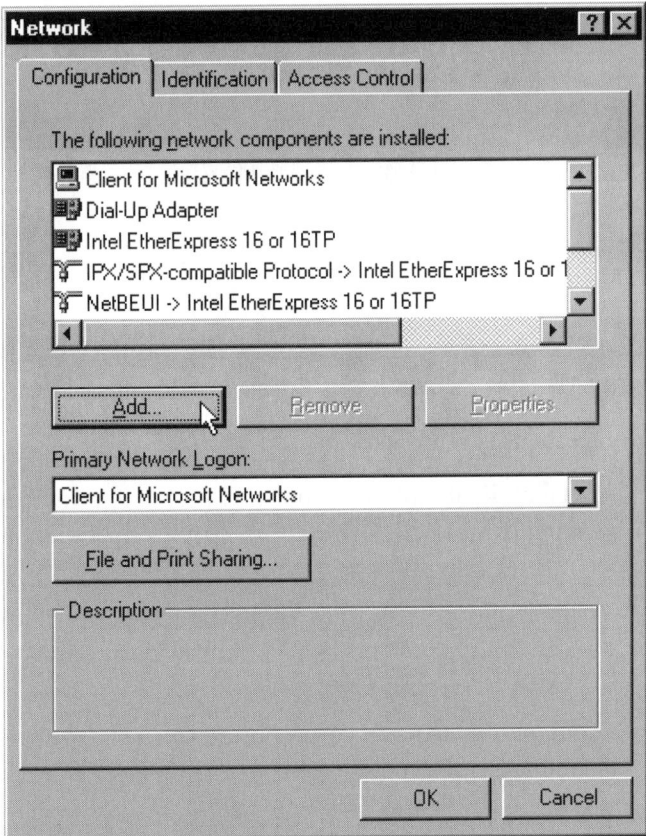

Figure 31-1: *The Configuration tab of the Network dialog box.*

3. If you see *TCP/IP* in the list of installed components, skip ahead to the section on "Configuring the TCP/IP Software for a Permanent Connection" or the one on "Configuring the TCP/IP Software for a Dial-Up Connection."

4. Click the Add button below the list of installed network components. The Select Network Component Type dialog box, shown in Figure 31-2, will appear.

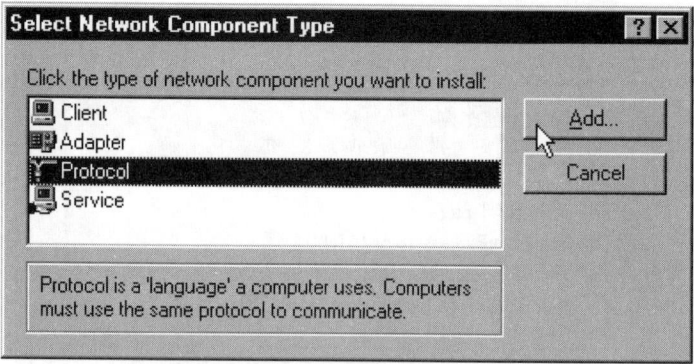

Figure 31-2: *The Select Network Component Type dialog box.*

5. Click Protocol in the list and then click the Add button (or just double-click Protocol) to open the Select Network Protocol dialog box.

6. In the Manufacturers list in the left panel, click Microsoft. In the Network Protocols list in the right panel, click TCP/IP, as shown in Figure 31-3.

7. Click OK to save your changes and return to the Network dialog box.

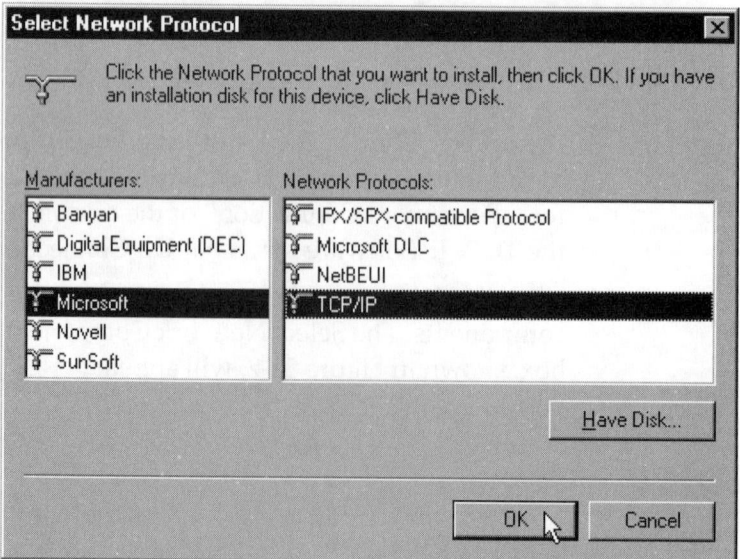

Figure 31-3: *The Select Network Protocol dialog box, with Microsoft and TCP/IP selected.*

That takes care of the installation steps. Leave the Network dialog box open so that you can configure TCP/IP for your connection. If you'll be using a permanent connection, follow the steps in the next section. If you'll be using a dial-up connection, skip ahead to the section "Configuring TCP/IP for a Dial-Up Connection."

CONFIGURING TCP/IP FOR A PERMANENT CONNECTION

Assuming that you've installed TCP/IP and have all the information listed in Table 31-1, you're ready to configure TCP/IP for a permanent connection to the Internet. In the following steps, you'll plug in the TCP/IP settings your network administrator gave you earlier (refer to Table 31-1):

1. Starting from the Configuration tab of the Network dialog box, click *TCP/IP* in the installed components list, then click the Properties button (or just double-click TCP/IP). You'll see the TCP/IP Properties dialog box.

2. Click the IP Address tab of the dialog box (if the tab isn't selected already), click the Specify An IP Address option button, and enter your IP Address and your Subnet Mask in the appropriate fields. When you've finished, the screen will resemble Figure 31-4.

TIP

IP addresses and subnet masks typically consist of four parts. Each part contains up to three digits, and a period (.) separates each part from the next. If the subpart you're typing has three digits, the cursor will jump automatically to the next subpart. If the subpart has fewer than three digits, you'll need to press the period key to move the cursor to the next subpart. You can use the left and right arrow keys on your keyboard and other standard text editing methods also to move the cursor through the IP Address and Subnet Mask entries as necessary.

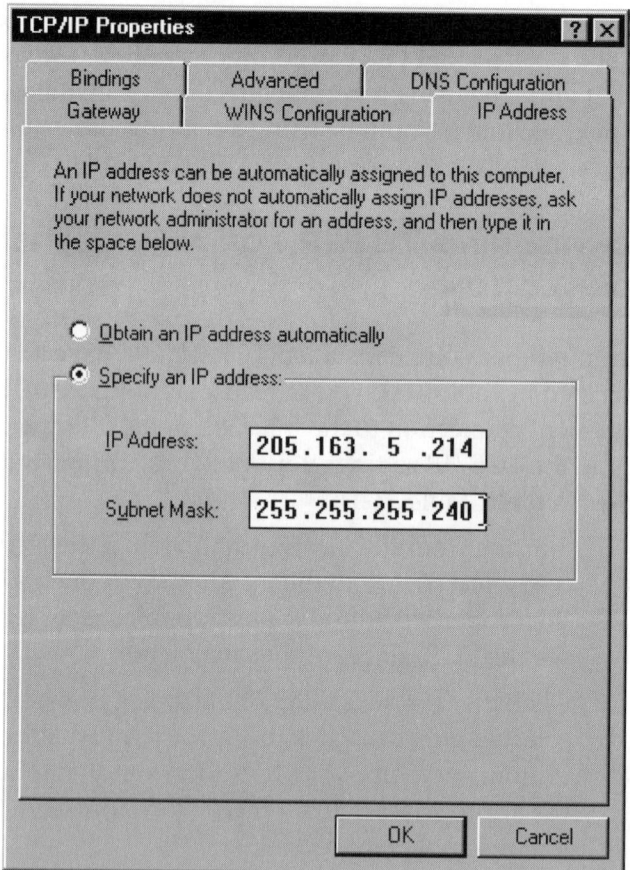

Figure 31-4: *A completed IP Address tab.*

3. Click the WINS configuration tab, click the Select the WINS configuration tab, and then click the Disable WINS Resolution option button, unless your network administrator has told you otherwise.

4. Click the Gateway tab. Then, enter your gateway IP address in the New Gateway box, and click the Add button.

5. Click the Bindings tab. The Client For Microsoft Networks box is checked by default (leave this box checked). If necessary, check any additional clients that are required.

6. Click the Advanced tab and be sure that Set This Protocol To Be The Default Protocol is selected (checked).

7. Click the DNS Configuration tab and then click the Enable DNS option button. Fill in the following items, so that your screen resembles Figure 31-5.

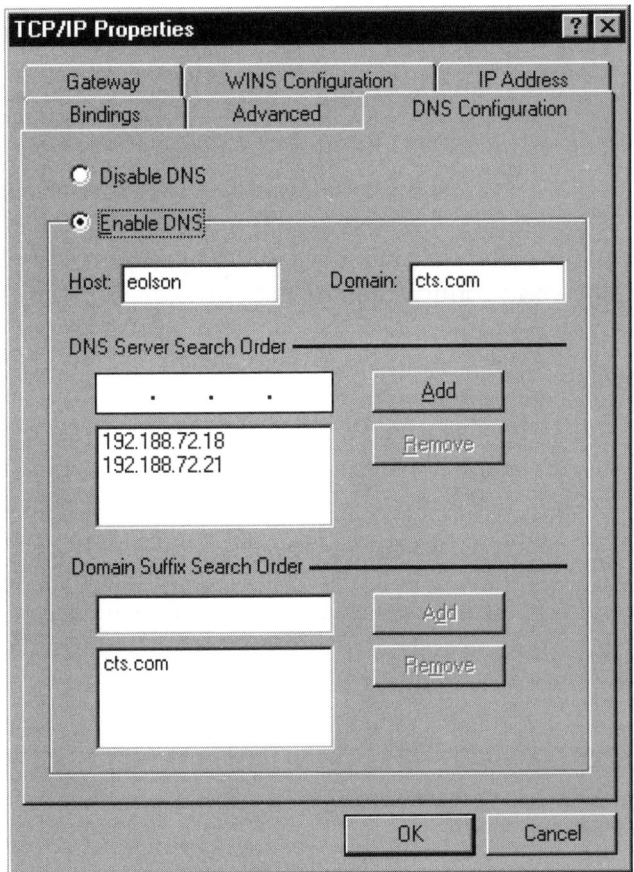

Figure 31-5: *The completed DNS Configuration tab.*

- In the Host box, enter your user name.
- In the Domain box, enter your company's domain name.

- In the DNS Server Search Order box, type your company's main DNS server IP address, and click the Add button.

- If your network administrator has provided your company's alternate DNS server IP address, type that address in the DNS Server Search Order box and click the Add button.

- In the Domain Suffix Search Order box, type your company's domain suffix and click the Add button.

8. Click OK to return to the Configuration tab of the Network dialog box.

Congratulations! You've configured your TCP/IP settings. Now, stay in the Network dialog box so that you can do the next step—installing and configuring the network adapter software.

TRAP

After configuring your TCP/IP settings to access the Internet over a local area network, you may receive the error message, "This DHCP client was unable to obtain an IP network address from a DHCP server. Do you want to see future DHCP messages?" If this happens, click No in the message box, and continue working normally. The message should not bother you again. For more information, check out the Microsoft Knowledge Base article at http://www.microsoft.com/kb/peropsys/win95/q139805.htm.

INSTALLING & CONFIGURING THE NETWORK ADAPTER SOFTWARE

Your network card or network adapter is a hardware device that physically connects your computer to the network. Chances are that your adapter software (or driver) is already installed and configured properly. But just in case it isn't, the next two sections explain how to install and configure the software for a permanent connection to the Internet.

INSTALLING THE NETWORK ADAPTER SOFTWARE

Follow these steps to install the network adapter software:

1. If you're not already viewing the Configuration tab in the Network dialog box (refer to Figure 31-1), open the Network option in Control panel by repeating Steps 1 and 2 of the previous section on "Installing TCP/IP."

2. If you see the name of your network adapter in the list of installed components, skip ahead to the next section on "Configuring the Network Adapter Software."

3. If the network adapter isn't in the installed components list, click the Add button. You'll see the Select Network Component Type shown earlier in Figure 31-2.

4. Click Adapter in the list, then click the Add button (or just double-click Adapter) to open the Select Network adapters dialog box.

5. In the Manufacturers list in the left panel, click the manufacturer of your network card. In the Network Adapters list in the right panel, click the exact model of your card (see Figure 31-6 for an example).

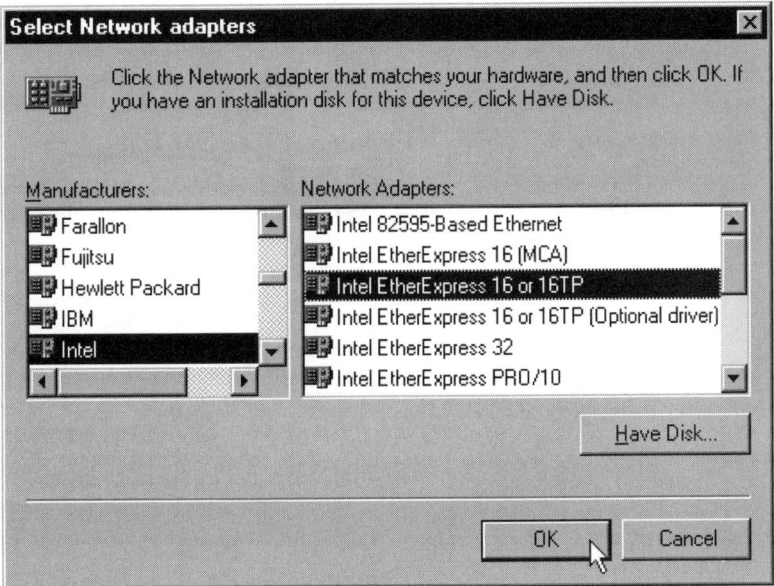

Figure 31-6: *The Select Network adapters dialog box, with a sample manufacturer and network adapter selected.*

6. Click OK to save your changes and return to the Network dialog box.

You've now installed the network adapter software. Again, leave the Network dialog box open so that you can configure the adapter, as explained next.

CONFIGURING THE NETWORK ADAPTER SOFTWARE

Here are the steps for configuring your network adapter software. Again, you'll be plugging in the settings your network administrator gave you (refer to Table 31-1):

1. Starting from the Configuration tab of the Network dialog box, click the name of your network adapter in the installed components list, and then click the Properties button (or just double-click the name). You'll see a Properties dialog box for your adapter, similar to the one shown in Figure 31-7. The title bar and tabs in the dialog box will be specific for the network card you've installed.

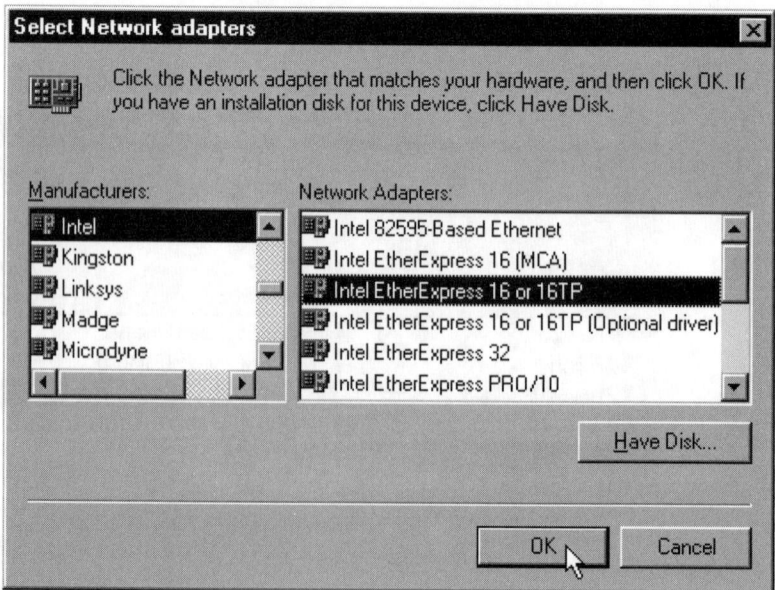

Figure 31-7: *Properties dialog box for an Intel EtherExpress 16 or 16TP adapter.*

2. Click the Bindings tab and select (check) the TCP/IP and NetBEUI check boxes. Also check the boxes next to the names of any other necessary protocols for your LAN.

3. Click OK to return to the Configuration tab.

When you've finished changing the Network settings, click OK to exit the Network Properties dialog box. Windows 95 will ask whether you want to reboot your system. Click Yes and take a quick break while your system restarts.

That's it! You're ready to fire up Netscape Navigator and cruise the Net.

SETTING UP DIAL-UP NETWORKING

If you're using a modem to connect to the Internet, the setup steps are a little more complicated than those for setting up a permanent connection. Still, if you just take each step, one at a time, you'll find the job less intimidating than you might expect.

1. Gather the setup information from your ISP and jot it down in Table 31-2 (or make a copy of the table and then write the info on the copy).

TRAP

For obvious security reasons, you might not want to write down your computer's password in Table 31-2, especially if other people might be peeking at your answers.

Your IP address:	
Your subnet mask:	
Your gateway IP address:	
Your computer's user host name:	
Your ISP's domain name:	
Your ISP's primary DNS server IP address:	
Your ISP's secondary DNS server IP address (if any):	
Your ISP's domain suffix:	
Your ISP's telephone number:	
Your computer's login name:	
Your computer's password:	

Table 31-2: *What you'll need to know to set up a dial-up connection.*

2. Set up your modem as explained in Chapter 30, "Getting Online (for Newbies)."

3. Install the Dial-Up Networking software. (See the "Installing Dial-Up Networking" section that follows.

4. Install the TCP/IP software, as explained earlier in "Installing TCP/IP."

5. Configure the TCP/IP software for dial-up networking. (See the "Configuring TCP/IP for a Dial-Up Connection" section that follows.)

6. Create and configure a connection to the computer you want to dial into. (See the "Installing & Configuring a Dial-Up Connection" section that follows.)

7. Connect to the Internet, as explained later in "Connecting to the Internet."

8. Disconnect from the Internet, as explained later in "Disconnecting from the Internet."

9. Create a script to automate the dial-up connection. This step is optional, but it can save you the trouble of typing a user name and password each time you connect to your ISP. (See the "Creating a Dial-Up Script" section that follows.)

GETTING CONNECTED TO THE INTERNET WITH MICROSOFT'S INTERNET JUMPSTART KIT

Microsoft's Internet Jumpstart Kit is a handy set of utilities and extensions to Windows 95 that makes it easier for you to configure Windows 95 for Internet access. Here's what you'll find in the Internet Jumpstart kit:

Internet Setup Wizard: A tool that makes it easier to set up Windows 95 for use on the Internet. The Internet Setup Wizard simplifies the whole process of setting up your system for SLIP or PPP access to the Internet.

Internet Explorer: Microsoft's World Wide Web browser for Windows 95.

SMTP Mail Provider: Adds features to Microsoft Exchange's Inbox, so that it can send and receive Internet mail using POP3 post offices.

Internet Extensions: Extra goodies to enhance the integration between Windows 95 and the Internet.

You can download the Internet Jumpstart kit (free) if you haven't already purchased Windows Plus! (which also contains the kit, plus some fun desktop themes and sounds, enhanced disk compression, and a cool 3D pinball game). You'll find the Internet Jumpstart kit software on the Microsoft Network (MSN), at *ftp://ftp.microsoft.com* and on other online services, such as CompuServe.

Installing Dial-Up Networking

Dial-Up Networking is the component of Windows 95 that lets you attach to your Internet Service Provider via SLIP or PPP. Just in case you didn't install Dial-Up Networking when you first installed Windows 95, you can do so now by following these steps. You might want to gather up your original Windows 95 floppy disks or CD-ROM for this procedure, in case you need to install some software:

1. Double-click My Computer on the Windows 95 desktop, then double-click Control Panel (or choose Start | Settings | Control Panel). The Control Panel window will open.

2. Double-click the Add/Remove Programs icon to open the Add/Remove Programs Properties dialog box.

3. Click the Windows Setup tab, shown in Figure 31-8.

Figure 31-8: *The Windows Setup tab of the Add/Remove Programs Properties dialog box.*

4. Click the Communications entry and click the Details button to open the Communications dialog box, shown in Figure 31-9.

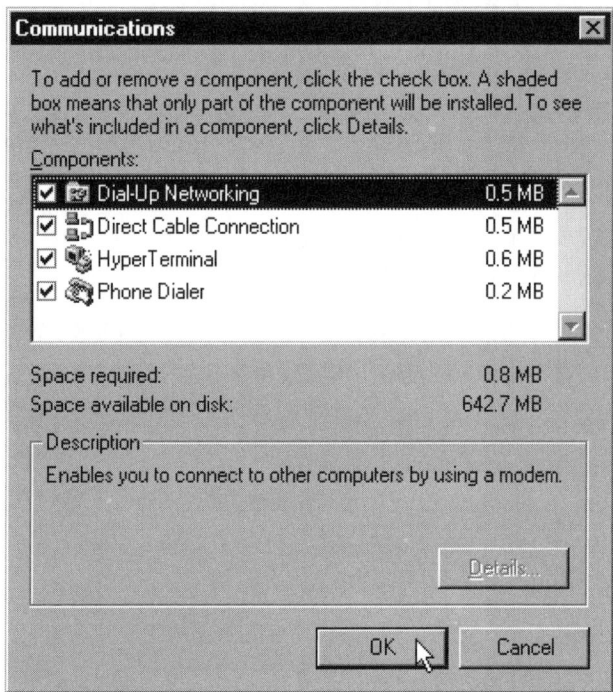

Figure 31-9: *The Communications dialog box, with all the communications components selected.*

5. If Dial-Up Networking is checked, click Cancel until you return to the Windows 95 desktop. Otherwise, click the Dial-Up Networking check box to select it, and click OK twice.

6. Follow any prompts that appear on your screen and restart your computer when prompted to do so.

Well, that's over with. Now, on to configuring TCP/IP for a dial-up connection to the Internet.

ADDING SLIP & DIAL-UP SCRIPTING SUPPORT

Windows 95 supports PPP, but it doesn't support SLIP right out of the box. If you have the CD-ROM version of Windows 95, however, SLIP support is easy to add. Here are the steps to follow:

1. Insert the original Windows 95 CD into your CD-ROM drive.

2. Double-click My Computer on the Windows 95 desktop, then double-click Control Panel (or choose Start|Settings|Control Panel). The Control Panel window will open.

3. Double-click the Add/Remove Programs icon to open the Add/Remove Programs Properties dialog box.

4. Click the Windows Setup tab and then click the Have Disk button. The Install From Disk dialog box appears.

5. Click the Browse button and you'll see the Open dialog box. Use the Drive's drop-down list to choose your CD-ROM drive. Then use standard navigation techniques to locate the file *admin\apptools\dscript\rnaplus.inf* and click OK until you see the Have Disk dialog box.

6. In the Components list of the Have Disk dialog box, select (check) SLIP and Scripting for Dial-Up Networking, and click the Install button. SLIP, CSLIP, and a handy feature called dial-up scripting will be added to your system. You'll learn more about dial-up scripting later in this chapter.

By the way, if you don't have the CD-ROM version of Windows 95, all is not lost. You can download (or get a friend to do it for you) dial-up SLIP and scripting support software at *http://www.microsoft.com/windows/software/admintools.htm*.

CONFIGURING TCP/IP FOR A DIAL-UP CONNECTION

Assuming that you've already installed TCP/IP on your computer, you're now ready to configure it. During these steps, you'll be plugging in most of the information you recorded earlier in Table 31-2. Are you ready? Here goes:

1. Starting from the Configuration tab of the Network dialog box, click *TCP/IP->Dial-Up Adapter* in the installed components list, then click the Properties button (or just double-click TCP/IP->Dial-Up Adapter). You'll see the TCP/IP Properties dialog box.

2. Click the IP Address tab of the dialog box (if the tab isn't selected already).

3. If your Internet Service Provider assigns IP addresses dynamically, select the Assign An IP Address Automatically option button, and skip to Step 4. Otherwise, click the Specify An IP Address option button and enter your IP Address and your Subnet Mask in the appropriate fields (refer to Figure 31-4).

4. Click the Gateway tab. Then, enter your gateway IP address in the New Gateway box and click the Add button.

5. Click the DNS Configuration tab and then click the Enable DNS option button. Fill in the following items, so that your screen resembles Figure 31-5.

   - In the Host box, enter your computer's user host name.

   - In the Domain box, enter your ISP's domain name.

   - In the DNS Server Search Order box, type your ISP's primary DNS server IP address and click the Add button.

   - If your ISP has provided a secondary DNS server IP address, type that address in the DNS Server Search Order box and click the Add button.

   - In the Domain Suffix Search Order box, type your ISP's domain suffix and click the Add button.

8. Click OK to return to the Configuration tab of the Network dialog box.

9. Click OK again to exit the Network Properties dialog box. Windows 95 will ask whether you want to reboot your system. Click Yes and wait patiently while your system restarts.

If you'd like to take a breather, now might be a good time. But if you're game to set up the dial-up connection to your Internet Service Provider, go ahead to the next section.

INSTALLING & CONFIGURING A DIAL-UP CONNECTION

Telling Windows 95 how to connect to your Internet Service Provider is really quite easy. As usual, I'll first explain how to install the connection, then I'll show you how to configure it with the finishing touches.

INSTALLING A NEW DIAL-UP CONNECTION

Here's how to install a new dial-up connection:

1. Double-click My Computer on the Windows 95 desktop, then double-click the Dial-Up Networking icon. The Dial-Up Networking window will open.

2. Double-click the Make New Connection icon to start the Make New Connection Wizard, shown in Figure 31-10.

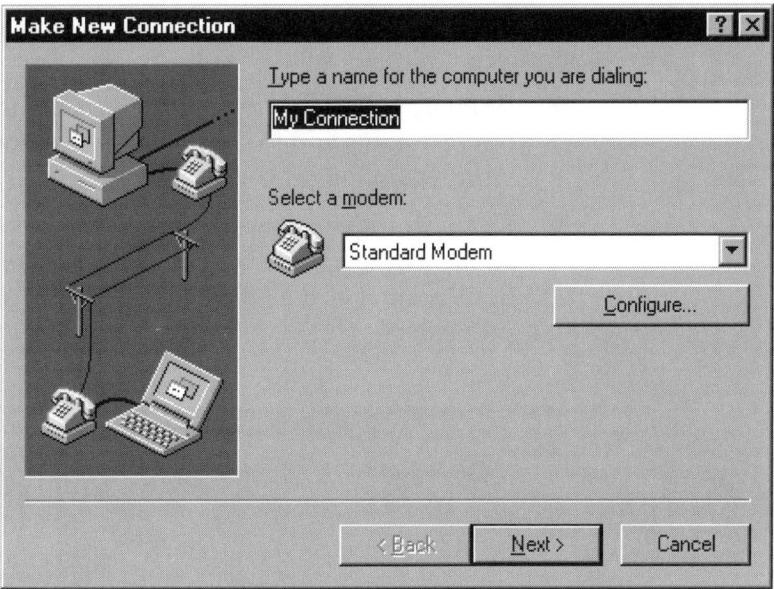

Figure 31-10: *The Make New Connection Wizard dialog box.*

3. Type the name of your Internet Service Provider in the Type a name for the computer you are dialing text box. For example, I'd type **CTS Net**, the name of my service provider.

4. Be sure that the name of your modem appears in the Select a modem drop-down list box. If it doesn't, select your modem's name from the drop-down list.

5. Click the Configure button to display the properties for your modem. If necessary, you can adjust the options shown on the General tab, though you probably won't need to.

6. Click the Options button in the Properties dialog box. Figure 31-11 shows the dialog box after Step 7 is completed.

7. On the Options tab, select (check) *only* the following two options:

- Bring up terminal window after dialing (checking this option allows you to supply your user name and password when logging on to your ISP).

- Display modem status (checking this option displays a status window that shows the progress of your connection and makes it easier to troubleshoot connection problems).

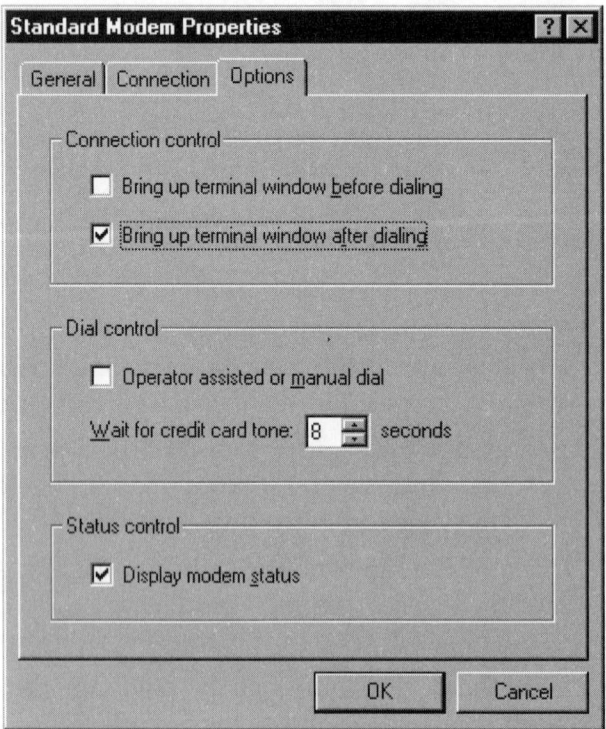

Figure 31-11: *The Options tab, with the required options checked.*

8. Click OK to return to the Make New Connection dialog box, and click Next to continue.

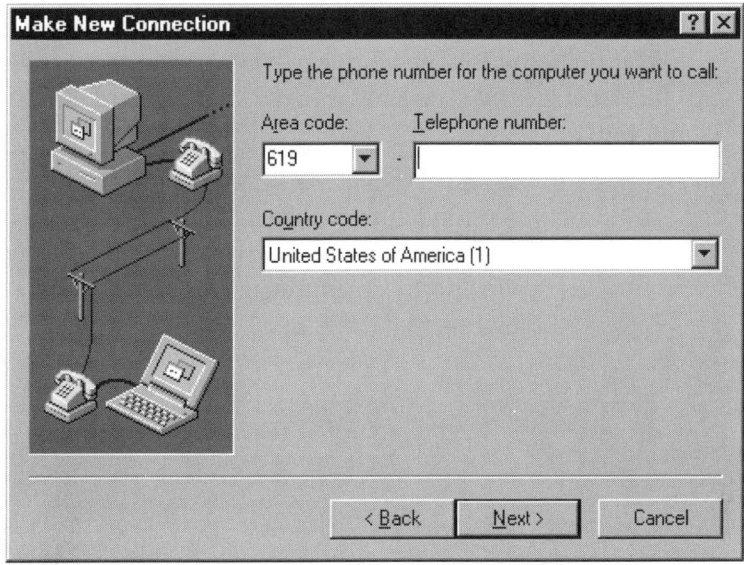

Figure 31-12: *The phone number page of the Make New Connection dialog box.*

9. In the phone number page, shown in Figure 31-12, type the correct information for your ISP and click Next.

10. Follow any other instructions that appear and then click the Finish button.

A new connection icon appears in your Dial-Up Networking window, looking something like the example in Figure 31-13.

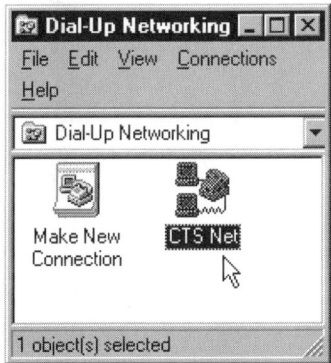

Figure 31-13: *The Dial-Up Networking window, with a new connection.*

CONFIGURING THE DIAL-UP CONNECTION

The finishing touches for your dial-up connection are pretty easy to add, especially if you have Table 31-2 handy. Here are the steps to follow:

1. In the Dial-Up Networking window, right-click the dial-up connection icon you want to configure (CTS Net, in my example) and choose Properties. Or, click the icon and choose File | Properties from the menu bar. Figure 31-14 shows the dialog box that pops up.

Figure 31-14: *The General tab of the dialog box for your connection.*

2. Click the Server Type button. You'll see the Server Types dialog box, which (when you've finished filling it in) should resemble Figure 31-15.

   ■ From the Type Of Dial-Up Server drop-down list, choose a server type. Unless you are certain that you are not connecting through a PPP connection, choose *PPP: Windows 95, Windows NT 3.5, Internet.*

   ■ In the Advanced Options area, select (check) only En-able software compression. (If you have problems with communications later, ask your ISP whether to clear this option.)

   ■ In the Allowed network protocols area, make sure that TCP/IP is selected.

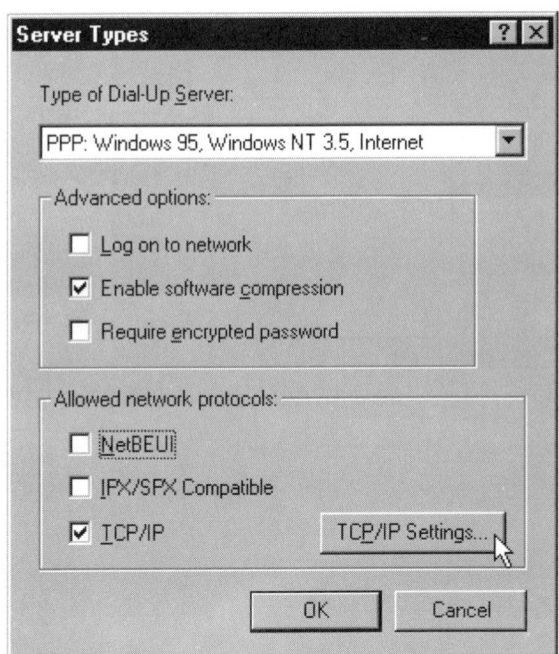

Figure 31-15: *The completed Server Types dialog box.*

3. Click the TCP/IP Settings button to open the TCP/IP Settings dialog box. A completed example appears in Figures 31-16 and 31-17.

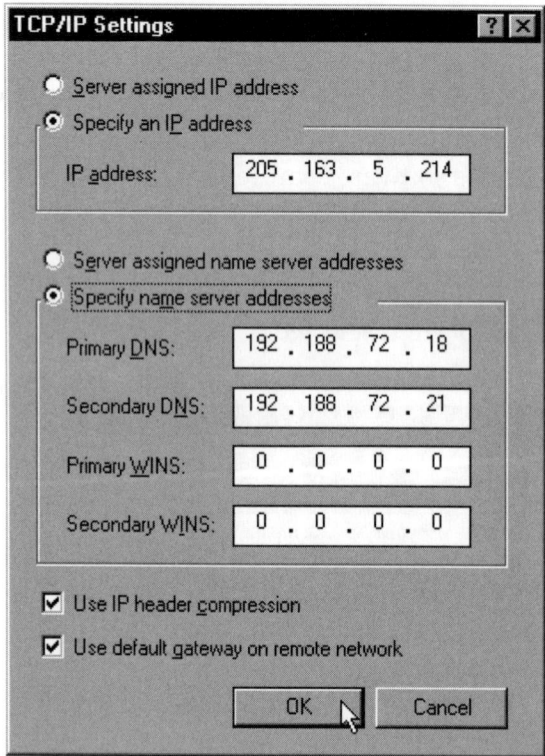

Figure 31-16: *The completed TCP/IP Settings dialog box for fixed IP and DNS addresses.*

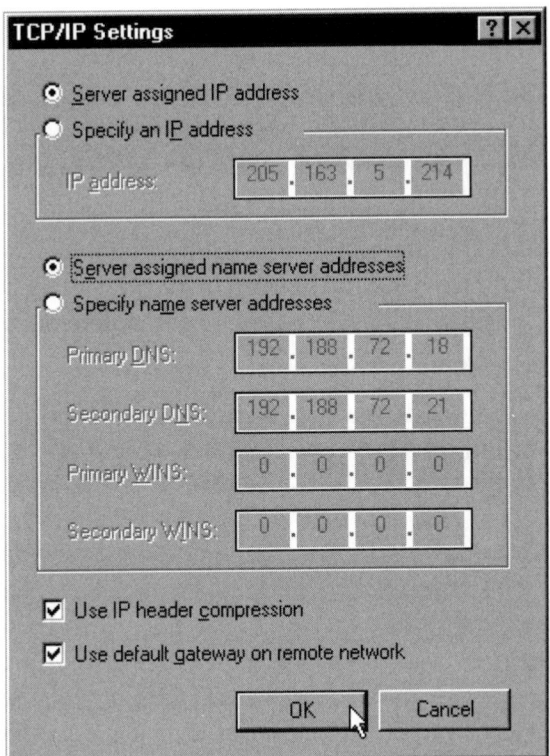

Figure 31-17: *The completed TCP/IP Settings dialog box for dynamically assigned IP and DNS addresses.*

4. If your ISP assigns you an IP address each time you dial in, select the Server assigned IP address option button. Otherwise, select the Specify an IP address option button, and type your IP address in the IP address box.

5. Assuming that your ISP hasn't given you other instructions, click the Specify name server addresses option button. Then enter your ISP's primary DNS server IP address in the Primary DNS box. If your ISP has a secondary DNS server IP address, enter it in the Secondary DNS box. (Ignore the Primary WINS and Secondary WINS boxes.)

6. Assuming that your ISP hasn't given you other instructions, be sure to check the bottom boxes (Use IP header compression and Use default gateway on remote network).

7. Click OK until you return to the Windows 95 desktop.

Cool! You're finally ready to surf. All that remains is to follow the simple connection steps in the next section.

TIP

To make your connection icon even more convenient, create a shortcut to the connection icon on your desktop. Simply hold down the Ctrl key while you drag the connection icon from the Dial-Up Networking window to your desktop. If you want to add the shortcut to your Start menu also, hold down the Ctrl key while you drag the connection icon from the Dial-Up Networking window to the Start button on the taskbar.

CONNECTING TO THE INTERNET

The drudgery is over and you don't need to worry about doing all those silly setup steps anymore. Now jumping onto the Internet with your dial-up connection is just a hop, skip, and a click away:

1. Double-click the icon for your ISP in the Dial-Up Networking window or on your desktop (or click the Start button on the taskbar and choose the appropriate option from the Start menu).

2. The Connect To dialog box will appear (see Figure 31-18). Go ahead and type your User name and Password (even though you'll have to enter them again later). If you're calling from a different location than usual, you may need to choose a different Phone number, Dialing from location, or Dial Properties.

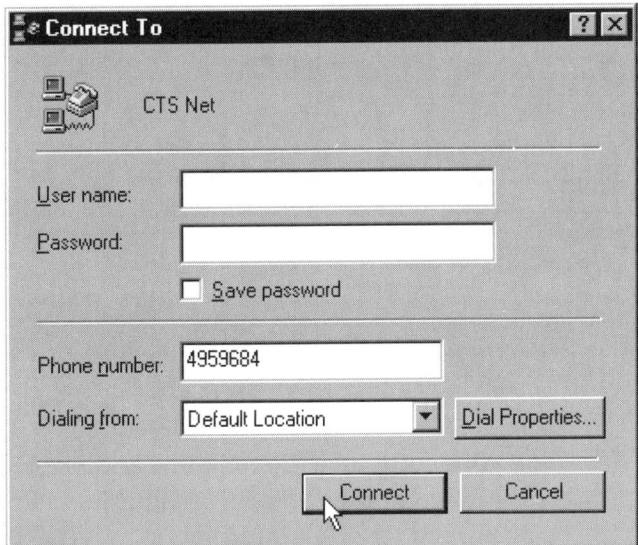

Figure 31-18: *The Connect To dialog box.*

3. Click the Connect button. A Connecting To... message will appear and your modem will click and clack away. Soon you'll see a Post-Dial Terminal Screen window similar to the example shown in Figure 31-19.

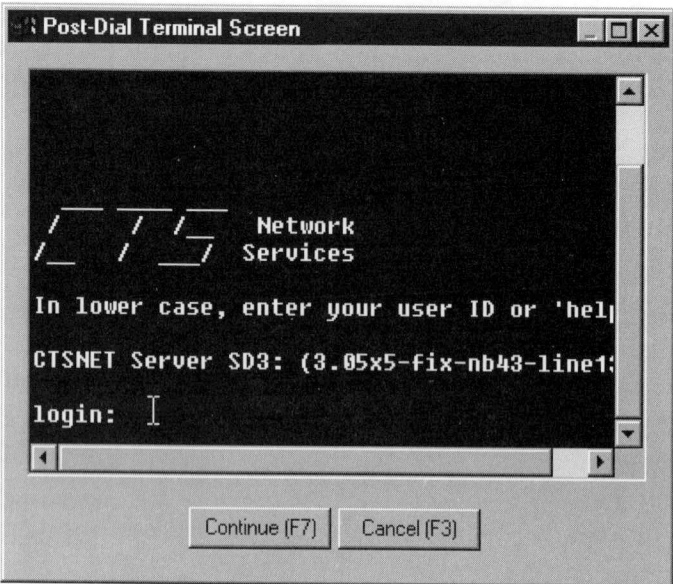

Figure 31-19: *The Post-Dial Terminal Screen window.*

4. Type your computer's login name and press Enter. Then type your computer's password and press Enter. You may be prompted for other information as well. If the host system assigns you an IP address or displays other important information, be sure to write it down. (Don't worry if you see some gobbledygook on the screen; that's normal.)

5. Click the Continue button or press F7.

6. If your ISP dynamically assigns you a different IP address every time you log in, you may be asked to verify or enter your IP address. Enter the IP address you just jotted down, and click OK to continue.

After a few moments, you'll see the Connected To dialog box shown in Figure 31-20. That means you're on! Now you can minimize the Connected To dialog box, if you want, and start Netscape Navigator or any other Internet client program.

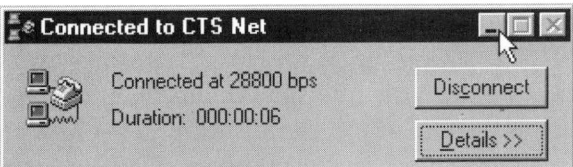

Figure 31-20: *The Connected to CTS Net dialog box.*

TIP

> *You can use the dial-up scripting feature (described in a moment) to automate the log on process so that you don't have to type your user name and password each time you connect to your ISP's computer. Setting up the script is fairly easy and it's definitely worth the effort.*

AUTOMATIC DIAL-UP WHEN YOU NEED IT!

If you've installed Microsoft's Internet Explorer or the Internet Jumpstart kit on Microsoft Plus!, you get an added bonus—Dial-Up Networking will run automatically whenever you start an Internet client program such as Netscape Navigator and you're not currently connected to your ISP. Moreover, if you're idle for 20 minutes, you'll be disconnected automatically. Combine these features with the dial-up scripting feature discussed later in the chapter and you'll be dialing into cyberspace almost as fast as your permanently connected friends do.

You can turn the autodial feature off or on, increase or decrease the autodisconnect idle time, and adjust other Internet settings, if you want. Open My Computer and double-click Control Panel (or choose Start|Settings|Control Panel). Then double-click the Internet icon, click the Connection tab, make the necessary changes to the settings, and click OK.

By the way, you can download Internet Explorer for free! For more information, visit Microsoft's Internet Explorer Web site at *http://www.microsoft.com/ie/*.

DISCONNECTING FROM THE INTERNET

Disconnecting from the Internet is a breeze. If the Connected To dialog box is minimized, click its button in the taskbar so that you can see the Disconnect button shown in Figure 31-20. Now, click the Disconnect button. The Connect To dialog box will disappear, and you'll be disconnected from your ISP.

TRAP

If you forget to disconnect from your ISP's computer, you're likely to rack up unwanted connect charges. Netscape Navigator and most other Internet client programs do not disconnect automatically when you exit them. Always check the taskbar to see whether a forgotten connection button is still lurking around. If it is, click the button in the taskbar and then click the Disconnect button in the Connect To dialog box.

CREATING A DIAL-UP SCRIPT

If you've installed the Dial-Up Scripting Tool that comes with the Windows 95 CD-ROM, you can create a little script that will automatically supply your login name and password when you dial into your ISP's computer. This is fairly easy to do and like most setup procedures, you only need to do it once. Invest a little time now and you'll save a bunch of time later.

ADDING THE CLIENT FOR MICROSOFT NETWORKS

The first step is to add "Client for Microsoft Networks" to the Network dialog box in Control Panel, if it isn't there already. Here's how:

1. Double-click My Computer on the Windows 95 desktop, then double-click Control Panel (or choose Start | Settings | Control Panel).

2. In the Control Panel window, double-click the Network icon and make sure that the Configuration tab is selected (refer to Figure 31-1).

3. If the Primary Network Logon drop-down list on the Configuration tab includes the option Client For Microsoft Networks, skip to Step 7. Otherwise, continue with Step 4.

4. Click the Add button to open the Select Network Component Type dialog box (refer to Figure 31-2).

5. Double-click the Client option in the network component list (or click the Client option, and then click the Add button). The Select Network Client dialog box will appear (it's similar to the Select Network Adapters dialog box shown in Figure 31-6).

6. In the Manufacturers list in the left panel, click Microsoft. In the Network Clients list in the right panel, click Client For Microsoft Networks. Click OK.

7. Click OK to return to the Control Panel window.

INSTALLING THE DIAL-UP SCRIPTING SOFTWARE

Now, follow the steps in the sidebar, "Adding SLIP & Dial-Up Scripting Support," earlier in this chapter. Those steps will add the dial-up scripting software to your computer.

CREATING THE DIAL-UP SCRIPT

Creating the dial-up script is the only tricky part of this whole business. To make life as simple as possible, grab a piece of paper and a pencil, then log on to the Internet manually. Jot down *exactly* what appears on your screen, including any blank spaces, just before you type your user name and password, and jot down *exactly* what you type in response—including any presses of the Enter key. For example, when I log in manually I first see this (the underline character represents a blank space):

```
Login:_
```

I type my login name and press Enter.
Then I see

```
Password:
```

I type my password and press Enter.

When I'm successfully connected, a message that ends with the word *enabled* appears on my screen.

Now I need to create a dial-up script that waits for *ogin:_* (where the underline represents a space). When the script sees that, it needs to type my user ID, and then press Enter. Next, the script needs to wait for *word:* to appear on the screen. Then it needs to type *mypassword,* and press Enter. The script can stop when it sees the word *enabled* on the screen.

You no doubt noticed that I plan to have the script wait for just the last few characters of the first prompts. Sometimes, the first character sent might have some attribute assigned to it, such as an underscore, which the program that plays the script won't recognize. By typing just the last few letters of each prompt, I'm less likely to run into any problems with those special characters.

Anyway, the next step is to fire up Notepad (Start | Programs | Accessories | Notepad) and express the logon procedure in *scripting language,* in which

- **waitfor** tells the script player what characters to wait for
- **transmit** tells the player what character to send
- **^M** represents a press on the Enter key

In this example, I would type the script *exactly* as it's shown in Figure 31-21. Note that I've included the space that comes after the *Login:* prompt. The $USERID part tells the script to the User Name from the Connect To dialog box shown back in Figure 31-18. $PASSWORD tells it to use the Password from that same dialog box.

TRAP

You must select the Save Password check box in the Connect To dialog box if you want the script to automatically type your password for you.

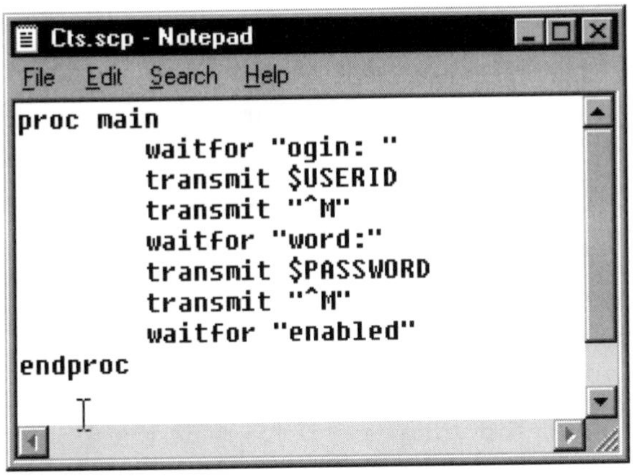

```
Cts.scp - Notepad                    _ □ ×
File  Edit  Search  Help
proc main
        waitfor "ogin: "
        transmit $USERID
        transmit "^M"
        waitfor "word:"
        transmit $PASSWORD
        transmit "^M"
        waitfor "enabled"
endproc
```

Figure 31-21: *A sample dial-up script.*

To save your script in Notepad, choose File | Save As. Now, navigate to the \Program Files\Accessories folder and save the file as *myscript*.scp (*myscript* is any valid filename you want).

HOOKING UP THE SCRIPT TO YOUR DIAL-UP NETWORKING ICON

Now you need to tell your dial-up networking icon to use the new script. Here's how:

1. Double-click My Computer on the Windows 95 desktop and then double-click the Dial-Up Networking icon.

2. In the Dial-Up Networking window, right-click the icon you use for dial-up networking, and choose Properties; or click the icon, and choose File | Properties from the menu bar. You'll see the General tab of the dialog box for your connection (refer to Figure 31-14).

3. Click the Server Type button to open the Server Types dialog box (refer to Figure 31-15).

4. In the Advanced Options area, select (check) Log On To Network, and choose OK to return to the dialog box for your connection.

5. Click the Configure button and then click the Options tab. Your screen will resemble Figure 31-11, shown earlier.

6. In the Connection Control area, deselect (clear) the Bring Up Terminal Window Before Dialing and the Bring Up Terminal Window After Dialing options.

7. Click OK until you return to the Dial-Up Networking window.

8. Open the Dial-Up Scripting Tool by choosing Start | Programs | Accessories | Dial-Up Scripting Tool.

9. Click the Browse button, then locate and double-click the *myscript*.scp you previously created in the \Program Files\Accessories folder. Figure 31-22 shows the screen after this step has been completed.

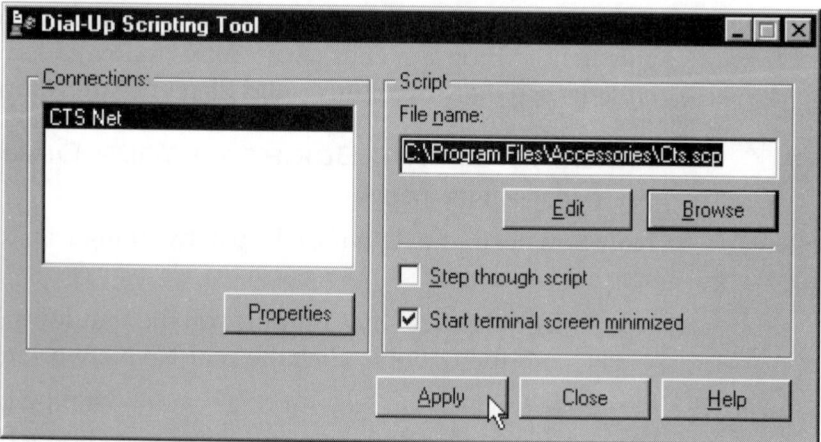

Figure 31-22: *The Dial-Up Scripting Tool, after the script filename has been specified.*

10. Click the Apply button and then click Close.

That's it! The dial-up script setup is complete.

> ### TIP
>
> *The Dial-Up Scripting command language offers many more com-*
> *mands than those shown in the simple script in Figure 31-21. For ex-*
> *ample, it includes commands that can capture and set dynamic IP ad-*
> *dresses. To learn more about the dial-up scripting command language,*
> *click the Help button in the Dial-Up Scripting Tool dialog box.*

QUICK CONNECTING TO THE INTERNET

Now that you've installed your dial-up script, you can dial into the
Internet the quick-and-easy way. Here are the much shorter connection steps:

1. Double-click the icon for your ISP in the Dial-Up Networking window or on your desktop (or click the Start button on
   the taskbar, and choose the appropriate option from the
   Start menu). The Connect To dialog box will appear (refer to
   Figure 31-18).

2. If the information is not already visible in the dialog box,
   type your User Name and Password, and select (check) the
   Save Password check box.

3. If you're calling from a different location than usual, choose
   a different Phone Number, Dialing From location, or Dial
   Properties, as necessary.

4. Click the Connect button.

The rest of the logon process takes place automatically—no more
annoying prompts for your user name and password.

SETTING UP WINDOWS 95 TO USE ISDN

Integrated Services Digital Network (ISDN) is the buzzword on
everyone's lips today. It's a high-speed digital telephone service
that can operate at speeds up to 128,000 bits per second, which
is about five times faster than today's fastest analog (28.8kbps)

modems. Using ISDN can speed up Internet download times dramatically and call setup is almost instantaneous. But ISDN doesn't come cheap and it's not available everywhere. To use ISDN, you need *all* of the following:

- ISDN service from a telephone company
- ISDN hardware to connect your PC to ISDN
- ISDN software to enable your ISDN hardware
- Internet or LAN connection that supports ISDN

Until recently, ISDN was both frightfully expensive and nearly impossible to install—if you could even get the service. With its increasing popularity, ISDN prices are falling, it's getting easier to install, and it's available in more places than ever before.

The specific steps for setting up ISDN service vary, but the basics are as follows:

1. Find out whether your ISP supports ISDN. If the answer is "No," stop right here. You can't use ISDN with your current ISP.

2. Find out what hardware your ISP has tested with its ISDN connection. It's essential to choose hardware that's compatible with your ISP's equipment.

3. Find out whether your telephone company (or *telco*) supports ISDN. If the answer is "No," stop right here.

4. Send your ISDN order to your telco the easy way—with Microsoft's Get ISDN Now! Web site at *http://www.microsoft.com/windows/getisdn/default.htm*. With the help of a simple fill-in-the-blanks form, you can find out which telcos can offer you ISDN, check whether the necessary ISDN is installed in your area, get pricing information for the ISDN packages available from your telco, send your telco an electronic order request for ISDN service, and automatically tell the telephone company how to configure your ISDN line. How's that for incredible?

5. Download Microsoft's free ISDN Accelerator Pack from *http://www.microsoft.com/windows/software/isdn.htm*, if necessary. The ISDN Accelerator Pack enables Windows 95 to make dial-up network connections over ISDN lines. You'll need this software only if you've installed an internal ISDN adapter. External adapters look like modems to your PC, and don't need any additional software.

6. Install your ISDN adapter and get your telco to wire you up.

7. Try it out!

If you have any problems, check first with your Internet Service Provider. They're your best resource for getting any kinks out of your ISDN connection to their computers.

Moving On

By now you should be able to get connected to the Internet, fire up Netscape Navigator, and start cruising the World Wide Web, as discussed in Chapter 2, "Browsing the Web, Gold Style." If you have any problems, or just want to tweak Netscape Navigator to better suit your own personal tastes, you can refer to the next chapter on Personalizing Netscape Navigator.

Personalizing Netscape Navigator

There are many ways to personalize Netscape Navigator so that it better fits your working style. You don't have to be connected to the Internet to personalize Navigator—you can customize the program whenever you want.

In this chapter, I discuss many personalization features that aren't covered elsewhere in the book, and I point you to other chapters where you can learn to personalize the Netscape editor, e-mail and news window, and various security features. Topics covered in this chapter include the following:

- Quick tour of the features for personalizing Netscape
- How to change Netscape's appearance
- How to improve Netscape's performance

CRUISING THE OPTIONS MENU

The Options menu (see Figure 32-1) on the Netscape browser menu bar contains all the options you'll need for personalizing Netscape. To personalize just about anything in Netscape, follow these general steps:

1. Pull down the Options menu on the Netscape browser menu bar, and choose the command you want.

The Options menus on the Netscape Mail menu bar and the Netscape News menu bar are similar to the Options menu discussed in this chapter. Those other Options menus, however, do offer a few extra commands as discussed in Chapter 27, "Doing E-Mail With Gold," and Chapter 28, "Cruising the Newsgroups With Gold."

2. If a Preferences dialog box appears, click the tab for the settings you want to change, update the settings as necessary, and click OK.

For more details about any option in a Preferences dialog box, click the tab that contains the settings you want to change, then click the Help button at the lower-right corner of the dialog box. You can look up appropriate topics also in the Netscape Handbook (Help | Handbook).

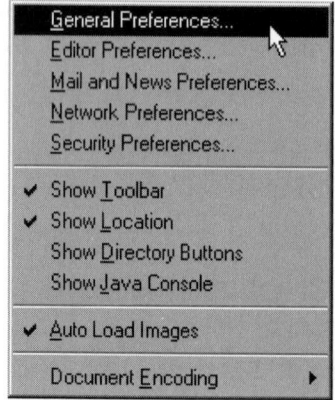

Figure 32-1: *The Options menu on the Netscape browser menu bar.*

The next few sections briefly describe the General Preferences, Editor Preferences, Mail and News Preferences, Network Preferences, and Security Preferences commands on the Options menu. In the later section on "Changing the Look of Your Browser," you'll learn more about the "Show...", Auto Load Images, and Document Encoding commands on the Options menu.

GENERAL PREFERENCES

Choosing Options | General Preferences takes you to the Preferences dialog box shown in Figure 32-2. Here's what you'll find:

- The Appearance, Fonts, Colors, and Images tabs control the general appearance of Netscape and the pages that appear when you browse the Web. See "Changing the Look of Your Browser," later in this chapter, for details.

- The Apps tab specifies the location of supporting applications for Telnet and TN3270 (see Chapter 29, "FTP, Gopher & Telnet"), for viewing HTML source code (see Chapter 15, "Tuning HTML Tags"), and for changing the directory Netscape uses for storing temporary files.

- The Helpers tab controls the way Netscape interprets various file formats (see Chapter 29). You'll rarely need to change the options on this tab.

- The Language tab indicates (to a server) which language Netscape will accept. You'll rarely need to change the options on this tab either.

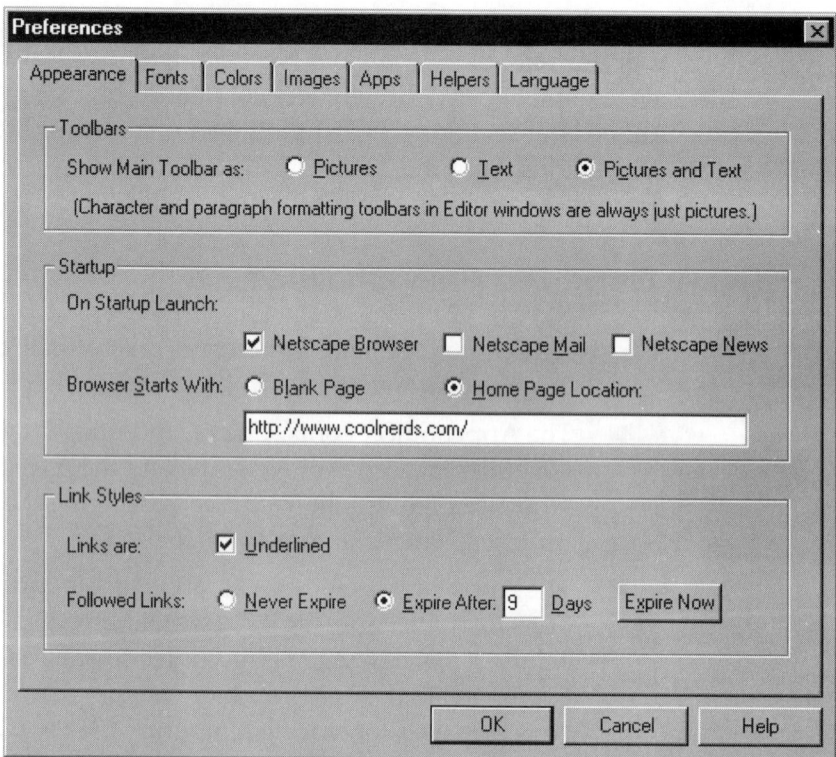

Figure 32-2: *Choose Options | General Preferences and click the Appearance tab to see this Preferences dialog box.*

EDITOR PREFERENCES

Choosing Options | Editor Preferences takes you to the Editor Preferences dialog box shown in Figure 32-3. The Editor Preferences options affect Web pages that you create in Gold's editor, as discussed in Parts I and II in this book. External editors for HTML Source and Image are covered in Chapter 15, "Tuning HTML Tags," and Chapter 14, "Power Image Publishing," respectively.

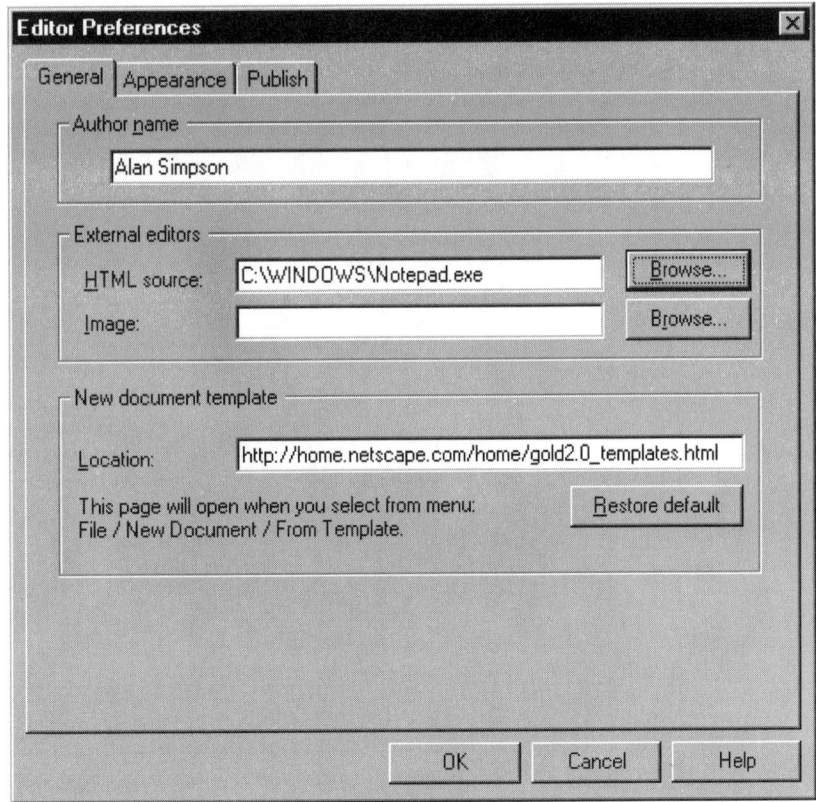

Figure 32-3: *Choose Options | Editor Preferences, and click the General tab to see this Editor Preferences dialog box.*

MAIL AND NEWS PREFERENCES

Figure 32-4 shows the Preferences dialog box that appears when you choose Options | Mail and News Preferences. You'll need to set up some mail and news preferences before you can use Netscape for electronic mail and newsgroups. (See Chapter 27, "Doing E-Mail With Gold," and Chapter 28, "Cruising the Newsgroups With Gold.")

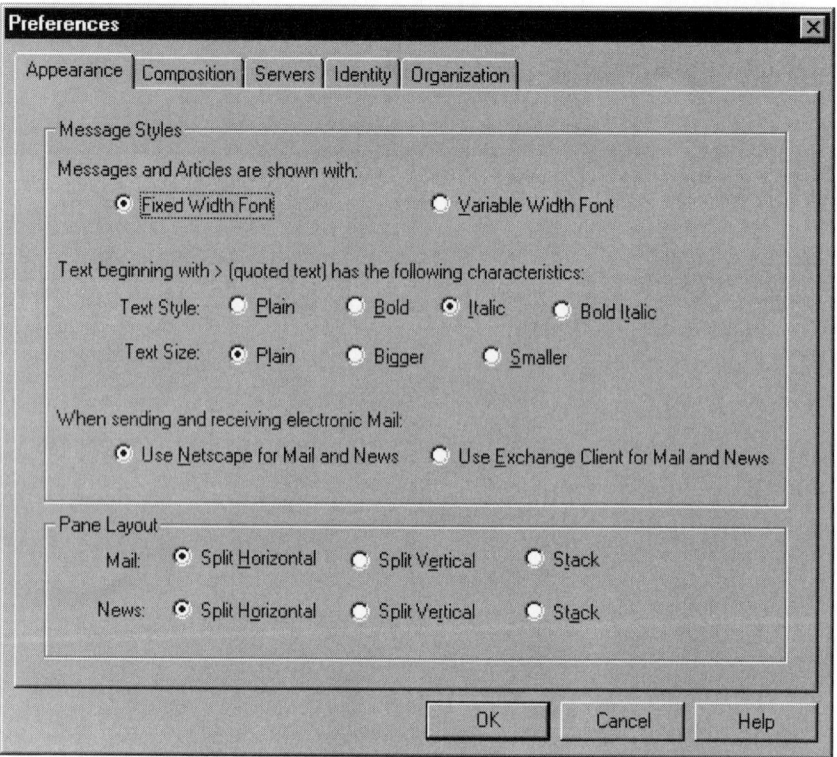

Figure 32-4: *Choose Options | Mail and News Preferences, and click the Appearance tab to see this Mail and News Preferences dialog box.*

NETWORK PREFERENCES

Choosing Options | Network Preferences takes you to the Preferences dialog box shown in Figure 32-5. You'll learn about the *Cache* and *Connections* tabs later in this chapter (see "Speeding Up Your Browser"). What about the other tabs in this dialog box? Here's a quick summary of their purpose:

■ The Proxies tab specifies the location of your proxy server, if you have one. You do not need to configure proxies if you have a direct connection to the Internet.

- The Protocols tab specifies whether to show an alert before accepting a cookie or submitting a form by e-mail. It also specifies whether to submit your e-mail address as an anonymous FTP password (see Chapter 29, "FTP, Gopher & Telnet").

- The Language tab specifies whether to enable Java and JavaScript.

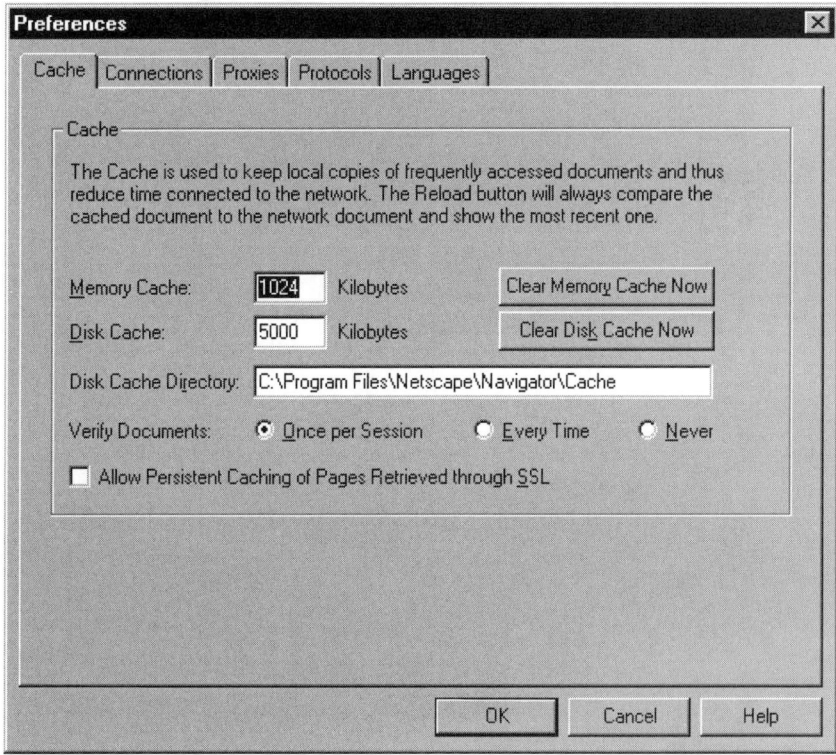

Figure 32-5: *Choose Options | Network Preferences, and click the Cache tab to see this network Preferences dialog box.*

SECURITY PREFERENCES

In Figure 32-6, you see the Preferences dialog box that appears when you choose Options | Security Preferences. Netscape's many security features help to protect sensitive information as it flies across cyberspace. (See Chapter 20, "Doing Money on the Internet," for details.)

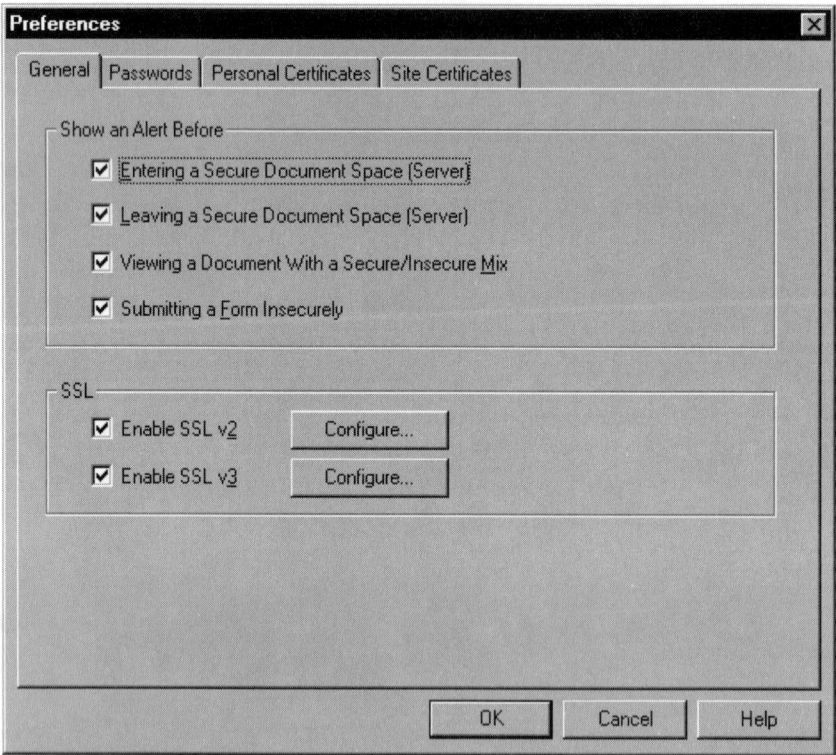

Figure 32-6: *Choose Options | Security Preferences, and click the General tab to see this security Preferences dialog box.*

A SPECIAL KIT FOR NETSCAPE ADMINISTRATORS

If you're in charge of distributing and managing Netscape client software in a large organization, you may want to purchase the $19.95 Netscape Administration kit. This kit makes it easier for you to specify settings in one copy of Navigator and then distribute copies, with those settings, to multiple users in your company. You can also lock the settings so that the other users cannot change them.

For example, you can choose the startup home page, proxy server configurations, outgoing SMTP mail server, incoming POP mail server, News NNTP server, and preferences for leaving e-mail on the server for your entire organization in one fell swoop. You also can use the kit to redefine the description and underlying URLs for nonrequired entries on the Directory and Help menus, to change the button labels and underlying URLs for Netscape's directory buttons, and to modify the browser's animation and logo.

To learn more about the Netscape Administration Kit, visit *http://home.netscape.com/comprod/products/navigator/version_3.0/enterprise/index.html.*

CHANGING THE LOOK OF YOUR BROWSER

As the next few sections explain, there are many ways to change the look of the Netscape browser and the Web pages you view.

SHOWING OR HIDING THE ONSCREEN "DOODADS"

You can view the Netscape window with or without the toolbar, the Location box, the directory buttons, and the Java Console. To turn these features on and off, choose any of the following options, as necessary:

- Options I Show Toolbar
- Options I Show Location
- Options I Show Directory Buttons
- Options I Show Java Console

These are toggle options. You check an option to display the corresponding doodad, and you clear or uncheck an option to hide the doodad.

Figure 32-7, shows a sample Web page in which the toolbar, the Location box, the directory buttons, and the Java Console are turned off. As you can see, the screen has an uncrowded look and more space is available for displaying the Web page. Figure 32-8 shows the same page with all the onscreen doodads turned on.

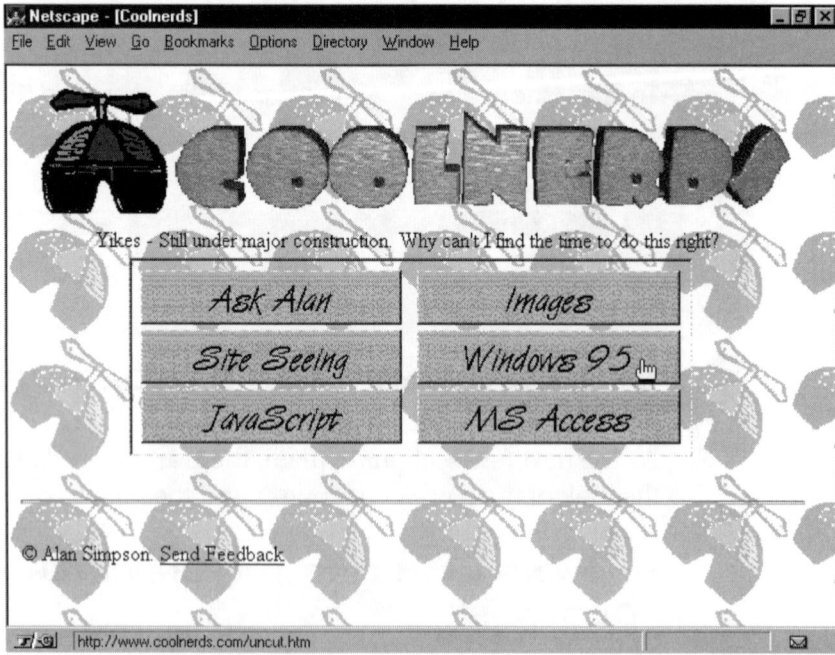

Figure 32-7: *A Web page with all onscreen doodads turned off.*

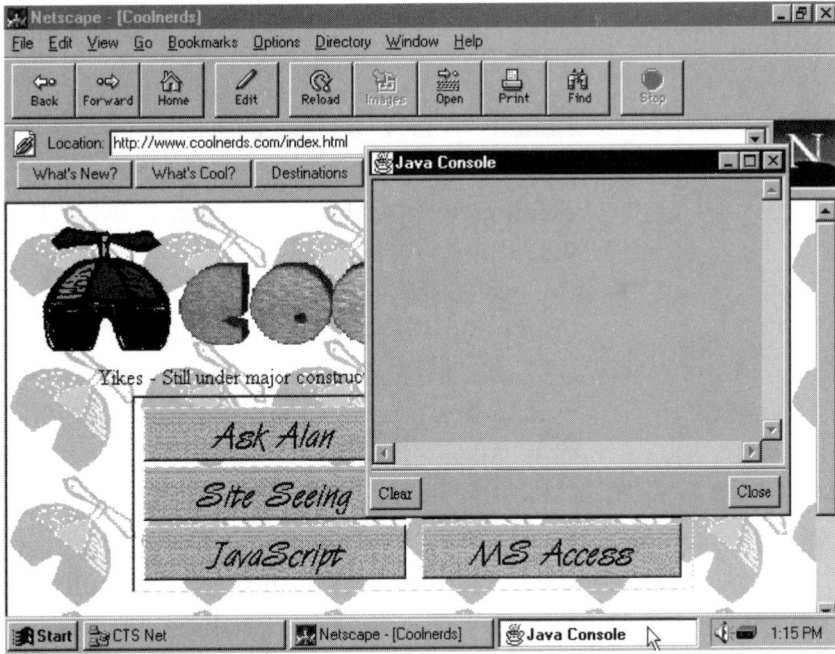

Figure 32-8: *A Web page with all onscreen doodads turned on.*

If you've turned off the toolbar, you can use the following menu commands and shortcut keys instead of the toolbar buttons:

- Choose Go | Back, or press Alt+left arrow, instead of clicking the Back button to view the previous document in the history list.

- Choose Go | Forward, or press Alt+right arrow, instead of clicking the Forward button to view the next document in the history list.

- Choose Go | Home instead of clicking the Home button to return to your browser's home page.

- Choose File | Edit Document instead of clicking the Edit button to edit the current document.

- Choose View | Reload, or press Ctrl+R, instead of clicking the Reload button to reload the current document.

- Choose View | Load Images, or press Ctrl+I, instead of click-
  ing the Images button to reload the current document's images. (This option makes sense only if you've unchecked
  Options | Auto Load Images, as discussed later in the chapter.)

- Choose File | Open Location, or press Ctrl+L, instead of
  clicking the Open button to open a URL in the browser window or the editor window.

- Choose File | Print, or press Ctrl+P, instead of clicking the
  Print button to print the active document.

- Choose Edit | Find, or press Ctrl+F, instead of clicking the
  Find button to search for text in the current document. Press
  F3 to repeat the current search.

- Choose Go | Stop Loading, or press Esc, instead of clicking
  the Stop button to interrupt the current transfer.

If you've turned off the Location box, you still can visit a differ-
ent URL. Simply choose File | Open Location (or press Ctrl+L), type
the URL you want to visit, and press Enter.

And if you've turned off the directory buttons (which usually
appear below the Location box), you can choose equivalent options
from the Directory menu. From left to right, the Directory menu
options that correspond to the directory buttons are What's New?,
What's Cool?, Netscape Destinations, Internet Search, and People.
The last button, Software, corresponds to the Help | Software com-
mand on Netscape's menu bar.

CHANGING NETSCAPE'S GENERAL APPEARANCE

Figure 32-2 showed the Preferences dialog box that appears when
you choose Options | General Preferences and click the Appearance
tab. From this dialog box you can choose various toolbar, startup,
and link style options, as described next:

- In the *Toolbars area* of the dialog box, specify whether to
  show the main toolbar as Pictures, Text, or Pictures And
  Text.

- In the *Startup area*, choose the window and home page that
  should appear when you start Netscape. You can choose to
  launch the Netscape Browser window, the Netscape Mail

window, or the Netscape News window, and you can choose whether to start with a Blank Page or a specific Home Page Location. If you choose Home Page Location, specify the URL for the home page of your choice in the text box just below the Home Page Location option.

■ In the *Link Styles area*, choose whether links are Underlined and how long Netscape remembers links that you've followed. Your options for remembering followed links are Never Expire (Netscape always remembers followed links) or Expire After the number of Days you specify (initially, 9 days). To erase Netscape's memory of unvisited links, click the Expire Now button, and click OK.

CHANGING THE BROWSER'S FONTS

Your browser—not the author of the Web page—determines the font used to display text on a page. By default, Netscape uses the Times Roman font to display proportional text and the Courier New font to display fixed font text.

TIP

In a proportional font, each letter takes up only as much space as it needs. For example, the letter i is narrower than the letter m. The text you're reading now is printed in a proportional font. Fixed-width fonts look more like typewriter text—where each letter takes up the same space. For example, the letter i uses as much width as the letter m. In most Web pages you view, the main text will be displayed in a proportional font. Fixed-width fonts might be used to display sample programming code, text in columns, or other special situations.

You're not stuck with these default font settings! In fact, you can use any fonts that are installed on your computer as the proportional and fixed fonts, and you can choose a different combination of proportional and fixed fonts for different *document encoding* settings.

For example, in Figure 32-9, I've chosen the Traditional Chinese (Big 5) document encoding to display my Web pages. Previously, I had assigned the Tahoma font to the proportional text on Traditional Chinese (Big 5) encoded documents. Figure 32-10 shows the same page displayed with the Western(Latin1) document encoding; because I didn't change the fonts for that encoding, Netscape uses the default Times Roman proportional font.

TIP

> *The document encoding simply connects a particular name (such as Traditional Chinese (Big 5) or Western(Latin1)) to a specific combination of proportional and fixed font settings. My choice of Traditional Chinese (Big 5) and Western(Latin 1) in Figures 32-9 and 32-10 was completely arbitrary. I could have chosen any document encoding that Netscape offers, or I could have picked a User Defined document encoding.*

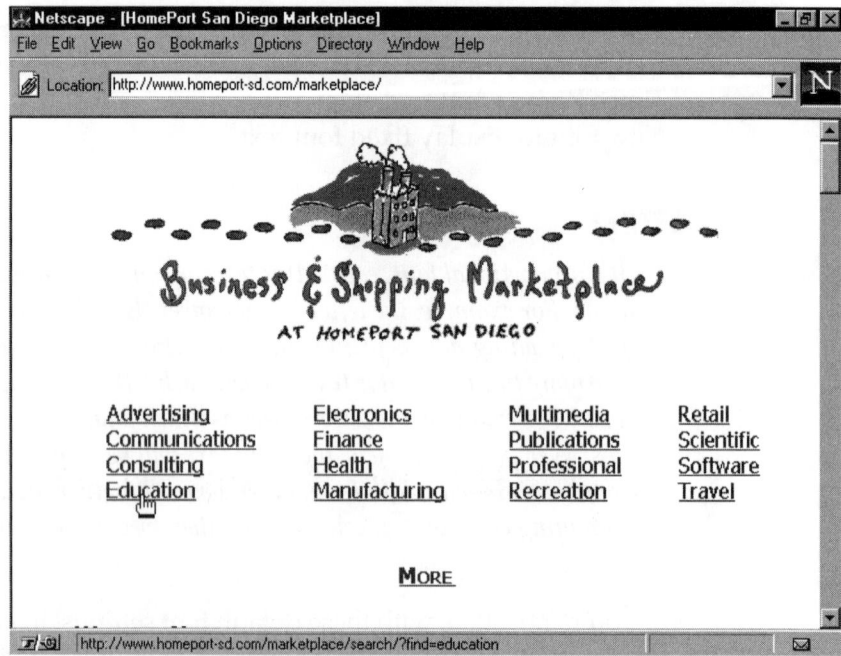

Figure 32-9: *Here I've chosen Traditional Chinese (Big 5) as the document encoding; earlier, I assigned Tahoma as the proportional font for the Traditional Chinese (Big 5) document encoding.*

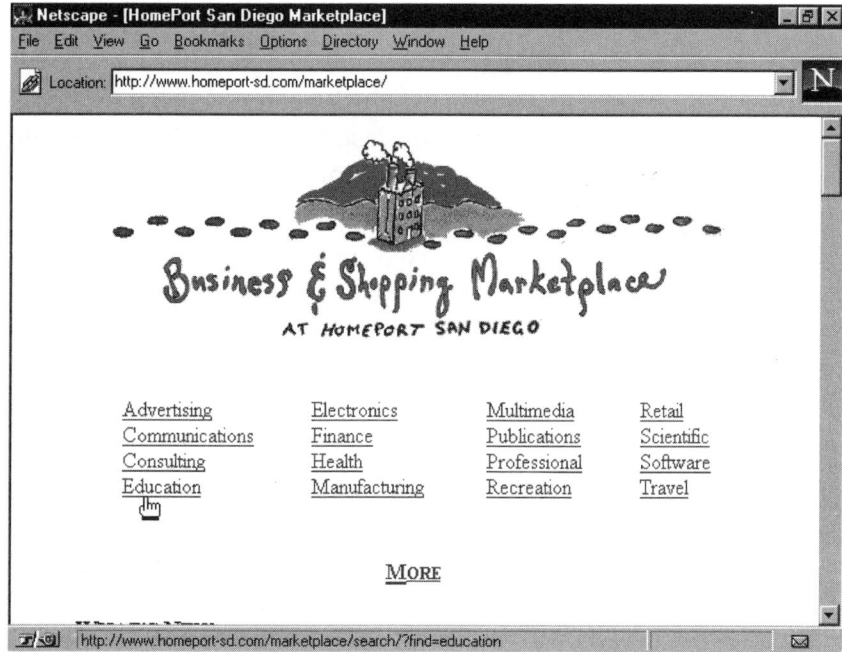

Figure 32-10: *Here I've chosen the Western(Latin1) encoding, which uses Times New Roman as the proportional font.*

To choose the proportional and fixed fonts for a particular document encoding, follow these steps:

1. Choose Options | General Preferences, and click the Fonts tab (see Figure 32-11).

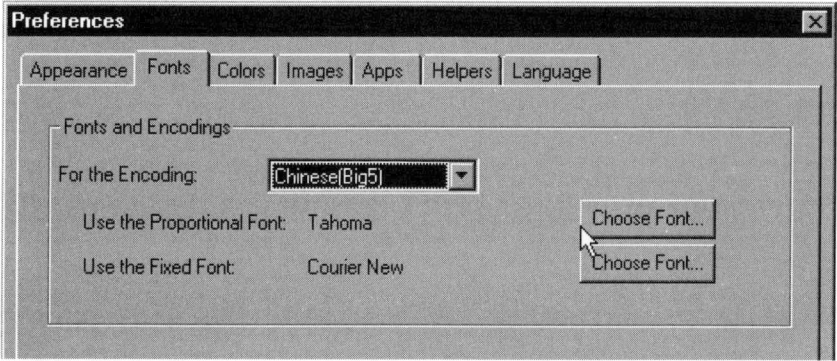

Figure 32-11: *Use the Fonts tab of the Preferences dialog box to assign a proportional font and a fixed font to a specific document encoding.*

2. Choose the encoding name you want from the For The Encoding drop-down list.

3. To assign a proportional font, click the Choose Font button across from the Use The Proportional Font option, select the Font, Size, and Script options you want for the base proportional font, and choose OK.

4. To assign a fixed font, click the Choose Font button across from the Use The Fixed Font option, select the Font, Size, and Script options you want for the base fixed font, and choose OK.

5. Click the OK button at the bottom of the dialog box to save your settings.

To select the document encoding you want to use for displaying documents as you browse the Web, choose Options I Document Encoding, and select an encoding option from the menu shown in Figure 32-12. The current document and any future documents you view *during the current session* will use whatever fonts are assigned to the selected document encoding. Of course, you can choose a different document encoding whenever you want. If you exit and restart Netscape, the display will revert to the default document encoding and its font settings.

TIP

Netscape's default document encoding is Western(Latin 1), which initially uses Times New Roman for the proportional font and Courier New for the fixed font. To change the default document encoding, first choose the document encoding you want to use as the default (via the Options I Document Encoding menus); then choose Options I Document Encoding I Set Default.

Figure 32-12: *The Options | Document Encoding submenu.*

CHANGING THE BROWSER'S COLORS

The Netscape browser usually controls the color of links, followed
links, text, and the background (but Web page authors can change
these colors, if they want). To change the browser's default color
settings, choose Options | General Preferences, and click the Colors
tab (see Figure 32-13). Then, do any of the following:

■   To set a custom color for Links, Followed Links, or Text,
    click the Choose Color button next to the option you want to
    change, click the color you want in the Color dialog box that
    appears, and choose OK. After you choose a color, Netscape

automatically checks the appropriate Custom check box. To return to Netscape's default color, simply clear the appropriate Custom check box.

■ To change the background color, choose Custom (next to the Background option), click the Choose Color button next to the Custom option, pick a color, and choose OK. If you want to return to Netscape's default background color, choose the Default option.

■ To choose an image instead of a background color, choose Image File, and then either type the filename of the image you want to use or click the Browse button and then locate and double-click the image filename. You can choose any GIF, JPG, or JPEG image that's available on your hard disk.

■ To always use the colors and background choices you've assigned, rather than the ones the Web page author has assigned, select (check) the Always Use My Colors, Overriding Document check box. To use whatever colors and background options the Web page author has selected (or the choices shown on the Colors tab, if the author hasn't chosen anything special), clear the check box.

When you've finished making changes, click the OK button at the bottom of the dialog box to save your settings.

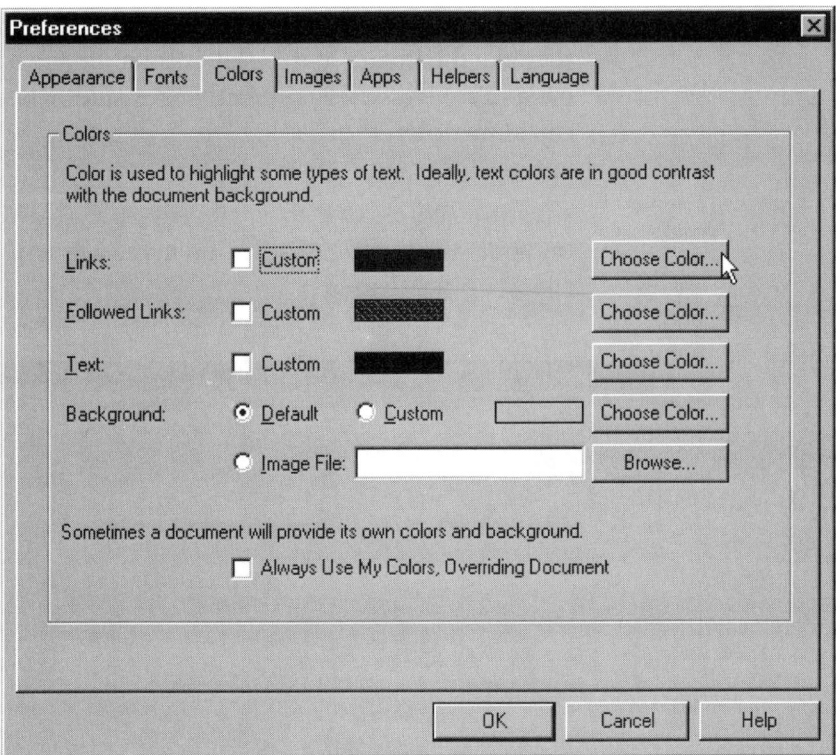

Figure 32-13: *The Colors tab of the Preferences dialog box.*

CONTROLLING THE APPEARANCE OF IMAGES

You can control the way Netscape displays colors and images. To begin, choose Options I General Preferences and click the Images tab (see Figure 32-14). Then, to pick the method Netscape uses to display colors, choose one of the following options in the Choosing Colors area:

■ Automatic lets Netscape figure out the best method for displaying colors (this is the default, and usually the best, setting).

- Dither uses a color-approximation technique called *dithering* to make the image match the original image's intended colors as closely as possible. Dithering gives truer colors but can slow down the display.

- Substitute Colors uses a simpler method than dithering to substitute colors that most closely match the colors available on your computer. Substitution gives less true colors but can speed up the display.

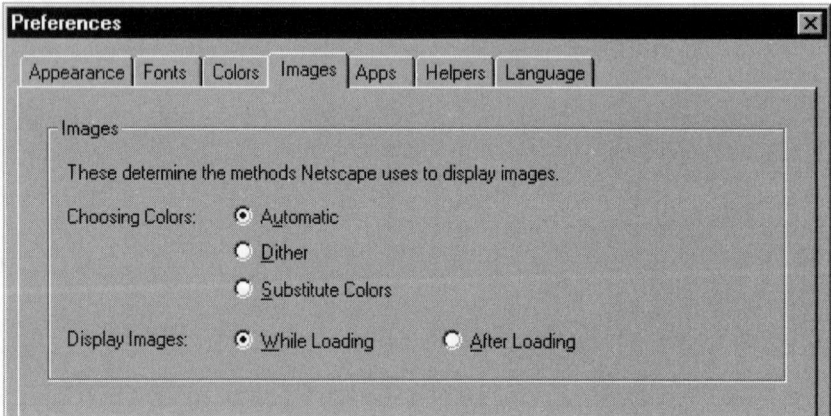

Figure 32-14: *The Images tab of the Preferences dialog box.*

To control when Netscape displays images as it downloads a page, choose either of these options from the Display Images area:

- While Loading displays images incrementally while the page is downloading. This method gives you some feedback as the transmission progresses, but it can be a little slow.

- After Loading displays images after the page has finished downloading. This method gives you no feedback for the image as the transmission progresses, but it can be a little faster on a fast network connection.

When you've finished making changes, click the OK button at the bottom of the dialog box to save your settings.

SPEEDING UP YOUR BROWSER

There are several ways to speed up Netscape, as the next few sections explain.

SPEEDING UP THE IMAGE DISPLAY

One of the easiest ways to speed up browsing on the Web is to turn off the images. Of course, turning off images makes the pages less interesting, but if you're mainly interested in reading text and moving quickly, you might want to try it.

To turn automatic loading of images off or on, choose Options | Auto Load Images from the menu bar. This is a toggle option. When Auto Load Images is checked on the Options menu, images load automatically; when it isn't checked, images do not load.

TIP

If there's a copy of a Web page in your disk cache, you still may see the images on the page, even if you've turned off the Auto Load Images option. The next section discusses caching.

When automatic image loading is turned off, images appear as crumpled or fractured image icons, as shown in Figure 32-15.

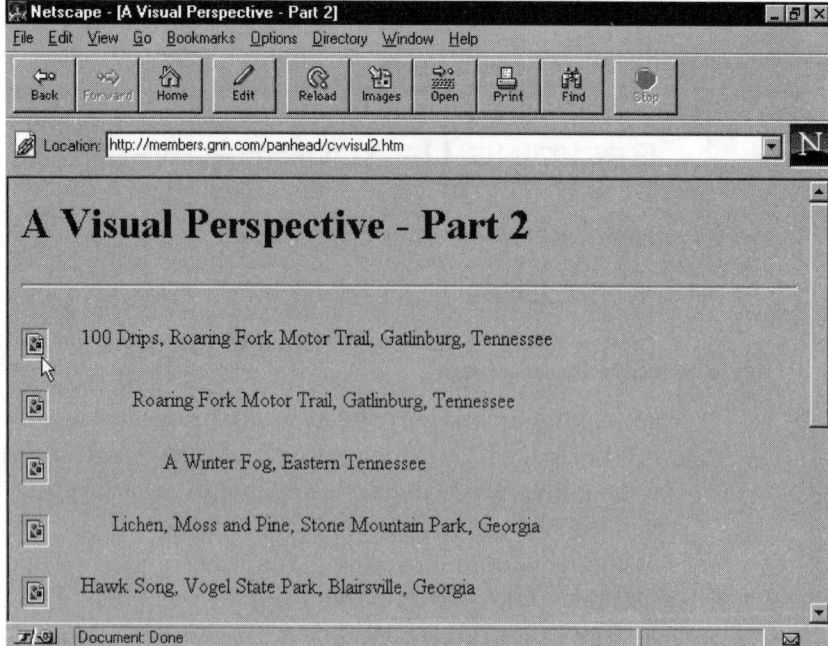

Figure 32-15: *Images appear as little icons when you've turned off the Auto Load Images feature.*

Even if you've turned off the automatic loading of images, you can easily view any or all images on the page. Here's how:

■ To view a particular image, simply click its fractured icon. Or, right-click its icon and choose View Image.

■ To view all the images on the page, click the Images button on the toolbar, or choose View | Load Images, or press Ctrl+I.

TIP

Another way to speed up the image display a little is to choose the Sub-stitute Colors and the After Loading options on the Images tab, as ex-plained earlier in "Controlling the Appearance of Images."

KEEPING YOUR CACHE ON HAND

Netscape uses both a memory cache (pronounced *cash*, like the green stuff) and a disk-based cache to keep local copies of documents that you access frequently. Your browser's home page is an example of a frequently used document.

If your computer has lots of memory, you may want to increase the size of the memory cache for faster access. Likewise, if your computer has lots of disk space, you can increase the size of the disk cache to access documents from the disk rather than downloading them (disk access usually is faster than downloading). By contrast, if your computer is short on memory or available disk space, you might get better performance by reducing the cache size.

TIP

Netscape cleans up its disk cache when you exit the program. If exiting seems to take a long time, try reducing the size of the disk cache.

To adjust Netscape's cache options, choose Options | Network Preferences, and click the Cache tab. (Flip back to Figure 32-5 to see the options on the Cache tab.) Here's how to set each option:

- Memory Cache: Specify the size of the memory cache in kilobytes. The default memory cache is 1024 kilobytes (1MB). If you want to clear the memory cache, click the Clear Memory Cache Now button, and choose OK.

- Disk Cache: Specify the size of the disk cache in kilobytes. The default disk cache size is 5000 kilobytes (5MB). If you want to clear the disk cache, click the Clear Disk Cache Now button, and choose OK. Then, exit Netscape and restart it.

- Disk Cache Directory: Specify the directory (or folder) in which to store the disk cache. The default directory is C:\Program Files\Netscape\Navigator\Cache.

- Verify Documents: Specify how often to check whether a page in cache has changed on the network server. Your options are Once Per Session (the best tradeoff between fast performance and accurate pages), Every Time you visit the URL for the page (slower, but the pages will be accurate), and Never (quick, but pages can be inaccurate).

TIP

Whenever you want to, you can force Netscape to check the network server to determine whether a page has changed, regardless of the Verify Documents settings. To do this, click the Reload toolbar button, or choose View | Reload from the menu bar, or press Ctrl+R. If the page has changed on the server, Netscape will reload it. Consider reloading if you've chosen the Never or Once Per Session option under Verify Documents and you suspect the page is out of date. Reload is handy also when a page appears to be garbled or hung up.

- Allow Persistent Caching of Pages Retrieved Through SSL: Clear this option if you're concerned about security. If security isn't important, you can speed things up a bit by selecting (checking) this option. The option is cleared by default.

STREAMLINING YOUR NETWORK CONNECTIONS

Figure 32-16 shows the Preferences dialog box that appears when you choose Options | Network Preferences and click the Connections tab. You can use options on this tab to change the number of network connections Netscape can open to your Internet server, and to change the size of the buffer that Netscape uses during data transmission.

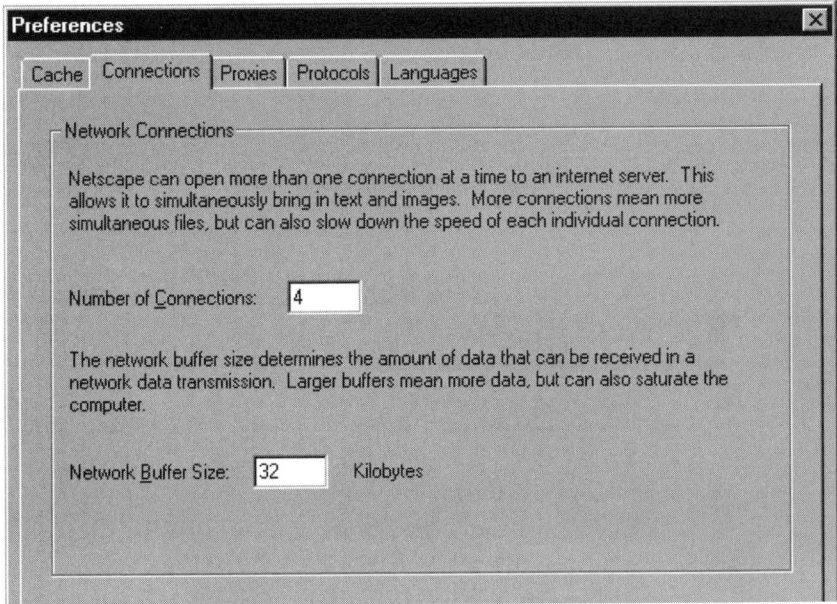

Figure 32-16: *The Preferences dialog box, after choosing Options | Network Preferences and clicking the Connections tab.*

The text on a Web page and each image on a page are stored in distinct files. To display the page on your screen, Netscape must open (for each file) a separate connection to the Internet server. Increasing the setting in the Number of Connections text box lets Netscape open more simultaneous connections to the server; however, this increase in the number of connections can decrease the speed of each individual connection. The default setting is 4 simultaneous connections.

Another factor that affects transmission speed is the size of the buffer that's used to receive network data. Larger buffers allow more data in each transmission, but they can saturate the computer. The default buffer setting is 32K.

TRAP

The default settings on the Connections tab should be fine for most people. Tweaking things too much can slow down performance for you and for others. It's a good idea to check with your network administrator before you change these settings.

THE END

I don't expect many people to read a 900+ computer/Internet book from cover-to-cover, like a novel. But in case you did that I want to say Congratulations on your new found Internet / World Wide Web Publishing Guruhood. You can now browse and publish with the best of them!

Where do you go from here? Well, there are still more areas you can explore. Perhaps JavaScript if you'd like to add some more interactivity to your Web site. Or check out some of the newly emerging capabilities for Web publishers, including ActiveX controls and Cascading Style Sheets (CSS). On the other hand, you can just spend some time to see what you've already learned and build one heck of a great Web site!

Thanks for reading. And let me know how things are going.

Alan Simpson
alan@coolnerds.com

PART VII:

Appendices

Appendix A

About netscapepress.com

Netscapepress.com is where you will find the most up-to-date information about Netscape Press. Please visit the site at **http://www.netscapepress.com/.** Netscapepress.com features a catalog of other Netscape Press titles, technical support information, and updates to the book as needed.

Netscapepress.com is the home of *Navigate!,* the official electronic publication of Netscape Press. *Navigate!* is a monthly online publication that offers a wide range of articles and reviews aimed at Netscape users. *Navigate!* features interviews with industry icons and experts, as well as articles excerpted from upcoming Netscape Press titles. Learn how to improve your Web site or to use the best search engines online. Stay abreast of the latest technological innovations and impress your friends with your intimate knowledge of the world's most popular Internet browser.

Netscape Press is a joint effort between Ventana and Netscape Communications Corporation, and serves as the publishing arm of Netscape.

Appendix B

About the Companion CD-ROM

The CD-ROM included with your copy of the *Official Netscape Navigator 3.0 Gold Book, Windows Edition,* contains valuable software programs.

To view the CD-ROM using:

- **Windows 3.1/Windows 95/Windows NT:** Double-click on the LAUNCHME.EXE file from your Windows Explorer or File Manager.

You'll see a menu screen offering several choices. See "Navigating the CD-ROM" below for your option choices.

NAVIGATING THE CD-ROM

Your choices for navigating the CD-ROM appear on the opening screen. You can quit the CD, view the software, browse the Hot Picks, or learn more about Ventana.

The software section lists all of the software programs on the CD. You can install the items one at a time to your hard drive.

If the Ventana Viewer does not run properly on your machine, you can access the material on the CD directly through File Manager (Windows 3.1x) or Windows Explorer (Windows 95).

Program	Description
Acrobat Reader 3.0	This pre-release version of Acrobat Reader 3.0 (previously code-named "Amber") allows you to view Adobe Acrobat portable document format files inside Netscape. Acrobat files can be created by any program that supports PostScript and retains all the formatting, text styles, and graphics of the original document in a format perfect for Web publishing.
Gold Wave	Sound editor, player, and recorder for MS-Windows. A great audio processing tool.
WebWhacker	WebWhacker downloads the HTML code for Web pages, along with all the associated images. This allows users to store pages locally and update them only occasionally, reducing connect time and costs.
Map This!	Utility for creating image maps.
Paint Shop Pro 3.12	A shareware product with a wide variety of useful features for manipulating images.
CoolEdit	CoolEdit is a digital sound editor for Windows that enables you to "paint" with sound: tones, pieces of songs and voices and miscellaneous noises, sine waves and sawtooth waves, noise, or just pure silence. CoolEdit also gives you a wide variety of special effects to "touch up" your sounds: reverberation, noise reduction, echo and delay, flanging, filtering, and many others.
LView Pro	LView Pro is a powerful and easy to use image viewer/editor, very popular on the Internet. LView Pro is marketed by Mmedia Research Corp, please visit our Web page at http://world.std.com/~mmedia.

RTF to HTML	Converts RTF documents to HTML allowing you to publish Microsoft Word, Word-Perfect, FrameMaker, Claris Works, and other word processing documents on the World Wide Web.
WebForms	WebForms™ provides users with the ability to create forms and retrieve their responses without the use of CGI. The benefit of this to an ISP is that it allows you to offer forms capability without taxing your server.
WinZip	WinZip compresses and decompresses Windows files for transmission. It's an excellent graphical zipping utility.

TECHNICAL SUPPORT

Technical support is available for installation-related problems only. The technical support office is open from 8:00 A.M. to 6:00 P.M. Monday through Friday and can be reached via the following methods:

Phone: (919) 544-9404 extension 81

Faxback Answer System: (919) 544-9404 extension 85

E-mail: help@vmedia.com

FAX: (919) 544-9472

World Wide Web: **http://www.vmedia.com/support**

America Online: keyword *Ventana*

LIMITS OF LIABILITY & DISCLAIMER OF WARRANTY

The author and publisher of this book have used their best efforts in preparing the CD-ROM and the programs contained in it. These efforts include the development, research, and testing of the theories and programs to determine their effectiveness. The author and publisher make no warranty of any kind expressed or implied, with regard to these programs or the documentation contained in this book.

The author and publisher shall not be liable in the event of incidental or consequential damages in connection with, or arising out of, the furnishing, performance, or use of the programs, associated instructions, and/or claims of productivity gains.

Some of the software on this CD-ROM is shareware; there may be additional charges (owed to the software authors/makers) incurred for their registration and continued use. See individual program's README or VREADME.TXT files for more information.

Appendix C

Installing Netscape Navigator Gold

This appendix is about getting Netscape Navigator Gold, version 3.0, installed on your hard disk. Typically, you can just follow the instructions that came with your package. Or, if you download a copy, you can just follow Netscape's downloading instructions. If you don't have either of those handy, you can follow the instructions presented in this chapter.

WHAT YOU NEED TO RUN GOLD

To use Netscape Navigator Gold 3.0, you'll need at least the following:

- A PC or compatible with a 486 or Pentium Processor
- At least 6MB RAM (preferably 8MB)
- A hard disk with at least 5MB of disk space available
- Windows 95 installed
- A connection to the Internet: Either a dial-up account (if you're an individual) or a permanent LAN connection (if you work for a large organization).
- If you'll be connecting online via a dial-up account, you'll also need a modem.

BUYING NETSCAPE NAVIGATOR GOLD 3.0

You can purchase Netscape Navigator Gold, version 3.0, from traditional sources such as computer stores and mail-order houses. Or, if you already have access to the Internet, you can purchase Gold online. Just point your Web browser to http://home.netscape.com, and choose General Store from the navigation bar on the screen. When you get to the General Store (see Figure C-1), choose Navigators. Choose whichever Netscape Navigator Gold package seems best for you and follow the download and installation instructions that appear on the screen.

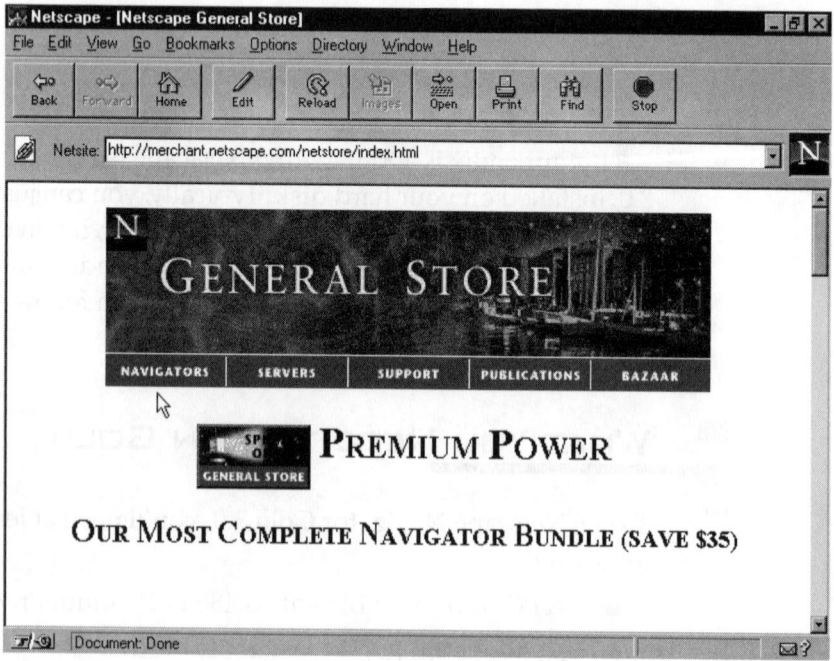

Figure C-1: *If you already have an Internet connection, you can buy Gold from Netscape's General Store.*

INSTALLING NETSCAPE NAVIGATOR GOLD 3.0

If you downloaded your copy of Netscape Navigator Gold 3.0, just follow the installation instructions that were presented during the download. (Typically, you just have to double-click the name of the file that you downloaded.)

If you're installing Netscape Navigator Gold 3.0 from floppy disks or a CD-ROM, follow these steps to install the program:

1. Insert the setup disk (#1) in your computer's a: drive or CD-ROM drive.

2. Close all open programs, so that you're at the Windows 95 desktop.

3. Click the Windows 95 Start button and choose Settings | Control Panel.

4. Double-click the Add/Remove Programs icon.

5. Click the Install button, then click Next.

6. The Command line... box should already point to the appropriate drive and program name (e.g., a:\setup.exe or d:\setup.exe). Just click the Finish button, then follow the instructions on the screen.

From this point on, the exact steps presented onscreen will vary slightly, depending on whether you're installing from floppies or a CD-ROM. Generally, however, a Wizard will take you through the complete installation procedure.

Along the way, you'll probably encounter the prompt shown in Figure C-2.

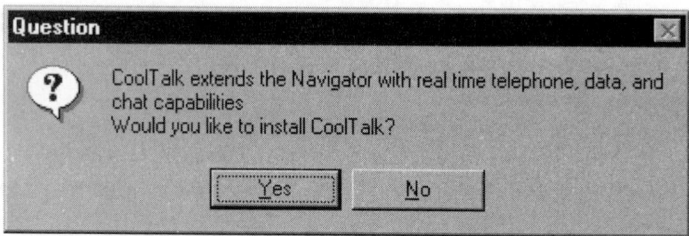

Figure C-2: *Install CoolTalk?*

I suggest you choose Yes and install CoolTalk now. You'll then see the prompt shown in Figure C-3.

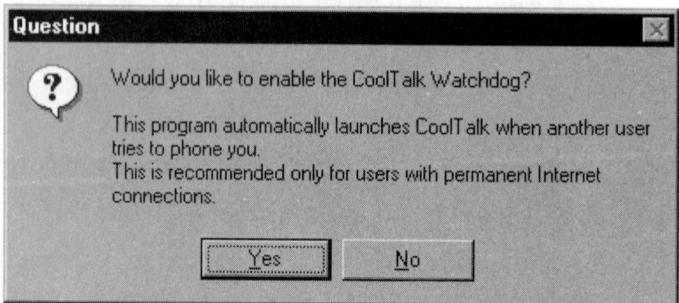

Figure C-3: *Install CoolTalk Watchdog?*

As the instructions say, you should choose Yes only if you have some kind of permanent, dedicated connection to the Internet. If you dial up to the Internet via a modem, choose No.

Continue the installation. When you've finished installing all of Netscape Navigator 3.0, you can refer to Chapter 26, "CoolTalk: Talking on the Net," at any time to learn about CoolTalk.

You'll be presented with the message shown in Figure C-4. It's not necessary to connect to Netscape's site and continue the setup. If you have no way to connect to the Internet right now, don't worry about it. Just choose No to continue the installation offline.

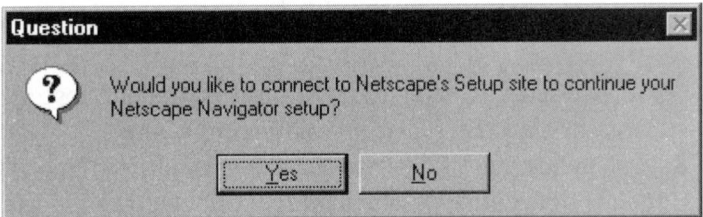

Figure C-4: *Don't worry if you can't answer Yes to this question.*

Eventually, you'll come to the dialog box shown in Figure C-5, which lets you know that Netscape Navigator Gold is now installed on your computer.

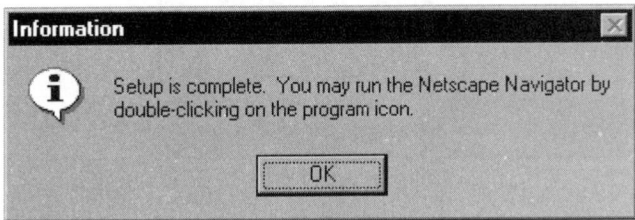

Figure C-5: *Setup is complete.*

STARTING NETSCAPE NAVIGATOR GOLD

You can start Netscape Navigator Gold in the same way you'd start any other Windows 95 program. In this case, however, you need to decide whether you want to work online (connected to the Internet/World Wide Web), or offline. If you want to work online, get connected first, as appropriate for your situation. For example, double-click My Computer, double-click Dial-Up Networking, then double-click the icon that connects you to your ISP. Enter your login name and password, if necessary.

Then start up Netscape Navigator by double-clicking the short-cut icon on your Windows 95 desktop. Or, if you don't have that shortcut icon, choose Start | Programs, then choose the option(s) necessary to start Netscape Navigator Gold.

Be aware that if you see the message shown in Figure C-6, it just means that you are not currently connected to the Internet. If you click OK, you'll still be taken into Netscape Navigator, where you can work offline creating your own Web pages or whatever.

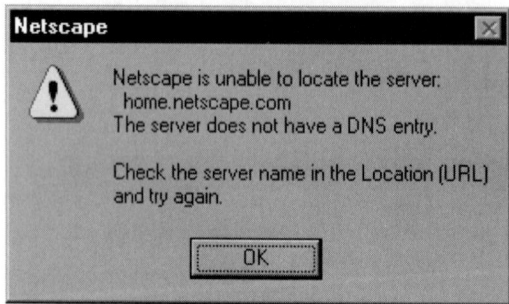

Figure C-6: *Choosing OK lets you use Navigator offline.*

TIP

If you plan to work offline often, consider starting Navigator with a blank page. See "Changing Netscape's General Appearance" in Chapter 32.

If you have any problems, be sure to check the instructions that came with your copy of Netscape Navigator Gold, as well as the logging on instructions from your Internet Service Provider. America Online and CompuServe users should check the appropriate areas of those services, as discussed in Chapter 30, "Getting Online (for Newbies)."

Appendix D

Special & Foreign Characters

There are two ways to type special and foreign characters into your Web pages while using Gold's Editor:

- Copy a character from the Windows Character Map
- Type the special "ampersand tag" right into the page source.

We'll look at each method here.

USING THE WINDOWS 95 CHARACTER MAP

When you're working in the Gold Editor, you can copy a character from the Windows 95 Character Map into your Web page. Follow these steps:

1. Make sure you're in the Navigator Editor (not "browse" mode).
2. Click at where you want to insert the special character.
3. Click the Windows 95 Start button, and point to Programs | Accessories | Character Map.

IF YOU DON'T HAVE THE CHARACTER MAP

If you can't find the Windows 95 Character Map, you've probably just never installed it. If you want to install it, you should first save your document and close all open windows. You should also gather up your original Windows 95 floppy disks or CD (unless Windows 95 came preinstalled on your PC). Then, to install Character Map:

1. Click the Start button and choose Settings I Control Panel.

2. Double-click Add/Remove Programs.

3. Click the Windows Setup tab.

4. Click on Accessories, then click the Details button.

5. If Character Map is not already selected, select it now (so it has a checkmark).

6. Choose OK (twice) and follow any instructions that appear on the screen.

4. In the Font drop-down list choose Times New Roman as in Figure D-1.

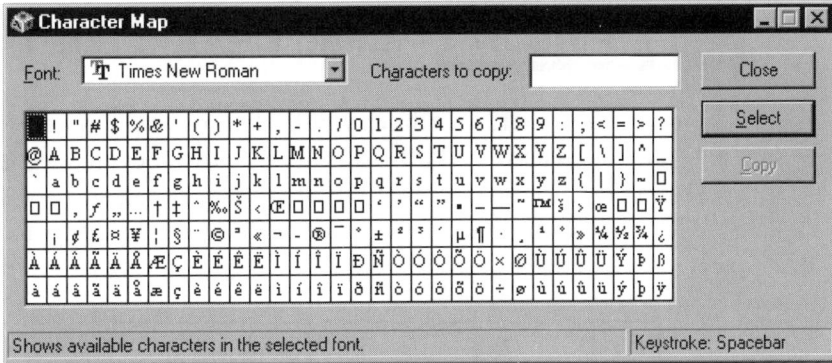

Figure D-1: *The Windows 95 Character Map with Times New Roman as the font.*

5. Click on the character you want to copy, then click the Select button. You can repeat this step to copy multiple characters.

6. Click the Copy button to copy the selected characters to the Windows clipboard. Then click the Close button. You should be back in Gold's Editor.

7. Click where you want to insert the special characters and then click the Paste button in the toolbar, or press Ctrl+V, or right-click and choose Paste, or choose Edit | Paste from the menu bar.

To verify the special characters, click the View in Browser button or choose File | Browse Document.

TYPING IN SPECIAL CHARACTER TAGS

If you're working directly with the document source in a text editor, such as WordPad, you can type the special &*tag*; symbol directly into the document. Note that each tag starts with an ampersand (&) and ends with a semicolon (;) as listed in Table D-1. Be sure to use the same upper/lowercase letters listed in the table.

Ch	Tag	Name
		Non-breaking space.
"	&quot;	Double quotation
&	&amp;	Ampersand
<	&lt;	Less than
>	&gt;	Greater than
©	&copy;	Copyright
®	&reg;	Registered trademark
½	&frac12;	One half
¾	&frac34;	Three fourths
¶	&para;	Paragraph symbol
±	&plusmn;	Plus/minus
£	&pound;	Pound
À	&Agrave;	Capital A, grave accent
à	&agrave;	Small a, grave accent
Á	&Aacute;	Capital A, acute accent
á	&aacute;	Small a, acute accent
Â	&Acirc;	Capital A, circumflex accent
â	&acirc;	Small a, circumflex accent
Ã	&Atilde;	Capital A, tilde
ã	&atilde;	Small a, tilde
Ä	&Auml;	Capital A, dieresis or umlaut mark
ä	&auml;	Small a, dieresis or umlaut mark
Å	&Aring;	Capital A, ring

Ch	Tag	Name
å	å	Small a, ring
Æ	Æ	Capital AE diphthong (ligature)
æ	æ	Small ae dipthong (ligature
Ç	Ç	Capital C, cedilla
ç	ç	Small c, cedilla
_	Ð	Capital Eth, Icelandic
∂	ð	Small eth, Icelandic
È	È	Capital E, grave accent
è	è	Small e, grave accent
É	É	Capital E, acute accent
é	é	Small e, acute accent
Ê	Ê	Capital E, circumflex accent
ê	ê	Small e, circumflex accent
Ë	Ë	Capital E, dieresis or umlaut mark
ë	ë	Small e, dieresis or umlaut mark
Ì	Ì	Capital I, grave accent
ì	ì	Small i, grave accent
Í	Í	Capital I, acute accent
í	í	Small i, acute accent
Î	Î	Capital I, circumflex accent
î	î	Small i, circumflex accent
Ï	Ï	Capital I, dieresis or umlaut mark
ï	ï	Small i, dieresis or umlaut mark
Ñ	Ñ	Capital N, tilde
ñ	ñ	Small n, tilde
Ò	Ò	Capital O, grave accent
ò	ò	Small o, grave accent
Ó	Ó	Capital O, acute accent
ó	ó	Small o, acute accent
Ô	Ô	Capital O, circumflex accent

Ch	Tag	Name
ô	&ocirc;	Small o, circumflex accent
Õ	&Otilde;	Capital O, tilde
õ	&otilde;	Small o, tilde
Ö	&Ouml;	Capital O, dieresis or umlaut mark
ö	&ouml;	Small o, dieresis or umlaut mark
Ø	&Oslash;	Capital O, slash
ø	&oslash;	Small o, slash
ß	&Szlig;	Small sharp s, German (sz ligature)
Ù	&Ugrave;	Capital U, grave accent
ù	&ugrave;	Small u, grave accent
Ú	&Uacute;	Capital U, acute accent
ú	&uacute;	Small u, acute accent
Û	&Ucirc;	Capital U, circumflex accent
û	&ucirc;	Small u, circumflex accent
Ü	&Uuml;	Capital U, dieresis or umlaut mark;
ü	&uuml;	Small u, dieresis or umlaut mark
Y	&Yacute;	Capital Y, acute accent
y	&yacute;	Small y, acute accent
ÿ	&yuml;	Small y, dieresis or umlaut mark
_	&THORN;	Capital THORN, Icelandic
_	&thorn;	Small thorn, Icelandic

Table D-1: *Special and foreign characters.*

Appendix E

Color String Literals & Triplets

When inserting HTML tags and JavaScript code manually into a Web page, you can use the color names and triplets shown in Table E-1. Most browsers support the triplets. So you might want to use them rather than the string literals.

If you'd like to see how pairs of colors look together on the screen, check out my Color Schemer JavaScript applet. Point your Web browser to http://www.coolnerds.com and follow the links to Web Publishing >> JavaScript >> Color Schemer. There are also two great Web sites at which you can find colors based on their hexidecimal values: http://www.webmotion.com/Websurfshop/ Colorcode/and http://www.infi.net/wwwimages/colorindex.html

Color String Literal	Triplet	Color String Literal	Triplet
aliceblue	F0F8FF	darkred	8B0000
antiquewhite	FAEBD7	darksalmon	E9967A
aqua	00FFFF	darkseagreen	8FBC8F
aquamarine	7FFFD4	darkslateblue	483D8B
azure	F0FFFF	darkslategray	2F4F4F
beige	F5F5DC	darkturquoise	00CED1
bisque	FFE4C4	darkviolet	9400D3
black	000000	deeppink	FF1493
blanchedalmond	FFEBCD	deepskyblue	00BFFF
blue	0000FF	dimgray	696969
blueviolet	8A2BE2	dodgerblue	1E900FF
brown	A52A2A	firebrick	B22222
burlywood	DEB887	floralwhite	FFFAF0
cadetblue	5F9EA0	forestgreen	228B22
chartreuse	7FFF00	fuchsia	FF00FF
chocolate	D2691E	gainsboro	DCDCDC
coral	FF7F50	ghostwhite	F8F8FF
cornflowerblue	6495ED	gold	FFD700
cornsilk	FFF8DC	goldenrod	DAA520
crimson	DC143C	gray	808080
cyan	00FFFF	green	008000
darkblue	00008B	greenyellow	ADFF2F
darkcyan	008B8B	honeydew	F0FFF0
darkgoldenrod	B8860B	hotpink	FF69B4
darkgray	A9A9A9	indianred	CD5C5C
darkgreen	006400	indigo	4B0082
darkkhaki	BDB76B	ivory	FFFFF0
darkmagenta	8B008B	khaki	F0E68C
darkolivegreen	556B2F	lavender	E6E6FA
darkorange	FF8C00	lavenderblush	FFF0F5
darkorchid	9932CC	lawngreen	7CFC00

Color String Literal	Triplet	Color String Literal	Triplet
lemonchiffon	FFFACD	moccasin	FFE4B5
lightblue	ADD8E6	navajowhite	FFDEAD
lightcoral	F08080	navy	000080
lightcyan	E0FFFF	oldlace	FDF5E6
lightgoldenrodyellow	FAFAD2	olive	808000
lightgreen	90EE90	olivedrab	6B8E23
lightgrey	D3D3D3	orange	FFA500
lightpink	FFB6C1	orangered	FF4500
lightsalmon	FFA07A	orchid	DA70D6
lightseagreen	200B2AA	palegoldenrod	EEE8AA
lightskyblue	87CEFA	palegreen	98FB98
lightslategray	778899	paleturquoise	AFEEEE
lightsteelblue	B0C4DE	palevioletred	DB7093
lightyellow	FFFFE0	papayawhip	FFEFD5
lime	00FF00	peachpuff	FFDAB9
limegreen	32CD32	peru	CD853F
linen	FAF0E6	pink	FFC0CB
magenta	FF00FF	plum	DDA0DD
maroon	8000000	powderblue	B0E0E6
mediumaquamarine	66CDAA	purple	800080
mediumblue	0000CD	red	FF0000
mediumorchid	BA55D3	rosybrown	BC8F8F
mediumpurple	9370DB	royalblue	4169E1
mediumseagreen	3CB371	saddlebrown	8B4513
mediumslateblue	7B68EE	salmon	FA8072
mediumspringgreen	00FA9A	sandybrown	F4A460
mediumturquoise	48D1CC	seagreen	2E8B57
mediumvioletred	C71585	seashell	FFF5EE
midnightblue	1919700	sienna	A0522D
mintcream	F5FFFA	silver	C0C0C0
mistyrose	FFE4E1	skyblue	87CEEB

Color String Literal	Triplet
slateblue	6A5ACD
slategray	708090
snow	FFFAFA
springgreen	00FF7F
steelblue	4682B4
tan	D2B48C
teal	008080
thistle	D8BFD8
tomato	FF6347
turquoise	40E0D0
violet	EE82EE
wheat	F5DEB3
white	FFFFFF
whitesmoke	F5F5F5
yellow	FFFF00
yellowgreen	9ACD32

Table E-1: *Color string literals and triplets.*

Appendix F

JavaScript Reserved Words & Case

This appendix lists every JavaScript word in its proper upper/lowercase letter. Reserved words are also included. Do no use any of the words in this appendix as variable names.

abs	boolean	cos	final
abstract	break	Date	finally
acos	button	default	fixed
action	byte	defaultChecked	float
alert	case	defaultSelected	floor
alinkColor	catch	defaultStatus	focus
anchor	ceil	defaultValue	fontcolor
anchors	char	do	fontsize
appCodeName	charAt	document	for
appName	checkbox	double	form
appVersion	checked	E	forms
Array	class	elements	forward
asin	clear	else	frame
atan	clearTimeout	encoding	frames
back	click	escape	function
bgColor	close	eval	getDate
big	confirm	exp	getDay
blink	const	extends	getHours
blur	continue	false	getMinutes
bold	cookie	fgColor	getMonth

getSeconds	method	round	title
getTime	min	search	toGMTString
getTimezoneOffset	name	select	toLocaleString
getYear	native	selected	toLowerCase
go	navigator	selectedIndex	top
goto	new	self	toUpperCase
hash	null	setDate	transient
hidden	onBlur	setHours	true
history	onChange	setMinutes	try
host	onClick	setMonth	typeof
hostname	onFocus	setSeconds	unescape
href	onLoad	setTime	userAgent
if	onMouseOver	setTimeout	UTC
implements	onSelect	setYear	value
import	onSubmit	short	var
in	onUnload	sin	vlinkColor
index	open	small	void
indexOf	options	sqrt	while
instanceof	package	SQRT1_2	window
int	parent	SQRT2	with
interface	parse	static	write
isNaN	parseFloat	status	writeln
italics	parseInt	strike	
lastIndexOf	password	string	
lastModified	pathname	sub	
length	PI	submit	
link	port	substring	
linkColor	pow	sup	
links	private	super	
LN10	prompt	switch	
LN2	protected	synchronized	
location	protocol	tan	
log	public	target	
LOG10E	radio	text	
LOG2E	random	textarea	
long	referrer	this	
Math	reset	throw	
max	return	throws	

Glossary

Access provider—Just another term for Internet Service Provider (ISP), a company that can give you access to the Internet.

AOL—America Online. A large commerical online service that also offers Internet access.

Argument—A value or expression inside a function's parentheses. For example in history.go(–1) the –1 is an argument.

BTW—By the way.

Cache—Pronounced "cash," refers to copies of Web pages that are automatically stored locally on your own hard disk, to speed access to those pages when you re-access them with the Back and Forward buttons. When you close Navigator, text from pages remain in the cache. However, pictures, which consume a lot of disk space, are not saved. Thus if you access a cached page without being online, the page will appear with icons in place of pictures.

Chat—The general term used to describe communicating with other people on a network, live, by typing messages back and forth.

CIS—CompuServe Information Service. A large commerical online service that also offers Internet access.

Client—A computer that acts as a "consumer" on the Internet. For example, when you're browsing the World Wide Web from your PC, your PC is playing the role of the client. The machines that hold the information you're browsing are called *servers*.

Client pull—A technique that allows a downloaded page to automatically send instructions back to the server. For example, a page might contain programming code that says "reload this page in five minutes."

Code—The generic term for instructions written for a computer to follow. HTML tags and JavaScript commands would be considered code.

Codec—A program that *com*presses audio or visual data for faster transfer across a network, and can also *de*compress the data after it has reached its destination.

com—At the end of a Web site address, indicates that the Web site is a commercial site (as opposed to a government or educational site). For example, http://www.coolnerds.com is a commercial site and is not affilitaed with any government agency or school.

Content—The general term for the information (text and pictures) in a Web page.

Control—A single button, check box, text box, or changeable "blank" on a fill-in-the-blank form. Also called a *field*.

Cyberspace—A slang term for the Internet, originated in the novel *Neuromancer* by William Gibson.

Dial-up—A non-permanent connection to the Internet where you connect. A *dial-up account* is one where you connect to the Internet via telephone lines and a modem.

Directory—A place on a disk where a bunch of related files are stored. Called a *folder* in Windows 95.

Dithering—If a printer doesn't have a color or shade of gray built into its palette, it can approximate a color or gray shade by mixing availabe colors or shades. The act of mixing these colors or shades is called *dithering*.

Document—A general term for something you create and save using a computer program. With Netscape Navigator Gold's editor, the documents you create are Web pages, which can be viewed by any Web browser.

Domain name—A nickname for a Web site address. Behind the scenes, IP addresses are numbers like 123 45 67 890. A domain name lets you come up with an easier to remember an alternative, such as "coolnerds."

Download—To copy a program or some other file(s) from a larger server computer on the Internet down to your own personal PC (the client).

External—Generally refers to an image, sound clip, or video that's not presented to the reader immediately. But rather, the page displays a link that, when clicked, displays the picture, sound clip, or video.

Field—A single blank on a fill-in-the-blank form.

Fixed Width—A fixed width font is one in which every letter is exactly the same width. For example, the letter *I* takes up just as much space as the letter *m*. Sometimes called a typewriter font, or monospaced font. Courier is a common fixed width font.

Flame—To send nasty, angry e-mail or newsgroup articles.

Folder—A place on a disk where files are stored. Also called a *directory*.

Font—A particular style of print consisting of a typeface (style), weight (bold, italic, and so forth), and size measured in points.

GIF—Graphics Interchange Format. A format for storing pictures electronically for fast transmission over networks.

Home page—The first page you see (or your readers see) when first connecting to a Web site.

Host—(n) Refers to a server machine on the Internet. (v) An ISP that hosts your Web site is one that gives you space to publish your Web pages on the Internet.

HTML—HyperText Markup Language. A set of tags that tell a Web browser how to present text in a Web page. For example, the tags <b>...</b> tell the Web browser to "display all text between the <b> and </b> in boldface.

http—HyperText Transfer Protocol. The protocol (set of "rules") used by the World Wide Web.

Hyperlink—A hot spot in a document that, when clicked, takes the reader to another document, or to a specific place (i.e., a Named Anchor) within a document. Also called *link*, for short.

Image—Another name for picture or graphic. On the World Wide Web, usually refers to a picture that's stored in GIF or JPEG format.

Information Superhighway—Another name for the Internet.

Inline—An object that's displayed automatically when a reader opens a page. Can be an image, sound, or video. Inline images are displayed with an <IMG> tag. Inline sound and video require <embed> tags.

Internaut—A person who cruises the Internet (slang).

Internet Access Provider—Just another term for Internet Service Provider (ISP), a company that can give you access to the Internet.

InterNIC—The organization that keeps track of domain names and registers new domain names. They can be reached through a Web browser at http://ds.internic.net.

IRC—Internet Relay Chat. A service of the Internet that lets users communicate by typing messages back and forth. CoolTalk (Chapter 6) also offers a Chat tool.

IS411—InSoft's (IS) Directory Assistace (411) server for finding people who use CoolTalk. Avialable when you click the Start Conference button in CoolTalk.

ISDN—Integrated Services Digital Network. A special type of phone connection that provides fairly fast access to the Internet. Requires special arrangements with your local phone company, an ISP that can support ISDN, and a special modem called a *terminal adapter*.

ISP—Internet Service Provider. A company that can give you access to the Internet.

JPEG—A format for storing photograph-quality figures in a compressed format that allows for reasonably fast transmission over a network. Developed by the Joint Photographic Experts Group.

LAN—Local Area Network. A collection of computers within a single room, department, or building that are connected by cables to form a small, local network.

Link—Short for hyperlink. A hot spot in a Web page that, when clicked, takes the reader to some other Web page, or area within a Web page.

Method—In JavaScript, an action that some object can perform.

Modem—A simple device that connects a PC to the telephone lines.

Mozilla—Name of Netscape's dragon mascot, and also a general name they use for their Navigator products.

MPEG—A highly compressed format of video that can move (relatively) quickly across the Internet. The format was designed by the Motion Pictures Experts Group.

MSN—The Microsoft Network. A large commercial online service hosted by Microsoft Corporation. Also provides Internet access.

Multimedia—The use of multiple communications media—any combination of text, pictures, sound, and video—in a single presentation.

Newbie—A beginner. Someone who is new to the Internet.

Object—In JavaScript, a "thing" on the screen that you can detect and manipulate using JavaScript code. For example, the current document, the Navigator window, and forms are all manipulable objects.

Offline—Using your PC without being connected to the Internet.

Online—Connected to the Internet.

Pixel—A single dot on a computer screen. As a unit of measurement, 100 pixels equals about an inch, or about 1/6th the width of a screen at 640 x 480 resolution.

Point—(v) To rest your mouse pointer on something. (n) The unit of measure for measuring the height of letters, where 1 point equals roughly 1/72 inch.

PPP—Point-to-Point Protocol. If you're connecting to the Internet from your PC and don't already have access to the Internet through a large company or organization, you'll want to find an Internet Access Provider that can give you PPP access.

Property—A characteristic of an object. For example "background color" is a property of a document (object).

Proportional—A proportional font is one in which every letter takes up only as much space as it needs. For example, the letter *I* is narrower than the letter *m*. Most professionally typeset print (including what you're reading right now) is displayed in a proportional font, such as Times Roman.

Server—A computer that's connected to the Internet 24 hours a day, 365 days a year, that contains Web pages and other materials for people to access.

Server push—Keeps the HTTP connection between client and server open for an indefinite period of time.

SLIP—Serial Line Interface Protocol. One of the protocols used for dial-up phone connections to the Internet. The other protocol, PPP, is newer and is supported by Windows 95.

Smiley—A little face typed from characters. For example if you look at this :-) sideways, it looks like two eyes, a nose, and a mouth. Means "hooray" or "just kidding."

Snail mail—The new, not-so-flattering term for traditional mail, which takes a few days, rather than a few seconds, to reach the intended recipient.

Spam—Internet junk mail or advertising.

String—A chunk of text, such as "Hello there," as opposed to a number, such as 123.45.

TCP/IP—The protocol (set of rules) used by the Internet that allows all those computers to "talk to" one another. Also called the Internet Protocol. TCP/IP capabilities are built into Windows 95 and Windows NT.

Telco—Short for telephone company—your local "Baby Bell."

TIA—Thanks in advance.

URL—Uniform Resource Locator. The address of a specific specific site on the Internet, usually in a format like http:// www.somename.com.

Virtual hosting—A service offered by some ISPs that allows your Web site to have its own custom URL, in the simple www.*yournamehere*.com format.

VRML—An acronym for Virtual Reality Markup Language, the "language" used to create 3D virtual worlds on the Internet.

Web browser—A program used to browse pages in the World Wide Web. Netscape Navigator—the main topic of this book—is a Web browser. (Many would say it's *the* Web browser!)

Web page—A document on the World Wide Web that contains text and HTML tags. Can be downloaded and viewed by any Web browser.

Web site—A presentation on the World Wide Web. When you go to an URL through your Web browser, you're actually visiting a Web site.

WhoIs—An Internet service that lets you look up "taken" domain names, as well as who is adminstering every domain. To get there, point your Web browser to gopher://rs.internet.net/7waissrc:/rs/whois.src.

World Wide Web—One of the services offered by the Internet. Perhaps the most popular because it provides access to text, graphics, multimedia, and 3D virtual worlds.

WWW—World Wide Web. Often used in Web site addresses e.g., http://www.coolnerds.com.

Index

the online magazine for Netscape™ users

Empower

yourself with up-to-date tools for navigating the Net—in-depth reviews, where to find them and how to use them.

Enhance

your online experience—get to know the latest plug-ins that let you experience animation, video, virtual reality and sound...live, over the Internet.

Enliven

your Web pages—tips from experienced Web designers help you create pages with punch, spiced with multimedia and organized for easy navigation.

Enchant

your Web site visitors—learn to create interactive pages with JavaScript applets, program your own Internet applications and build added functionality into your site.

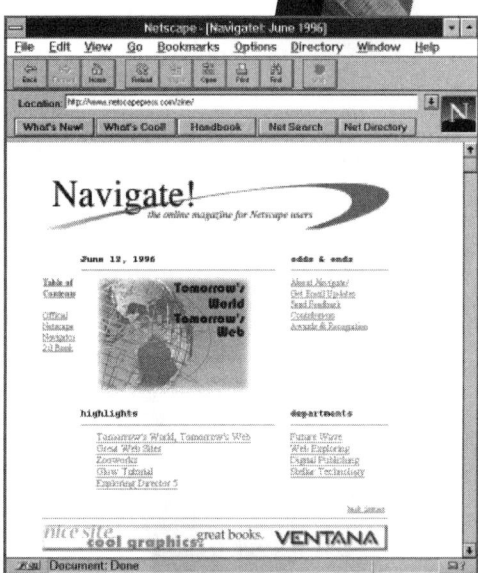

http://www.netscapepress.com/zine

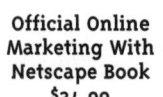

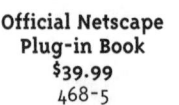

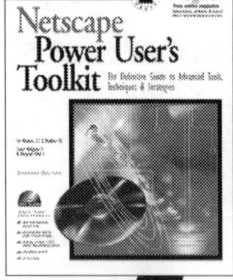

Follow the leader!

250,000+ in its first edition!

Hot on the heels of the runaway international bestseller comes the complete Netscape Press line—easy-to-follow tutorials; savvy, results-oriented guidelines; and targeted titles that zero in on your special interests.

All with the official Netscape seal of approval!

Add Power to Web Pages

Official Netscape JavaScript Book

$29.99, 520 pages, illustrated, part #: 465-0

Add life to Web pages—animated logos, text-in-motion sequences, live updating and calculations—quickly and easily. Sample code and step-by-step instructions show how to put JavaScript to real-world, practical use.

Java Programming for the Internet

$49.95, 806 pages, illustrated, part #: 355-7

Create dynamic, interactive Internet applications. Expand the scope of your online development with this comprehensive, step-by-step guide to creating Java applets. Includes four real-world, start-to-finish tutorials. The CD-ROM has all the programs, samples and applets from the book, plus shareware. Continual updates on Ventana's *Online Companion* will keep this information on the cutting edge.

The Comprehensive Guide to VBScript

$34.99, 408 pages, illustrated, part #: 470-7

The only encyclopedic reference to VBScript and HTML commands and features. Complete with practical examples for plugging directly into programs. The companion CD-ROM features a hypertext version of the book, along with shareware, templates, utilities and more.

Books marked with this logo include a free Internet *Online Companion*™, featuring archives of free utilities plus a software archive and links to other Internet resources.

Make it Multimedia

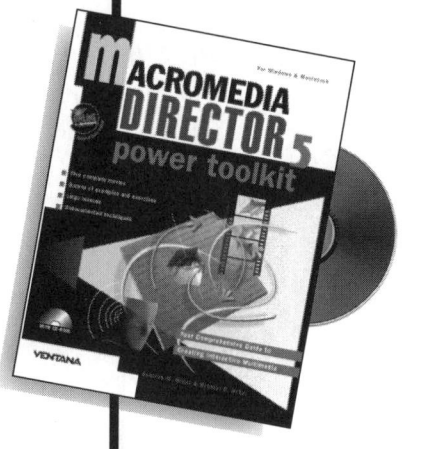

Macromedia Director 5 Power Toolkit

$49.95, 800 pages, illustrated, part #: 289-5

Macromedia Director 5 Power Toolkit views the industry's hottest multimedia authoring environment from the inside out. Features tools, tips and professional tricks for producing power-packed projects for CD-ROM and Internet distribution. Dozens of exercises detail the principles behind successful multimedia presentations and the steps to achieve professional results. The companion CD-ROM includes utilities, sample presentations, animations, scripts and files.

Shockwave!

$49.95, 400 pages, illustrated, part #: 441-3

Breathe new life into your web pages with Macromedia Shockwave. Ventana's *Shockwave!* teaches you how to enliven and animate your Web sites with online movies. Beginning with step-by-step exercises and examples, and ending with in-depth excursions into the use of Shockwave Lingo extensions, *Shockwave!* is a must-buy for both novices and experienced Director developers. Plus, tap into current Macromedia resources on the Internet with Ventana's *Online Companion.* The companion CD-ROM includes the Shockwave player plug-in, sample Director movies and tutorials, and much more!

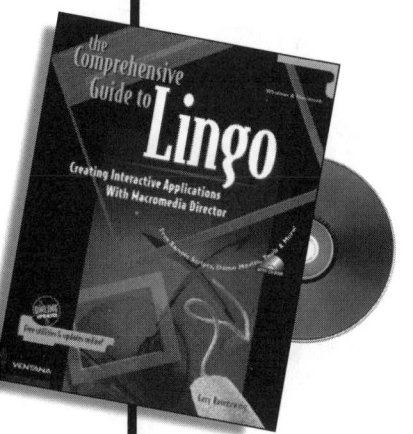

The Comprehensive Guide to Lingo

$49.99, 700 pages, illustrated, part #: 463-4

Master the Lingo of Macromedia Director's scripting language for adding interactivity to presentations. Covers beginning scripts to advanced techniques, including creating movies for the Web and problem solving. The companion CD-ROM features demo movies of all scripts in the book, plus numerous examples, a searchable database of problems and solutions, and much more!

Web Favorites

Looking Good Online

$39.99, 400 pages, illustrated, part #: 469-3

Create well-designed, organized web sites—
incorporating text, graphics, digital photos, backgrounds
and forms. Features studies of successful sites and design
tips from pros. The companion CD-ROM features samples
from online professionals; buttons, backgrounds, templates
and graphics.

News Junkies Internet 500

$24.99, 500 pages, illustrated, part #: 461-8

Quench your thirst for news with this comprehensive listing
of the best news and most useful sites and sources on the
Web. Includes business, international, sports, weather,
law, finance, entertainment, politics and more. Plus rated
reviews of site strengths, weaknesses, design and
navigational properties.

Walking the World Wide Web, Second Edition

$39.95, 800 pages, illustrated, part #: 298-4

More than 30% new, this book now features 500 listings
and an extensive index of servers, expanded and
arranged by subject. This groundbreaking bestseller
includes a CD-ROM enhanced with Ventana's exclusive
PerpetuWAVE technology; updated online components that
make it the richest resource available for web travelers;
Netscape Navigator; and a hypertext version of the book.

TO ORDER ANY VENTANA TITLE, COMPLETE THIS ORDER FORM AND MAIL OR FAX IT TO US, WITH PAYMENT, FOR QUICK SHIPMENT.

TITLE	PART #	QTY	PRICE	TOTAL

SHIPPING

For all standard orders, please ADD $4.50/first book, $1.35/each additional.
For software kit orders, ADD $6.50/first kit, $2.00/each additional.
For "two-day air," ADD $8.25/first book, $2.25/each additional.
For "two-day air" on the kits, ADD $10.50/first kit, $4.00/each additional.
For orders to Canada, ADD $6.50/book.
For orders sent C.O.D., ADD $4.50 to your shipping rate.
North Carolina residents must ADD 6% sales tax.
International orders require additional shipping charges.

SUBTOTAL = $ _____

SHIPPING = $ _____

TAX = $ _____

TOTAL = $ _____

Or, save 15%–order online. http://www.vmedia.com

Mail to: Ventana • PO Box 13964 • Research Triangle Park, NC 27709-3964 ☎ 800/743-5369 • Fax 919/544-9472

Name _____

E-mail _____ Daytime phone _____

Company _____

Address (No PO Box) _____

City _____ State _____ Zip _____

Payment enclosed ___ VISA ___ MC ___ Acc't # _____ Exp. date _____

Signature _____ Exact name on card _____

Check your local bookstore or software retailer for these and other bestselling titles, or call toll free:

800/743-5369

All technical support for this product is available from Ventana.
The technical support office is open from 8:00 A.M. to 6:00 P.M. (EST) Monday through Friday and can be reached via the following methods:

World Wide Web: http://www.netscapepress.com/support

E–mail: help@vmedia.com

Phone: (919) 544-9404 extension 81

FAX: (919) 544-9472

America Online: keyword **Ventana**